Present Tense

To our students, from whom we've learned a lot!

Present Tense

The United States Since 1945

Third Edition

Michael Schaller
University of Arizona

Robert D. Schulzinger
University of Colorado, Boulder

Karen Anderson
University of Arizona

WADSWORTH
CENGAGE Learning™

Australia • Brazil • Japan • Korea • Mexico • Singapore • Spain • United Kingdom • United States

WADSWORTH
CENGAGE Learning™

Present Tense: The United States Since 1945, Third Edition

Michael Schaller, Robert D. Schulzinger and Karen Anderson

Editor in Chief: Jean L. Woy

Senior Development Editor: Frances Gay

Senior Project Editor: Christina M. Horn

Senior Production/Design Coordinator: Jennifer Meyer Dare

Senior Designer: Henry Rachlin

Senior Manufacturing Coordinator: Marie Barnes

Senior Marketing Manager: Sandra McGuire

Credits appear on page I-28, which constitutes an extension of the copyright page.

Cover Image: Peter Holt/Illustration Works, Inc./Getty Images.

For product information and technology assistance, contact us at **Cengage Learning Customer & Sales Support, 1-800-354-9706**

For permission to use material from this text or product, submit all requests online **www.cengage.com/permissions** Further permissions questions can be emailed to **permissionrequest@cengage.com**

Library of Congress Control Number: 2001133341

ISBN-13: 978-0-618-17037-1

ISBN-10: 0-618-17037-5

Wadsworth
20 Channel Center Street
Boston, MA 02210
USA

Cengage Learning is a leading provider of customized learning solutions with office locations around the globe, including Singapore, the United Kingdom, Australia, Mexico, Brazil, and Japan. Locate your local office at **www.cengage.com/global**

Cengage Learning products are represented in Canada by Nelson Education, Ltd.

To learn more about Wadsworth, visit **www.cengage.com/wadsworth**

Purchase any of our products at your local college store or at our preferred online store **www.CengageBrain.com**

Printed in the United States of America
8 9 10 11 12   14 13 12 11 10

Contents

6 The Dream of a Great Society

7 The Vietnam Nightmare

8 The Politics and Culture of Protest

Maps and Charts

Preface

In the 1990s, many Americans displayed what some admirers and a few critics called "triumphalism." The end of the Cold War, the collapse of the Soviet Union, and the strong performance of the U.S. economy seemed proof that the nation's values and institutions had met the test of the post–World War II decades. Many Americans expected that as the world's one remaining superpower, the United States could refocus its attention away from international concerns and toward meeting domestic challenges. But the catastrophic terrorist attacks of September 11, 2001, revived the centrality of international issues. Fear of terrorism, combined with renewed ethnic violence around the world, growing discontent with economic globalization, climate change, and rising energy prices demonstrated that the world remains a dangerous and complicated place. The beginning of the new millennium provoked fresh anxieties and undermined the boast that American prosperity, security, and world dominance were assured.

The third edition of *Present Tense* builds on the balanced account of domestic politics, social and cultural change, economic trends, and foreign affairs of the earlier editions but focuses on the many challenges faced by the United States to its institutions, ideals, and physical security during the past few decades. A new last chapter covers events through spring 2003, including the election of 2000, events since September 11, and the war in Iraq. Several chapters highlight the changing face of American immigration; capital movements and labor politics; the debate over globalization; clashing notions of the role of government in managing people's lives; the ways in which race, class, and gender divide Americans; and the evolving role of the United States in the post–Cold War world.

Each chapter contains a new extended essay called "American Trends and Issues" that traces a theme of special importance over several decades. Among the trends and issues discussed are the development of broadcast journalism, the impact of globalization, the rise of the military-industrial complex, the politics of scandal, education-reform movements, the fallout shelter craze, modern architecture, the social impact of high-tech medicine, the massive growth of prisons, stock-market booms and busts, and the social and cultural factors that impinge on the lives of working women and mothers. In addition, the chapter bibliographies, illustrations, and photographs have all been updated.

We welcome a new coauthor, Karen Anderson, to the *Present Tense* team. A specialist in the history of women, work, family, and minority groups, Karen has written extensively on women defense workers during World War II and ethnic women in twentieth-century America, and she is completing a book on the Little Rock school desegregation crisis of 1957.

Friends, colleagues, and students at the universities of Arizona and Colorado have assisted us in conceiving, writing, and improving this book. In addition, many readers have sent along useful suggestions on ways to improve the text. To all, we extend our appreciation. Their interest has helped make this a better book. We also thank the following reviewers who provided many useful comments on the book that guided us in the revision process: Jeffrey Charles, California State University, San Marcos; Walter L. Hixson, University of Akron; Margaret Paton-Walsh, Albright College; Joel M. Roitman, Eastern Kentucky University; and Victoria W. Walcott, St. Bonaventure University.

M.S.   R.D.S.   K.A.

New Deal and World War: Into the Modern Era

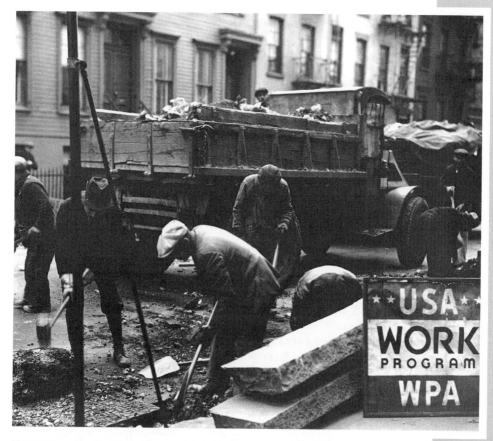

Men employed by the Works Progress Administration, a New Deal work relief program, widen a street. / © Bettmann/CORBIS

One day in 1936, Farm Security Administration photographer Dorothea Lange was driving on a California highway trying to reach home before it got very late. She saw a sign that said "Pea Pickers' Camp," passed it, drove for a while, and then turned back. At the camp, she took the most famous photograph of her career and provided the American public with a poignant picture of the devastation wrought by the Great Depression. The photograph, with the caption "Migrant Mother," appeared in the *San Francisco News* the next day to illustrate a story describing the 2,500 migrant farm workers stranded in Nipomo, California, without work, food, or income. The photograph of "Migrant Mother" generated intense public sympathy. On the same page, the *News* ran an editorial entitled "What Does the 'New Deal' Mean for This Mother and Her Child?" The picture of Florence Thompson and three of her children came to represent the suffering, despair, and quiet strength of those victimized by the nation's worst economic crisis. Within a few days, the federal government sent 20,000 pounds of food to the distressed workers. By the time the aid arrived, however, Thompson and her family had left Nipomo in search of work elsewhere.

For many then and since, Thompson has epitomized the plight of rural families displaced by the "Dust Bowl" and the Depression. Her story, however, is much more complex. A native of Oklahoma, Thompson had migrated to California in the 1920s with her Mississippi-born husband and their three children. Her poverty had multiple causes. Although she was widely perceived to be white by those who saw the photograph, Thompson was actually a Cherokee whose family had been displaced from tribal lands. Widowed in 1931 with five small children and a sixth on the way, she supported her family working in the fields by day and in a restaurant at night. After the birth of an out-of-wedlock child, she returned to Oklahoma with her children. By the mid-1930s, she and her family had joined the "Okie" migration to California, where she established a common-law relationship that led to four more children. Eking out a living as farm workers, theirs was a precarious existence. In the postwar period, Thompson married a more stable wage earner and left farm labor.

During World War II, the migration of poor people from the rural areas of Oklahoma, Texas, Arkansas, and Missouri to California continued at a high volume. These "defense Okies" were joined by other migrants seeking work in defense plants. In California, many of those who had come before the war experienced decreased hostility from the local population and economic improvement as they moved from rural work to industrial and construction jobs. No longer seen as a relief burden and valued now for their contributions to the war effort, they overcame much of the stigma associated with their origins as poor rural southerners. For them as others, the defense boom meant higher wages (often in unionized jobs), low unemployment rates, and the labor of wives, which brought many families out of the economic distress of the 1930s.

As Thompson's story suggests, the administration of Franklin Delano Roosevelt, who served as president from 1933–1945, had mixed implications for her and other Americans. Her family's plight indicates the tattered nature of the safety net for poor Americans before and after the New Deal. Indeed, many in the "Okie" migration came because New Deal agricultural policies and politics had cost them their work as tenant farmers. Her photograph was part of a government publicity campaign to generate sympathy and public assistance for those displaced, and it helped prompt a new role for government in the lives of Americans.

Our current powerful federal government, which touches the life of every American in myriad ways, evolved during the years of Roosevelt's presidency. Direct government intervention in the economy, government provision of extensive social services, government involvement in and support for science and industry—all these are by-products of the Great Depression and World War II. For white women and people of color, these years brought some expansions in opportunity, primarily during the war years, along with rising hopes and frustrations that had a great effect on postwar society. Most dramatically, the United States assumed a new, all-important position in international relations. By the end of the Roosevelt era, the United States had become a superpower—a difficult, uneasy role that has shaped the nation's history ever since.

When Farm Security Agency photographer Dorothea Lange took this picture of Florence Thompson and three of her children, she gave a poignant human face to the millions of Americans struggling to survive in Depression-era America. / AP/FSA/Wide World

Economic Crisis

Franklin D. Roosevelt's inauguration in March 1933 occurred in the midst of the Great Depression, with the American economy perched on the threshold of collapse. Following the dramatic stock market crash on October 24, 1929, over 13 million workers—one-fourth of the labor force—had lost their jobs, while many others faced drastic reductions in their wages and work hours. In the same period, industrial production and national income had fallen by half, and foreign trade had declined by two-thirds. The collapse of 5,000 banks wiped out 9 million savings accounts. The ensuing panic created a run on solvent banks as well. Hundreds of thousands of homeowners and farmers faced foreclosure when financial institutions called in loans. On one day in 1932, one-fourth of the land in the state of Mississippi was sold at auction. Millions of homeless throughout the United States slept in makeshift camps derisively called "Hoovervilles," after the incumbent president, Herbert C. Hoover, who seemed paralyzed by this national crisis. The title of a popular song asked plaintively, "Brother, Can You Spare a Dime?"

Unprecedented in its magnitude and duration, the Great Depression forced the American people and their elected officials to face the problems of poverty more directly than at any time in the country's history. Accustomed to ignoring the destitution and distress of the chronically poor—immigrants, people of color, the elderly, and rural inhabitants—Americans took poverty seriously when millions of urban white men in their prime earning years experienced long-term unemployment and downward mobility. Ironically, their problems also focused policymakers' attention on the plight of those historically consigned to economic marginality. Lorena Hickok, journalist and New Deal insider, wrote to Harry Hopkins, a professional social worker and one of the president's closest confidantes, that their investigation of poor people had "uncovered for the public gaze a volume of chronic poverty, unsuspected except by a few students and by those who have always experienced it."

People of color, for whom poverty had been an enduring problem, faced even more severe destitution as a result of the economic crisis, and at times, as a result of New Deal policies themselves. Before World War II, over three-fourths of all African Americans lived in the South, where they were employed mainly in agriculture or as domestic workers. In the North, they occupied the lowest rung of industrial and service jobs and eked out a precarious living. The Great Depression left them with nowhere to turn because desperate white workers took many of their jobs, many white families fired domestic workers to cut expenses, and New Deal agricultural policies prompted landowners to discharge large numbers of white and black tenant farmers and sharecroppers in the South. In the Southwest, state and local governments "repatriated" 400,000 Mexican and Mexican American workers to Mexico to spare themselves relief expenses and in response to the idea that the jobs these workers held belonged to (white) "Americans." Many middle-class people of color faced ruin, and their hardships increased the economic power of whites in racial ethnic communities. In Harlem, the proportion of property that African Americans owned or managed declined from 35 percent of the total in 1929 to 5 percent in 1935.

White women workers did not experience occupational displacement to the same degree as African American women mostly because many employers were not willing to replace women with men workers and because men were often reluctant to take work labeled "women's" or to settle for the wages that were usually paid to women. Employers believed that certain jobs required skills they assumed to be feminine and were not willing to replace experienced women with inexperienced male workers. This situation did not mean, however, that the jobs held by women were "Depression-proof." Some journalists, business leaders, and public officials even suggested that the "cure" for unemployment was to fire all married female workers to open slots for jobless men! As the Depression deepened, women's unemployment rates increased dramatically. This trend was caused by increased employer discrimination against women workers, especially those who were married; public policies that focused almost exclusively on increasing male employment; cutbacks in public sector jobs, including those of public school teachers; and greater numbers of women seeking jobs to be able to contribute to their families' support. One federal relief official complained, "your average businessman just won't believe there are any women who are absolutely self-supporting." The fact that some Americans believed unemployment would be solved if women relinquished their jobs to men indicates the degree to which women served as scapegoats for the nation's economic woes.

Older workers also faced a critical situation in the economic crisis. Historically, most had worked or relied on relatives for their livelihoods because very few had access to corporate or government pensions. Although many had families to support, they were among the first fired and, as the Depression dragged on, they faced the likelihood that they would never secure full-time employment again. Many of these workers were very frightened and demoralized. Harry Hopkins concluded that they had "gone into an occupational oblivion from which they will never be rescued by private industry." When Francis Townsend, a California doctor, mobilized older citizens to secure government pensions, his grassroots movement scared policymakers into support for a much less drastic plan that became part of the Social Security Act of 1935.

The Depression had significant effects on family life. Unable to support families, young people deferred marriage. In many cases, economic hardship heightened family stress and conflict by disrupting customary divisions of labor and authority within families, exacerbating dissension over economic issues, and forcing relatives to move in together and thus pool resources. When male breadwinners lost their jobs, wives and children often provided income for their families. In some cases, they assumed some of the prerogatives Americans had associated with the provider role, provoking conflict. One jobless man reported that there "certainly was a change in our family . . . —I relinquished power in the family. I think the man should be boss in the family. . . . But now I don't even try to be the boss. She controls all the money. . . . The boarders pay her, the children turn in their money to her, and the relief check is cashed by her or the boy. I toned down a good deal as a result of it." At times, wives refused sex to unemployed husbands because they worried about bringing more children into a household already in grim economic circumstances and convinced that they did not owe sex to a mate who was not meeting his traditional family responsibilities. Conflicts over money, power, and sex sometimes escalated to domestic violence.

The decline in marriages caused by the Depression was mirrored by a decline in the birth rate. The economic crisis, in fact, occasioned a substantial change in public, medical, and political views regarding birth control and abortion. Some Americans, saw their difficulties as deriving in part from poor family planning. "I could have avoided my present status," one man noted, "if I had taken precautions to have fewer children. Before the depression I never gave a thought to birth control. Both my wife and I were against it, and let the children come as they would. Had we been able to foresee the depression, we would have felt differently about it. I'm convinced now that birth control is a good thing." The demand for reproductive services led the American Birth Control League and the federal government to open birth control clinics in large numbers. Although official medical authorities continued to condemn abortion, many doctors changed their views and added economic circumstances to medical indicators as legitimate reasons for abortions. Abortions remained illegal throughout the United States, but increasing numbers of women obtained them in the 1930s. In Chicago, one doctor performed abortions for over 18,000 women between 1932 and 1941. Reflecting changed medical attitudes, over 200 other physicians in the area referred women patients to her for the illegal procedure.

Women responded to their families' material and emotional problems in other ways, too. In all social groups, women used their labor to reduce family expenses. They grew and processed food, made and mended family clothing, learned how to prepare meals more economically, and exchanged goods and services with their neighbors. They also used their interpersonal skills to reduce the stresses of new family arrangements and reduced incomes. Extended families may appear idyllic when viewed through the lens of nostalgia, but having large numbers of relatives occupying crowded households often led to conflict.

Not all families managed to weather their crises. In the early years of the Depression, divorces declined because unhappy spouses could not afford the legal costs of a formal divorce. Desertions increased, however, followed later by rising divorce rates and a related growth in the number of female-headed families. These families and many others would find that the traditional institutional practices of the economy and those of government and private charities would be inadequate for ensuring their survival.

The Roosevelt Revolution

In the United States, "good government" had traditionally meant "minimal government," with the greatest authority remaining in the hands of state and local officials. Unlike the developed nations of Europe, the United States had no tradition of a federal government actively committed to solving social and economic problems. Yet minimal government had failed to stem the ravages of a massive depression with both national and international origins. Reliance on state and local governments and private charities—a favorite solution of Hoover and other conservatives—could not begin to counter the effects of the Depression. Faced with declining tax revenues, most local governments fired workers and cut already meager assistance programs. In Chicago, unemployment cost workers approximately $2 million per day in lost wages, and public and private local and state agencies there provided about $100,000 per day in assistance.

In Roosevelt's view, the time had come when government had to save capitalism from its own folly by ensuring every American the "right to make a comfortable living." He predicted that a violent revolution of the Right or Left "could hardly be avoided if another president failed as Hoover has failed." His apprehensions may have been exaggerated. American citizens, in the words of one contemporary observer, appeared more in the grip of "fathomless pessimism" than of revolutionary fervor. Still, it seemed likely that disillusion with democracy and capitalism would spread rapidly if government failed to combat the Depression. The fear that desperate times might lead to desperate measures prompted policymakers to provide more rights and benefits to workers than they would have done otherwise.

Accepting the Democratic presidential nomination in 1932, Roosevelt promised a "new deal" for the American people, and in his inaugural address the next March, he sought to break the mood of despair. "The only thing we have to fear," he proclaimed, "is fear itself." He made it clear that he intended to deliver what the nation demanded: "action and action now." Should Congress fail to respond to the challenge, he would seek "broad executive power to wage a war against the emergency, as great as the power that would be given to me if we were in fact invaded by a foreign foe."

As Roosevelt's words hinted, his "new deal" required a federal government that would take a direct and prominent role in the economy and American society. Roosevelt favored an active federal government that would safeguard the public welfare within a vibrant system of free enterprise. Throughout the 1930s, he sought to rescue capitalism by curbing its excesses through reform and regulation. This approach was a new phenomenon in American history—it was almost a revolution. Within a few years, Roosevelt's administration enlarged the federal government's size and scope to an extent previously unimaginable. The new federal government touched more people in more ways than ever before.

Until 1933, the only routine interaction between the federal government and most citizens was the delivery of mail by the post office. Policies set in Washington rarely affected the everyday lives of ordinary people. There was no pension system, no federal unemployment compensation, no aid to dependent children programs, no federal housing support, no stock market or banking regulations, no farm subsidies, no withholding of payroll taxes, and no minimum wage—to name only a few federal activities now taken for granted.

The New Deal reflected Roosevelt's complex personal background. Born an only child to a socially prominent Anglo-Dutch family in upstate New York, Roosevelt never had to struggle for money, status, security, or dignity. Like many young men of patrician roots, he viewed self-made millionaires and industrialists as unscrupulous. Roosevelt had an easy self-assurance that disarmed almost everyone he met. Although not a deep thinker, he relished fiery intellects and recruited them as his advisers. His broad but undisciplined mind sought practical solutions rather than detailed theoretical analyses of vexing social problems. Supreme Court Justice Oliver Wendell Holmes succinctly described Roosevelt as a "second-class intellect, but a first-class temperament."

After serving Woodrow Wilson as assistant secretary of the navy during World War I and running unsuccessfully as the Democratic nominee for vice president in 1920, Roosevelt suffered a crippling attack of polio. Several years of therapy beginning in 1921 failed to restore the use of his legs, but his struggle with polio "humanized" Roosevelt. Previously considered something of an upper-class dandy who dabbled in politics as a hobby, Roosevelt had now suffered the kind of tragedy that afflicts ordinary people. When he re-entered politics to run for governor of New York in 1928, he related to people in an intimate way. His emotional vigor overshadowed his physical handicap. He could stand only with the aid of braces and generally sat in a wheelchair, but his handicap never emerged as a serious liability, even in an age when such disabilities often ended public careers. He charmed the press corps so effectively that they refrained from writing about or taking pictures of his legs.

Unlike the cautious Hoover, Roosevelt was determined to take quick action to meet the national emergency. During the so-called First Hundred Days following his inauguration in March 1933, Roosevelt mobilized the federal government. He worked with an eclectic group of university professors, socially conscious lawyers, and social workers known as his "Brain Trust," and the new administration rapidly drafted legislation and figured out how to administer it. Although not anticapitalist, most members of the Brain Trust believed that, in a complex economy dominated by large industrial corporations, government must force big business to share its power and, in Roosevelt's words, "distribute wealth more equitably." Congress gave the president most of what he sought, and even initiated some programs of its own.

Within a short time, the New Deal produced a score of recovery programs that boosted prices and employment while shoring up banking and financial institutions. The National Industrial Recovery Act (NIRA) encouraged businesses to form associations that would raise prices and profits, in the hope that this move would create new jobs. The Agricultural Adjustment Act (AAA) sought to raise farm prices by limiting crop production in return for cash subsidies. Other new laws regulated banking and provided federal insurance for individual deposits, supervised the stock market, provided funds for refinancing home mortgages, and insured private loans for new construction projects. To preserve basically sound industries that faced ruin unless assisted by the government, the Reconstruction Finance Corporation (started by Hoover) loaned about $10 billion to the private sector. This influx of capital saved millions of jobs and kept factories operating. The Tennessee Valley Authority (TVA)—an ambitious and unique new agency—undertook vast flood-control and electrical-power projects in the Upper South. Various government bureaucracies launched massive dam-building ventures in the West, thus remaking the economy and ecology of the entire region.

In the next few years, the new administration would break dramatically with the laissez-faire tradition, crafting its policies in a context of persisting economic crisis and recurring popular mobilizations. The latter ranged from the anti-eviction actions of urban Unemployed Councils to union drives and strikes by rural and industrial workers alike. In Arkansas and Texas, for example, impoverished tenant farmers and sharecroppers formed the Southern Tenant Farmers' Union (STFU) to increase their power relative to the planters who had exploited them economically and politically for many decades. Because they had used racial divisions to secure their power and profits in the past, the planters understood that the STFU's ability to bring black and white farmers into its fold posed as much of an economic threat to their interests as it did its goal of claiming a larger share of the proceeds from farm production. Ultimately, the planters relied on violence and their right to evict tenants to destroy the STFU.

The growth and transformation of the American labor movement in the 1930s reveals the reciprocal relationship between the changes in public policies and the grassroots organizing efforts that sometimes developed during the New Deal. In 1933, section 7(a) of the NIRA provided ground rules for labor relations and attempted to establish the federal government as a mediator between workers and employers, which was a change from its past position as the ally of management. Under the law, however, the government had no legal authority to act when management intimidated or fired workers for supporting unions or broke other NIRA rules designed to secure workers' right to organize. Despite this lack of federal intervention, militant union drives occurred in many industries, encouraged by workers' conviction that Roosevelt and his administration supported their efforts. John L. Lewis, president of the United Mine Workers, capitalized on this belief by urging his organizers to tell coal miners that "the President wants you to join a union."

By 1934, workers across the country had organized to address long-term grievances against their employers and to counter the Depression's devastating effects. In most cases, management fought bitterly to retain its power over workers by using its traditional repertoire of tools: violence, blacklisting and firing of union activists, and other forms of intimidation. From California to the Carolinas, union activists fought pitched battles against employers' security forces, police, and National Guardsmen, which sometimes resulted in serious injuries and deaths. The federal government was occasionally able to encourage mediation, as in the case of the San Francisco longshoremen's strike. When a businessman there requested federal intervention, charging that the strikers wanted to "destroy our most sacred institutions and traditions," Secretary of Labor Frances Perkins responded that "the only 'sacred tradition' which the strike leaders sought to destroy were low wages and graft-ridden hiring halls."

In the textile industry, long a bastion of low wages, long hours, and child labor, the United Textile Workers of America mobilized hundreds of thousands of workers in New England and the South for an industrywide strike in 1934. In addition to their desperate poverty, the workers particularly objected to the "stretch-out," a practice requiring workers to attend several machines at a time. One worker described the physical exertion this practice required: "When you get out, you're just trembling all over." Local police in the South brutalized union leaders, driving some out of town, while employers surrounded the plants with machine guns to fend off union activists, most of whom were women and children. Embracing the violent strategies of industry leaders, a textile trade publication declared that "a few hundred funerals will have a quieting influence." Company officials evicted strikers from company housing. Although federal policies permitted the provision of public assistance to striking workers, local welfare officials denied support to union members. One observer reported, "Some of these folks are literally starving." In the end, the workers gained nothing because they were overcome by the employers' power and the federal government's timidity and lack of authority.

Faced with a militant workers' movement and aware of the inadequacies of the labor provisions of the NIRA, Congress passed the National Labor Relations Act, also known as the Wagner Act, in 1935. The act recognized the right of workers to organize into unions and to bargain collectively with employers as a means of improving their wages and working conditions. Even so, it took a series of strikes and other militant actions for the new Congress of Industrial Organizations (CIO) to organize in basic industries such as steel, coal, and automobile manufacturing. Because the CIO organized on an industrywide basis, it was able to incorporate more women and minority workers than the American Federation of Labor (AFL), which organized only skilled crafts workers. It also mobilized workers at the grassroots level, a tactic that encouraged women to participate. However, union leadership remained in the hands of white men, who often failed to recognize that unions had a responsibility to address race and sex discrimination in the workplace.

With local agencies overwhelmed by the number of unemployed, the New Deal replaced reliance on private, local charity for the needy with a system of social rights, or entitlements. The Social Security Act (SSA) of 1935 created a national system to administer pensions, unemployment insurance, and aid for the blind and handicapped. It replaced the mothers' pension laws passed in some northern and western states with a program of Aid to Dependent Children (ADC). For the first time, the federal government took primary responsibility for alleviating the impact of unemployment and poverty on individual Americans.

The benefits of the SSA were not extended equally to all citizens. The unemployment compensation and pension programs excluded workers in agriculture, domestic service, government, and other occupations held disproportionately by white women and people of color. Almost 90 percent of African American women workers were ineligible for these sources of support. The unemployment compensation and pension programs were not means tested and did not regulate the lives of their recipients. The ADC program, which mainly benefited single mothers and their children, gave great discretion to the states in determining stipend levels and administering eligibility requirements and provided a lower level of federal contribution. The result was very low stipends for these families and a systematic pattern of racial discrimination in southern and western states. Local officials used casework methods to monitor the lives of recipients to ensure that they kept clean houses, sent their children to church, and did not keep company with men. The policies designed for men did not incorporate oversight of their morals, a fact that prompted historian Linda Gordon to conclude that policymakers responsible for those programs "considered the supervision inherent in casework unneeded, demeaning, [and] an attack on a (largely unconscious) masculinity."

Eager to alleviate economic hardship and to jump-start the economy, the Roosevelt administration also broke new ground by adopting programs to assist the unemployed. A host of agencies, such as the Federal Emergency Relief Administration (FERA), the Works Progress Administration (WPA), and the Civilian Conservation Corps (CCC), provided grants to states for welfare benefits or directly employed the poor in federal works projects. These programs hired the unemployed to build highways, municipal buildings, schools, seaports, airports, zoos, parks, and dams throughout the United States. Artists were commissioned to paint murals in public buildings; writers were commissioned to write travel guides. In New York City alone, the WPA employed more people than the entire American army. At its peak, the WPA had a national work force of 3 million.

African American schoolchildren in an art class sponsored by the WPA in Florida. / Franklin D. Roosevelt Library

The Roosevelt administration broke with a century-long tradition of government interference in the private lives of Native Americans by instituting the Indian New Deal in 1934. Under the leadership of John Collier, who became the new commissioner of Indian Affairs in 1933, the government abandoned the policy of allotment that had been central to its assimilation efforts since 1887. Under the old policy, the government divided communal Indian lands into small individual holdings and sold much of the remaining Indian lands to white settlers at bargain basement rates. In the 1930s, the federal government tried to stimulate economic development on the reservations by encouraging crafts production and other market-based strategies. These tactics did little to alleviate the destitution that haunted the reservations, however. Still, Collier tried to undo the legacy of indifference and exploitation that had previously characterized federal policies. Christian ministers criticized him bitterly for lifting the ban on traditional Indian religious ceremonies and for dropping efforts to force cultural and religious assimilation.

Many in Roosevelt's inner circle justified their vigorous government action by citing the theories of an iconoclastic British economist, John Maynard Keynes. Keynes believed that active state intervention was fundamental to the success of mature capitalism. The depression of the 1930s had so shaken business confidence, he argued, that recovery without government intervention was unlikely. Corporations and entrepreneurs would not make new investments until consumer demand reappeared. To increase consumer demand, public money had to be pumped into the economy.

Government money could enter the economy in several ways. By hiring unemployed workers to build bridges or roads, for example, the government could generate demand for raw materials and machinery. Workers receiving government paychecks would be able to pay for rent, food, and clothing, thus creating a market for consumer goods. This government intervention would create sufficient consumer purchasing power to restore the confidence of the private sector and to enable government to collect higher taxes when economic conditions improved. As the economic system returned to normal, the government could withdraw its participation from the marketplace.

Orthodox economists and political conservatives bristled at the idea of government intervention in the economy, and they considered deficit spending a heresy. Even Roosevelt hesitated to support the massive federal spending and central planning that Keynes and his followers believed were necessary to overcome the depression. Roosevelt also feared making citizens too dependent on the government as an employer of last resort. Nevertheless, his pragmatic approach to the crisis brought profound changes to the American economy and government.

Many of the New Deal programs and agencies had expired by the end of World War II. Several, including the Securities and Exchange Commission, the Federal Deposit Insurance Corporation, the TVA, and the Social Security Administration, survive today. Most important, the New Deal established the principle that the federal government should intervene in the country's economic and social life on behalf of its citizens.

Along with the revolution in the size and scope of government came a change in the profile of federal appointees. Most federal officials had been white, Anglo-Saxon men from the business community. The New Deal reached out to Catholics, Jews, African Americans, and women with professional experience in social work, labor unions, and universities. Some of Roosevelt's closest advisers, such as Thomas Corcoran, James Farley, Henry Morgenthau, Jr., and Felix Frankfurter, came from Irish or—even more controversial—Jewish backgrounds. Labor Secretary Frances Perkins, the first woman in a presidential cabinet, played a critical role in promoting new social legislation. Harry Hopkins, the first professional social worker to serve a president, became a frequent and influential adviser on both domestic and foreign affairs. First Lady Eleanor Roosevelt, a political activist who represented a national network of progressive women, also influenced Roosevelt's views on social issues. Between 1933 and 1945, she transformed the role of First Lady as she vigorously promoted the New Deal agenda. Unfettered by the political restrictions that bound her husband, she pushed various progressive measures. Trade unionists, sharecroppers, and women's groups considered her their pipeline into the government. She also emerged as the administration's leading advocate for the rights of African Americans. At a segregated meeting in Alabama, she insisted on sitting in the "colored only" section. When the Daughters of the American Revolution refused to rent a concert hall to African American singer Marian Anderson, Eleanor Roosevelt resigned from the organization in protest. She then secured the grounds of the Lincoln Memorial for the performance.

African American employment at all levels in the federal government tripled between 1933 and 1945, with most of the gains made during the war years. Roosevelt's new federal agencies caused a sensation by abolishing segregated cafeterias and offices in their Washington headquarters. An informal "Black Cabinet" of prominent African American citizens consulted regularly with agency heads and, on occasion, with the president. Eleanor Roosevelt, especially, championed the efforts of racial minorities. She met regularly with African American leaders like Mary McLeod Bethune, an official of the National Youth Administration; invited them to the White House; and legitimized their concerns. She supported civil rights legislation and federal laws against lynching and the poll tax. Her more cautious husband, fearful of the power exercised by southern Democrats in Congress, refused even to speak on such issues.

This multiplicity of voices enriched Roosevelt's presidency and brought the concerns of diverse groups and classes to national attention. For women and African Americans, however, the politics of representation employed in the New Deal had important limitations. Almost all policymakers, men and women alike, believed that a family wage economy, in which men supported women and children, would ensure women's economic well-being. They ignored the historic multiple-earner strategy in working-class families and women workers' need for increased opportunities and higher wages, in part because they were reluctant to help women become economically independent from men and because they assumed that women took jobs that legitimately belonged to men. By 1940, many African Americans were beginning to believe that the "Black Cabinet" strategy of the administration offered them symbolism rather than substantive change in state policies.

To a large degree, Roosevelt relied on his appeal to the "forgotten man" to stimulate widespread interest in New Deal programs. Part of his effectiveness stemmed from his ability to speak to the American people en masse. Few national leaders have used the mass media—in his case, radio—as effectively to bond with the public. Roosevelt initiated "fireside chats": live radio broadcasts through which he addressed millions of listeners in their living rooms. His audience considered the president a guest in their homes and planned their evening activities around his broadcasts.

Roosevelt's appeal transcended traditional factions and was particularly strong for working-class people. The New Deal coalition included not only the traditional Democratic Party machine but also labor unions and voters from almost every ethnic and minority group. The children of immigrants and minorities, helped by New Deal social programs, developed a greater sense of belonging and self-worth. These supporters contributed to Roosevelt's landslide re-election in 1936 and then to his re-election in 1940 and 1944.

Millions of Americans experienced tangible benefits from New Deal programs. Some people were put to work; others received farm support payments or were able to refinance mortgages. Rural residents could recall the day on which electric power, funded by the federal government, first came to their homes and farms. Above all, Roosevelt's programs and personality restored hope to vast numbers of Americans and countered the lure of fascism and communism. Yet there were signs, even in the heady early days of the New Deal, that it would not be an unqualified success. Although the unemployment rate fell dramatically from its high of 25 percent in 1933, it still hovered at 16.9 percent in 1936 (compared to just 3.2 percent before the stock market crash in 1929) and continued at an unacceptably high level throughout the 1930s. And many people fell through the gaps in the New Deal assistance programs.

Because federal programs operated through and depended on the cooperation of local authorities, government administrators often bowed to local racial prejudices and distributed benefits in blatantly unequal proportions. This situation created more hardship and inequity in the South, where local officials ensured that agriculture, relief, and jobs programs maintained racial and class inequalities. Although federal regulations stated that landowners were to share their federal subsidies for crop reductions with their tenant farmers and sharecroppers, the dominance of local AAA positions by southern white landowners meant that this distribution did not occur. The displacement of many poor farmers from the land occasioned by crop reductions meant that poor whites and blacks had nowhere to turn for other work in the underdeveloped South. Racial discrimination in relief worsened the already desperate situation of African Americans. Local white officials also fought to ensure that the money gained through federal relief and jobs policies did not exceed the very low pay usually accorded to Mexican Americans in the Southwest and African Americans in the South. In Mississippi, where over half the population was African American, 98 percent of the jobs with the Civilian Conservation Corps went to whites. In 1938, the president declared that the South was "the nation's number 1 economic problem."

Organizations like the National Association for the Advancement of Colored people (NAACP), the National Urban League, and the National Negro Congress protested the denial of work-relief benefits to African Americans and fought against the delegation of power to local authorities. They lobbied politicians and mobilized African American voters in the North to demand change. They found important supporters among left-wing political groups, the CIO, and white liberals. But Roosevelt was not willing to anger the southern wing of the Democratic Party, which held disproportionate power in Congress and was already wary of the liberal bent of New Deal programs, even though some of those programs enriched the planters who controlled Democratic officeholders from the South. Because of disfranchisement in the South, most African Americans could not vote, and southern Democrats controlled key committees in Congress.

The New Deal civil rights record gradually improved. Top federal work-relief administrators hired growing numbers of minorities. Although officials in the South resisted these moves and segregation in federal programs remained common, African Americans appreciated these efforts by Democratic New Dealers. As one leading black newspaper commented, "[W]hat administration within the memory of man . . . had done a better job . . . considering the imperfect human material with which it had to work? The answer, of course, is none."

The positive effect of New Deal policies on the racial climate in the United States, however incomplete, attracted millions of new voters into the Democratic coalition. In the 1932 presidential election, over two-thirds of African American voters (nearly all in the North) supported the Republican candidate, Herbert Hoover, over Franklin Roosevelt. In 1940, over two-thirds of them voted for the Democratic ticket, and this number grew in later decades.

Throughout the 1930s, groups and individuals on both the Left and the Right promoted radical alternatives to FDR's reforms. These groups and individuals included the American Communist Party as well as demagogues like Father Charles Coughlin, Gerald L. K. Smith, Francis Townsend, and Louisiana senator Huey Long. Each blamed "conspirators"—industrialists, bankers, Jews or other minorities—for America's problems. In the end, however, none offered a credible alternative to the New Deal.

Despite Roosevelt's landslide re-election in 1936 and the establishment of large Democratic majorities in Congress, the New Deal's struggles increased in the president's second term. Roosevelt caused one problem himself with a bungled attempt to pack the Supreme Court. Through 1937, a group of four conservative justices, joined by Chief Justice Charles Evans Hughes and Justice Owen Roberts, formed a majority that struck down New Deal legislation such as the NIRA and the AAA and thus threatened the entire New Deal program.

The conservatives insisted that not even a national economic emergency justified government interference in private economic matters such as the setting
of wages and the sanctity of contracts. In fact, the Supreme Court had been
the most conservative part of the American government since the 1780s, defending slavery and big business against almost all challengers.

Fearing further judicial assaults on his programs, Roosevelt asked Congress in 1937 for the authority to appoint up to six additional Supreme Court
justices. It refused to do so. In mid-1937, however, one justice who usually
voted with the conservatives switched sides, and another announced plans to
retire. An emerging liberal majority on the Court upheld the Wagner Act, the
minimum wage law, and key provisions of the Social Security Act. The Court
had turned a decisive corner. From 1937 on, the federal government exercised
broad regulatory power over private contracts and commerce without fear of
judicial intervention.

Roosevelt's judicial appointments had a lasting impact on civil rights.
With the exception of James F. Byrnes, Roosevelt's eight appointees to the
Supreme Court sympathized with efforts to dismantle legal segregation. By the
late 1940s, they had struck down state laws excluding minorities from juries,
established the rights of workers to picket against discrimination in employment, outlawed racially restrictive covenants in housing, challenged segregation on interstate public transportation, forbade the peonage of farm workers,
and outlawed the system that barred nonwhites from voting in the all-
important southern Democratic primaries. These Supreme Court rulings
provided momentum for additional legal challenges to segregation and for the
civil rights movement of the late 1940s through the 1960s.

But just as the Supreme Court began affirming the right of the government to intervene extensively in the economy, a severe recession in 1937 and
1938 caused an increase in unemployment and shook popular confidence in
Roosevelt's leadership. Roosevelt's influence with Congress had waned, and he
barely managed to shepherd the landmark Fair Labor Standards Act through
Congress in mid-1938. The act banned child labor, established a federal minimum wage, and limited the workweek to forty hours for many occupations. It
exempted agricultural, retail, clerical, domestic, and other service workers—
groups that were represented disproportionately by white women or people of
color—from its wages and work hours provisions. Until the 1960s, when social movements forced changes in the law, significant numbers of employed
white women and people of color routinely received below-minimum wages
for their labor.

In the 1938 congressional elections, Republicans picked up eighty-one
House and eight Senate seats. They joined conservative Democrats in blocking
additional New Deal innovations. They demanded balanced budgets, curbs on
labor unions, and—under the banner of states' rights—no federal help for
racial minorities. Many of the additional goals of the Roosevelt administration
would not be addressed until the 1960s.

The conservative bloc in Congress created the House Un-American Activities Committee, which later achieved notoriety in the postwar years. The

committee charged that Roosevelt's "left-wing followers in the government are the fountainhead of subversive activities." Under attack from politicians whose support he needed to deal with growing threats from Germany and Japan, and hoping to repair his tattered relations with business leaders, Roosevelt backed away from reform. Soon the outbreak of war pushed social progress even further into the background.

America and the World Crisis

Until the late 1930s, the focus on the Great Depression limited public concern with foreign affairs. Roosevelt barely mentioned world events in his first inaugural address in 1933. He did promise that the United States would act as a "good neighbor," especially in dealing with Latin America, and this policy resulted in the removal of occupation troops from Haiti, the lowering of tariffs, and the extension of trade credits to Latin American countries.

Early in his first term, Roosevelt extended diplomatic recognition to the Soviet Union. Since the Russian Revolution in 1917, the United States had refused to recognize the Soviet government. Public school teachers had been urged not to mention the name Soviet Union, and many maps showed the country as a blank spot. The president hoped that recognition would boost trade with the newly industrialized country and ally the Soviets with the Western democracies against Nazi Germany and Imperial Japan. Lingering suspicions of communism, disputes over payment of Czarist debts, and revulsion toward Joseph Stalin's brutal collectivization of agriculture and his political purges prevented much cooperation before 1941.

By the mid-1930s, the spirit of isolationism was widespread. Many Americans, including a substantial number in Congress, believed that the United States should have little to do with conflicts between foreign countries. Congressional hearings of the mid-1930s focused on charges that British and French propagandists and U.S. arms manufacturers (the "merchants of death") had hoodwinked the United States into entering World War I. These charges increased the public's distaste for foreign affairs and led Congress to pass neutrality acts between 1935 and 1937. These acts restricted the president and private Americans from giving economic assistance to foreign nations at war.

These laws, which did not distinguish between aggressor and victim, coincided with belligerence by Germany, Japan, and Italy. All three countries were ruled by Fascist or ultranationalist regimes that claimed special rights, frequently on the basis of race, to conquer their neighbors. The Italian invasion of Ethiopia in 1935, the Italian and German support of the 1936 Fascist revolt in Spain, German remilitarization, Germany's annexation of Austria from 1936 to 1938, and Japan's invasion of China in 1937 evoked little more than tongue-clicking from the U.S. government.

In September 1938, when Adolf Hitler demanded the partition of Czechoslovakia, Roosevelt supported the decision by the British and French governments to appease Hitler's appetite, delay war, and possibly turn the German dictator's wrath toward the Soviet Union. After the fateful meeting in Munich, in which the British and French sealed the fate of the Czechs by agreeing to Hitler's demands, Roosevelt cabled two words to British Prime Minister Neville Chamberlain: "Good man." Only later, when Hitler turned his fury on the West, did the Munich agreement and the term appeasement take on the aura of cowardly capitulation.

Like most Americans (and many Europeans), Roosevelt hoped to preserve the world balance of power while taking as few risks as possible. He hoped that other nations would take the responsibility for containing the advances of aggressor nations. After Hitler violated the Munich agreement by seizing all of Czechoslovakia and then demanded Polish territory, the British and French finally abandoned their policy of appeasement. In the months after Munich, Roosevelt got Congress to increase funding for a critical buildup of American air and naval forces.

In September 1939, after signing a nonaggression pact with the Soviet Union, Hitler invaded Poland. Britain and France responded by declaring war on Germany. By June 1940, Germany's Blitzkrieg ("lightning war") victories in Western Europe had left only Britain resisting Nazi power. (Russia remained neutral until it was attacked by Germany in June 1941.) Japan, which by then occupied large portions of China, joined Germany and Italy in the Axis Alliance and began threatening European and American colonies in Asia.

Just weeks after the outbreak of war in Europe, the president received a stark indication of the growing German threat. Nuclear physicist Albert Einstein, himself a Jewish refugee from the Nazis, sent Roosevelt a letter warning that German scientists had taken the first steps toward harnessing atomic power for military use. If German scientists developed an atomic bomb, Einstein predicted, Hitler would win the war.

Roosevelt authorized a group of high-level officials to begin an atomic weapons program, later code-named the Manhattan Project. By 1945, about 150,000 people were working on some phase of the $2 billion project to construct the ultimate weapon. Many of the project's participants realized that the bomb would have a profound effect on the world, both during and after the war. The massive development project also marked a coalition of government, science, and industry that became a hallmark of post-1945 national security policy, as well as a force for social transformation of the nation.

As Germany stepped up its attacks against Britain, Roosevelt stretched his constitutional powers to the limit. He transferred warships to the British and ordered the American navy to prevent German submarines from entering a large portion of the Atlantic. The American army at that time was comparable in budget ($500 million) and size (185,000 men) to the Bulgarian army and desperately needed to expand. Prodded by Roosevelt, Congress reluctantly passed the nation's first peacetime draft in 1940, despite charges from his opponents that labeled him a warmonger.

Roosevelt promised the voters in 1940 that he would not send America's youth into any foreign wars. After his election to an unprecedented third term

(cont. on page 21)

The Rise (and Fall) of Broadcast Journalism

World War II almost created broadcast journalism. Radio news reports, especially from overseas, barely existed before Edward R. Murrow signed up with the fledgling Columbia Broadcasting System (CBS) to cover London during the 1940–1941 German air force *blitz* that tried to bomb Britain into surrender. Speaking in a deep, reassuring voice, with air-raid sirens and audible explosions in the background, Murrow began his radio reports with the line "This . . . is London." For millions of Americans, his description of the resilience of ordinary Londoners was proof that the Nazi war machine had not crushed the one nation that stood between Hitler and the United States.

With the rise of television in the early 1950s, Murrow became the driving force in the CBS news division. Nightly network news remained a brief, fifteen-minute summary of events until it expanded to a half hour in 1963. Before then, Murrow pioneered the use of television documentaries to bring weighty issues to a mass audience. During the 1950s, he hosted *See It Now,* television's first weekly show with a news magazine format and the forerunner of shows such as *60 Minutes.* Produced in partnership with Fred Friendly, *See It Now* explored complex and controversial issues. In 1954, for example, Murrow broke the taboo on critical coverage of Senator Joe McCarthy by examining both the brutal methods and dubious results of the senator's anticommunist crusade. In 1955, Murrow (himself a chain smoker) devoted two shows to a special investigation of the several recent scientific studies linking cigarette smoking and lung cancer. Other episodes examined the development of the Salk polio vaccine, the environmental threat posed by pesticides, and the impact of the Red Scare on American life.

Murrow and his corporate sponsors also recognized the market for "middlebrow" entertainment. His *Person to Person* show featured interviews with actors, sports figures, and creative artists. Walter Cronkite, a Murrow protégé, made his mark at CBS with a show called *You Are There* that featured mock interviews with historical figures, such as Brutus in the Roman Forum at the moment he assassinated Julius Caesar or George Washington at Valley Forge.

In 1960, Murrow and Friendly began a new documentary series called *CBS Reports.* An early episode, "Harvest of Shame," chronicled the harsh lives and miserable working conditions of migrant farm laborers. Its impact has been compared to John Steinbeck's classic novel, *The Grapes of Wrath.* Murrow's popularity prompted the NBC and ABC networks to upgrade their news divisions to compete with CBS.

In 1961, President John F. Kennedy appointed Murrow to head the U.S. Information Agency (USIA), the bureau that presented government news and information programs abroad. Although he generally shared Kennedy's outlook, Murrow chafed at the escalation of the Vietnam War and found the role of official propagandist limiting. Shortly after Kennedy's death, the veteran newsman resigned so that he could return to broadcast journalism. Ironically, the journalist who did so much to alert the public to the risks of smoking fell ill with lung cancer and died in early 1965.

In some ways, Murrow's legacy lived through his successors. Walter Cronkite became the CBS evening news anchor in 1963 and was soon described by pollsters as "the most trusted man in America." In 1968, in the wake of the Tet Offensive in Vietnam, when he publicly questioned the value of continuing the war, President Johnson was stunned. "If I've lost Cronkite," he lamented, "I've lost middle America."

Beginning in the 1970s and accelerating after 1990, broadcast journalism faced a wide range of commercial and technological challenges. Corporate conglomerates pur-

CBS wartime correspondent Edward R. Murrow in London, 1940. His live broadcasts reassured Americans that Hitler's air force had not subdued England. / AP/Wide World

chased most locally owned radio and television stations while giant corporations such as Disney, General Electric, and Viacom acquired the ABC, NBC, and CBS networks. New corporate owners, their stockholders, and financial analysts cared less about the content of news and entertainment shows and more about their immediate profitability. Broadcast executives had to minimize costs (by lowering production expenses) and maximize advertising revenue (by expanding audience size or attracting more "desirable," i.e., younger, viewers) to keep their jobs. The proliferation in the late 1980s first of cable news stations such as CNN and then of Internet news sites meant that the number of people watching traditional network news shows was steadily dwindling. In the early 1980s, for example, the evening news shows on the three networks attracted 84 percent of the viewing audience. By 2002, that number fell to barely 43 percent. Even more troubling, television audiences became more demographically fragmented as cable and Internet outlets siphoned off groups of younger, older, male, and female viewers most interested in, say, sports, financial news, health matters, music, and so on.

Americans who remained tuned to network news averaged about sixty years old and were considered just a step away from the grave by youth-centered advertisers fixated on the eighteen- to twenty-four-year-old market. The commercial products advertised during network news—Pepcid, Viagra, Polident, and Depends—illustrate the point. Market fragmentation, the loss of a wider viewing audience, and pressure for profits made radio and television news divisions desperate to hold onto what remained of their viewer base, even if it required "dumbing down" their coverage.

Technological change also reshaped the news. Previously, a news show might feature a discussion of the root causes of a war or refugee crisis abroad. Now, a small crew with a mobile video camera fed to a satellite link could show starving refugees or a volcanic eruption in nearly real time. The effect was dramatic. In 1993, for example, CNN broadcast video that showed eighteen U.S. soldiers who were part of a peacekeeping mission being killed by a mob in Somalia. This incident, the basis of the book and film *Black Hawk Down,* prompted a public outcry that led the Clinton administration to withdraw troops from the U.N. peacekeeping mission. The images and the public outrage they fostered, not the real value to the national interest of the intervention, shaped policy.

Closer to home, technology drove news coverage in other ways. In the late-1970s, as mobile minicameras mounted on helicopters became available, television stations in Los Angeles calculated they could afford either to maintain traditional news bureaus in the state capital, Sacramento, or buy the camera-equipped aircraft. While testing the cameras, one helicopter happened upon a police chase on an L.A. freeway. The helicopter tracked and simultaneously broadcast the chase. Other local television stations promptly reduced the number of reporters in the field and acquired camera-equipped helicopters that roamed the sky in search of the "chase of the day." O. J. Simpson's celebrated freeway drive was merely the best known of these incidents. As live video of fires, crime scenes, and car chases proliferated, broadcasters cynically adopted the phrase "if it bleeds, it leads."

Network executives engaged in the equivalent of buying camera-equipped helicopters by shifting news budgets from "hard" to "soft" coverage. At first, this change meant promoting more programs with news magazine formats and reducing the number of journalists stationed abroad. *60 Minutes* segued into *48 Hours.* From there, it was a short jump to the tabloidlike *Dateline, 20/20,* and *Entertainment Tonight.* In place of Edward R. Murrow, Geraldo Rivera became the most visible "investigative journalist" on television. Soon, hucksters like Jerry Springer put Geraldo to shame with "investigations" that consisted of social deviants pummeling each other in front of cheering audiences. One network promoted celebrity boxing matches as part of its public affairs offering. Not all of these shows found a large audience, but each appealed to a segment of the fragmented media market.

Cable and Internet news faced a special challenge. Because they broadcast continuously, they required a constant stream of words and images to fill the screen. Programmers relied on celebrity gossip and sex scandals. For a decade beginning in 1991, scandals involving O. J. Simpson, the murder of Jon-Benet Ramsay, Bill and Hillary Clinton, Paula Jones, and Monica Lewinsky dominated the airwaves. In 2001, obsessive coverage of an affair between California Congressman Gary Condit and a missing intern, Chandra Levy, seemed poised to replace the Clinton-era sex scandals until it was preempted by the terrorist attacks on the World Trade Center and Pentagon. In the "new economy," news had become just another commodity.

---

in 1940, however, he declared that if England or China surrendered, Americans would be "living at the point of a gun." To prevent this predicament, he proposed a massive aid program, called Lend-Lease, that would make America the "arsenal of democracy." In a "fireside chat," the president compared the aid to lending a fire hose to a neighbor whose house was in flames to keep the sparks from spreading. In March 1941, Congress passed legislation, by a lopsided vote, to provide $7 billion in military aid for nations resisting Germany and Japan.

This aid package was nearly as large as the entire federal budget at that time. Secretary of War Henry Stimson referred to the Lend-Lease bill as a "declaration of economic war" against Berlin and Tokyo.

Roosevelt sent American troops to occupy Greenland and Iceland and ordered navy ships in the Atlantic to hunt down German U-boats. By the autumn of 1941, the German and American navies were engaged in an undeclared war that led to the sinking of an American destroyer. When Nazi armies invaded the Soviet Union in June, Roosevelt quickly approved Lend-Lease to the Soviets. He did so despite earlier American fury at Stalin for signing the 1939 nonaggression pact with Hitler, which freed the Soviets to seize the Baltic republics and eastern Poland.

With American attention turned toward the crisis in Europe, Japan took the opportunity to seize southern French Indochina, demand special access to oil from the Dutch East Indies, and insist that Washington stop military aid to China. In response, Roosevelt shifted naval units to the Pacific and imposed a trade embargo on Japan, leaving Tokyo with only a few months' reserve of petroleum. Roosevelt insisted that Japan had to quit the Axis Alliance with Germany, withdraw its forces from China and Indochina, and make a nonaggression pledge before he would lift the oil embargo. Japan, under the de facto leadership of General Tojo Hideki, demanded the immediate resumption of oil sales and a cutoff of aid to China before considering any pullback.

When discussions broke off on November 26, 1941, American officials expected a Japanese attack in Southeast Asia or on the American-controlled Philippines; they sent warnings to commanders there and in Hawaii. American intelligence had been intercepting Japanese diplomatic communications, but they were unaware of Japan's plan to target the Pacific fleet at Pearl Harbor, Hawaii.

On December 7, 1941—a date, Roosevelt said, would "live in infamy"—Japan mounted a surprise air attack on the U.S. fleet and airfields at Pearl Harbor. The assault killed over 2,400 sailors and soldiers, damaged or sank eight American battleships, and destroyed a large number of planes. Suddenly, war had come to the United States. At Roosevelt's request, Congress promptly declared war on Japan. On December 10, Japan's allies—Germany and Italy—declared war on the United States. As Japan rolled to a string of easy victories in Southeast Asia, shock and humiliation shook an American citizenry that had previously felt immune from the war. But Germany and Japan had sown the seeds of their own doom by engaging America's vast military-industrial potential. Within a short time, America was producing more ships and planes each month than were lost to the Japanese during the sneak attack on Pearl Harbor.

Pearl Harbor ended domestic dissent over participation in the war. On New Year's Day in 1942, the United States, Great Britain, the Soviet Union, and twenty-three other partners issued a "Declaration of the United Nations," a pledge to fight for victory against the Axis. Roosevelt and his military advisers resolved that the United States would provide additional Lend-Lease aid to Britain, Russia, and China to help them carry the bulk of the fighting against Germany and Japan. As soon as possible, British and American armies would open a second front to invade Western Europe and relieve the pressure on the Soviets (who would face about two-thirds of all German forces alone until 1944). Roosevelt's "Europe-first" strategy anticipated that once the Allies crushed Germany, the Soviets would then join in the final assault on Japan.

Supply problems, British stalling, the competing demands of the war against Japan, and other factors delayed the Allied entry into France until June 6, 1944. The massive invasion of Normandy on that date (see Map 1.1) quickly broke the power of the Nazis in Western Europe. By then, the Soviets had pushed German forces out of Russia and into Poland, at a cost of more than *20 million* civilian and military dead. Given the Western allies' long delay in opening the second front, Stalin remained deeply suspicious of them. He believed they would fight Germany to the last Russian and then move to control Europe themselves.

The behavior of Soviet leaders tended to arouse similar fears in London and Washington. Beginning in 1942, for example, Stalin demanded that Roosevelt and Churchill approve the transfer of parts of prewar Poland and southeastern Europe to the Soviet Union. Although Western leaders believed such a concession would violate the rights of Poland and the other nations involved, they also recognized that the Soviets had a justified interest in creating a security zone in Eastern Europe, the route of two German invasions since 1914. Churchill and Roosevelt eventually accepted the Soviet demands in return for Stalin's promise to respect the political independence of the rest of Eastern Europe. Some American policymakers believed that at times Churchill seemed more interested in safeguarding British interests in the Mediterranean than in defeating Hitler. Like the Soviet Union, Britain also worried about America's power in the postwar world.

Roosevelt hoped that wartime trust and cooperation would create support for a new world political order. At a series of summits held between 1941 and 1945, the president sketched plans for a postwar international organization, the United Nations, to be monitored by what he sometimes called the "Four Policemen"—the United States, the Soviet Union, Great Britain, and China. Each nation would police a particular sphere of interest that was important to it and would work toward opening up world trade, decolonizing its own empire, and rehabilitating Germany and Japan to encourage their formation of democratic societies. The United Nations was chartered in 1945, shortly after Roosevelt's death. By then, however, growing mistrust between the United States and the Soviet Union frustrated efforts to have the United Nations serve as an international peacekeeper.

Although the diplomatic and strategic logic of the war often seemed confused, a pattern had emerged by 1945. As Stalin remarked, "[W]hoever occupies a territory also imposes on it his own social system." Thus, the Western Allies gradually established pro-Western, anticommunist regimes in North Africa, Italy, Greece, France, western Germany, Japan, and southern Korea. As American forces advanced across the Pacific, Washington took possession of hundreds of islands formerly in the possession of Japan, declaring them "strategic trusteeships." The United States also became more involved in the

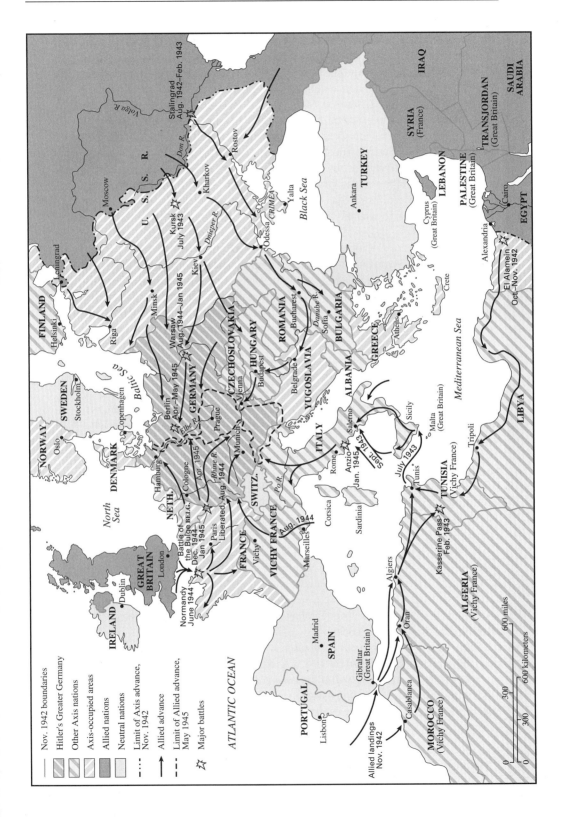

Middle East, an area of immense petroleum reserves. Roosevelt met with the ruler of Saudi Arabia, King Ibn Saud, in 1943 and began a cooperative relationship that provided American access to Saudi oil for the rest of the twentieth century.

In truth, all the Allies looked after their own interests, even while pursuing common goals. The British, French, and Dutch rushed to recolonize Southeast Asia as Japan retreated (see Map 1.2). As Russian forces pushed the Nazis toward Berlin, Stalin similarly imposed pro-Soviet regimes in most of Eastern Europe. Roosevelt, who was hardly naïve, preferred delaying most bargaining until the war's end, when he thought the U.S. position would be stronger.

But by February 1945, the Allies could no longer defer discussing postwar issues. Roosevelt and Churchill joined Stalin for a crucial meeting at Yalta, a Soviet city on the Black Sea. There the "Big Three"—Great Britain, the United States, and the Soviet Union—agreed to participate in the new United Nations and to exact industrial reparations from Germany. They also agreed that the Soviets would enter into the war against Japan three months after Hitler's defeat. In exchange, Roosevelt granted Stalin certain concessions. Critics of the Yalta agreements later charged that Roosevelt acceded to Stalin's demands out of naïveté, deteriorating health, or perhaps even communist sympathies. Why else would he sanction a dominant Soviet role in Poland or grant Stalin special economic privileges in Manchuria? "Yalta" became shorthand, especially among Republicans, for appeasement of Soviet territorial demands.

In fact, the Yalta agreement merely recognized what Stalin had already taken in Eastern Europe and the Baltic states. The Soviets were poised to invade Germany and would soon be able to attack Japan through Manchuria. Thus, Roosevelt did not give away anything. Furthermore, American military leaders feared high casualties in the last stages of the war against Japan and pressed Roosevelt to make concessions to Stalin to get Stalin into the Pacific War. The three leaders pledged cooperation in restoring democratic government in the liberated territories.

Roosevelt believed that the accord was the best he could do under the circumstances. Without continued Soviet cooperation, Roosevelt knew the Western Allies would face a far bloodier road to Berlin and Tokyo. Soviet domination of Eastern Europe and northeast Asia—which Stalin could impose with or without Western permission—seemed a reasonable price for saving American lives and shortening the war. Even American hard-liners did not seriously recommend fighting the Soviets to move them out of Poland. Most Americans rejoiced, in fact, when the Russians captured Berlin and when Germany surrendered on May 8, 1945. On the basis of earlier agreements, the Soviet Union turned over part of the German capital and other territory to its allies.

It is important to realize that when the war ended, the United States and its Western Allies dominated most of the industrialized world. The Soviets occupied much of Eastern Europe and a fourth of Germany, but their spoils did

◀ **Map 1.1**
The Allies on the Offensive in Europe, 1942–1945

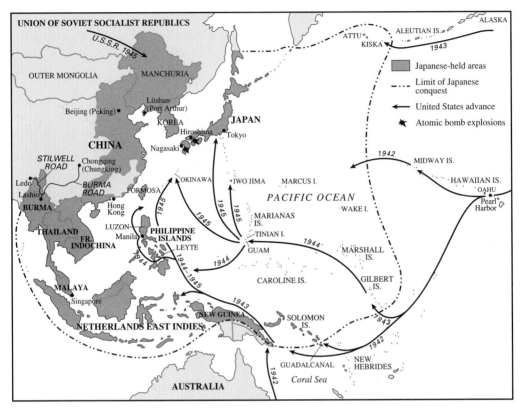

Map 1.2
The Pacific War

little to enhance their industrial or economic power. This fact, more than any other, ensured American supremacy after 1945. Among the warring powers, the United States had made the smallest human sacrifice—about 400,000 dead, compared to a worldwide total approaching 50 million—and had gained the most. Russian civilian deaths during the three-year siege of Leningrad—just one city—exceeded the total number of military deaths sustained by the United States. The United States emerged from the war with the world's strongest economy and armed forces, as well as a monopoly on atomic power. When the killing stopped, the United States, with only 6 percent of the world's population, produced half the world's goods. This relative level of power and economic well-being was not surpassed in the subsequent half-century. As one contemporary noted, "[W]hile the rest of the world came out bruised and scarred and nearly destroyed, we came out with the most unbelievable machinery, trade, manpower, and money."

War on the Home Front

The war years brought most New Deal social programs to a halt. Even though the New Deal was gone, the war itself acted as a catalyst for far-reaching social and economic change. In 1941, the United States still had many characteristics of a rural and small-town society. Of 132 million Americans, only about 74 million lived in cities with more than 10,000 inhabitants. About one-third of dwelling units lacked indoor plumbing, and two-thirds lacked central heating. Only 40 percent of adults had an eighth-grade education. One-fourth had graduated from high school; one-tenth had attended college, and only half of these had completed a college degree. Over half of all wage-earning men and three-fourths of wage-earning women earned $1,000 per year or less. In January 1941, about 9 million workers, or 15 percent of the labor force, still had no job. Private investment stood 18 percent below the 1929 level. The gross national product (GNP) barely surpassed the 1929 figure.

All of this changed dramatically during the war years. Unemployment almost disappeared, and ordinary Americans felt the shadow of the Great Depression finally lift from their lives. Private investment quickly surpassed the 1929 level and then continued to soar. GNP swelled from a prewar level of $90 billion per year to over $212 billion in 1945. Mass population shifts occurred as millions of Americans moved to cities. By the end of the war, the United States had taken a giant leap from its lingering small-town past toward the urbanized, high-tech present.

The most obvious economic effect of the war was the surge in federal spending. The Lend-Lease program alone, which cost a total of $50 billion during the war years, was an enormous sum compared to the total federal budget of $9 billion in 1939. The annual federal budget increased tenfold, to more than $95 billion, between 1939 and 1945. Not surprisingly, this budget increase led to a rapid rise in the national debt, despite efforts to fund a significant proportion of war costs through increased taxes.

In addition to raising money, the government had to mobilize U.S. industry for war. For this task, Roosevelt turned to the business executives he had once denounced as selfish plutocrats. Thousands of corporate executives agreed to guide the national economy; they were called "dollar-a-year men" because they kept their business salaries and received only a token payment from the government. These "war lords of Washington," as one critic called them, exercised unprecedented control over the national economy by deciding what should be built, where, and by whom.

Corporations were initially reluctant to invest the huge amounts of money needed to convert from civilian to military production. For example, it would cost General Motors a fortune to retool plants to produce tanks and jeeps instead of cars. Who would pay for conversion (and reconversion when the war ended), and how could profits be guaranteed? Should private businesses invest in costly, experimental technology that might have no peacetime application? To encourage industrial production, the Justice Department relaxed antitrust enforcement. Washington offered manufacturers the innovative "cost plus a fixed fee" contract whereby the federal government paid research and production costs and purchased items at a guaranteed markup. As a result, corporate after-tax profits swelled from $6.4 billion in 1940 to $10.8 billion in 1944.

Defense mobilization led to other innovations. Before 1941, the federal government spent little on scientific research. By 1945, Washington funneled $1.5 billion annually into research and development, not counting the $2 billion spent on atomic bomb research and the billions more used to construct plants to manufacture steel, synthetic rubber and other products. Radar, electronic computers, jet engines, synthetic fibers, wonder drugs like sulfas and penicillin, nuclear weapons, napalm, and ballistic missiles were all products of wartime research. The government used the war to justify experiments on American citizens, including injecting unwitting people with radioactive substances as part of the research connected to the Manhattan Project.

The War Department's Office of Scientific Research and Development (OSRD) poured $2 billion into the vast, highly secret atomic bomb project. In three new "atomic cities"—Oak Ridge, Tennessee; Hanford, Washington; and Los Alamos, New Mexico—nearly 150,000 people conducted research, refined uranium, and produced weapons. The facilities rivaled the entire automobile industry in size. In 1950, Congress created the National Science Foundation to institutionalize its basic research, especially research related to defense.

Overall, the administration's policies spurred military production that was little short of miraculous. In recognition of the importance of industrial output to Allied victory, Soviet leader Joseph Stalin once toasted Roosevelt by remarking that "Detroit was winning the war." Aircraft plants, which had produced barely 2,000 planes a year before the war, turned out nearly 100,000 in 1944. By 1945, American industry had produced over 100,000 tanks, 87,000 ships of all types, 2.5 million trucks, 5 million tons of bombs, and 44 billion rounds of ammunition. As a result, Allied soldiers had a three-to-one advantage in arms over their Axis enemies. A story was told at the time of a ship christening at which a woman at dockside was handed a bottle of champagne to do the honors. "But where is the ship?" she asked. "Just start swinging, lady," a worker remarked. "We'll have the ship there in time."

On the negative side, the war production gave birth to what later critics, including President Dwight D. Eisenhower, would call the military-industrial complex. In 1940, the hundred largest American companies produced only 30 percent of the goods manufactured in the United States. But wartime spending on high technology benefited large firms more than small ones. By 1945, the "Big 100" American companies produced 70 percent of the country's defense output, and the ten largest corporations accounted for nearly one-third of all war production. The close relationship between the military and large defense contractors would continue after the war, and the economic health of many U.S. communities would depend on military appropriations.

As big business prospered during the war years, so did its traditional antagonists, the labor unions. For both patriotic and practical reasons, most labor leaders worked closely with government and business leaders. Buoyed by rising wages, most major unions took a no-strike pledge during the war, and this willingness to cooperate enhanced their emerging role as part of the economic and political establishment. Among factory workers, union membership increased dramatically, from 10.5 million in 1941 to 15 million in 1945. This number represented one-third of the nonfarm work force and the all-time peak of union membership.

At first, the combination of defense spending, full employment, and shortages of civilian goods fueled inflation. Agencies like the National War Labor Board and the Office of Price Administration imposed various wage and price controls, along with rationing. Consumers needed ration coupons to buy items like gasoline, meat, and sugar. Children were encouraged to collect old cans, tires, and fat, which could be recycled into war goods. City dwellers cultivated millions of tiny victory gardens to supplement their diet.

While ordinary people conserved sugar and saved cans, a remarkable process was occurring. The war years brought about the most dramatic rise in income for working Americans in the twentieth century. With adjustment for inflation, real factory wages rose from $24 to near $37 per week during the war, largely because the greatest growth in employment occurred in unionized, high-wage manufacturing jobs. The share of the national wealth held by the richest 5 percent of Americans declined from 23.7 percent to 16.8 percent. The number of families with an annual income below $2,000 fell by half, while the number with annual incomes over $5,000 increased fourfold.

In addition to its economic impact, the war had a dramatic effect on where Americans lived and worked (see Map 1.3). The most obvious change was the fact that 16 million men and 250,000 women entered military service between 1941 and 1945. Almost all eligible men between the ages of eighteen and thirty-five served in the armed forces. Over 12 percent of the total American population spent time in uniform. Many GIs were sent to parts of the country they had never seen before, and often they liked what they saw. The military thus broke down regional barriers.

An upheaval among civilians also took place. Six million rural Americans headed for war work in the cities, while as many urban residents moved to jobs in new cities. Many of the migrants were African Americans who left the states of the old Confederacy in the South for jobs in the North and West. With shipbuilding, aircraft manufacturing, and other war industries concentrated on the east and west coasts and in the upper Midwest, these areas grew rapidly. Many cities, however, could not readily absorb such rapid increases in population, which led to severe overcrowding caused by housing shortages. As white officials, realtors, and residents sought to retain prewar patterns of segregation in housing, racial conflicts increased and African Americans faced extreme overcrowding and neighborhood deterioration. The federal government's housing program for war workers built few projects for blacks.

The Sunbelt—the warm states of the South and Southwest—began its rise during the war years. Not only war workers but tens of thousands of military personnel migrated to cities in the West—like San Diego, Los Angeles, and Seattle—and decided to remain there as permanent residents. California's population grew by over one-third during the war, when 2 million people came from the South and from rural areas to work in the aircraft and

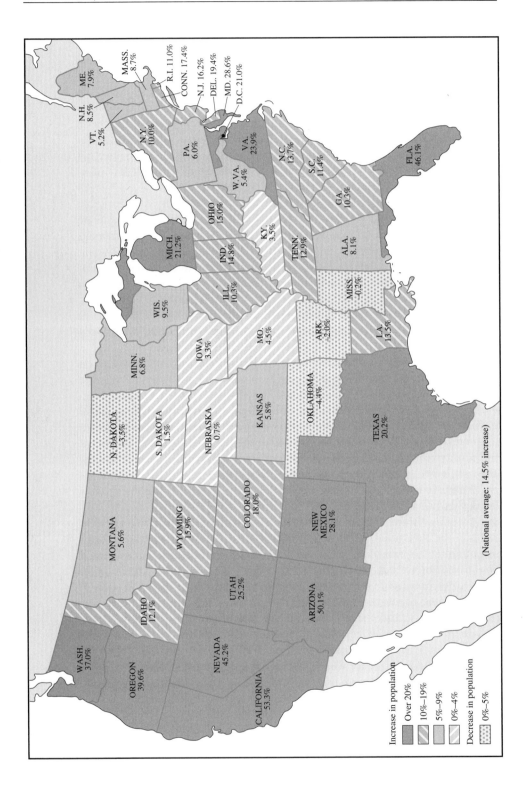

MASS. 8.7%
R.I. 11.0%
CONN. 17.4%
N.J. 16.2%
DEL. 19.4%
MD. 28.6%
D.C. 21.0%

ME. 7.9%
N.H. 8.5%
VT. 5.2%
N.Y. 10.0%
PA. 6.0%
VA. 23.9%
N.C. 13.7%
S.C. 11.4%
FLA. 46.1%

W.VA. 5.4%
OHIO 15.0%
KY. 3.5%
TENN. 12.9%
GA. 10.3%
ALA. 8.1%

MICH. 21.2%
IND. 14.8%
ILL. 10.3%
MISS. -0.2%

WIS. 9.5%
IOWA 3.3%
MO. 4.5%
ARK. -2.0%
LA. 13.5%

MINN. 6.8%
OKLAHOMA -4.4%
TEXAS 20.2%

N. DAKOTA -3.5%
S. DAKOTA 1.5%
NEBRASKA 0.7%
KANSAS 5.8%

MONTANA 5.6%
WYOMING 15.9%
COLORADO 18.0%
NEW MEXICO 28.1%

IDAHO 12.1%
UTAH 25.2%
ARIZONA 50.1%

WASH. 37.0%
OREGON 39.6%
NEVADA 45.2%
CALIFORNIA 53.3%

(National average: 14.5% increase)

Increase in population
Over 20%
10%–19%
5%–9%
0%–4%
Decrease in population
0%–5%

shipbuilding industries. The population of the West grew by 40 percent between 1940 and 1950, with much of that explosive growth a direct result of the war.

Women's roles changed dramatically during the war, too, even though gender-based inequality remained deeply ingrained. In 1940, about 27 percent of all women worked outside the home, but only 15 percent of married women did so. Most women in the labor force held low-paying jobs in light manufacturing, service, and clerical areas. Employers justified the exclusion of women from many occupations on the basis of stereotypes about women workers, including the belief that they could not handle work that was technical, physically arduous, or managerial.

With the wartime labor shortage came a shift in public policy and private attitudes toward women in the labor force. Women were encouraged to work and to take jobs traditionally held by men—at least for the time being. A War Department pamphlet put it succinctly: "A women is a substitute—like plastic instead of metal." The Office of War Information (OWI), an agency that produced radio plays, films, and posters in an attempt to mold public attitudes, added its encouragement for women to join the work force. Such appeals swayed public opinion. Before the war, 80 percent of surveyed Americans opposed wives working outside the home; in 1942, 80 percent approved.

By 1945, over 6 million additional women, including 4 million who had been housewives before the war, had entered the industrial work force and accounted for one-third of the total. They worked as riveters, welders, assembly line workers, aircraft fabricators, and in numerous other positions previously held only by men. Steelyards, shipyards, and aircraft plants employed almost no women before 1942, but three years later women made up as much as 40 percent of the work force in key defense plants. Despite the persistence of racism in employment, African American women contributed to the trend, entering manufacturing and clerical work in significant numbers for the first time.

Despite the wartime labor shortage, women were often assigned to gender-segregated tasks, received lower wages than men for the same work, and found few support services such as daycare for children. In a few cases, social workers discovered babies sleeping in cars outside defense plants because their working mothers had nowhere else to leave them. Business and political leaders offered various rationalizations for denying women equal pay and access to daycare. Women were encouraged to think of factory work as a temporary expedient, to keep their sights on the home, and to be prepared to resume the roles of housewife and mother when the war ended.

Many of these women, however, had different expectations. Surveys by the Labor Department found that, although many women resented unequal pay and sexual harassment on the job, they found the new opportunities and

◀ **Map 1.3**
Americans on the Move During the 1940s

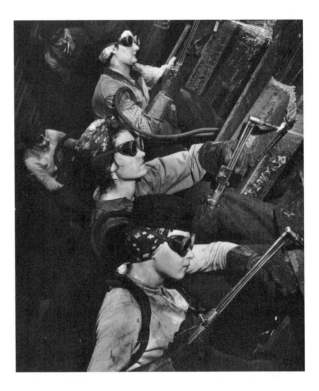

Women welders at a Gary, Indiana, steel plant prepare armor plating for tanks. / Margaret Bourke-White, © Life Magazine, Time Inc.

responsibilities exciting. Women enjoyed spending and saving their higher earnings, valued the independence and self-confidence that came with earning an income, and liked acquiring new skills. Most employed women hoped to continue working when peace returned—but they did so, as we will see in Chapter 3, under changed rules. Some men found the wartime changes unsettling. Max Lerner, a popular columnist, voiced a common male complaint that war work had created a "new Amazon" who could "outdrink, outswear, and outswagger the men."

When they sought defense work, women of color faced additional obstacles stemming from racist treatment by management and coworkers. In the Southwest, Mexican American women achieved their greatest access to defense jobs in the aircraft industry of southern California. Elsewhere in the region, discrimination confined most to service work and traditional industrial work, especially in garment production. Similarly, Native American women left reservations in large numbers but found jobs primarily in service work. African American women entered defense work in large numbers mostly outside the South and did so in part as a result of their own activism. When denied defense work, they held protests at plant gates, worked with civil rights organizations and unions to combat discrimination, and filed complaints with the federal government.

As men entered military service, women's responsibilities increased in many ways beyond that of wage earner. Women became the center of family life as never before. They also assumed responsibility for critical unpaid work in service to the wartime state. They served as Red Cross nurses, canteen volunteers, and actresses on tours sponsored by the United Service Organizations (USO). These contributions were celebrated in films like *Stage Door Canteen*, the tale of three USO hostesses who struck up romances with soldiers on leave. Hollywood's romanticized images of women's unpaid work notwithstanding, most women discovered that their domestic labor was more difficult and time-consuming as a result of consumer shortages, overcrowded housing, the need to do volunteer work for the war effort, and inadequacies in public services.

The war also fostered important changes in race relations because minority communities' dissatisfaction with the pace of change increased. The United States was fighting enemies who proclaimed the right to enslave or exterminate "inferior" races. Presumably, American citizens were united in detesting such hateful ideologies. Yet minorities in the United States and in the armed forces still faced discrimination and abuse. Law and tradition segregated them in school, at the workplace, and in numerous aspects of social life.

In 1941, as defense orders poured into factories, African American leaders expressed outrage that employment on military production lines opened new opportunities almost exclusively for white workers. A. Philip Randolph, head of the Brotherhood of Sleeping Car Porters, a union composed mostly of African Americans, challenged racial economic discrimination directly. That spring, he announced plans for a mass march on Washington to demand equal employment rights.

To avert a racially explosive protest march, Roosevelt issued Executive Order no. 8802, which created a presidential Fair Employment Practices Committee (FEPC) to investigate complaints of discrimination in the defense industry. Even though the FEPC lacked enforcement power, it pressed formerly segregated industries to hire about 600,000 additional African American workers by 1945. The lure of these new jobs contributed to the migration of about 2 million African Americans from the South to other regions during the 1940s.

African American leaders supported the war effort, seeking what they called a double victory—a victory over Nazi racism abroad and discrimination at home. The NAACP urged its members to "persuade, embarrass, compel, and shame" the federal government into acting against racism. Migration, employment in industry, and military service created a strengthened desire among African Americans for the full rights of citizenship long denied them. Higher wages and the wartime activism of African American women in particular also led to tremendous growth in the membership of the NAACP. Nevertheless, segregation and racism remained the norm, both in the military and in civilian life, during and after the war.

Ironically, the shared experience of war helped remove old ethnic barriers between whites. On the battlefields and in the canteens, white Americans from various ethnic and religious backgrounds mingled and got to know one another. But the black-white barrier was much harder to crack. Although the military drafted 1 million African Americans, it segregated them and placed most of them in menial positions such as cook, driver, or laborer. The Red Cross maintained segregated blood banks. African American troops were often stationed in the South and commanded by Southern white officers who treated them harshly.

Still, African American soldiers pressed ceaselessly for greater responsibilities and often challenged the racism they encountered in the military and in the communities adjacent to military bases. For example, a young lieutenant named Jackie Robinson—who would later become the first black player in major league baseball—refused to sit in the segregated section of a bus. He was court-martialed for his defiance, but he successfully defended himself and the charge was dismissed. Although his rebellion was not at all unusual, he was fortunate in his treatment. Throughout the war years, hostile white communities responded to the concentration of large numbers of black soldiers in their area with limitations on the soldiers' access to off-base recreation and freedom of movement. When they fought back against racist treatment, black soldiers faced violence at the hands of military and civilian police, which often led to bloody encounters that sometimes involved people from local African American communities. As General Benjamin Davis, the highest ranking black army officer, noted, "[M]ilitary training does not develop a spirit of cheerful acceptance of Jim-Crow laws and customs." Unwilling to desegregate the military, the War Department responded with more on-base recreation for African Americans and better training for military police. Ultimately, only the transfer of large numbers of black troops to combat areas abroad reduced the military's racial tensions.

At home, African American anxieties were confirmed by several violent wartime race riots, most notably in Detroit in 1942 and in Harlem in 1943. In Detroit, a black-white fight at a park sparked the riot; in Harlem, the violence started with the shooting of a black soldier by a policeman. White resentment of blacks seeking homes in white-only neighborhoods and applying for factory jobs previously reserved for whites contributed to the intensity of these conflicts.

In spite of such outbreaks of racial hatred, the war years generally had a positive effect on the struggle for equality and civil rights largely because war occasioned shifts in the consciousness and political mobilization of people of color. Military service, even in a segregated system, brought soldiers from minority communities a certain sense of empowerment. New employment opportunities, exposure to the world outside the rural South and Southwest, migration to new places, and growing membership in civil rights organizations also gave a tremendous boost to people of color. The wartime generation was unwilling to suffer silently in the face of discrimination; both their militancy and their expectations were on the rise. These people and their children would play a critical role in the postwar challenge to segregation.

Mexican immigrants and Mexican Americans also experienced hardship during the war. Since the early twentieth century, Mexicans had migrated in large numbers to the United States. After 1941, as large numbers of agricultural workers entered the armed services or sought more lucrative defense work, farm managers experienced severe labor shortages. In 1942, the federal government negotiated a contract labor program with Mexican authorities that continued, in various forms, until 1964. Under this so-called *bracero* (laborer) program, the U.S. government promised to supervise the recruitment, transportation, and working conditions of large groups of Mexican farm workers. During the war, this agreement brought in about 1.75 million farm and railroad laborers. However, the proposed supervision of working conditions was incredibly lax, *braceros* were paid as little as 35 cents per day (despite a mandated minimum wage of 30 cents an hour), and many lived under miserable conditions. The program did not stem the continued migration of many undocumented workers during and after the war.

The nearly 2.7 million Mexican Americans faced additional problems. Living mostly in the Southwest, they were confronted with segregation in schools, housing, and employment. New social tensions flared in communities such as Los Angeles, where rapid growth inflamed latent racism. Mexican American youth gangs members dressed in flamboyant clothes called zoot suits. They were frequently harassed by the police and by white servicemen, who often cruised the barrios in search of zootsuiters and attacked and humiliated them by stripping off their clothes. Police often charged the zootsuiters instead of the servicemen with disturbing the peace. To many Chicanos, the distinctive clothing was a way to assert their ethnic identity and to flout white culture.

The tensions exploded in June 1943, when hundreds of sailors and marines went on a several-day rampage, attacking Mexican Americans, African Americans, and Filipinos in East Los Angeles. Because local police participated in the attacks, military police were needed to quell the riot. The *Los Angeles Times* reported the incidents with headlines such as "Zoot-Suiters Learn Lesson in Fight with Servicemen." When Eleanor Roosevelt suggested that long-standing discrimination against Mexican Americans might have provoked the riots, the paper accused her of promoting racial discord.

The consequences of racism were, of course, nowhere more savage during the war than they were for European Jews. The Holocaust was a tragedy the United States did little to avert. In November 1938, after the German government had stripped German Jews of most civil and economic rights, Nazi mobs attacked Jewish businesses, synagogues, and homes, smashing and looting in an orgy that quickly became known as *Kristallnacht*, or Night of the Broken Glass. Shortly after that incident, German police sent 20,000 Jews to concentration camps, which later became the sites of mass extermination. Roosevelt remarked that he could "scarcely believe that such things could occur in a twentieth-century civilization." As the Nazis conquered Eastern Europe, the murder escalated.

European Jews who attempted to flee confronted legal barriers everywhere. Since 1924, the United States' National Origins Act had restricted nearly all immigration from Eastern and southern Europe. Even Jews who qualified under the unfilled German quota faced a maze of bureaucratic red tape that made it nearly impossible to obtain an entry visa.

Fear of competition for scarce jobs added to anti-Semitism in the United States, creating little sympathy for, and much agitation against, the immigration of even token numbers of Jewish refugees. Roosevelt, who worked closely with many Jewish advisers, was already the target of anti-Semitic remarks. Bowing to this pressure, he allowed the State Department to place impediments in the path of would-be immigrants seeking sanctuary.

Evidence surfaced in 1942 and 1943 that the Nazis planned to exterminate millions of Jews with poison gas. Yet even after the plans became known, U.S. and British strategists rejected the idea of bombing the death camps and the rail lines leading into them. Such diversions from more important missions, Allied leaders argued, would delay victory. Congress rebuffed efforts to allow Jewish children into the United States. American officials even opposed granting temporary refuge to the few thousand European Jews who had slipped away from Nazi control.

In 1944, Roosevelt finally created a War Refugee Board to establish camps in neutral countries and U.S.-occupied territory overseas. These centers eventually helped save the lives of a few hundred thousand refugees. Only 1,000

The liberation of the Bergen-Belsen concentration camp— Americans confront the Holocaust. / Imperial War Museum

refugees were admitted directly into the United States. As one scholar wrote, "Franklin Roosevelt's indifference to so momentous an historical event as the systematic annihilation of European Jewry emerges as the worst failure of his presidency."

Roosevelt's failure to champion the cause of Jewish refugees must be seen in light of the strong anti-Semitism in American culture. An opinion poll taken in 1942 found that many U.S. citizens believed that Jews posed nearly as great a threat to national security as did Germany and Japan. Leaders of the American Jewish community anguished over the horrors of Nazi persecution but feared a backlash among Christian Americans if they spoke out forcefully. As a result, most Jewish organizations refrained from pressing politicians to rescue Holocaust victims. Instead, they called for creating a Jewish homeland in Palestine for those lucky enough to survive.

Meanwhile, the Japanese American community was singled out for special persecution in the United States. Not only was Japan a wartime enemy, but the United States also had a century-long tradition of anti-Asian agitation and hysteria. The surprise attack on Pearl Harbor, followed by Japan's initial victories in the Pacific, spurred exaggerated fears that Japanese Americans would conspire to aid the enemy. Although almost no members of the Japanese American community committed sabotage or illegal acts before or after 1941, their mere existence aroused public hysteria. Journalists such as Westbrook Pegler demanded that every Japanese man, woman, and child be placed under armed guard. Congressman Leland Ford of California insisted that any "patriotic native-born Japanese, if he wants to make his contribution, will submit himself to a concentration camp." General John DeWitt, head of the Western Defense Command, declared that Japanese of any citizenship were enemies. A popular song was entitled "We're Gonna Find a Feller Who Is Yeller and Beat Him Red, White, and Blue."

In February 1942, President Roosevelt issued Executive order no. 9066, which was quickly backed by Congress. The order declared that parts of the country were "military areas" from which any or all persons could be barred. Nearly every politician in the West applauded the move. Although the regulations also targeted German and Italian aliens (most Italians were later exempted), all persons of Japanese ancestry, regardless of their citizenship, were affected. In May, the War Relocation Authority ordered 112,000 Japanese to leave the West Coast in a matter of days. In Hawaii, unlike California, the dangers of a Japanese invasion were much more real, but residents of Japanese descent made up such a large portion of the Hawaiian population and were so vital to the economy that only a few individuals were interned.

Nearly all those affected by the forced relocation orders complied without protest, abandoning their homes, farms, and personal property to speculators. Bleak internment camps were hastily established in several Western states. While not equivalent to incarceration in the Nazi death camps, this mass imprisonment marked the greatest violation of civil liberties in wartime America.

Japanese American families at the Manzanar War Relocation Center in California line up for "mess call." / AP/Wide World

Families lived in rudimentary dwellings and were compelled to do menial work under armed guard.

In 1944, the Supreme Court addressed the policy of forced relocation in a case against Fred Korematsu, a citizen who had refused to leave a designated war zone on the West Coast. The Court's decision in *Korematsu* v. *United States* affirmed the government's right to exclude individuals from any designated area on the basis of military necessity. The majority claimed that the defendant's race was irrelevant because the government could, if it chose, exclude groups besides those of Japanese ancestry. In a powerful dissent, Justice Frank Murphy denounced the *Korematsu* verdict as a "legalization of racism" based on prejudice and unproven fears.

Despite the restrictive relocation orders and the degradation of life in the internment camps, Japanese Americans contributed significantly to the U.S. war effort. Many male internees volunteered for military duty and served in Europe, achieving recognition for their bravery in action. Others worked in the Pacific theater as translators, interpreters, or intelligence officers. A few Japanese American men chose to resist the draft, declaring that they would not assume the obligations of citizenship until they had been given their full rights as citizens. As the war progressed, some internees were permitted to leave the relocation camps if they agreed to settle in eastern states. By the summer of 1945, all could leave. A fortunate few found that friends had protected their homes or businesses; the rest lost the work of a lifetime.

Despite growing recognition that internment had been a grave error, Congress and the courts hesitated to make formal redress. Congress offered a token payment in 1948, but it was not until the 1980s that several Japanese Americans convicted of wartime offenses successfully reopened their cases. Files from the Justice Department and the Federal Bureau of Investigation revealed that prosecutors had withheld evidence showing that no danger existed to justify relocation. Congress then made a formal apology and offered compensation of about $20,000 per surviving internee.

Wartime Politics

As the wartime economic boom gradually erased memories of the Great Depression, many Americans felt that the reform programs of the New Deal no longer mattered. The 1942 congressional elections increased the number of seats held by Republicans and conservative southern Democrats. The new Congress proceeded to end several New Deal agencies, including the WPA and the CCC.

The president's chief of mobilization, James F. Byrnes, gloated that the war had helped elbow the "radical boys out of the way [and] more will go." His prediction proved accurate, and nervous Democratic Party leaders blamed electoral losses on the left-leaning vice president, Henry A. Wallace. Unlike his more cautious boss, Wallace actively promoted civil rights and had called for postwar economic intervention by the government. Witnessing Roosevelt's obvious physical decline, the party barons feared that Wallace might assume the presidency after Roosevelt's death or retirement. Bowing to their complaints, in mid-1944 Roosevelt agreed to replace Wallace with Senator Harry S Truman, a moderate from Missouri. The Democratic candidates faced a Republican ticket headed by New York Governor Thomas E. Dewey. Roosevelt won easily, though by his smallest majority yet (53.4 percent). He got significant assistance from organized labor, which created the first political action committee, or PAC, to raise campaign funds.

Despite the political challenges and his own concentration on winning the war, Roosevelt made some effort in his last years to impart a vision for postwar reform. In his 1944 State of the Union address, he called for drafting a "second Bill-of-Rights under which a new basis of security and prosperity can be established for all." He described a government committed to providing jobs, housing, education, and health and retirement insurance for all Americans.

In a draft speech dictated on April 11, 1945, and as victory in Europe loomed, Roosevelt appealed to the American people to "conquer the fears, the ignorance and the greed" that made the horror of world war possible. But the next day, April 12, the president died of a cerebral hemorrhage. Roosevelt's death and the imminent victory over the Axis forces marked the threshold of the postwar era.

Conclusion

The Roosevelt years, stretching from the Great Depression to the last months of World War II, brought vast changes to the nation and increased its role on the world stage. Those years molded the postwar world in fundamental ways that continue to affect us today.

Both the Depression and the war prompted rapid growth in the federal government's size and scope of action. For the first time in the nation's history, the U.S. government had a direct and frequent effect on the daily lives of ordinary citizens. The government managed the economy to an unprecedented degree. It began to provide relief to the needy and the elderly, but it did so within the limits imposed by an economy that discriminated against white women and people of color. It funded scientific research that changed U.S. industry and made possible the high-tech society in which we now live.

The Great Depression and the war put Americans on the move, literally as well as figuratively. During the war, millions of rural and small-town Americans packed their bags and headed to the major industrial cities. African Americans left the rural South in huge numbers, many making their new homes in the North and West. The *bracero* program, and the high level of immigration by undocumented workers that accompanied it, contributed to a substantial influx of Mexican workers. The Sunbelt and the West Coast began their rise to prominence.

For women, the years of the Depression and war meant the continuation of labor discrimination and of the idea that women's identities and work should be particularly focused on home and family. The war tested those patterns, however, giving women a chance to take jobs traditionally reserved for men and to demonstrate their capacity for work in heavy industry. This change constituted a first step toward the revolution in women's lives that is still occurring today. For ethnic minorities, these years were times of mingled hope, fear, and disappointment. The wartime internment of Japanese Americans left a blot on the nation's record that no later compensation could remove. The government's failure to help European Jews escape the Holocaust seemed almost incomprehensible to later generations. Yet the Roosevelt era also brought a rising concern for the rights of minorities and new hopes that protest could lead to improvement—crucial ingredients for the civil rights movement of the postwar years.

The generation dubbed America's "greatest" by journalist Tom Brokaw thus left a mixed legacy for the future. Its economic reforms and assistance programs saved capitalism in the United States, while leaving those Americans most vulnerable to private-sector discrimination—people of color and white women—outside its most important protections. Those reforms owed as much to the pressures provided by grassroots activists as to the political capacities of politicians in Washington. The military victory in World War II was hardly won single-handedly by the United States, which relied heavily on its Allies to carry the burden before it entered the war and to bear the brunt of the fighting in Europe throughout the war. The most important military contributions provided by the United States were its industrial production and technical advances in warfare, most notably the development of nuclear weapons.

Finally, as a direct consequence of the war, the United States emerged in 1945 as the world's leading military and economic power. Europe was devastated. The Soviet Union, though a mighty wartime ally and future competitor, had suffered terrible losses. In the postwar world, the history of the United States would be shaped by its demanding new role as a superpower and by the conflicting ideas of it citizens about how that role should be played.

F U R T H E R • R E A D I N G

On the Depression and New Deal, see Michael A. Bernstein, *The Great Depression: Delayed Recovery and Economic Change in America, 1929–1939* (1988); Anthony J. Badger, *The New Deal: The Depression Years, 1933–40* (1980); William E. Leuchtenberg, *Franklin D. Roosevelt and the New Deal* (1963); Kenneth S. Davis, *FDR: The New Deal Years, 1933–1937* (1986); Suzanne Mettler, *Dividing Citizens: Gender and Federalism in New Deal Public Policy* (1998); Alan Brinkley, *Voices of Protest: Huey Long, Father Coughlin, and the Great Depression* (1982); Harvard Sitkoff, *A New Deal for Blacks* (1978); James N. Gregory, *American Exodus: The Dust Bowl Migration and Okie Culture in California* (1989); Lizabeth Cohen, *Making a New Deal: Industrial Workers in Chicago, 1919–1939* (1991); Susan Ware, *Holding Their Own: American Women in the 1930s* (1982); Steven Fraser, *Labor Will Rule: Sidney Hillman and the Rise of American Labor* (1991); Steve Fraser and Gary Gerstle, eds., *The Rise and Fall of the New Deal Order, 1930–1980* (1989). **On American society during World War II,** see Doris Kearns Goodwin, *No Ordinary Time: Franklin and Eleanor Roosevelt: The Home Front During WWII* (1994); Daniel Kryder, *Divided Arsenal* (2000); John M. Blum, *V Was for Victory: Politics and American Culture during World War II* (1976); Karen Anderson, *Wartime Women (1981);* Susan Hartmann, *The Homefront and Beyond* (1980); Peter Irons, *Justice at War: The Story of the Japanese-American Internment Cases* (1982); Roger Daniels, *Prisoners Without Trial* (1993); Gerald D. Nash, *The American West Transformed: The Impact of the Second World War* (1985); Studs Terkel, *"The Good War": An Oral History of World War II* (1984). **On military strategy and foreign policy,** see Robert Dallek, *Franklin D. Roosevelt and American Foreign Policy* (1979); Warren Kimball, *The Juggler: Franklin D. Roosevelt as Wartime Statesman* (1991); Russell D. Buhite, *Decisions at Yalta* (1986); David Wyman, *The Abandonment of the Jews: America and the Holocaust, 1941–45* (1984); Michael Sherry, *The Rise of American Air Power* (1987); John Dower, *War Without Mercy: Race and Power in the Pacific War* (1986); Martin J. Sherwin, *A World Destroyed: The Atomic Bomb and the Grand Alliance* (1975); Michael C. C. Adams, *The Best War Ever: America and World War II* (1994); William O'Neill, *A Democracy at War: America's Fight at Home and Abroad in W.W. II* (1993). **On broadcast journalism,** see A. M. Sperber, *Murrow: His Life and Times* (1998); Steven M. Barkin, *American Television News: The Media Marketplace and the Public Interest* (2003); Leonard Downey, Jr., and Robert J. Kaiser, *The News About the News: American Journalism in Peril* (2002); Eric Alterman, *Sound and Fury: The Triumph of the Punditocracy* (2002), and *What Liberal Media? The Truth About Bias and the News* (2003).

2

From Atomic War to Cold War: Victory and Containment at Home and Abroad, 1945–1952

The death of a city and the birth of a symbol: Atomic bomb destroys Nagasaki, Japan, August 9, 1945. / © CORBIS

J ack Short of Poughkeepsie, New York, was barely twenty years old when he landed in France soon after D-Day in June 1944. Over the next ten months, the men in his unit raced toward Berlin, pushing the German army back across the Rhine. On the eve of the Nazi surrender in May 1945, Short and his comrades came upon a concentration camp at Nordhausen, Germany. The bodies of the dead and dying, he recalled, were "stacked up like cordwood." Decades later, he sometimes reviewed the photographs he took that day as a testament to the horrors he encountered.

In spite of this painful memory, Jack Short told interviewer Studs Terkel how the war had actually improved his life. Born into a working-class family, all Short's relatives worked in factories. None had ever gone beyond high school. But after three years in the military and meeting people from different backgrounds, Jack aspired to more. Almost miraculously, the government's new GI Bill helped turn his dream into reality. "It paid for 99 percent of your college expenses and gave you money each month to live on," the veteran explained. In 1950, Jack Short became the first of his family to graduate from college, and he took a job with the emerging computer giant, IBM. "Everything in my life since the war," he believed, "has been positive."

World War II transformed Jack Short's life and the lives of most Americans, whether or not they served in the military. Although no one intended or expected it, the most destructive, human-caused event in history revitalized the nation's economy and propelled it into the position of the world's leading power. The year 1945 would also witness the death of Franklin Roosevelt, the birth of the nuclear age, and the beginning of the so-called Cold War that defined international relations for the next half century.

Truman Takes Charge and Prepares for the First Atomic War

On April 12, 1945, Vice President Harry S Truman relaxed with congressional friends in the office of House Speaker Sam Rayburn. After chairing a tedious Senate debate on a water treaty, the vice president savored a stiff bourbon. Abruptly, a phone call from presidential press secretary Steve Early summoned him to the White House. There, Eleanor Roosevelt delivered a somber greeting: "Harry, the president is dead." Truman asked if there was anything he could do for her. "Is there anything we can do for you?" she replied; "you are the one in trouble now."

Since 1933, Franklin D. Roosevelt had dominated public life in America. To millions of working men and women, he personified their restoration of faith in democracy and capitalism; he steered the country through the shoals of depression and war, only to be struck down cruelly on the threshold of victory over evil. Even those who resented Roosevelt's political accomplishments, especially his expansion of the power of the federal government, recognized him as a giant whose passing left a void in American public life. An ordinary soldier spoke for millions when he remarked, "America will seem a strange place without his voice, talking to the people when great events happen." Nearly everyone recognized that FDR was a tough act to follow.

Truman, a former haberdasher, county judge, and senator and widely disparaged as a political nobody, was suddenly in charge of concluding the war, preserving the Grand Alliance, converting the war economy to peacetime production, and nurturing the liberal goals of a still unfulfilled New Deal. Organized labor, ethnic Americans, racial minorities, and women hoped to expand the vistas of opportunity partially opened to them by Franklin Roosevelt. Business interests and conservatives in both the Democratic and Republican parties celebrated Roosevelt's passing as a chance to reassert their traditional power over society.

The new president came from a modest farming family near Independence, Missouri. During World War I, he commanded an artillery battery in Europe. After the armistice, he returned to Missouri, married Bess Wallace, and opened a clothing store in Kansas City. When the business failed, he turned to politics.

For most of the 1920s and early 1930s, Truman served as an elected judge in Jackson County, adjacent to the area controlled by "Boss" Tom Pendergast's corrupt Kansas City political machine. Despite his friendship with Pendergast, Truman earned a reputation for competence and honesty. In 1934, riding the early crest of Roosevelt's popularity, he won election to the U.S. Senate as a Democrat.

The future president's youthful social outlook mirrored the bigotry common in midwestern border states. "I think one man is just as good as another," he wrote his fiancé, "so long as he's honest, and decent, and not a nigger or a Chinaman." As a senator and president, he modified these views and expressed support for civil rights and liberties.

Truman left few footprints in the Senate before he achieved modest fame for investigating war profiteering. During the three months he served as vice president, he had little contact with Roosevelt. Either because he could not reckon with his own mortality or because he had a low regard for Truman, Roosevelt had kept his deputy in the dark about the development of the atomic bomb, the growing strains among the Allies, and his postwar plans. Truman resented the fact that he was surrounded by better-informed men reluctant to admit him into Franklin Roosevelt's inner circle. Commenting on the staff and cabinet he inherited, Truman lamented that there was not a "man on the list who would talk frankly." The "honest ones were afraid and the others wanted to fool me."

During his first year in the Oval Office, Truman pushed out nearly all Roosevelt's intimates, replacing many old New Dealers with advisers closely linked to big business and the military. Even though Truman later proposed several New Deal–style reform programs, many rank-and-file progressives considered him a lukewarm liberal. By the same token, Republicans and conservative Democrats criticized him as too liberal and shook the political tightrope on which he wobbled, hoping to make him tumble.

As Allied armies neared Berlin in April 1945, Truman had to respond rapidly to military and diplomatic problems he knew little about. In his determination to appear as a forceful leader, he sometimes made snap judgments. Just hours after taking office, for example, he asserted to aides that, unlike his former boss, he would "stand up to the Russians," implying that Roosevelt had been too easy on Stalin.

Several of Roosevelt's more anti-Soviet advisers, including ambassador to Moscow Averell Harriman, Secretary of the Navy James Forrestal, chief of staff Admiral William Leahy, and Undersecretary of State Joseph C. Grew encouraged Truman's suspicions of Stalin. All had urged Roosevelt to demand a larger role for non-Communists in the new governments of Poland and Eastern Europe. Truman accepted their advice more readily than his predecessor.

Following Roosevelt's death, Harriman had flown from Moscow to Washington to brief Truman on Soviet behavior. The ambassador blamed the tensions between the allies on Stalin's effort to expand the Soviet sphere in Eastern Europe, in violation of the Yalta accords. Harriman condemned the advance of Russian armies as a "barbarian invasion of Europe." Communism, he told Truman, confronted America with an ideological threat "just as vigorous and dangerous as Fascism or Nazism." Truman accepted at face value Harriman's warning that failure to resist Stalin would resemble the nearly fatal appeasement of Hitler in the 1930s.

On April 23, 1945, the president used what he called "words of one syllable" to accuse visiting Soviet foreign minister Vyacheslav M. Molotov of violating pledges to allow free elections in Poland. When the envoy complained about the president's language, Truman recalled that he gave Molotov a "straight one-two to the jaw," yelling, "[c]arry out your agreements, and you won't get talked to like that." In private, however, he wondered if he had done right.

Verbal fireworks had little impact on Soviet policy, in Poland or elsewhere. Stalin responded to Truman's charge of treaty violations with a blunt statement: "Poland borders with the Soviet Union," he observed, which "cannot be said of Great Britain or the United States." The Soviet dictator noted that just as the Western allies imposed friendly governments in areas they liberated from the Nazis, he would forge a security zone in Eastern Europe, even if it caused a rupture in the Grand Alliance. British Prime Minister Winston Churchill complained that Stalin had erected an "iron fence" (anticipating the term *iron curtain*) across Europe by installing brutal puppet regimes in Poland, Bulgaria, and Rumania—much as Hitler had done before him.

In the time-honored tradition of Russian czars, Stalin measured Soviet security by the weakness of neighboring states and the degree of control that Moscow exercised over them. Also, like most Russians, he really did fear a revived Germany and Japan. Because most Eastern Europeans resented Soviet pressure, they would, if allowed free elections, form governments that sought Western protection. This resentment further complicated matters and convinced Stalin that nothing short of total Soviet control could ensure that Eastern Europe remain a buffer against a revived Germany. By imposing harsh control over Eastern Europe, however, Stalin aroused the very hostility he feared from the capitalist West—including the eventual decision to rebuild western Germany and Japan. When Germany formally surrendered on May 8, 1945, the Allies partitioned Germany and its capital into occupation zones. No one yet knew whether these divisions would be temporary or permanent. The German problem became more complicated when the Soviet Union annexed a swath of land along the Soviet-Polish border and compensated Poland by grafting on to it a portion of eastern Germany. This swap moved the Soviet border closer to Central Europe. Meanwhile, the expulsion of ethnic Germans from Poland and Czechoslovakia in 1945 forced 11 million refugees into occupied Germany.

As the jockeying for power in Europe began, the conflict with Japan raged on. Despite American hopes and aid, Nationalist China under Jiang Jieshi (Chiang Kai-shek) contributed little to the war against Japan. Instead, U.S. navy, army, and marine forces fought their way across the Pacific, seizing islands from which to mount additional naval and air attacks. By early 1945, Japan was surrounded, cut off from its several million troops in China and Southeast Asia, running out of raw materials, and subject to relentless air attack. In March, for example, army air force planes launched incendiary raids on Tokyo, which killed over 100,000 civilians and burned much of the city. Japanese troops on islands close to the homeland, such as Iwo Jima and Okinawa, fought desperately, often using suicide *kamikaze* tactics to resist the Americans.

By the summer of 1945, Japan was defeated, but the militarists in power refused to surrender. They clung to the belief that by continuing to fight, they could win better terms of surrender. Although many civilian leaders wanted to negotiate a cease-fire, the Japanese emperor wavered. U.S. military planners dreaded the prospect of invading either China (where several million Japanese troops remained) or the Japanese home islands. They urged Roosevelt and then Truman to seek Soviet help, even if it meant that Stalin gained an Asian foothold.

Allied leaders held what proved to be their final wartime summit conference in mid-July 1945. Truman, Churchill, and Stalin met in Potsdam, the once opulent suburb of bombed-out Berlin. (Midway through the conference, voters in Britain tossed Churchill out of office and replaced him with Labor Party leader Clement Attlee. The new prime minister promised a better life for British workers but shared Churchill's strong anticommunist views.) Amid the rubble of what was to have been Hitler's Thousand-Year Reich, the "Big Three" spent nearly two weeks arguing over German and Polish boundaries, the make-up of eastern European governments, and reparations from Germany to the Soviet Union. Truman came to Potsdam hoping to get a renewed Soviet pledge to join the war soon against Japan. Stalin agreed to do so by mid-August.

On July 16, amidst these discussions, Truman received a coded message that an atomic bomb had been tested successfully at the Trinity site in New Mexico—a remote location near the Los Alamos laboratory. The news cheered Truman considerably because the new weapon might end the war quickly, thus saving American lives and reducing the Soviet role in the defeat of Japan. Truman casually mentioned to Stalin that American scientists had developed a powerful, new weapon. Although the term *atomic bomb* was not used, Stalin understood. His Western Allies had tried to keep the atomic project secret from him, but Soviet spies had learned about it and Stalin had already begun his own nuclear program. The Soviet leader's outward calm led Truman to gloat mistakenly that he had "fooled Mr. Russia."

At the conclusion of the conference, British and American officials issued the Potsdam Declaration. Unless Japan surrendered promptly, they warned, "[I]t may expect a rain of ruin from the air the likes of which has never been seen on this earth." Still hoping to negotiate better terms, the Japanese government vowed to fight on.

Truman ordered that the two available atomic bombs, code-named Fat Man and Little Boy, be used as soon as possible. On August 6, a B-29 named *Enola Gay* (for pilot Paul Tibbets's mother) flew from the island of Tinian and dropped the first bomb on the city of Hiroshima. Residents had rejoiced over their having been spared the conventional bombing attacks inflicted on most other cities. In fact, war planners had purposely kept Hiroshima "virgin," as they put it, to demonstrate more forcefully the power of the new weapon. Two days later, the Soviet Union declared war on Japan and sent the Red Army into Japanese-occupied Mongolia and Manchuria. On August 9, an American plane obliterated Nagasaki with a second atomic bomb. About 150,000 civilians, including many Korean laborers and a few American POWs, perished in the attacks. Radiation sickness later claimed more victims.

Since these events, scientists, historians, politicians, and ordinary citizens in Japan and the United States have debated the decision to use the atomic

The devastation of Hiroshima after the use of the atomic bomb. / © Dennis Brack/Black Star

bombs. Critics wondered if anti-Asian sentiment played a role, along with Truman's desire to keep the Soviets out of Asia and to force them to back down in Eastern Europe. Many speculated that a desperate Japan would have soon quit fighting anyway, if only the United States had offered better terms or demonstrated the bomb's power on, say, an uninhabited island off Japan's coast. Others disputed claims by Truman and his aides that using the bomb averted one-half million or more U.S. invasion casualties. (Actual estimates projected 50,000 deaths.)

While critics raise valid questions, most historians have come to accept the logic of Truman's decision to use the atomic bombs. Publicly, Truman never voiced doubt about his motives. In announcing the first attack, he thanked God for giving him a weapon that saved "thousands and thousands of American lives." Privately, Truman criticized "crybaby" scientists who had wanted to inform Japan in advance of an atomic attack. At the time he decided to go forward, Truman privately called the Japanese "savages, ruthless, merciless and fanatic." When "you have to deal with a beast," he wrote, "you have to treat him like a beast." Other prominent Americans issued calls for "gutting the heart of Japan with fire," killing "about half the civilian population," and even "sterilizing every damn one of them so that in a generation there would be no more Japs."

Truman and advisers like Secretary of State James F. Byrnes did hope that the impact of the atomic bomb would end the war before Soviet armies gained a foothold in China or Japan. When news of the atomic test reached Byrnes at Potsdam, he told an aide that the president no longer needed to haggle with Stalin over details. He could issue an ultimatum "giving the Japs two weeks to surrender or face destruction." A "secret weapon" would be ready by then.

Truman and those closest to him had multiple rationales for using the bomb. Even if the president did not expect a half million casualties from an invasion, he probably believed that even one avoidable American death justified an atomic strike. The United States possessed only three or four atomic bombs in August, so it seemed risky to chance a "demonstration shot" that the Japanese might well ignore. If Truman could end the war quickly, reduce American deaths, and limit Soviet expansion in Asia, he saw no reason *not* to seize the opportunity. After all, how could he justify having spent $2 billion constructing the weapon if he hesitated to use it?

Although anti-Japanese sentiment was rampant, U.S. strategists had planned to use the atomic bomb against German targets if the weapon had been available before the Nazi surrender. British and American firebombing of German and Japanese cities was as deadly to civilians as the new weapon. The indiscriminate slaughter of civilians had become so common by 1945 that few moral objections were raised in public. Truman and his aides believed that, given the structure of Japan's government, probably nothing short of combat use of the bomb would compel surrender on acceptable terms.

American officials knew that military hard-liners in Japan rejected even the most minimal surrender terms insisted upon by the United States. These terms included military occupation and disarmament, the trial of war criminals, and strict limits on the Japanese emperor's power. Secretary of War Henry Stimson, although deeply troubled by the moral dimensions of the bomb, favored its use because he thought it would "produce exactly the kind of shock on the ruling Japanese oligarchy" that would "strengthen the position of those who wished peace" and would "weaken . . . the military party." Recent evidence suggests that he guessed correctly. The bomb, one high-ranking Japanese official remarked just after its use on Hiroshima, "drastically altered the whole military situation and offered the military [in Japan] grounds for ending the war."

Following the destruction of Hiroshima, the Japanese emperor and his civilian aides agreed that Japan "must now bow to the inevitable," especially if it hoped to avoid a revolt by ordinary Japanese. The Soviet declaration of war on August 8 reinforced their belief. Even after these events, however, the Japanese army high command still believed that Japan could secure better surrender terms by hanging tough. The destruction of Nagasaki on August 9 broke the deadlock by creating a "psychological shock" that allowed both the Japanese emperor and Japan's militarists to save face. Several of Japan's key army leaders convinced themselves that America's "scientific prowess," not its military skills or bravery, had overwhelmed them. "We lost a scientific war," explained one of Hirohito's army aides. Under this circumstance, "the people will understand" and be forgiving. In a letter to his son shortly after the surrender, the emperor complained that his generals had placed "too much significance on spirit, and were oblivious to science." Rationalizing defeat as a surrender to "science" also served as a prelude to Japan's postwar emphasis on science, technology, and trade.

On August 10, a day after the destruction of Nagasaki, the emperor acted decisively. "Since the appearance of the atomic bomb," he told his cabinet, "continuation of the war spelled needless suffering for his subjects and Japan's ruin as a nation." He ordered his aides to accept the Potsdam Declaration, with the proviso that he remain on the throne. Anxious to end the war and slow the Soviet advance in China, Truman agreed on August 14 to modify the original peace terms. If the emperor personally ordered his troops throughout Asia to surrender, the United States would permit him to remain on the throne, subject to the authority of the American occupation commander, General Douglas MacArthur. The next day, Hirohito addressed his country via radio and called on all Japanese to cease resistance.

The awful destruction of Hiroshima and Nagasaki may have had an unintended positive consequence. Pictures and descriptions of what happened to these cities and their inhabitants, such as John Hersey's harrowing account of nuclear death in *Hiroshima* (1946), appeared around the world. Despite the saber-rattling of the Cold War, Soviet and American leaders recognized the special nature of nuclear weapons and used their atomic arsenals as a deterrent and as weapons of last, not first, resort.

Victory over Japan ended nearly a decade and a half of world lawlessness and confirmed the United States' place as the world's leading economic and military power. With a mere 6 percent of the earth's population, the United

States produced over half of the world's goods and controlled more than half of its wealth. Not surprisingly, Americans celebrated their wartime accomplishments, and many shared the view articulated by Henry Luce, the influential publisher of *Time* and *Life* magazines. The "American experience," Luce wrote in 1945, "is the key to the future. America must be the elder brother of the nations in the brotherhood of man." The notion that this country had a special historic mission was not new. Now, however, the nation had a uniquely powerful position. To the Soviets—and to other critics of U.S. policy in the postwar years—an attitude of the sort expressed by Luce smacked of arrogance and provoked a volatile mix of gratitude and hostility.

Demobilization and Building Peace: The GI Bill and New Deal Legacy

In 1946, Hollywood released a film with the ironic title *The Best Years of Our Lives*. It told the poignant story of three veterans—one actor was an actual GI who lost his hands in the war—returning home and making a sometimes painful readjustment to civilian life. Although the film won the Academy Award for best picture, within a few years several artists who worked on the project were accused of being Communists and using the movie as a vehicle to undermine society. For most Americans, the early postwar years were uncertain but compared to the previous period of depression and war, the postwar period really turned out to be the best years of their lives.

After Japan surrendered, Americans were eager to turn their attention to domestic matters. Young people looked forward to obtaining peacetime jobs and starting new families. With money in their pockets, they began moving to new suburbs and having children in record numbers. After a decade and a half of privation, they also went on a spree of consumer buying, snapping up home appliances, automobiles, and new gadgets called televisions.

Americans hoped that victory in World War II would ensure prosperity, not a return to depression. Many worried that the mustering out of 12 million men from military service, along with the abrupt cancellation of war orders that displaced 2 million workers, might create massive unemployment. Soldiers and sailors stationed around the world demanded to be shipped home as soon as possible. They sometimes demonstrated to protest delays. A point system, based on length of service, brought order to the process. In less than two years, the number of men in uniform fell by 90 percent.

Veterans had less difficulty finding jobs than many experts anticipated. A large number of veterans replaced women workers, 3 million of whom were laid off in the aftermath of victory. Both bosses and labor leaders took their lead from a senator who called on Congress to force "wives and mothers back to the kitchen." Private employers and civil service boards gave veterans preference over other job seekers. Even though 75 percent of women who wished to continue working eventually found postwar jobs, they often had to settle for clerical, sales, and light assembly work rather than the more lucrative skilled factory labor available during the war. In 1950, about 33 percent of women held paying jobs, up from 27 percent before the war. Their wages decreased from a wartime level of about $50 to $37 per week for white women, and to half that for African American women. Men experienced only a small drop in pay.

The American economy performed better than most people predicted. Between 1945 and 1952, the gross domestic product (GDP) rose an average of 4 percent annually. A huge savings pool built up during the war fueled an inflationary surge during 1945–1946, but the conversion of war plants soon began to satisfy consumer demand for a range of goods that had been in short supply before 1945 or, in many cases, had not existed earlier. The number of working Americans increased from a wartime high of 53 million to 60 million in 1948, and to 64 million by 1952.

Many labor unions came out of the war determined to push for both wage increases and a greater say in company policy. The United Automobile Workers (UAW), for example, staged a long strike against industry giant General Motors during 1946. In addition to higher wages and more benefits, the UAW wanted a seat on the GM governing board in order to influence corporate policy. Ultimately, the UAW, like many other industrial unions, settled for a contract that provided more money but little say over workplace rules. Because labor unions won a bigger slice of the pie, and as the Cold War intensified and government and employers brought pressure on the labor movement to cooperate, most labor unions became less militant and more accommodating.

Before 1945, the American government had never treated its war veterans generously. Aside from token pensions for the disabled or their widows, the federal government lost interest in its soldiers once they had finished serving their country. The sheer dimensions of World War II changed that pattern. Sixteen million men and about 350,000 women served in the armed forces, which meant that nearly every American family had a son, father, or close relative in service. In 1944, President Roosevelt and the otherwise anti–New Deal American Legion formed an alliance to push Congress to reward military service through a comprehensive entitlement program. FDR and liberals saw this as a unique opportunity to enact one last great New Deal reform. Conservatives considered the expanded aid a patriotic obligation. Together, the coalition outmaneuvered opponents such as Democratic Representative John Rankin of Mississippi, who feared that federal aid to African American veterans would challenge segregation. Ultimately, the 1944 Servicemen's Readjustment Act, or GI Bill of Rights, as everyone called it, benefited millions of veterans and their families and influenced where they worked, lived, and studied. In the next chapter, we will see how government and private financing of veterans' home mortgages literally reshaped the urban and suburban landscape.

The GI Bill provided unemployment pay for veterans, hiring preferences in civil-service jobs, new hospital and health benefits, low-interest loans to start businesses and purchase homes, and tuition and living stipends for college and vocational education. Demobilized soldiers unable to find work received $20 per week—more than the minimum wage of 40 cents per hour—

for up to one year. Participation in the so-called 52-20 club put spending money in veterans' pockets, gave them a sense of dignity, and enabled them to search for jobs as they readjusted to civilian life. This program paid out nearly $4 billion in the postwar years.

Except for those attending religious or teacher training schools, few Americans of moderate means attended college before 1945. The GI Bill offered students who enrolled in college or a trade school $110 per month to live on, plus additional money for books, fees, tuition, and dependents' support. The resulting surge of veterans into both public and private universities created a far larger and more democratic system of higher education—a change with great social consequences for the rest of the century. In the late 1940s, over 2 million students, half the total male enrollment at institutions of higher learning, attended college on the GI Bill. Nearly half the veterans in school were married, which forced colleges to drop their prohibitions or strict control over married students. Family housing units replaced all male dormitories; diapers, rather than team pennants, hung out of windows. Freshman hazing, a common experience before the war, almost ceased. One battle-hardened veteran of the Iwo Jima campaign recalled how he and his friends handled demands from younger upperclassmen that they wear beanies and perform menial chores: the veterans formed a platoon and chased the would-be hazers off campus. College professors judged the GI generation, which was determined to get degrees quickly and begin careers, as the most motivated students they had ever encountered.

As students flooded into crowded facilities, state legislatures were pressured to fund public universities more generously. By 1947, the total federal outlay for veterans' education reached $2.25 billion. When the program ended in 1956, the Veterans Administration (VA) had spent $14 billion. The professionals and technicians trained during these years earned far higher incomes than unskilled laborers, thus allowing the government to recoup much of its outlay in increased tax revenues.

Because only a small number of women had served in uniform, they received modest benefits from the GI Bill. Still, the number of women attending college increased after 1945. They were often steered away from careers that placed them in competition with men, however. Tacit or explicit sex discrimination and quotas led to a drop in the number of women enrolled in law, medical, and business schools. Harvard Business School did not admit a female student until 1963.

These attitudes were often bolstered by experts who insisted that women had to leave the work force and return to the home, for their own good and for the health and well-being of the nation. As sociologist Ferdinand Lundberg and psychiatrist Marynia Farnham explained in their 1947 bestseller, *Modern Woman: The Lost Sex*, "[W]omen are the pivot around which much of the unhappiness of the day revolves, like a captive planet. To a significant extent they are responsible for it. . . . Women as a whole (with exceptions) are maladjusted, much more so than men. For men have appropriate means to social adjustment: economic, political, and scientific power, and athletic prowess." Farnham and Lundberg saw no point in eliminating the employment and professional barriers that inhibited women. Instead, they urged women to seek happiness in the domestic realm by pursuing the traditional roles of homemaker and mother.

Popular Culture and the Age of Television

During the first half of the twentieth century, mass-circulation periodicals, motion pictures, and the radio dominated popular culture. When the war ended, most adult Americans read daily newspapers (usually in the evening); 34 million households (out of 38 million) owned at least one radio that they used to listen to music, comedy, sports, and soap operas; and the average American still went to a movie theater at least once each week. Soon, however, a new electronic medium—television—began to displace other forms of popular entertainment.

Because its large size made it difficult to distribute a newspaper widely, the United States lacked any truly "national" newspapers before the technological revolution in printing in the 1970s. In the years just after World War II, most households subscribed to local newspapers. Aside from a few big city dailies, reporting focused on local social events, sports, weather, crime, and gossip. Except for the staff members of a handful of newspapers that served black communities in cities like New York, Chicago, and Pittsburgh, nearly all journalists were white males. In the 1950s, the *Washington Post* hired its first African American reporter, but forced him to use a segregated washroom. The few female journalists were usually assigned to cover fashion and homemaking.

Radio remained more popular than newspapers or movies until the early 1950s. People tuned into four national networks and numerous local stations. Most programming consisted of popular music, sporting events, radio dramas that focused on romance or adventure, quiz shows, and situation comedies.

Since the 1920s, five major Hollywood studios dominated the movie production industry and owned most of the theaters that showed films. Hollywood also dominated the global movie industry before World War II and for decades afterward. Domestic audiences grew larger during the war, and by 1945, the typical urban American viewed two movies per week. Industry production codes regulated the sexual and moral content of films, stipulating how long a kiss might last, and meted out punishment to those who broke the law or acted immorally. Films typically portrayed people of color as servile and lazy, Asians as suspicious, and women as the "weaker sex" whose lives should revolve around husbands and families.

Beginning in 1948, television revolutionized popular culture, eclipsing radio, motion pictures, newspapers, and magazines. Although the technology had been pioneered in the 1920s—and Franklin Roosevelt had even appeared in an experimental broadcast in 1939—television did not flourish until the price of receivers was reduced as a result of wartime production techniques, and broadcasters received permission to charge for commercials. In 1946, the Federal Communications Commission (FCC) licensed twenty-six television stations, which began airing shows the next year. In 1948, both the Democrats and the Republicans held their presidential nominating conventions in Philadelphia because the city possessed a cable hookup that allowed viewing by an audience of 10 million. By 1949, about 1 million homes, mostly in large cities, watched television on sixty-nine local stations. After that, the number of viewers increased exponentially. The percentage of homes with TV sets grew from 0.4 percent in 1948 to 9 percent in 1950, from 23.5 percent in 1951 to 34.2 percent the next year.

At first, most TVs were purchased by taverns and wealthy families. Bars took out newspaper notices encouraging patrons to come and watch television while drinking. Well-off families often flaunted their wealth by hosting neighborhood "TV parties" for those unable to afford sets of their own. By the early 1950s, prices declined and television ownership became common. Parents with young children were especially eager to acquire the new technology, either as a form of in-house babysitting for the kids or evening relaxation for the exhausted adults.

Airwaves were soon filled with visual versions of radio shows. Comedy-variety, situation comedies, westerns, soap operas, quiz shows, sporting

Television's first star, "Uncle Miltie" (Milton Berle), hoofs it with Ethel Merman, about 1950. /
© Bettmann/CORBIS

events, and police dramas became—and have remained—standard TV fare. Uncle Miltie (Milton Berle), starred in the first big television hit, *The Milton Berle Show*, which debuted in 1948. The show was so popular that stories spread of water pressure in cities plummeting during commercial breaks when millions of viewers rushed to the bathroom. Although television was not the sole cause, its radically growing popularity cut deeply into the size of audiences that attended vaudeville and movies or read newspapers. Films and television shows, especially in the 1950s, both reflected and perpetuated various cultural stereotypes.

The Origins of the Cold War and the Birth of Containment

In September 1946, a year after the Japanese surrendered aboard the battleship *Missouri* in Tokyo Bay, former vice president and Commerce Secretary Henry A. Wallace addressed a crowd in New York's Madison Square Garden. The escalating war of words between Washington and Moscow deeply troubled Wallace. President Truman, he feared, had fallen under the spell of anti-Soviet hard-liners such as Secretary of State James F. Byrnes and Navy Secretary James Forrestal, both of whom urged a get-tough policy. But "getting tough," Wallace declared, "never brought anything real and lasting—whether for school yard bullies or businessmen or world powers. The tougher we get, the tougher the Russians will get." Instead, he urged both nations to modify their behavior, perhaps by adopting a spheres-of-influence approach that accepted each other's special interests.

Whether right or wrong, Wallace sought a middle ground where none existed. His audience, which included many members of the American Communist Party, booed him for suggesting that the Soviet Union had any need to mend its ways. Truman similarly rejected the notion that the United States bore any blame for tensions with its former ally. The president fired Wallace from his cabinet, complaining to an aide that the "Reds, phonies, and 'parlor pinks' . . . seem to be banded together and are becoming a national danger. I am afraid they are a sabotage front for Uncle Joe Stalin."

Months before this incident, the president ruminated that he was "tired of babying the Soviets." Unless "Russia is faced with an iron fist and strong language," he reasoned, "another war is in the making." With considerable insight, he told his wife and daughter that a "totalitarian state is no different whether you call it Nazi, Fascist, or Communist." In fact, he claimed to see no difference between the Soviet regime, its Czarist predecessor, "or the one Hitler spoke for."

As World War II ended, the national security policies of Washington and Moscow were on a collision course. Stalin was determined to forge a security sphere around the Soviet Union by dominating Eastern Europe. He crushed all political movements he could not control. Although Stalin offered little encouragement to communists outside this sphere, his prediction of a coming world revolution terrified Western audiences, who had looked forward to a world of political pluralism, reduced trade barriers, and reconciliation with the defeated Axis powers.

At the same time as Americans came to fear Soviet expansion abroad, an anticommunist hysteria erupted at home. Fueled by legitimate worries about the Soviet Union as well as by political opportunism, the domestic Red Scare distorted national politics and culture for almost a decade. Even at the time, it was clear that communism was no threat *in* the United States. Prodded by political demagogues, however, the federal and state governments as well as private industry conducted a political witch hunt in search of real and imaginary Reds. This activity frustrated efforts by progressives—including, to some degree, President Truman himself—to expand social reforms of the New Deal. It also led to political intolerance and the suppression of civil liberties. The outbreak of the Korean War in June 1950, and its bloody but inconclusive nature, invigorated the Red Scare and set the stage for the Republican Party's return to national power.

The Cold War dominated American foreign policy from 1945 until the Soviet Union collapsed in 1991. It produced a high level of tension between the United States and its communist rivals. It also spurred a nuclear arms race, divided much of the world into antagonistic alliances, and led to competition for influence in the poor, postcolonial nations of Africa, Asia, the Middle East, and Latin America, collectively known as the Third World. The Cold War shaped the foreign and domestic policies of the two superpowers, including their political, economic, and military institutions. It provided justification for American leaders to exercise power far away from home, and gave Soviet leaders, from Joseph Stalin to Mikhail Gorbachev, an external enemy that justified their internal repression. Wars fought by the United States in Korea and Vietnam were in part proxy contests to frustrate perceived threats from the Soviets and Chinese communists.

Although six great industrial powers (the United States, Germany, Japan, France, Great Britain, and the Soviet Union) fought World War II, only the Soviet Union and the United States emerged from the conflict with enhanced strength or additional territory. The United States was powerful, judged by economic, technological, and military measures and by the fact that it controlled much of the world's energy supply. The Soviet Union controlled more territory in 1945 than it had in 1941, but its devastating wartime losses—of at least 25 million people and much of its farm equipment and factories—gave it an economic base only one-quarter in size compared to the United States. Like those of the United States, the Soviet armed forces demobilized rapidly after 1945. The Soviet Union also lacked much of an air force or navy and, until 1949, did not possess atomic bombs. In terms of power, the Soviet Union was a distant second to the United States.

American anxiety about Soviet intentions in 1945 and 1946 derived in part from the fact that the Red army occupied much of Eastern Europe and Germany and well as northeastern China. These positions placed Soviet power close to the industrial heartland of Western Europe and Japan. Few American

(cont. on page 60)

The Rise of the Gunbelt

When Japanese troops surrendered on August 15, 1945, journalist Edward R. Murrow remarked that "seldom, if ever, has a war ended leaving the victors with such a sense of uncertainty and fear, with such a realization that the future is obscure and that survival is not assured." The threat of nuclear annihilation made the half-century of peace after World War II a uniquely uncertain period. In the 1954 film *Strategic Air Command*, actor Jimmy Stewart personified the sacrifices demanded of Americans in the Cold War. Stewart's character, "Dutch" (also Ronald Reagan's nickname), abandoned a promising career as a major league baseball pitcher to serve in the Air Force. When his wife protested, arguing that no war was being fought, Dutch spoke for a generation of Americans: "But there is a kind of war. We've got to stay ready to fight without fighting. That's even tougher. That's why I made this decision."

On the eve of the war, U.S. military spending would hardly count as a "rounding error" in today's federal budget. Massive defense outlays during World War II segued into the forty-year-long Cold War arms race, punctuated by hot wars in Korea and Vietnam. Before the collapse of the Soviet Union in 1991, military spending peaked at around $300 billion. After a small decline during the 1990s, spending rose sharply under President George W. Bush. Following the September 2001 terrorist attacks on the United States, Bush requested a $400 billion defense budget. By comparison, America spends about $10 billion annually on foreign aid.

Military spending has never been about only national security or the size of the armed forces. Nuclear weapons, computers, and aerospace technology required close cooperation among the Pentagon, private industry, and universities. Astronomers, mathematicians, computer programmers, physicists, and oceanographers played as large a part in modern warfare as generals and foot soldiers.

The huge sums of money directed toward specific technologies, industries, and regions have reshaped the political and economic landscape of post–World War II America. Just as journalists and geographers refer to the Sunbelt, Frostbelt, and Rustbelt to characterize the climate and economic conditions in different regions, defense spending has created wholly new industrial complexes in parts of California, the Pacific Northwest, New England, Texas, Arizona, New Mexico, Georgia, Florida, Utah, and Colorado. This flow of dollars into what some have called America's Gunbelt contributed to the deindustrialization of what, in earlier times, had been the nation's Midwest industrial heartland. President Eisenhower voiced concern over this phenomenon when he left office in 1961, cautioning Americans about the costs and risks of an immense "military-industrial complex."

During and after World War II, the federal government recognized the value of pure and applied research by establishing several national laboratories such as those in Los Alamos and Sandia, New Mexico; Livermore, California; Brookhaven, New York; Oak Ridge, Tennessee; and Argonne, Illinois. Defense research money also flowed into institutions such as the Massachusetts Institute of Technology (MIT), the California Institute of Technology (Cal Tech), the University of California, and the University of Chicago. During World War II, these universities created special units that focused on the development of atomic power, radar, rocketry, and proximity fuses. During the 1950s and 1960s, government funds allowed MIT and Cal Tech to create major research programs in defense-related areas such as particle physics, materials science, and optical sciences. By the 1970s and 1980s, the Defense Department, National Science Foundation, and Energy Department sponsored university research in areas such as recombinant DNA, superconductors, supercomputers, and robotics.

Nike missile production line in Santa Monica, California, 1955. With so many defense plants, southern California became the "buckle on the Gunbelt." /
© Bettmann/CORBIS

Most defense dollars—especially the lucrative aerospace and electronics contracts—flowed to New England, the South, the Southwest, and the West. Until the 1990s, about a dozen large defense contractors dominated the field. Then, many merged; in effect, only a handful of giant companies actually build planes, missiles, ships, and other equipment for the Department of Defense. Winning or losing a contract to build a new fighter plane can make or break the fortunes of both a contractor and a community like San Diego, Seattle, or Houston.

Moreover, defense spending had a significant impact on gender, race, and class relations. Military production for items like rockets and airplanes tends to be more capital than labor intensive—requiring more money and a smaller number of highly trained workers than equivalent civilian production. As a consequence, defense spending often channels money away from industries relying on less skilled blue-collar workers. As recently as 1990, women made up only 15 percent and minorities just 3 percent of the aerospace work force.

Corporations have invested more of their own resources in technology and plants likely to attract defense dollars. This, in turn, meant less investment in older plants in midwestern and northeastern cities that employed a more diverse industrial work force. Contributing to the loss of blue-collar jobs in older cities, the flow of military contracts and employment to the Gunbelt had an especially negative effect on African American workers in cities like Detroit, Philadelphia, Cleveland, Chicago, and Milwaukee.

Los Angeles and southern California boast the nation's biggest concentration of military contractors and defense-supported universities. In 1941, barely 5 percent of America's academic and other research scientists received federal grant money. By the early 1960s, about half of the nation's scientists relied on government research support. These funds had a huge impact on local business conditions. In the early 1990s, for example, following the collapse of the Soviet Union, the decline in military procurement dealt a sharp blow to the California economy.

Defense contractors, university researchers, military leaders, and politicians have promoted increasingly complicated and expensive weapons systems. The two most costly and controversial programs of the past few decades have been the Stealth, or B-2 bomber, and the antimissile system (called the Strategic Defense Initiative [SDI] by supporters and Star Wars by critics). Both systems were conceived in the late 1970s. Eventually, the Air Force acquired a few dozen Stealth bombers at a cost of about $1 billion per plane. Difficult to fly and expensive to maintain, the B-2 is combat-ready barely one-third of the time. Although designed as a strategic weapon for use against the Soviet Union, it found a niche role as a tactical bomber in the military operations in Kosovo and Afghanistan. In the two decades since President Reagan proposed building an antimissile shield, the government has spent $100 billion on missile defense but has yet to deploy a workable system. If the technological problems can be solved, a missile defense will cost several hundred billion dollars more to deploy.

The best known, most cost-effective, and longest lasting Cold War weapon, the B-52 bomber, was conceived at the inception of that struggle and continues to play a key role in military operations. The plane has "starred" in several films, including *Dr. Strangelove*. The B-52 "Stratofortress," as its manufacturer called it, was conceived over a weekend in 1947, when Boeing engineers responded to a call to design a plane capable of reaching the Soviet Union from the United States and delivering a massive nuclear payload. The swept-back wing design for the long-range bomber was eventually applied to a new generation of large commercial jets such as the 707.

The first B-52s rolled off assembly lines in 1952 and the last models were built a decade later. The plane's immense dimensions made it appear like some flying prehistoric creature as it rumbled down extra-long runways. Forty feet tall and 185 feet from wingtip to wingtip, the B-52's eight jet engines allowed it to fly at 650 miles per hour, and as high as 50,000 feet or as low as 300 feet. It could deliver a 70,000-pound nuclear or conventional payload a distance of 9,000 miles. The planes were produced for the remarkably cheap price tag of $8 million each (about $50 million in today's dollars), and Boeing built 744 of the aircraft, of which nearly 100 are still flying. Originally, the plane was designed to last for about five thousand hours of flying before metal fatigue set it. The use of upgraded components has more than tripled its life expectancy. The B-52 has received three major overhauls, and its avionics and electronics are periodically upgraded. These modifications led wags to joke that Boeing figured out how to sell the same plane to the Air Force three times.

Air Force and civilian planners recognized the awe-inspiring physical and psychological power of the B-52. Originally on alert twenty-four hours a day to deter or retaliate against an aggressor, the warplane was never used for its intended mission—dropping hydrogen bombs on the Soviet heartland. But it has played major roles in every regional conflict since the 1950s. The B-52 was used extensively to drop conventional bombs during the Vietnam War. It served as a workhorse during the conflicts in the Persian Gulf in 1991, in Kosovo in the late 1990s, in Afghanistan after September 2001, and in the war with Iraq in 2003. When a B-52 is deployed, a pilot recalled, "the other side knows you're serious."

Military officials have mothballed many of the more expensive weapons systems built since the 1980s, but the B-52 remains airworthy and can be kept operational until 2037, more than eighty years after the first models flew. In fact, the B-52 may be the first operational warplane that the *grandchildren* of the original pilots might fly in combat. When Eisenhower cautioned about the influence of the military-industrial complex, he also called for weapons that delivered "more bang for the buck." The B-52 certainly fit the bill.

leaders expected Stalin to seize these areas by force. Instead, they worried that the physical, economic, social, and political weakness in Asia and Europe would create a vacuum into which Soviet power would inevitably flow. To make matters worse, radical nationalist groups were competing for power in parts of Asia and the Middle East, areas that had or soon would gain independence from the British, French, Dutch, and Japanese. U.S. officials worried that if the Soviet Union controlled the industrial potential of Western Europe and Japan or the resources of the Third World, it could become strong enough to alter the global balance of power.

Although both the United States and the Soviet Union nursed mutual fears extending as far back as the Bolshevik Revolution of 1917, leaders in neither Washington nor Moscow had a master plan for world domination after 1945. Nevertheless, each side defined security in ways that threatened the other. Thus, Stalin's determination to extract reparations from Germany and to protect Soviet borders by forcibly creating puppet buffer states in Eastern Europe struck many Americans as both brutal and provocative. Similarly, American desires to rebuild the economies of Europe and Japan and to construct overseas military bases looked to Stalin like a plan to encircle and threaten the Soviet Union. During 1946, when Washington blocked the flow of industrial reparations from western Germany to the Soviet Union, Moscow responded by squeezing resources out of eastern Germany and its new satellites in Eastern Europe. Stalin invoked the fear of "capitalist encirclement" in a speech to the Russian people in February 1946, when he called for greater sacrifices to meet the outside threat.

Political leaders on both sides of what soon became called the Iron Curtain often found it useful to overdramatize the immediacy of the threat. For example, former British prime minister Winston Churchill encouraged anti-Soviet sentiments as part of a campaign to secure a multibillion-dollar loan from the United States. Speaking to an audience that included President Truman in Fulton, Missouri, on March 5, 1946, Churchill declared that "from Stettin [Poland] in the Baltic to Trieste [Italy] in the Adriatic, an Iron Curtain has descended" that separated the free and slave world. He proposed an alliance of all English-speaking peoples, backed by the atomic bomb that "God has willed to the United States."

Churchill ignored the fact that while brutal, the Iron Curtain was as much a defensive barrier for a weak Soviet Union to hide behind as a starting block for future expansion. In fact, Stalin used the rigid division of Europe in part to hide from the people of Eastern Europe and Russia the truth about the backwardness of the Soviet empire. This isolation allowed Stalin to pump up the threat of "capitalist encirclement" and call on his subjects to work harder for defense in place of seeking greater liberty or more consumer goods.

In the aftermath of these accusations, the Soviet Union rejected membership in two American-sponsored international economic organizations: the World Bank and the International Monetary Fund. These institutions were designed to stabilize currencies and to promote world trade and economic development. The U.S. dollar, redeemable for gold at $35 per ounce, served as the world's benchmark currency until 1971.

Stalin, who pushed his scientists to develop an atomic bomb, also rejected the so-called Baruch Plan, an American proposal made to the United Nations in 1946 for placing all forms of nuclear power under a U.S.-controlled international commission. In the midst of the U.N. debate over the plan, the United States conducted a series of dramatic atomic bomb tests on the Pacific atoll of Bikini, a name quickly popularized by a French bathing suit designer. Even though the odds of a nuclear deal at the United Nations were slim to begin with, the provocative Bikini tests made them almost impossible.

The two sides exchanged accusations, and each jockeyed for position. As noted above, the Americans halted the dismantling of German and Japanese industry for shipment as reparations to Russia. At Nuremberg, Germany, and Tokyo, Japan, the Soviets and Americans joined in the trial and punishment of a small number of Axis leaders as war criminals. But cooperation soon faded. Washington had initially refused to employ Nazis for scientific work. But soon Americans began recruiting hundreds of German rocket scientists, physicists, and physicians to work in or for the United States. "Operation Paperclip," the project's code name, found a home for physicians who had conducted horrible medical experiments on concentration camp inmates, as well as for engineers like Wernher von Braun, who worked slave laborers to death while he supervised the development of the deadly V-1 and V-2 rockets. Japanese doctors who conducted germ warfare tests on Allied POWs were given immunity from prosecution after they provided their data to American scientists. The Soviets, who had suffered so gravely under the Nazi assault, adopted similar recruitment practices.

In 1946, the Americans responded to what they saw as Soviet threats against Iran and Turkey. During World War II, the Allies had deposed the pro-Nazi shah and jointly occupied Iran. British and American forces departed early in 1946, but the Soviets lingered, demanding oil concessions like those held already by the British. To force action, they backed a separatist movement in northern Iran. Moscow also pressed Turkey to grant it joint control over the Dardenelles, a strategic strait connecting the Mediterranean and Black seas. Some American diplomats feared a Soviet sweep across Turkey and Iran, which would give it control over much of the Middle East and its oil reserves.

Declaring that the United States might as well find out now rather than later whether Stalin was bent on world conquest, Truman issued tough warnings against Soviet meddling and sent a naval task force into the Mediterranean. In fact, Stalin had limited goals in the region and no desire to fight the far stronger United States. When he backed off, some Americans leaders concluded that the Soviet dictator had expansionist goals that could only be curbed with superior strength. Meanwhile, American oil companies used the opportunity to muscle in on the British and gain concessions in Iran, Saudi Arabia, and Kuwait.

In spite of angry rhetoric and regional disputes, both the Soviet Union and the United States sharply reduced the size of their armed forces and their military budgets after 1945. Americans possessed an atomic monopoly but built few atomic bombs in the immediate aftermath of the war and mothballed many of its long-range aircraft. The Soviets retained a larger ground force than the Americans and the British but devoted much of it to internal police duties. American pressure may have influenced Soviet actions in Iran and Turkey, but Stalin also voluntarily withdrew troops from Manchuria, parts of Norway, Finland, Hungary, and Czechoslovakia. As of 1947, the two antagonists probably lacked the capacity or desire to initiate a major war.

During the two years following the end of the war, economic chaos and political instability afflicted much of the world. In Europe and Japan, the physical destruction of war; the uncertainties of military occupation; and a shortage of money, fuel, and raw materials stalled economic recovery. Rebellions and civil war in French Indochina, India, the Dutch East Indies, and China impeded the flow of raw materials to Western Europe and Japan. A nearly bankrupt Great Britain had to abandon India and Palestine. To stem starvation in occupied Germany and Japan, the United States spent nearly $1 billion per year. Even though the Soviet Union did not cause these problems, Americans feared Stalin would benefit from them.

George F. Kennan, then second in command at the U.S. embassy in Moscow, sent his superiors a report early in 1946 analyzing the worsening world situation. In his so-called long telegram (that he published as an article anonymously in 1947), Kennan argued that Stalin purposely provoked tension with the West to justify his harsh repression of the Soviet people and the captive eastern Europeans. Although Soviet power remained "impervious to the logic of reason," it was "highly sensitive to the logic of force." Rather than trying to placate the Kremlin, Kennan asserted, Washington should implement a policy of "long-term, patient but firm and vigilant containment." This suggestion soon became the operating principle behind American foreign policy.

Like several of Truman's advisers, Kennan recognized that the immediate threat to Europe and Japan was not Soviet military power but a growing economic crisis or "dollar gap." This gap constituted the difference between the value of American exports and the amount of dollars that foreign customers had available to pay for them. As 1947 began, the gap stood at about $8 billion and threatened to halt world trade. Foreign trade—including American exports—could continue only if the U.S. government and private lenders provided credit. They would risk doing so only as long as Europe and Japan showed signs of recovery. Once credits disappeared, foreign nations would be unable to trade with the United States or import the industrial raw materials they needed to spur recovery. This could quickly bring on the kind of global economic collapse that fed the Great Depression and led to World War II. The Soviets, American leaders feared, might take advantage of such chaos by using the carrot of economic assistance and the stick of military intimidation to gain control of vulnerable areas of Europe and Asia. If the Soviets harnessed European and Japanese industry and Middle Eastern petroleum to their own economy, Kennan warned, they could tip the balance of world power in their favor.

Containment, in short, depended on the reconstruction of the German and Japanese economies, what Undersecretary of State Dean Acheson called the "great workshops of Europe and Asia." Yet Congress, controlled by Republicans since 1946, balked at long-term foreign aid, which was a new idea at the time. When GOP critics accused Truman of promoting New Deal–type welfare programs abroad, the plan stalled.

Since 1944, a brutal civil war had raged between conservative Greek monarchists and the left-wing National Liberation Front (EAM). EAM included both communists and noncommunists. Britain had supported the monarchists, but on February 21, 1947, the financially hard-pressed government in London informed Washington that it could no longer aid Greece. The State Department's Dean Acheson took charge of selling a Greek aid program to Congress, with the hope that it would pave the way for a far larger, more comprehensive assistance package.

In discussions with the president and members of Congress, Acheson insisted that the United States and the Soviet Union were divided by an "unbridgeable ideological chasm." In this battle between democracy and dictatorship, any shirking of responsibility would prove fatal. If the United States walked away from Greece, then like "apples in a barrel infected by one rotten one," the "corruption . . . would infect Iran and all to the east." Greece's struggle was portrayed as a proxy battle between Soviet and Western interests.

Republican Senator Arthur Vandenberg, chairman of the Foreign Relations Committee, urged Truman to make a dramatic case to Congress if he wanted GOP support for foreign aid. According to legend, Vandenberg declared that if the Democrats wanted to provide a WPA-style welfare program to Greece, Truman needed to "scare the hell out of the American people."

When Truman spoke to Congress on March 12, 1947, he highlighted the "global struggle between freedom and totalitarianism." Portraying all communists as Soviet-directed enemies of economic and political freedom, the president declared that it must be the "policy of the United States" to "support free peoples who are resisting attempted subjugation by armed minorities or by outside pressure." Galvanized by this so-called Truman Doctrine, Congress approved $400 million for aid to Greece and Turkey.

As it turned out, Joseph Tito, the Communist leader of Yugoslavia—rather than Stalin–was the main supporter of the Greek rebels. Tito hoped to build his own mini-empire by adding parts of Greece to his proposed Balkan federation. Stalin took a dim view of empire-building by his puppets and had discouraged support for the Greek communists in order to avoid provoking the United States. Angered by his underling's provocative actions, the Soviet leader denounced Tito as a renegade and tried to topple him. The desperate Tito cut off support to the Greek rebels and soon solicited American aid. The lack of support from Tito for their rivals coupled with U.S. military assistance led to victory by the conservative Athens government.

The real impact of the Truman Doctrine, however, was felt elsewhere. On June 5, 1947, speaking at Harvard University, Secretary of State George C. Marshall proposed an ambitious plan for economic recovery that soon took his name. To prevent the Soviets from taking advantage of economic collapse, Marshall called on Congress to fund a multiyear reconstruction program for Western Europe and Japan. During the next few months, this idea evolved into a $27 billion aid request.

The Republican-controlled Congress hesitated to fund what became known formally as the European Recovery Program (informally as the Marshall Plan). Fortunately for Truman, Stalin helped ensure positive action. The Soviet leader worried that if U.S. aid succeeded in rebuilding Western Europe and Japan, pressure would build in communist-controlled and nonaligned parts of Eastern Europe to join an American-led trade and military bloc. To discourage this development, Stalin pressed the large communist parties and labor unions in France and Italy to oppose the aid scheme. In February 1948, when the Czech government showed interest in aid through the Marshall Plan, Stalin ordered a coup by local communists that pulled neutral Czechoslovakia behind the Iron Curtain. In March, the commander of American forces in Germany warned of a "subtle change in Soviet behavior" that might indicate plans to launch a war with "dramatic suddenness." Truman then called on Congress to fund the Marshall Plan quickly, before Moscow gobbled up Europe (see Map 2.1).

Congress passed a trimmed-down aid program that included funds to rebuild the Japanese economy. Over the next several years, the United States provided more than $15 billion in reconstruction aid (around $100 billion in 2003 dollars) in the form of credits, raw materials, and agricultural commodities. The American commitment also spurred greater regional cooperation among European and Japanese leaders.

At this time, Congress also enacted the National Security Act of 1947, which reformed the squabbling military and intelligence agencies. The act created a unified Department of Defense, led by a civilian cabinet secretary, and a National Security Council (NSC) to advise the president on foreign policy matters. It also provided for a Central Intelligence Agency (CIA) to gather and analyze information and conduct secret, or covert, missions abroad. Along with a new military draft, Congress authorized expansion of the atomic arsenal from fifteen weapons to over two hundred bombs by 1950.

Stalin reacted to these events by imposing tighter economic and political controls in areas under his rule. He purged the few independent-minded leaders in Eastern Europe and also tried to drive the Western powers out of Berlin by blockading land routes into the city. A prosperous West Berlin, located deep inside the Soviets' East German occupation zone, shone as a tempting beacon of liberty. When the United States announced a currency reform for the Western zones of Germany and Berlin, Stalin attempted to force the Western powers out of the city. Claiming that the currency reform violated earlier agreements, he voided Western rail and road access privileges into West Berlin. However, the Soviets did not impede air corridors into the encircled city because these access routes were guaranteed in a separate agreement.

During the1948 Berlin Blockade, children cheer a U.S. cargo plane carrying supplies. Some pilots dropped candy as they landed. / © Bettmann/CORBIS

Occupation commander General Lucius Clay feared the imminent fall of Berlin and warned that "western Germany will be next." He urged Truman to allow him to shoot his way through Soviet barriers. Truman made a symbolic show of force by sending sixty atomic capable B-29 bombers—without nuclear weapons—to airfields in Britain. But rather than challenge the Soviet blockade directly, he opted to airlift food and fuel into Berlin. The president guessed, correctly, that Stalin did not want war. In fact, Soviet forces did not impede the airlift.

To Stalin's disappointment and Truman's delight, the yearlong Berlin blockade and airlift proved a public relations disaster for Moscow. On their final landing approach to Berlin, American pilots threw Hershey bars and chewing gum to children gathered at the ends of the runways, and the city and its people were transformed from former Nazi enemies into symbols of resistance to Soviet bullying. In May 1949, the United States convinced western Europeans to support the creation of a powerful new west German state, the Federal Republic of Germany. Even Stalin realized that his actions were counterproductive. Belatedly, the dictator called off the blockade and a month later, in June 1949, created a puppet German Democratic Republic in the former Russian occupation zone.

At this point, the United States was well on the way to winning the Cold War. As reconstruction aid poured into Western Europe and Japan, the European and Japanese economies came to life. American policy promoted regional

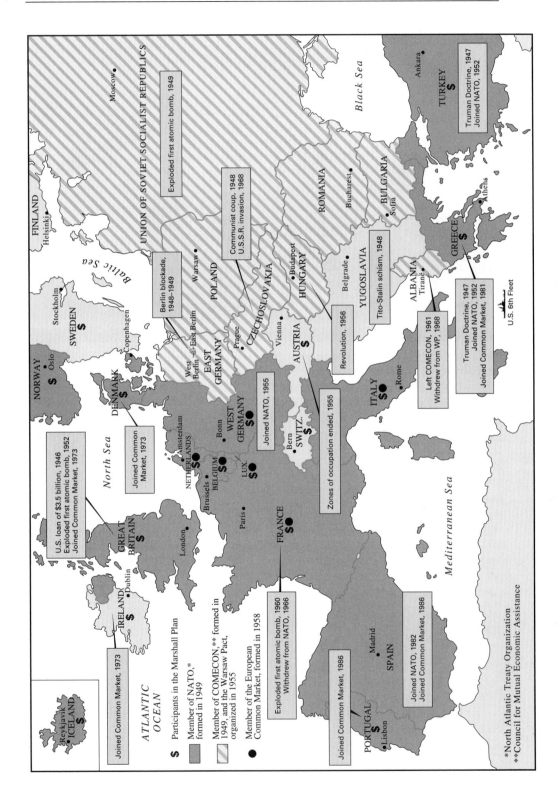

economic and political cooperation that broke down many of the barriers between West Germany and its neighbors. As living conditions improved, the influence of communist parties in France, Italy, and Japan declined. Stalin's effort to keep Europe and Japan weak, divided, and isolated from the United States had backfired. In April 1949, now Secretary of State Dean Acheson oversaw the creation of the North Atlantic Treaty Organization (NATO), which bound Britain, France, Belgium, the Netherlands, Italy, Portugal, Denmark, Iceland, Norway, and Canada to the United States in a common defense against Soviet attack. Over the following decades, Greece, Turkey, West Germany, and Spain joined the alliance. After the collapse of the Soviet Union, several of its former East European satellites joined as well. As Acheson boasted to Congress, America now enjoyed a "preponderance of power" over the Soviet Union.

It seems a cruel irony that charges of "softness on communism" stuck to the Democratic Party and the Truman administration. As historian Stephen Ambrose observed, the president and his party "forced the Russians out of Iran in 1946, came to the aid of the Greek government in 1947, met the Red Army's challenge in Berlin and inaugurated the Marshall Plan in 1948, joined the North Atlantic Treaty Organization in 1949, and hurled back the Communist invader of South Korea in 1950, all under the banner of the Truman Doctrine which had proclaimed American resistance to any advance of Communism anywhere."

National Politics in the Early Cold War and the Origins of the Red Scare

Many Americans felt politically adrift after Roosevelt's death in April 1945. As noted earlier, Truman assumed the presidency almost unknown to the public. Just weeks after Japan surrendered, Truman asked Congress to enact twenty-one domestic programs, including an increase in the minimum wage; more expenditures for hospitals, small businesses, and agricultural price supports; and a full-employment bill. A coalition of Republicans and southern Democrats buried most of these proposals. The full-employment bill would have committed the federal government to a policy of economic planning and management designed to ensure jobs for all. When finally passed, the Employment Act of 1946 created a presidential Council of Economic Advisers but merely endorsed the goal of maintaining full employment and production.

During the first year and a half of peace, most Americans were more troubled by inflation than unemployment. Wartime savings and veterans benefits, along with new jobs in the private sector, sustained purchasing power and prevented high levels of unemployment. But shortages of food and consumer goods such as automobiles and vacuum cleaners drove up prices. Major strikes

◀ **Map 2.1**
  Divided Europe

in the automobile, electrical, coal, and transportation industries created additional bottlenecks. Truman flip-flopped on the question of maintaining wartime price controls, and many Americans blamed him for the combination of shortages and high prices.

On the eve of the November 1946 congressional election, pollsters reported that only one-third of the public approved of Truman's job performance. Republicans captured the nation's mood in a campaign slogan that asked "Had Enough?" Most voters had. They elected eleven new Republicans to the senate and fifty-six to the House. For the first time since 1930, the GOP controlled both houses of Congress. Republican presidential prospects seemed bright. One poll taken in 1947 found that only 3 percent of Americans listed Truman among the most admired leaders of recent decades.

Despite promises by Republican leaders such as Ohio Senator Robert Taft to unravel the New Deal, Republicans made only tepid efforts to restore an unregulated economy. They did roll back some important labor rights by passing the Taft-Hartley Act of 1947. Enacted over Truman's veto, the law abolished the closed shop (which compelled workers to join a union), barred secondary boycotts, made unions liable for monetary damages, established procedures to decertify unions, and gave the president power to impose an eighty-day cooling-off period in labor disputes before a strike could be called. The Taft-Hartley Act also required union officers to take a noncommunist oath.

The law bolstered conservative labor leaders and made union-organizing drives more difficult, especially in the South. The Taft-Hartley Act encouraged state legislatures in the Sunbelt to pass right-to-work laws that barred making union membership a requirement for employment. To get out of union contracts, many labor-intensive industries, such as textiles, relocated to the Sunbelt.

In the run-up to the 1948 election, Truman seemed almost as unpopular within his party as he did among Republicans. When asked who the Democrats might run in 1948, some joked, "[W]e'll dig somebody up," a grim reference to Franklin Roosevelt. The president found comfort in an analysis prepared by his young adviser, Clark Clifford. In November 1947, Clifford urged Truman to step up his attack on Republican efforts to unravel New Deal reforms while offering a liberal program of his own.

During 1948, Truman vetoed sixty-two Republican-sponsored bills, damning them as efforts to kill the New Deal. He rallied the New Deal coalition by proposing programs to aid small farmers, raise the minimum wage, liberalize immigration policy, enhance civil rights, reduce taxes for workers, and increase Social Security benefits. As Republicans voted down each proposal, Truman's standing rose among key Democratic voting blocs. Organized labor appreciated his depiction of the Taft-Hartley Act as a "slave labor act." Jewish Americans and others of east European origin applauded his support for the Displaced Persons (immigration) Act and his prompt recognition of Israel. African Americans cheered his creation of an advisory Committee on Civil Rights and his endorsement of its call for federal laws against lynching and the poll tax and the creation of a Fair Employment Practices Commission. Small farmers admired his effort to raise commodity price supports. The president's sponsorship of the Truman Doctrine, Marshall Plan, and Berlin airlift convinced the public that he offered the right mix of liberalism at home and resistance to communism abroad.

At the same time as Truman reached out to labor and minorities, liberal Democrats moved closer to the political center by taking a stand against communism. Labor leaders such as Walter Reuther and David Dubinsky; public figures such as Eleanor Roosevelt and her son, Franklin, Jr.; and influential theologians and academics such as Reinhold Niebur and Arthur Schlesinger, Jr., organized the Americans for Democratic Action (ADA) in 1947. Although many ADA members did not especially admire Truman, they preferred him to Henry Wallace, whom they dismissed as a misguided apologist for the Soviet Union.

At the Democratic nominating convention in July 1948, Truman hoped to mollify both African Americans and southern Democrats by endorsing a bland civil rights platform. But liberals, led by Minneapolis mayor Hubert H. Humphrey, insisted on a stronger civil rights agenda. This infuriated segregationists, such as Senator James O. Eastland of Mississippi, who accused Humphrey of trying to "mongrelize" America and complained that Truman was "kissing the feet of minorities."

Some outraged southern delegates bolted the convention and organized their own States' Rights, or "Dixiecrat," party. They nominated Governor Strom Thurmond of South Carolina as their presidential candidate. Thurmond, like many who gravitated to his party, combined populism with bigotry. For example, they complained that Truman's support for foreign aid made him a tool of Wall Street millionaires and monopolists, while his advocacy of civil rights made him a pawn of communists, Jews, and African Americans. The Dixiecrats, Thurmond declared, stood for the "deepest emotion of the human fabric—racial pride, respect for white womanhood, and superiority of Caucasian blood." He condemned civil rights as a Red plot.

While segregationist Democrats attacked Truman from the right, Henry Wallace and his supporters accused Truman of abandoning New Deal principles and provoking a Cold War with the Soviet Union. Wallace ran for president on the ticket of the Progressive Party. With the Democrats split three ways, it seemed likely that Progressive voters in the North and Dixiecrats in the South could tip enough states to push the election into the House of Representatives or ensure a GOP victory.

Republicans maximized their appeal by moving toward the political center. Instead of the party's most prominent conservative, Senator Robert Taft, they nominated a moderate, New York Governor Thomas Dewey. The GOP candidate began the 1948 campaign with a fifteen-point lead over Truman in the opinion polls. One prominent Republican ridiculed Truman as a "gone goose." Dewey and his team felt so certain of victory that they spent more time planning his inauguration than outlining an agenda of their own or rebutting Truman's campaign rhetoric.

In a spirited campaign mounted on a special train that crisscrossed the country, Truman delivered hundreds of combative speeches. Relieved of any need to placate the Wallace or Thurmond factions of the party, Truman appealed to anticommunists as well as black urban voters. Boasting that he did not want the support of "Henry Wallace and his Communists" or Thurmond and avowed racists, Truman blasted the GOP-led "do-nothing Eightieth Congress." These "gluttons of privilege" stuck a "pitchfork in the back of the farmers" and "tried to enslave totally the working man." Republicans, he bellowed, would do a "real hatchet job on the New Deal" and bring back the Depression. Crowds at whistle-stops cheered, "Give 'em hell, Harry!"

Although most pollsters and many journalists had lost interest in the campaign, Truman's appeals took hold. When the tally came in November, Truman beat Dewey by 24 million votes to 22 million, one of the most dramatic upsets in the history of presidential contests. Wallace and Thurmond each received around 1 million popular votes. Even though the Dixiecrats won the electoral votes of four states (South Carolina, Louisiana, Alabama, and Mississippi), they and the Progressive Party faded away.

Now elected in his own right, Truman emerged from Franklin Roosevelt's shadow by introducing his own reform program, the Fair Deal. During 1949, he called on Congress to pass legislation providing national health insurance, public housing, expanded Social Security benefits, a higher minimum wage, support for civil rights, higher support payments for small farmers, and the repeal of the Taft-Hartley Act. Even though Democrats reclaimed control of the House and Senate in 1948, few of these measures even came to a vote in Congress. The enduring coalition of Republicans and southern Democrats tied up most Fair Deal proposals in committee. Only a modest expansion of Social Security and a weak public housing bill passed. Truman's new administration had barely begun before the expanding dimensions of the Cold War at home and abroad inflamed public suspicion of liberal social policies.

During the decade following World War II, a growing anticommunist movement convulsed American politics. It was linked to, but somewhat separate from, the Cold War confrontation between the two superpowers. American anticommunism stretched back to the Bolshevik Revolution of 1917. It revived in the 1930s, when left-wing elements of the Democratic Party, the labor movement, and American intellectualism squared off against centrists and conservatives who abhorred the Soviet Union and anyone who defended it. Before the Pearl Harbor attack ended debate, Republicans tried to make political headway against New Dealers by accusing them of an affinity for communism and disloyalty. Cold War anxieties after 1945 fed a Red Scare that reached a fever pitch by the end of the decade. Eventually, Joseph McCarthy, a Republican senator from Wisconsin, gave his name to the movement, but it was well under way by the time he emerged as a national figure in 1950.

Communism had a small but growing following in the United States during the 1930s. The American Communist Party reached its zenith during World War II, when nearly 100,000 people paid membership dues. Within a few years, party rolls declined by 50 percent, and by the mid-1950s, only about 25,000 Americans remained formal Communists. Most rank-and-file American Communists supported Soviet policy and ignored evidence of Stalin's brutality. But few advocated violence to overthrow the U.S. government and most were really more reformers than revolutionaries. Party leaders were more rigid apologists for Stalin and had a cynical view of democratic civil liberties, except in defense of their own activities. In any case, the FBI had infiltrated the party so thoroughly that it could barely organize a picnic, no less a revolution, in secrecy. European democracies, such as France and Italy, had far larger communist parties and lived much closer to the Soviet "threat." Although they excluded communists from a role in government, their societies experienced no comparable Red Scare. In the United States, government and private anticommunist efforts were wildly disproportional to the actual danger posed.

During and right after the war years, Republican political leaders, business groups, opponents of civil rights, and other conservatives discovered the advantage of linking Democratic liberals and progressive policies to "the Reds." Labeling someone or their ideas as communist effectively discredited them. In 1946, the chair of the Republican National Committee told voters that in the upcoming congressional election, they would have to choose between "Communism and Republicanism." In 1950, Senate candidate Richard Nixon charged that Helen Gahagan Douglas, his Democratic opponent, was "pink right down to her underwear." The American Medical Association denounced Truman's 1948 proposal for national health insurance by labeling it a "monstrosity of Bolshevism."

As early as 1942, southern Democrats were fearful of a postwar push for civil rights and condemned as communist those opposed to segregation. Representative Martin Dies, Democrat of Texas, deplored the fact that "throughout the South today, subversive elements are attempting to convince the Negro that he should be placed on social equality with white people." J. Edgar Hoover's FBI promoted this alleged link throughout the Cold War. In 1951, for example, the FBI chief approved a script for the film *I Was a Communist for the FBI* that included party members taking credit for inciting race riots in Detroit and New York. "To bring about Communism in America," one party boss asserts, "we must incite [more] riots." Soviet officials, the film explains, used African Americans as pawns.

In 1948, *Life* magazine highlighted the alleged nexus between communism, race, and sex in a report on smart "party girls" dangled in front of maladjusted young men by Communist leaders. These decoys preyed upon sexually inadequate males by flattering their vanity and providing sexual gratification. "The party girls were wonderful," *Life* explained. They talked, recruited, and "went to bed" with their marks. Worse still was the ploy of using white party girls to "enfold likely Negroes," even arranging interracial marriages to recruit blacks.

In 1946, the committee on socialism and communism of the U.S. Chamber of Commerce called for barring not just communists, but liberals, socialists, and other undesirables from teaching in schools, working in radio or television, or working in any "opinion forming agencies." In an effort to blunt union drives, the committee also recommended barring people with unacceptable ideas from large factories. After this position became formal U.S. Chamber of Commerce policy in 1952, the group called on local volunteers to monitor the ideas and actions of public officials.

There were, of course, real subversives, spies, and traitors in the United States. To acquire technology and military information, the Soviets utilized professional agents, disgruntled employees, and occasionally communist sympathizers or actual party members. Based on VENONA, the code name for FBI intercepts of Soviet communications during the 1930s and 1940s, historians estimate that a few hundred American citizens provided classified information to Moscow. American Communist leaders knew about these activities, even if most ordinary party members did not. Politically motivated spies were especially active during the 1930s and early 1940s, when democracy appeared on the ropes and the Soviet Union was an ally in the fight against fascism. After 1945, Soviet spies found it difficult to recruit communist sympathizers in the United States. By 1950, a top Soviet intelligence official reported to the Kremlin that because of the shortage of American recruits, he was forced to rely on newspaper clippings for information.

Most of the real traitors unearthed during the Red Scare had actually ceased spying at the end of World War II, and many of their names were already known to the FBI. Nevertheless, grandstanding politicians made few distinctions between past and present subversion and ignored the fact that most espionage was carried out by Soviet professionals utilizing Americans with a personal grudge against an employer or the government. College professors, actors, or even most diplomats were of little use or interest to Moscow.

Congress, especially the House Un-American Activities Committee (HUAC), played a large role in stirring up the Red Scare. The most strident committee members during the 1940s were conservative southern Democrats and like-minded Republicans. Democrats such as John S. Wood (Georgia) and John Rankin (Mississippi) used HUAC as a platform to criticize New Deal programs, especially those relating to civil rights. Rankin took pride in bringing to the nation's capital a law modeled on those in twenty-two states that banned interracial marriage. He condemned the Red Cross for "mongrelizing" the nation by removing racial labels from blood bank bottles, and warned of conspiracies among "alien-minded communistic enemies of Christianity," his code for Jews.

Truman attempted to deflect charges that he waffled on the Red threat by creating a Temporary Commission on Employee Loyalty in November 1946 and, the following March, a Federal Employee Loyalty Program. These organizations required all federal employees to undergo an investigation to determine if they posed a risk to national security. Hearsay, wiretaps, and anonymous denunciations could be used to discredit someone. Aside from the Communist Party itself, Attorney General Tom Clark compiled a list of eighty-two suspect organizations linked to subversion. Congressional committees identified over 600 such groups. Membership in any one of these organizations could, by itself, justify dismissal of "pinkos" and "fellow travelers" from government service. Communists, Clark warned, "are everywhere—in factories, offices, butcher shops, on street corners, in private businesses—and each carries with him the germs of death for society."

Investigations of federal employees were conducted by FBI agents, whose long-serving director, J. Edgar Hoover, had been chasing Reds since 1919. Hoover and many of his agents despised communists, African Americans, homosexuals, and most kinds of political or social nonconformity. By the early 1950s, over 5 million government employees had undergone some form of security check. Several thousand quit in protest, and a few hundred were fired for belonging to groups on the attorney general's list. Yet these probes uncovered almost no bona fide spies.

Anticommunists often viewed sexual "perversion" as linked to disloyalty, a handy option because there were few actual communists to catch. Senator Kenneth Wherry, Republican of Nebraska, considered it nearly impossible to "separate homosexuals from subversives." As a leader of the so-called Lavender Purge, Wherry urged action to secure major coastal cities "against sabotage through conspiracy of subversives and moral perverts in government establishments." Like many Americans, Wherry feared that "deviants" not only lacked patriotic fiber but also were susceptible to Red blackmail. A 1950 Senate report on the "Employment of Homosexuals and Other Sex Perverts in Government" warned that 3,750 gays worked for the federal government in Washington, D.C., including 400 in the State Department, and that "one homosexual can pollute a government office." Between 1947 and 1953, over 400 employees of the Department of State were dismissed or forced to resign for being homosexuals, a rate nearly double that of those fired as subversives. "Commies and queers," as Senator Joe McCarthy put it in 1950, were fair game.

Several memoirs by ex-communists connected their secret political and illicit sexual lives. The most important of these, Whittaker Chambers's *Witness* (1952), explicitly linked homosexuality and treason, and portrayed religious faith as the key to redemption. None of the confessionals, however, had the raw power or generated the mass appeal of novelist Mickey Spillaine. Beginning with his first novel *I the Jury* (1947), which introduced private detective Mike Hammer, Spillaine published seven books in six years that sold over 17 million copies. Hammer, a fictional World War II veteran, becomes a private eye to escape the "pansy" bureaucracy that emasculates real police work. He despises intellectuals, homosexuals, communists, and the Mafia and does his best to exterminate them. The hero boasts of killing "commies, queers, and dames" who "should have died long ago." The string of bestsellers stopped in 1952, when Spillaine became a Jehovah's Witness and dedicated himself to church work.

Nearly every case of actual espionage prosecuted in the 1940s and 1950s was the product of criminal investigations by the FBI, not congressional probes. J. Edgar Hoover was no civil libertarian, but unlike some members of Congress, he retained at least a minimal commitment to notions of evidence and cause and effect. Headline-grabbing politicians did little but sow confusion and fear. Still, a few high-profile cases of alleged treason involving communists, their sympathizers, and members of the Roosevelt administration created the impression among the public that a cabal of disloyal Americans threatened the nation.

When Republicans won control of Congress in 1946, Representative J. Parnell Thomas of New Jersey became HUAC's chair, and the committee soon announced that the Red plot against America "had its headquarters in Hollywood." The movie industry provided an almost irresistible target to the publicity-seeking committee. East European, Jewish immigrants headed most of the major film studios. Although they anglicized their names and made movies that celebrated American life, anti-Semites on HUAC, especially Representative John Rankin, were anxious to pillory them. The films produced by Hollywood studios dominated popular culture, and Rankin, like chair Thomas, realized the public would savor a glimpse at the private lives of celebrities.

There were, of course, "real" communists in Hollywood. A small number of writers, for example, formed the left-wing Screen Writers Guild that battled studio executives over salary and creative issues. In retrospect, what stands out about their scripts is the lack, not abundance, of political messages. Nervous studio bosses, such as Jack Warner and Sam Goldwyn, hoped that by cooperating with HUAC's probe they could demonstrate their own patriotism and crush the bothersome union.

HUAC held hearings in both Hollywood and Washington at which "friendly witnesses," such as Warner and actor Ronald Reagan, were encouraged to pledge their cooperation by instituting procedures to bar the employment of self-professed communists or of those who refused to tell Congress what it wanted to hear. When pressed for examples of Red messages in films, studio executives cited the sympathetic treatment of Apache chief Cochise in "Broken Arrow," kindly black servants, and the smiles depicted on the faces of Russian soldiers in a film produced during World War II.

The committee focused on a group of ten "hostile" writers and directors, including Dalton Trumbo, Ring Lardner, Jr., and John Howard Lawson. Several in this group were past or current communists. All ten refused to answer the committee's questions about their political beliefs, citing the First Amendment's protection of free speech and political association. They were cited for contempt and later jailed after the Supreme Court upheld HUAC's right to inquire into communist activities. Meanwhile, publications such as *Red Channels* and *Counterattack* soon appeared. They contained the names of hundreds of actors, writers, and directors accused of left-wing leanings who found themselves unemployable due to an informal blacklist. Following the HUAC probe, Hollywood studios produced a few dozen stridently anticommunist films, including *The Iron Curtain* (1948), *The Red Menace* (1949), *The Red Danube* (1949), *Conspirator* (1950), *My Son John* (1952), and *Big Jim McLain* (1952). With wooden plots and moral posturing, all these films were critical and commercial flops.

HUAC launched its most famous inquiry in 1948. For several years, Whittaker Chambers, an editor at *Time* magazine, had told various government officials that in the 1930s he had been part of a Soviet spy ring that received material from members of the Roosevelt administration. After 1937, Chambers explained, he broke with communism, became a devout Christian, and finally confessed his sins to Representative Richard Nixon, Republican of California, and other members of HUAC.

In 1950 Congressman Richard Nixon took grim satisfaction from learning that a federal jury had convicted Alger Hiss of perjury. / © UPI/Bettmann/CORBIS

In his first public appearance before the committee in August 1948, Chambers claimed that Alger Hiss, a former high official of the State Department, had been a fellow communist, although not a spy. Later, when Hiss filed a libel suit, Chambers upped the ante and named Hiss as a coconspirator. Unlike the sinister-looking Chambers, Hiss seemed a paragon of charm, eloquence, and professional accomplishment. He had worked for several New Deal agencies, had attended the wartime Yalta conference, and after the war became head of the prestigious Carnegie Endowment for International Peace.

When Hiss persuasively denied knowing Chambers, several HUAC members decided to drop the case. But Nixon, a freshman who had won election in 1946 by charging that his Democratic opponent, Jerry Voorhees, was procommunist, refused to give in. He arranged a face-to-face meeting between Chambers and Hiss, and coaxed an admission from Hiss that he had indeed met his accuser in the 1930s but knew him then by a different name.

After Truman's unexpected election victory in November, frustrated Republicans pushed the case with renewed vigor. Chambers, with FBI prompting, recalled additional details of his past misdeeds. He now charged that Hiss had passed secret documents to him as late as 1938. To prove this claim, he and Nixon brought reporters to Chambers's Maryland farm, where they produced a hollowed-out pumpkin that held documents and several rolls of microfilm. The FBI determined that the material (dubbed the pumpkin papers), were actually secret reports, some of which had been copied on a typewriter that matched a machine in the Hiss household. Because the statute of limitations on espionage had lapsed, Hiss was indicted only for perjury: lying to Congress about his communist affiliations and relationship with Chambers.

A trial in 1949 resulted in a hung jury, but in January 1950, a second jury found Hiss guilty. He went to jail for several years and spent the next forty years of his life maintaining his innocence and blaming the FBI for framing him. Chambers went on to a highly public career as a professional anticommunist. In his bestselling memoir, *Witness*, Chambers boasted that "when I took up my little sling and aimed at Communism, I also hit something else . . . that great socialist revolution, which, in the name of liberalism . . . has been inching its ice cap over the nation for two decades." Ronald Reagan, then in the process of changing his own political stripes from liberal to conservative, credited Chambers for helping him see the light. Thirty years later, President Reagan designated Chambers's farm and pumpkin patch a "national historic site" and Cold War shrine. Nixon parlayed his fame into winning a senate seat in California in 1950 and two years later won election as vice president.

Most historians now believe that Hiss did pass information to Moscow and lied about his actions. But the Chambers-Hiss case became more important as a political morality play. Republicans felt they had proved the link between New Dealers and the communist conspiracy. When Truman and Secretary of State Dean Acheson initially defended Hiss, Republicans went wild. Nixon called their actions "disgusting," adding that Acheson suffered from "color blindness—a form of pink eye toward the Communist threat in the United States."

In February 1950, a month after Hiss's conviction, British police arrested a German émigré scientist, Klaus Fuchs, who confessed to participating in a spy ring at the nuclear lab in Los Alamos, New Mexico, during World War II. Many suspected that Fuchs not only helped the Soviets get the atomic bomb but also may have given them data on the still undeveloped hydrogen bomb. In the summer of 1950, the FBI arrested a New York couple, Julius and Ethel Rosenberg, and charged them with conspiring to steal the "secret" of the atomic bomb.

The Rosenbergs had been Communist Party members in the 1940s. Unlike Fuchs, they denied their guilt, even when Ethel's brother, David Greenglass, who worked at Los Alamos, admitted his role in the conspiracy. After sifting the evidence for years and gaining access to Soviet materials, historians generally agree that Julius Rosenberg plotted to pass both atomic and other technological data to Moscow. The evidence against his wife was less clear, and fifty years after her conviction, Ethel's brother David admitted he had concocted some of his testimony about her role. She was the mother of two young sons, and it appears the government charged her in an effort to force her husband to confess. Ultimately, both Rosenbergs were convicted and died in the electric chair in 1953. Fuchs and several other confederates went to prison.

While Congress probed for spies, a federal jury convicted twelve leaders of the American Communist Party in October 1949 of violating the Smith Act.

This 1940 law made it a crime to advocate the overthrow of the government by force or to belong to a group advocating such action. The verdict, upheld by the Supreme Court in 1951 in *Dennis* v. *United States*, was handed down despite the fact that no evidence tied the party leaders to efforts to overthrow the government.

By the time the Supreme Court decided that communism was a violent and illegal conspiracy, Congress had passed new, restrictive laws. The Internal Security Act of 1950 (called the McCarran Act after Senator Pat McCarran, a Nevada Democrat) declared that communism was an international conspiracy posing an immediate threat to the United States. The law stopped short of outlawing the Communist Party but ordered "Communist affiliated" groups and individuals to register with a Subversive Activity Control Board or face a $10,000 fine and five years in prison. Communists were denied passports and barred from working for the government or in the defense industry. The law permitted the deportation of naturalized citizens and the detention, without trial, of people considered security threats in time of emergency.

In the climate of the early Cold War, immigration was perceived as a potential threat. The quota system adopted in the 1920s favored immigrants from Western Europe and excluded nearly everyone else. After 1945, the tragic condition of more than a million displaced persons in Europe evoked concern. These refugees included several hundred thousand Jewish Holocaust survivors and even more ethnic Germans, Latvians, Estonians, and Lithuanians who had fled Soviet control in Eastern Europe. After intense lobbying by citizens' groups, in June 1948 Congress passed the Displaced Persons Act, opening two hundred thousand special immigration slots for these people. An extension of the law in 1950 let in an equal number.

Congress deferred dealing with broader immigration problems until 1952, when it passed the McCarran-Walter Act. Senator McCarran believed that the country already had too many "indigestible blocs" and fought efforts to liberalize the strict quotas passed in the 1920s. The new law repealed the almost complete ban on Asian immigration but set an absurdly low annual quota of one hundred persons from each Asian-Pacific nation. It continued to favor Western Europe and to exclude most eastern Europeans. The law barred suspected communists, along with homosexuals and other "undesirables," from even visiting the United States. Naturalized citizens were subject to deportation if they were accused of subversive acts. Passed over Truman's veto, the law set basic immigration policy until 1965.

Thirteen states followed Congress's lead and established their own HUAC-type committees. They spent much of their efforts castigating labor unions and civil rights organizations, and imposing a web of loyalty oaths. Several southern state legislatures labeled even centrist civil rights organizations like the NAACP as Red fronts and barred their members from serving as public school teachers or working in civil-service jobs. Many states required public employees or those seeking licenses to pledge their loyalty. Loyalty pledges were often required to get a driver's license or even a business permit. Pharmacists in Texas, professional wrestlers in Indiana, and those seeking fishing permits in New York were required to affirm their opposition to communism and loyalty to the United States. Texas required that authors of school textbooks not only sign anticommunist oaths but also include in their books accounts of "our glowing and throbbing history of hearts and souls inspired by wonderful American principles and tradition."

The Expanding Dimensions of the Cold War

Despite the success achieved by American efforts in Western Europe and Japan, the Cold War overflowed its early boundaries. Soviet development of an atomic bomb led Washington to reassess its own security needs. Communist victories in China and Vietnam prompted demands for more extensive involvement in Asia. Meanwhile, the Republican drumbeat about spies and subversives grew louder.

In September 1949, American reconnaissance planes collected air samples that revealed an atomic explosion had recently occurred inside the Soviet Union. Coming several years earlier than many Americans expected, the detonation spurred fears that Stalin would be emboldened to challenge the United States. The Soviet bomb triggered both a search for spies who may have given away nuclear secrets as well as a debate over whether to build a super-, or hydrogen, bomb a thousand times more powerful than the weapons used against Japan. Whereas atomic bombs derived their energy from the splitting, or fission, of uranium atoms, the proposed new weapon would use the energy released by the fusion, or bonding together, of hydrogen atoms.

Some powerful voices protested this new venture. J. Robert Oppenheimer, a central figure in the creation of the atomic bomb, and diplomat George Kennan both argued against expanding the arms race. They did not believe that the Soviet atomic bomb gave Stalin much of an advantage, especially because atomic bombs could be made much more powerful anyway and the Soviets lacked the means to deliver a weapon directly against the United States. Before rushing into an expensive race to build a hydrogen bomb, they urged a renewed effort to negotiate an arms control pact with Moscow. If Stalin balked, the United States could still build a hydrogen bomb (an H-bomb).

The politically charged atmosphere in Washington poisoned debate. Truman's advisers used Oppenheimer's opposition to the hydrogen bomb as an excuse to remove him from his position as a government weapons consultant. Later, he was declared a "security risk" and barred from doing any classified work. Kennan, the so-called Father of Containment, was also sidelined. Secretary of State Acheson replaced him as head of policy planning with hard-liner Paul Nitze, an advocate of building the superweapon and sharply increasing military spending. Truman approved development of the H-bomb in January 1950. The United States tested a prototype device in November 1952, and the Soviets followed with their own the next August.

In October 1949, just a month after confirming the Soviet atomic test, Communist leader Mao Zedong established the People's Republic of China

Jiang Jieshi and Mao Zedong at an American-sponsored peace conference in 1945. Civil war soon followed. / Jack Wilkers, © Life Magazine, Time Inc.

(PRC). Jiang Jieshi's Nationalists fled to the island of Taiwan. The "loss of China," as Republicans described it, disheartened Americans who remembered the World War II alliance with Jiang and thought of China as America's favorite charity. Even though the United States had provided over $2 billion in military and economic aid to Jiang since 1945, his government's corruption and unpopularity nullified its effect. As one American military observer put it, Nationalist troops abandoned positions "they could have defended with broomsticks." In 1946, Truman had sent General George C. Marshall to mediate the conflict, but he abandoned the effort in 1947, criticizing both the Nationalists and Reds.

When Marshall returned to Washington to become secretary of state, the Truman administration largely washed its hands of China. Military aid seemed pointless because Nationalist commanders either fled or sold their weapons to the Communists. Privately, Truman called Jiang a "crook" and even Republican senators agreed in private that aid to China was "money down a rat hole." The president hoped that once Mao took power, he would distance himself from the bullying Soviets and act flexibly toward the United States.

In August 1949, Truman and Secretary of State Acheson tried to calm Americans by issuing a massive report, *The China White Paper*, detailing how Jiang's government, not the United States, had "lost" China. The administration criticized the Communists as well but made it clear that it would not defend Taiwan and would consider establishing diplomatic ties with the Communist regime once the "dust had settled" in China's civil war.

In January 1950, Acheson announced that the Truman administration would turn its attention away from China and concentrate on securing the "Great Crescent," the Asian-Pacific lands that stretched from Japan through Southeast Asia to India. Japan's industrial capacity and the raw materials of Southeast Asia, he explained, were much more important to American and European economic security than was the vast poorhouse of China. Ignoring this strategy, Republicans labeled *The China White Paper* a whitewash and criticized the administration for not offering military protection to either Taiwan or South Korea.

Early in 1950, the United States began to assist French forces fighting a Communist-led uprising in French Indochina (Vietnam, Laos, and Cambodia). During World War II, Vietnamese guerrilla leader Ho Chi Minh—a Communist but also a dedicated fighter against colonial rule—had cooperated with Americans against Japan. In 1945, he appealed for U.S. support in gaining Vietnamese independence. Earlier, Roosevelt had pressed the French to loosen their grip on Vietnam, but Truman worried more about keeping France a strong, anticommunist, and pro-American ally in Europe and Asia. Although some junior American diplomats sympathized with Ho Chi Minh's Vietminh independence movement, Secretary of State Acheson ended debate when he declared that in colonial areas, "all Stalinists masquerade as nationalists."

In an effort to undercut Ho Chi Minh's nationalist appeal, the State Department urged Paris to appoint a Vietnamese to lead their colony and to promise eventual independence. France selected Bao Dai, a dissolute playboy descended from Vietnamese royalty, as their puppet emperor. One irreverent U.S. diplomat complained that Bao Dai's entire political following in Vietnam consisted of "a pimp and three prostitutes." Nevertheless, in February 1950, after China and the Soviet Union recognized Ho Chi Minh's insurgent government, U.S. officials held their noses and extended official recognition to Bao Dai's puppet regime. That spring, the first American military aid and advisers were sent directly to Vietnam, a down payment on what would become a multibillion-dollar investment that eventually cost 58,000 American lives.

In the wake of the Soviet A-bomb and the Chinese Revolution, Truman ordered a comprehensive review of security policy. Acheson tapped his aide, Paul Nitze, to coordinate the study. The resulting top-secret document, given to Truman by the National Security Council (NSC) in April 1950 and known as NSC-68, presented a grim outlook. In a departure from Kennan's argument that the Soviet challenge was primarily economic and political, Nitze warned that the Soviets posed a real military threat and that Stalin's "fanatical" actions showed a new boldness that "borders on the reckless." By 1954, the report claimed, the Soviets would possess the nuclear capacity to destroy the United States. To counter Moscow's attempt to "impose its authority on the rest of the world," NSC-68 proposed a steep increase in both nuclear and conventional military spending.

Even Acheson described the report privately as overkill. But he defended it as required to "bludgeon the mass mind of government" into action. Some of the president's economic advisers argued that larger defense expenditures would supplement the Marshall Plan and boost industrial output and employment, both at home and among America's allies. Truman endorsed NSC-68 in principle but worried about its enormous price tag. With the administration under Republican attack and uncertain how to meet perceived communist threats, policy gridlock gripped Washington. But then, one high official later recalled, "Korea came along and saved us."

Conclusion

"I suppose," Truman told the American people a few days before he left office in 1953, "that history will remember my term . . . as the years when the Cold War began to overshadow our lives. I have had hardly a day in office that has not been dominated by this all encompassing struggle—this conflict between those who love freedom and those who would lead the world back into slavery and darkness."

During the Truman years, the basic outlines of American Cold War policy, at home and abroad, were established. The United States committed itself to the containment of Soviet power globally and to the promotion of world trade. It had established the principle that America would intervene with aid, advisers, or troops wherever it appeared that the Soviet Union, China, or any of their clients were trying to extend communist influence. Stalin and Truman, while certainly not moral equivalents, both oversimplified complex problems and blamed each other for many of the uncertainties of the post-1945 world order. In Western Europe and Japan, the United States largely succeeded in "winning" the Cold War by 1950. But soon, the frustrations of the Korean conflict, along with the fierce anticommunism spawned by both Truman and his Republican opponents, contributed to the Democrats' fall from power in 1952 and passed on a legacy of global competition between the United States and the Soviet Union.

F U R T H E R • R E A D I N G

On the Truman presidency and early postwar years, see Lizabeth Cohen, *A Consumers' Republic: the Politics of Mass Consumption in Postwar America* (2003); Robert J. Donovan, *Conflict and Crisis: The Presidency of Harry S Truman, 1945–1948* (1977) and *Tumultuous Years: The Presidency of Harry S Truman, 1949–1953* (1982); Alonzo S. Hamby, *Man of the People: A Life of Harry S Truman* (1995); David McCullough, *Truman* (1992); Norman D. Markowitz, *The Rise and Fall of the People's Century: Henry A. Wallace and American Liberalism, 1941–48* (1973); Zachary Karball, *The Last Campaign: How Harry Truman Won the 1948 Election* (2000). **On the origin of the Cold War,** see Melvyn Leffler, *A Preponderance of Power: National Security, the Truman Administration, and the Cold War* (1991); Arnold Offner, *Another Such Victory: President Truman and the Cold War, 1945–53* (2002); Martin Sherwin, *A World Destroyed* (1975); Gregg Herken, *The Winning Weapon* (1981); Paul Boyer, *By the Bomb's Early Light* (1990); David Holloway, *Stalin and the Bomb* (1994); John L. Gaddis, *The United States and the Origin of the Cold*

War, 1941–1947 (1972), *Strategies of Containment: A Critical Appraisal of Postwar American National Security Policy* (1982), and *We Now Know: Rethinking Cold War History* (1997); Norman Naimark, *The Russians in Germany: A History of the Soviet Zone of Occupation, 1945–1949* (1995); Carolyn Eisenberg, *Drawing the Line: The American Decision to Divide Germany, 1944–1949* (1996); Michael J. Hogan, *The Marshall Plan* (1987); Daniel Yergin, *A Shattered Peace* (1977); Walter Isaacson and Evan Thomas, *The Wise Men: Six Friends and the World They Made* (1986); Robert D. Dean, *Imperial Brotherhood: Gender and the Making of Cold War Foreign Policy* (2001). **On domestic communism and the Red Scare,** see William L. O'Neill, *A Better World: Stalinism and American Intellectuals* (1983); Harvey Klehr and John Earl Haynes, *The American Communist Movement: Storming Heaven Itself* (1992); Harvey Klehr, John Earl Haynes, and Kyrill M. Anderson, *The Soviet World of American Communism* (1998); John Earl Haynes and Harvey Klehr, *Venona: Decoding Soviet Espionage in America* (1999); Harvey Klehr and Ronald Radosh, *The Amerasia Case: Prelude to McCarthyism* (1996); Allen Weinstein, *Perjury: The Hiss-Chambers Case* (1997), and *The Haunted Wood: Soviet Espionage in America: The Stalin Era* (1999); Sam Tanenhaus, *Whittaker Chambers: A Biography* (1997); Ronald Radosh and Joyce Milton, *The Rosenberg File* (1997); Sam Roberts, *The Brother: The Untold Story of Atomic Spy David Greenglass and How He Sent His Sister Ethel Rosenberg to the Electric Chair* (2001); David Caute, *The Great Fear* (1977); Athan Theoharis, *Seeds of Repression: Harry S Truman and the Origins of McCarthyism* (1971); Richard Gid Powers, *Secrecy and Power: The Life of J. Edgar Hoover* (1987), and *Not Without Honor: The History of American AntiCommunism* (1995); Richard M. Freeland, *The Truman Doctrine and the Origins of McCarthyism* (1972); Richard Fried, *Nightmare in Red: The McCarthy Era in Perspective* (1990), and *The Russians Are Coming! The Russians Are Coming! Pageantry and Patriotism in Cold War America* (1998); David M. Oshinsky, *A Conspiracy So Immense: The World of Joe McCarthy* (1983); Thomas C. Reeves, *The Life and Times of Joe McCarthy* (1982); Ellen W. Schrecker, *No Ivory Tower: McCarthyism in the Universities* (1986), and *Many Are the Crimes: McCarthyism in America* (1998). **On immigration policies,** see David M. Reimers, *Still the Golden Door: The Third World Comes to America* (1992); Leonard Dinnerstein, *America and the Survivors of the Holocaust* (1982). **On the Korean War and the expanding dimensions of the Cold War,** see Bruce Cummings, *The Origins of the Korean War*, 2 vols. (1981, 1990); William W. Stueck, *The Road to Confrontation: American Policy Toward China and Korea, 1947–1950* (1981), and *The Korean War: An International History* (1995); Burton I. Kauffman, *The Korean War* (1986); Michael Schaller, *The American Occupation of Japan: The Origins of the Cold War in Asia* (1985), and *Douglas MacArthur: The Far Eastern General* (1989); John W. Dower, *Embracing Defeat: Japan in the Wake of World War II* (2000); Mark Bradley, *Imagining Vietnam and America: The Making of Post Colonial Vietnam, 1919–1950* (2000); Robert M. Blum, *Drawing the Line: The Origin of the American Containment Policy in East Asia* (1982). **On the military industrial complex,** see Ann Markusen, Peter Hall, Scott Campbell, and Sabina Deitrick, *The Rise of the Gunbelt: The Military Remapping of Industrial America* (1991); James Fallows, *The National Defense* (1981).

3

America at Home, 1953–1960

This scene of workers emptying moving vans in a new suburb of Los Angeles captures the mobility, materialism, and family norms that transformed postwar America's urban and social landscapes. / J. R. Eyerman, © Life Magazine, Time Inc.

In 1955, thousands of invited guests walked down Walt Disney's vision of Main Street for the first time as Disneyland opened in Anaheim, California. Imagined as a new kind of amusement park, it offered its visitors an entertaining and idealized view of nature and society. Its planners called that view "Disney Realism," explaining that they intended to "program out all the negative, unwanted elements and program in the positive elements." Their efforts started in their publicity, which targeted middle-class American families who embraced the consumer and domestic values that dominated the postwar period. They continued at the gates, where ticket prices and security guards ensured that only those who met the standards for appearance and demeanor would be admitted.

Once inside, visitors could enjoy the rides and marvel at their experiences in Tomorrowland, Adventureland, Frontierland, and Fantasyland. These park areas incorporated familiar characters and themes from Disney's films and television shows. Guests encountered Mickey Mouse, Donald Duck, and other favorites from Disney's cartoons on Main Street and in Fantasyland. They also attended exhibits provided by corporate sponsors, who were assured by Disney's promoters that "in this environment, visitors are more susceptible to the messages" they sought to convey. The amusement park touted nationalism and Cold War values, claiming "Disneyland could happen only in a country where freedom is a heritage and the pursuit of happiness a basic human right." In 1959 its managers reinforced the "Americanism" of such values when they defied the government's request to close the park to the public for a day to accommodate a visit by Soviet premier Nikita Khrushchev.

Disneyland's embrace of the corporate and consumer culture of the postwar period also extended to its personnel policies, which were designed to ensure a wholesome and pleasant experience for the customers. Disneyland employees learned at the outset that the company's culture required close conformity to its rules. The company handbook made this clear, expressing to its workers the "hope that you enjoy thinking our way." According to film critic Richard Schickel, Disney's employees had to "spend a few hard days in the 'University of Disneyland,' which [trained] them in the modern art forms—pioneered by the airlines—of the frozen smile and the canned answer delivered with enough spontaneity to make it seem unprogrammed." Indeed, Disney workers had to display the other-directed personality of the organization men described by the social critics of the time. Workers who had contact with the public were all white, prompting historian John Findlay to conclude that "race relations inside the theme park were far from futuristic."

As the success of Disneyland suggests, Americans in the 1950s accelerated the trends they pursued in the immediate aftermath of the war. The economy continued to grow. With money in their pockets, Americans rushed to new homes in suburbia, had children in record numbers, and went on a consumer buying spree, snapping up home appliances, automobiles, televisions, and a plethora of other goods and services. Most Americans believed they had entered an era of well-deserved stability and prosperity, a message widely reinforced in popular culture. Dwight D. Eisenhower was a popular president who brought a sense of security to American life. Especially for the white middle class and unionized blue-collar workers, confidence in material progress and the perfectibility of American society coexisted alongside a fervent anticommunist ideology and anxiety about nuclear destruction.

Beneath the surface stability, however, the 1950s were years of change and upheaval. Continued population movement and the automobile, television, and advanced technology weren't the only factors to change the face of American life. Critics began to complain that the apparent consensus of American society was hollow. In the age of *Father Knows Best* and trips to Disneyland, American youth developed its own subculture centered on rock 'n' roll music, which alarmed their elders. Meanwhile, the civil rights struggle erupted in the South, which forced Americans to confront issues that had too long been ignored.

The Affluent Society

Beginning in the late 1940s and continuing well into the 1990s, the most dramatic population growth occurred in American suburbs, the new rings of residential communities outside larger cities. Until the 1960s, people of color were barred by custom, law, or restrictive lending practices, but white Americans flocked in growing numbers to large subdivisions built on former farmland. Americans had begun leaving cities in the nineteenth century, but only after 1945 could the United States be called a suburban nation. Between 1940 and 1970, the proportion of suburban dwellers increased from 19.5 to 37.6 percent (see the table). An associated phenomenon was the rise in suburban shopping centers, or malls; their number increased from eight to four thousand in the first postwar decade.

Until 1945, the housing industry had focused on building custom homes or urban multifamily buildings. During the Depression and war years, housing construction almost ceased. Now, 16 million veterans and their new families clamored for homes and apartments. These homes did not exist, however, or cost more than most could afford. In New York City, for example, several

Geographic Distribution of U.S. Population, 1930–1970

Year	Central Cities	Suburbs	Rural Areas and Small Towns
1930	31.8%	18.0%	50.2%
1940	31.6	19.5	48.9
1950	32.3	23.8	43.9
1960	32.6	30.7	36.7
1970	31.4	37.6	31.0

Source: Adapted from U.S. Bureau of the Census, *Decennial Censuses, 1930–1970* (Washington, D.C.: U.S. Government Printing Office).

veterans and their brides slept each night in the beds in the show windows of Macy's department store. Their plight was only partly a publicity stunt because little affordable housing was available. More typically, new couples roomed with relatives.

Meanwhile, the National Association of Home Builders and the National Association of Realtors were lobbying to shape federal housing policies. By tradition, banks and other private lenders had followed restrictive mortgage procedures, often demanding 50 percent of the purchase price as a down payment and repayment of the balance within ten years. Following the war, however, the Federal Housing Administration (FHA) began insuring thirty-year bank mortgages with only a 5 to 10 percent down payment. Under the GI Bill, qualifying veterans could often take title for a token $1 down payment. By guaranteeing loan repayment, the FHA and Veterans Administration (VA) persuaded private lenders to relax mortgage terms.

The result was a housing boom, particularly in suburbia, where large areas of inexpensive land could be developed. Housing starts jumped from 114,000 in 1944 to 1.7 million in 1950. By then, federal agencies insured more than one-third of all mortgages. In addition to FHA and VA loan guarantees, the government's tax policy promoted housing growth by allowing a deduction for mortgage interest. Veterans' demands and the new federal policies meshed with a new trend in the construction industry: the increasing dominance of large construction firms, which had discovered that they could operate profitably by building a great number of similar homes on large tracts of land.

Levittown, named after builder William Levitt, became a synonym for suburban development. Levitt, a builder of luxury homes before 1941, pioneered prefabrication techniques for navy housing during the war. In 1947, he decided to mass-produce private homes that GIs would be able to afford. The first Levittown, a planned community of 10,000 homes, sprang from a 1,200-acre potato field on Long Island, New York. Larger projects followed in Pennsylvania and New Jersey.

Levitt harnessed mass-production techniques to home construction, making a "factory of the whole building site." Materials were precut and preassembled by teams of semiskilled laborers and moved to lots when needed. Instead of hiring union painters and carpenters, Levitt trained workers to do specific tasks, such as spray painting or using power tools, on an assembly-line basis. The company bought its own forests, milled its own lumber, and convinced appliance companies to manufacture new, standard-size washers, dryers, and refrigerators at reduced prices. At the height of Levittown construction, a house was completed every sixteen minutes. Construction costs were $10 a square foot, 30 percent below the industry standard. With a VA loan, a veteran could move into a new home for $56 per month, which was often less than the cost of renting an apartment. When one subdivision opened in 1949, 1,400 units sold in a single day.

The Levittown house, like Henry Ford's Model T, set an affordable standard that made homeownership a reality for the postwar middle class. But

Levittown was only the most conspicuous example of a widespread trend. Surrounding cities across the United States, new suburbs of similar, middle-class houses began to appear. In a chaotic world, the freestanding, single-family, self-contained, all-electric suburban home was presented as a refuge in which the female homemaker could take charge of housework and childcare, while appliances did the hard work.

Architectural critics condemned the cookie-cutter appearance of these new communities. Social commentators worried about conformist pressures, such as the rule that lawns be mowed weekly or that homes could be painted only with approved colors. But most new residents who had shared cramped quarters with resentful in-laws were thrilled to move into a three-bedroom house equipped with luxuries such as a washer, dryer, and refrigerator. Suburbia also homogenized white society by mixing ethnic, social, and political groups that formerly had lived in separate urban neighborhoods. New institutions such as churches and civic clubs replaced extended families and kinship networks.

Levittown and its many imitators made homeownership a reality for the white postwar middle class. Houses originally priced in the $7,000 range would be worth $300,000 or more fifty years later. Some "Levittowners" used their home equity gradually to trade up to fancier homes; others held on to their homes for decades and used the equity to finance college for their children or to fund their own retirement.

Suburbs tended to be ethnically diverse but racially segregated. Suburbanization actually increased the separation of races in most parts of America. In 1950, for example, only 1 million of the 20 million Americans living in suburbs were nonwhite. During its first several years, Levittown, like many planned subdivisions, barred "members of other than the Caucasian race" from buying homes. Meanwhile, in cities where most racial minorities were concentrated, federal agencies and private lenders provided few loans to build or improve homes.

By 1946, the nation was experiencing a baby boom that would last into the 1960s. The average number of children born to an American family increased from 2.4 to 3.2 between 1945 and 1957, when the boom peaked (see Figure 3.1). The American population surged by 30 million in the 1950s, reaching 180 million by the end of the decade. When births peaked at 4.3 million in 1957, one-third of all Americans were age 14 or younger. This demographic feature created exceptional demands for new housing, appliances, toys, and schools. Between 1950 and 1960, total school enrollment in kindergarten through twelfth grade increased from 28 million to 42 million.

In previous decades, parenting manuals had described infants as nasty tyrants who would grow up with grave character disorders if they were indulged or overstimulated. Pediatrician Benjamin Spock challenged these assumptions in his 1946 *Book of Baby and Child Care*. Spock urged parents to have fun with their kids. He encouraged physical contact and emotional nurturing as keys to healthy development. The book sold over 20 million copies in ten years, and 40 million copies by 1990.

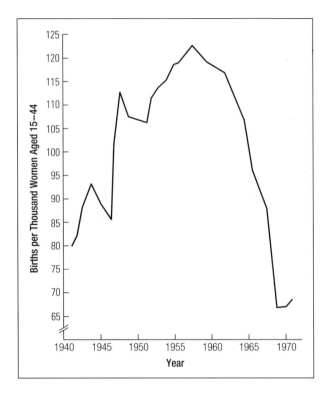

Figure 3.1
Birth Rate, 1940–1970

As young parents in suburbia read Dr. Spock and enjoyed their electric kitchens, the same policies that promoted suburban growth were causing serious problems for cities, the poor, and minorities. The FHA gave preference to subsidizing single-family, detached homes in the $7,000 to $10,000 range. Until the 1960s, the FHA provided few loans to assist buyers in racially mixed neighborhoods or to improve existing multifamily housing. In making these decisions, the FHA followed the color-coded rating system devised by the federal Home Owners Loan Corporation, which classified neighborhoods (from green to red) according to the loan default risks they were presumed to pose for mortgage lenders. These redlining practices kept many African Americans and other people of color out of the housing market and living in older, decaying urban neighborhoods. Meanwhile, minorities were barred from most suburban homes.

Public and private discrimination contributed to drawing a "white noose" around the increasingly nonwhite cities. As businesses and white families left the cities for the suburbs, they took with them the jobs and income that had contributed to urban tax revenues and employment. The growth of suburbs around a city usually resulted in the decline of the city's economy. By 1960, the suburban population of 60 million equaled that of all urban areas. Except for the South and West, where rural-to-urban migration continued, most large cities either lost population or barely held steady during the 1950s.

At first, almost all suburbanites commuted to jobs in central cities, but by 1960 many worked closer to home. Suburban employment and manufacturing rose dramatically, while employment in the twenty-five largest U.S. cities declined about 7 percent during the decade. Downtown commercial districts lost business to suburban shopping centers surrounded by acres of parking lots.

The American population continued to shift west and south, with California, Florida, and Texas attracting many newcomers. The gains in urban population in the West and suburban population in the Northeast came partly at the expense of rural America. The number of agricultural workers fell to barely 6 percent of the population, down two-thirds since America entered World War II.

The rise of the suburbs had other lasting effects as well. One was the increased demand for cars and better roads. Between 1946 and 1950, domestic automobile production jumped from 2 million to 6 million annually. By 1960, America had nearly 70 million vehicles on the road. In Los Angeles County alone, more cars traveled the freeways than in all of Asia or South America. By the 1950s, the highway lobby—an umbrella group of automakers, highway construction companies, and trucking firms—began to pressure the federal government for a national highway system. Nine out of ten suburban families owned a car, compared to only six out of ten urban households. Women driving station wagons full of children became emblems of suburban life.

These cars were not the staid models of the 1940s. Detroit built bigger, gaudier, more expensive machines than ever before. The public adored two- and three-tone models, tail fins, and wraparound windshields. Innovations like

By the 1950s, American culture was car culture. / Picture Research Consultants

power steering, automatic transmission, and air conditioning made cars more comfortable and convenient. Auto tourism became a major form of family leisure. Bobby Troupe's hit song "Get Your Kicks on Route 66" reflected Americans' love of the road. Families took cross-country trips to national parks and new amusement parks like Disneyland. Motel chains proliferated. So did other spin-off industries such as fast-food restaurants and drive-in theaters.

Responding to demands from business, local governments, and automobile owners, the federal government decided to upgrade the nation's inadequate highways. By 1956, a bipartisan movement in Congress, supported by organized labor, the highway lobby, and civil-defense advocates (who argued that better roads would speed the evacuation from cities in times of war), won passage of the National System of Defense Highways. This massive building program authorized the construction of forty thousand miles of new highways. Washington paid 90 percent of the initial $50 billion tab through excise taxes levied on tires and fuel, and the states paid the rest. The massive road-building program prompted one leading Democrat to quip that "the New Dealers had been replaced by the car dealers."

The interstate highway system dwarfed anything built by the New Deal. And although the title of the bill suggested that highways were needed primarily for defense purposes, the most important effects of interstate highways were social. By subsidizing the car culture with six thousand miles of city-to-suburb freeways, while denying funds for inner-city mass transit, government promoted suburban development at the cities' expense.

The public's enthusiasm for the automobile allowed manufacturers to ignore the poor safety records and nonexistent fuel efficiency of their products. The mounting highway death toll (forty thousand in 1959) elicited little concern, although a young Harvard law student, Ralph Nader, worried enough to begin investigating auto safety as early as 1957. But the big Detroit automakers either ignored their few critics or dismissed them as deviants.

By the early 1960s, many urban planners and ordinary Americans began to question the wisdom of chopping up cities with smog-producing freeways while permitting mass transit to decay. But during the 1950s, nearly everyone celebrated public road subsidies for private automobiles. Gasoline was cheap, highways were "free," and America's future was on the road.

Leisure and entertainment in general were becoming big business. Television's influence on American life was soon evident in ways both large and small. The television industry expanded quickly in the early 1950s, when the Federal Communications Commission (FCC) sped up licensing procedures. As the size of televisions increased, quality improved and prices fell to an average of $200. By the time Eisenhower took office in 1953, half of all American homes had a television. For the rest of the decade, sales ranged between 5 million and 7 million units annually. By 1956, two-thirds of all American homes had one or more televisions, and Americans viewed programs on over 600 stations, nearly all of which were affiliated with a national network. By the early 1960s, 90 percent of all homes had at least one receiver. As early as 1956, Americans spent more time watching television than working for wages.

Some early comedy-variety offerings, like Sid Caesar's *Your Show of Shows* (1950–1954), provided quality writing and acting. A fair amount of sophisticated live drama aired through the mid-1950s on shows such as *Kraft Television Theater, Playhouse 90,* and *Studio One.* But toward the end of the 1950s, Hollywood began selling old movies to television and producing low-budget, made-for-TV movies. This switch effectively removed most original drama from television.

Among the most successful comedy shows of the 1950s was *I Love Lucy,* which became a model for many subsequent situation comedies, or sitcoms. Lucille Ball played Lucy Ricardo, the scatterbrained wife of Cuban-born bandleader Ricky Ricardo, played by Desi Arnaz, her real-life husband. Each week Lucy and her friend Ethel Mertz schemed to get jobs, impress their husbands, and achieve respect. Their plans usually backfired, forcing Ricky and Fred Mertz to rescue their wives. Although the show's endings reinforced the assumption that traditional gender roles best suited the capacities of women and men, Lucy's ambition, energy, and resourcefulness came through strongly, undermining the psychological explanations of women's discontent that dominated other media.

Because of technical limitations on live broadcasts and remote filming, news coverage was not a staple of television until the early 1960s. Still, Edward R. Murrow, a pioneer of radio and TV investigative journalism, produced some exceptional work for CBS, including an exposé of Senator Joseph McCarthy on *See It Now* and a pioneering probe of the link between smoking and lung cancer in 1955. But most television news came in a fifteen-minute format. As innovations such as the video camera made it possible to follow breaking stories, the networks expanded nightly news coverage to half-hour broadcasts in 1963 and promoted the programs heavily to win audience share.

Television generally provided entertainment, not intellectual enlightenment. *Howdy Doody,* a lighthearted romp using marionettes and mock Indians, set the tone for children's programming. Westerns like *Hopalong Cassidy* and *The Lone Ranger* played to young viewers before adult westerns such as *Gunsmoke* and *Maverick* came into vogue. Soap operas and quiz shows dominated the daytime airwaves. Inexpensive to produce, they appealed to busy housewives, who could break up the household routine with television viewing. *Queen for a Day,* in which bedraggled women told hard-luck stories in return for prizes, merged the soap-opera and quiz-show formats.

In the evening, family-oriented sitcoms proliferated. The decade's big hits included *The Adventures of Ozzie and Harriet, Leave It to Beaver, Father Knows Best,* and *The Honeymooners.* Except for the last, in which bus driver Ralph Kramden (Jackie Gleason) and his sewer-worker buddy Ed Norton (Art Carney) schemed to get rich, these were middle-class fables in which white suburban families with a homemaker mother and a breadwinning father lived pleasant lives. People of color appeared only as servants. Television's need to attract mass audiences and thus earn advertising revenue ensured that its content would appeal to the greatest possible number and that complex social or economic issues would not be discussed.

The rarity of African Americans on television made the inclusion of any blacks noteworthy. Henry Louis Gates, Jr., who was raised in West Virginia in the 1950s, remembers that the neighbors would shout, "Colored, colored, on Channel Two," from their front porches or get on the phone to tell their friends. Even *Amos and Andy*, widely criticized for its stereotypical black characters, was popular in his neighborhood because the world of the show "was *all* colored, just like ours." The inclusion of black professionals on the show gave African Americans images of different lives. Like other Americans, blacks found that the "TV was the ritual arena for the drama of race" unfolding in American society, from Montgomery to Little Rock and beyond.

A quiz-show scandal in 1959 tarnished television's reputation as the purveyor of clean values. In 1955, a few prime-time quiz shows with large cash prizes, such as *The $64,000 Question* and *Twenty-One*, captured the public's fancy. In dramatic encounters, one or more contestants, isolated in glass booths, competed for cash prizes. To heighten the suspense, the questions were kept in bank vaults and brought to the studio by armed guards. Each week's winner proceeded to a new round, tougher questions, and bigger prizes. These shows attracted huge audiences and earned large profits for both the networks and sponsors. Producers often coached contestants on how to smile, grimace, fidget, and knit their brows while pondering the questions. Some contestants secretly received additional help, including the answers to questions.

In 1956, Charles Van Doren, a young, articulate English professor at Columbia University, won $129,000 on *Twenty-One*—a great improvement on his $4,400 academic salary. NBC hired him as a consultant for $50,000 annually. Parents and teachers wrote to praise Van Doren as a role model for children. Two years later, the bubble burst. In 1958, the man dethroned by Charles Van Doren complained to New York journalists that Van Doren had received the answers in advance. Both a grand jury and a congressional subcommittee investigated the scandal. Van Doren first maintained his innocence, but eventually he broke down and gave the investigating committee details of his cheating. The prospect of wealth and fame had corrupted him, Van Doren explained. In the wake of this scandal, networks canceled most of the quiz shows.

The scandal made some question the value of television. After all, TV had invaded the American home, taking center stage in the American living room. What happened when this new focus of family life lied to viewers? Should it be admired as a source of entertainment and information, despised as cultural pabulum, or feared for its demagogic potential? Just as social commentators disagree about television's worth in today's society, historians have mixed feelings about its contribution to the 1950s. Newton Minow, newly appointed chair of the Federal Communications Commission (FCC), shocked a gathering of broadcast executives in 1961 by describing their industry as a vast wasteland. Forty years later, quiz shows, sitcoms, sports, and police dramas (rather than westerns) still dominated television programming.

Nowhere was the impact of television on popular culture clearer than in the area of sports. After World War II, professional and college sports assumed a growing significance in American life. By the late 1940s, professional leagues in basketball and ice hockey had joined those in baseball and football to provide increasing sports entertainment for an avid public. Sports took on the trappings of a secular religion as people gave vast significance to the fortunes of their favorite teams. In the suburbs, Little League baseball and football, modeled on the professional leagues, enrolled millions of boys.

Television was part of this change because it elevated players to unprecedented fame and gave fans a new and closer look at their idols. Initially, TV cameras worked best in small arenas and other venues in which a single camera could pan the playing area. Boxing, wrestling, and roller derby fared well on TV, as did baseball. As the technology evolved, multiple and remote cameras improved the coverage of football and basketball, and sports occupied a growing portion of the TV schedule. By the 1960s, sports had become a major part of broadcasting. Television also became the key to sports profits because television payments soon exceeded the revenue from ticket sales.

Desegregation proceeded slowly in professional and college athletics. After Jackie Robinson broke baseball's color line in 1947, professional teams began to hire black athletes, but the pace varied from one sport to another. Some southern college basketball teams refused to recruit African Americans or play against teams that did. Because the segregated sports programs gradually became uncompetitive, they were eventually forced to recruit blacks as well as whites.

As the nation's population shifted toward the West and the Sunbelt, the owners of professional teams began to move franchises to these areas, often provoking outcries from loyal fans. When baseball owner Walter O'Malley took his Brooklyn Dodgers to Los Angeles after the 1957 season, New Yorkers decried his betrayal and demanded a congressional investigation. But during the next decade, many teams relocated. The old fans protested, but fans in the new cities hastened to the stadiums and arenas or watched the games on television.

The Politics of Moderation

By the beginning of the 1950s, it was clear that national politics were swinging to the right. The question was, how far right? General Dwight D. Eisenhower, widely known by his nickname Ike, chose politics as a second career at age sixty-two. Despite this late beginning, he became one of the most popular and successful presidents of the postwar era. The public was reassured by his calm, grandfatherly style and seldom questioned his rather disengaged stewardship of domestic policy. Veteran journalist Walter Lippmann remarked, "Ike could be elected even if dead. All you would need [to do is] to prop him up in the rear seat of an open car and parade down Broadway."

Eisenhower was born in 1890 in Denison, Texas, into a large, pious, and poor family. He grew up in Abilene, Kansas, and attended West Point despite his parents' pacifism. He graduated in 1915, but because few promotions were available during the interwar period, he had risen only to the rank of major by 1939. With the start of the war in Europe, however, Eisenhower quickly ascended to prominence, helped by army chief of staff General George C. Marshall, who considered him among the most promising men in the army. By 1944, Eisenhower was a four-star general and commander of the Allied forces in the European theater. His ability to manage and conciliate the Allied armies sped victory and won him acclaim as a talented and humane leader.

After the war, Eisenhower served successively as army chief of staff, president of Columbia University, and the first supreme commander of NATO during the Korean War. Ambitious but wary of politics, he rebuffed both Democratic and Republican invitations to seek the presidential nomination in 1948. Four years later, he still coveted the White House but disdained the idea of campaigning for office, seeking instead a "draft" that would nominate him by acclamation.

Despite Eisenhower's wartime ties to Roosevelt, he held fairly conservative views on economics and social programs, favoring private enterprise over government intervention as a solution to most problems. He was at the same time a confirmed internationalist who supported the containment of communism, the Marshall Plan, and the "Europe-first" orientation of the Truman administration. Eisenhower resented and feared the anti-NATO, Asia-first ideas of Republican presidential aspirants such as senators Robert Taft and Joseph McCarthy and General Douglas MacArthur. Early in 1952, Eisenhower made his decision: he resigned his NATO command and entered the Republican primaries, securing enough delegates to defeat his chief rival, Taft, at the party's nominating convention. Eisenhower placated the Republican right by tapping California senator Richard M. Nixon as his vice-presidential running mate.

Cracks in the Picture Window

While Eisenhower exuded his aura of political stability, American life was changing in significant ways. Technology continued the boom begun during World War II, and the economy reached new heights of prosperity in spite of three recessions. The home and family were increasingly the center of popular values, reinforced by a widespread revival in church membership. But critics surveying the social landscape began to insist that important flaws lay beneath the surface of prosperity and contentment.

Economic growth during the 1950s averaged more than 4 percent annually, despite recessions in 1954, 1958, and 1960. Inflation remained below 2 percent and unemployment remained below 5 percent. The gross national product (GNP) nearly doubled between 1950 and 1960, to $500 billion (see Figure 3.2). Measured in constant 1954 dollars, this represented a per capita increase of about 25 percent (from $2,096 to $2,536). Median family income grew from about $3,000 to $5,657. Real wages rose by 30 percent.

With high employment and higher incomes, Americans found more ways to spend their wages. Lenient bank lending policies and the advent of the credit card also stimulated consumer spending. The Diners Club and American Express credit cards were both introduced during the 1950s, followed by oil company, hotel chain, and department store credit cards. Sears promoted its cards

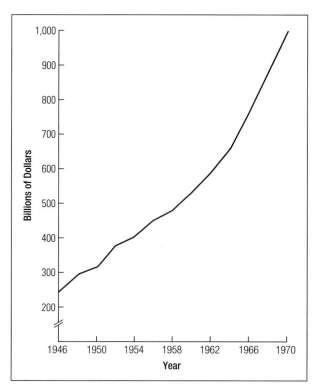

Figure 3.2
Gross National Product,
1946–1970

so aggressively that by 1960, over 10 million Americans held them. As a record number of young families furnished homes and clothed children in the 1950s, private debt climbed from $73 billion to $200 billion. That debt financed a mountain of consumer goods as Americans sought the new, the disposable, and the modern. Encouraged by advertising to equate consuming with personal freedom and "the good life," Americans used natural resources as though the supply was infinite and littered newly created landfills with tons of disposable goods. The 1950s witnessed the creation of the throwaway society, complete with TV dinners in aluminum containers or "boil-in bags," and a plethora of paper products—from napkins to dresses—that could be discarded after one use. In 1951, *House Beautiful* asked women "Is Your Grandmother Standing Between You and Today's Freedom?" while offering them information on the use of new household products. At the end of the decade, *Look* provided similar training and extolled the new "kitchen freedom" being offered to women.

The profile of industry and business also changed. Mergers accelerated, with the result that the two hundred largest corporations controlled over half of all business assets by the end of the decade. Some corporations were beginning to expand across national borders. Traditional industries such as iron, steel, textiles, and mining shrank, while chemicals, aviation, drugs, plastics, fast-food chains, discount retailers (such as Kresge's, later Kmart), and electronics expanded. Overall, heavy industry and manufacturing declined, partly a result of automation, which cost an estimated 1.5 million jobs from 1953 to 1959. New job growth clustered in the service, clerical, and managerial sectors. By 1956, white-collar workers outnumbered blue-collar workers for the first time.

Throughout the 1950s, the number of American farm families continued to decline. Increased mechanization, cheap chemical fertilizers, and new herbicides and pesticides allowed farmers to boost crop yields significantly. The increased production of grains, vegetables, and dairy products benefited urban consumers but created a surplus that drove agricultural commodity prices down. Congress responded by adopting a complex price support system that paid some farmers to grow less, paid others a subsidy to cover their costs, and promoted agricultural exports through subsidies or as food aid to poor countries. But even as the number of farmers declined in the decades after World War II, productivity grew and, as in industry, a growing proportion of farms were owned by corporate agribusiness and worked by employees. Small farmers found it increasingly difficult to compete against these conglomerates and foreign producers.

Meanwhile, the labor movement struggled, with only partial success, to hold its own. Once the war was over, it pushed for a law making the federal government responsible for securing employment for all job seekers who were able to work. The 1946 Full Employment Act, gutted in passage by Congress, promised only "maximum employment," an ambiguous term that left plenty of room for shifting views of what represented an acceptable unemployment rate. In 1955, the American Federation of Labor and the Congress of Industrial Organizations overcame their long-time rivalry and merged to form the AFL-CIO. But congressional investigations into union ties to organized crime, along with the federal conviction of Teamsters Union president Dave Beck, tarnished labor's image and led to the passage of the Landrum-Griffin Act of 1959. It created new legal restrictions on the labor movement, including additional limits on boycotts and picketing.

Although the number of union members remained fairly steady, the unionized proportion of the total work force declined with the loss of jobs in heavy industry, and unions faced new challenges as they sought to extend their power in the blue-collar sector. Corporate leaders used relocation and automation to reduce the power of unions. The automobile industry, for example, moved many plants to suburban locations, some in the Detroit area, and to new areas in the Midwest and California. In the South, redbaiting, management pressures, and local hostility to unions made growth difficult in a region where new service and manufacturing jobs (mostly for whites only) were rapidly replacing jobs lost in the rural areas. The unions that managed to penetrate the white-collar sector, such as the American Federation of State, County, and Municipal Employees (AFSCME), accounted for a growing percentage of union membership.

Throughout the decade, some progressive business leaders and economists boasted of creating a "people's capitalism" that ensured the equal distribution

(cont. on page 100)

High-Tech Medicine

The baby-boom generation was raised by three doctors: Dr. Spock, Dr. Salk, and Dr. Seuss. Dr. Benjamin Spock's advice to anxious parents alleviated stresses of childcare. Dr. Seuss (Theodore Geisel) wrote miraculous stories such as *The Cat in the Hat* and *Green Eggs and Ham* that put a generation of children to bed while instilling in them a love of reading. Dr. Jonas Salk's vaccine banished the terror of paralytic polio, a disease that had haunted America since the 1920s. The biotechnological revolution of the 1940s and 1950s ushered in an era when Americans looked to science and medicine to eliminate infectious disease, regulate birth, and mitigate the effects of aging. They also heard frequent warnings from public health authorities about the risks of smoking and obesity.

Today, Americans suffering from a diversity of maladies treat the problem with a pill or shot. Before World War II, few such treatments existed, and aspirin was about as high-tech as medicine got. World War II spurred a revolution that transformed the treatment of illness and produced the modern pharmaceutical industry.

Most physicians accepted the germ theory of disease, but science had produced few treatments before 1930. In 1929, British bacteriologist Arthur Fleming reported that the common *penicillium notatum* mold produced a substance that killed bacteria in a laboratory dish. But for a decade, no one followed up on this observation. In 1939, as war began in Europe, British and American researchers began to study the antibiotic, or germ-killing, properties of the mold.

Penicillin, as scientists called the mold's active ingredient, proved difficult to extract. It took a year to gather one-tenth of a gram of penicillin, just enough to test on an infected mouse. A human treatment required at least 30 grams. But, spurred on by the war, in 1941 a team of researchers discovered that penicillin could be produced through a bulk fermentation process that utilized a molasses-like by-product of corn. They enlisted private industry to start a massive production effort, and by 1942, several companies opened "bottle plants" that contained 100,000 one-liter fermentation containers. A federal "penicillin czar" oversaw the production and distribution of millions of doses of the miracle drug that destroyed the germs that caused such common killers as pneumonia, tuberculosis, and staphylococcus. After the war, many of the penicillin pioneers left government for university or private laboratories, where they developed new antibiotics.

Initially, few researchers realized that by killing off natural forms of bacterium, antibiotics cleared the path for the emergence of new drug-resistant strains. As drug-resistant "staph" and "strep" proliferated, pharmaceutical companies raced to develop new antibiotics. These new drugs, in turn, opened the bacteriological environment for new resistant strains in a never-ending antibiotic war.

Americans alive in the 1940s and 1950s dreaded few things more than the annual spring onset of the polio season. Each summer since 1916, the disease struck tens of thousands of victims, killing or paralyzing several thousand. In a futile effort to stop the plague, municipal pools and beaches closed and parents kept children at home. Everyone knew someone who, like Franklin D. Roosevelt in 1921, had gone to bed with a headache and never walked again. Their tragedy was captured in poignant photographs in *Life* and *Look* magazines that displayed hospital wards full of children and adults in bulky metal breathing devices called iron lungs. The most severe polio outbreak occurred in 1952, when 60,000 Americans fell seriously ill. About 3,000 died and about 9,000 suffered some degree of paralysis. Influenza, heart disease, and cancer took a higher toll, but no disease conjured up more fear than polio.

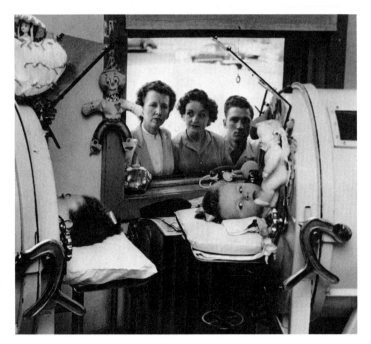

As polio epidemics grew more severe in the early 1950s, every parent's nightmare was that his or her child might die or end up in an "iron lung." / ©Bettman/CORBIS

Until the twentieth century, the virus that caused poliomyelitis afflicted relatively few people. Most babies were exposed to the virus shortly after birth, when it caused only a mild infection and conferred lifelong immunity. But in the United States, improved sanitation often delayed exposure to the virus, whose symptoms became more virulent as age increased. Babies raised in middle- and upper-class homes were more likely to avoid exposure in infancy and thus suffer from later infection.

The fight against polio became an American obsession during the 1930s to 1950s, in part because Franklin D. Roosevelt, whose legs were crippled by the disease in 1921, became president in 1933. Roosevelt projected a new public vision of the polio survivor as someone who triumphed over adversity through struggle. He and his former law partner, Basil O'Connor, organized the National Foundation for Infantile Paralysis in 1938. Although a private organization, it benefited from a close association with

FDR's New Deal. The foundation's "March of Dimes" annual fundraiser selected a poster child whose image helped bring in as much as $67 million each year by the 1950s for polio treatment and research.

The postwar baby boom intersected with a rising incidence of polio. The disease struck at the very essence of a middle-class, child-centered society, and at a faith that science could vanquish all problems. If scientists could harness nuclear power and build rockets and computers, surely they could conquer a primitive virus.

In 1949, Dr. Jonas Salk, a research physician based at the University of Pittsburgh (also home to Dr. Spock), received support from the National Foundation for Infantile Paralysis to develop a polio vaccine. Salk applied techniques developed by others who had discovered how to grow poliovirus in a test tube. He concentrated on creating a vaccine derived from "killed" viruses, while other researchers favored a vaccine from weakened, or "attenuated," live viruses.

After a small-scale test showed promise, Salk and his foundation sponsors launched a massive field trial. In 1954, 220,000 volunteers, 20,000 physicians, and 64,000 public health workers recruited 2 million elementary schoolchildren, called "polio volunteers," for the largest test ever of an experimental drug. To ensure accuracy, children from all races had to be included in the experiment. Segregation remained so strong in southern states, however, that black children were denied entry into the white-only schools where the shots were given. Instead, they lined up in parking lots for the test.

By April 1955, the results were conclusive. Newspaper headlines trumpeted "Polio Threat Conquered by Salk Vaccine." Salk became a global hero. He was featured on Edward R. Murrow's television show *See It Now* and was given a congressional medal. Although it would cost only $140 million to inoculate all Americans under age twenty-one, both the Eisenhower administration and the American Medical Association (AMA) opposed full public funding as a dangerous move toward "socialized medicine." The AMA distrusted Salk when he refused to claim sole ownership of the vaccine, saying to do so would be like "patenting the sun." After much squabbling, federal, state, and private funds supported a mass-vaccination campaign that almost banished paralytic polio and the terror that accompanied it.

In the early 1960s, country music diva Loretta Lynn recorded a hit entitled "The Pill." She crooned how "All these years I've stayed at home while you've had all your fun/And every year that's gone by another baby's come/There's gonna be some changes made right here on Nursery Hill/You've set this chicken your last time 'cause now I've got the Pill." The lyric reflected the fact that starting in 1960, for this first time in history, women had access to a relatively safe, effective, and legal oral contraceptive. The Pill was added to the list of American scientific triumphs

by many—and blamed by some for the nation's "moral decline."

Three male scientists (Drs. Gregory Pincus, Chang Min-chueh, and John Rock) are credited with developing and testing the Pill. But they were prodded, inspired, and funded by two remarkable women, Margaret Sanger and Katherine McCormick. Sanger, the founder of the Planned Parenthood Federation of America, had long crusaded for legal, effective birth control. She challenged many state and federal laws dating from the 1800s that barred birth-control counseling or even the sale of diaphragms and condoms. McCormick, one of the first women to earn a science degree from the Massachusetts Institute of Technology (MIT), was active in the women's suffrage movement. She used her fortune (from marrying into the McCormick farm implement family) to fund research on several illnesses as well as on human fertility.

Sanger believed a birth-control pill would ensure voluntary motherhood in advanced countries and control the so-called population explosion in poor countries. Her views were tinged with eugenics (the notion that society should limit the breeding of inferior humans) as well as Cold War concerns that overpopulation in the Third World would breed communism.

Sanger and McCormick turned for help to Dr. Pincus, a specialist in mammal physiology, who set up a private research institute after being denied tenure at Harvard University in the 1940s. The G.D. Searle pharmaceutical company had funded his effort to synthesize the hormone cortisone. But when another scientist won the race, Searle cut Pincus off. Sanger and McCormick then offered him support to develop a pill to prevent unwanted pregnancy. Federal agencies refused to fund contraceptive research.

Pincus, along with Chang and Rock, focused on the role played by the female sex hormones progesterone and estrogen in regulating fertility. Some early tests on humans were performed on involuntary female mental patients. Field trials took place among women on Puerto Rico and Haiti in the late 1950s.

Once the Pill showed promise, companies like G.D. Searle eagerly marketed the discovery. Searle received Food and Drug Administration (FDA) approval for Enovid, the brand name for the oral contraceptive, in 1960, even though thirty states still outlawed or severely restricted contraceptives. Women rushed to their physicians to get prescriptions for the Pill and it quickly became the most commonly used contraceptive in the United States. Partly because of the expense and the need for a doctor's referral, white, middle-class women have always been the biggest users of the pill. Despite opposition from their Church, about 30 percent of Catholic women of childbearing age used the Pill within a few years of its appearance.

By the close of the twentieth century, researchers developed an arsenal of medicines to treat not only infections, but also chronic health conditions. Pharmaceutical companies spend about $30 billion annually on research and development. It takes about eleven years to take a drug from the laboratory to the market.

The cost of drug treatment has grown not just because a single dose of medicine is expensive. Rather, a patient with high blood pressure now treats the condition with medicine that he or she will take for decades. In 2001, Americans spent $155 billion on prescription drugs. Nearly $80 billion went for just a few drugs that alleviate the symptoms of depression, allergies, diabetes, hypertension, and sexual dysfunction. Twelve percent of each health dollar now goes for drugs, an amount likely to double in ten years.

The high cost of long-term drug treatment is a growing burden to elderly patients and the healthcare system. When Congress passed the Medicare program for seniors in 1965, it did not include a prescription drug benefit because few medications existed to treat age-related illness. Today, drugs constitute one of the most expensive components of healthcare, especially among the elderly. Congress has refused to defray their cost for them or for the nearly 25 percent of working Americans with no health insurance.

---

of abundance and erased class divisions. Others, however, stressed economic growth, not income redistribution, as the means to economic well-being. They engaged in a sustained campaign using the media and economic "education" programs for their employees to persuade workers and the general public that Americans could rely on corporate leadership, unfettered by the countervailing power of unions or by government regulation, to create the material abundance they sought. This campaign characterized unions as obstacles to consumers' goals, discrediting their participation in strikes, in corporate decisions, and in national political life. It equated state action with communism, charging that state intervention led to tyranny and inefficiency.

Despite business leaders' protestations that increased productivity would benefit all, wealth remained highly concentrated, as it had throughout the century. In 1960, the richest 1 percent of the population possessed one-third of the nation's wealth, and the top 5 percent controlled over half its wealth. Half of all families had no savings account, and almost one-fourth of the population lived near or below the poverty line (then figured as an income of $3,000 per year for a family of four). The poverty rate was especially high among the elderly, racial minorities, and rural Americans.

Superficially, Americans seemed a content lot, and they became increasingly devout. By the end of the decade, two-thirds of the population claimed formal church membership, up from 48 percent before World War II. Ninety-seven percent professed a belief in God. Religious popularizers like Billy Graham became media celebrities, appearing in newspapers, on radio and television, and on bestseller lists. A new translation of the Bible sold millions of copies. For those without time to read it, *Reader's Digest* issued an abridgment. Congress added the words *under God* to the Pledge of Allegiance and put the motto "In God We Trust" on the nation's paper money.

Christianity, like parenthood and the suburban nuclear family, became a measure of Americanism and a rejection of atheistic communism. Surveys revealed that a large majority of Americans considered atheism a subversive threat. Like Eisenhower, few people stressed doctrinal differences or weighty theological issues; rather, religion served to unify society. As Will Herberg, a professor of Judaic studies, noted in his incisive 1955 study *Protestant-Catholic-Jew*, the nation's religions, especially in suburbia, tolerated almost any content in their observances—or lack thereof. Rather than reorienting life to God, religion served a social function in the new communities.

Religious and secular opinion leaders agreed emphatically on one issue—the need for a strong American family founded on traditional values. There was as much novelty as tradition in postwar family values, however. The conviction that the nuclear family could meet all the emotional and practical needs of its members was new, although the idea that women were responsible for seeing that it did so successfully derived from older beliefs. According to popular media, when a woman subordinated her needs and ambitions totally to her family's well-being, she would ensure that families would be happy and stable.

Reinforcing this view, advice columns, television shows, and schools emphasized traditional gender roles, placing the husband at work and the wife in the home. Indeed, the popular media used its version of Freudian psychology to urge women to accept their femininity, meaning subordination to men, domesticity, and economic dependence. To do otherwise was understood as a socially dangerous form of emotional maladjustment. Indeed, experts interpreted women's dissatisfaction with these prescriptions as unhealthy masculinist strivings, code language for penis envy. In some cases, women were institutionalized and subjected to electric shock treatments for failure to conform their values and behavior to these precepts.

Clearly, experts in the 1950s produced a great deal of advice literature designed to repress women's discontent by labeling it deviant. Those women who found society's expectations impossible to meet or unrewarding felt compelled to deny, hide, or seek panaceas for their unhappiness. One suburban housewife later described her life in these years as one of "booze, bowling, bridge, and boredom." When *Redbook* magazine asked its readers to explain "Why Young Mothers Feel Trapped," the editors received an astonishing twenty-four thousand replies. The popularity of a new drug—tranquilizers—marketed in the mid-1950s attested to women's sense of uneasiness with their lives. In 1959, Americans, mostly women, consumed 1.15 million pounds of the pills.

At the same time, American women appeared to embrace the domesticity touted by 1950s popular culture. During the decade, they reversed a hundred-year trend by marrying younger and having more babies. Changes in courtship and sexual practices contributed to these trends. In the postwar period, young couples radically changed dating practices, shifting from an emphasis on popularity, evidenced by casual dates with different people, to going steady. The development of emotionally intense and sexually freighted long-term relationships among teenagers frightened their parents, who worried particularly about premarital pregnancies. Their fears were well placed because the 1950s spawned the highest teen pregnancy rates in U.S. history and witnessed an increase of more than 100 percent in the proportion of white brides who were pregnant on their wedding day. As historian Stephanie Coontz concluded, "Young people were not taught how to 'say no'—they were simply handed wedding rings."

Pregnant women who did not marry faced constrained choices. Parents and public officials strongly encouraged white women to leave town for the duration of their pregnancies, usually spending that time in homes for unwed mothers, and then to put their babies up for adoption. Doing so enabled the young women to undergo a kind of moral rehabilitation, first, by hiding the pregnancy from public view at home and, second, through counseling. These policies enabled many white couples to fulfill their family goals by becoming adoptive parents. Most white officials, however, viewed African American women as incapable of moral change and expected them to keep their babies. Few adoption services were available to them, and the enduring poverty of African American families meant that most did not meet the economic standards for adoption developed by whites. The women's families generally offered assistance and acceptance to them and their children. African American women's increasing use of Aid to Families with Dependent Children to help support their children prompted a backlash among whites, who saw the mothers as immoral and the children as economic liabilities.

Abortion remained illegal but had become somewhat safer with the introduction of antibiotics in the 1940s. Escalating police crackdowns on abortion providers, often accompanied by sensationalist coverage by the local press, made securing the illegal procedure more difficult. Even so, large numbers of women had abortions and many, especially those who were poor, died as a result. The situation was hardly invisible because big-city hospitals created special wings to treat women suffering from infections and other complications. Middle-class women could sometimes secure safe, legal abortions if a hospital committee agreed that continuing the pregnancy would cause them serious physical or emotional harm. Those who tried to do so, however, were likely to be turned down on the grounds that their desire for an abortion might itself be a symptom of a profound maladjustment whose cure would include motherhood.

Despite society's conviction that women, men, and children were happiest when women focused on full-time homemaking, the domestic authority exercised by women generated cultural anxieties about "the overfeminization of schools and households." In 1954, *Life* magazine announced "the domestication of the American male" and worried that it might lead to emasculation. Family experts saw a solution to this threat in men's greater involvement with their children, particularly their sons. In an article urging men to take a more active role in their sons' lives, *Better Homes and Gardens* worried about whether Americans were "staking our future on a crop of sissies" and sympathized with fathers' fears: "You have a horror of seeing your son a pantywaist, but he won't get red blood and self-reliance if you leave the whole job of making a he-man of him to his mother." *Rebel Without a Cause,* a film starring James Dean that focused on a young man's alienation and rebellion, associated juvenile delinquency and children's unhappiness with inverted general roles in a family where the mother had too much authority and the father (seen at one point wearing an apron) too little.

A fear of sexual chaos, brought on by the Cold War, also emerged as a common theme. Popular literature discussed the dangers posed by "loose women" and "sex perverts" who might be in league with the Soviet Union. Senator Joseph McCarthy, whose close aide Roy Cohn was a closeted homosexual, joined Republican Party chair Guy Gabrielson in warning that "sexual perverts [had] infiltrated our government" and were "perhaps as dangerous as real Communists." Even the admirable Joseph Welch, counsel to the army in the hearings that finally exposed McCarthy's mania, was not above gay-baiting. When confronted with evidence obviously doctored by McCarthy's associates, he taunted Cohn, "Do you suppose fairies put it there?"

The dominant domestic ideology of the period, which Betty Friedan dubbed "the feminine mystique" in her 1963 book of that title, defined women as wives and mothers. But in fact, one-third of all women worked for wages, and total female employment grew in the 1950s from 16.5 million to 23 million, a number representing one-third of the work force. The rapid growth of the clerical and service sectors of the economy created many new jobs for women. Not only were employers dependent on women's paid labor, many working-class families pieced together a livelihood and others achieved middle-class status because of the income added by working wives. In many households, economic necessity and postwar consumerism trumped domesticity as women made decisions about work and family. Nevertheless, in popular thinking, women belonged at home, raising children and erecting a bulwark of social stability.

Despite warnings from self-declared experts that higher education inhibited fertility, a growing number of women attended college. Educated women, however, still faced discouragement. Adlai Stevenson exhorted women at Smith College not to feel frustrated by their distance from the "great issues and stirring debate" for which their education prepared them. A woman could be a good citizen, he claimed, by helping her husband find value in his work and by teaching her children the uniqueness of each individual. Increasingly, critics insisted that women be taught primarily those subjects designed to prepare them for domesticity and assumed that a college education was more important for men. Indeed, male high school graduates were twice as likely to earn a college degree as their female counterparts.

Prodded by such assertions from civic leaders and the media, it is not surprising that the average mother of the 1950s had between three and four children, usually by age thirty. As noted earlier, the birth rate continued to rise until 1957. At the same time, contraception, accepted by all the major faiths except the Roman Catholic Church, became common as a method for spacing pregnancies and limiting births.

Sexual Anxieties, Popular Culture, and Social Change

In spite of the formal sexual orthodoxy of the era, there were portents of a more emancipated future. Notably, sex was more openly discussed and displayed during the 1950s than in most earlier periods. Popular science provided a vehicle for sexual openness in 1953 when Dr. Alfred C. Kinsey published his bestselling *Sexual Behavior in the Human Female*, which suggested that women, like men, engaged in a wide variety of sexual acts, both before and after marriage. In the climate of the times, many people considered this finding "dirty" and offensive. Many had reacted similarly to his earlier finding that homosexual encounters were common and that many gay men did not look or act in stereotypical ways.

Kinsey's reports did not reduce prejudice against gay men and lesbians, who formed an urban subculture and their own political organizations in the postwar years. They did so in the face of political attacks from anticommunists and heightened police harassment that were enabled, ironically, by the proliferation of bars and other public areas frequented by gays and lesbians. In 1951, a small group of leftist gay men formed the Mattachine Society and in 1955, Del Martin and Phyllis Lyon created the Daughters of Bilitis, the first lesbian organization. Although the formation of gay and lesbian communities and political groups enabled mutual support and some efforts at public education, the conviction that homosexuality was dangerous and abnormal retained its hold on the general public.

Sexual conservatism did not prevent artistic representations of sex from becoming more open in the 1950s. In the film industry, for example, the Hollywood Production Code had long barred the use of words like *virgin* and *seduction* and restricted the sexual content of films. Even married couples were shown sleeping in separate beds. By the mid-1950s, the code was relaxed. The movies did not necessarily improve, but the sex in them became more graphic than before.

During the same years, the Supreme Court overturned several state laws restricting publication of serious erotic literature, such as D. H. Lawrence's *Lady Chatterley's Lover*. Such books became more widely available, and writers of less renown also offered some steamy reading. The decade's most popular novel, *Peyton Place* (1956), sold almost 10 million copies. The book jacket promised that author Grace Metalious, a young housewife, "lifted the lid off a small New England town, exposing lust, rape, incest, alcoholism, murder, and hypocrisy."

Playboy magazine was surely the most influential erotic publication of the decade. Its glossy centerfolds brought bare-breasted women into millions of homes, displaying them like one more consumer product. When Hugh Hefner first published *Playboy* in December 1953, he featured the rising starlet Marilyn Monroe as "Playmate of the Month." Slick, upscale, and replete with the hedonist Playboy philosophy, selections from serious writers, and airbrushed photographs of busty women, *Playboy* represented a quantum leap from the grimy "girlie" magazines of the past. By 1956, its circulation had reached one-half million per month.

Besides pressuring women into domestic roles, the massive profamily propaganda of the fifties stifled many men, who found that *Playboy*, which described marriage as a trap for unwary men, provided a rationale for their avoidance of family. Hefner pitched his magazine to college students and young status-conscious men who wanted to date, not marry, the centerfold models. Willing to spend their salary on the expensive stereos and pricey liquor advertised in *Playboy*, they dreamed of worry-free sex with no mortgages or children to complicate their lifestyle.

Young girls, by contrast, were urged to develop the bodies and behaviors that would inspire young men to date and eventually marry them. Advice literature in the popular media told adolescents and young women the taboos of dating. For girls, they included going "dutch" (letting each person pay his or her own expenses), opening your own doors, showing too much intelligence, and ordering your own food in a restaurant. In a letter to *Scholastic Magazine*, a boy from Missouri summed up the rationale for codes designed to reinforce the idea that men were in control in heterosexual relationships: "[P]aying the girl's way gives me a responsible and important feeling. It makes me feel superior to my date." Women also had to present acceptable bodies to signify their conformity to 1950s gender prescriptions. Encouraging and capitalizing on the popularity of Marilyn Monroe, American advertisers promoted devices and creams designed to increase breast size, while the clothing industry propelled young women into "training bras" and girdles in the name of "junior figure control." Historian Joan Jacobs Brumberg concluded that these practices constructed young girls as sex objects and "foreshadowed the ways in which the nation's entrepreneurs would accommodate, and also encourage, precocious sexuality."

The emerging art form of rock 'n' roll touched a deep chord in American youth. Before the advent of rock, mainstream 1950s music featured fatuous songs like "How Much Is That Doggie in the Window?" But as television gave radio increasingly stiff competition, radio stations became less profitable, and this prompted many of them to change their formats. In some large cities, radio stations began targeting a new audience, African Americans. African American popular music of the time, often called "race music," vibrated with religious and sexual energy. But white audiences had little exposure to it. To make the distinctive black style more acceptable, some disc jockeys called it rhythm and blues, or R&B. After 1945, R&B began to influence southern hillbilly and western cowboy music, creating the hybrid country-and-western style. And by the mid-1950s, increased exposure of R&B paved the way for its evolution into rock 'n' roll. This dynamic new musical form, along with improved recording technologies and the emergence of a large cohort of teenagers with money to spend, created a vast new commercial market in music.

In 1952, Cleveland disc jockey Alan Freed premiered an R&B radio show called "Moondog's Rock 'n' Roll Party." Like the term *jazz, rockin' and rollin'* originally referred to sexual intercourse. To appeal to his white audience, Freed downplayed this reference, connecting the words *rock 'n' roll* to the style of dancing associated with the music. From then on, the barriers between white and black music began to tumble. White audiences heard black music at the same time the civil rights movement was challenging the racism of white society.

In 1954, Bill Haley, a portly, nearly middle-aged white bandleader, recorded "Rock Around the Clock," an exuberant tune that became the theme song of the popular film *Blackboard Jungle* (1955). The movie chronicled the struggle of a young teacher in a run-down inner-city high school who tried to motivate alienated, poor youth. It touched on problems of race, class, and delinquency—unusual themes in commercial art of the time. The film's message—crime does not pay, and middle-class values are a salvation—is scarcely remembered. But "Rock Around the Clock," critics and audiences agreed, gave *Blackboard Jungle* its "insurrectionary power" and brought white middle-class youth to their feet. Theater owners reported spontaneous dancing in the aisles.

The record industry was especially eager to appeal to white youth because they represented an enormous market. Teenagers, a relatively recent term for those who enjoyed a prolonged adolescence before entering the labor force, formed an expanding group during the 1950s. Their numbers and economic impact grew steadily, so that by 1959, the teenage market—including money spent by parents on teenagers and by teenagers on themselves—topped $10 billion per year. With so much at stake, record producers hustled to find more white recording artists who employed the black sound in a form acceptable to white teenagers.

The biggest find was a nineteen-year-old part-time truck driver from Tupelo, Mississippi—Elvis Presley. Born poor, he had taught himself the guitar and learned the R&B style. His first record in 1954 earned him appearances on regional radio shows, and within a year he was a star throughout the South. In live performances, he aroused his fans, both female and male, by undulating his body and thrusting his hips in a style he attributed to revivalist preachers. Presley almost created the image of the hypersexed male rock star, replete with long hair, leather jacket, a sneering expression, and a sultry demeanor.

By 1956, Presley had become a national sensation. He released a series of hits, including "Heartbreak Hotel," "Don't Be Cruel," "Love Me Tender," and "I'm All Shook Up," that sold over 14 million records that year. He appeared on Ed Sullivan's popular TV variety show, where the cameras focused above the waist to conceal the young man's suggestive thrusts. Over 80 percent of all American viewers watched this performance, a number unsurpassed until the Beatles made their television debut in 1964.

Between early 1956 and March 1958, when the army drafted him, Presley released fourteen consecutive million-seller records. By 1966, he had sold 115 million records. Presley's success not only set a standard for other white rock singers, but also spurred white acceptance of African American artists such as Ray Charles, Chuck Berry, Little Richard, and Fats Domino.

While the young went wild over rock 'n' roll, parents recoiled at its influence. Some rock lyrics made fun of middle-class values. Besides its generally sensual, even sexual emphasis, rock music ridiculed work ("Get a Job"), downplayed schools ("Don't Know Much About History"), mixed religion with sex ("Teen Angel"), scoffed at authority ("Charlie Brown, He's a Clown"), and celebrated irresponsibility ("Rock Around the

Elvis Presley in 1956. His exuberant singing style shocked adults and excited youths. / UPI/Bettmann/CORBIS

Clock"). Popular music had never before so blatantly defied social mores or so distinguished youth from older generations.

Adult fears, and the discontents that gave rise to concern, emerged plainly in films like *The Wild One* (1953), *Rebel Without a Cause* (1955), and *Blackboard Jungle* (1955). These three movies featured actors Marlon Brando, James Dean, and Sidney Poitier, respectively, as young toughs who oozed anger, sexuality, and contempt for their elders. Their fictional characters presented an even stronger challenge to the social order than did Holden Caulfield, the alienated teenage hero of J. D. Salinger's popular novel *Catcher in the Rye* (1951). Despite the films' overt messages that violence and immorality were wrong, most teenagers who flocked to see Brando, Dean, and Poitier cheered the unrepentant rebels, not the characters who accepted their elders' advice.

Among parents who had just experienced World War II, peace and quiet seemed a good bargain. Young people, however, wanted something more. A youth subculture was emerging, and many parents worried about it. They blamed its music, movies, books, and comics, and even the television programs that would seem so innocent to later generations. Some people invoked the communist specter. Early in the decade, Justice Department officials helped one Hollywood studio produce a film warning that "throughout the

United States today, indeed throughout the free world, a deadly war is being waged." The "Communist enemy," the film declared, was trying to subvert American youth by spreading drugs and encouraging obscenity in the mass media.

Education and Mass Society

Many political liberals and professional educators attributed juvenile delinquency and a host of other social ills to the lack of federal aid to public schools. Without more money for buildings, equipment, and libraries, they argued, teachers could not cope with surging enrollments and the constant accumulation of new information. Only higher salaries, paid for by taxes, would lure talented college graduates into teaching. Many academics also criticized the schools for emphasizing social adjustment and conformity, rather than skepticism and individuality, and for inadequate attention to the traditional, subject-based academic curriculum.

Conservatives, on the other hand, were wary of plans to increase the federal government's role in education. They blamed the educational establishment itself, including teacher training colleges and unions, for poor student performance. The right wing believed that John Dewey's popular ideas of "progressive education," with their emphasis on social relevance, democratic ideals, and pragmatism, had undermined respect for the acquisition of basic skills, traditional values, and culture. They called for a return to basics, more classroom discipline, and the teaching of religious values. These debates were not new and would continue to the present day.

Neither liberal nor conservative critics fully acknowledged that part of the problem lay in the changing nature of mass education. Before World War II, relatively few students finished high school, and even fewer went to college. Public primary schools sought merely to instill some basic discipline and rudimentary reading and arithmetic skills. The wealthy attended private schools, middle-class students received a standard liberal arts curriculum in public high schools, and most working-class children dropped out to help support their families or sought vocational training.

Postwar prosperity resulted in many more working-class youths attending high school. As blacks and Hispanics migrated to urban areas, they became a major presence in public schools, increasing the cultural and social diversity there. Tension within this newly varied population, combined with the baby boom and the rapid expansion of the suburbs, put education at all levels under stress. Schools were expected to teach job skills, citizenship, and a sophisticated science, math, and literature curriculum to a broader cross section of students than ever before.

In the postwar period, educators adapted to these developments by locating schools carefully to ensure that student populations came from homogeneous class and racial backgrounds; using standardized tests to assign students to different tracks (college or vocational) in secondary schools; and emphasizing education for citizenship and social adjustment, rather than academic training, for students on the vocational or general tracks. Under this system, educators assumed that tests accurately reflected academic promise and interests and that students who came from disadvantaged groups should generally be prepared for blue-collar jobs. They also hoped that their focus on adjustment would prevent working-class alienation from schools and other social institutions and practices and thus help to prevent crime and radicalism.

Whatever their level of performance on IQ and achievement tests, girls found themselves increasingly relegated to commercial curricula designed to prepare them for clerical and service jobs. In the mid-1950s, only 48 percent of high school girls, compared to 66 percent of boys, were in academic or general curricula. Encouraged by guidance counselors, the girls chose clerical work or marriage as their desired occupations and took typing, shorthand, and other vocational classes. Among those whom the Educational Testing Service rated as able to do college work, 78 percent of the boys and only 62 percent of the girls planned to attend college.

By tradition, American schools are locally funded and controlled, making it difficult to promote change at the national level. Criticism of American education reached new heights after October 1957, however, when the Soviet Union launched the first artificial satellite, Sputnik I (see Chapter 4). Anxiety over the Cold War added fuel to the crisis in education. Journalists and politicians described the Soviet Union as the model of successful mass education. Communism, it seemed, had won the space race by winning the education race. What would Moscow win next?

In fact, Soviet success in education was greatly exaggerated. Nevertheless, Sputnik forged a national consensus in the United States in favor of federal aid to education. Before the crisis, southern Democrats opposed federal spending for education, fearing it would erode local control and spur integration. Northern liberal Democrats worried about opening public coffers to parochial schools. Parochial schools feared that higher school taxes would affect parents' ability to pay tuition and would thus erode their client base. Most Republicans simply opposed spending money on social programs. But the clamor to catch up with the Russians changed the debate.

Senator Lyndon B. Johnson of Texas, Democratic majority leader and presidential aspirant, chaired an investigating committee assessing the impact of Moscow's space coup. Long an advocate of federal support for education, he now warned of a widening science and technology gap. Congress and President Eisenhower cooperated in September 1958 to pass the National Defense Education Act (NDEA), a billion-dollar package, supplemented by state grants, to provide aid to schools and universities. It granted funds for construction; student loans and scholarships; and the teaching of science, mathematics, and foreign languages. In the following two decades, the NDEA and successor programs had a huge impact on American education at all levels, from the primary grades through graduate and professional schools. As with the GI Bill of the decade before, loans and fellowships allowed many more students to pursue advanced degrees. By 1960, the United States granted ten thousand doctorates annually, three times the pre–World War II number. Foreign students flocked to American universities, making the United States a world center of higher education.

With educational assistance provided by the NDEA, a record number of students enrolled in college during the 1960s. The large group of confident, intellectually curious students hitting college campuses coincided with growing American military involvement in Vietnam. Not surprisingly, this generation of college students would play a major role in challenging the Vietnam War in the 1960s.

The 1950s role models for college rebels were the Beats, a small, loosely defined group of iconoclastic writers who captured the public attention late in the decade. Their defiance of social and literary convention, as well as their dabbling in drugs, Eastern mysticism, and homosexuality, outraged the middle class and excited many teenagers and young adults. Beatniks, as they became known, disparaged Christianity, work, materialism, family life, patriotism, and interest in winning the Cold War.

The Beat writers included poets Allen Ginsberg and Gregory Corso and novelists Jack Kerouac and William S. Burroughs. Most began writing in New York City early in the decade and later drifted toward San Francisco. Ginsberg gained national attention in 1956 when San Francisco police charged him with obscenity for publishing his poem *Howl*, a highly personal cry against American materialism. The Beats achieved additional fame in 1957 with Kerouac's bestseller *On the Road*, a raucous, thinly fictionalized account of the author's cross-country travel with his unconventional friends.

Despite such rumblings of rebellion, most social commentators agreed that the United States had solved the major problems afflicting society. Persistent pockets of poverty, such as among African Americans, were seen as minor embarrassments rather than as major problems. An influential analysis published by Daniel Bell near the end of the decade, *The End of Ideology*, argued that the passionate ideological crusades of earlier years no longer had relevance. The United States had mastered the production of abundance and now had only to decide how to allocate the wealth.

Nevertheless, some critics began to question the social mores and culture that arose from this decade of calm prosperity. Books such as David Riesman's *The Lonely Crowd* (1950), Sloan Wilson's *The Man in the Gray Flannel Suit* (1955), William H. Whyte, Jr.'s *The Organization Man* (1955), John Keats's *The Crack in the Picture Window* (1957), and Richard Gordon's *The Split Level Trap* (1960) turned a critical eye on the 1950s and its definition of successful masculinity. Riesman and Whyte discussed the eclipse of the inner-directed personality that they deemed appropriate for men. Instead of relying on internal drives and values, they charged, Americans had become other-directed: little more than sheep who sought approval and rewards from their peers and the corporate hierarchy. Wilson worried that corporate success required that men develop the arts of ingratiation and subordination (usually associated with femininity) not those of individuality. According to Whyte, the bureaucratic structure of big business stifled a healthy competitive spirit in men. No longer spurred by drive and vision, the organization man looked to "the group as the source of creativity."

Critics also attacked the pervasive consumer culture. In a trilogy of best-sellers criticizing the advertising industry—*The Hidden Persuaders* (1957), *The Status Seekers* (1959), and *The Waste Makers* (1960)—journalist Vance Packard blamed mass marketing and the concept of planned obsolescence for turning citizens into insatiable consumers of overpackaged, unnecessary, and often shoddy products. According to Packard, American families spent an average of $500 a year just for packaging costs. He singled out the automobile industry in particular for its reliance on new models each year to increase car sales and for creating bigger and bigger cars that used increasing amounts of steel and other materials, guzzled gas and oil, and wore out parts at an accelerated pace. When economists from MIT, the University of Chicago, and Harvard examined his charges, they found that more than one-fourth of the price of new cars could be accounted for by the costs of designing and producing new models each year.

Only a few social critics claimed to find basic structural flaws in American society. One of these was sociologist C. Wright Mills, whose book *The Power Elite* (1956) asserted that a small group of military, business, and political leaders controlled the country in such a way that the majority of Americans were left powerless. Herbert Marcuse, a German émigré philosopher, blended Freudian psychology and Marxism in his *Eros and Civilization* (1956), which argued that a tiny minority manipulated the lives of most people and developed unique forms of psychological repression. In *Growing Up Absurd* (1960), Paul Goodman criticized schools and other institutions for stifling creativity and individualism. These critics offered evidence that America's problems had not disappeared or been forgotten. Their dissent foreshadowed the radical challenges that emerged in the 1960s.

Continuing Struggles: Civil Rights and Civil Liberties

At a time when so many Americans enjoyed abundance, African Americans were still denied basic human rights and opportunities. In the rural South, farm mechanization pushed black sharecroppers off the land. Because the Social Security Act excluded farm laborers from its benefits, these displaced workers were not eligible for unemployment compensation. Desperate for employment, some went to southern cities like Atlanta and Birmingham. More went north and west (see Map 3.1). They entered urban labor markets at the bottom, as unskilled laborers and service workers.

The migrants did not find residential integration in their new communities. Just as they arrived, white Americans were leaving the cities for the suburbs. By 1960, over half of all African Americans lived in the largely poor and mostly black inner cities. There, they faced great shortages of affordable housing, caused in part by restrictive covenants that forbade occupants to sell to people of color as well as federal mortgage loan policies that excluded black

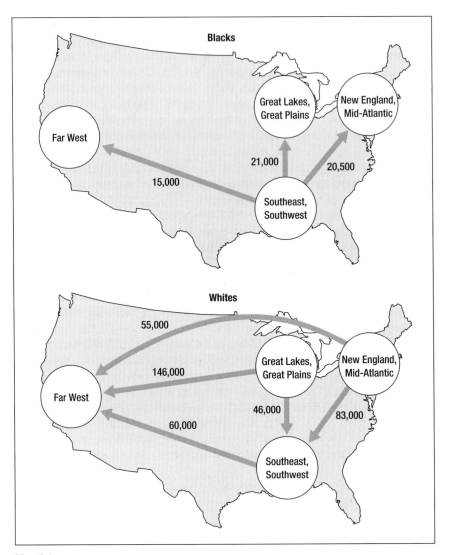

Map 3.1
Average Annual Regional Migration, 1947–1960

neighborhoods from coverage. Landlords in these neighborhoods subdivided units, leading to greater overcrowding; refused to make repairs; and charged exorbitant rents for the scarce housing. Blacks generally paid more than whites for worse housing. As the cities deteriorated, the new suburban communities remained nearly all white. The poor housing conditions in black communities convinced many whites that integrated neighborhoods would deteriorate and many bankers that home loans to blacks were high risk. In the North, whites organized protests when they thought homes in their areas would be sold to blacks.

In the South, segregation came under sharp attack from African American activists. Court decisions, boycotts, and new laws undermined the legal and social pillars of racism. Led in many cases by war veterans, African Americans organized voter-registration drives in the South, where they encountered white hostility and sometimes outright violence. After hearing reports of blacks killed for daring to assert their voting rights, President Truman acted. Even though he privately rejected social equality among the races, he established the President's Committee on Civil Rights in late 1946 to recommend steps for the federal government to take to ensure basic civil rights for all Americans. The panel urged government action to guarantee equal opportunity in education, housing, and employment. It called for federal laws against lynching and poll taxes, the creation of a permanent Fair Employment Practices Commission, and a strong Civil Rights Division within the Justice Department.

When Congress declined to act, Truman used executive authority to bolster civil rights enforcement by the Justice Department. He also appointed a black federal judge and made several other minority appointments. When labor leader A. Philip Randolph threatened in July 1948 to organize a boycott of the draft to protest the segregated armed forces, Truman issued an executive order calling for desegregation in the services. Still, the armed services moved so slowly that desegregation took another six years.

As the government inched forward, African Americans pursued nonviolent direct action inspired by India's Mohandas Gandhi. Two women staged the first sit-in in Washington, D.C., during the war. (One of them, Patricia Harris, later became a cabinet secretary in the Carter administration.) After the war, the Congress of Racial Equality (CORE) carried out sit-ins at lunch counters in northern cities and organized a "swim-in" at Palisades Park in New Jersey. Although mobs beat the participants, the amusement park and many lunch counters were desegregated as a result of these demonstrations. These small and hard-won victories convinced activists of the importance of direct action for mobilizing their communities and maintaining political pressure on the white establishment.

In the legal realm, too, progress was being made. In *Smith* v. *Allwright* (1944), the Supreme Court overturned the whites-only primary system that prevailed in many southern states. Two years later, in *Morgan* v. *Virginia* (1946), the Court held that racial segregation on interstate buses violated federal law. In 1947, CORE organized the first freedom ride to test the ruling. The group made it as far as Durham, North Carolina, before being arrested and sentenced to thirty days on a chain gang. In *Shelley* v. *Kraemer* (1948), the justices ordered that state courts could not enforce restrictive clauses in private contracts. On hearing of the new ruling, a furious congressman declared "there must have been a celebration in Moscow last night."

Nothing symbolized the unequal status of African Americans more powerfully than school segregation. At the time, 53.9 percent of white college students in the South attended state universities supported by taxpayers, while only 8.9 percent of black college students did so. The region provided only three law schools for African Americans but had thirty-one for whites.

In various decisions, the U.S. Supreme Court did not outlaw segregation or overturn the separate-but-equal rule dating from 1896 (*Plessy v. Ferguson*). But a majority of justices seemed willing to chip away at segregation by forcing states to honor the "equal" part of the "separate but equal" doctrine. Their rulings encouraged Thurgood Marshall, chief counsel of the National Association for the Advancement of Colored People (NAACP), to escalate the attack on school segregation, placing the system under constant judicial siege. By 1952, the NAACP was pressing five suits before the Supreme Court against public school segregation.

These five suits were eventually combined under the heading of one key case involving Linda Brown of Topeka, Kansas. Each morning, she had to walk past a nearby white-only school to catch the bus that would take her to a colored-only school. Marshall decided to abandon his piecemeal strategy. He likened the "separate-but-equal" doctrine to the "black codes" established after the Civil War to restrict the rights of African Americans. The doctrine could be sustained, Marshall argued, only if the Supreme Court agreed "that for some reason Negroes are inferior to all other human beings." Marshall insisted that segregation violated the Fourteenth Amendment, and he submitted research by psychologist Kenneth Clark suggesting that African American children educated in single-race schools suffered lasting emotional and intellectual damage.

The Supreme Court heard arguments in *Brown v. Board of Education* late in 1952, but they delayed ruling. Chief Justice Fred Vinson, like several associate justices, had misgivings about segregation but thought states had a right to set their own school policies, discriminatory though they may be. In September 1953, in the midst of the Court's deliberations, Vinson died. Associate Justice Felix Frankfurter privately quipped that Vinson's timely demise was "the only proof I've ever seen of the existence of God." A year before, presidential candidate Eisenhower had secured support from Governor Earl Warren of California by promising him the first opening on the Supreme Court. Eisenhower had some qualms about appointing Warren to the most influential seat on the Court, but he honored his promise. Neither Eisenhower nor most other Americans imagined how fateful this appointment would become. Warren viewed the Supreme Court as a unique force for protecting the weak, the oppressed, and the disadvantaged. His vision and activism brought the Court into the center of national politics and made him the most influential chief justice in over a century.

Warren ordered a rehearing of *Brown* in December 1953. Then he persuaded all eight associate justices to join him in a unanimous opinion, issued in May 1954, that struck down segregation in public education. Warren rejected the *Plessy* decision of 1896 and put forth an essentially new interpretation of the Fourteenth Amendment. For Warren, the issue was simple justice. To segregate schoolchildren solely on the basis of race, he wrote, "generates a feeling of inferiority . . . that may affect their hearts and minds in a way unlikely ever to be undone. . . . Segregation with the sanction of law, therefore, has a tendency to retard educational and mental development of Negro children." In education, he declared, "separate but equal has no place. Separate educational facilities are inherently unequal."

Critics charged that the ruling misconstrued the Constitution and relied on dubious sociological data. Others accused the Supreme Court of usurping congressional and state power by making, rather than interpreting, the law. A young minister in Lynchburg, Virginia, named Jerry Falwell claimed he saw "the hand of Moscow" behind the *Brown* decision. He further stated that "[i]f Chief Justice Warren and his associates had known God's Word, I am confident that the . . . decision would never have been made." According to Falwell, the Bible taught that blacks "were cursed to be the servants of the Jews and Gentiles" and not their constitutional equals. Warren's defenders retorted that the *Brown* decision yielded the morally correct verdict. In fact, the Supreme Court had taken action—reluctantly—to resolve a moral, legal, and political issue that neither Congress nor the president would confront. Civil rights had been stuck in a political gridlock that only the Supreme Court seemed capable of unraveling.

In practice, the *Brown* decision affected only public schools, not the comprehensive web of segregation laws that prevailed in twenty-four states and the District of Columbia. The Supreme Court delayed implementing its ruling and called for consultation between local authorities and judges. During 1954 and 1955, while the Court heard the NAACP demand "integration now," southern states requested delays and demagogues called for "segregation forever." During this interim period, the Court's delay and President Eisenhower's uneasiness over the desegregation ruling helped fuel a massive resistance movement.

Warren again spoke for a unanimous Court in May 1955 when he ruled in a case called *Brown II* that school segregation must be ended everywhere in the nation. Although desegregation should begin with "all deliberate speed," the Court issued no timetable. Southern officials hoped that federal district judges would wink at delays and, as a Georgia official remarked, define a "reasonable time as one or two hundred years." When district judges insisted on early action, however, segregationists dug in their heels. In several southern states, white citizens' councils sprang up to intimidate black parents and white school boards attempting to integrate the schools. Designed to provide a respectable form of resistance, these groups of middle-class citizens—the "uptown Ku Klux Klan"—formally disavowed violence while tacitly encouraging it. Indeed, they took out newspaper ads providing the names of blacks who had registered to vote or engaged in other civil rights activities. Southern politicians hurried to inform white citizens that the Court's decision was illegitimate, and therefore white southerners would not have to comply with it. Over one hundred members of Congress signed a Southern Manifesto opposing the *Brown* decision. Senator Harry F. Byrd, a Democrat from Virginia, called for massive resistance, and several state legislatures in the South declared that they would defy the "unconstitutional" Supreme Court rulings.

In the next few years, these states passed over 450 laws designed to interpose state authority between the federal government and local school officials, forbid officials to carry out any action that would mix races in public schools, and provide state money (usually in the form of vouchers) to support all-white private academies. In addition, several states curtailed or abolished public schools. At one point, Mississippi and South Carolina actually amended their state constitutions to abolish public education, and Virginia closed public schools for several months. In 1957, their efforts received support from conservative spokesperson William F. Buckley, who wrote in the *National Review* that "the White community in the South is entitled to take such measures as are necessary to prevail, politically and culturally, in areas where it does not predominate numerically. . . ." It had the right to do so, he argued, because "for the time being, it is the advanced race . . . It is more important for any community, anywhere in the world, to affirm and live by civilized standards, than to bow to the demands of the numerical majority."

In the short run, the passage of these laws enabled southern politicians to delay implementation of school desegregation by creating enormous legal confusion, to cost the NAACP and other litigants a great deal of time and money as they challenged the laws in court, and to claim that the laws represented legitimate public authority—unlike the Supreme Court's decisions— because they reflected the popular will of the South. While doing so, they clogged the courts with cases involving laws that would eventually be declared unconstitutional. Because of this resistance and hostility, most schools in the South and many in the North remained as segregated in 1960 as before. Far from being resolved, the issue would become the focus of public debate again and again in later decades.

President Eisenhower did little to promote the Supreme Court rulings. As army chief of staff in 1948, he had defended military segregation, arguing that "if we attempt to force someone to like someone else, we are just going to get into trouble." Of course, equality under the law, not the "liking" of minorities, was the real issue. Pressed by the contending factions to endorse or denounce the *Brown* ruling, Eisenhower privately blamed Earl Warren for the crisis and called his appointment of the judge "the biggest damn fool mistake I ever made." Although the president accepted the desegregation decision, he declined to endorse it. He told Booker T. Washington's daughter, "We cannot do it by cold law-making, but must make these changes by appealing to reason, by prayer, and by constantly working at it through our own efforts." NAACP executive director Roy Wilkins reacted to the president's hesitant approach by observing that "President Eisenhower was a fine general and a good, decent man, but if he had fought World War II the way he fought for civil rights, we would all be speaking German today."

One of Eisenhower's earliest tests came in 1955, when a fourteen-year-old African American boy named Emmett Till was murdered in Mississippi for violating southern racial mores. Till, who lived in Chicago, had come to the delta area of Mississippi to visit relatives there. In an attempt to impress local black children, he claimed to have had white girlfriends in the North. In response, they goaded him to prove himself by flirting with a white woman named Carolyn Bryant, who was working in her family's store in the town of

Money, Mississippi. In the South, where whites assumed that black men were sexual aggressors determined to pursue white women, the defense of white women's sexual and racial purity was the defense of the color line itself. Although Bryant did not tell her husband, Roy, of the incident, he heard of it from others. With his half-brother, J. W. Milam, he took Till from the home of the boy's uncle, brutally murdered him, and dumped the body in the Tallahatchie River.

Although southern white officials initially condemned the murder, Mississippi whites rallied around the accused when northerners reacted with horror to the event. That horror was intensified when Till's mother, Mamie Till Bradley, declared that she wanted "the world [to] see what they did to my boy" and kept the casket open at the funeral. Initially published in *Jet* magazine, the photograph of his body, which had been mutilated almost beyond recognition, was soon reprinted widely in white publications. At the trial in Sumner, Bradley testified that the victim was her son, while lawyers for the defense argued that the body was not that of Till. They also wanted to include testimony from Carolyn Bryant regarding the incident in the store, which would invite the jurors to conclude that Till had "asked for it," but the judge forbade her to testify in front of the jurors on the grounds that the information she presented was not relevant. The sheriff, Harold Strider, testified that the body had been in the water too long to be that of Till, leaving it to the defense attorneys to try to explain the presence of Till's ring on the body in question. After the jury had acquitted the defendants, Strider said that he wanted to "tell all of those people who've been sending me those threatening letters that if they ever come down here, the same thing's gonna happen to them that happened to Emmett Till."

Till's murder occurred in the poorest region of the poorest state in the union. African Americans, who were a majority of the area's population and the backbone of its plantation labor force, counted no registered voters in their ranks. Mississippi was the birthplace of the white citizens' councils. Through the use of violence and economic threats and reprisals, their members had significantly reduced the already small number of blacks on the voting rolls in the state and elsewhere and had created a climate of terror for any who sought racial change.

The national media attention focused on the murder combined with national outrage at the acquittals put the Eisenhower administration in a difficult position. The president refused public comment on the case. Convinced that only state laws had been violated in the case, administration officials claimed that they were powerless to act. The Civil Rights Acts of 1866 were the only ones on the books at the time designed to provide federal protection for civil rights. They had been eroded by conservative Court decisions in the 1940s and were always hindered by the refusal of white jurors in the South to convict whites accused of crimes against blacks. Even so, the administration had little enthusiasm for using them when it had strong legal grounds or for strengthening them in order to protect the lives and civil rights of African Americans. In 1955, local U.S. attorneys received orders from the Justice

Department not to investigate disorders that impeded the execution of federal integration decrees, even though federal jurisdiction was clear in these cases. A year later, FBI director J. Edgar Hoover, who had believed that the outcry over the Till case had been communist inspired, argued against strengthening the civil rights laws on the grounds that to do so would impair social harmony in the South.

Eisenhower's greatest effort on behalf of change came in response to a direct challenge to federal authority in Little Rock, Arkansas. In 1957, the Little Rock school board, which had voluntarily put forward its own desegregation plan in 1955, began implementation by choosing nine African American students to enroll in the city's Central High School. But Governor Orval Faubus called out the National Guard to block them. When a federal court ordered the troops to withdraw, a white mob surrounded the school, taunting and threatening the blacks attempting to enroll. Faced with massive local revolt against a federal court order and unable to persuade the defiant Faubus to offer state assistance in protecting the black students, Eisenhower reacted as he would to an insubordinate junior officer. Embarrassed by Soviet propaganda publicizing American racism—which found a wide audience in the Third World—he sent one thousand army troops and ten thousand National Guardsmen to ensure the students' safety, maintain order, and support the authority of the federal government.

Fifteen-year-old Elizabeth Eckford endured the taunts and threats of hostile white students as she attempted to desegregate Little Rock's Central High School in September 1957. Under orders from Arkansas governor Orval Faubus, National Guard troops barred her entrance. / Bettmann/CORBIS

The troops stayed a year, although their presence in the school did not deter a systematic campaign of harassment of the African American students orchestrated by a group of segregationist white students. In an effort to prevent integration, Governor Faubus closed the Little Rock public high schools in September 1958 under a new state law that required voters to approve the continuation of integration or close the affected schools. Despite the efforts of local African Americans, a few ministers, and some white women activists, voters strongly rejected integration. A year later, a federal court disallowed this move and local voters, disillusioned with closed schools, removed the segregationists who had opposed reopening the schools from the Little Rock school board. The whole episode, including vivid pictures of the howling mob and the frightened but dignified African American students, became an international embarrassment to the United States.

The administration tried to mollify critics by introducing a civil rights bill to Congress in 1957. Attorney General Herbert Brownell pushed the legislation while Eisenhower recuperated from an illness. Brownell had political motives for pressing a civil rights bill: he hoped that a debate on the question would divide the northern and southern wings of the Democratic Party and curb the influence of presidential hopeful Lyndon Johnson. The ploy failed when Johnson used his talents of persuasion to convince a majority of Democrats to support the Civil Rights Act of 1957, an amended version of the administration's bill that declared support for black voting rights but left enforcement in the hands of southern juries.

In passing the 1957 Civil Rights Act, Congress was responding to a rising tide of grassroots activism on the part of African Americans. Shortly before Christmas in 1955, Rosa Parks, a tailor's assistant in Montgomery, Alabama, who was also secretary of the local NAACP branch, boarded a bus to ride home. When ordered to move to the rear so that a white passenger might sit, she refused. Parks declared that she had decided to discover "once and for all what rights I had as a human being and, a citizen." Besides, she added, "my feet hurt." For her trouble, she was arrested for violating the law requiring the separation of whites and blacks on public buses.

Rosa Parks was not the first black woman to be arrested for breaking this law; in three recent cases, the city of Montgomery had dropped charges to avoid a legal challenge. The Women's Political Council, a group of African American professional women, knew of Parks's good reputation in the community and her support for civil rights causes. They considered her case an ideal test case. The council conferred with other community leaders, including E. D. Nixon, a local NAACP official, and decided to mobilize grassroots support for a challenge to the law. They enlisted the help of Baptist ministers, including Ralph Abernathy and Martin Luther King, Jr., in organizing a black boycott of Montgomery buses.

King, then a twenty-seven-year-old preacher, was new to the community. He came from a prominent family in Atlanta. His father, Martin Luther King, Sr., ministered to a large congregation and encouraged his talented son to pursue a broad education, including a doctorate in theology from Boston University.

This woman joined about fifty thousand other African Americans in Montgomery, Alabama, who walked to work, to stores, and to church for over a year to protest the city's segregated bus system. / Don Cravens, © Life Magazine, Time Inc.

Martin Luther King, Jr., did not initiate the challenge to racism in Montgomery, but he gradually emerged as its leader because of his talents and passionate oratory. He told local and national audiences that "there comes a time when people get tired . . . of being segregated and humiliated, tired of being kicked about by the brutal feet of oppression." The time had come for his people to cease tolerating "anything less than freedom and justice." Influenced by his reading of Thoreau and Gandhi, King applied the principles of nonviolent civil disobedience to the boycott. He would soon become the nation's most prominent African American leader.

For a year, about fifty thousand African Americans walked or rode in car-pools rather than ride the segregated buses of Montgomery. Led by JoAnn Gibson Robinson, African American women sparked, organized, and staffed the Montgomery campaign. Boycott leaders did not insist on full integration, asking only that passengers be seated on a first-come, first-served basis, with blacks seating themselves from the rear to the front and whites from the front to the rear. Despite the modest nature of this request, city officials responded by indicting protest leaders for violating state antiboycott laws and by banning car-pools as a public nuisance. Terrorists bombed churches and the homes of activists, including King's. But in November 1956, the Supreme Court overturned the Alabama bus segregation law under which Parks had been arrested. This decision left the city and the bus company no legal recourse and a financial disincentive to resist integration. Thus, the combination of grassroots and judicial activism achieved victory.

The boycott illustrates the critical role that churches and ministers played in the early civil rights crusade. Because segregation excluded blacks from political activity, churches offered the one permissible setting for community organization. They provided a base of support, local leadership, some financial resources, a common language and culture, and a sense of empowerment that could be turned toward meeting political goals. Ministers such as King and Abernathy molded African American religions into a political weapon by portraying heroes like Moses and Jesus as social revolutionaries. Just as the biblical Jews reached the Promised Land after long tribulation, African Americans could win freedom, these ministers told their congregations, through faith and a commitment to struggle.

Many other African Americans had challenged segregation, independently and collectively, by the end of the decade. College students in the South took the boldest initiative. In February 1960, four students from the North Carolina Agricultural and Technical College, after shopping in a Greensboro, North Carolina, Woolworth's, sat down at the lunch counter to order coffee. When the manager refused to serve them, they stayed there until the store closed, when they were arrested.

This tactic spread quickly. Lunch counter sit-ins occurred in over thirty cities in seven states. Many protesters were arrested, and some were beaten. Most adopted a strategy of nonviolence in the face of assaults. The effort yielded notable successes, with many national chains integrating their lunch counters. Some of the student activists followed Ella Baker into the Student Non-Violent Coordinating Committee (SNCC), which she organized in 1960. Over the next few years, SNCC would play a major role in challenging segregation.

Despite these important achievements, most African Americans still attended predominantly segregated schools and lived in single-race neighborhoods at the close of the 1950s. Few blacks in the South could vote. Many more personal sacrifices by civil rights activists, and the intervention of a sympathetic federal government, would be necessary to effect real change.

The civil rights movement brought together diverse Americans who had fought long and hard against discrimination. Mexican Americans also organized on their own behalf in the postwar period. Groups such as the League of United Latin American Citizens (LULAC) and the GI Forum resisted discrimination and segregation in the West, mounting legal challenges that overturned school segregation in California and banned the exclusion of Mexican Americans from Texas juries. Such organizations emphasized the rights of Mexican Americans to be treated as full citizens, but they distanced themselves from Mexican immigrants coming into the country—both legally and illegally.

At the same time, many western Mexican Americans, Native Americans, and other people of color resisted Anglo calls for cultural assimilation. They sought to maintain the languages and traditions that made their groups distinctive. The tension between the desire for equal rights and the demand for legal and cultural distinctiveness remains an issue for people of color in the West today.

Even as the federal government and the courts began to support African Americans, the Eisenhower administration and Congress imposed several well-intentioned but ultimately calamitous policies on Native Americans. Reversing New Deal efforts to expand assistance to American Indian tribes, the federal government adopted the policy of termination: gradually eliminating many Indian reservations and social services. Native American nations were also required to turn properties held communally by the respective tribes into private holdings in the hands of individuals or corporations. The administration and Congress justified these measures as ways to reduce costs, protect states' rights, and expand the rights of individual Native Americans. Indeed, congressional supporters of the policy routinely referred to it as one that would offer freedom to American Indians. This freedom, however, was understood in terms of autonomy from certain forms of government rather than as self-determination. Indeed, most Native Americans opposed termination, and government regulation of their economic activities and personal lives increased.

Between 1954 and 1960, the federal government withdrew benefits from sixty-one tribes. Many reservations were absorbed by the states in which they were located, becoming new counties. The tribes now had to pay state taxes and conform to state regulations. To raise the cash required for taxes, many tribes and individuals had to sell land and mineral rights to outside interests. For example, the Klamaths of Oregon, enticed by offers from lumber companies, sold off most of their ponderosa pine forests. The Menominees of Wisconsin sold much of their reservation to wealthy Chicagoans, who built vacation cabins on former tribal land.

The financial gains from these deals proved fleeting. The loss of returns from tribal enterprises to white economic interests and the persistence of Native American poverty took their toll. Individuals who needed assistance through Aid to Families with Dependent Children had to liquidate their assets, including the bonds they had received as compensation for termination, in order to qualify for benefits. Within a few years, the tribes were worse off than before. An increasing number of American Indians abandoned the former reservation lands. By the end of the 1960s, half the Native American population had relocated to urban areas, assisted by a federal program that provided them with one-way tickets to various cities. There, the Native Americans found the same limited opportunities encountered by other people of color entering urban economies.

Starting in 1956, the Supreme Court began unraveling the restraints on free speech and political action that had been spun during the Red Scare. The Court nullified antisubversion statutes in forty-two states with the 1956 *Pennsylvania* v. *Nelson* decision. Speaking for the majority, Chief Justice Warren ruled that only federal, not state, laws could make it a crime to advocate the overthrow of the federal government. In 1957, in *Jencks* v. *United States*, the Court dealt a blow to government witch hunts by insisting that accused persons had the right to examine the evidence gathered against them. That same year, in *Yates* v. *United States*, the Supreme Court overturned the conviction of fourteen midlevel Communist Party officials sentenced for violating the Smith Act. The justices ruled that verbal calls for toppling the government did not constitute a crime. To be illegal, an act must involve the attempt to "do something now or in the future."

The Court, however, did not extend its liberal premises to sex discrimination cases. In the 1961 case of *Hoyt* v. *Florida*, it upheld states' rights to limit women's participation on juries to ensure that they did not neglect their domestic responsibilities. In Florida, women were exempted from jury service unless they registered their willingness to serve with the court and passed the subjective criteria on jury service applied by local officials. The defendant in the case, Gwendolyn Hoyt, was accused of murder in the death of her husband, whom she accused of infidelity and physical abuse. Her lawyers argued that hers was a crime of passion and that she could not receive a fair trial if she were "forced to trial by jury with an all-male panel who do not have the same passions and understanding of females and their feelings as other women would have." The state of Florida contended that the defendant was seeking not a fair jury, but one that included "female friends," and defended the state law on the grounds that women were the "only bulwark between chaos and an organized and well-run family unit. . . ." The Supreme Court agreed that Florida's law was reasonable because the Constitution "does not entitle one accused of crime to a jury tailored to the circumstances of the particular case, whether relating to the sex or other condition of the defendant" and because ". . . woman is still regarded as the center of home and family life."

Eisenhower's Second-Term Blues

As Eisenhower entered the final year of his first term, the public seemed at ease with his casual style of leadership. The Korean War had ended, Senator McCarthy was a spent force, Stalin's successors called for peaceful coexistence, and the economy was robust. Only Eisenhower's health worried voters. He suffered a serious heart attack in September 1955 and a disabling attack of ileitis, followed by surgery, the next June. His speedy recovery, however, quieted most fears. Eisenhower decided to run again.

Eisenhower harbored doubts about keeping Vice President Richard Nixon on the ticket. He had never liked the brash young man, and now he pondered ways to ease Nixon out. When Nixon balked, Eisenhower relented rather than provoke the wrath of the Republican right. But his misgivings about Nixon undermined the vice president's stature and hurt his presidential candidacy in 1960.

The Democrats renominated Adlai Stevenson, following a challenge from Senator Estes Kefauver, who then beat Senator John F. Kennedy for the vice-presidential slot. Stevenson raised serious questions about poverty, the lack of a national health program, and the administration's refusal to fund public schools. Stevenson also favored ending the draft and halting the open-air testing of atomic weapons; however, he condemned Eisenhower for losing half of Indochina to communism and for not building as many long-range bombers as the Soviets. Nevertheless, as one journalist commented, "The public loves Ike. . . . The less he does the more they love him."

On Election Day in November 1956, Eisenhower gathered 58 percent of the popular vote, over 35 million ballots to Stevenson's 26 million. The public liked Ike far more than it liked his party, however. The Democrats maintained a four-seat majority in the Senate and a twenty-nine-seat majority in the House.

In November 1957, Eisenhower suffered a mild stroke. Although his mental powers were intact, his slurred speech made his public communication less effective than before. That autumn, several foreign and domestic events called his leadership into question. After his dispatch of troops to Little Rock, Arkansas, to protect the black students at Central High School, critics called his actions either too great or too modest a response. The clamor over Sputnik prompted Democrats to ridicule Eisenhower for starving education and for spending too little money on space and defense projects. The new Soviet leader, Nikita Khrushchev, began making whirlwind tours of the Third World, offering aid and winning praise for his country's support of emerging nations. In 1958, Eisenhower's powerful chief of staff, Sherman Adams, resigned amid allegations that he had accepted expensive fur coats from a contractor. Democrats in Congress took the lead in funding the NDEA and space research. To many Americans, Eisenhower began to seem disengaged.

By 1960, political discontent was percolating just beneath the surface. The third recession since Eisenhower took office along with new challenges from Moscow, a communist revolution in Cuba, and a sense that America needed younger, more dynamic leadership gave the Eisenhower administration a tired, somewhat shabby appearance. Yet Eisenhower remained a hero to most Americans. They credited him with ending the Korean War and delivering peace and prosperity. His bland, comfortable stewardship, like that of the typical father in the era's sitcoms, had reassured most middle-class Americans that they would be allowed to get on with their lives.

Conclusion

In the postwar period, American society changed in significant areas of social and cultural life: greater numbers of Americans went to college, including particularly white, working-class men; many white, middle-class Americans moved from cities to suburbs; minorities concentrated in the inner cities largely because of housing and employment discrimination at the hands of private economic interests and public policymakers; interest in consumer products such as home appliances and televisions surged; and Americans of all social groups created a baby boom that, by the late 1950s and 1960s, would lead to an increasingly youth-oriented culture.

For women, the heroic wartime days of Rosie the Riveter were gone. Once government no longer needed her workplace services, experts and the media transformed the working woman from a patriot to a subversive threat with dizzying speed. This switch justified a return to discriminatory practices in the workplace and the insistence that women were to stay home with their families. Although many women managed to return to work, they generally had to settle for lower-paying jobs. More women attended college than before the war, but men's educational advantage increased and women faced especially high barriers in fields such as law and business.

For ethnic minorities, these years brought similarly mixed results. Native Americans faced difficulties brought on by the policy of termination. Mexicans continued to migrate to the United States, but like the Mexican Americans already in the country, they faced persistent discrimination. Mexican Americans and Native Americans grappled with the tension between seeking equality and maintaining their cultural distinctiveness. African Americans made significant progress in establishing civil rights through voter-registration drives, legal challenges, nonviolent demonstrations, and symbolic acts like sit-ins and freedom rides. Sometimes the activists encountered bloody resistance, and the legislative and executive branches took only small and slow steps to help. Yet crucial court victories set the scene for the major civil rights victories of the 1960s.

In retrospect, the 1950s seem a curiously contradictory period in American life. Eisenhower practiced the politics of moderation, churches increased their membership, and conservative family values appeared dominant. Middle-class suburban families embraced the trappings of prosperity—the automobile, home appliances, television, sports, jet travel, and other new miracles of consumerism. But young people, inspired by their own emerging subculture, entered a period of ferment. Despite the emphasis on traditional family structures, sex was discussed more openly. Women went to work in greater numbers, not quite fulfilling their idealized role as housewives and mothers. Intellectuals challenged the era's conformity and consumerism, and the Beat writers dared to suggest that drugs, sex, and alternative religious experiences might be more important than patriotism.

Perhaps the biggest contradiction of all was that despite the overall prosperity, one in four Americans lived near or below the poverty line at the end of the decade. And despite government inaction, some economists had begun to pay serious attention to this problem. By then, too, the civil rights revolution was under way; the African American struggle to end segregation and claim equal rights was in the process of transforming the social landscape. American women's discontent with constrained lives was also coming to the surface, posing a threat to all fundamental institutions. With all of these developments interacting, the 1950s was a period of considerable change beneath a guise of security and stability.

F U R T H E R • R E A D I N G

On Eisenhower, business, and the politics of the 1950s, see Charles Alexander, *Holding the Line* (1975); Stephen E. Ambrose, *Eisenhower: The President* (1984); Barbara B. Clowse, *Brainpower for the Cold War: The Sputnik Crisis and the National Defense Education Act of 1958* (1981); Fred L. Greenstein, *The Hidden Hand Presidency* (1982); Elizabeth A. Fones-Wolf, *Selling Free Enterprise: The Business Assault on Labor and Liberalism, 1945–60* (1994). **On social change and popular culture,** see Keith W. Olson, *The G.I.*

Bill, the Veterans, and the Colleges (1974); Kenneth Jackson, *Crabgrass Frontier: The Suburbanization of the United States* (1985); Herbert J. Gans, *The Levittowners* (1967); John M. Findlay, *Magic Lands: Western Cityscapes and American Culture After 1940* (1992); Richard Schickel, *The Disney Version: The Life, Time, Art and Commerce of Walt Disney* (1968); Erik Barnouw, *Tube of Plenty* (1982); Mark H. Rose, *Interstate: Express Highway Politics, 1941–56* (1979); Susan Strasser, *Waste and Want: A Social History of Trash* (1999). **On gender, families, and sexualities,** see Elaine T. May, *Homeward Bound: American Families in the Cold War Era* (1988); Rickie Solinger, *Wake Up, Little Susie* (1992); Leslie J. Reagan, *When Abortion Was a Crime: Women, Medicine, and Law in the United States, 1867–1973* (1997); Stephanie Coontz, *The Way We Never Were: American Families and the Nostalgia Trap* (1992); Beth Bailey, *From Front Porch to Back Seat: Courtship in Twentieth Century America* (1988); Joan Jacobs Brumberg, *The Body Project: An Intimate History of American Girls* (1997). **On civil rights,** see Stephen J. Whitfield, *A Death in the Delta: The Story of Emmett Till* (1988); Nicholas Lemann, *The Promised Land: The Great Black Migration and How It Changed America* (1991); Mark V. Tushnet, *The NAACP's Legal Strategy Against Segregated Education* (1987); Taylor Branch, *Parting the Waters: America in the King Years, 1954–63* (1988); David J. Garrow, *Bearing the Cross: Martin Luther King, Jr., and the Southern Christian Leadership Conference* (1986); Richard Kluger, *Simple Justice* (1975); Michal Belknap, *Federal Law and Southern Order: Racial Violence and Constitutional Conflict in the Post-Brown South* (1987); Mario Garcia, *Mexican Americans: Leadership, Ideology, and Identity, 1930–1960*. **On high-tech medicine and polio,** see Jane S. Smith, *Patenting the Sun: Polio and the Salk Vaccine* (1990); Andrea Tone, *Devices and Desires: A History of Contraception in America* (2001).

4

Generals and Presidents:
U.S. Foreign Policy in the 1950s

They liked Ike: President Dwight D. Eisenhower flashes his trademark smile. /
© Bettmann/CORBIS

Shortly after the arrest in England of spy Klaus Fuchs in February 1950, Senator Homer Capehart, an Indiana Republican, rose from his seat in the Senate chamber to ask, "How much more are we going to have to take? Fuchs and Acheson and Hiss and hydrogen bombs threatening outside and New Dealism eating away at the vitals of the nation. In the name of Heaven, is this the best America can do?" In a speech before the Republican Women's Club of Wheeling, West Virginia, on February 9, Capehart's colleague from Wisconsin, Joseph McCarthy, explained why the nation faced such grim prospects. America risked defeat in the Cold War, McCarthy asserted, because Secretary of State Acheson, a "pompous diplomat in striped pants and a phony British accent," employed over two hundred communists in the State Department. These miscreants had already "lost" China and were poised to betray the remainder of the free world.

As we saw earlier, during the first months of the 1950s, the American public was whipsawed by countervailing claims of victory and defeat in the Cold War. President Truman and his top aides insisted that the Marshall Plan and the NATO Alliance had stabilized Western Europe and Japan, effectively denying Stalin the real prizes he sought. Republicans countered that the Truman administration, riddled with security risks and spies, looked the other way while Soviet and Chinese agents gained ground in Asia, Africa, the Middle East, and Latin America. As politicians traded charges, ordinary citizens worried that traitors had penetrated the nation's vital institutions. Truman and Secretary of State Acheson tried to refute these charges, but events at home and abroad soon overwhelmed them. Amid lurid claims of what he called "twenty years of treason," Senator McCarthy added his name to the rogue's gallery of American politics. A relative latecomer to the Red Scare, he so dominated public attention from 1950 to 1954 that *McCarthyism* became a catchword for the era. A stalemated war in Korea and growing doubts about Truman's leadership contributed to the election of the first Republican president since Herbert Hoover. Although General Dwight D. Eisenhower campaigned on a pledge to clean out the federal government and to liberate people in the "enslaved nations of the world," he presided over an administration characterized by moderation at home and abroad. In fact, Eisenhower worked behind the scenes to restrain the arms race and explore cooperation with a new generation of Soviet leaders.

McCarthyism and the Korean War

Joseph McCarthy served as a county judge in Wisconsin before entering the Marine Corps during World War II. While a desk officer stationed in the Pacific, McCarthy flew a few routine missions in the tail gunner's seat of a combat aircraft. In 1946, campaigning as "tail gunner Joe," he won election to a seat in the U.S. Senate. During his first years in Washington, both colleagues and journalists considered him an affable buffoon, quick with a joke or a drink. In 1950, in search of a hot issue, McCarthy pieced together information provided by friends such as Representative Richard Nixon into an indictment of the Truman administration.

The speech he gave on February 9, 1950, in Wheeling, West Virginia, with its claim that Secretary of State Acheson employed hundreds of communist agents bent on betraying America, catapulted McCarthy from obscurity to international prominence. Over the next few months, McCarthy often changed the number of traitors and their exact roles. In an unguarded moment while drinking with several reporters, he confided that he had no idea if there were two or two hundred spies in Washington. "What I have," he gloated, "is a bucket of shit, and I know just where to spread it." Ultimately, he labeled as spies and traitors the "whole group of twisted-thinking" New Dealers who "led America to near ruin at home and abroad."

McCarthy was a cynic and opportunist who came to believe his own ravings. During a Senate probe into his charges, he clowned and bullied his way around the evidence. His sensational claims were shown to be either fantasies or recycled information. McCarthy quibbled over the number of alleged Reds in government because it suggested that the Democrats questioned only his details, not the basic facts of his case. Several leading Republicans in Congress saw through his antics but valued him as a wrecking ball who undermined public faith in the Democratic Party. Many ordinary Americans found comfort in McCarthy's conspiracy theories, which provided simple answers to complex

As lawyer Joseph Welch (hand on brow) listens, Senator Joseph McCarthy lectures a special Senate committee about the supposed Communist conspiracy in the United States. / UPI/Bettmann/CORBIS

questions. The country had no need for expensive aid programs and entangling foreign alliances such as the Marshall Plan and NATO. A purge of Reds at home would set everything right.

Journalists such as George Reedy felt guilty about devoting coverage to McCarthy. Reedy recalled that "Joe couldn't find a Communist in Red Square" and "didn't know Karl Marx from Groucho." But as a senator, he commanded a degree of attention from the press. Blessed with a good sense of timing, McCarthy often made inflammatory charges just before radio, TV, or press deadlines. This timing put his accusations in front of the public for a day or more, while his hapless victims struggled to play catch-up.

The North Korean invasion of South Korea on June 25, 1950, transformed the Cold War into a hot one. By the time the fighting stopped three years later, U.S. defense spending had quadrupled, over forty thousand Americans (and many more Koreans and Chinese) had been killed, and U.S. forces were stationed around the globe. Violence within and between the rival Koreas killed tens of thousands even before the outbreak of formal war.

In August 1945, the United States and the Soviet Union had divided Korea, a Japanese colony since the early twentieth century, into temporary occupation zones north and south of the 38th parallel (see Map 4.1). Plans to unify the country collapsed as the Cold War intensified. The Soviets sponsored a communist regime, the Democratic People's Republic of Korea led by Kim Il Sung, in the north. South of the 38th parallel, the United States promoted a conservative government, the Republic of Korea, led by Syngman Rhee, a prominent Korean nationalist who had lived in the United States for decades. Soviet and U.S. forces departed in 1949, leaving behind advisers to rival regimes that each claimed the right to rule all Korea.

Korea had no special strategic importance, but American officials worried that abandoning the South Korean government might be seen as deserting an ally. Despite their own doubts about Rhee's authoritarian regime, Truman and his advisers reacted quickly to the North Koreans' attack. They considered the invasion a Soviet test of U.S. resolve, not a bona fide civil war. The relationship between Stalin and North Korea's Kim Il Sung, one U.S. official remarked, was "the same as that between Walt Disney and Donald Duck."

The facts were murkier. The Soviets, and to a lesser extent China, had provided support and advice for the North Korean assault. But Stalin approved the venture largely in response to Kim's pleas for assistance and his assurance that northern forces would be welcomed as liberators. They would sweep to victory, Kim insisted, before the United States could respond. Stalin and Mao viewed the attack as a low-risk move to create a unified, communist-friendly Korea that would help counterbalance nearby Japan, then being rebuilt and rearmed by the United States. No one anticipated a major war.

Once fighting began in 1950, the Truman administration rushed to support the beleaguered South Korean government. The U.N. Security Council

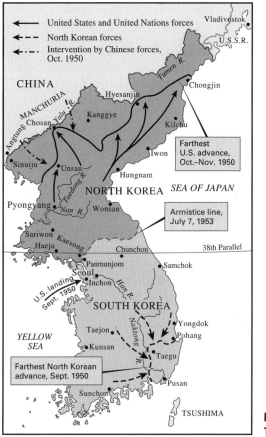

Map 4.1
The Korean War

(which the Soviets were boycotting to protest its refusal to seat a delegation from the People's Republic of China) adopted an American resolution that called upon member states to assist South Korea. On June 27, Truman ordered U.S. air and naval forces into action. Fearing a wider threat to the Asia/Pacific area, Truman also expanded aid to French forces fighting communist guerrillas in Indochina (Vietnam) and sent the U.S. 7th Fleet to protect the Chinese Nationalist–held island of Taiwan from Chinese communist assault. Three days later, he dispatched ground combat forces to Korea under the command of General Douglas MacArthur, who already served as occupation commander in nearby Japan. Congress was informed of these actions but not asked to declare war. Truman soon referred to the intervention as a police action. American soldiers made up the large majority of U.N.-sponsored troops in Korea.

For two months, U.S. and South Korean forces struggled to maintain a toe-hold around the city of Pusan on the southern tip of the Korean peninsula. On September 15, 1950, MacArthur assembled a large force that mounted a daring amphibious assault at Inchon, a port in South Korea behind North Korean lines. In barely two weeks, triumphant American soldiers had cleared South Korea of Northern invaders and achieved the U.N. and U.S. goal of re-establishing the South Korean government.

The deceptively easy victory at Inchon gave MacArthur the appearance of infallibility and prompted Truman to expand American goals. In place of restoring the prewar border, Truman ordered MacArthur to cross the 38th parallel to destroy the North Korean army and to unify the country under the Rhee regime. The strategy of rolling back communist influence had wide appeal. Truman hoped it would send a tough message to Stalin as well as to Republicans at home who questioned his leadership. MacArthur guessed that a victory in Korea might open the way for a wider crusade against communism in China and, possibly, clear a path for him to the White House. The president worried about the general's loose talk of a bigger war and several times considered firing him. But as a World War II hero and the darling of the Republican Party who had twice sought the GOP presidential nomination, MacArthur could not be removed without provoking a backlash among many Americans who considered him a living legend.

Truman sought a military victory in Korea without provoking a wider war with China or the Soviet Union. Yet he discounted several warnings from China during October that American forces should not move north of the 38th parallel or approach the Yalu River, which separated North Korea from Manchuria, China's industrial heartland. Truman took China's threats to intervene more seriously than did MacArthur—who may well have wanted to provoke a major conflict—and flew to Wake Island in the Pacific to confer with the general. MacArthur claimed the war was nearly over and that if the Chinese dared to intervene, there would be the "greatest slaughter." The prophecy proved true, but not exactly as he supposed.

In late November, MacArthur ordered an all-out push to the Yalu River, predicting that American troops would be "home by Christmas." Chinese soldiers stunned the U.S. commander by crossing into North Korea and launching an offensive that drove American forces back to and then south of the 38th parallel. MacArthur responded by accusing Truman and the Joint Chiefs of Staff of tying his hands in this "entirely new war." After China entered the fighting, the American commander demanded massive reinforcements, called on Truman to seek help from anticommunist Chinese on Taiwan, and proposed attacking China, perhaps with atomic bombs.

Truman and nearly all his civilian and military advisers rejected these ideas. They wanted to defend South Korea, not start World War III by provoking an even bigger fight with Moscow and Beijing. Nor did they see any role for the atomic bomb on Korean battlefields or against Chinese cities. Because the real Cold War prizes remained in Europe and Japan, it made no sense to get sucked into a major war in a strategic backwater. Instead, Truman reverted to the original war aim of restoring separate North and South Korean regimes.

Still, many Americans were intoxicated by MacArthur's grandiose rhetoric and had difficulty understanding why American soldiers should "die for a tie." After less than a year of fighting, two-thirds of the public disapproved of how Truman handled the war. In March 1951, MacArthur sabotaged the president's attempt to start truce talks with China. He followed this tactic by sending a letter to Republican congressman Joseph Martin, in which he implied that by not fighting for a clear win, Truman was responsible for the pointless murder of American boys. MacArthur asserted, "[T]here is no substitute for victory."

Truman finally had enough. On April 11, 1951, he sacked MacArthur, whom he privately called a "flim-flam artist" and a "bunko man." The president named General Matthew Ridgway, the respected commander of the 8th Army in Korea, as theater commander as well as MacArthur's replacement in Japan. Republicans condemned the president and predicted that firing MacArthur would lead to a communist conquest of all Asia. Senator Nixon claimed Truman had made the communists "the happiest people in America." Senator McCarthy insisted that Truman must have been drunk when he fired the general. Crowds in several cities burned effigies of Truman, and many newspapers demanded his impeachment.

MacArthur returned to a series of parades in his honor, followed by an invitation to speak before Congress. In his memorable speech of April 19, 1951, the general repeated his charge that Truman was an appeaser and called for military victory in Korea and all Asia. He closed with the lyrics of an old army song, "Old Soldiers Never Die, They Just Fade Away." As one seasoned journalist noted of the audience, there was not a "dry eye among the Republicans, nor a dry seat among the Democrats."

Obviously, MacArthur hoped he would not fade away. But, in fact, he did so rather quickly. Lengthy Senate hearings into the military situation in Korea revealed that no senior U.S. military commanders agreed with MacArthur's strategy. As General Omar Bradley, chairman of the Joint Chiefs, put it, expanding the conflict in Korea or fighting China would be the "wrong war, in the wrong place, against the wrong enemy." Unable to score political points in his testimony, MacArthur began a nationwide speaking tour, paid for by a pair of conservative Texas oil millionaires. Crowds at arenas where he spoke cheered the general. But when he began calling for a rollback not only of Asian communism but also of petroleum taxes paid by his patrons, the crowds thinned and he soon cancelled the remainder of the tour. A year later, Republicans nominated a heroic World War II general as their presidential candidate, but his name was Eisenhower, not MacArthur.

The public's love affair with MacArthur also lapsed because his successor, General Ridgway, halted China's offensive in Korea and restored the battle lines near the 38th parallel without using atomic weapons or widening the war. In July 1951, China and North Korea began armistice talks with the United States. The talking, and fighting, continued for two more years.

Political and Economic Consequences of the Korean War

When the Cold War turned hot in Korea, conservatives of both parties escalated their attacks on liberalism. Senator Pat McCarran, a Nevada Democrat, competed with Joe McCarthy for the title of chief Red hunter. After giving his name to the anticommunist McCarran Act (discussed in Chapter 2), he took over the chair of the new Senate Internal Security Subcommittee (SISS), which launched a series of lengthy political probes into the alleged loss of China by subversive diplomats and organizations. Some State Department officials specializing in Asian affairs were subjected to as many as ten loyalty hearings and then finally fired. Within a few years, so many China experts were purged that a senior official called the Far Eastern Division of the State Department a "disaster area filled with human wreckage."

Energized by the Korean stalemate, the Red Scare continued through the late 1950s. Between 1950 and 1956, various House and Senate committees launched over 100 probes of alleged communist activity by public employees, labor unions, and voluntary organizations, and within particular industries such as Hollywood. Left-leaning unions—such as the Mine, Mill and Smelter Workers; the Longshoreman's Union; the United Electrical Workers; and the New York Teachers Union—were favorite targets. Several corporations that were eager to rid themselves of bothersome demands for higher wages and improved working conditions used allegations of communist control to refuse to negotiate contracts with suspect unions. They sometimes justified this stance by saying that the federal government would refuse to place military orders with industries whose workers were represented by communists or "fellow travelers."

Individuals suspected of political unorthodoxy or who simply refused to sign loyalty oaths could be fired by local, state, and federal agencies. In New York, for example, 300 public school teachers were fired for political reasons during the 1950s. Nationally, about 100 college professors lost their jobs. As noted earlier, several thousand federal employees quit or were fired in the face of loyalty hearings.

In 1956, America's most prominent playwright, Arthur Miller, was indicted for contempt of Congress when he refused to tell the House Un-American Activities Committee (HUAC) the names of people whom he had seen at communist meetings decades before. Miller, whose play about the Salem witch trials, *The Crucible*, was a thinly veiled allegory of Cold War political hysteria, had refused a deal offered by HUAC. If he permitted his wife, actress Marilyn Monroe, to pose in suggestive photographs with the committee chair, he would be let off with a slap on the wrist. Fortunately for Miller and Monroe, a judge later quashed the indictment.

Popular expressions of anticommunism appeared on television and in magazines, film, and popular books. Herbert Philbrick's 1952 memoir, *I Led Three Lives*, aired as a weekly TV show from 1953 to 1956. In 1956, J. Edgar Hoover assisted the publication of a bestselling history of his agency, *The FBI Story*, written by Don Whitehead, which also ran in 170 newspapers and was made into a movie. Hoover published his own bestselling exposé of communism, *Masters of Deceit* (1958), which went through twenty-nine printings by 1970.

The Korean War also had other, lasting economic and political consequences. Defense spending at home and abroad fueled rapid economic growth that lasted nearly two decades. Before the war began, American defense expenditures were just under 5 percent of the annual gross national product (GNP). After the fighting erupted in Korea, military spending rose to over 13 percent of GNP in 1953 and averaged 10 percent for the rest of the decade. This high rate of military spending forged a consensus that joined Democrats and Republicans in support of big government spending. The defense budget served as a kind of national economic policy for the United States, promoting advances in electronics and aerospace technology. It also continued the process begun during World War II of shifting the country's manufacturing base from the Northeast and Midwest to the South and West. By 1957, for example, over one-half of all industrial jobs in southern California were linked to military production. Later, when geographers began using the term Sunbelt to refer to much of the South and the West Coast, some argued that these areas really ought to be called the Gunbelt.

War-generated spending also spurred economic growth in Western Europe and Japan, where the United States placed military orders. Prosperity promoted closer economic and political integration in Western Europe. Six western European countries established a coal and steel community in 1951, eliminating trade barriers in these basic commodities. In 1957, the six-nation Treaty of Rome created the European Economic Community (EEC), the forerunner to the Common Market. A decade of strong growth in Europe and Japan undercut the waning appeal of left-wing political parties.

The economic growth promoted by military spending lay in the future. As of 1952, the political mood in the United States remained sour. The stalemate in Korea, the redbaiting by both Republicans and conservative Democrats, and the charges of petty corruption in Washington doomed the Truman administration as the 1952 election neared. The GOP campaign slogan that denounced the Democrats as the party of "Korea, Communism, and Corruption" proved brutally effective.

Eisenhower Takes Command

Shortly after taking office in 1953, President Dwight D. Eisenhower gathered a group of military and diplomatic specialists in the White House sun parlor and asked them to reassess Cold War strategy. In a project dubbed Operation Solarium, the experts weighed the policy of containment against more radical proposals, including threatening Moscow with nuclear war should it cross a demarcation line, and attempting to push back existing areas of Soviet control through political, psychological, economic, and covert military pressure. Discussion even touched on launching a pre-emptive attack on the Soviet Union.

As a candidate, Eisenhower had pledged he would never rest until he had liberated the "enslaved nations of the world." John Foster Dulles, the newly appointed secretary of state, had denounced the existing containment policy as a "treadmill, which at best might keep us in the same place until we drop exhausted." Both men had criticized Truman's foreign policy because it was not designed to win a conclusive victory, and Republican campaign rhetoric had castigated the Democrats for "abandoning people to Godless terrorism."

Nevertheless, the new president approved continuation of the containment policy much as it had been received from his predecessor. With the campaign's rhetoric behind him, Eisenhower pursued a relatively moderate foreign policy during his two terms in office. His precise approach to foreign affairs was not easy to categorize. Although he had declared that America could never rest until the communist yoke had been lifted from Eastern Europe and China, he resisted calls from the Pentagon and Congress to increase defense spending, fearing that large budget deficits would be as destructive as war in the long run. He was willing to threaten other countries with nuclear weapons, but he avoided full-scale conflict and never employed America's expanded nuclear arsenal against an enemy. Under Eisenhower's leadership, the United States and the Soviet Union gradually learned how to coexist.

Eisenhower's choice for secretary of state, the formidable John Foster Dulles, seemed a marked contrast to the avuncular president. A powerful corporate lawyer active in the Presbyterian church, Dulles had long been touted as the Republicans' chief foreign policy expert. He often wore a sour expression, and he delivered frequent lectures on Christian virtue and communist sin. He was so noted for his toughness against communism—in Asia and elsewhere—that Winston Churchill joked he was the only "bull" who carried around his own "China closet."

During Ike's two terms, Dulles and Vice President Richard Nixon made frequent bellicose and controversial statements, creating the impression that they, not Eisenhower, were the real forces behind the administration's foreign policy. In fact, as historians have come to realize, Eisenhower kept both men on a short leash. He used them to float controversial ideas, warn adversaries, and appease Republican hard-liners. They acted as lightning rods to draw criticism away from the president, whose views were less extreme.

The administration's 1953 strategic plan, called NSC 162/3, placed a greater emphasis than before on the use of atomic bombs, both as weapons and as bargaining chips in the Cold War. For the president, this approach had economic as well as military benefits. By relying more on nuclear weapons and the air force, the United States could slash the size of its costly ground forces. Unlike military officials who wanted enough troops, ships, and conventional munitions to achieve a decisive superiority over the Soviet Union, Eisenhower favored sufficient striking power to deter or, if necessary, destroy the Soviet Union, but no more than was needed. Attempting to match the Soviets "man for man, gun for gun," he warned, would lead to national bankruptcy. On one public occasion he noted that "every gun that is made, every warship launched, every rocket fired, signifies, in a final sense, a theft from those who hunger and are not fed, those who are cold and are not clothed." Eisenhower managed to reduce military expenditures from about $52 billion annually to about $36 billion at the end of his first term, even if none of the savings went to the hungry, the cold, or the poorly clothed. During his second term, military spending increased again because of congressional pressure and renewed competition with the Soviet Union.

Eisenhower and Dulles christened their strategy the New Look. The strategy depended on what Dulles called the threat of "massive retaliation" against Soviet or Chinese provocation. The administration had inherited a nuclear arsenal of about one thousand bombs. Over the next eight years, this stockpile grew to eighteen thousand weapons. An important addition to the military's arsenal was the huge, eight-engine B-52 bomber. Small, tactical nuclear

Cartoonist Herblock depicted the anxiety many Americans felt about the Eisenhower-Dulles foreign policy. / From *Herblock's Special for Today,* Simon & Schuster, 1958

weapons as well as intercontinental ballistic missiles (ICBMs) and submarine-launched missiles were under development. By the time Eisenhower left office in 1961, the United States had enough air-, sea-, and ground-launched nuclear weapons to destroy Soviet targets many times over—far surpassing Eisenhower's own goal of sufficiency. The Soviets played catch-up and soon acquired their own "overkill" capacity.

Some critics, especially Democratic politicians and career army officers, argued that the New Look and the doctrine of massive retaliation locked the United States into an all-or-nothing response to foreign threats. Eisenhower and Dulles responded with three measures designed to meet the all-or-nothing dilemma. First, the administration entered into anticommunist military alliances with numerous countries, promising American materiel support for local troops fighting in small wars. Second, for situations short of war, the president authorized the CIA to carry out covert military operations against unfriendly regimes or groups. Finally, the administration pushed the development of tactical atomic weapons for battlefield use. These explosives, small enough to be fired in artillery shells, were intended to counter a conventional attack by Soviet or Chinese forces without escalating to global thermonuclear war. The army even developed a 58-pound atomic bomb that commandos could carry in their packs and use to blow up bridges, factories, or military depots.

Eisenhower saw no reason why atomic artillery shells should not be used "exactly as you would use a bullet or anything else." He approved a policy stating that, in the event of hostilities with the Soviet Union, the United States would "consider nuclear weapons to be as available for use as other munitions." In part because of his military background, however, Eisenhower was wise enough to fear a nuclear showdown. In 1954, when South Korean strongman Syngman Rhee wanted him to threaten Russia and China with war in order to unify Korea, Eisenhower replied that "if war comes, it will be horrible. Atomic war will destroy civilization." Clearly, the president hoped to avoid a nuclear conflict, and he saw the atomic arsenal as a deterrent. If deterrence failed, however, Eisenhower was prepared to "push the button."

The policy of relying more heavily on the nuclear threat received its first test in Korea, where fighting continued near the 38th parallel despite two years of peace talks. A major unsettled point was China's demand that the United States observe international law by returning all Chinese and North Korean prisoners of war (POWs) held in South Korea, including several thousand who had sought asylum. Like Truman before him, Eisenhower feared a domestic backlash if he agreed to repatriate POWs to China against their will.

Determined to break the deadlock, Eisenhower ordered a study to consider the use of tactical atomic weapons in Korea. To his surprise, most military and diplomatic experts doubted that atomic weapons would do much good. As the Truman administration had realized, there were few suitable targets to bomb in North Korea. Inconclusive use of the bomb might "depreciate the value of our stockpile," strategists warned. Attacking urban and industrial targets in China would cause huge civilian losses, something Eisenhower opposed. In a bluff, American officials spread the rumor that Eisenhower planned to use the atomic bomb. When an armistice was achieved in July 1953, Dulles claimed that he had made it known to the Chinese that they faced a nuclear threat, and that fear of it compelled them to accept the U.S. demand for voluntary prisoner returns.

In reality, several factors contributed to the breakthrough. Joseph Stalin's sudden death from a stroke on March 5, 1953, brought to power Soviet leaders eager to improve relations with the United States. China had grown weary of the costly war and sought better ties with the West. Even before Washington had dropped hints about escalating the war, Chinese and American negotiators had made progress on a partial exchange of sick and wounded prisoners. They then compromised on the broader issue. POWs resisting repatriation would be remanded to a neutral commission to determine their ultimate fate. When South Korean president Syngman Rhee opposed this deal, an enraged Eisenhower threatened to depose him. Thus, diplomacy and Stalin's death, as much as atomic threats, led to the Korean cease-fire.

During the dictator's final years, Stalin had expanded Soviet military power and initiated bloody new purges to stamp out imagined conspiracies within his inner circle. After his death, a triumvirate composed of Georgi Malenkov, Nikolai Bulganin, and Nikita Khrushchev assumed power. The three new leaders promised Soviet citizens a better life. Despite their rivalries, they agreed to do away with Stalin's network of terror and to seek improved relations with the West. Malenkov announced that no dispute—even with the United States—was so bad it could not be settled peacefully through negotiations.

By 1955, Khrushchev's skills at inner-party intrigue allowed him to oust his colleagues and emerge as the first among equals. In 1956, he shocked his country and the world by denouncing Stalin's crimes. Downplaying his own role as one of the dictator's henchmen, the new party boss charged that Stalin's "personality cult" had distorted communism and led to the slaughter of several million loyal Bolsheviks and Soviet citizens.

Changes within the Soviet Union posed challenges. Should Washington trust Soviet talk of "peaceful coexistence," or should it increase pressure on Moscow now that a less oppressive regime held power? Did the new Kremlin leaders really seek cooperation with the West? Should the United States try to break up the Sino-Soviet alliance? If so, should it maintain a rigid policy toward China or act more flexibly? Some Western leaders, such as Winston Churchill, urged Eisenhower to meet with the new Kremlin bosses and to allow commercial ties with China; restrained by Dulles, Eisenhower at first reacted cautiously to changes in the communist camp. Either from fear of a political backlash, a preference to wait passively for the demise of communism, or conflicting advice from his aides, the president hesitated to open a dialogue with Soviet leaders.

The Ebbing of McCarthyism

The Red Scare at home also influenced Eisenhower's approach to foreign policy. During 1953 and 1954, Senator Joseph McCarthy continued to attack supposed Reds in American government. Although Eisenhower personally found McCarthy vile, he had done little during the presidential campaign to alert the public to McCarthy's excesses. Even when McCarthy labeled General George C. Marshall a traitor who had perpetrated "a conspiracy so immense as to dwarf any previous such venture in the history of man," Eisenhower refused to condemn the senator or defend the general—the World War II chief of staff, architect of the Marshall Plan, and the man who raised Ike from military obscurity to the heights of wartime command. Eisenhower merely told aides he would not "get into the gutter" with McCarthy.

Eisenhower made other concessions to Republican extremists. In 1953, he refused to block the execution of Ethel and Julius Rosenberg, who were convicted of espionage for Moscow, even though he harbored doubts about Ethel's guilt. In another high-profile case, Eisenhower approved stripping physicist J. Robert Oppenheimer of his security clearance in retaliation for his opposition to the development of the hydrogen bomb. Eisenhower allowed Dulles to appoint Scott McLeod, a McCarthy protégé, to purge China specialists in the State Department who had predicted victory by Mao's communist forces in 1949. Foreign Service officers had to demonstrate "positive loyalty,"—an indefinable quality—to keep their jobs. Dulles ordered that books by "Communists, fellow travelers, et cetera" be removed from U.S. Information Agency libraries abroad. "Et cetera" included works by such "radicals" as Mark Twain. During Eisenhower's administration, about fifteen hundred federal employees in various agencies were fired as security risks, and another six thousand were pressured to resign.

But McCarthyism was on the wane after 1954, the year McCarthy began to self-destruct. Early in that year, piqued at the army's refusal to give his staff aide David Schine a draft deferment and other special treatment, McCarthy charged the army with coddling communists. The bizarre allegation focused on a dentist, Irving Peress, who had been drafted, promoted, and honorably discharged despite his admitted communist sympathies. When high-ranking army officials, acting on the president's orders, refused to apologize or give personnel records to the senator, McCarthy charged them with incompetence and treason. The Wisconsin Republican declared he "did not intend to treat traitors like gentlemen."

With Eisenhower's backing, army leaders countercharged that McCarthy had tried to blackmail them into giving David Schine special treatment. In April 1954, the Senate launched an inquiry. At this time, television journalist Edward R. Murrow aired a segment of his show *See It Now* that highlighted some of McCarthy's most unsavory actions. Soon several members of the Senate began to question their colleague's behavior. During a dramatic, televised Senate inquiry known as the Army-McCarthy hearings, 20 million viewers had their first close look at McCarthy's vicious attacks on the loyalty of all who resisted him. Army counsel Joseph Welch, the soul of telegenic respectability, parried McCarthy's shrill tirades and refused to be provoked by the slashing attacks of Roy Cohn, the senator's legal aide.

Although only a small number of observers realized it at the time, a sexual undercurrent was present in an exchange between Cohn, a closeted homosexual who ridiculed gay men as perverts and subversives, and Welch. When Cohn could not explain how certain evidence he had placed in the record had been tampered with, Welch taunted Cohn by suggesting that "fairies"—common slang for gay men—had been responsible. By hinting broadly that Cohn was homosexual, Welch implied that McCarthy's villainy even extended to hiring deviants. In the timbre of the times, homosexuality was considered so unsavory that even liberals and civil libertarians felt free to use allegations of it to attack the redbaiters.

After weeks of failing to prove any Red plot within the army, a frustrated McCarthy charged that Frederick Fisher, a young lawyer who worked for Welch's Boston firm but was not a member of the army's legal team, had communist leanings. Welch, who had anticipated the accusation, responded to McCarthy's mudslinging with a sad shake of the head, saying, "I think I never really gauged your cruelty or your recklessness." Unable to stop himself, the senator resumed his attack on Fisher. Finally, Welch could tolerate McCarthy's slander no more. He declared that McCarthy's forgiveness would "have to come from someone other than me." The lawyer then issued a historic query: "Have you no sense of decency, sir, at long last? Have you left no sense of decency?"

Even though the Army-McCarthy hearings rendered no formal verdict, the senator had failed a critical media test. Opinion polls taken during and after the televised sessions revealed a dramatic slide in McCarthy's approval rating, from nearly 50 percent at the beginning of 1954 to only 30 percent in June. By December, the Senate voted to censure him for "unbecoming conduct." Eisenhower, who took a bit more credit for the senator's humiliation than was warranted, hosted Welch at the White House and remarked that "McCarthyism had become McCarthywasim." The senator's slide gave Eisenhower more freedom to maneuver. McCarthy never recovered from these public defeats. Shunned by old friends, he increased his legendary drinking, lost political influence, and died of alcohol-related illness in 1957.

America and the Challenges of the Third World

In the fifteen years following the end of World War II, thirty-seven nations emerged from colonialism to independence, eighteen during 1960 alone. Most of these new states were nonwhite, poor, nonindustrialized, and located in Asia, Africa, or the Middle East (see Map 4.2). Many had gained independence through armed struggle; in some, the violence continued after independence. They had much in common with other poor nations, especially those in Latin America, where political unrest often became armed rebellion. During the 1950s, at least twenty-eight prolonged guerrilla insurgencies were under way.

Most of these emerging and underdeveloped nations, loosely called the Third World, existed outside the bloc of the industrialized democracies (the First World) and the communist nations (the Second World). Few had democratic governments. Most sought to remain neutral in the Cold War while pursuing economic development and soliciting aid from both sides. Poor nations both envied and resented American power. They often employed the rhetoric of socialism, even as they sought the material rewards of capitalism. Under Stalin, the Soviet Union had ignored or criticized most noncommunist liberation movements. Khrushchev proved more adroit, offering economic and military assistance to emerging nations whether or not they adhered to Moscow's line.

The United States shared Moscow's concern with the Third World. The emerging nations contained vast raw material wealth and a huge population. Eisenhower and Dulles worried that the Third World's criticism of imperialism and capitalism would provide a wedge for Soviet influence. And many Americans mistrusted any model of national development that deviated from the U.S. experience.

Competition for influence in the Third World also affected domestic policy. For example, American diplomats and intelligence officials reported that communist propagandists had a field day publicizing racial violence in the United States. Stories and pictures of lynchings, Klan rallies, and race riots during the 1950s were frequently distributed by the Soviets in Asia and Africa. Several times in the 1950s, African Americans filed appeals with the United Nations demanding international action to defend the basic rights of black Americans.

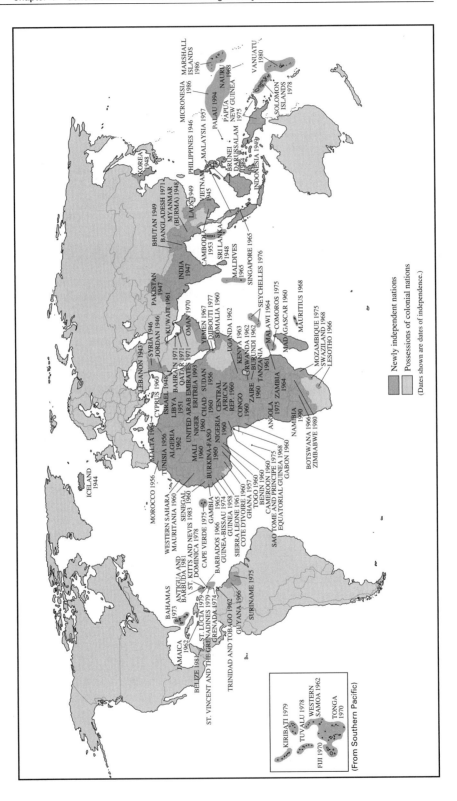

KOREA 1948

MARSHALL ISLANDS 1986
MICRONESIA 1986
PALAU 1994
NAURU 1968
VANUATU 1980
PAPUA NEW GUINEA 1975
MALAYSIA 1957
SOLOMON ISLANDS 1978
PHILIPPINES 1946
BRUNEI DARUSSALAM 1984
INDONESIA 1949

BHUTAN 1949
BANGLADESH 1971
MYANMAR (BURMA) 1948
LAOS 1949
VIETNAM 1945
CAMBODIA 1953
SRI LANKA 1948
SINGAPORE 1965
MALDIVES 1965

PAKISTAN 1947
INDIA 1947

SYRIA 1946
JORDAN 1946
KUWAIT 1961
BAHRAIN 1971
QATAR 1971
OMAN 1970
YEMEN 1967
DJIBOUTI 1977
SOMALIA 1960

LEBANON 1943
CYPRUS 1960
ISRAEL 1948

SEYCHELLES 1976
COMOROS 1975
MADAGASCAR 1960
MAURITIUS 1968

UGANDA 1962
KENYA 1963
RWANDA 1962
BURUNDI 1962
TANZANIA 1961
MALAWI 1964

LIBYA 1951
MALTA 1964
TUNISIA 1956
ALGERIA 1962

ERITREA 1993
SUDAN 1956
CHAD 1960
NIGER 1960
CENTRAL AFRICAN REP. 1960
ZAIRE 1960
CONGO 1960
ZAMBIA 1964
MOZAMBIQUE 1975
SWAZILAND 1968
LESOTHO 1966

ANGOLA 1975
NAMIBIA 1990
BOTSWANA 1966
ZIMBABWE 1980

ICELAND 1944

MOROCCO 1956
WESTERN SAHARA
MAURITANIA 1960
SENEGAL
MALI 1960
BURKINA-FASO 1960
NIGERIA 1960

UNITED ARAB EMIRATES 1971

GAMBIA 1965
GUINEA-BISSAU 1974
GUINEA 1958
SIERRA LEONE 1961
COTE D'IVOIRE 1960
GHANA 1957
TOGO 1960
BENIN 1960
CAMEROON 1960
SAO TOME AND PRINCIPE 1975
EQUATORIAL GUINEA 1968
GABON 1960

CAPE VERDE 1975

BAHAMAS 1973
ANTIGUA AND BARBUDA 1981
ST. KITTS AND NEVIS 1983
DOMINICA 1978
ST. LUCIA 1979
ST. VINCENT AND THE GRENADINES 1979
BARBADOS 1966
GRENADA 1974
BELIZE 1981
JAMAICA 1962
TRINIDAD AND TOBAGO 1962
GUYANA 1966
SURINAME 1975

☐ Newly independent nations

☐ Possessions of colonial nations

(Dates shown are dates of independence.)

KIRIBATI 1979
TUVALU 1978
WESTERN SAMOA 1962
FIJI 1970
TONGA 1970

(From Southern Pacific)

Significantly, the first meeting between Vice President Nixon and Martin Luther King, Jr., took place in 1957 in Ghana, one of the newly independent African nations. The violent reaction in 1957 to court-ordered integration of Central High School in Little Rock, Arkansas, was front-page news in the Soviet press, which showed pictures of a mob surrounding black teenager Elizabeth Eckford and screaming "Lynch her." President Eisenhower, who had tried to avoid taking any direct stand in defense of civil rights, finally acted by dispatching federal troops to enforce the integration order lest it become a propaganda victory for America's Cold War rival.

To avoid embarrassment, the State Department urged officials in southern states to treat visiting African and Asian diplomats, tourists, and students as "honorary whites" exempted from Jim Crow laws. Partly to counteract communist charges of American racism, during the 1950s government agencies began sending abroad prominent African Americans, such as jazz musician Louis Armstrong and the Harlem Globetrotters basketball team, as informal "ambassadors of goodwill."

The main strategy of the Eisenhower administration to halt communist inroads in the Third World included forging numerous anticommunist alliances based loosely on NATO. These alliances included the Central Treaty Organization (CENTO) in the Middle East and the Southeast Asia Treaty Organization (SEATO), as well as bilateral defense agreements with Taiwan, South Korea, Spain, and the Philippines. Unlike NATO, most of these pacts committed Washington to provide only aid and consultation in cases of aggression. The agreements had more psychological and political than military value because when American interests abroad were threatened, the United States usually acted on its own.

Foreign aid also played a growing role in the administration's effort to influence the Third World. Under Truman, nearly all foreign economic assistance had been sent to Western Europe and Japan. Eisenhower first called for eliminating most aid, offering two-way trade as the best way to help poor countries. But because the poorest nations had little to export and no money to buy foreign goods, two-way trade would not substantially help them. Eventually the Eisenhower administration not only increased overall aid levels but also sent most of its assistance—surplus food, credits to buy American products, military equipment, construction loans—to emerging nations.

Critics pointed to faults in the aid programs for developing nations. For example, providing surplus grain under the Food for Peace program fed the hungry and helped American farmers dispose of surplus crops, but it also undermined enactment of sound agricultural policies in needy countries. Construction loans were frequently squandered on glamorous projects like sports arenas, while basic necessities like rural irrigation systems and clinics went unfunded.

◄ **Map 4.2**
Nations Achieving Independence, 1943–1980

In 1958, writers William J. Lederer and Eugene Burdick highlighted these problems in their bestselling novel, *The Ugly American.* They described a fictional Southeast Asian country (one resembling Vietnam) in which arrogant American diplomats knew nothing about their host nation and lived in an isolated "golden ghetto." They contemplated grand development schemes but ignored the plight of the peasant farmers. The unconventional hero defied the stereotype by learning the local language, associating with ordinary people, discovering their real needs, and successfully defending the nation against communism.

When aid programs did not suffice, the Eisenhower administration countered communist influence in the Third World by supplying military advisers and authorizing covert actions by the CIA. During the 1950s, Eisenhower deepened American involvement in Vietnam, and soon the United States was intervening in Iran, Guatemala, the Congo, and Cuba as well.

During his first term, Eisenhower appointed General James Doolittle to chair a secret study of the CIA's ability to counter Soviet activities. The resulting report warned that America faced "an implacable enemy whose avowed objective is world domination by whatever means and at whatever cost." There were "no rules in such a game," because "previously acceptable norms of human conduct" no longer applied. Americans "must learn to subvert, sabotage and destroy our enemies by more clever and sophisticated and more effective methods than those used against us."

Using the CIA to conduct secret operations had a strong appeal to American leaders. Covert actions provided the opportunity to achieve foreign policy goals without the direct costs of war or the scrutiny of public debate. The secrecy of CIA operations also permitted the government to act in ways that the American public found too uncomfortable to admit or to discuss, be it overthrowing governments or testing mind-altering drugs on unsuspecting citizens.

Eisenhower inherited the war in French Indochina and passed it on to his successors. In 1953 and 1954 (and in later years), policymakers worried that if the communist Vietminh guerrillas won in Vietnam, first all of Southeast Asia and then resource-starved Japan would "fall like dominoes." After this fall, Eisenhower predicted, the Pacific Ocean would "become a Communist lake."

Since 1950, the United States had spent over $1 billion in Vietnam, providing about 70 percent of the cost of France's war against the Vietminh and its leader, Ho Chi Minh. As American analysts admitted, however, French rule was unpopular in Vietnam and unlikely ever to be accepted. Eisenhower and Dulles hoped that if the French granted real power to noncommunist Vietnamese rather than the puppet emperor Bao Dai, the war would change from a colonial struggle to a battle against communism. Defending the "freedom" of an independent Vietnam would prove more popular among Americans—and presumably Vietnamese—than saving a colony.

In the spring of 1954, the war in Indochina reached a climax. Vietminh guerrillas trapped twelve thousand French troops at Dienbienphu, a valley in northern Vietnam. Washington again urged the French to grant Vietnam independence as a way of building support for expanded American and British military aid. Eisenhower compared the threat in Vietnam to the dangers posed by the Axis powers before World War II. As in the 1930s, he complained, the French were "a hopeless, helpless mass of protoplasm."

As the battle for Dienbienphu climaxed late in April, Dulles, Nixon, and the heads of the armed services formulated plans for American air strikes against the Vietminh. General Nathan Twining proposed dropping three small atomic bombs around the battle zone to clean out the communists. Eisenhower urged restraint, declaring, "You boys must be crazy. . . . We can't use those awful things against Asians for the second time in ten years." Eisenhower did consider a conventional air strike, however, and he allowed Dulles to threaten atomic retaliation if China sent combat troops to help the Vietminh. But when Britain declined to commit troops to aid the French and congressional leaders proved unenthusiastic, Eisenhower refused to intervene.

Early in May 1954, the Vietminh overran Dienbienphu. In Paris, a new prime minister, Pierre Mendes-France, pledged to negotiate a quick end to the Indochina war during talks that summer at an international conference in Geneva. Eisenhower sent an American observer to the Geneva talks, and Dulles also attended briefly. When asked if he planned to meet with Chinese representative Zhou Enlai, Dulles responded, "[O]nly if our cars collide." The United States feared that whatever arrangement emerged from Geneva would merely enhance communist power and prestige.

To the surprise of Americans, China and the Soviet Union actually played a moderating role at the Geneva talks. Eager to win points with the West, the major communist states pressed Ho Chi Minh to accept a temporary division of Vietnam rather than taking immediate total control. The Geneva Accords, reached in July, drew an armistice line, intended as a temporary military division, along the 17th parallel, with French forces moving to the South and Vietminh troops to the North. The key provision called for the departure of all French forces from Vietnam by 1956, followed by free national elections. No foreign forces were to replace the French. As the French withdrew from Indochina, they also granted independence to Laos and Cambodia, which bordered Vietnam.

American leaders were hopeful about the two-year hiatus before the proposed elections, which Ho Chi Minh would probably win. Dulles warned European leaders that the West must never surrender Southeast Asia. To bolster the wobbling dominoes, he flew to Manila in September 1954. There, he signed the SEATO alliance, essentially a Western pact to police Asia. Only two southeast Asian nations, Thailand and the Philippines, were signatories. Dulles also negotiated a defense treaty with Taiwan.

Meanwhile, the United States began providing substantial economic and military assistance, as well as military advisers, directly to noncommunist groups in southern Vietnam. As the French departed, American personnel, many working for the CIA, backed Ngo Dinh Diem, a Vietnamese Catholic (in a largely Buddhist nation) who had lived for several years in Europe and the United States. Attracted by his pro-Western rhetoric, his Christianity, and his anticommunism, army and CIA officers helped Diem organize a government and army in Saigon. To expand Diem's base of support, the CIA encouraged

Vietnamese Catholics, many of whom lived north of the 17th parallel, to move south. About 1 million did so.

In 1956, with American approval, Diem canceled the scheduled national unity election. Instead, he staged a pair of elections below the 17th parallel that deposed Emperor Bao Dai and substituted himself as president of the new Republic of Vietnam. Washington recognized this republic, better known as South Vietnam, as an independent nation. American diplomats and journalists applauded Diem's "one man democracy" and sent another $1 billion in aid to the regime. By 1960, however, a powerful communist-led guerrilla movement was threatening to topple what Senator John F. Kennedy called "our offspring."

Fear of the People's Republic of China (usually called Red China in the 1950s) boosted America's interest in the fate of Vietnam. In 1954 to 1955 and again in 1958, the United States and China came close to war over the fate of several small Nationalist Chinese–held islands in the Taiwan (Formosa) Strait. The most important of these, Quemoy and Matsu, lay only a few miles off the coast of China. The pro-American Chinese Nationalist government on Taiwan (Formosa) stationed troops on these islands and often used them as staging areas for commando raids against the mainland. In retaliation, and in hope of taking over Taiwan, the Chinese began shelling Quemoy in September 1954. The United States responded by signing a mutual security pact with Taiwan.

In private, both Eisenhower and Dulles had little respect for Jiang Jieshi (Chiang Kai-shek) and ridiculed his claim to the Chinese mainland. Yet both felt compelled to assist Jiang, in part because they had criticized the Democrats for deserting him but also because they feared additional Chinese expansion if Taiwan fell. The administration convinced Congress early in 1955 to approve the Formosa Strait Resolution, which empowered the president to use force to protect the security of Taiwan and "related positions and territories in that area." The president and secretary of state also issued a veiled warning of atomic retaliation if Chinese forces invaded Quemoy or Taiwan.

The 1955 crisis ended when China seized a few minor islands in the Taiwan Strait but abandoned efforts to capture Quemoy. Washington and Beijing then began diplomatic talks in Warsaw and Geneva that continued, sporadically and with little success, for fifteen years. Tensions resumed in 1958 when China renewed its shelling of Quemoy and Eisenhower ordered the American navy to resupply Nationalist troops on the island. After some tense moments, the Chinese declined to shoot at the American ships. The Americans convinced Jiang to stop provoking China. The Chinese artillery gradually abated, first firing only on odd-numbered days and soon after that substituting shells filled with propaganda leaflets.

Eisenhower used the CIA to deal with various threats in both the Middle East and Central America. The agency played an especially important role in deposing regimes that challenged American or Western domination of raw materials and in situations where the Soviets were not directly involved. Examples of these situations occurred in Iran, Guatemala, and Cuba.

During World War II, American oil companies began to displace British, French, and Dutch control of Arab and Persian Gulf petroleum. Inexpensive oil played a major part in the postwar economic growth of the United States, Western Europe, and Japan. When Eisenhower took office, he inherited a smoldering dispute over control of Iranian oil. In 1951, Iran's nationalistic (but noncommunist) prime minister, Mohammed Mossadeq, seized the holdings of the Anglo-Iranian Oil Company without fully compensating its (mostly British) owners. In retaliation, major European and American oil companies organized a boycott, refusing to purchase, transport, or refine Iranian petroleum. In May 1953, as the boycott caused economic havoc in Iran, Mossadeq cabled Eisenhower that, unless the boycott ended, he might seek Soviet assistance. Eisenhower rejected Iran's request for support and urged Mossadeq to reach a "reasonable settlement" along the lines demanded by the British.

Shah Mohammed Reza Pahlavi, Iran's nominal monarch, had played only a minor role in the nation's politics since succeeding his father during World War II. The young shah resented Mossadeq's influence and saw the crisis as an opportunity to gain power by playing up the Soviet threat. His interests coincided with those of American diplomats and oil companies, who hoped to preempt Britain's dominant role in the Iranian oil industry. To prevent any Soviet role in Iran and to preserve access to the region's petroleum, Eisenhower authorized the CIA to cooperate with British agents in a coup to topple Mossadeq and put the shah in control.

Kermit Roosevelt, grandson of Theodore Roosevelt and a veteran spy, played a key role in the coup. Arriving in Teheran in August 1953, he contacted the shah and a general in the Iranian army, Fazollah Zahedi. Roosevelt financed violent demonstrations against Mossadeq, enlisting mobs led by circus performers along with army and police personnel. The shah fled briefly to Rome while the army moved to restore order. Zahedi's forces stormed the parliament and arrested Mossadeq, and the general became prime minister. The shah returned to power, and Washington promptly extended $45 million in aid to his government.

An American delegation sent by Eisenhower mediated a deal between Iran and the British oil companies. The settlement allowed Iran to retain control of its oil fields as long as it agreed to market its petroleum at a low price through a consortium, in which American companies were granted a 40 percent stake. The British discovered that the cost of calling in the United States included losing a large measure of its oil monopoly.

Aside from Iran, the Middle East remained in political turmoil throughout the 1950s. Arabs felt humiliated by Israel's military victory in 1948 and the continued ability of the tiny Jewish state to defeat its numerous Arab neighbors. Although at the time Britain and France, rather than the United States, provided most of Israel's weapons, American Jews, with Washington's blessing, made substantial private contributions to Israel. Many Arabs considered Israel a vestige of Western colonialism; they also found it a useful scapegoat for their own problems.

(cont. on page 151)

Oil

Oil for planes, ships, tanks, and trucks helped the Allies win World War II. Petroleum became even more important after 1945 as Americans drove cars, flew in commercial aircraft, ate food produced by industrial agriculture, and used a vast array of plastics crafted from petroleum. Throughout the post–World War II era, Americans developed an almost unquenchable thirst for oil and petroleum-based products. At the same time, they regularly distrusted and feared, and they occasionally loathed, large oil companies and their executives.

Led by the United States, worldwide demand for oil encouraged the growth of the biggest, richest business on the planet—the petroleum industry. In the postwar period, the rising demand for oil-based products and the increasingly complicated relationships among multinational oil companies, petroleum-producing nations, and world powers like the United States and the Soviet Union set the tone for much of international relations and domestic political and economic affairs.

Before the 1950s, the oil industry had been relatively simple, even though it had always been a central player in the world economy. The United States produced and consumed much of the world's oil domestically, and a small number of American (Amoco, Esso [later Exxon], Mobil, Texaco, and Chevron), British (British Petroleum), Dutch (Shell), and French (Total and Elf) multinationals controlled the international oil industry.

In the decade after World War II, American cars rode for ten miles on a gallon, but with the price of gasoline at only 20 cents per gallon, few people worried about the efficiency of internal combustion engines. Although gas was cheap and plentiful, Americans did resent the influence of the oil companies. These behemoths managed to avoid paying corporate income taxes.

If the driving public was blissfully unconcerned about the future of oil supplies during the 1950s, oil-company executives and government officials believed that expanding American access to cheap, reliable sources of foreign oil was vital to the country's prosperity and power. In the race for influence, the United States and the Soviet Union eyed oil-rich nations such as Saudi Arabia, Iraq, Iran, and Libya as key to long-term success.

More than most industries, the petroleum industry has been closely intertwined with governments and international affairs. For oil-producing nations, their economies and international status depended on their success at extracting the "black gold" and setting its price. By the time Eisenhower took office, the first postwar oil crisis had erupted over who controlled Iranian oil. Iran's new prime minister, Mohammed Mossadeq, seized control of oil production, and major British and American oil companies responded with a well-orchestrated boycott that wreaked havoc on the Iranian economy. Mossadeq turned to President Eisenhower for help ending the boycott in 1953, suggesting that, without it, he might be forced into the arms of the Soviets. Eisenhower ignored him. Instead, he authorized a CIA-sponsored coup to oust Mossadeq and return to power Shah Mohammed Reza Pahlavi. Once the coup succeeded, Eisenhower offered the Shah financial aid and mediated a settlement between British oil companies and the Iranian government. The deal, which called for a consortium to market the country's petroleum, assured American companies a significant portion of future Iranian oil profits.

America's need to maintain its oil supply continued to shape its relationship to countries in the Middle East. In 1956, for example, the dictator of Egypt, Colonel Gamal Abdel Nasser, sparked a global crisis when he appropriated the Suez Canal from Anglo-French control in an attempt to rid his country of the lingering influence of its former colonial rulers. The canal provided Western

Europe with vital access to the majority of its oil supply, and Great Britain and France loathed the idea of relinquishing control to Nasser. Along with Israeli forces, British and French troops temporarily seized the waterway. The invasion failed when the United States, motivated by its own need to maintain a steady supply of oil, cut off emergency oil reserves from Britain and France and suspended financial support for Israel. The three powers withdrew their armies from the canal and the Sinai Peninsula.

In 1960, five oil-rich countries—Iran, Iraq, Kuwait, Saudi Arabia, and Venezuela—met in Baghdad and formed the Organization of Petroleum Exporting Countries (OPEC) in an attempt to wrest pricing power from the multinationals who had controlled the industry until that time. They demanded that companies consult with member countries on all future pricing matters. Over the next decade, OPEC and the multinationals negotiated the price of oil for the world market. In 1970, a barrel of oil sold for $2.00 on the world market, about the same as ten years before. At the end of the 1960s, however, the OPEC countries had raised the royalty payments they demanded and received from the multinationals to the point where $0.50 of every dollar went to OPEC members.

OPEC seized international attention in 1973 when the member states raised the price of oil from $2.00 to $8.00 a barrel after the outbreak of the Yom Kippur War. It followed this surprising action with an even bolder one, however, one that changed the balance of power in the region and wiped away all remaining vestiges of the notion that corporations and superpowers were in control: OPEC instituted an embargo against the United States and other countries supporting the Israelis in the war. The effects were devastating: lines formed at gasoline stations; motorists cursed each other, government officials, and oil industry leaders. Americans began demanding more fuel-efficient cars. They turned away from cars made by the Big Three domestic man-

Refinery pipeline: America's dependence on oil has increased steadily since World War II. Well over half of the oil now consumed—mostly by automobiles—is imported. / © Hulton-Deutsch Collection/ CORBIS

ufacturers (General Motors, Ford, and Chrysler) and scrambled to buy Japanese and German vehicles. Executives of the Big Three waited until it was almost too late to roll out their own smaller, lighter, more fuel-efficient vehicles.

For the next several years, OPEC decisions dominated the direction of international oil markets and, by extension, the world economy. Industrialized nations worked to diminish their dependence on OPEC products. Beginning in the late 1970s, the development of oil production on Alaska's North Slope, in Mexico, and especially in the North Sea (sites that had been identified as new sources of oil but not developed prior to 1973) offered some alternatives in the international marketplace.

The scramble to identify and exploit other new sources of oil consumed the industry in the decades that followed as multinational oil companies redirected their exploration efforts to stable, westernized areas. This trend only increased as political instability took hold in Middle Eastern nations and sparked additional panic in world markets following the 1979 Iranian revolution. The price of oil shot up once more—to $32.00 dollars a barrel. A gallon of gasoline cost over $1.00, and long gasoline lines appeared again in the United States. The federal government restricted car owners to buying gas no more than four days a week. The old popular disdain for the oil industry, symbolized by the contempt that many Americans had held for John D. Rockefeller, the founder of Standard Oil in the early twentieth century, intensified. *Dallas,* a prime-time soap opera featuring a family of crude, conniving oil billionaires, became the most popular show on television for several years in the late 1970s.

The rise of the environmental movement—the green movement—beginning in the 1970s affected the American oil industry. In some paradoxical ways, the green movement has encouraged the growth of the petroleum industry. The movement's focus on clean air and water provided an impetus for American corporations and consumers to switch from coal- to oil-based fuel. More often than not, however, environmentalists have adversely affected the industry and its reputation. When the supertanker *Exxon Valdez* ran aground in Alaska's Prince William Sound in 1989 and spilled over 240,000 barrels of oil into the water, environmentalists seized on the event as evidence that the world needed to focus on environmental protection over energy consumption, and people around the world responded.

Oil remained a constant element in U.S. foreign and domestic policy. During the Gulf War of 1991, the United States led a multinational force of thirty-seven countries to reverse Iraq's attempt to annex the tiny, oil-rich country of Kuwait. Oil remained cheap throughout the rest of the 1990s. The price of gasoline fell to about $1.10 per gallon.

When inflation was taken into account, fuel in the late 1990s was cheaper than at any time since 1960. After the oil crises of 1973 and 1979, Congress mandated a doubling of the efficiency of internal combustion and electric engines. By 1995, everything from cars to boats to airplanes to refrigerators to furnaces required less than half the fuel that they had used in 1975 to produce the same amount of work.

Unfortunately for the hopes of energy conservationists, Americans inevitably forgot their earlier concern about fuel efficiency with the onset of low gasoline prices in the mid-1990s. Passenger cars remained efficient, but consumers deserted the sedan and rushed to buy heavy sports utility vehicles (SUVs), many of which got less that 12 miles per gallon. SUVs offered comfort; they seemed safer than smaller cars; and owners thought their rugged good looks made the occupants look tough, outdoorsy, and free spirited. The auto manufacturers loved them too. The Big Three and Japanese automakers earned three times as much on every SUV sold than they did on the average car. Because of a quirk in the federal fuel-efficiency standards, regulators considered SUVs to be light trucks, not cars, and therefore exempted them from the strictest fuel-economy standards. America's dependence on foreign oil reached 60 percent of annual consumption.

By 2000, energy policy became an issue in the presidential election campaign. The Republican candidates George W. Bush and Dick Cheney both had close ties to the Texas oil industry. They proposed drilling for oil in the Arctic National Wildlife Refuge (ANWR), a vast area of pristine wilderness adjacent to the nearly played-out oil field of Prudhoe Bay. Al Gore, the Democratic candidate, advocated conservation and a major research effort to wean Americans from dependence on the internal combustion engine.

In 2001, the Bush administration put Vice President Cheney in charge of a task force charged with developing a new national energy policy. Cheney's task force met in secret for months. Oil-industry executives found an open door, while environmentalists had little influence. By the time the Bush administration unveiled its energy plan in the summer of 2001, public opinion had once more turned sharply against the oil industry. Following a wave of mergers in the oil industry in the late 1990s, oil prices rose again—to an average of about $1.75 per gallon. In San Francisco and Chicago, prices hit $2.40 per gallon in the summer of 2001. As a result of these mergers, Exxon had gobbled up Mobil, and Chevron bought Texaco. In the previous fifteen years, Amoco, Gulf, Diamond Shamrock, and Sinclair had all disappeared as independent companies. Americans believed that the major oil companies colluded to keep supplies tight and prices high. Public anger at big oil surged even more when the Houston energy-trading firm Enron collapsed under a mountain of bad debt and shady accounting practices in 2001.

Congress declined to endorse additional drilling in ANWR, but it also declined to demand higher fuel-efficiency standards for SUVs. The 280 million people living in the United States, about 4 percent of the world's population, consumed about 25 percent of the world's oil production. Americans continued to fret about the price and availability of oil, a commodity they desperately needed and whose suppliers they often despised.

Such was the situation when Gamal Abdel Nasser, an Egyptian army officer, toppled the inept, pro-British King Farouk in 1952. Nasser emerged as a popular and ambitious leader who envisioned Egypt as the center of a revived Arab world. He bought arms from the Soviet bloc; but at the same time he sought economic assistance from the West to finance construction of the immense Aswan Dam across the Nile. The dam was designed to provide electricity and water for Egyptian farmlands. Dulles initially favored American financing for the project, but he canceled the aid in July 1956 when Nasser extended diplomatic recognition to communist China. By this time, the Eisenhower administration feared that Nasser's appeal to pan-Arab nationalism would destabilize the oil-rich region—even though Egypt had little oil of its own—thus opening a path for Soviet influence or endangering the West's supply of cheap petroleum.

Nasser retaliated for the withdrawal of American support by nationalizing the British-owned Suez Canal, through which much of Europe's oil supply passed. Egypt's seizure of the canal enhanced Nasser's image among Arabs and provided tolls that would help pay for the Aswan Dam. The British and French governments decided to send forces to recover the canal (and, they hoped, topple Nasser). They coordinated their plans with Israel, which feared the popular Egyptian's influence on other Arabs.

In accordance with the joint plan, on October 29, 1956, the Israeli army attacked and defeated the Egyptian army on the Sinai Peninsula and camped just east of the canal. Britain and France then announced the dispatch of troops, with the stated goal of protecting the Suez Canal from destruction. The European powers demanded that both Egyptian and Israeli armies withdraw from either side of the waterway and return it to European control.

These actions by America's allies infuriated Dulles and Eisenhower. They feared that European intervention in the Suez dispute would strengthen Arab radicals and distract world attention from the crisis in Hungary, where Soviet forces were crushing an uprising. The fact that America's two close friends, England and France, had acted secretly both embarrassed and angered the American leaders. The United States therefore joined the Soviet Union in condemning the Suez attack, and the otherwise rival superpowers supported a U.N.-mandated cease-fire. With sunken vessels blocking oil shipments through the canal, Dulles pressed Latin American exporters to embargo petroleum sales to Britain and France until the European forces left Egypt. Washington also threatened to block private American aid to Israel. By December 1956, the invaders had left Egypt, Nasser had claimed a victory over imperialism, and British prime minister Anthony Eden had resigned in disgrace.

Following this fiasco, Britain and France moved to accommodate Arab sentiment by distancing themselves from Israel, and the United States took a more active role in the Middle East. In January 1957, Eisenhower got Congress to approve a resolution giving him the power to use force, if necessary, to "block Communist aggression" in the region. Washington hoped to woo conservative Arab rulers in Saudi Arabia, Jordan, and Iraq by posing as their protector against both Soviet influence and Nasser's radical followers.

The so-called Eisenhower Doctrine held that the United States would intervene in the Middle East if any nation there requested help to resist a communist takeover. During 1957, a series of plots, coups, and countercoups swept Syria, Jordan, and Iraq. In 1958, Nasser forged an alliance among Egypt, Syria, and Yemen, creating the United Arab Republic. In July, a pro-Nasser officer, General Abdel Karim Kassim, toppled the pro-Western King Faisal of Iraq and considered allying his new government with Egypt.

American officials feared that Nasser and his followers throughout the region would block the world's access to Middle Eastern oil, forcing the United States, Europe, and the Soviet Union to bargain with them for petroleum. Determined to block Nasser's influence, the Eisenhower administration made a show of strength in the tiny country of Lebanon, where a political crisis had shaken the government for months.

Before abandoning control of Lebanon during the 1940s, France imposed on the Lebanese a constitution that gave greater political power to the Maronite Catholic minority than to the Muslim majority. As the number of Muslims grew, so did their resentment at their second-class status; many were attracted to Nasser's vision of a unified, Arab Middle East. In July 1958, Lebanese president Camille Chamoun, a Maronite, outraged Muslims by suggesting he might stay in office when his term expired a few months later. Egypt urged Muslims to depose the Christian-dominated government in Beirut, and rioting erupted. When Chamoun looked to the United States for assistance, Eisenhower saw an opportunity to intimidate Nasser.

The president believed that Nasser's true aim was to gain control of vital Middle East petroleum supplies in order to destroy the Western world. Dulles feared that unless American forces intervened in Lebanon, all governments in the Middle East not affiliated with Nasser would be overthrown. The impact would be felt worldwide, he worried, as people surmised that the United States was "afraid of the Soviet Union."

On July 14, 1958, Eisenhower ordered fourteen thousand marines, with tactical nuclear capability and backed by a large fleet, to suppress what he called a "Communist-inspired" threat to Lebanon. Ironically, by the time the marines landed in Beirut, most of the rioting had ended. Sunbathers gaped in awe as landing craft disgorged troops prepared to fight their way ashore.

The operation achieved its basic aim of limiting Nasser's influence over Middle East oil supplies. The Lebanese factions patched together a compromise, and Chamoun surrendered his office to another Christian. Iraq dropped plans to ally with Egypt and promised to protect Western-owned oil facilities. Even Nasser backed off after receiving word from Khrushchev that the Soviet Union would not assist him in any direct challenge to the United States. Although the Middle East remained chronically unstable and the Arabs and Israelis would fight several more wars, Eisenhower's show of force held the line through the end of the decade.

The Eisenhower administration was also greatly concerned about blocking communist influence in Latin America. In Senate testimony in 1953, the secretary of state described a growing communist conspiracy in the region. In the past, Dulles explained to his brother Allen, director of the CIA, Washington could afford to ignore turmoil in Latin America. Now, however, unrest and upheaval would lead to control by communists.

Most U.S. aid to Latin America took the form of military advice and equipment. For example, the army established special training programs in Panama and elsewhere for Latin American military officers. By paying lip service to democracy, ignoring the region's social problems, and aligning itself with repressive regimes, Washington showed that it opposed communism in Latin America, but it turned a blind eye to the dictatorships and poverty there. In 1953, Eisenhower and Dulles identified the major crisis in Latin America as the "Communist infection" in Guatemala, one of the region's poorest nations.

In 1944, a group of reform-minded Guatemalan army officers had overthrown long-time dictator Jorge Ubico. After a relatively fair election in 1945, reformer Juan Jose Arevalo became president. He inherited a desperately poor country in which the European-descended elite held nearly feudal control over the large Indian population. About 2 percent of the population controlled 70 percent of the land. In addition, the American-owned United Fruit Company, a banana grower, held vast tracts of farmland, much of which remained uncultivated. United Fruit also controlled railroads, ports, and communications infrastructure. Although United Fruit was not the most exploitative employer in Guatemala, its American employees lived in relative luxury while its peasant workers eked out a living on a dollar a day. Arevalo abolished forced Indian labor, extended voting rights, imposed a minimum wage, and began a modest land-reform program. In 1951, Arevalo's elected successor, President

Jacobo Arbenz Guzman, ordered the redistribution of large uncultivated land-holdings to the poor and sponsored new labor and wage reforms. In the Guatemalan context, these actions were revolutionary. Arbenz drafted plans to build new roads and ports that would break United Fruit's monopoly over the transportation system. He also expropriated 400,000 acres of uncultivated company land, offering compensation of $3 per acre, a figure based on the declared tax value of the property.

United Fruit demanded $75 per acre and got the Eisenhower administration to intercede on its behalf. The State Department—several of whose top officials had past business associations with United Fruit—claimed that the issue was neither social justice nor land reform but a communist assault on private property. American officials cooperated with United Fruit publicists in a propaganda campaign that labeled Arbenz a communist dupe. By casting the dispute over compensation for banana plantations as a battle between communism and Western-style democracy, the administration and United Fruit created a pretext for intervention. By removing Arbenz, Dulles told the president, Eisenhower would achieve a "Czechoslovakia in reverse." He was referring, of course, to the Soviet military pressure that toppled the noncommunist government in Prague in 1948. Washington prodded several key Latin American nations to join it in a declaration that no nation in the Western Hemisphere had a right to a communist government.

In the summer of 1953, Eisenhower authorized a CIA plan to stage a coup in Guatemala. To undermine Arbenz's support within the military, Washington cut off aid to the Guatemalan army and increased assistance to neighboring states. From bases in Honduras and Nicaragua, the CIA organized a small Guatemalan exile force under Carlos Castillo Armas. It began a disinformation campaign, using pamphlets and radio broadcasts to confuse the Guatemalan people. The broadcasts declared that a large rebel army would soon attack. When Arbenz purchased a small arms shipment from communist Czechoslovakia in May 1954, American officials immediately described it as part of a "master plan of world communism" that threatened the Panama Canal.

In June, one thousand or so CIA-directed exiles entered Guatemala and set up a base camp. CIA radio stations broadcast reports of a massive invasion. A few small planes dropped anti-Arbenz leaflets in the capital while the pilots threw sticks of dynamite out of their cockpits. In a panic, Arbenz tried to arm a peasant militia. The regular army feared fighting the United States or being supplanted by peasants. Fooled into thinking he faced a large invasion and deserted by his army, Arbenz resigned on June 27, 1953. As the CIA had planned, Castillo Armas and his comrades took over.

Eisenhower considered the Guatemalan coup a model Cold War triumph. At a dinner in their honor, Eisenhower told a gathering of key CIA participants that, thanks to them, America had averted the establishment of a Soviet beachhead in the Western Hemisphere. The new Guatemalan rulers restored United Fruit's lands and rolled back most other reforms. Over the next three decades, a succession of military governments slaughtered an estimated

100,000 Indians, labor organizers, students, and intellectuals who challenged the ruling elite.

Eisenhower later approved CIA operations to overthrow President Sukarno of Indonesia, General Rafael Trujillo of the Dominican Republic, and Premier Patrice Lumumba of the Congo. Although Sukarno survived a botched coup attempt, Trujillo and Lumumba both fell to assassins' bullets. American agents encouraged these assaults but did not take a direct role.

The Cuban Revolution of 1959 presented a greater challenge than had Guatemala. Since Franklin Roosevelt, American presidents had tolerated Cuba's long-lived military dictator, Fulgencio Batista, because he protected foreign investments and supported the United States in the Cold War. As a reward, Cuban sugar producers enjoyed privileged access to the American market. This profited wealthy landowners, among them many Americans, but few benefits trickled down to plantation workers.

Batista's regime collapsed in January 1959 when Fidel Castro led a guerrilla army into Havana. The son of a well-to-do Cuban family, Castro had lived for a time in New York, where he dreamed of pitching for an American baseball team. Trained as a lawyer, he led a failed rebellion in the early 1950s, spent time in a Cuban prison, and launched a second revolt in 1956. Castro called initially for socialist reform but had no specific Marxist program or links with the Soviet Union.

At first, Washington took a wait-and-see attitude. Castro legalized Cuba's small Communist Party, made anti-American speeches, ousted moderates

Fidel Castro with Richard Nixon in April 1959 during his visit to the United States. / AP/Wide World Photos

from his movement, postponed promised elections, and publicly executed about five hundred of Batista's henchmen. During a visit to Washington in April 1959, Castro insisted he wanted good relations with America. But he later signed a trade deal with Russia and expropriated foreign-owned plantations, paying the owners with bonds rather than cash at a price based on deflated tax valuations. Eisenhower decided the Cuban leader was a dangerous pro-Soviet puppet.

Although Castro lost his popularity among the wealthy, many poor and nationalistic Cubans admired his bold challenges to Uncle Sam. Castro's spunk in standing up to the United States also made him something of a hero elsewhere in Latin America. To counter his appeal, Eisenhower approved long-term economic aid to Latin America, a program President John F. Kennedy later dubbed the Alliance for Progress.

After cutting trade and diplomatic ties with Cuba, Eisenhower decided in mid-1960 to eliminate Castro. He authorized the CIA to undermine Castro's image and regime covertly and to train an army of exiled Cubans to invade the island. Mindful of the overthrow of Guatemala's Arbenz, Castro organized a popular militia armed with Soviet weapons. A year later, the CIA plan led to the disastrous Bay of Pigs invasion, for which the next president, John F. Kennedy, took the principal blame.

The Hungarian Uprising and Refugee Politics

Although the Eisenhower administration intervened in Third World countries to counter communist influence, it avoided challenging the Soviets in regions they already controlled. This fact was clear during the 1956 uprising in Hungary. Inspired by Khrushchev's recent speech denouncing Stalin, Hungarian citizens as well as local communist officials revolted against Soviet domination in the autumn of 1956. A reformist faction gained control of the Hungarian Communist Party and began to dismantle the totalitarian apparatus. Moscow held back at first but intervened brutally when reformer Imre Nagy declared that Hungary intended to quit the Warsaw Pact, the military agreement that bound eastern European states to Moscow. Early in November, in the middle of the Suez crisis, Khrushchev sent Russian tanks into Budapest to crush this heresy.

Although CIA-supported Radio Free Europe had urged eastern Europeans to revolt, when the Hungarians did rise against the Soviets, Washington refused to help. Eisenhower feared that American intervention would destroy Hungary rather than free it. "[The] Russians are scared and furious," he noted, and "nothing is more dangerous than a dictatorship in that frame of mind." The president even barred sending to Hungary a group of CIA-trained exiles prepared for guerrilla operations.

The uprising in Hungary created a major refugee problem for the United States. About 200,000 people, mostly noncombatants, fled the reimposition of

Soviet control. Because the 1952 McCarran-Walter Act barred most immigration from Eastern Europe, few could enter the United States. As President Truman had predicted, the law was a slap in the face to those "fleeing barbarism."

In 1953, Eisenhower had persuaded Congress to enact the Refugee Relief Act. This law allocated about 200,000 special visas outside the quota system, with half reserved for "escapees" from "Communist-dominated" areas of Europe. A few Chinese also came under its provisions. Except for this one-time relaxation, however, strict immigration quotas remained in place. Senators William Revercomb of West Virginia and Pat McCarran of Nevada warned that refugees might be Communist "sleeper agents," and many Americans complained that too many foreigners had already entered the country. In 1954, Eisenhower responded to complaints about large numbers of illegal Mexicans by authorizing the deportation of 1 million undocumented migrants during a nationwide sweep called Operation Wetback.

The mass Hungarian exodus prompted the United States to bend its rigid immigration policy. Eisenhower found a loophole in the existing law that permitted the attorney general to grant refugees "parole," a legal status that allowed them to enter the United States "for emergency reasons or for reasons deemed strongly in the public interest." This provision had been written to accommodate individual hardship cases, not large groups. Nevertheless, Congress approved use of the parole power to admit 38,000 Hungarians; it also voted special aid for them. Most of the 160,000 others who fled Soviet reprisals settled in Europe.

Lawmakers and the public showed selective compassion toward this group. The Hungarians were seen both as victims of Soviet oppression and as an easily assimilated group. The situation repeated itself in 1959 and 1960, when over 125,000 middle- and upper-class Cubans fled Castro's revolution. By utilizing the special parole provision, Congress avoided pressure to liberalize restrictive immigration quotas.

Policymakers viewed refugees from communist regimes not merely as victims but as public relations assets in an ideological struggle. Mexicans were deported as unworthy "economic refugees," while Hungarians and Cubans were welcomed as symbolic freedom fighters. The situation repeated itself in later decades when the federal government routinely welcomed Cuban "boat people" while simultaneously towing boatloads of desperate Haitians out to sea.

The Space Race

In October 1957, the Soviet Union captured world attention by launching a basketball-size satellite, Sputnik 1. A White House spokesperson dismissed the achievement as an "outer space basketball game." A month later, however, the Russians launched the one-thousand-pound Sputnik II carrying a dog into orbit. Senator Lyndon Johnson of Texas, chair of the Armed Services Committee's Preparedness Subcommittee, expressed astonishment that another nation achieved a technological victory over the United States. Like millions of Americans, he wondered what it would mean if a Sputnik satellite carried a nuclear bomb instead of a dog. Senator Henry Jackson of Washington called for a National Week of Shame and Disgrace. *Life* magazine added to the panic when it described the Soviet satellite as a major defeat for the United States.

The space and missile race had begun during World War II with the German V-2 rocket. After 1945, both Moscow and Washington eagerly recruited German scientists—including some guilty of terrible crimes against humanity—to help develop rocket programs. After a slow start, Eisenhower's New Look strategy, with its stress on atomic weapons, provided a budget and mission boost for the American rocket program. The new president was also keen to use rockets for launching reconnaissance satellites capable of providing reliable visual intelligence on Soviet capabilities. By observing what the Russians really had, the United States could avoid arming too lightly or too heavily.

But even with increased funding, spy satellites would take years to develop. As a stopgap, Eisenhower approved constructing the secret U-2 spy plane. A brilliant team of aircraft engineers designed and built the U-2 prototype in only three months at a secret site run by Lockheed Aviation. In 1956, the high-flying spy plane began crisscrossing the Soviet Union at 80,000 feet, photographing rocket test sites and allowing intelligence analysts to keep close tabs on their rivals' progress.

The U-2, Eisenhower explained, produced intelligence "of critical importance to the United States." Besides revealing what the Soviets *did* have, it revealed what they did *not* have. The spy plane, Eisenhower said, "provided proof that the horrors of the alleged 'bomber gap' and the later 'missile gap' were nothing more than the imaginative creations" put forth by irresponsible Americans who wanted to build more weapons than U.S. security needs required.

When Sputnik 1 went aloft, Eisenhower assured his cabinet that it posed no threat and hinted at a closely guarded secret: U-2 pictures revealed that, despite the success with Sputnik, the Soviets possessed only a small and unreliable rocket arsenal. The president urged his colleagues to play down Sputnik, lest public hysteria force an unnecessary boost to America's space budget.

Administration spokespersons therefore belittled the Russian achievement as a gimmick and attributed it to the skills of German scientists working for the Soviets rather than communist technological superiority. But this talk did little to quell public anxiety. Democrats, educators, journalists, and military contractors alike charged in the media that the Russians had humiliated the United States and threatened its national security. Each of these groups used Sputnik as leverage to achieve its own agenda: to embarrass the administration, to secure more funding for education, or to force an increase in defense spending. At the Senate committee hearings chaired by Lyndon Johnson, a parade of critics claimed that the Soviets had achieved the scientific equivalent of the Japanese attack on Pearl Harbor. On television, stand-up comics asked what the first Americans to reach the moon would discover: "Russians," came the punch line.

In response to this pressure, Eisenhower advanced the date for launching an American satellite. In December 1957, in the middle of the Senate hearings on the space race, a hastily prepared Vanguard rocket exploded on takeoff as live TV caught the mishap. Critics promptly dubbed it Flopnik. Eisenhower then approved the use of a military rocket, which launched a satellite a few months later.

As the Senate hearings wound down, Johnson warned of widening gaps between the United States and the Soviet Union in aircraft, missiles, submarines, and high technology. Because the United States stood on the verge of losing the "battle of brainpower," he called for increases in space and military appropriations as well as massive federal funding for education. Eisenhower responded by appointing a White House science adviser and increasing funding for the National Science Foundation. He worked with Congress to create the National Aeronautics and Space Administration (NASA), with an initial budget of $340 million. As noted earlier, he also supported passage of the National Defense Education Act (NDEA), a billion-dollar package of federal grants for schools and universities.

Shortly after Sputnik's launch, a high-level advisory panel, the Gaither Commission, reported to Eisenhower on the expanded Soviet threat. Hoping to force Eisenhower's hand, the authors used inflammatory language like that contained in the NSC-68 report of 1950 and leaked their conclusions to journalists. Headlines warned that the United States was about to become a second-class power exposed to immediate danger from a Soviet Union bristling with missiles. The Gaither report predicted that the Soviets would soon deploy hundreds of nuclear-tipped, long-range missiles, thus threatening America's survival. The authors called for accelerating American missile production, increasing military spending by 25 percent, and building a massive system of fallout shelters (at a cost of $30 billion) to protect civilians. Democratic presidential hopefuls, among them senators Stuart Symington, John F. Kennedy, and Lyndon Johnson, warned that the administration ignored a perilous "missile gap." This charge was bogus because the United States possessed a far more advanced technology base and was about to deploy a new array of land- and sea-based missiles.

Stirrings of Détente

Even as the space race joined the arms race in heightening public anxiety in America and creating new reasons for disagreement with the Soviets, a countervailing trend began to emerge. Eisenhower and Khrushchev took significant steps toward détente, talking with each other at summit meetings and establishing a temporary moratorium on nuclear tests. Although these efforts produced no lasting agreement, they did set a precedent for future negotiations.

The relaxation of tensions stemmed in part from the fact that by 1955, the Soviets possessed a substantial atomic arsenal. The Cold War rivals had struck a balance of power, or of terror: either side could greatly damage or destroy the other. Eisenhower acknowledged that under these circumstances, there was little possibility of victory, only varying degrees of mutual devastation, in a full-scale war. In spite of Dulles's boast that his willingness on several occasions to go "to the brink of war" had forced China and the Soviet Union to back down, Soviet leader Nikita Khrushchev probably hit the mark when he explained that Dulles "knew how far he could push us, and he never pushed us too far."

By the mid-1950s, growing prosperity in Europe and the changing of the Kremlin guard had taken some of the edge off the Cold War. The creation of an independent West German army and its inclusion in NATO in 1955 formalized the postwar division of Europe. The Soviets responded by creating their own military alliance, the Warsaw Pact, which was mostly a mechanism for controlling, not defending, Eastern Europe. But otherwise they accepted Western moves. The Soviets surprised the United States in 1955 by accepting American terms for a treaty ending the joint occupation of Austria that had begun in 1945.

Prodded by the NATO allies and his own desire to lessen the nuclear threat, Eisenhower agreed, in July 1955, to meet the Soviet leadership at a summit conference in Geneva. At the gathering, Eisenhower stunned the Soviets by calling for a policy of "open skies," whereby each side would be free to conduct aerial reconnaissance of the other's military facilities. The United States had little to lose and much to gain from such an arrangement. The Russians dismissed the proposal as a "bald espionage plot," and it went nowhere. Eisenhower, of course, soon approved development of the U-2 spy plane. Despite the lack of formal agreement, both sides left the summit praising the "spirit of Geneva"—a willingness between opposing blocs to talk.

During Eisenhower's final three years as president, he tried harder to reach some form of accommodation with the Soviet Union. For example, the perennial problem with Berlin re-emerged in 1958. Since the early 1950s, about 300,000 East Germans had fled communist rule annually, most of them through Berlin. Faced with this population hemorrhage, Khrushchev demanded the withdrawal of Western forces and the creation of a "free" (meaning East German–controlled) city. He announced a six-month deadline for the removal of Western troops, prompting members of Congress to demand an increase in defense spending. Eisenhower told the Soviets that American forces would stay in Berlin; at the same time, however, he informed Khrushchev that if the deadline for Western withdrawal were set aside, a superpower summit could be arranged. Khrushchev dropped his threat and accepted an invitation to visit America in the fall of 1959.

In July, before the scheduled visit, Eisenhower sent Vice President Richard Nixon on a goodwill trip to the Soviet Union. During an impromptu debate with Khrushchev, held in a model American kitchen at a Moscow trade fair,

Nixon proposed shifting the terms of the superpowers' competition. During what journalists dubbed the kitchen debate, the vice president boasted that most Americans owned houses stocked with appliances that made life easier for homemakers. A flustered Khrushchev dismissed these "useless gadgets" but insisted that Soviet housewives had even better washing machines. Confident that America had the edge in the appliance race, Nixon asked, "Would it not be better to compete in the relative merits of washing machines than in the strength of rockets?" Influential Democrats lambasted this effort to encourage nonmilitary competition. Senator John F. Kennedy, positioning himself as a presidential candidate, ridiculed what he labeled Nixon's femalelike "experience in kitchen debates" as a prime example of the administration's weakness and the reason for its failure to build more missiles.

A few months later, the Soviet leader visited the United States. When he conferred with Eisenhower at Camp David, Maryland, the absence of the hard-liner Dulles, who was terminally ill with cancer, lightened the atmosphere. As in the earlier summit meeting between Eisenhower and Khrushchev, no formal agreements emerged. But the two leaders found it useful to take each other's measure, and both spoke of a "spirit of Camp David," which observers took to mean an informal reduction in tensions. Khrushchev accepted the president's idea that he travel through the United States. Among other places, he visited a Hollywood movie studio and an Iowa corn farm. Although angry that security concerns blocked a stop at Disneyland, where Mrs. Khrushchev had hoped to meet Mickey Mouse, the Soviet leader enjoyed himself and agreed to meet Eisenhower in Paris the following spring.

To Eisenhower, these summits offered a chance to reduce the danger of nuclear war and to slow the development in America of a garrison state obsessed with security. The president believed that massive defense spending had contributed to America's emerging international trade deficit and to the economic recession of 1958. Khrushchev hoped that a reduction in tension would improve his ability to hold off Soviet hawks, including members of the military establishment who demanded greater missile production. For both Khrushchev and Eisenhower, one of the central issues was an agreement to limit nuclear testing.

In December 1953, Eisenhower had proposed an Atoms for Peace program to secure international cooperation in expanding the peaceful use of atomic technology. Congress passed legislation assisting construction of domestic nuclear power plants, but the proposal had little effect on curbing the arms race. In fact, for the rest of the decade, both the United States and the Soviet Union produced tens of thousands of additional nuclear weapons. In the United States, this increase required a crash effort to expand uranium mining, plutonium production, and weapons testing, mostly in western states, in Alaska, and on Pacific islands.

In the red rock mesas and valleys of Arizona, for example, government engineers descended on Navajo villages and convinced sheepherders to take up uranium mining "in defense of the nation." Hundreds of small mines, employing over 1,500 Navajos, were opened during the 1950s and 1960s. The miners were offered good wages, but they were never warned about the dangers of breathing uranium dust. By the 1970s, many of the miners were ill with various fatal cancers. In some families, two or three generations of fathers and sons died from mining-related cancers.

Uranium ore was turned into weapons-grade material at processing facilities in Hanford, Washington, and Rocky Flats, Colorado. Many small subcontractors, like the Albecroft Machine Shop, which was located in a residential neighborhood of Oxford, Ohio, also built bomb components. Under pressure to produce enriched uranium and plutonium at an accelerating pace, such facilities observed few environmental safeguards. Radioactive residue was dumped into streams, vented into the air, or buried in the ground. When Albecroft closed in the 1960s, it left behind polluted ponds that local children used as swimming holes. Five of six girls in one family living adjacent to the abandoned plant died of cancer. As one Defense Department official admitted in 1980, "[T]he army considered what was inside the fences [of the nuclear facilities] our problem, and no one should know about that."

Between 1945 and 1963, atmospheric test blasts were conducted at sites in Nevada and the South Pacific. During these tests, thousands of soldiers and sailors were stationed as close as three miles from ground zero. In Nevada, infantry units were often marched to the detonation point within an hour of the explosion; the intent was to "train military units to become familiar with new weapons and their characteristics." Soviet troops underwent similar training. From a present-day perspective, the ignorance of the hazards of radiation is astounding.

Atomic dummies at Yucca Flat, November 1955. To study the effects of an atomic blast on suburbia, weapons designers placed lifelike dummies inside Levittown-style homes at nuclear bomb test sites. / Loomis Dean, © *Life Magazine,* Time Inc.

Thousands of Americans living in small towns in Nevada, Utah, and Arizona—the so-called downwinders—were exposed to high levels of wind-blown fallout following each test. In 1955, the government distributed brochures to people living near the test sites. It informed them that "you are in a very real sense active participants in the nation's atomic test program." Many residents recall having family picnics outdoors to watch the giant plumes of colored clouds from the explosions. Little did they know that "active" participation would eventually be measured by high rates of leukemia and other cancers from radioactive fallout.

Similar misfortune plagued the Bikini islanders, whose Pacific atoll was selected as the location for the first full-scale hydrogen bomb test in 1954. The Defense Department moved the population to another island, but this relocation failed to protect them when the unexpected power of the bomb and shifting winds dusted them with radioactive debris. Fifty years later, Bikini remains uninhabitable. A Japanese fishing boat, the *Lucky Dragon,* sailed too close to the test area and was contaminated by what its crew called "the ashes of death." This incident caused a crisis with the Japanese government after one of the sailors died. The dramatic mushroom cloud from the Bikini explosion was featured in the 1954 Japanese horror film *Godzilla,* designed as a parable for adults about the dangers of nuclear weapons. When released and re-edited in the United States two years later, the film's antinuclear message was toned down in order to attract a teenage audience.

While most early cases of radioactive contamination were caused by ignorance, accident, or the desire to cut corners and thus speed weapons production, cases of willful injury also occurred. Beginning in 1945 and continuing through the early 1970s, medical scientists at government laboratories and in prominent research institutions subjected unsuspecting patients to injections of plutonium and other radioactive substances. Generally these patients were poor prison inmates and minorities or were already suffering from grave illnesses. Most had no idea of the risks involved. Several hundred pregnant women, for example, were offered free prenatal "care" that included injections of small amounts of plutonium to determine its effects on fetal development. The purpose of many of these experiments was to determine "safe" radiation dosages for workers in the nuclear industry.

Before the 1970s, the Atomic Energy Commission (AEC), citing national security, downplayed the danger from all forms of radiation, even though by the late 1950s, its own studies had confirmed the injury to the miners, soldiers, and downwinders. The AEC actually promoted routine use of X-rays in shoe stores to fit children. Soldiers at the Nevada test site were instructed merely to avoid breathing sand. The downwinders were told to dust off their clothes and brush off their shoes if debris fell on them. The best action, according to the AEC, was "not to be worried about fallout." Navajo miners and workers at Rocky Flats and other weapons plants were not even provided with paper face masks when digging ore or sweeping plutonium dust. Cartoons featuring Bert the Turtle assured American schoolchildren that they would be safe from nuclear bombs if they remembered to "duck and cover" beneath their desks.

In 1990, as medical evidence mounted about the devastating health effects of exposure to radiation, Congress passed the Radiation Exposure Compensation Act. Under its provisions, uranium miners, military personnel, workers in government nuclear arsenals, and downwinders who had suffered certain types of cancer were eligible for between $50,000 and $100,000 in compensation. In many cases, however, the eligibility criteria were so complex that victims had difficulty making a case. For example, by 1990, most of the Navajo uranium miners had died. Many of their widows could not produce marriage certificates or employment stubs from forty years earlier and were barred from collecting damages. After long delays, Congress and the Energy Department moved to rectify some of these problems in 2001.

By the late 1950s, growing public anxiety over nuclear fallout led a growing number of scientists and citizen activists to urge a halt to nuclear tests. Eisenhower sympathized with some of their concerns but would not agree to a test ban unless the Soviets permitted on-site inspection. When Moscow hinted that it might relent, American hard-liners panicked. Dr. Edward Teller told Eisenhower that if he were allowed to conduct tests a while longer, he could build a fallout-free weapon. Although misleading, Teller's claim slowed negotiations on a ban. In 1958, however, the president changed tack when his newly appointed science adviser, James Killian, introduced him to several scientists who refuted Teller's views. They argued that atmospheric testing was not needed to maintain a nuclear arsenal, especially if underground testing continued. To assuage fears that the Soviet Union might sign a test-ban treaty and then continue testing secretly, American scientists assured Eisenhower that a network of seismic stations could detect most nuclear explosions, even those underground. While their subordinates worked on the terms of a treaty, Khrushchev and Eisenhower agreed to an informal test moratorium, effective in October 1958. To placate hardliners, both leaders approved a round of massive test explosions just before the moratorium.

Eisenhower proposed banning fallout-producing atmospheric explosions but allowing small underground tests. The smaller tests were difficult to detect and, as American hard-liners noted, they were useful in designing new types of weapons. Khrushchev surprised American negotiators by proposing a comprehensive ban on all testing, coupled with limited on-site inspection within the Soviet Union to guard against cheating. Although uncertainties remained, a compromise agreement at the upcoming Paris summit seemed possible.

However, the May 1960 Paris summit proved a fiasco. On the eve of the conference, an American U-2 spy plane crashed inside the Soviet Union. It was brought down by a combination of engine failure and a Soviet missile. Eisenhower had approved this risky mission in the hope of gathering photographic evidence confirming that, despite Khrushchev's bluster, the Soviet Union had not deployed many long-range rockets. Such data would give the president greater flexibility in arms control discussions. The failed U-2 mission proved disastrous for this cause.

After American officials released a cover story about a missing weather aircraft, Moscow announced that in fact it had brought down a spy plane.

The Soviet trial of captured U-2 plane pilot Francis Gary Powers. Powers was later exchanged for a Soviet spy, only to die in a crash while flying a traffic helicopter. / © Bettmann/CORBIS

The CIA had assured Eisenhower that neither the aircraft nor its pilot could survive a crash. This assertion led Ike to deny that any such aircraft existed. Khrushchev then stunned Washington by displaying the well-preserved wreckage of the U-2. He then trotted out a live and contrite U-2 pilot, Francis Gary Powers, who confessed to espionage. The president was so depressed about this turn of events and their undermining détente that he considered resigning.

When the two world leaders met in Paris a few weeks later, Khrushchev demanded that Eisenhower apologize to the Soviet people for the U-2 mission. Eisenhower refused, and the summit broke up. An important opportunity to limit nuclear testing and slow the arms race had slipped away. The informal moratorium on nuclear testing lasted until the fall of 1961, when both the Soviets and the Americans resumed their tests.

Conclusion

By the end of his presidency, Eisenhower sensed the limitations of his achievements in foreign policy. He also worried that American society would face increased regimentation as the nation remained shackled to its huge and growing defense budget. His reflections on these matters were evident in his remarkable farewell address of January 1961, which has been quoted repeatedly ever since. Eisenhower warned against the temptation to solve domestic problems through "some spectacular and costly action" abroad. The old general deplored the view that a large increase in defense spending would create a miraculous solution to the nation's troubles. The greatest threat to democracy, he observed, came from a new phenomenon, the "conjunction of an immense military establishment and a large arms industry." Americans needed to guard against the unwarranted influence of this "military-industrial complex." With this turn of phrase, the former military man had sounded a warning that would ring down the decades. It had little immediate effect, however, on the administrations that followed.

Eisenhower began his presidency proclaiming the New Look, which emphasized the use of nuclear weapons and the doctrine of massive retaliation. Accordingly, he presided over a dramatic buildup of the nuclear stockpile, including the development of ICBMs. He also intervened repeatedly in Third World conflicts, often employing the CIA to undermine governments that he considered dangerous. He deepened the American involvement in Vietnam, which would have tragic consequences in the 1960s and 1970s.

Nevertheless, most historians see Eisenhower as a president who basically kept the peace. After ending the Korean War, he avoided direct conflicts with the Soviet Union or China. Although he and Dulles brandished nuclear weapons as the ultimate threat, he never authorized a nuclear attack. In the early years of his administration, he made significant efforts to restrain defense spending, and in his second term, he took steps toward détente with the Soviet Union. The next chapter will examine how his immediate successor, John F. Kennedy, handled issues such as the space race, missiles, détente, and unrest in the Third World.

F U R T H E R • R E A D I N G

On foreign policy, the arms race, and the Cold War during the 1950s, see Stephen E. Ambrose, *Eisenhower: The President* (1984), and *Ike's Spies* (1981); H. W. Brands, Jr., *The Cold Warriors* (1988); Robert A. Divine, *Eisenhower and the Cold War* (1981); Richard Immerman, *John Foster Dulles and the Diplomacy of the Cold War* (1990), *John Foster Dulles: Piety, Pragmatism, and Power in U.S. Foreign Policy* (1999), and *Waging Peace: How Eisenhower Shaped an Enduring Cold War Strategy* (1998); Richard Rhodes, *Dark Sun: The Making of the Hydrogen Bomb* (1995); Howard Ball, *Justice Downwind: America's Nuclear Testing Program in the 1950s* (1986); Robert A. Divine, *Blowing on the Wind: The Nuclear Test Ban Debate, 1954–60* (1978); Tad Bartimus, *Trinity's Children: Living Along America's Nuclear Highway* (1991); Jonathan Weisgall, *Operation Crossroads: The Atomic Tests at Bikini Atoll* (1994); Carole Gallagher, *American Ground Zero* (1993); Kenneth D. Rose, *One Nation Underground: The Fallout Shelter in American Culture* (2001); Walter A. McDougall, *The Heavens and the Earth: A Political History of the Space Age* (1985); Ellen Schrecker, *No Ivory Tower: McCarthyism and the Universities*

(1986) and *Many Are the Crimes: McCarthyism in America* (1998); Mary Dudziack, *Cold War Civil Rights: Race and the Image of American Democracy* (2000); Thomas Borstelmann, *The Cold War and the Color Line: American Race Relations in the Global Arena* (2002); Philip Taubman, *Secret Empire: Eisenhower, the CIA, and the Hidden Story of America's Space Espionage* (2003). **On recent studies of the Soviet Union and China in the Cold War,** see V. M. Zubok, *Inside the Kremlin's Cold War: From Stalin to Khruschev* (1996); Chen Jian, *China and Mao's Cold War* (2001). **On U.S. policy in the Third World,** see Stephen G. Rabe, *Eisenhower and Latin America: The Foreign Policy of Anti-Communism* (1988); Nick Cullather, *Secret History: The CIA's Classified Account of Its Operations in Guatemala, 1952–1954* (1999), and *Illusion of Influence: The Political Economy of United States—Philippine Relations, 1942–1960* (1994); Mark Bradley, *Imagining Vietnam and America: The Making of Post-Colonial Vietnam, 1919–1950* (2000); George McT. Kahin, *Intervention: How America Became Involved in Vietnam* (1986); Robert Schulzinger, *A Time for War: The United States and Vietnam, 1941–1975* (1997); David L. Anderson, *Trapped by Success: The Eisenhower Administration and Vietnam* (1991); John Gaddis, *The Long Peace* (1987); Michael Beschloss, *Mayday* (1986); Thomas Paterson, *Contesting Castro: The United States and the Triumph of the Cuban Revolution* (1994); Qiang Zhai, *China and the Vietnam Wars, 1950–1975* (2000); Gordon Chang, *Enemies and Friends: The United States, China, and the Soviet Union, 1948–1972* (1989); Michael Schaller, *Altered States: The United States and Japan Since the Occupation* (1997); Barry M. Rubin, *Paved with Good Intentions: The American Experience and Iran* (1981); Robert McMahon, *The Cold War on the Periphery* (1994); Elizabeth Cobbs, *The Rich Neighbor Policy* (1992); Richard Immerman, *The CIA in Guatemala* (1982); Douglas Little, *American Orientalism: The United States and the Middle East Since 1945* (2002). **On the growth of the oil industry,** see Hooshang Amirahmadi, ed., *The Caspian Region at a Crossroad: Challenges of a New Frontier of Energy and Development* (2000); Michael Economides and Ronald Oligney, *The Color of Oil: The History, the Money and the Politics of the World's Biggest Business* (2000); Roger Owen and Sevket Pamuk, *A History of Middle East Economies in the Twentieth Century* (1999); Ahmed Rashid, *Taliban: Militant Islam, Oil, and Fundamentalism in Central Asia* (2000); Daniel Yergin. *The Prize: The Epic Quest for Oil, Money and Power* (1991).

5

The New Frontier at Home and Abroad, 1960–1963

President John F. Kennedy and Soviet leader Nikita Khrushchev meet in Vienna, June 1961. / © Bettmann/CORBIS

On a sweltering Monday afternoon in late July 1962, President John F. Kennedy, Secretary of State Dean Rusk, and National Security Adviser McGeorge Bundy spent a few minutes discussing the qualities the president wanted in the officials who would represent the United States abroad. "You never want to generalize," the president cautioned, but he could not get over what he thought was an appalling lack of "spine" among Foreign Service officers. He disliked one ambassador because he did not present "a very virile figure." Kennedy chuckled that "maybe that work doesn't require it." Yet he clearly believed that diplomats needed to be forceful in arguing the American case. "These days," he told his key foreign policy lieutenants, "you're talking to so many people who are dictators, who sort of come off in a hard and tough way [and] I don't think it makes much of an impression on them if some rather languid figure" from the Foreign Service presents the American point of view. Not that Kennedy wanted to rely on brute force. "I know that you get this sort of virility over at the Pentagon and you get a lot of . . . admirable nice figures, without any brains." He wanted something else—tough-minded, disciplined, intelligent, and curious representatives to explain the American cause.

He was not alone. By 1960, many Americans wanted something more. Not only had President Eisenhower's grandfatherly style begun to seem unexciting, but social and political attitudes were also evolving. Among many young people, the ideal of a stable, secure, middle-class family in the suburbs was giving way to a desire for more adventure, a greater challenge, and service to people or causes greater than themselves. Among African Americans, who represented approximately 10 percent of the country's population, the degrading system of legal segregation had become intolerable. A new civil rights movement spread across the South, where more than half the African American population lived. In politics, many people admired a style of action and engagement rather than the cautious consensus of the 1950s. Americans who embraced these new challenges and sense of promise found a leader to suit their tastes in the wealthy, witty, and optimistic John F. Kennedy.

Often known informally as Jack or JFK, the young Massachusetts Democratic senator was elected as the nation's first Catholic president by a tiny margin in 1960. Kennedy embodied urbane masculinity. He combined a dazzling smile, a youthful appearance, a probing intelligence, and abundant curiosity with what his admirers called toughness—the ability to act decisively without expressing agonizing self-doubt. The Kennedy style captivated the mass media and, through them, the public. Kennedy's presidency raised the expectation that problems could be solved by wit, intelligence, knowledge, energy, and skillful management. Many middle-class Americans felt more optimistic about their country's social, spiritual, and economic prospects during the one thousand days of Kennedy's presidency than they did for years thereafter. His murder on November 22, 1963, permanently wounded the American outlook.

Seen in retrospect, however, Kennedy's administration loses some of its luster. In the decades after 1963, more and more of the dark side of the Kennedy years came to light. The president's sunny optimism sometimes seemed to be reckless risk taking. His compulsive womanizing and his disregard for civil liberties were judged more critically in later years. Kennedy's toughness, knowledge, and energy alone could not meet many of the challenges facing the country. His principal skills were those of technique and style. He had less success outlining a compelling vision for the future. Kennedy was a splendid public official. He connected with people; he made them look forward to the future. But he was not an advocate of any particular cause. He and his supporters considered it a source of strength and a sign of their maturity that they treated public affairs coolly and dispassionately.

In domestic affairs, Kennedy's often detached, pragmatic attitude made the federal government slow to respond to important emerging issues. During his presidency, an energetic civil rights movement gathered strength across the American South. Scenes of bloody attacks on black and white Freedom Riders sickened many people across the country. The effort to integrate the University of Mississippi led to another violent confrontation. The demand for civil rights pushed the Kennedy administration into supporting legislation banning legal discrimination. Public concern over the desperate conditions of the one-quarter of Americans living in poverty also revived in the early 1960s. Kennedy responded with some sensitivity to the problems of the poor, but his legislative agenda remained unfulfilled at the time of his death. Some of Kennedy's reluctance to passionately embrace causes of social reform stemmed from the narrowness of his electoral victory over Republican Vice President Richard M. Nixon in 1960. Kennedy did not want to get too far in front of public opinion. But he also remained deeply suspicious of expressing too much passion for any social cause.

In foreign policy, the United States continued the policy of containment that had been established more than a decade earlier. Kennedy's belief in the need for toughness with the Soviet Union encouraged him to take more risks about the possibility of nuclear war than his predecessors had done. Although the public backed him at the time and remembered him fondly for decades afterward, historians have taken a more measured view of his foreign policy. They have balanced admiration for his intelligence, engagement, and energy with disappointment over his assertive waging of the Cold War. If only he had dared to think more imaginatively about improving relations with the Soviet Union, or if he had had more time, the United States and the world might have been spared decades more of anxiety.

American Society and Politics in 1960

Americans expressed a yearning anxiety about their lives in 1960. The post–World War II economic boom was real, but it also left many people looking for something more. By 1960, Americans were more educated than ever before. In 1960, females stayed in high school through the eleventh grade; males stayed in high school through the tenth. (Ten years earlier, males and females had left school in the tenth and ninth grades, respectively, on average.)

In 1950, about 1.56 million men were enrolled in higher education, compared with 721,000 women. In 1960, 2.26 million men and 1.3 million women were in college. Graduation rates for the genders were far different, though. About 37 percent of women graduated, compared with 55 percent of men. Even starker differences between the genders showed up when one considers the attainment of postgraduate degrees. In 1960, 8,000 men received doctorates, compared with 1,028 women.

Women continued to enter the work force in the 1950s, reversing the trend of the immediate post–World War II years. In the decade between 1950 and 1960, 5 million more women worked outside the home, raising the percentage of working women to 38 percent (from 34 percent at the beginning of the decade).

About 50 percent of African Americans lived in poverty in 1960. Throughout the 1950s, blacks continued to leave the South, where the demeaning system of legal segregation remained the norm. By 1960, only about 53 percent of African Americans lived in the states of the Old Confederacy. In the South, African Americans experienced daily humiliations. Schools, restaurants, buses, beaches, drinking fountains, and swimming pools were segregated. Whites addressed African American men as "boy," or "George," or "Jack." African American women were called "Aunt" or by their first names. Whites in the South never addressed African Americans as Miss, Mrs., or Mr. Racial discrimination was more subtle in the North, but it still ran deep.

Unemployment rates among blacks were twice as high as for whites. Employers discriminated against African Americans in hiring, wages, and promotions. Housing discrimination intensified in northern cities. The major cities of the North designed massive urban-renewal projects that tore down black neighborhoods and forced African Americans into dilapidated neighborhoods or huge, forbidding, high-rise housing projects. By 1960, social critics began characterizing African American neighborhoods in northern cities as ghettos. Blacks who sought to migrate to the suburbs were blocked at almost every turn.

In 1960, social critic Paul Goodman published *Growing Up Absurd*, a series of essays decrying what he characterized as the mindless consumerism of the 1950s. Like many cultural critics in the late 1950s, Goodman complained about the conformity, blandness, sameness, and lack of adventure of suburban life. The election of 1960 crystallized many of the hopes Americans had for the new decade. It demonstrated how much American politics had changed since World War II. Democrats expected that the New Deal coalition of liberals, working-class people, Catholics, southerners, and racial minorities would continue to give them an advantage in presidential elections. They believed that the idea of an activist government, promoted by the New Deal, had been accepted by a majority of Americans. They explained away the popularity of Dwight D. Eisenhower as a reflection of his personal appeal rather than an endorsement of the Republican Party. However, the 1960 election results revealed serious limits to the New Deal coalition and the public's acceptance of government activism. The Democrats barely won with John F. Kennedy, a moderate candidate from the party's center. Richard Nixon, the Republican candidate, did so well that he remained an important figure in American politics. White southerners continued their flight from the Democratic Party, preparing the way for future Republican and conservative triumphs.

Only forty-two years old when he announced his candidacy for the presidency in January 1960, Massachusetts senator John F. Kennedy shook up Democratic Party professionals, who dismissed him as a brash outsider. But these leaders were unaware of the advantages Kennedy's celebrity would bring to the 1960 election. He was already well known to the public thanks largely to the tireless efforts of his father, former ambassador to Great Britain Joseph P. Kennedy. The Ambassador, as he liked to be called, had amassed a fortune in real estate and the movies in the 1920s. A fiercely proud Irish American Catholic, Joseph Kennedy took various positions in the New Deal. He hoped to succeed Roosevelt and become president in 1940. That ambition dashed, he planned to have his first-born son, Joseph, Jr., elected the first Catholic president, but Joe, an Army Airs Corps pilot, died when his plane was shot down over France in 1944. The Ambassador then decided that his second son, John, would carry the family's ambitions to the White House. Joseph Kennedy helped plant laudatory stories about his son John in newspapers and magazines in the 1950s. He helped garner the 1957 Pulitzer Prize for his son's 1956 book *Profiles in Courage*. John Kennedy made a favorable impression by nearly winning the Democratic Party's nomination for vice president in 1956. His fresh, youthful appearance stood in sharp contrast to Eisenhower's age and apparent passivity—a difference Kennedy planned to emphasize in his campaign. Kennedy looked like the picture of good health—his face tanned, his hair abundant, and his teeth a radiant white. Appearances told only part of the story, though. Kennedy suffered from a disorder of his adrenal gland, for which he took a mixture of cortisone and amphetamines. The pills produced a mild euphoria, which heightened the sense of hope and optimism he wanted to project.

Kennedy also believed that his moderate stance on the controversial issues of the 1950s would distinguish him favorably in voters' minds from the party's liberal wing. He astutely concluded that the public mood had become more conservative since the New Deal, and that voters would respond best to a candidate who projected energy and managerial competence rather than passionate commitment to causes. The growing influence of television bolstered Kennedy's approach. He mastered the medium, appearing in people's living rooms as intimate, friendly, and approachable. His father's Hollywood background helped. "We're going to sell Jack like soap flakes," Joseph Kennedy declared. Some observers marveled at the young senator's command of the small screen. The journalist Stewart Alsop, one of FDR's greatest admirers, thought Kennedy was his equal. "Kennedy is his own secret weapon," Alsop wrote. Others thought Kennedy was shallow. The independent leftist journalist I. F. Stone complained about the "phony smell of advertising copy" hanging over the Kennedy campaign.

Although party professionals and most liberals had their doubts about the young candidate, they could not agree on an alternative. Kennedy dashed the

Enthusiastic crowds greeted Massachusetts Democratic senator John F. Kennedy wherever he campaigned for president in 1960. / © Bettmann/CORBIS

hopes of the older men by winning victories in seven presidential primaries. His victory in West Virginia, an overwhelmingly Protestant state, proved that his Catholicism would not provoke a significant voter backlash. By the time the Democratic convention met in July, only Senate majority leader Lyndon Johnson of Texas could mount a last-ditch campaign against Kennedy.

Johnson's bid came so late, and Johnson had opposed so many liberal initiatives, that his attempt to gain the nomination fizzled. Kennedy won on the first ballot. He then astonished his own staff—and disturbed party liberals—by offering the vice-presidential nomination to Johnson. Much to Kennedy's surprise, Johnson accepted. Two days later, Kennedy addressed fifty thousand Democrats at the Los Angeles Coliseum. He announced that "we stand on the edge of a New Frontier—the frontier of the 1960s—a frontier of unknown opportunities and perils—a frontier of unfulfilled hopes and threats." The crowd cheered when he offered not "a set of promises [but] a set of challenges." Kennedy's New Frontier came with "the promise of more sacrifice instead of more security," and the public was intrigued.

Nevertheless, Richard Nixon, the Republican candidate, had the advantages of experience in national office and the inherited mantle of the popular president Eisenhower. Nixon's steadfast loyalty to the president helped him win the Republican nomination over a last-minute challenge from New York governor Nelson Rockefeller, who had spent the previous two years on ambitious public works projects in the Empire State. Shortly before the Republican nominating convention, Nixon met Rockefeller and agreed to lead a much more activist government than Eisenhower had directed.

To win the presidency, Kennedy had to demonstrate that he was Nixon's equal. A key element in the campaign was a series of four face-to-face televised debates. The first Kennedy-Nixon debate proved crucial because most voters had never seen Kennedy before, whereas Nixon had been a familiar figure for the last eight years. Instead of seeing an inexperienced youth easily defeated by his opponent, viewers saw Kennedy as a knowledgeable, self-assured, handsome candidate. His crisp, fact-filled delivery made him appear Nixon's equal, erasing experience as an edge for the incumbent vice president. Nixon, on the other hand, looked tired and haggard. Sweat poured down his face. Each candidate's appearance affected audience perceptions of who had won the debate. People who watched the debate on television considered Kennedy the clear winner, whereas those who listened to it on the radio thought Nixon did a better job.

During the campaign, each man tried to convince voters that he would confront the communist threat with greater conviction than his opponent, and both indicated that they would oppose the Soviet Union more vigorously than had Eisenhower. Nixon vowed to defend Quemoy and Matsu, two small islands off the coast of the People's Republic of China, which Eisenhower and Dulles had protected. Kennedy responded with an attack on Eisenhower and Nixon for tolerating a "Communist outpost" in Cuba, just ninety miles from Florida. Shortly before the final debate, Kennedy's office released a statement promising "to strengthen the non-Batista democratic anti-Castro forces." Nixon, aware that the CIA had already developed plans for an invasion of Cuba, feared that Kennedy had deliberately revealed a plot to overthrow Castro. Nixon characterized such a plan as a violation of international law that would rouse anti-American passions throughout the Western Hemisphere.

No Catholic had ever been elected president. In 1928, the Democratic Party had nominated New York's governor Al Smith, who had gone down to an ignominious defeat. Millions of Protestants, who customarily voted for Democratic candidates, deserted Smith. They expressed the fear that a Catholic president would show greater allegiance to the pope than to American interests. Kennedy deftly turned the issue of his Catholicism to his advantage, neutralizing anti-Catholic sentiments and winning the hearts of his fellow Catholics. He gave a brilliant televised performance before the Houston Ministerial Association—a highly skeptical audience of several hundred Southern Baptists—telling them, "I am not the Catholic candidate for President, I am the Democratic candidate, who happens to be Catholic." He promised to resign if he was ever forced to choose between violating his conscience and violating the Constitution.

Another brilliant gesture helped him secure the votes of blacks. African Americans had been cool toward Kennedy because of his noticeable lack of interest in civil rights legislation during his years in Congress. Kennedy and his brother Robert melted the animosity with two telephone calls in late October 1960. Civil rights leader Martin Luther King, Jr., had been sent to a rural Georgia jail to serve a four-month sentence on trumped-up charges involving a demonstration against a segregated lunch counter at an Atlanta department store. John Kennedy called the prisoner's wife, Coretta Scott King, to express his interest in her husband's welfare. His brother and campaign manager Robert secured King's release by calling the judge and telling him that the harsh sentence made the state of Georgia look bad. The judge relented and ordered King's release. In gratitude, King's father, Martin Luther King, Sr., a Baptist minister, withdrew his earlier endorsement of Richard Nixon and proclaimed that the mostly Protestant African Americans had no reason to fear the election of the Catholic Kennedy. The Kennedy campaign then distributed 2 million copies of a booklet describing the Kennedy brothers' efforts on King's behalf.

In the November election, Kennedy won a razor-thin plurality, beating Nixon by only 118,574 votes out of a total of 68,334,888 votes cast. And even that narrow victory was tainted by charges of voter fraud in several key states where Kennedy won by a small margin. Sixty-four percent of Americans cast votes, the largest proportion since 1920. The issue of Kennedy's religion reduced his popular-vote margin, but it actually helped him win electoral votes. Although he lost the backing of about 1 million Protestants who had supported Democrats in earlier elections, these people were concentrated in midwestern farm states that customarily voted Republican anyway. Among Catholics, Kennedy won 80 percent of the vote, up from the approximately 63 percent who had voted for Democratic candidates since Roosevelt, and this gain proved important in the electoral college. African Americans also helped Kennedy win key northern industrial states such as New York, Pennsylvania, and Michigan. Although most blacks still could not vote in the South, those who did provided crucial victory margins in North Carolina, South Carolina, and Texas. The presence of Texas senator Lyndon Johnson on the ticket also helped the ticket carry traditionally Democratic states of the Old Confederacy.

The Kennedy Presidency

Kennedy took the oath of office under a brilliant blue sky on a bitterly cold January 20, 1961. The handsome young president captured his listeners with his stirring phrases and his calls to sacrifice in his inaugural address. The speech included what were probably Kennedy's most famous words: "And so my fellow Americans, ask not what your country can do for you—ask what you can do for your country."

The stylish inauguration set the tone for the one thousand days of the Kennedy administration. He and his family projected a sexy image of vigor and refinement to which the nation responded. The president's staff participated in bone-wearying fifty-mile hikes; the nation's public schools began requiring physical education. Intellectuals felt valued, in sharp contrast to the harassment they had experienced during the McCarthy era. Jacqueline

Kennedy touched a similar nerve with her efforts to refurnish the White House with authentic antiques.

At every opportunity, Kennedy sought to distinguish his freewheeling management approach from the military-style hierarchy of the Eisenhower years. The new president sought advice from anyone in or out of government. His brother Robert operated a running seminar on public policy at his sprawling home across the Potomac in Virginia. Many old Washington veterans heard echoes of the exciting days of the early New Deal. Some people thought the newcomers were far too brash. "They've got the damned bunch of boy commandos running around," complained former Democratic presidential candidate Adlai Stevenson.

In choosing his advisers and key administrators, Kennedy appointed a group that writer David Halberstam would later call "the best and the brightest." Relatively young, often educated in the most distinguished colleges and universities, many of them boasting fine records in business or academia, these new stars in Washington added to the Kennedy aura. Kennedy assembled a cabinet of men who shared his view that managerial competence, not commitment to any particular program, mattered most in the conduct of public affairs. Feeling the need for continued counsel from his closest adviser, he named his thirty-six-year-old brother Robert as attorney general. He included two Republicans in his cabinet: C. Douglas Dillon as treasury secretary, to reassure business leaders, and Robert S. McNamara, the young president of Ford Motor Company, as secretary of defense. McNamara—ferociously intelligent, impatient with ignorance, a numbers-and-facts kind of man—set the tone of the New Frontier. If information could not be summarized numerically, McNamara would not use it.

Kennedy also chose a Republican to fill an important post outside the cabinet. McGeorge Bundy, forty-one-year-old dean of the faculty at Harvard and a long-time friend, became national security adviser. Kennedy believed that Eisenhower's disengaged style had hampered the nation's conduct of foreign affairs; he wanted to elevate the importance of the national security adviser to help make the president the central figure in foreign policy. Under Kennedy, the influence of the secretary of state—a cabinet position—declined. After a long search for a secretary of state, Kennedy settled on Dean Rusk, formerly Truman's assistant secretary of state for Far Eastern affairs.

At the same time that he sought to strengthen his control of foreign policy, Kennedy limited his options in domestic affairs by retaining J. Edgar Hoover as director of the Federal Bureau of Investigation. From the beginning, Hoover and Robert Kennedy fought bitterly. Hoover refused to acknowledge the existence of the Mafia; Robert wanted the FBI to infiltrate it. The attorney general also pressed Hoover to obtain evidence against Jimmy Hoffa, president of the Teamsters Union, but Hoover resisted that idea as well. The FBI director, in turn, forced Robert into approving wiretaps on African American civil rights leader Martin Luther King, Jr., whom Hoover detested and suspected of ties to the Communist Party of the United States. With these tapes, Hoover compiled lurid evidence of King's many extramarital sexual encounters. Yet the Kennedys had to keep Hoover in office because the FBI chief had in his files damaging tape recordings that proved a 1941 sexual liaison between twenty-three-year-old navy lieutenant John F. Kennedy and a woman who may have worked for Nazi intelligence. Although President Kennedy often seemed to flaunt his extramarital encounters, he feared that Hoover's files could destroy him.

Kennedy's Foreign Policy

Like his predecessors, Kennedy pursued a policy of containing the Soviet Union and opposing revolutionary change in the Third World. In 1961 and 1962, the United States confronted the Soviet Union and its Third World clients as assertively as ever before, hoping for a decisive Cold War victory. In the Cuban missile crisis of October 1962, the world came close to a nuclear war. In the aftermath of the missile crisis, ordinary citizens and policy planners looked for alternatives to their permanent competition. This early détente, or relaxation of tension, did not last, however.

Fidel Castro was like a toothache to the new president: the pain would not get better and Kennedy could not take his mind off the Cuban dictator. In 1960, under President Eisenhower, the CIA had begun planning an invasion of Cuba by armed exiles. By the time Kennedy took office, the operation was nearly ready. When the CIA presented its plans for the invasion, most of Kennedy's inner circle of advisers approved. CIA chief Allen Dulles informed the president that the prospects for success in an invasion of Cuba were greater than they had been in 1954, when the agency had sponsored an invasion of Guatemala. Dulles predicted that once the exile force landed, a general uprising would sweep over Cuba, expelling Castro from the island.

Kennedy's main concern was for the administration's ability to maintain "plausible deniability" of its involvement. In response, the CIA changed the proposed landing site to the remote, swampy Bay of Pigs, and the president banned the U.S. Air Force from providing cover to the invaders. Some analysts later claimed that these alterations doomed the operation but, in fact, the plan was flawed from the beginning. Castro was broadly popular among poor Cubans throughout the island. Castro's large, well-supplied army of peasant supporters was ready for an attack. Indeed, some of Kennedy's own advisers doubted that the plan would work. The invasion went forward anyway because it seemed easier to continue than to cancel an advanced plan. The president feared looking weak should word leak out that he had scrapped a plan prepared by the Eisenhower administration. He worried that if the members of the brigade were forced to return to the United States from their bases in Guatemala, they would inform the media of the plan, making it appear that Kennedy's toughness was just a pose for the election.

The invasion began at first light on April 17, 1961 (see Map 5.1). The brigade hit the beaches shortly after a CIA broadcast from Honduras entreated Cubans to rise against Castro. That plea had no effect, but Castro's own call to arms for his 200,000-man militia worked perfectly. The Cuban defenders sank

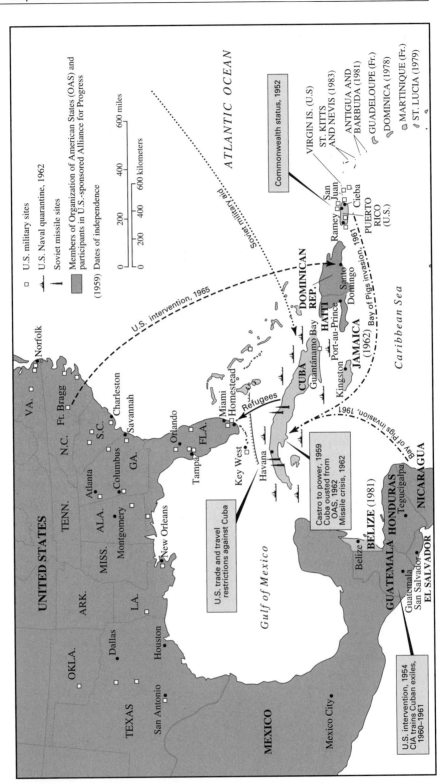

U.S. military sites

U.S. Naval quarantine, 1962

Soviet missile sites

Members of Organization of American States (OAS) and participants in U.S.-sponsored Alliance for Progress

(1959) Dates of independence

0   200   400   600 miles
0   200   400   600 kilometers

Soviet military aid

U.S. intervention, 1965

U.S. intervention, 1954
CIA trains Cuban exiles,
1960–1961

U.S. trade and travel
restrictions against Cuba

Castro to power, 1959
Cuba ousted from
OAS, 1962
Missile crisis, 1962

Bay of Pigs invasion, 1961

Commonwealth status, 1952

ATLANTIC OCEAN

Caribbean Sea

Gulf of Mexico

UNITED STATES

MEXICO

TEXAS
OKLA.
ARK.
LA.
MISS.
TENN.
ALA.
GA.
FLA.
S.C.
N.C.
VA.

San Antonio
Houston
Dallas
New Orleans
Montgomery
Atlanta
Columbus
Orlando
Tampa
Miami
Homestead
Key West
Savannah
Charleston
Ft. Bragg
Norfolk
Mexico City

Refugees

Havana
CUBA
Guantánamo Bay
JAMAICA
Kingston
HAITI
Port-au-Prince
DOMINICAN
REP.
Santo
Domingo
PUERTO
RICO
(U.S.)
Ramey
San
Juan
Cieba

VIRGIN IS. (U.S)
ST. KITTS
AND NEVIS (1983)
ANTIGUA AND
BARBUDA (1981)
GUADELOUPE (Fr.)
DOMINICA (1978)
MARTINIQUE (Fr.)
ST. LUCIA (1979)

BELIZE (1981)
Belize
GUATEMALA
Guatemala
San Salvador
EL SALVADOR
HONDURAS
Tegucigalpa
NICARAGUA

many of the invaders' landing craft. Attackers who made it ashore became easy targets for Castro's tanks and fighter planes. By the evening of the first day, officials in Washington knew that the operation had failed. Within seventy-two hours, the Cuban army had captured 1,189 invaders and killed 114; only about 150 escaped death or capture.

In the aftermath of the Bay of Pigs debacle, Kennedy set about restoring the image he had tried to craft of a decisive, successful, active leader. He embarked on a public relations offensive against Castro, implying that the United States would look for other ways to end Castro's regime. In a speech before the American Society of Newspaper Editors, Kennedy blamed the victim, explaining that American "restraint" toward Cuba was "not inexhaustible." He pledged never to "abandon . . . the country to communism." The public loved Kennedy's tough reaction. A Gallup poll taken the week after Kennedy's speech revealed that 71 percent approved of his overall handling of the presidency, and over 80 percent backed his Cuban policy.

Kennedy's obsession with Cuba continued after the failure of the Bay of Pigs invasion. The American government ransomed the approximately twelve hundred captured Cuban exiles with $120 million worth of drugs, medical supplies, trucks, tractors, and agricultural implements. Veterans of the brigade were given a tumultuous reception in Miami's Orange Bowl. Kennedy accepted one of their battle banners and promised to return the flag "in a free Havana." All the while, his administration proceeded with efforts to discredit, overthrow, or kill Fidel Castro and drafted plans to invade the island once more.

In late 1961 the CIA initiated Operation Mongoose, the code name for various schemes to oust or assassinate the Cuban leader. The CIA developed a series of fantastical plans. Psychological warfare experts suggested that a full beard represented sexual potency in Cuban culture, so agents tried to drop depilatory powder in Castro's boots. Another scenario involved agents slipping him cigars either laced with LSD to make him incoherent or injected with poison to kill him. At various times, would-be assassins tried to poison him, spear him with harpoons as he snorkeled in the Caribbean, or induce him to don a wet suit rigged with explosives. None of these attempts worked.

In frustration, the CIA turned to the Mafia, hoping to tap its assassination expertise. Mafia chiefs had helped the Eisenhower administration in its efforts to kill Castro because they hoped to regain control of the casinos closed by the revolutionaries. Eventually, the connection between the U.S. government and the criminals became too hot for top Kennedy administration officials, and the partnership was severed. One of the president's several mistresses also shared a bed with the boss of the Chicago Mafia. FBI director Hoover knew of this bizarre triangle, and he ultimately persuaded Robert Kennedy that any exposure of this connection could severely embarrass the administration. Kennedy stopped the affair. Castro learned of the American-sponsored plots on his life and sought

◀ **Map 5.1**
   The United States in the Caribbean and Central America

help from his patrons in Moscow. Nikita Khrushchev responded with Soviet troops equipped to repel another U.S. invasion. In mid-1962, the Soviets also agreed to station in Cuba a few dozen intermediate-range ballistic missiles (IRBMs) armed with nuclear bombs. This action soon provoked a major crisis.

Elsewhere in the developing world, the Kennedy administration used various methods—some far gentler than Operation Mongoose; some equally violent—to encourage people and governments to support the United States in its global competition with the Soviet Union. During the election campaign of 1960, Kennedy accused the Eisenhower administration of indifference to poverty in Latin America and a lack of support for independence movements in Africa and Asia. Eisenhower, he said, had ignored the winds of change sweeping the Third World and had opened the way for the Soviet Union to gain advantages there. The new administration sought to restore America's prestige among the poor or newly independent states of Latin America, Africa, and Asia by helping to build modern societies in those areas of the world.

Fearing that many Latin American states, racked by poverty, social inequality, and political repression, stood on the verge of revolutions similar to Cuba's, the Kennedy administration developed a foreign assistance program called the Alliance for Progress. Kennedy obtained from Congress a down payment of $500 million to eradicate illiteracy, hunger, and disease in the Western Hemisphere. Over the next eight years, the United States provided about $10 billion in assistance to Latin American governments; an additional $8 billion came from private agencies. Kennedy also promised to advance political and social reform in Latin America by pressuring the region's political leaders to revise tax and land laws that favored the rich.

The hopes inflated by the Alliance for Progress made disappointment almost inevitable. Creating just and prosperous societies in the Western Hemisphere proved far harder than restoring modern, industrial European countries to the prosperity they had enjoyed before World War II. Throughout Latin America, economic growth stalled at an unimpressive average of 1.5 percent per year during the 1960s. Unemployment rose, and the average figures for life expectancy, infant mortality, adult illiteracy, and the amount of time that children spent in school remained the same.

The Kennedy administration found it harder to practice concern for democracy and social justice than to preach it. Kennedy produced a mixed record in his efforts to promote popular, elected governments. The administration did hasten the end of Rafael Trujillo's dictatorship in the Dominican Republic, and it supported constitutional regimes in Venezuela, Colombia, and Mexico. But it allowed military coups in Argentina, Guatemala, Honduras, and Haiti. The CIA also secretly funded moderate and conservative candidates in Chile to undermine the Socialist candidate, Salvador Allende Gossens, in the presidential race of 1964. In most cases, a government's attitude toward Castro determined the American response to it. Governments that opposed Castro received American aid. Those that expressed sympathy for him or questioned U.S. actions in the Bay of Pigs were suspected of leftist sympathies and denied Alliance for Progress funds.

Another program, which did not involve covert actions, had a more lasting benefit. The Peace Corps, a project arising from the Kennedy administration's desire to encourage active commitment among American young people, became one of the most popular government programs in recent history. Like the Alliance for Progress, the Peace Corps originated from Cold War preoccupations and a sense that Eisenhower had done too little to oppose communism abroad. The day after his inauguration, Kennedy asked his brother-in-law, Sargent Shriver, to organize the Peace Corps. Congress created the new organization in September 1961. In the remaining twenty-seven months of the Kennedy administration, about seven thousand Peace Corps volunteers, most under age twenty-five, went to work in forty-four countries in Asia, Africa, and Latin America. More than half worked in education, fighting adult illiteracy and teaching children. The rest helped with community development, public works, healthcare, and agricultural programs.

A Peace Corps volunteer in the West African nation of Mali helps with the planting. / Courtesy of the Peace Corps

Most recipients of the aid admired the earnest young Americans, but to the surprise of some Peace Corps volunteers, they did not choose to transform their culture into one based on an American model. Peace Corps members learned from the exchange of ideas that the Peace Corps promoted. The personal impact of their service lasted for decades. Service in the Corps became a grand adventure. A volunteer wrote home: "Well, I got it—malaria!" He carried a secret microphone in his breast pocket when he met his hero, President Kennedy. "I got it all on tape," he wrote his parents. His eyes were opened to the appalling poverty of rural Colombia. He carried a small boy down a mountainside from a remote village to a doctor who would operate on his crushed foot. ("Have you ever tried to convince a little boy that he really doesn't need his little toe?") Sophisticated volunteers returned home with a heightened appreciation for other cultures. Many came to question the anticommunist assumptions that had created the Peace Corps in the first place. Instead of seeing the problems of poorer lands in terms of the competition between the United States and the Soviet Union, many returning volunteers believed that the United States should try to understand poorer countries in terms of their own culture and history.

Africa was only a slightly higher priority to Kennedy than it had been to Eisenhower. And when the administration did act decisively in Africa, it assisted conservative elements. For example, in the former Belgian Congo, a nation that had been independent since mid-1960, the Kennedy administration spent two years trying to install an anticommunist labor leader as head of the government. The CIA bribed the Congolese legislature into electing Washington's choice, a move Rusk hailed as a "major Soviet defeat." The victory proved ephemeral, however, and the Congo sank into civil war. During this conflict, the United Nations tried to arrange cease-fires and create stability, but Washington resented these efforts, fearful that they would interfere with American efforts to promote an anticommunist faction.

Obsessive anticommunism and preoccupation with events elsewhere also hampered American efforts to advance independence in Portugal's African colonies of Angola and Mozambique. At first, the Kennedy administration backed a U.N. resolution condemning Portuguese rule. Later, however, Portugal's dictator threatened to tear up the lease for American military bases on the Azores, a group of islands in the mid-Atlantic. Portugal's friends in the United States argued that the bases were vital outposts in the Cold War. Faced with stiff opposition, the Kennedy administration gradually dropped its support for self-determination and independence from European rule for the remaining colonies in Africa.

In addition to challenging Fidel Castro and attempting to fend off further leftist gains in the Third World, the Kennedy administration also intensified direct American opposition to the Soviet Union. The frigidity in U.S.-Soviet relations that began with the U-2 incident and the collapse of the Paris summit in May 1960 continued throughout the first year of the new administration. Hoping to demonstrate his mastery of foreign affairs, Kennedy met Soviet Communist Party General Secretary Nikita Khrushchev at a hastily arranged summit conference in Vienna in June 1961. The meeting took place less than two months after the catastrophe at the Bay of Pigs. Although the American public had rallied around their young president after the Cuban debacle, Kennedy's standing abroad had suffered. Earlier reservations among world leaders regarding his youth and lack of experience in foreign affairs seemed to have been borne out by the fiasco in Cuba. Thus, Kennedy went to Europe in June to reassure French president Charles de Gaulle that he could recover from his blunder and also to impress Khrushchev with how tough he could be.

The stop in Paris buoyed the president. The First Lady charmed the aging President de Gaulle, and Kennedy's knowledge and his ability to speak clearly and cogently relieved French suspicions. But in Vienna, instead of the get-acquainted session he had expected, the president found himself caught up in a dangerous conflict with Khrushchev over the future of Berlin.

The former capital of the Third Reich had been occupied by the four victorious Allies (the United States, the Soviet Union, Great Britain, and France) since 1945. Emerging Cold War tensions had blocked progress on a formal peace settlement with Germany, leaving the future of Berlin unresolved. The city was divided into eastern and western sectors, and the entire municipality was completely surrounded by the German Democratic Republic (East Germany). Created by German Communists in 1949, East Germany maintained its capital in the part of Berlin controlled by the Soviet Union. The Western powers, however, refused to recognize the sovereignty of the German Democratic Republic or its control over East Berlin. The Federal Republic of Germany (West Germany), also established in 1949, had installed its capital in the quiet Rhine town of Bonn. Since its inception, West Germany had insisted that the two Germanys must eventually be reunited and that East Germany was a puppet of the Soviet Union. Meanwhile, the Western powers had retained their rights to supervise the affairs of Berlin.

At the Vienna summit, Khrushchev raised the issue of Berlin as a way of bolstering the sagging legitimacy of East Germany. He had complained about the West's refusal to acknowledge East German sovereignty at the Camp David summit with Eisenhower in September 1959, but the situation had persisted. In the interim, the East German government had pressed the Soviets to do something to boost its prestige. Now, at his meeting with Kennedy in Vienna, the Kremlin leader insisted that the Allies finally resolve the German problem by signing a peace treaty recognizing the legitimacy of East Germany, with a capital at East Berlin. If no progress occurred soon, he threatened, the Soviet Union would sign a separate peace treaty with East Germany, ceding to that government control over land and air access to Berlin. Under such a treaty, East Germany would be in a position to strangle West Berlin because the city's economy depended on trade with the rest of West Germany, 120 miles away. The Western powers had been strongly committed to West Berlin's existence ever since they had airlifted supplies to the city in 1948. The loss of West Berlin, many feared, would erode faith in Washington's ability to defend other friendly areas challenged by the Soviet Union.

In addition to his tough stand on Berlin, Khrushchev surprised Kennedy by affirming Soviet support for what he called "wars of national liberation" in Southeast Asia and Latin America. Kennedy responded to Khrushchev's unexpected demands by expressing hopes for friendly relations with the Soviets, but he clearly had been caught off guard. Robert Kennedy felt that his brother's failure to crush Cuba had led Khrushchev to believe Kennedy was a weak president.

In the aftermath of the Vienna summit, the United States came close to war with the Soviet Union over Berlin. Within hours after returning to the United States, Kennedy delivered a somber, televised report on his encounter with Khrushchev. He told the public that meeting the Soviet leader had been a frightening experience. He explained that Khrushchev believed "the tide of history was moving his way" and "the so-called wars of national revolution supported by the Kremlin would replace the old method of direct aggression and invasion."

Behind the scenes, Kennedy prepared U.S. forces for a showdown with the Soviets over Berlin. He recognized that Khrushchev had manufactured the Berlin crisis in order to demonstrate his own toughness to the Soviet military and to assure the East German government of his support. Nevertheless, the United States behaved as if the crisis could turn into a war. To prevent the

Soviets from making good on their threat to limit access to Berlin, Kennedy let them know that Washington no longer felt bound by its pledge not to unloose a preemptive nuclear strike. He decided that Khrushchev "won't pay attention to words. He has to see you move."

On July 25, 1961, Kennedy further defied the Soviets with a bellicose speech. "If we do not meet our commitments to Berlin, where will we later stand?" he asked the American public. He reactivated some reserve units, which were to go immediately to Germany, and increased the armed forces by over 200,000 troops by doubling draft calls and dropping the exemption for married men. The next day, he asked Congress for an additional $3.5 billion for military outlays. Included in that figure was $207 million more for civil defense—an amount that prompted morbid speculations among ordinary citizens about the likelihood of nuclear war. Seventy-one percent of those questioned in a Gallup poll agreed that Americans should fight their way into Berlin if access were blocked.

While American anxieties grew, events in Germany in early August changed the course of the crisis. The constant stream of refugees from East to West Germany became a flood in July. That month, more than thirty thousand of the best-educated and most skilled East Germans left their dreary police state for the robust economic opportunities of the West. The East German government responded to the exodus on the night of August 13 by beginning construction of a concrete and barbed wire fence between East and West Berlin. Within three days, the Berlin Wall became an almost impenetrable barrier that prevented East Germans from fleeing to West Berlin. The wall would remain in existence for almost three decades, and hundreds of East Germans would be shot trying to escape through it or over it. Yet in 1961, despite the moral outrage in the West, construction of the Berlin Wall actually defused the crisis. It allowed the Soviets and East Germans to stop the flow of refugees without a diplomatic confrontation with the West. Khrushchev spoke no more about a separate peace treaty.

The Berlin Wall caught the Kennedy administration completely by surprise. Its construction demonstrated that the American military buildup had not intimidated the communists. Nor had it left the United States with the kind of flexible options that the Kennedy administration had wanted. On the other hand, many of Kennedy's advisers privately accepted the logic of the solution. Although Kennedy drew cheers from hundreds of thousands when he spoke at the wall in June 1963, declaring "Ich bin ein Berliner" ("I am a Berliner"), it is clear that his Berlin policy did not present the flexible, skeptical approach to world politics that his intellectual supporters expected from him.

The Kennedy administration adopted a more complex mixture of military threat and diplomatic bargaining during the Cuban missile crisis of October 1962, one of the most pivotal and dangerous episodes of the Cold War. In the end, the United States forced the Soviet Union to remove missiles and manned bombers from Cuba, but for thirteen days, from October 15 to 28, 1962, the United States and the Soviet Union approached the brink of thermonuclear war.

(cont. on page 188)

Nuclear Fallout Shelters—A Blast from the Past

In the wake of the September 11, 2001, terrorist attack against the World Trade Center and the Pentagon, and amidst fears that the nation's enemies might next use biological or atomic weapons, the Bush administration dusted off an emergency plan devised at the height of the Cold War. In the event of Washington's destruction, it provided for a shadow government in secret locations staffed by key officials. The largest of nearly one hundred underground facilities, built in White Sulfur Springs, West Virginia, could accommodate the 535 members of Congress and support staff. Although conceived to stymie a Soviet nuclear barrage, the shadow government took shape again after the September 11 attacks.

Since the first atomic bombs were used against Japan, numerous American writers speculated on how a nuclear attack might affect the United States. Three of the best-selling novels in the 1950s, Nevil Shute's *On the Beach* (1957), William M. Miller, Jr.'s *A Canticle for Liebowitz* (1960), and Pat Frank's *Alas, Babylon* (1959), contained apocalyptic themes of nuclear war that threatened all life on earth.

The anxiety over atomic war grew more intense after 1954, when the newly tested hydrogen bomb produced a vastly more powerful explosion than its atomic cousin. The accidental irradiation of a Japanese fishing boat in 1954 and later of several small towns in southern Utah from test explosions added to the widespread fear that radioactive strontium-90 had contaminated the nation's milk supply.

In response, some Americans formed citizens groups such as the Committee for a Sane Nuclear Policy to demand an end to nuclear testing. Filmmakers in Hollywood and Tokyo produced dozens of "creature features" like *Godzilla* and *Them* that depicted rampaging monsters created by nuclear tests. The federal government, acting through the Federal Civil Defense Administration (FCDA), tried to reassure the public that nuclear weapons were not so terrible.

Among its most celebrated actions was OPERATION ALERT, a series of mass evacuations begun in 1954. The best-known drill occurred in Washington, D.C., in 1955, when President Dwight D. Eisenhower and fifteen thousand federal employees were taken to thirty-one secret sites in a mock evacuation. Another demonstration took place in Mobile, Alabama, where civil defense officials transported thirty-seven thousand schoolchildren to secure locations. Most of these exercises proved so chaotic that officials privately admitted that civil-defense agencies "couldn't cope with a brushfire threatening a dog house in the backyard." None of the tests treated the threat of radioactive fallout seriously and many urban officials dismissed the notion of evacuating large cities as "so much moonshine."

During the 1950s and 1960s, public school students routinely performed "duck and cover drills." After watching a Walt Disney film about *Our Friend the Atom*, pupils read a pamphlet or viewed a cartoon featuring Bert the Turtle. He reassured children that they would be safe if they hid beneath a school desk and tucked their heads between their knees. Some young cynics subverted the exercise by chanting, "Now we put our head between our knees and kiss our ass goodbye." Their skepticism was justified. Federal blueprints for "nuclear-safe" schools included plans for large morgues in each building. A secret 1958 Defense Department *Emergency Plans Book* concluded that a Soviet nuclear and/or biological-chemical attack, even if directed only against military and industrial targets, would kill 30 million Americans outright, with at least 10 million more soon dying of radiation exposure. In the wake of such an attack, the planners concluded, the economy, law and order, and healthcare would collapse.

The nuclear family: the federal government encouraged families to build fallout shelters such as this prototype. Despite fears of nuclear war, very few did so. / © Bettmann/CORBIS

President Eisenhower and Congress dealt with these threats by utilizing them to build support in 1956 for the largest federal construction program ever: the National System of Defense Highways. The new coast-to-coast interstates, designed to accommodate the public's love of the automobile, were also promoted as a network to speed the movement of military vehicles and the evacuation of urban areas.

The Soviet Union's launch of the Sputnik satellite in October 1957 rekindled public fear of sudden nuclear attack and prompted resumed calls for defense. Reports issued by two blue-ribbon panels, the Gaither Committee and the Rockefeller Brothers Fund, urged the Eisenhower administration to spend billions of dollars to construct a vast network of blast and fallout shelters. The RAND Corporation, a private think tank linked to the Defense Department, proposed building an immense shelter under Manhattan to house 4 million people. Defense expert Herman Kahn, author of the controversial book *On Thermonuclear War* (1960) and the model for Dr. Strangelove in Stanley Kubrick's 1962 film of that name, insisted that most Americans could survive a nuclear conflict if they had shelters. In a short time after the bombs fell, he claimed, life would return to "normal." New York governor (and presidential hopeful) Nelson Rockefeller pressed his state legislature to make fallout shelters mandatory in new homes and buildings. Shelter advocates argued that besides saving lives in a war, civil-defense measures would deter an enemy attack.

These claims failed to sway President Eisenhower or the American public. Eisenhower balked at the immense expense and dubious value of shelter construction. If individuals wanted to build their own shelters, he told aides, they should do so. The government should offer advice (like the quaintly named Grandmother's Pantry program of guidelines for stockpiling food) but no funding. Eisenhower insisted that a credible threat of "massive retaliation" remained the best way to deter a Soviet attack.

The public also resisted calls to go underground. Many intellectuals publicly criticized the notion of retreating underground as barbaric, war mongering, or a poor use of money. Ordinary Americans focused on the "gun-thy-neighbor" problem. Journalists, teachers, theologians, and tele-

186

vision scriptwriters speculated over how to handle people without a shelter trying to gain entry into one built by their neighbor or a stranger. Would a shelter owner be justified in shooting intruders? The press printed threats by some of the few people who actually built shelters to blast away at interlopers. By the end of 1960, only about 1,500 home shelters had been constructed.

In 1961, President John F. Kennedy tried to breathe new life into the civil-defense crusade. That May, JFK spoke of shelters as "insurance." In July, he responded to a Soviet threat to drive the Western powers out of Berlin by announcing that he would defend the divided city. He also called on Congress to fund a shelter system. In a crisis mode, Congress appropriated over $200 million for a crash program to identify and stock existing structures as temporary fallout shelters while a new Office of Civil Defense developed a broader program.

Kennedy persuaded the editors of *Life* magazine to rally support for his plan. *Life* devoted its September 15, 1961, issue to promoting shelters, claiming that they could save the lives of 97 percent of all Americans. In December, the Office of Civil Defense printed millions of copies of a pamphlet entitled "Fallout Protection: What to Know and Do About Nuclear Attack." A nuclear war would be "terrible beyond imagination," the writers admitted. Then, in a shift of tone, they assured Americans that with proper precaution, "it need not be a time of despair."

Kennedy endorsed the creation of a vast shelter construction industry and proposed federal funding for community and school shelters. Cheered on by Herman Kahn, physicist Edward Teller ("father of the H-bomb"), and Governor Rockefeller, public agencies placed prototype shelters on display in parks, schools, and at state fairs.

Critics raised many of the old moral objections and argued that only middle- and upper-class homeowners could afford private shelters. Willard Libby, former head of the Atomic Energy Commission, retorted

that a "poor man's shelter" could be built with railroad ties and bags of dirt for less than $100. To prove his point, he constructed a prototype near Los Angeles, only to have it destroyed almost immediately by a brushfire. Atomic scientist turned peace activist Leo Szilard described this incident as "proof not only that there is a God, but that he has a sense of humor."

To Kennedy's consternation, support for a federal shelter program faded in 1962 as the Berlin crisis abated. The whole idea, one critic noted, led to "more introspection than excavation." As talk turned to the basic question of whether survivors' lives would be worth living, shelter advocates recanted. In January 1962, *Life* retracted its earlier claim that civil defense could save nearly all Americans. Shelters, the magazine now advised, "would somewhat increase the chances of survival" under "certain ghastly circumstances." The New York legislature, which in November 1961 adopted Governor Rockefeller's plan for mandatory shelters in new buildings, reversed course a few months later when the press reported that several state politicians had financial ties to construction companies. Congress rejected Kennedy's proposal that the federal government underwrite the cost of school and community shelters. Not even the brief terror stoked by the Cuban missile crisis of October 1962 revived interest in civil defense. With the signing of the limited nuclear test ban treaty in 1963, most Americans turned their attention away from the issue of civil defense. As of 1965, private homeowners had built only about 200,000 fallout shelters, most of them little more than reinforced corners of existing basements.

In 1982, as part of his plan to confront the Soviet Union, President Reagan revived talk of bomb shelters. He claimed—incorrectly—that the Soviets had invested heavily in civil defense in order to survive a nuclear war. Deputy Undersecretary of Defense T. K. Jones predicted that the United States could easily protect its population and recover quickly from an all-out nuclear war if people simply took time to "dig a hole, cover it with a couple of doors, and then throw three feet of dirt on top. . . ." Everybody, he proclaimed, is "going to make it if there are enough shovels to go around."

Again, the public balked at the notion of going underground. Jones's remarks provoked congressional hearings, angry editorials, and a revived antinuclear movement. Jonathan Schell's 1982 bestseller, *The Fate of the Earth*, retold what would happen if a hydrogen bomb hit New York. In 1983, 100 million viewers tuned into an ABC docudrama, *The Day After,* that portrayed the gruesome aftermath of a nuclear war in a midwestern town. The public's refusal to embrace civil defense prompted Reagan to shift direction in favor of an antimissile system that he called the Strategic Defense Initiative, and that critics dubbed Star Wars.

Until the 2001 terrorist attacks on American soil, civil defense had faded as an issue. President George W. Bush then revived the antimissile program as a pillar of his defense agenda. The president also created an Office of Homeland Security to defend against both terrorists and "rogue states" armed with atomic, biological, or chemical weapons. The next step, some have speculated, may be a call for construction of underground shelters.

In the summer of 1962, the Cubans believed that another American-sponsored invasion of their island might be launched at any time. Their fears were realistic: the Defense Department had already drafted plans for a second, larger attack on Cuba. In July, Raul Castro, Fidel's brother and Cuba's minister of defense, visited Moscow and pleaded for Soviet help against the CIA's Operation Mongoose. In response to this plea, Khrushchev supplied Cuba with intermediate-range ballistic missiles (IRBMs) and the technicians to operate them. The missiles were capable of delivering nuclear warheads to targets in the eastern third of the United States. By this time, the Soviets had also stationed manned bombers and an estimated ten thousand to forty thousand troops in Cuba to repel another invasion.

Missiles offered little effective protection against the small-scale harassment of Operation Mongoose, but the weapons served Soviet interests in several ways. They retaliated against the United States, which had stationed its own IRBMs, aimed at the Soviet Union, in Turkey. The weapons would probably make Castro feel safer and more grateful than ever for Moscow's help. Most of all, Khrushchev believed that sending the missiles to Cuba had little cost. They really had not increased the threat to the United States, a fact noted at the height of the crisis by Secretary of Defense McNamara. "A missile is a missile," he said at the time. "It makes no difference if you are killed by a missile fired from the Soviet Union or from Cuba." Applying the same reasoning, Khrushchev did not expect that the United States would risk world war to force the missiles out.

Khrushchev did not reckon on America's obsession with Cuba and the emphasis that would be placed on the Cuban missile crisis as the fall congressional campaigns approached election day. Even before Kennedy knew the exact extent of the missile buildup, some Republicans, led by Senator Kenneth Keating of New York, claimed that the Soviets had installed IRBMs capable of launching a nuclear attack at any moment. (Keating's information came from a group of anti-

Castro Cubans.) On October 10, 1962, Keating declared that the Soviets in Cuba had the "power to hurl rockets into the American heartland." Fearful of a public outcry and of charges that the Democrats were "soft," Congress passed a resolution promising "by whatever means may be necessary, including the use of arms . . . to prevent in Cuba the creation or use of an externally supported military capability endangering the security of the United States."

On the night of October 15, the CIA developed photographs taken by a U-2 spy plane that showed the construction fifteen miles south of Havana of a launching site for missiles with a range of about two thousand miles. The president saw the pictures at nine o'clock the next morning and exploded, saying that he had been "taken" by the Soviets, who had assured him in September that only defensive anti-aircraft missiles would be situated in Cuba. The missiles had to be removed, he said. Otherwise, the United States would be vulnerable to attack, the public would be terrified, and "Ken Keating will probably be the next president of the United States."

An executive committee consisting of the administration's principal foreign policy and defense officials met secretly over the next twelve days. Their task was to force the Soviets to back down without igniting a world war. Robert Kennedy chaired most of the meetings. The president attended some of them, but he usually kept quiet to allow uninhibited deliberations. The

In October 1962, U.S. ambassador to the United Nations Adlai Stevenson presents to the Security Council photographs showing Soviet missile installations in Cuba. / © Bettmann/CORBIS

president was keenly aware of the historic significance of the executive committee meetings, and he ordered secret tape recordings of the proceedings. When the tapes were made public in the 1990s, they revealed Kennedy's probing intelligence. Throughout the crisis, the president and his brother sought the removal of the Soviet missiles without resorting to war. From the beginning, the participants agreed that the missiles presented an unacceptable threat. Allowing them to stay in Cuba would represent a humiliating setback for an administration committed to waging the Cold War more aggressively than the apparently cautious Eisenhower had.

Although the advisers were united in their refusal to tolerate the missiles, they were divided on tactics. They weighed the risks and potential opportunities offered by a blockade of Cuba or air strikes against the missile installations. As the discussions proceeded, a majority of the executive committee members, prodded by Robert Kennedy, began to endorse the idea of a quarantine of Cuba as a way of forcing the Soviets to remove the missiles. The committee eventually recommended a blockade.

By Sunday, October 21, 1962, the Washington press corps was abuzz with speculation. On Monday, the blockade began; 108 U.S. Navy ships patrolled the Atlantic Ocean and the Caribbean Sea, intercepting and inspecting the cargo of any vessel bound for Cuba to make certain it was not carrying offensive weapons. At 7 P.M. that evening, Kennedy appeared on television to deliver one of the most somber speeches any president had ever given. He announced the existence of the CIA photographs, explaining that they showed "a series of offensive missile sites . . . now in preparation on that imprisoned island."

Americans anxiously waited out the next several days. When the president received news that Soviet ships were steaming toward the navy's blockade line, the tension seemed too much to bear. Robert Kennedy remembered that his brother's face was drawn, his eyes squinting in anguish. A few hours later, however, navy officials radioed that the Soviet vessels had stopped without challenging the blockade. The U.S. navy allowed only tankers and passenger ships through. As a symbolic gesture, sailors from two U.S. destroyers boarded a cargo ship chartered by the Soviets. Finding no forbidden weapons, the navy allowed the ship to pass through to Cuba.

The blockade succeeded in preventing movement of additional weapons to Cuba because neither the Americans nor the Soviets wanted the situation to deteriorate into war. The quarantine did not, however, settle the matter of the missile sites already under construction. In a series of telegrams to Khrushchev and in several secret, face-to-face meetings in Washington between U.S. and Soviet representatives, Kennedy pressured the Soviet leader to demolish the sites and remove the missiles already in Cuba. At one point, a Soviet representative in Washington offered to remove the missiles and bombers. Khrushchev confirmed the offer in a telegram, but he added a condition: he would act only if the United States removed its IRBMs from Turkey. Kennedy ignored the offer of an exchange, and he also did not respond when Khrushchev seemed to reverse himself in a later telegram. Instead, Kennedy repeated that the Soviet missiles had to be eliminated, and he focused on Moscow's initial offer to remove them. Faced with overwhelming American military might and astonished that the young American president would actually risk a nuclear war over a largely symbolic issue, Khrushchev capitulated. He wired Kennedy that he had instructed his officers to "discontinue construction of the . . . facilities, to dismantle them, and to return them to the Soviet Union."

It appeared to relieved Americans that Kennedy had won a great victory. In the aftermath of the crisis, the United States quietly removed its missiles in Turkey. Washington also promised never to invade Cuba. In return, the Soviets took their manned bombers out of Cuba and pledged never to install offensive weapons on the island.

Fidel Castro felt betrayed by Khrushchev's surrender; the suspension of Operation Mongoose a few days after the end of the crisis did little to mollify him. He believed that the United States still wished him dead and that now he had no protector. His anxieties had a factual basis. The next spring, the State Department created a secret Cuban Coordinating Committee to bring down Castro's government. In October 1963, the committee approved sabotage operations against twenty-two targets on the island.

During the crisis and for years afterward, Kennedy won high praise for his grace under pressure and the way he sifted conflicting advice and made decisions. By skillful diplomatic initiatives that allowed Khrushchev room to maneuver, he forced the Soviet Union to retreat without a fight. The eventual removal of American missiles from Turkey offered the Soviets a small satisfaction. Yet Kennedy had risked nuclear war to show his toughness toward Khrushchev and Castro. The missiles in Cuba never threatened the security of the United States to the extent the president had indicated at the time. As his trusted aide Theodore Sorensen later observed, "[T]he United States was already living under the shadow of Soviet missiles, which could be launched from Soviet territory or submarines, and, therefore, there was no real change in our situation that required any kind of drastic action."

The Cuban missile crisis sobered both the Americans and the Soviets, encouraging officials and ordinary citizens in both countries to look for ways to avoid future confrontations. In the aftermath of the showdown, relations between the superpowers began to improve. In the next six months, the two governments agreed to install a direct communications link—a Teletype hot line—connecting the Kremlin with the White House. Kennedy abandoned some of his harsh anticommunist rhetoric and urged other Americans to do the same. Americans and Soviets had a mutual interest in ending the arms race, the president declared: "We all breathe the same air. We all cherish our children's future."

In 1963, the United States and the Soviet Union signed the first limited test ban treaty, ending the aboveground nuclear tests that had resumed in 1961. The treaty banned explosions of atomic devices in the atmosphere, in outer space, and under the ocean. The two sides promised to work on a more comprehensive treaty banning underground nuclear explosions as well.

New Frontiers at Home

On the domestic front, the Kennedy administration tried to shake the torpor of the Eisenhower years by promoting an expanding American economy. Kennedy's efforts to improve economic conditions began slowly, but they gained momentum over time. Administration officials initially resisted endorsing efforts to redistribute wealth, fearing that such programs would provoke antagonism from wealthy and middle-class Americans. At first, the Kennedy administration paid more attention to the economic and social concerns of the white middle class than to the deprivation of the poor or the hardships endured by people of color. In 1963, the last year of his life, Kennedy adopted a more liberal position, calling for aggressive government action to eliminate poverty.

The president's curiosity and his wide reading eventually made him alert to the previously hidden crises of widespread poverty and the degradation of the environment. Kennedy and his principal advisers had come of age politically in the late 1940s and 1950s—a time when leaders were expected to stress the positive aspects of American society as it confronted the Soviet Union in the Cold War. In the early 1960s, however, Americans looked more critically at their country's shortcomings. Kennedy had spoken eloquently during the 1960 presidential campaign about the need for vigorous action both at home and abroad, and although he did not develop many specific details for a domestic program, it was to his credit that he grew intellectually as president by recognizing the flaws and inequities in American society. By late 1962, the Kennedy administration had begun to lay the foundations of the major domestic reforms that would be undertaken by his successor.

When Kennedy promised in 1960 to get the country moving again, to a large extent he was promising to engineer an economic recovery. Economic growth had averaged about 3 percent annually from 1953 to 1960, but the averages masked wild yearly swings, from declines of 2 percent in some years to growth of 5 percent in others. And although prices had increased little during the Eisenhower years, the country had suffered sharp recessions in 1954, 1958, and 1960. Rising unemployment had helped Kennedy win some important industrial states in the Midwest in the presidential election of 1960.

Kennedy's efforts to bolster economic growth worked slowly, but eventually the economy expanded robustly. Rather than stimulating the economy directly by creating government programs to aid depressed areas, as liberal advisers urged, the Kennedy administration decided that a safer course was to adjust taxes to encourage private investment. In April 1961, Kennedy urged Congress to eliminate the complicated system of tax deductions, or loopholes, that had arisen since 1945. At the same time, he stated that businesses would invest more if Congress enacted investment tax credits to encourage businesses to modernize their plants and equipment. At first, the proposed legislation received little attention because concern over the Bay of Pigs and heightened tensions with the Soviets preoccupied Congress. When Congress resumed work on the tax issue in the summer of 1963, it preserved most of the tax loopholes while giving more preferences to corporations than Kennedy had originally requested. The revised bill finally passed in the early months of the Johnson administration.

The economy improved overall in the Kennedy years, though its performance fell short of what had been promised. In contrast to the fluctuations of the 1950s, economic growth was steady at 3 percent per year. Unemployment began to decline from 6 percent to under 5 percent. In 1961 and 1962, inflation, as measured by the consumer price index (CPI), fell to a nearly negligible rate of 1 percent per year. Business leaders were reassured by the administration's resistance to policies designed to redistribute wealth and income.

Public concern grew over the plight of one-fifth of the American population—approximately 25 million people—living in poverty. Largely forgotten since the end of World War II, the poorest Americans lived in decaying cities and remote rural areas. Eighty percent of them were white; the remainder were ethnic minorities. The poorest of the poor were people over the age of sixty-five living in rural areas. The Democrats of the 1950s and early 1960s, heirs of the New Deal but eager for acceptance from the business community, had mostly ignored their needs. In 1962, Michael Harrington, a former social worker, challenged this indifference in his book *The Other America*. Harrington decried a vicious cycle in which "there are people in the affluent society who are poor because they are poor; and who stay poor because they are poor." He spoke directly to the country's leaders, explaining to them, "the fate of the poor hangs on the decisions of the better off."

The Other America made a deep impression on intellectuals and opinion makers. Kennedy found in Harrington's book a troubling critique of his own timid efforts to revitalize the American economy and to make the New Frontier reach everyone in the country. He asked the chair of the Council of Economic Advisers to develop plans for a more vigorous assault on poverty. Before a program was ready, however, Kennedy was murdered.

The Push for Civil Rights

The popular movement to eliminate discrimination based on race reached its peak in the 1960s. By the end of the decade, the efforts of thousands of African Americans and their white allies ended the degrading system of legal segregation. America underwent a revolution in race relations. This so-called Second Reconstruction altered the American racial landscape even more than the first Reconstruction, which took place in the decade after the Civil War. African Americans had mobilized against segregation for years; by the 1960s, their efforts commanded the attention of most white Americans, provoking both support and resistance. As public officials gradually realized how important it was to end legally sanctioned segregation, the Kennedy administration began to take steps to aid the effort.

In 1961, six years after the Supreme Court ruled that segregation in the public schools had to end "with all deliberate speed," separation of the races remained a fact of life across the nation, especially in southern and border regions (including Washington, D.C.). Not only were many public schools and universities closed to blacks, so were many public transportation vehicles, bathroom facilities, and parks, as well as privately owned restaurants and hotels. The National Association for the Advancement of Colored People (NAACP), the most prominent of the black civil rights organizations, had sought to build on the victory in the landmark *Brown* v. *Board of Education* case by persuading the courts to order quicker desegregation and encouraging Congress to pass civil rights legislation protecting black voters. The NAACP desegregated some school districts and saw passage of a civil rights law in the late 1950s, but progress was painfully slow. As noted in Chapter 4, President Eisenhower did not speak out against racial discrimination, and he only belatedly ordered federal troops to Little Rock, Arkansas, in 1957 to ensure the safe admission of black students to that city's Central High School. The modest Civil Rights Act passed that year did not outlaw discrimination in public or privately owned accommodations as African Americans had hoped it would. After the sit-in at a Greensboro, North Carolina, lunch counter in 1960, the sit-in movement spread, along with marches, demonstrations, and other protests against legally sanctioned discrimination. Many of these actions involved the newly formed Student Non-Violent Coordinating Committee (SNCC). Participation in demonstrations, sit-ins, and mass marches sent waves of energy through African American young people. "You find out," said one, "the difference between being dead and alive." Poor blacks were thrilled to see African American college students take the lead. "We were all excited about these young people," a woman recalled, "because they treated us so nice." Martin Luther King, Jr., said that the civil rights workers were "trying to save the soul of America."

As a senator, John Kennedy had taken few positions on racial discrimination. During the presidential campaign of 1960, he became somewhat bolder, but he continued to walk a narrow line on civil rights, hoping to retain the support of traditional white southern Democrats while also winning the votes of blacks. He refrained from endorsing new civil rights laws but condemned Eisenhower for his timidity in not putting the moral authority of the presidency on the side of victims of racial prejudice. The president, Kennedy said, could end discrimination in public housing "with the stroke of a pen" by signing an executive order. He promised that his protection of minorities would be more vigorous, and blacks believed that the Kennedy brothers' telephone calls on behalf of the jailed Martin Luther King, Jr., signaled sympathy with their cause.

At first, however, Kennedy's administration did little to advance civil rights. Particularly galling to those blacks who had supported him was Kennedy's failure throughout 1961 to sign an executive order ending discrimination in public housing. By the end of the year, the Congress of Racial Equality (CORE), a rival of the NAACP that favored more militant action, sought to shame Kennedy into making good on his promise. CORE organized the Ink for Jack campaign, in which supporters of civil rights mailed thousands of ballpoint pens to the White House. Eventually, in 1962, Kennedy signed an executive order outlawing racial discrimination in public housing.

The Ink for Jack campaign represented only a small part of the civil rights effort. Many ordinary citizens believed that much more was required to achieve civil rights and that the government would not act unless pressured from below. In the spring of 1961, blacks and whites joined together in a campaign of civil disobedience to force the federal government to take a more aggressive stand. In early May, two busloads of blacks and whites left Washington, D.C., bound for New Orleans, with interim stops scheduled along the way throughout the South. Calling themselves Freedom Riders, the travelers demanded the enforcement of a 1960 Supreme Court decision striking down state laws prohibiting mixed seating on interstate buses and requiring public accommodations along the way to maintain whites-only and colored-only facilities. In practice, such laws meant nonwhites could not enter most restaurants or relieve themselves in most public restrooms.

At first, the Freedom Riders encountered icy stares from white people and found bus stations mysteriously closed when they arrived. This silent resistance was difficult enough, but when the travelers reached Alabama, the opposition proved much more dangerous. In Anniston, Alabama, a mob of two hundred whites attacked one bus with pipes, slashed the tires, and demanded that the Freedom Riders leave the bus. Although the local police escorted the bus and its passengers out of town, the gang continued its pursuit in fifty cars. After the bus's tires went completely flat, the mob surrounded it, and someone threw a bomb through the window. When the Freedom Riders ran out of the bus, the mob beat them. One white Freedom Rider was punched in the face while others stomped on his chest until he lost consciousness. A Howard University student on the bus said, after being hit in the head, "I see what Martin Luther King means when he says suffering *is* redemption."

When the buses reached Montgomery, the police gave a howling mob of five hundred to one thousand fifteen to thirty minutes to run rampant. They first went after TV and newsweekly crews, smashing their cameras. Then they turned their fury on the Freedom Riders. Women screamed, "Kill the nigger-loving son of a bitch," at the first white man to leave the bus. John Siegenthaler, President Kennedy's personal emissary, tried to help two women escape. He was then knocked unconscious and lay on the ground for thirty minutes because no white ambulance would pick him up. FBI agents also did not intervene. Siegenthaler later complained, "[I]t galls me to think that the FBI stood there and watched me get clubbed."

This inexcusable refusal by public authorities to protect U.S. citizens goaded Kennedy into action. The violence had been photographed and shown in newspapers and on television, shocking many Americans. Scenes of the howling mob attacking unarmed Freedom Riders also offered a propaganda boost to the Soviet Union on the eve of the Vienna summit. The president, sickened by the sight of this violence, ordered U.S. marshals to Alabama to protect the Freedom Riders, and the Justice Department enjoined racist organizations from further interference with the buses.

At the same time, the reluctance of the administration to take decisive action was evident. Only 24 percent of Americans said that they supported the

During the violence against the Freedom Riders in Montgomery, Alabama, Attorney General Robert F. Kennedy consults with Byron White, a Justice Department official he had sent to Montgomery to head a force of four hundred U.S. marshals to restore calm. / © Bettmann/CORBIS

Freedom Riders, but 70 percent said that they approved of Kennedy's sending marshals to keep the peace in Montgomery. No matter how offensive the attacks on Freedom Riders became, Washington officials remained reluctant to antagonize southern whites, who had been an essential element of the Democratic Party's coalition. Robert Kennedy asked for a cooling-off period of 100 days to let tempers subside. James Farmer, executive director of CORE, acidly replied, "We've been cooling off for one hundred years. If we got any cooler we'd be in the deep freeze." Accordingly, CORE ignored advice to stop the demonstrations and continued to arrange Freedom Rides for the rest of the summer of 1961. Federal marshals offered protection against physical assaults on the buses and riders. At the same time, Robert Kennedy sought unsuccessfully to persuade the Freedom Ride organizers that voter registration, rather than public demonstrations, would do more for the cause of civil rights.

Like many other white northerners, the Kennedy brothers gradually developed greater concern over racial discrimination as the demonstrations continued. They expressed their greatest commitment to civil rights in September 1962, during a confrontation with Mississippi governor Ross Barnett over the enrollment of James Meredith, a black man, at the state's university in Oxford. Meredith, an air force veteran, had applied for admission to the University of Mississippi in January 1961. A high school graduate and resident of Mississippi, he was entitled to admission to the state university, but it refused to enroll him. He appealed the decision in federal court, and on September 13, 1962, Supreme Court Justice Hugo Black, a native of Alabama and former member of the Ku Klux Klan, ordered the university to admit him. Mississippi's state legislature responded by making Governor Barnett a temporary registrar of the university. Playing to strong racist sentiments throughout the state, Barnett vowed not to surrender to "the evil and illegal forces of tyranny." He promised that Meredith would never register.

The president and attorney general spoke several times on the telephone to Barnett. For a while, it appeared that a compromise had been arranged: the governor would save face by resisting the federal marshals who had been sent to Oxford to escort Meredith into the university, but Meredith would be allowed to register later. That deal fell through, however, as hundreds of whites converged on the college town, intent on chasing Meredith away. When Meredith and his escort of federal marshals finally reached the campus, over one thousand white demonstrators blocked their path, screaming, "Go to Cuba, nigger lovers, go to Cuba!" They threw rocks and bottles at the line of marshals. Then several members of the mob, now numbering over two thousand, opened fire with shotguns and rifles, killing an English reporter and wounding a marshal and a U.S. border patrolman.

In the midst of this violence, Kennedy addressed the nation. He spent more time calming the fears of white Mississippians than explaining the evils of racial discrimination. He appealed to that state's "great tradition of honor and courage, won on the field of battle." He urged the university's students, most of whom had not been involved in the demonstrations, to continue to stay on the sidelines, because "the eyes of the nation and the world are upon you and upon all of us." At the same time, Kennedy ordered 23,000 army troops to Oxford to quell the rioting and to ensure that Meredith could enroll for classes and study in relative peace. Five hundred troops remained stationed in Oxford until Meredith graduated in June 1963. Martin Luther King, Jr., thought the Kennedy brothers had helped the cause of civil rights but that they did not fully appreciate how much work remained to be done.

In 1963, Martin Luther King, Jr., sought to increase the momentum of the civil rights movement. In May, he helped organize demonstrations for the end of segregation in Birmingham, Alabama. The protesters found the perfect enemy in Birmingham's police commissioner, Eugene "Bull" Connor, whose beefy features and snarling demeanor made him seem a living caricature of a racist southern sheriff. Connor's police used clubs, dogs, and fire hoses to chase and harass the demonstrators. Kennedy watched the police dogs in action on television—along with the rest of the country—and confessed that the brutality made him sick. He later observed, "the civil rights movement should thank God for Bull Connor. He's helped it as much as Abraham Lincoln." The president dispatched the head of the Justice Department's civil rights division to Birmingham to try to work out an arrangement between King's demonstrators and local business leaders that would permit desegregation of lunch counters, drinking fountains, and bathrooms. The president made several calls to the business leaders himself, and they finally agreed to his terms.

Birmingham, Alabama, police use dogs against civil rights marchers, May 1963. / AP/Wide World

On June 10, 1963, during a national address focusing on civil rights, Kennedy acknowledged that the nation faced a moral crisis. He rejected the notion that the United States could be the land of the free "except for the Negroes." Reversing his earlier reluctance to request civil rights legislation, he announced that he would send Congress a major civil rights bill. The law would guarantee service to all Americans, regardless of race, at all establishments open to the public—hotels, restaurants, theaters, retail stores, and the like. It would also grant the federal government greater authority to pursue lawsuits against segregation in public schools and universities and would increase the Justice Department's powers to protect the voting rights of racial minorities.

African American leaders found Kennedy's commitment to legislation encouraging, but they wanted assurances that the president would follow through. To maintain pressure on Congress, several civil rights leaders revived the idea, first presented in 1941, of a march on Washington to promote civil rights. The Kennedy administration was not in favor of such a march. Already public opinion polls indicated that a plurality of voters thought the president was pushing integration too fast, and Kennedy worried about the political cost of endorsing the black push for equality.

The March on Washington went forward anyway, on August 28, 1963. A crowd of about 300,000 people, mostly black but including people of all races, filled the mall facing the Lincoln Memorial. Led by folk singer Joan Baez, they sang the spiritual "We Shall Overcome," which had become the unofficial anthem of the civil rights movement. They heard other songs and listened to speeches. John Lewis, a leading Freedom Rider, prepared a militant address that was toned down by march organizers before he delivered it. He spoke of "blacks" rather than "Negroes," a change in terminology that took hold over the next few years.

The climax came when Martin Luther King, Jr., offered to the watching world an inspiring vision of the future: "I have a dream that one day all God's children, black men and white men, Jews and Gentiles, Protestants and Catholics, will be able to join hands and sing in the words of the old Negro spiritual, 'Free at last! Free at last! Thank God Almighty, we are free at last!'" Although he had invoked these images many times before, much of white America was listening to him for the first time. President Kennedy watched on television and told an aide in admiration, "He's damn good." But within three months, Kennedy was dead, and the civil rights legislation advocated by the March on Washington needed the support of a new president.

Scientific, Technological, and Cultural Changes in the Early 1960s

Americans had developed a new appreciation for the benefits of technology by the early 1960s. They believed that much of their prosperity came from exciting new developments in electronics, space research, medicine, and transportation. By the time Kennedy was murdered in November 1963, however, fears had grown about the potential negative impact of modern science and engineering on everyday life. In April 1961, days before the defeat at the Bay of Pigs, a Soviet cosmonaut, Yuri Gagarin, became the first man to orbit the earth. Americans felt ashamed and frightened. The shock of the 1957 Sputnik launch was still fresh in everyone's mind. Members of the joint congressional committee on space demanded that the Kennedy administration make good on its campaign pledge to restore the country's flagging prestige. One member of the committee told the director of the National Aeronautics and Space Administration (NASA), "[T]ell me how much money you need, and this committee will authorize all you need." A newspaper concluded that Soviet successes in space had "cost the nation heavily in prestige" and that "neutral nations may come to believe that the wave of the future is Russian."

In this atmosphere, the Kennedy administration wanted to act quickly. NASA's own reports indicated that the United States led the Soviet Union in every area of space science, but in the tense aftermath of Gagarin's flight and the Bay of Pigs, Americans wanted a definitive victory in the space race. The president told a press conference that he was tired of the United States being second best. He made Vice President Lyndon Johnson chair of the Space

Council and instructed him to look for ways of "beating the Russians." In late May, the president went before Congress to announce a goal of "landing a man on the moon, and returning him safely to earth . . . before the decade is out." Privately, Kennedy expressed doubts about whether the race to the moon would yield many scientific breakthroughs, but he remained convinced that getting to the moon before the Soviets carried its own rewards.

To fulfill this lunar mission, Congress encouraged NASA to create the Apollo program. Johnson made certain that friends in Texas and nearby states received the lion's share of the scientific and construction contracts for Apollo. The Apollo complex followed the contours of the Gulf of Mexico, from Texas to Florida, providing jobs, income, and a stake in federal projects to traditionally poor but fast-growing southern states. Johnson called it a "second Reconstruction" for the area. In four years, the number of workers employed directly by NASA had grown from 6,000 to 60,000. Another 411,000 scientists, engineers, technicians, and clerical staff flocked to the region to work for private firms under contract to NASA.

While the Apollo scientists worked feverishly preparing for the moon mission, NASA tried to top Gagarin's orbital flight. In the summer of 1961, two astronauts, Alan Shepard and Virgil Grissom, made space flights lasting about fifteen minutes in capsules launched by Atlas ICBMs. Then, in February 1962, ten months after Gagarin's orbit, Marine Lieutenant Colonel John Glenn was strapped into Friendship 7 and blasted into orbit. In the next five hours, Glenn made three trips around the globe. His success buoyed Americans, who had seen too many events that seemed to point to a decline in U.S. power, influence, and scientific preeminence. Glenn was a guest at the White House and enjoyed a ticker-tape parade down Manhattan's Broadway, the likes of which had not been seen since Charles Lindbergh returned in triumph after his solo flight from New York to Paris in 1927.

Americans also began to focus on another concern, which would become increasingly important in later years: the quality of the environment. In 1962, science writer Rachel Carson published *Silent Spring*, a lengthy indictment of the damage done to the environment by the pesticide industry. Use of synthetic pesticides, a product of technology developed during World War II, had increased 400 percent between 1947 and 1962. The United States now sprayed 650 million pounds of deadly chemicals per year over farms, gardens, and homes. As Carson wrote, these poisons did not distinguish among their victims and "should not be called insecticides but biocides." The chemicals remained in the environment, filtering through the soil, entering the groundwater, and eventually finding their way into the food chain, where they contaminated animals and humans alike.

Carson's work alarmed the American public. About 200,000 copies of her book were snatched up within a month, and members of Congress and newspapers were deluged with letters demanding federal action. Kennedy met Carson, and he instructed the President's Science Advisory Committee (PSAC) to study the pesticide problem. In May 1963, the PSAC reported that pesticides had done extensive damage to fish, birds, and other wildlife and that traces of toxic chemicals had been found in humans. The report urged elimination of the use of toxic pesticides. Pesticide manufacturers opposed the recommendations, but seven years later, the newly formed Environmental Protection Agency (EPA) banned the use of DDT, the most harmful pesticide, in the United States. A new environmental movement arose in the West in response to the explosive growth of cities. Western environmentalists tended to be city people who wanted to protect the wilderness areas where they sought recreation and renewal. In the 1960s, they often focused on issues involving water and the wilderness. The Sierra Club, led by David Brower, successfully fought the construction of a dam at Echo Park on the Colorado River, which would have flooded part of Dinosaur National Monument in Utah, and managed to prevent the construction of dams that would have flooded parts of the Grand Canyon. Their victories, however, were sometimes Pyrrhic.

Instead of building a dam at Echo Park, for example, the Bureau of Reclamation built one that flooded Glen Canyon, a place of such extraordinary grandeur that its loss would become the cardinal symbol of environmental degradation to a later, more militant generation of wilderness advocates. And when the Sierra Club argued against the Grand Canyon dams, they insisted that developers could instead garner electrical generating capacity by building coal-fired and nuclear power plants. As a consequence, the Black Mesa on the Arizona Navajo and Hopi reservations was strip-mined, and the coal-burning Navajo Power Plant was built at Page, Arizona. Such tradeoffs convinced more and more advocates of environmental protection that they would have to take a more systemic, ecological view of their cause.

For all of the excited talk about the new decade of the 1960s representing a sharp break with the supposed dullness of the 1950s, people's personal lives changed slowly. Theodore Sorensen, Kennedy's aide, joked that "this administration is going to do for sex what the last one did for golf." The first birth-control pill was approved for use in May 1960. A sexual revolution was on its way, but it took its time gathering momentum. The same year, a poll of college women reported that over 50 percent of them were virgins. The same poll reported that 70 percent of male college students expected to marry virgins. Homosexual acts were against the law in nearly all states and municipalities. Abortion was illegal in every state. The words *rape* and *abortion* could not be spoken on NBC news. The *Saturday Evening Post* ran a story on abortion in 1961, and it received hundreds of letters condemning both abortion and the *Post*'s decision to carry the story.

Some attitudes toward sex, childhood, and family life did change in the early 1960s. In 1962, Helen Gurley Brown published *Sex and the Single Girl,* a manifesto for an end to the sexual double standard. She then took over the editorship of *Cosmopolitan* and altered its format to stress the pleasure of sex for young women. About the same time, Hugh Hefner, who had started *Playboy* in 1952, began publishing "The Playboy Philosophy" as a monthly column. No one would have mistaken Hefner's opinions about the joys of sex and the repressive outlook of traditional sexual morality for the deep thoughts of classic or contemporary philosophers, but he did capture a moment. The young women who read *Cosmopolitan* and the young men who looked at *Playboy* sensed that some of the truths of togetherness and suburban happiness of the 1950s were sheer hypocrisy.

It became fashionable in the Kennedy years to puncture the pretensions of the powerful. In 1961, Joseph Heller published *Catch-22*. This comic send-up of the absurdities and petty abuses of power in military life in World War II attracted a huge following among young readers. The phrase *Catch-22*, with its sense that many, if not most, rules in large organizations were developed by fools to humiliate decent people, caught on with young people. The next year, Ken Kesey published *One Flew Over the Cuckoo's Nest*, a novel set in a mental hospital where a brutal staff enforced a series of absurd rules. Kesey's young readers responded to his outrage at the arbitrary exercise of raw power.

The 1950s had seen its share of criticism of the banality of suburban life. Social critics had nearly ignored cities in that decade, possibly because few people thought cities interesting. But now cities seemed once more to hold out promise—if only the heavy hand of officialdom could be lifted. In 1961, Jane Jacobs published *The Death and Life of Great American Cities*. The book celebrated cities, not suburbs, as the centers of vibrant civilization. But Jacobs assailed generations of city planners, who had drained the natural vitality of the American urban landscape since the 1920s with their grandiose projects. She wrote that urban renewal had leveled living communities and replaced them with spiritually dead blocks of high-rise sameness where no one knew anyone. Her vision of urban blight sounded a warning for the decade. While many Americans appreciated Kennedy's optimism and sense of managerial expertise, more unruly, ecstatic, and rambunctious spirits were spreading. In the later years of the 1960s, this new exuberance, so challenging to authority, became a central feature of American life. (See Chapter 8.)

Assassination

Kennedy's endorsement of the civil rights movement during the fall of 1963 complicated his re-election chances in the South. As in 1960, a key state was Texas, where the Democrats feuded over policies and patronage. Governor John Connally, leader of the Texas Democrats' conservative faction, opposed Kennedy's plans for a civil rights bill. The governor was not on speaking terms with the state's liberal senator, Ralph Yarborough, and both Connally and Yarborough distrusted Vice President Lyndon Johnson, whose shifting positions did not satisfy either liberals or conservatives. Seeking to bolster his own standing in his home state, Johnson persuaded several prominent national officeholders, including the president, to visit Texas in the fall.

When U.N. ambassador Adlai Stevenson spoke in Dallas in October, he encountered ugly demonstrations organized by vocal conservatives. Handbills appeared with pictures of Kennedy labeled "Wanted for Treason." The mob swarmed around Stevenson, someone hit him in the face with a sign, and only the protection of a police squad got him out of the hall safely. The attack on

Stevenson was only the most recent in a series of violent protests against the administration. The Secret Service had compiled thirty-four credible threats on the president's life from the Dallas area since 1961. Many came from those who espoused extreme right-wing views, but the Secret Service also documented threats from leftists, anti-Castro Cubans, Puerto Rican nationalists, black militants, and several mentally disturbed individuals.

One month after Stevenson's encounter with the mob of Dallas demonstrators, on November 21, 1963, Kennedy flew to San Antonio with Jacqueline to begin a three-day swing through the Lone Star State. Johnson joined them later that day in Houston and the next day in Fort Worth, where the president addressed businesspeople about the importance of Texas defense contractors to the nation's military strength. At 11:20 A.M., Air Force One took off from Fort Worth for the brief flight to Dallas. The presidential jet landed in Dallas at noon, and Governor Connally, his wife Nellie, and President and Mrs. Kennedy entered an open-air limousine for a trip downtown, where Kennedy was scheduled to speak before another business group. The motorcade route had been published days before to ensure the largest crowd possible. Thousands lined the route, and most were smiling, cheering, and waving. Mrs. Connally told the president, "You can't say Dallas doesn't love you." Kennedy replied, "That's obvious." Seconds later, at 12:33 P.M., three shots rang out. Two bullets hit the president; one passed through his throat and the other exploded through the back of his head. In shock, Mrs. Kennedy rose and climbed onto the rear hood of the car. The motorcade raced to nearby Parkland Hospital, where Kennedy was pronounced dead at 1:00 P.M.

Later that afternoon, police arrested twenty-four-year-old Lee Harvey Oswald in a movie theater. A Marine Corps veteran and lonely drifter, Oswald had recently returned from a long stay in the Soviet Union. He worked in the Texas Book Depository, the building from which the shots were fired. Oswald had flitted among political causes of the left and right, making it difficult for later investigators to determine his motives. He had contacted the Cuban embassy in Mexico City earlier in 1963, but the Cubans had refused to speak with him, fearing that he was a provocateur sent by the CIA. To complicate matters further, Oswald had family ties to a Mafia member who had spoken of his desire to kill Kennedy in order to halt the Justice Department's investigations of organized crime.

The chances of ever discovering Oswald's true allegiances probably disappeared two days after the Kennedy assassination. That Sunday, most Americans sat glued to television sets, watching hundreds of thousands of grief-stricken mourners file past a closed casket in the Capitol rotunda. When the networks cut away to the basement of the Dallas police station to show Oswald being escorted to another jail, millions of viewers saw nightclub owner Jack Ruby step out of a crowd and kill Oswald with a bullet to the abdomen.

In December 1963, President Johnson appointed a special commission, chaired by Chief Justice Earl Warren, to investigate the assassination. Less than a year later, the Warren Commission filed a report concluding that

Two women stand grief-stricken outside Parkland Hospital in Dallas on the
afternoon of November 22, 1963, after learning of President Kennedy's death.
© Bettmann/CORBIS

Oswald, acting alone, had killed Kennedy. The Warren Commission worked
hastily because it believed a speedy report would still rumors of a conspiracy,
but that did not happen. For years afterward, many Americans, at times a majority of them, believed that a conspiracy was behind Kennedy's murder. The
list of suspected conspirators was varied and shifted from year to year: extreme
conservatives, the Mafia, the CIA, Fidel Castro, conservative Vietnamese, even
Lyndon Johnson. In 1979, a House committee concluded that more than one
person had fired shots at Kennedy's limousine, but FBI scientists rebutted the
committee's findings. In the decades after the Warren Commission's report, little tangible evidence has come to light to demonstrate that its conclusions
were flawed.

The persistence of the belief that Kennedy died at the hands of conspirators represented an effort to make sense out of a shocking act that deeply
shook many Americans' faith in their institutions. In the years following

Kennedy's death, other prominent figures fell to assassins, and shots were fired at other presidents in 1975 and 1981. Within five years of that fateful November afternoon, Americans had come to see their society as dangerous, violent, and led by people who lacked Kennedy's ability to inspire the nation. Many traced the beginning of their sense that America's public institutions did not work properly to the day Kennedy died.

Conclusion

After his death, Americans quickly elevated John Kennedy to martyrdom. His optimism, wit, intelligence, and charm—all of which encouraged the feeling that American society could accomplish anything its people wanted—were snuffed out in an instant. He was only forty-six years old. Within six months of his murder, journalist Theodore White bestowed on his administration the name Camelot. Popularized by the 1962 Broadway musical of that title, the term referred to the mythical kingdom of Arthur and his knights of the Round Table. In this view, Kennedy's 1,037-day administration represented a brief, shining moment during which the nation's political leaders spoke to Americans' finest aspirations.

The reality was more complicated. Kennedy and his advisers had been formed by the experiences of the postwar world. They represented a new generation, nurtured by the Cold War, an activist government, and the military-industrial complex. Skeptical of ideology and serenely self-confident, officials of the Kennedy administration and their circle of friends believed problems could be mastered and managed. That was their strength because it encouraged their curiosity about people, trends, and ideas. They learned from their setbacks and mistakes, and by 1963, their skepticism even extended to the beliefs they expressed in 1960 that the United States could vanquish the Soviet Union through sheer willpower. Their self-confidence offered Americans hope.

Yet the style of cool self-reliance favored by Kennedy and his advisers also betrayed their primary weakness. Their resistance to emotion and passion stunted their ability to empathize with groups that had been excluded from the bounty of American society. The Kennedy administration did more for civil rights than his predecessor had, but its principal efforts in this area came as a result of intense pressure and dramatic events that could not be ignored. On the questions of poverty and the environment, Kennedy took important first steps; whether his administration would have accomplished significantly more if he had lived longer, historians can only speculate. Overall, his domestic program reflected the politics of consensus, much like his predecessor's.

In foreign affairs, he also continued an earlier trend, the reflexive anti-communism of the Cold War, but with a particularly aggressive twist. His propensity for tough confrontation with the Soviets led the world to the brink of nuclear holocaust. Only after the near-disaster of the Cuban missile crisis did he begin to move toward détente.

Advocates of the New Frontier had promised the country a new youth and vigor in the White House, and the Kennedy administration provided these qualities in abundance. It was less successful in offering substance and new solutions. The burden of resolving many problems fell on Lyndon Johnson, a very different man, who was suddenly elevated to the presidency.

F   U   R   T   H   E   R   •   R   E   A   D   I   N   G

On politics and policies in the Kennedy administration, see Maurice Isserman and Michael Kazin, *America Divided: The Civil Wars of the 1960s* (2000); James N. Giglio, *The Presidency of John F. Kennedy* (2003); Robert Caro, *The Years of Lyndon Johnson*, Vol. 3, *Master of the Senate* (2002); Allan Matusow, *The Unraveling of America: A History of Liberalism in the 1960s* (1984); Philip Zelikow and Ernest May, eds., *The Presidential Recordings: John F. Kennedy, The Great Crises* (2001); Richard Reeves, *President Kennedy: Profile in Power* (1993); Thomas C. Reeves, *A Question of Character: A Life of John F. Kennedy* (1991); Theodore Sorensen, *Kennedy* (1965); Arthur M. Schlesinger, Jr., *A Thousand Days* (1966) and *Robert F. Kennedy and His Times* (1978); Theodore H. White, *The Making of the President, 1960* (1961); David Knapp and Kenneth Polk, *Scouting the War on Poverty: Social Reform Politics in the Kennedy Administration* (1971); Robert Dallek, *An Unfinished Life: John F. Kennedy, 1917–1963* (2003). **On Kennedy's assassination,** see Gerald Posner, *Case Closed: Lee Harvey Oswald and the Assassination of JFK* (1993). **On space policy,** see Walter A. McDougall, *. . . The Heavens and the Earth: A Political History of the Space Age* (1985). **On civil rights,** see Taylor Branch, *Parting the Waters: America in the King Years, 1954–1963* (1988) and *Pillar of Fire: America in the King Years, 1963–1965* (1998); David Garrow, *Bearing the Cross: Martin Luther King, Jr., and the Southern Christian Leadership Conference* (1986). **On environmentalism,** see Samuel P. Hays, *Beauty, Health, and Permanence: Environmental Politics in the United States, 1955–85* (1987); Marc Reisner, *Cadillac Desert: The American West and Its Disappearing Water* (1993). **On changing sexual mores,** see Lara V. Marks, *Sexual Chemistry: A History of the Contraceptive Pill* (2001); and Andrea Tone, *Devices and Desires: A History of Contraceptives in America* (2001). **On foreign policy,** see Thomas Zeiler, *Dean Rusk: Defending the American Mission Abroad* (2000); Ernest May and Philip Zelikow, *The Kennedy Tapes: Inside the Kennedy White House During the Kennedy Administration* (2001); Thomas Paterson, *Contesting Castro: The United States and the Triumph of the Cuban Revolution* (1994); Michael Beschloss, *The Crisis Years: Kennedy and Khrushchev 1960–1963* (1991); Montague Kern, Patricia W. Levering, and Ralph B. Levering, *The Kennedy Crises: The Press, the Presidency and Foreign Policy* (1983); Elizabeth Cobbs Hoffman, *"All You Need Is Love": The Peace Corps and the Spirit of the 1960s* (1998); John Lewis Gaddis, *Strategies of Containment* (1981); Trumbull Higgins, *The Perfect Failure: Kennedy, Eisenhower and the Bay of Pigs* (1987); Richard D. Mahoney, *JFK: Ordeal in Africa* (1983). **On nuclear fallout shelters,** see Kenneth D. Rose, *One Nation Underground: The Fallout Shelter in American Culture* (2001); Andrew W. Grossman, *Neither Dead Nor Red: Civil Defense and American Political Development in the Early Cold War* (2001); Paul Boyer, *Fallout: A Historian Reflects on America's Half-Century Encounter with Nuclear Weapons* (1998); Margo Henriksen, *Dr. Strangelove's America: Society and Culture in the Atomic Age* (1997).

6

The Dream of a Great Society

A mother holds her daughter in front of their home in poverty-stricken Appalachia. /
© Wally McNamee/CORBIS.

By the early 1960s, many Americans believed that the apparent prosperity of the postwar years masked serious flaws in their society. At least one-quarter of the population remained mired in grinding poverty. Racial segregation remained the law of the land. Some middle-class white college students caught glimpses of the brutality encountered every day by African Americans in the South. Allard Lowenstein, a civil rights activist, told an audience of thousands of rapt students on the Stanford University campus in the fall of 1963 that Mississippi was "a foreign country in our midst." It was a place where "you can't picket, you can't vote, you can't boycott effectively, can't mount mass protest of any kind, and can't reach the mass media."

Many African Americans already knew what Lowenstein was talking about. Throughout the South, blacks demanded an end to legal segregation, and they pressed for the right to vote. In the midst of the outpouring of grief over Kennedy's assassination, Robert Moses, a leader of the Student Non-Violent Coordinating Committee (SNCC), commented that most white people in the country did not comprehend how strong was the resistance to voting rights for African Americans in the Deep South. The daily violence—beatings, clubbings, and jailings—against civil rights workers was terrifying. Moses told a SNCC conference on the Howard University campus over Thanksgiving weekend in 1963 that volunteers across the South every day confronted "the problem of overcoming fear."

On Thanksgiving morning, Martin Luther King, Jr., preached in Atlanta. He referred only briefly to Kennedy's murder before surveying the history of two hundred years of slavery. "A low dirty, evil thing," he called it. He described "[m]en and women chained to ships like beasts. . . . They knew the rawhide whip of the overseer. Sizzling heat. Long rows of cotton." The congregation shouted, "Preach on." King did—with a high note: "We've broken loose from the Egypt of slavery!" Continuing the biblical metaphor, he said, "Caleb and Joshua have come back with a minority report. They are saying we *can* possess the land."

The new president, Lyndon Johnson, acknowledged the deeply felt desire to distribute the benefits of affluence to those who had been left behind. He had witnessed deprivation firsthand during the Great Depression and was strongly moved to erase it. Addressing Congress five days after Kennedy was shot, he said, "We have talked long enough in this country about equal rights. We have talked for a hundred years or more."

As president, Johnson articulated a vision of a "Great Society." And for a while he captured the public mood. He rode the crest of a wave of earnest popular demands to bring an end to racial discrimination, provide equal opportunity to all people, eliminate poverty, and provide all Americans with adequate healthcare. Yet the scale of this undertaking was so vast that disappointments were almost inevitable. Also, by 1966, the popular consensus in support of these goals began to erode under the weight of the war in Vietnam and a white backlash against government efforts on behalf of African Americans. Johnson's own shortcomings—his abrasiveness, untruthfulness, and manipulation of others—made him an unsuitable leader, however, for such times of political discord. When he lost congressional support for his initiatives, Johnson turned his back on the Great Society he had so eloquently promoted in his first years in office. He withdrew on occasion into passivity and a brooding paranoia.

The successes and failures of the Great Society reflected the triumphs and disappointments of political liberalism in general. From the time of the New Deal until the mid-1960s, the liberal ideal—expanding government power in order to improve social and economic conditions—dominated much of American political and social life. By the end of the 1960s, however, many Americans no longer believed that government programs, agencies, or officials delivered tangible benefits. The early 1960s were years of enormous hope and promise for many; by the end of the decade, however, a more somber mood prevailed. America's faith in liberalism became a casualty, to some extent, of liberalism's most ambitious endeavor.

Lyndon Johnson: The Man and the President

Lyndon Johnson went to Washington in 1931, during the depths of the Great Depression, as an aide to a newly elected Texas congressman. The congressman let Johnson run his office and decide how he should vote; within months, the young aide was congressman in everything but name. In 1933 Johnson persuaded his boss to drop his entrenched conservatism and support the New Deal. Two years later, in 1935, Johnson used the contacts he had made within the Texas congressional delegation to win appointment as the Texas director of the newly created National Youth Administration. In 1937 Johnson won a special election to Congress as a New Dealer. He took the courageous step for a Texas politician of courting black and Mexican American voters, telling the black leaders of Austin, Texas, that if they supported him he would someday back voting rights and perhaps a hot-lunch program.

Back in Washington, he mastered the rules of the House and faithfully voted for Roosevelt's programs. By 1948 Johnson wanted to be a senator. In keeping with the Truman administration's ambivalent attitude toward New Deal reforms, he tempered his earlier populism, ran a viciously negative campaign as a moderate against a conservative former governor, stuffed ballot boxes in some key precincts, and won the election by eighty-seven votes. From that point, he rose fast, becoming the majority leader in the Senate by 1955.

For the remaining six years of the Eisenhower administration, Johnson ran the Senate as no one had before him. He perfected the "treatment," a combination of flattery, cajolery, threats, empathy, blackmail, and horse trading, to get his way. His relations with the Eisenhower administration were excellent, but liberal Democrats came to distrust him as a Texas wheeler-dealer. He eliminated references in the 1957 civil rights bill to equal treatment in public accommodations, and he sided with business interests against labor unions in the debate over the Landrum-Griffin Labor Reform Act of 1958. Liberals were offended, seeing such actions as the work of a compromiser and perhaps even a reactionary.

Johnson toyed with the idea of a presidential run in 1960, but he hesitated. After Kennedy had won the nomination, Robert Kennedy, the candidate's brother and campaign manager, relayed word to Johnson that Kennedy wanted him as vice president. Eventually the senator from Texas, reviled by many of Kennedy's most ardent backers as a southwestern political fixer and manipulator, became the Democratic vice-presidential candidate. He accepted the nomination in order to win the election for the Democrats; his job during the campaign was to carry Texas and as much of the South as possible.

Johnson helped Kennedy carry Texas by forty-six thousand votes. His service during the campaign temporarily warmed the hearts of Kennedy's inner circle, but for Johnson it proved to be a curiously joyless victory. Johnson feared, with good reason, that he would have little power as vice president. When there were important decisions to make—on Berlin, Cuba, Vietnam, taxes, civil rights—Kennedy and his inner circle made them without consulting Johnson. Instead, the vice president chaired the newly created National Aeronautics and Space Council and the Presidential Committee on Equal Opportunity. In 1961, these positions seemed remote outposts of the New Frontier. They were, however, important proving grounds for Johnson's own presidency.

Johnson found solace in travel. When he left Washington for trips to Africa, Europe, and Southeast Asia, he was like a man released from jail. But by 1963, even the delights of travel had paled. Kennedy's staff could not stand Johnson, and he knew it. In the summer of 1963, some of Kennedy's aides

President Lyndon B. Johnson herding cattle on his Texas ranch. / © Bettmann/CORBIS

openly expressed the wish that Johnson—"Uncle Corn Pone," they called him—would voluntarily step down from the Democratic ticket in 1964. In early November 1963, a dispirited Johnson confided to an aide that his future as vice president seemed bleak, and he mused about a new career. It came in an unexpected way. On November 22, Kennedy was shot in Dallas, on a trip arranged to quell the endemic feuding among Texas Democrats.

Johnson took the oath of office aboard Air Force One with a stricken Mrs. Kennedy, her clothes splattered with the blood of the slain president, looking on. Many of Kennedy's most ardent supporters viewed Johnson as unworthy of the office held by a fallen hero. Unlike Harry Truman, who became president following the death of Roosevelt in 1945, Johnson asked his predecessor's staff to stay. But it was nearly impossible to cultivate harmony between Kennedy's circle and the assistants who had served Johnson in the vice presidency. The more inconsolable of the Kennedy people resented Johnson as a usurper. Johnson's aides believed Kennedy did not deserve his posthumous golden reputation. After all, Kennedy's domestic agenda had made little progress in Congress, but a legislative master like Johnson might turn the dreams of racial justice and expanded economic opportunity for the poor into law.

Initially Johnson rose above such pettiness. Immediately after Kennedy's funeral, he addressed Congress, calling for unity, consensus, and the continuance of Kennedy's vision. A few weeks later, he stood before Congress to deliver his first State of the Union address. In it, he pledged to continue Kennedy's program, but with a distinctly activist and legislative stamp. Along with civil rights—the basic moral issue of the day—he emphasized the need to eliminate the blight of poverty. "This administration today, here and now, declares unconditional war on poverty in America. . . . It will not be a short or easy struggle, but we shall not rest until that war is won."

After his stirring words to Congress, Johnson plunged immediately into the effort to pass the landmark civil rights bill advocated by the demonstrators in Washington in August 1963. Despite Johnson's best efforts, the bill languished in the Senate in the fall. The provisions outlawing segregation in privately owned restaurants, overnight lodgings, and transportation were anathema to southern senators, who complained that they interfered with property rights. Nevertheless, in 1964, the House of Representatives, with the assistance of the Johnson administration, added two additional provisions to the bill. One empowered the Justice Department to intervene and file suit when a person's civil rights had been violated. The other created the Fair Employment Practices Commission, giving it the power to enforce equal opportunity in hiring and promotion in firms employing more than one hundred people. The House also added a provision forbidding discrimination based on gender as well as race; this provision later had a dramatic impact in reducing discrimination against women. The bill sailed through the House on February 10, 1964, by a vote of 290 to 130. Representatives explained their votes as a tribute to John Kennedy.

Things were more difficult in the Senate, however, where southerners and other opponents of the bill threatened to defeat it with a filibuster. Johnson

went to work with his legendary "treatment" to force senators to vote for clo-
ture (an end to debate), in order to bring the legislation to a vote on the floor.
With the aid of Minnesota Democrat Hubert Humphrey, he wooed Everett
Dirksen, the Republican minority leader. They convinced Dirksen that the
party of Abraham Lincoln could not afford to be responsible for the defeat of
civil rights legislation. Finally, on July 2, 1964, two and a half months after
the filibuster began, the Senate passed the law by a vote of 73 to 27.

The act banned discrimination based on race in public accommodations—restaurants, theaters, hotels, motels, and rooming houses. State-
supported institutions such as schools, libraries, parks, playgrounds, and
swimming pools could no longer be segregated. The Justice Department now
had the right to intervene to protect those whose civil rights had been violated.
The Fair Employment Practices Commission could bring suit to end discrimination in private employment.

Johnson looked forward to signing more civil rights legislation after the
election of 1964. He told the new attorney general, Nicholas deB. Katzenbach
(who took over in the summer of 1964 after Kennedy resigned), "I want you
to write me the goddamndest, toughest voting rights act that you can devise."
Before submitting a voting-rights bill, however, Johnson wanted to be elected
president in his own right. He hoped not just to win, but to demolish the Republican nominee. As "president of all the people," he could emerge from the
shadow of John Kennedy's legacy. He believed that winning a wide majority
would enable him to preside successfully over a legislative program as rich as
the New Deal.

Johnson's task appeared to be made easier by recent changes within the
Republican Party. Since the New Deal, Republicans had suppressed their most
conservative inclinations during presidential campaigns, nominating nonideological, centrist candidates they hoped could win. Whatever else they believed in, Republican presidential candidates Dewey, Eisenhower, and Nixon all
accepted the basic premise of the New Deal: that the federal government had a
role to play in managing social and economic affairs. Party conservatives complained, but they were regularly outvoted at convention time.

By 1964, however, the more conservative Republicans, including Senate
minority leader Everett Dirksen, House minority leader Charles Halleck, old
supporters of Senator Robert Taft, members of far-right groups like the John
Birch Society, and various newcomers to the party (among them Ronald Reagan, a former president of the Screen Actors Guild), had had enough. Enraged
by what they considered the arrogance of "the Eastern Establishment," they
railed against Wall Street, international finance, Madison Avenue, Harvard,
the *New York Herald Tribune*, and Ivy League prep schools. One advocate of this
militant new conservatism, Phyllis Schlafly, complained that in the past "a
small group of secret king-makers, using hidden persuaders and psychological warfare techniques, [had] manipulated the Republican national convention to nominate candidates who had side-stepped or suppressed the key issues." Never again, vowed the conservatives, promising to nominate one of
their own for the presidency.

For their part, eastern Republicans such as governors Nelson Rockefeller of New York and William Scranton of Pennsylvania were contemptuous of the backwardness and ignorance of the people they called "primitives"—midwestern, southern, and western politicians who had never valued the role of government in modern society. Fighting for the nomination were Rockefeller, a man whose pedigree and career proclaimed "Eastern Establishment," and Senator Barry Goldwater of Arizona, standard-bearer for the new conservatives.

Goldwater was a product of the Sunbelt, the fast-growing region that had gained wealth, power, and population since World War II. He grew up in Phoenix, a city that had swelled from thirty thousand inhabitants in his youth to over eight hundred thousand by the 1960s. Freed, they hoped, from the crowding, dirt, crime, and zoning regulations of older cities, the residents of the Sunbelt adopted new political habits. They distrusted government—especially the federal government, which controlled hundreds of thousands of acres of land in the western states—and they resented easterners. Few of them publicly acknowledged that federally funded roads, dams, and electric power grids had made the Sunbelt's agricultural, industrial, and population growth possible.

Goldwater capitalized on the Sunbelt's animosity in his 1964 campaign. He sealed his nomination for the presidency with a narrow win over Governor Rockefeller in the California primary in early June. Goldwater quickly dashed moderate Republicans' hopes that he would soften his rhetoric and run as a centrist. His speech accepting the Republican nomination gave no quarter,

Arizona senator Barry Goldwater accepts the Republican Party's nomination for president in San Francisco, July 1964. / © Bettmann/CORBIS

saying that "those who do not care for our cause, we don't expect to enter our ranks." Finally, he dismissed party moderates with his famous pronouncement, "Extremism in the defense of liberty is no vice! . . . Moderation in the pursuit of justice is no virtue!"

In Goldwater, Lyndon Johnson found the perfect opponent. Choosing Senator Hubert Humphrey of Minnesota as his running mate, Johnson campaigned as a unifier and a builder of consensus. In contrast to Goldwater, who seemed sharp, divisive, and ultimately frightening to the public, Johnson looked conciliatory. The Arizona senator alarmed voters with talk of giving control over nuclear weapons to battlefield commanders. His proposals to make Social Security private and voluntary and to sell the Tennessee Valley Authority confirmed suspicions that he was a radical who wanted to dismantle the most popular programs of the New Deal.

Democrats capitalized on these fears with a series of hard-hitting television advertisements designed to portray Goldwater as untrustworthy. The most famous of the TV spots showed a young girl counting the petals on a daisy. The image of the girl faded as a solemn announcer counted backward from 10. The sight of a mushroom cloud rising from an atomic explosion filled the screen, and Johnson was heard in a voice-over: "These are the stakes. We must learn to love one another, or surely we shall die." Johnson refused to debate Goldwater, letting the mushroom cloud and other TV ads carry his message instead, with devastating effect.

Johnson summarized his goals as moving "not only toward the rich society and the powerful society, but upward to the Great Society." He defined the Great Society as "abundance and liberty for all . . . an end to poverty and racial injustice . . . a place where every child can find knowledge to enrich his mind and to enlarge his talents." Johnson drew huge, responsive crowds throughout the country, and a wide coalition—whites and blacks, business and labor, liberals and moderates, Democrats and Republicans—supported his campaign.

Johnson's victory represented the greatest presidential landslide since the previous century. He carried forty-four states and 60.7 percent of the popular vote (see Map 6.1). Nevertheless, there were some ominous signs for the Democratic Party when it came to the distribution of the popular vote. Throughout the South—the base of the Democrats' success in presidential elections since 1932—Johnson received only 51 percent of the white vote, a signal that his party's control of that region had slipped. In fact, this election would be the last time a Democratic presidential candidate would win a majority of the southern white vote. In the Deep South, Goldwater's conservative appeal was especially effective. In addition to his native Arizona, Goldwater carried South Carolina, Georgia, Alabama, Mississippi, and Louisiana. White voters in those states were enraged by the Civil Rights Act, and grave fissures had appeared in the New Deal coalition.

But in the aftermath of Johnson's dramatic victory, it was hard to predict any difficulties for the Democrats. Alongside the Johnson landslide, the Democratic Party added thirty-seven seats in the House and two more seats in the Senate. When the new Congress convened in January 1965, House Democrats

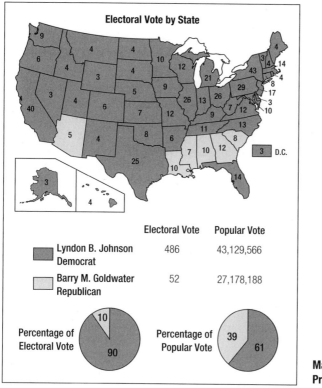

Electoral Vote by State

	Electoral Vote	Popular Vote
Lyndon B. Johnson Democrat	486	43,129,566
Barry M. Goldwater Republican	52	27,178,188

Percentage of Electoral Vote: 90 / 10

Percentage of Popular Vote: 61 / 39

Map 6.1
Presidential Election of 1964

outnumbered Republicans by 295 to 140. In the Senate were sixty-eight Democrats and only thirty-two Republicans. Not since Franklin Roosevelt's election of 1936 had either party assembled such massive majorities in Congress. Johnson appeared to have the congressional backing he needed to use the government to revitalize American society.

The Great Society: Success and Disappointment

Spurred by Lyndon Johnson, in 1965 and 1966, Congress enacted the most sweeping social reforms since the New Deal. Designed to win the War on Poverty and create the Great Society that Johnson had promised, these programs enhanced the role of the federal government in promoting health, economic welfare, education, urban renewal, and civil rights. The scope and content of the Great Society programs originated in the work of numerous social thinkers, reformers, and activists. In the late nineteenth and early twentieth centuries, progressive social reformers believed that the poor were mostly immigrants whose culture did not conform to that of the dominant white Protestant majority. The poor could be helped to achieve a stable position in American society by extending down to them the hands of the well-to-do and the intellectuals who studied their problems. In the 1960s, the federal government revived this approach. Intellectuals studied the conditions of poor Americans and sought solutions to their problems. Consultants came to Washington to help draft laws reflecting the ideas of social scientists from the past twenty years.

The Great Society was not limited to programs designed to eliminate poverty among the poorest quarter of the population; Great Society programs also served the needs of the three-quarters of Americans who were not poor. The creators of the Great Society hoped to give everyone a stake in its success. They wanted to avoid policies that appeared to take resources from one group and give them to another. By steering clear of redistribution of wealth, the Great Society was able to gain the support of white, middle-class Americans. Many, perhaps most, middle-class, white Americans endorsed the goals of the Great Society while the economy expanded, as it did for most of the 1960s. Even during the boom, however, middle-class whites began to worry about their own place in society. The effort to maintain a consensus carried substantial costs, and eventually support for the War on Poverty faded in the middle class.

These ambitious initiatives not only increased government spending but also required a greater number of government officials to administer them. In contrast to the 1930s and 1940s, however, the greatest need for new government employees was at the state and local levels (see Figure 6.1). Some of the new programs were very successful, but others left a legacy of disappointment and controversy.

Extending federally funded healthcare benefits was one of the first and most popular of the Great Society initiatives. In 1965, heeding the president's call to improve access to healthcare for elderly Americans, Congress enacted the ambitious program known as Medicare. Fulfilling a pledge made first by the Truman administration, the legislation created universal hospital insurance for Americans over age sixty-five who were covered by Social Security. Congress also included voluntary insurance to cover doctors' fees and nursing-home charges. Medicare did not, however, cover the cost of medicines prescribed outside hospitals. At the time, few medicines other than antibiotics and a limited number of pills for high blood pressure were in widespread use. Three decades later, medicines prescribed outside hospitals provided at least as much medical care as did hospital visits. A complementary program, Medicaid, was enacted in 1966; it allowed participating states to receive matching federal grants to pay the medical bills of welfare recipients of all ages. After a slow start, all states but Arizona agreed to participate in Medicaid. The creation of Medicare and Medicaid coincided with growing awareness of environmental and other human threats to health and well being. For example, public health concerns over the risk of cigarettes grew steadily after the January 1964 widely reported release of the Surgeon General's report that corroborated the long discussed links between smoking, lung cancer and heart disease.

Medicare and Medicaid gained wide popularity because they covered nearly everyone at one time or another in their lives. The programs substantially reduced the gap in medical treatment between the poor and the rich. By

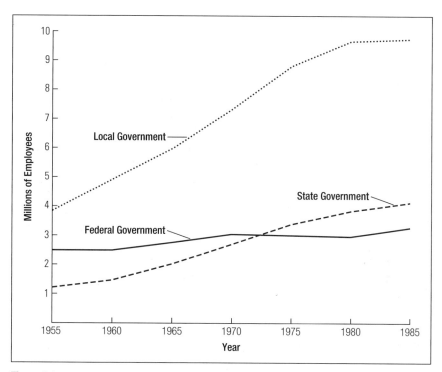

Figure 6.1
Growth of Government, 1955–1985

1970, the proportion of Americans who had never visited a physician fell from 19 percent to 8 percent. Prenatal visits increased, which helped lower the infant mortality rate by 33 percent. Among African Americans, the change in infant mortality was especially noticeable, declining from 4 percent of live births in 1965 to 3.1 percent in 1970 and 2.4 percent in 1975.

One problem, however, was the cost of these medical programs, which far outstripped original estimates. To overcome resistance from many medical doctors, the administration had agreed that medical services would continue to be provided by private doctors chosen by the patients themselves. Hospitals and physicians would receive "reasonable and customary" payments for their services. When the inflation rate climbed during the late 1960s, medical charges rose even faster. Partly as a result, the annual cost of these government programs soared from $3.4 billion to $18 billion in ten years. As the financial resources of Medicare became strained, the government encouraged medical professionals to restrict the amount of time that patients spent in hospitals. At the same time, numerous pharmaceutical innovations made it easier to treat ailments such as heart disease, diabetes, anxiety, depression, and even cancer outside hospitals. By the late 1970s, many private insurance plans included payments for prescription drugs, but Medicare did not.

In 1965, Congress also passed a spectacular array of measures aimed directly at reducing poverty. Many of these programs were designed to alleviate the urban poverty that had led to race riots in numerous American cities in the summer of 1965. Congress created the Office of Economic Opportunity (OEO) to supervise the War on Poverty. Johnson appointed Sargent Shriver, who had successfully headed the Peace Corps, as the first director of the OEO. Congress also created the food-stamp program, which provided assistance to people whose income fell below a level set by the government. The program worked well: ten years after its enactment, research indicated that government efforts were "almost fully effective in reducing flagrant malnutrition."

Because experts considered education a key element in helping young people climb out of poverty, Congress created the Head Start program to reach the preschool children of impoverished families. This program was also successful. Later studies revealed that Head Start children gained substantial advantages over poor children who did not enroll. They gained an average of seven points on IQ tests and were half as likely as nonparticipants to repeat grades in school or to be assigned to special-education classes. Long-term studies suggested that, as teenagers and young adults, Head Starters completed more years of school, worked more steadily, and engaged in less criminal behavior. Congress also provided grants to school districts with large numbers of poor children, and scholarships and loans for underprivileged college students.

Another step was the creation of the Job Corps, which was patterned on the Civilian Conservation Corps of the New Deal. Reformers believed Job Corps members would develop effective work habits that they would continue to use once they gained employment outside the government. The corps employed one hundred thousand young men and women from poor families. Eight years later, in 1973, Congress expanded the Jobs Corps with the Comprehensive Employment and Training Act (CETA). CETA provided on-the-job training for the chronically unemployed. For those who could not find positions with private employers, the government created full-time public service jobs for them. Although costly, this program met its goals.

To aid urban renewal, Congress created the Model Cities program, but this endeavor was less successful. Planners had originally hoped to concentrate on a few targets, mobilize local leadership, and try various methods to invigorate dying communities. If a few cities could be revitalized—their slums renewed and their residents provided with useful work—these demonstration projects would act as beacons for other places. Powerful members of Congress channeled the lion's share of the benefits to their own districts. The program could not even begin to fulfill the vision of its founders.

To oversee the distribution of grants for Great Society programs, Congress established the cabinet-level Department of Housing and Urban Development (HUD) and Department of Transportation (DOT). These departments made a start in reducing the grinding poverty in urban centers, but Congress did not fund them fully in the period from 1965 to 1967. By the time the Johnson administration asked for a new housing act in 1968, much of the enthusiasm for the Great Society had ebbed. The costs of the Vietnam War made Congress reluctant to fund programs designed to replace dilapidated inner-city tenements. Consequently, the president's request to build 6 million low-income dwellings was slashed to less than one-quarter of the original proposal.

Funding problems also bedeviled the OEO, headed by Sargent Shriver, who left the Peace Corps to take on the vastly more complicated job of directing the War on Poverty. The OEO was supposed to coordinate several other programs, including the Job Corps; Volunteers in Service to America (VISTA), a domestic version of the Peace Corps; and the Community Action Program (CAP). Despite Shriver's best efforts, the OEO had to oversee a vast proliferation of programs, with little increase in funds. There were organizational troubles as well. One task of CAP was to encourage recipients of government assistance to participate in administering government programs; the goal was defined as "maximum feasible participation." But this goal provoked clashes between local authorities and the neighborhood activists assisted by the OEO.

Such conflicts undermined congressional support for the OEO after 1966. The CAP's difficulties typified some of the Great Society's larger problems. The Johnson administration was trying to satisfy irreconcilable groups and factions. Johnson truly believed in building a consensus—a legacy of his congressional career—and he thought the way to foster consensus was to satisfy competing interest groups. But the antipoverty programs, as the historian Allan Matusow observed, "sought to appease vested interests that had resisted reform or occasioned the need for it in the first place." As time went on, administrators of Great Society programs came to believe that they had been underfunded and could not possibly meet the vast needs of the country's poor. Opponents of the programs, on the other hand, came to believe that they gave too much power to groups who previously had not had a voice. However modest this empowerment of the poor was, it threatened the political and social position of the people who had previously been dominant.

Despite the many flaws of the antipoverty programs and the resistance they sparked, they had some real successes. They helped reduce the percentage of people living in poverty by about 50 percent in a decade. Standards of medical care improved dramatically. Education reached impoverished rural and urban children in ways that had never before seemed possible. Job training provided a means of breaking out of the cycle of poverty. If the Johnson administration did not vanquish poverty in the United States, it at least gave many Americans an opportunity for a better life.

The issue of reform became inextricably bound up with race. Some of the most far-reaching changes created by the Great Society involved expanding the voting rights of people who had been persistently excluded from the polls because of their race. A series of demonstrations in Alabama helped set the stage for congressional action. For six weeks in early 1965, Martin Luther King, Jr., and the Student Non-Violent Coordinating Committee (SNCC) organized demonstrations in Selma for the right to vote. A city of 29,000 people, Selma had 15,000 African Americans of voting age. In 1965 only 355 of them were registered to vote. The board of registrars, which determined voting eligibility, met for a few hours, twice a month. It took great courage for any

African American to appear before the registrars, and when they did so, they found a board determined to keep them from the polls. African Americans were denied a place on the voting rolls for failing to cross a *t* or dot an *i* on the voter registration form. The registrars routinely asked African American applicants convoluted questions like, "What two rights does a person have after being indicted by a grand jury?"

In January and February 1965, demonstrators demanding the right to vote in Selma were clubbed and tear-gassed by Alabama sheriff's deputies who arrested and jailed over three thousand people. Sheriff Jim Clark wore a button reading "NEVER." At one point, deputies threw a woman to the ground and Sheriff Clark beat her with a club. The deputies used electric cattle prods on the demonstrators, singeing their skin and forcing them to their knees, vomiting in agony.

King and John Lewis of SNCC then organized a fifty-six-mile march from Selma to Birmingham. On Sunday, March 7, 1965, six hundred black demonstrators walked to the Edmund Pettis Bridge at the edge of town. State troopers and sheriff's deputies gave the marchers two minutes to turn back. A phalanx of uniformed officers then flew into the marchers. Swinging their clubs and hurling tear gas at the demonstrators, the officers advanced to the cheers of a white mob standing nearby. Sheriff Clark then ordered horse-mounted deputies to plunge into the crowd. They hit the demonstrators with bullwhips and rubber tubes wrapped in barbed wire. Seventy demonstrators went to the hospital. As he was carried off on a stretcher, SNCC leader Lewis said, "I don't see how President Johnson can send troops to Vietnam . . . and can't send troops to Selma." Television news ran film of the massacre that Bloody Sunday repeatedly. Across the country, editorials denounced the Alabama authorities and demanded congressional action on a voting-rights act. For the culminating march to Montgomery on Tuesday, March 9, thousands of people flew in.

Johnson seized the opportunity to deliver a moving speech before Congress on March 15. He recalled the poverty of the rural school where he had taught in 1928: "My students were poor and they often came to class without breakfast, hungry. They knew even in their youth the pain of injustice. . . . Somehow you never forget what poverty and hatred can do when you see its scars in the hopeful face of a young child." He had never expected to be in a position to do much about the problem. But now that he had the chance, he told Congress, he meant to use it: "I mean to be the president who educated young children . . . who helped to feed the hungry . . . who helped the poor to find their own way." He then linked these memories with a call for passage of the voting-rights act. If African Americans did not gain equal voting rights, Johnson declared, "we will have failed as a people and a nation." He asked his fellow citizens to "overcome the crippling legacy of bigotry and injustice." Adopting the slogan of the civil rights movement, he insisted "we shall overcome."

Congress obliged with the Voting Rights Act of 1965, which empowered the Justice Department to register voters directly in localities where discrimination existed. If fewer than 50 percent of the citizens of a district voted or were registered to vote in 1964, the Justice Department assumed that there had been discrimination at the polls. Literacy tests for voter registration were also outlawed. Over the next three years, the law resulted in the registration of an additional 740,000 black voters (see Map 6.2). The overall rate of registration among African Americans rose from 31 percent to 57 percent. About 70 percent of whites registered. The law eventually produced an increase in black officeholders as well. The number of blacks in the House of Representatives rose from five to seventeen in the next twenty years, and the total number of black public officials in the entire nation increased from 103 to 3,503. In the 1970s and 1980s, African Americans were elected to the mayor's office in cities ranging from Newark, New Jersey, and Gary, Indiana, to New York, Los Angeles, and Chicago. The change was even more startling in the Deep South: Atlanta, New Orleans, Birmingham, and even Selma elected black mayors.

Although the Great Society is remembered for its attempts to erase poverty and discrimination, it also sponsored programs that appealed directly to the American middle class. By funding the arts and humanities, promoting

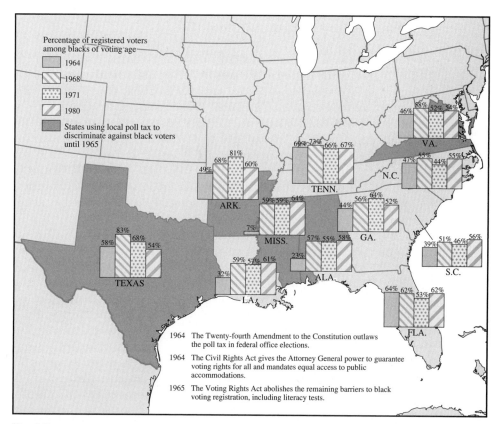

Map 6.2
Voting Rights for African Americans, 1964–1980

nonprofit television, and helping to clean up the nation's highways, the Johnson administration produced benefits even the wealthy could appreciate.

To fulfill his promise to "build a richer life of mind and spirit," Johnson sent Congress legislation to create the National Foundation for the Arts and Humanities, a smaller version of the National Science Foundation, which had been in existence since 1950. The new foundation consisted of two divisions: the National Endowment for the Arts (NEA) and the National Endowment for the Humanities (NEH). The Federal Council on the Arts and Humanities was created to supervise the two endowments. Both directly and through state councils, each endowment offered grants to individuals and to institutions such as universities, museums, ballet companies, and local arts centers.

The NEA and NEH sponsored conferences, produced films, offered fellowships for scholars and creative writers, and funded university courses and new curricula. In the beginning, the endowments grew slowly, from a budget of $2.5 million each in 1966 to roughly $6 million each in 1970. But ten years later, each endowment was spending $106 million per year. Together, the NEA and NEH had a profound effect on the arts and humanities throughout the nation. The proliferation of local theater and dance companies, the development of many young artists and writers, the expansion of scholarly research—all of these were made possible by the NEA and NEH.

The Great Society influenced American television, too. To offer American people an alternative to commercial programming, Congress in 1967 reserved 242 channels on the nation's airwaves for local public, noncommercial TV stations. It also provided direct federal subsidies for public programming with the creation of the Corporation for Public Broadcasting (CPB). Governed by a presidentially appointed board, the CPB distributed grants to produce TV shows and helped with the operating budgets of local public TV stations. Programs such as *Sesame Street*, an educational hour for preschoolers, and *Nova*, a highly regarded series on science, received support from the CPB. Five years later, in 1972, Congress added National Public Radio, a network of noncommercial radio stations. Those stations, and some of the programs they aired, received support from the CPB.

The Great Society also demonstrated a concern for the natural environment. Congress enacted legislation mandating improvements in air and water quality. The president's wife, known to the nation as Lady Bird Johnson, took the lead in fostering a more pleasant environment along the nation's roads. Deathly afraid of air travel, she commuted between Texas and Washington on the nation's highway system. She was appalled by the junkyards and unsightly billboards lining the interstates. She pressed her husband to submit to Congress the Highway Beautification Act, which was passed in 1965. By increasing the federal contribution to interstate highway construction from 85 to 90 percent for states that joined the program, the law encouraged states to ban billboards and remove roadside junkyards. Because the law allowed billboard companies wide latitude in adhering to regulations, it resulted in only minor improvements. Nevertheless, this early gesture toward beautification, along with the measures designed to clean up the air and water, set the stage for stronger environmental laws in the 1970s.

Johnson's Great Society had a profound influence on immigration as well. When Johnson took office, an immigration quota system dating from the 1920s was still in effect. In setting limits on entry for many foreign nationals, the quotas reflected deep-rooted racial and ethnic biases against Asians, Eastern Europeans, Catholics, and Jews. Hoping to erase the inequities of this system, President Kennedy had presented Congress with an immigration-reform package abolishing discrimination against immigrants on the basis of national origin.

The bill languished until Kennedy's death, but Johnson resubmitted it to the reform-minded eighty-ninth Congress in 1965. When it passed that year, it seemed only a moderate modification of America's immigration policy. It phased out the national quota system over the next three years. After 1968 there would be a total of 290,000 slots available each year, divided into 170,000 visas for immigrants from the Eastern Hemisphere and 120,000 for immigrants from the Western Hemisphere. In place of quotas based on national origin, Congress created seven categories to set priorities for granting entry. Two categories of immigrants received the highest priority: those holding desirable job skills and those with close relatives (parents and siblings) in the United States. Political refugees were given the lowest priority and accounted for the smallest number of visas. This situation was largely overlooked at the time but generated controversy later.

Because the law gave first preference to family members, Congress expected that the new mix of immigrants would closely resemble the old one. Although this reasoning made sense at the time, it failed to anticipate a profound change in immigration patterns in the next decade. For a few years, the law worked as planned, admitting immigrants from southern and Eastern Europe in large numbers.

By the middle of the 1970s, however, immigration patterns had changed due to worldwide economic trends. Job prospects brightened in Europe, making America less attractive. European immigrants made up 45 percent of the total in 1965 but only 15 percent in the late 1970s. During this period, immigration from Asia, the Caribbean, and South America shot up. Residents of these lands found the American economy extraordinarily attractive compared to the opportunities available in their own countries. This situation was especially true for educated people, whose skills qualified them for special preference under the terms of the 1965 law.

Congress did not envision that the family reunification provision would create an immigration chain. For example, a foreign student attending college in the United States could gain the skills needed to qualify for immigration preference. Within a short time, he or she could use the family reunification provision to bring over his or her parents, spouse, and children. As these relatives attained citizenship, they too became eligible to sponsor relatives. Thus, an ever wider network evolved, bringing many additional immigrants to the United States.

This pattern, which held true for immigrants from nearly every Asian nation except Japan, actually reduced poverty in the United States. Many Asian immigrants came from upper-class, highly educated backgrounds. Within a decade of the new law's passage, tens of thousands of Asian physicians and nurses entered the United States. They became the backbone of many public hospitals' staffs. So many professionals emigrated from South Korea, Taiwan, the Philippines, India, Pakistan, and the British colony of Hong Kong that officials in these countries sometimes accused the United States of promoting a "brain drain" of talent that they needed for progress at home.

By 1979 the seven largest groups of immigrants were all of non-European origin:

Mexico   52,000

Philippines   41,300

China, Taiwan, and Hong Kong   30,180

Korea   29,348

Jamaica   19,714

India   19,708

Dominican Republic   17,519

Refugees and undocumented aliens swelled these figures even further. All in all, the 1965 immigration act resulted in an unprecedented boom in non-European immigrants to the United States during the 1970s.

Changes in the National Economy

In the early years of his administration, when his Great Society programs were springing into action, Johnson's efforts were bolstered by the greatest peacetime economic boom since the end of World War II. The administration's strategy—adjusting government spending to encourage employment and growth and to dampen inflation—seemed to work. Unemployment fell to 3.7 percent of the labor force, its lowest level since the Korean War. Economic activity, as measured by changes in the gross national product (GNP), grew by over 4 percent per year from 1964 to 1966. (*Gross national product* was the term used in the 1960s to measure total output of goods and services. In the 1990s, the term was changed to *gross domestic product*.) Government expenditures and receipts were roughly in balance for these years.

The boom hastened the rise of the Sunbelt. Spending for the military and the space program continued to flow to the South and the West. California consolidated its position as the premier defense contracting state (it became known as "the buckle on the Sunbelt"), while Texas surpassed New York as the second. By the end of the 1960s, the federal payroll in the ten Sunbelt states amounted to $10 billion per year, double the amount in all other states combined.

Business prospered in the Sunbelt as well. For example, the oil industry, long headquartered in the Northeast, began to relocate to Texas, Oklahoma, and California. Getty, Union, Occidental, and Signal Oil, all based in Los Angeles, grew to prominence. Phillips Petroleum of Bartlesville, Oklahoma, and Tenneco, in Houston, challenged New York–based companies such as Mobil and Texaco.

The sixties also saw an explosion in banking in the Sunbelt. North Carolina National Bank grew the fastest, earning more money than any other bank in the country. San Francisco's Bank of America became the country's largest, with hundreds of branches serving retail customers. It heavily promoted its BankAmericard, the first bank credit card, sparking a new trend in consumer spending. In 1965, four big Chicago banks started MasterCard; two years later, four California banks created Master Charge. Ads urged consumers to use their plastic to purchase everyday items—gasoline, clothing, meals, televisions, lawn mowers. The banks made money from these cards in three ways: charging interest for purchases not paid for within a specified grace period, collecting fees from merchants accepting the cards, and licensing other banks to issue their own cards bearing the now famous BankAmericard, MasterCard, and Master Charge names. Bank of America eventually sold its credit-card business to a consortium of other banks, who changed the name of the card to VISA, and Master Charge merged with MasterCard, retaining the latter name.

Sunbelt banks also took the lead in developing bank holding companies, financial concerns that bought small local banks. The new entities, among them the United Bank of Los Angeles, Valley National Bank of Phoenix, and Columbia Savings and Loan of Los Angeles, had assets of over $1 billion each, a large sum for the time. They were able to provide loans for large real-estate and industrial-development programs, which had previously been forced to rely on major Wall Street firms for financing.

Wall Street also did well. Between 1963 and 1966, the New York Stock Exchange enjoyed its greatest growth since the 1920s, with prices more than doubling. One effect of this bull market was the development of industrial conglomerates. Audacious dealmakers, often from the Sunbelt, arranged for one firm to buy another in an unrelated industry. The parts of the resulting merged enterprise had little to do with one another economically, but the balance sheets showed increased profits. As if to emphasize the company rather than the product, the combined firms took names that had little intrinsic meaning. American Tobacco became American Brands. Ling Temco Vought became LTV. Some of these business arrangements joined highly unlikely partners. Litton Shipyards, renamed Litton Industries, acquired the Stouffer food company; the renamed LTV, a defense contractor, bought the Wilson meat-packing corporation.

But celebrations of the economic boom were premature. By 1966 the growing war in Vietnam (see Chapter 7) had unleashed unexpected and uncontrollable inflation. The inflation rate began to fluctuate between 2.5 percent and 4 percent per year. For people accustomed to the many years of price stability since the Korean War, this development was frightening. Keynesians explained the rise as a result of too much business demand in the wake of the

(cont. on page 230)

Big Dreams, Big Buildings

The Cold War was as much about culture as it was about international conflict. Americans sought to show people around the world the freshness, cleanliness, and openness of American society. In the 1950s, the government created the United States Information Agency (USIA) and expanded Voice of America and Radio Free Europe to broadcast American music and news over the radio to a global audience. The Eisenhower administration launched a new trade-fair program aimed at promoting American business interests abroad. The most famous occurred in Moscow in the summer of 1959. Vice President Richard M. Nixon and Soviet Communist Party General Secretary Nikita S. Khrushchev engaged in a heated impromptu debate over the merits of an all-electric kitchen installed by General Electric (GE). Nixon explained that Americans lived better than anyone. Khrushchev replied that Americans were too materialistic and lived in isolation.

By 1960, ninety-seven trade exhibits had been seen by more than 60 million people in twenty-nine countries. Visitors gaped at the vast array of postwar consumer products, from huge cars to electric ranges, automatic dryers, toasters, stereos, and TVs. Some overseas critics bemoaned the intrusion of American consumer culture as unsophisticated and threatening to local traditions. But the scoffers rarely came to the fairs. The millions who did mostly liked the bright smiles on the faces of the young American women and men who demonstrated the contemporary wares.

American businesses transmitted American culture and beliefs to host countries through other avenues, some quite unintended. Products as different as Hollywood movies, TV shows, Coke and Pepsi-Cola, McDonald's hamburgers, and Ford Mustangs and Chevrolet Corvettes created larger-than-life visions of the United States

that veered from powerful and generous to free and fresh, to wasteful and arrogant. Architecture too transmitted ideas about the American style to an international audience.

Buildings constructed by Americans abroad conveyed the idea that the United States was a new, modern, rich, and powerful country. Following the end of World War II, the State Department commissioned no fewer than two hundred projects in seventy-two countries. Most of these structures, developed for embassies and consulates, were designed like modern corporate architecture. Between 1954 and 1959, over fifty different architectural firms developed about fifty-eight high-profile buildings, including U.S. embassies in India, England, and Norway. The designers favored huge, open entryways. The façades used white stone and a lot of glass. While some criticized the results of the State Department's building program as ostentatious and others praised them as cutting-edge artistry, few could fail to see that these massive new structures transmitted the image of a thoroughly modern, glamorous, commanding, and rich United States. The London embassy project, for instance, was elevated from the street level on stilts and featured a controversial stone eagle with a thirty-five-foot wingspan perched atop its main entrance.

These public buildings drew their inspirations from the glass-and-steel skyscrapers built in American cities in the 1950s and 1960s. Philip Johnson, a prominent modern architect, set the tone with his design for New York's Seagram Building. When Seagram's headquarters opened, critics lauded it for its apparent weightlessness. The green glass seemed to float above the noisy, crowded city below. Modern buildings, like modern American, seemed unbounded, free, and clean. Architectural magazines hailed the new American embassies as admirable examples of the progressive-minded, friendly

The World Trade Center under construction in lower Manhattan, February 1971. / © Charles E. Rotkin/CORBIS

spirit of America, and contrasted them with the classic and pretentious architectural style of Soviet embassies that seemed as heavy as Russian food and unstylish as the suits favored by the stolid bureaucrats of the upper echelons of the Soviet government.

Commentators especially appreciated the way that the planners appropriated local architectural styles and transformed them into modernized, distinctly American structures. Such was the case in Ireland in 1959. Developers capitalized on that country's Celtic motifs and round building designs to deliver a trendy structure that included floor-

to-ceiling windows separated by precast concrete sections and the most up-to-date amenities. Buildings like this one, which offered updated versions of antiquated styles, successfully transmitted the idea that Americans were innovative—and in control.

While policymakers may have welcomed such a reputation, the designs of the new embassies were as likely to convey less flattering images of the United States. For instance, the new embassy in Morocco, completed in 1961, made a mockery of American innovation when it proved unlivable thanks to a long list of flaws: it was too hot in summer,

227

drafty and cold in winter; the roof leaked; stone floors and plazas cracked. Designers placed some of the windows in out-of-the-way crannies that made it impossible to clean the glass. An eight-foot-high wall and fence surrounded the enormous American embassy in Saigon, Vietnam, making it nearly impossible to see the buildings from the street. The American-designed presidential palace in Saigon opened in 1965. Its façade of gilt-colored, anodized aluminum looked cheap, and the palace itself resembled a Sunbelt municipal building.

On a broader level, critics condemned the grandiose scale on which the embassies were built, finding them out of step with the new attitudes of self-determination and frugality in ascendance around the world. By the mid-1960s, the State Department, having exhausted earlier funds and facing withering criticism from Congress, stepped back from its ambitious building program. The State Department building program then concentrated on low-profile embassies. By the 1980s, architectural styles had changed too. The most sought-after architects had tired of the open, glass-and-steel, high-rise style. Where once it appeared clean, architects now considered it sterile. Tall buildings soaring above the streets below now appeared isolated and lacking the human touch.

Structures erected by American businesses during the Cold War also conveyed the idea of a privileged, powerful United States through their architectural style. The physical presence of the sixteen glittering new Hilton hotels erected in sixteen cities—including Istanbul, Berlin, Tel Aviv, Cairo, and Athens—became beacons of the American way of life. Conrad Hilton makes clear in his autobiography, *Be My Guest*, that he viewed the internationalization of his hotel chain as an effective way to spread the American message of freedom and democracy around the world. The hotels featured luxurious amenities like wall-to-wall carpeting, high-speed express elevators, air conditioning, bars and restaurants on upper floors with views of the surrounding cities, and outdoor swimming pools where waiters brought Cokes, American beer, and hamburgers to lounging guests. These hotels provided an enviable American contrast to the traditional and sometimes dilapidated buildings of the host cities. In Athens, for instance, the imposing and luxurious Hilton proved a dramatic contrast to the crumbling Acropolis, leaving no doubt as to which country was currently on the rise.

The view of America as exceptional extended inside the hotel as well, where interiors offered sanitized versions of local art and culture so that guests could "experience" the unfamiliar. In Istanbul, for instance, the Hilton featured Turkish-vaulted architecture, a ladies' sitting area garnished with divans and lavish draperies to create an Arabian Nights effect, a mini-mall with locally produced items for purchase, and local cuisine. These attempts to re-create the local flavor stood in stark contrast to the glimmering coffee shops, green lawns, and American soda fountains that were prominent features of the usual international Hilton experience. Together, the juxtaposition of American modernity and native tradition created an idealized, Americanized version of foreign lands for Western consumption. Hilton hotels provided Americans safe havens from which to view foreign lands. For the most skeptical critics, a stay in an overseas Hilton was like a trip to Disneyland. Everything was clean and safe—and deeply false and misleading. But the guests appreciated a familiar setting in a strange land. Locals also started to use the American hotels as meeting places with visiting business executives. The Egyptians, Turks, Israelis, or Germans who used the hotels began to enjoy the comfort and efficiency they found there. They might become slightly annoyed by their own country's slower pace, but at the same time they became interpreters of the United States to their own countries, and vice versa.

Other U.S. corporations overseas sent an even more exclusivist message with the structures they developed. Oil conglomerates extracting oil from Middle East land, for instance, created elite compounds for their American employees that were strictly off limits to native workers. The California-based Arabian American Oil Company created a sprawling oasis of Americanism in Dhahran, Saudi Arabia, that featured a bowling alley, a golf course, air conditioning, cinemas, and elaborate landscaping. Its ostentation stood in stark contrast to the dirt floors, flimsy huts, and stinky latrines forced on the majority of the local work force. Some U.S. military installations took a similar approach, creating spaces that exuded a message of modernity and exclusivity. The bungalows at China Beach, about ten miles north of Da Nang, Vietnam, and a popular rest and recreation area for Americans during the Vietnam War, were an exact replica of an American beach club, with one exception, however. The eight-foot-high brick wall that ran along the beach was topped with rolls of barbed wire to keep out local Vietnamese, any one of whom the military feared might be a dangerous Viet Cong guerrilla. In the Middle East, the Sinai Field Mission, erected in 1976 as a permanent base for American troops charged with patrolling a U.N. buffer zone between Israeli and Egyptian forces, featured trendy, prefabricated, concrete modules like those used by a major hotel chain. As if to illustrate that American soldiers were a breed apart, the mission offered luxurious amenities such as tennis courts, carpeting, and air conditioning.

Since at least the 1960s, American structures have served as targets for those disgruntled with American policies and privileges. In 1969, for instance, right-wing militants bombed the Athens Hilton as a way of expressing their displeasure with American support of a rival political group. Embassies have repeatedly suffered attacks by militants hostile to American interests, from the 1975 chaotic takeover of the U.S. embassy in Saigon through the violent assault on the Tehran embassy by Iranian students in November 1979 and the 1998 bombings of U.S. embassies in Tanzania and Kenya by Islamic fundamentalists.

No buildings better symbolized the complex story of American architecture's place in global economics and culture than did the 110-story twin towers of the World Trade Center (WTC). When the WTC opened in 1972, the tide had already turned against the minimalist style of post–World War II commercial skyscrapers. Critics savaged the design as "two Kleenex boxes standing on their side." No longer did steel, concrete, and glass mean clean lines and the power of American enterprise. Instead, the critics said that the WTC was barren and dull. The whole idea of building a vertical city where 40,000 people would work every day appeared to be artificial. The windswept plaza of the entryway to the WTC seemed devoid of the vibrant street life it had replaced. But over the years, workers and tourists alike grew fond of the WTC. The food at Windows on the World might have been uninspired, but the view at night was breathtaking. So was the vista from the observation deck. The Islamic terrorists who tried to bring down the WTC in February 1993 by parking a bomb-laden Ryder truck in the basement perceived the building as a central symbol of American financial and commercial power. That bombing attempt failed. But on September 11, 2001, another group of terrorists succeeded when two commercial jetliners crashed into each of the twin towers in a span of twenty minutes. Within ninety minutes of the last plane crash, first the north and then the south tower collapsed in giant fireballs. Two thousand eight hundred people died. Tens of millions of shocked television viewers saw the buildings fall. The reverberations will last for years.

war in Vietnam. They urged the president to raise taxes in 1966 in order to pay for the war and to stem inflation. Johnson refused, fearing that if he emphasized the need to pay war bills, conservatives would force him to squeeze his Great Society budget. Liberals criticized him too when they saw how much the war hurt the reform effort. Wanting to satisfy everyone, Johnson believed that the country could afford both guns and butter. The administration did monitor price and wage increases, and it established guideposts for business and labor to follow. But it had little success in rolling back the increases that it considered excessive.

Interest rates soared in 1966. Banks began paying more than 5.5 percent interest on passbook accounts, more than savings and loan institutions were legally permitted to offer. Thereafter, owners of savings and loans lobbied Congress to relax the ceilings on what they could pay depositors. Rates on government securities, consistently below 3 percent in previous years, rose to 6 percent. The credit crunch, as it was called, also sent the stock market sprawling in 1966. All of this was supposed to slow the rise in prices, but it did not. In 1966 and 1967, prices rose by more than 4 percent per year; in 1968, inflation hit 6 percent.

Inflation hurt pensioners living on fixed incomes and small savers whose return was kept low by regulation. But in the beginning, it helped those poor people who had obtained jobs during the boom because wages for marginal workers rose faster than those for skilled workers. Businesses lost to inflation, however, as higher wages reduced profits, from 10.6 percent of the nation's income in 1966 to 7.2 percent in 1970. Inflation also took its toll internationally. Since 1945 the dollar had been the standard currency of international trade. As prices rose in the United States, European holders of dollars began redeeming their currency for gold. The United States Treasury obliged, but by 1968 the $20 billion U.S. gold reserve represented less than one-third of all dollars held by foreigners.

What seemed the worst about inflation were its persistence and its tendency to increase over time. A 3 percent rate of inflation might be tolerable if it went no higher. In the last years of the Johnson administration, however, the annual rate of inflation rose steadily, discouraging savings, making long-term investment difficult, and souring the public on additional costly programs to aid the poor.

The Supreme Court and Civil Liberties

While Lyndon Johnson promoted his Great Society, the Supreme Court was engaged in another sort of liberal reform: the expansion of constitutionally guaranteed rights. Still led by Chief Justice Earl Warren, the Court expanded on its work of the 1950s: protecting the rights of individuals, altering criminal law, and regulating national and state voting systems. Together, presidents Johnson and Kennedy appointed four justices to the Supreme Court. Byron White (1962–1993), named by Kennedy, became one of the more conservative members. But Arthur Goldberg (1962–1965), Abe Fortas (1965–1969), and

Thurgood Marshall (1967–1991) joined with Warren, Hugo Black, William O. Douglas, and William Brennan to consolidate the Court's liberal majority.

While acknowledging that the freedoms of speech, assembly, press, and religion guaranteed by the First Amendment sometimes had to be balanced against other interests, the Court's liberal majority required the government to show a compelling need to restrict liberty. If it could not, citizens' freedoms could not be abridged.

In *Bond* v. *Floyd* (1966), for example, the Court ruled that the Georgia House of Representatives could not refuse to seat an elected representative of the people, even though he expressed admiration for those who had opposed conscription for the war in Vietnam. A unanimous Court held that neither public officials nor private citizens could be punished for opinions that did not violate the law. The Court also offered protection to "symbolic speech." In *Tinker* v. *Des Moines School District* (1969), the Court ruled that students could not be expelled for wearing black armbands protesting the war in Vietnam. Writing for the majority, Justice Fortas argued that students did not lose their rights when they entered a schoolroom.

In *New York Times* v. *Sullivan* (1964), the Court loosened restraints on what the news media could write or broadcast about well-known figures. The Court ruled that public officials could not win a judgment of libel against a publication merely because a statement was untrue. The libel laws covered only "recklessly false statements" made with "actual malice." Justice Brennan held that "even a false statement may be deemed to make a valuable contribution to public debate." The decision emboldened the press, but it also resulted in a complete lack of privacy for public figures.

Nothing produced more public debate and more confusion on the Court than its efforts to define obscenity. From 1957 to 1968, the Court decided thirteen obscenity cases, issuing fifty-five separate opinions. It never did satisfactorily resolve the questions of what is obscene and how much latitude the government should have in restricting such material. Justice Brennan thought he had found an answer in *Roth* v. *United States* (1957), when he observed that expressions containing "the slightest redeeming social importance" could be protected by the First Amendment. The Court agreed that government could regulate as obscene any materials that "the average person, applying contemporary community standards," would regard as appealing to "prurient interests." For the next decade, the Court tried to write rules determining what materials fit that definition. It failed to do so, acknowledging that the process had to be subjective. Obscenity would remain a controversial issue for subsequent justices on the Supreme Court. Under Chief Justice Warren Burger (1969–1986), the Court changed the definition of obscene materials from "utterly without redeeming social value" to "lacking serious literary, artistic, political or social value." This definition permitted more government regulation, but it was no more successful than the earlier definition in creating a universally accepted standard.

The Warren Court won praise from civil libertarians and stirred opposition from traditionalists with a series of decisions interpreting the First Amendment's

Earl Warren, chief justice of the United States from 1953 to 1969, presided over a Supreme Court that greatly expanded individual rights. / © Bettmann/CORBIS

ban on the establishment of a state religion. In *Engel* v. *Vitale* (1962), the Court banned states and localities from instituting prayers in public schools. Justice Black, writing for the majority, said, "[I]t is no part of the business of government to compose official prayers for any group of American people." Over the next several years, the Court ruled that schools could not require devotional reading of the Bible. The justices also revived memories of the famous 1925 "monkey trial" of John Scopes in Tennessee when they struck down an Arkansas law requiring the teaching of "creation science" as a valid alternative to the theory of evolution. Such a law, the Court decided, was an unconstitutional attempt to establish a state religion.

Conservatives denounced these cases as examples of judicial lawmaking. One member of Congress complained that "they put the Negroes in the schools, and now they have driven God out." To a substantial minority of Christians, the Court's rulings were highly offensive. From 1963 through the mid-1980s, opponents of the rulings tried to pass constitutional amendments permitting prayers or Bible-reading in public schools. Although these efforts failed, they were a key element in the conservative tide that rose in the late 1970s. Many religious men and women who had once voted Democratic became ardent supporters of Ronald Reagan and the Republicans in 1980.

The Court also expanded the rights of citizens accused of crimes and set new procedural standards for law enforcement officers. In *Mapp* v. *Ohio* (1961), the Court forced all states to conform to the exclusionary rule, which holds that evidence gathered outside the specific terms of a search warrant cannot be used against a defendant. In another landmark case, *Gideon* v. *Wainwright* (1963), the Court observed that Clarence Earl Gideon, a man who had spent over half of his adult life in jail or prison, had never had a lawyer to defend him. The decision affirmed that a "fair trial" meant a right to qualified legal counsel. If a defendant could not afford an attorney, a state had to provide one.

In a more controversial, 5-to-4 ruling in *Miranda* v. *Arizona* (1966), the Warren Court extended the Fifth Amendment's ban against self-incrimination. Ernesto Miranda, arrested for burglary in Phoenix, had been coerced into confessing by police, who told him that if he remained quiet, judges would sentence him harshly. In its opinion on this case, the Warren Court set standards for police to follow when arresting suspects. Accused persons had to be informed in clear language (later called the Miranda warnings) that they had a right to remain silent and that anything they said could be used against them in a court of law. Police officers had to tell suspects that they had a right to a lawyer and that if they could not afford to hire one, legal counsel would be provided free by the state.

The Warren Court also enhanced the right to privacy in a decision that had profound reverberations both for individual behavior and for legal reasoning and scholarship. In 1965 the Court struck down an 1879 Connecticut law prohibiting the use of any contraceptive device and penalizing anyone giving advice on birth control. The law had long been ignored, but Planned Parenthood managed to bring it before the Court as a test case. In *Griswold* v. *Connecticut*, Justice Douglas held that the state's ban on contraception violated a long-established right to privacy. Although such a right is not specified in the Constitution, Douglas inferred it from other rights that are specified in that document. Three other justices—Brennan, Goldberg, and Warren—concurred, but they were troubled by what they saw as Douglas's invention of a new right. Instead of following Douglas's reasoning, therefore, they relied on the rarely used Ninth Amendment, which reserves for the people any rights not enumerated in the Bill of Rights. They argued that the right of privacy was ancient, older than the Constitution, and that the framers intended to incorporate it through the Ninth Amendment. One of the Court's liberals, Hugo Black, dissented. Black considered himself a strict constructionist, and he could find no specific guarantee to a right of privacy contained in the Constitution. Black's reservations gave some legal scholars pause, but the popular reaction to the *Griswold* decision was highly favorable—few people wanted state intrusion into their bedroom.

The Court also established new rules for elections, making them more representative and democratic. In *Baker* v. *Carr* (1962), the Court overruled earlier precedents when it declared that it and lower courts could decide if the boundaries of state congressional districts were fair. In many states, legislatures had not reapportioned the districts for decades. As a result, rural districts often contained fewer than one-fifth the population of their urban or suburban counterparts. City dwellers complained, but they were reminded that the U.S. Senate also did not represent voters proportionally. But after *Baker* v. *Carr*, underrepresented voters had a wedge with which to sue. They based their appeals on the simple rule of "one person, one vote," and the Court agreed with them.

By 1968 Earl Warren had been chief justice for fifteen years. He was seventy-seven years old and had presided over some of the most far-reaching decisions in the Court's history. In March of that year, Lyndon Johnson announced that he would not seek re-election. Because Warren wanted Johnson to have the opportunity to appoint a chief justice, he told the president that he intended to resign as soon as his successor could be confirmed. The president had a candidate in mind—Abe Fortas. An associate justice since 1965, Fortas was a long-time friend who had continued to give Johnson political advice after his appointment to the Court, often violating the tradition of judicial impartiality. During those three years, Fortas had become a stalwart member of Warren's liberal majority.

Fortas's nomination faced immediate difficulties in the Senate. Democrats still had a majority, but Republicans used several delaying tactics throughout the summer. They expected Richard Nixon to win the upcoming presidential election, and they wanted him to appoint the chief justice. Fortas's support for the Vietnam War, as well as his intimate ties to the now unpopular Johnson, had made him unattractive to some Democrats as well. During the confirmation hearings, the Senate Judiciary Committee learned that Fortas had received $15,000 for teaching some summer law courses; the money had been paid by men who might have had cases before the Court. Faced with charges of cronyism, Fortas asked Johnson to withdraw his nomination in October. Warren remained chief justice until 1969, when President Nixon named Warren Burger, a conservative federal judge from Minneapolis, to replace him. Fortas remained an associate justice until the spring of 1969, when further allegations of financial impropriety forced him to resign.

The end of the Warren Court marked the conclusion of a sixteen-year era of expanding individual rights and the curtailment of arbitrary government power. At the beginning of this period, the Court outlawed segregation in public schools; by the end, it had expanded First Amendment protection in ways that affected the daily lives of most Americans. It had validated the growing pluralism in American life. Yet its endorsement of social changes exacted a substantial price, in effect eroding the Court's own authority in the years that followed. Traditionalists who bemoaned the very pluralism that the Court had affirmed attacked the justices' work. Over the next twenty years, conservatives gained an advantage by deriding what they characterized as the social engineering and judicial activism of the Warren Court. While the subsequent Burger and Rehnquist Courts did not reverse most of the decisions of the Warren years, they curtailed many of their applications.

Decline of the Great Society

Despite the high hopes raised in 1964 and the amazing spate of Great Society legislation in 1965 and 1966, the good feelings lasted barely eighteen months. By late 1966, the impetus behind the Great Society had dwindled. Among the principal reasons for this decline were the war in Vietnam and a white backlash against the extension of civil rights.

Johnson's efforts to secure equality for all races peaked with the Voting Rights Act of 1965. That act, together with the Civil Rights Act of 1964, allowed the Johnson administration to put the weight of the federal government behind efforts to end formal, legal discrimination against racial minorities. Yet most observers realized that ending social and economic inequality between the races would require more than removing the legal barriers.

In the summer of 1965, while addressing the graduating class at predominantly black Howard University in Washington, D.C., Johnson spoke of the vicious cycle of "despair and deprivation" among African Americans. He explained that the Voting Rights Act was "the beginning of freedom . . . but freedom is not enough." He noted that the unemployment rate for blacks was now double that for whites, although thirty-five years earlier it had been the same. The unemployment rate for black teenage boys was 23 percent, compared to 13 percent for whites. The poverty rate for whites had fallen 27 percent, while that of blacks had diminished by only 3 percent.

The reasons for the increasing economic gap between whites and blacks were complex, Johnson said, mostly deriving from "ancient brutality, past injustice, and present prejudice." But Johnson placed some of the responsibility for black poverty on the current cultural norms of African Americans themselves. Drawing on a report called *The Negro Family: The Case for National Action*, by Assistant Secretary of Labor Daniel Patrick Moynihan, he emphasized the dreadful effects of "the breakdown of the Negro family structure." Assuming that this structure should consist of an adult male wage earner and a female homemaker, his argument implied a sentimental, idealized view of the family, hardly representative of the reality for either black or white Americans. Yet both Moynihan and Johnson ignored the complexity and variety of family life in their effort to demonstrate links between culture and poverty. "When the family collapses," Johnson said, "it is the children that are usually damaged," because of the absence of a strong father figure. "When it happens on a massive scale," the president explained, "the community itself is crippled."

Johnson's speech and Moynihan's report were supposed to set the agenda for additional government action to reduce poverty. Moynihan had expected that by concentrating on cultural reasons for African American poverty, the administration would be able to secure better antipoverty programs. But that was not to be. A White House conference met in November with the goal of expanding earlier civil rights legislation, but it broke up in acrimony over the Moynihan report. Some African Americans, expressing new feelings of racial pride and resenting what they perceived to be condescending meddling by white liberals, denounced Moynihan's conclusions as racist. Several critics concluded that the report blamed the victims of discrimination for their plight. Analysts found flaws in Moynihan's methods and described unique strengths in African American families and culture.

Despite its apparently condescending tone, the Moynihan report represented a serious attempt to address a complex problem. But the early criticism undermined support for it. The report left a contradictory legacy. Some people noted its attention to black male unemployment and advocated jobs and training programs. Conservatives and some moderates seized on the report's bleak condemnation of African American family structure to justify dismantling antipoverty programs, notably Aid to Families with Dependent Children. At the same time, Johnson was distracted by the growing problem in Vietnam. In July 1965, he committed U.S. ground forces to the war, and over the next years, as the war consumed more and more of the government's resources and the administration's attention, the problems of poverty and racial inequality received less priority.

Another problem also intervened. In the summer of 1964, race riots struck New York City and several other cities in New York and New Jersey.

Police responded to these outpourings of African American rage with gunfire. Dozens of mostly young black men were shot dead. These violent incidents proved to be only preludes to what was to come. In August 1965 a major uprising erupted in Watts, a predominantly African American section of Los Angeles. The insurrection sprang from economic frustration and black rage at the brutality of the all-white police force. Nevertheless, the events in Watts shocked moderate whites, who only five months before had been moved by the nonviolence and moral force of the demonstrators at Selma, Alabama. White support for racial equality began to erode.

Over the next year, whites began to resent the efforts of Martin Luther King, Jr., and other civil rights leaders to desegregate housing in northern cities. Suspicion was also aroused by the Supreme Court's extension of the rights of people accused of crimes. The race riots spread from one city to another after 1965; by 1968, Detroit, Newark, Washington, Cincinnati, and many other cities across the country had experienced major rioting. Whites were further alienated by the militancy of a newer generation of black leaders (see Chapter 8). By the time of the 1966 congressional elections, white anger at blacks was a key underlying issue.

In 1966, a Gallup poll reported that 52 percent of whites believed the administration was pushing too hard on civil rights, 20 percent more than four years ago. Some Republican candidates denounced "crime in the streets," a term for the African American uprisings. They opposed the Great Society's plans to desegregate public housing. Democrats, too, fanned white fears of blacks. The unsuccessful Democratic candidate for governor of Maryland ran on the slogan "Your home is your castle—protect it." One Democratic congressman from Chicago ruefully reported that in "any home, any bar, any barber shop" you will find people "talking about Martin Luther King and how they are moving in on us and what's going to happen to our neighborhoods."

The white backlash, along with voter dissatisfaction over the administration's handling of the Vietnam War (see Chapter 7), propelled a Republican gain of forty-seven seats in the House and three in the Senate in 1966. The backlash also had an effect at the state level. In California, conservative Republican Ronald Reagan, who condemned the Watts rioters, won the governorship with a margin of nearly 1 million votes. After the election results were in, the defeated Democratic governor, Edmund G. Brown, concluded that "whether we like it or not, people want separation of the races."

Over the next two years, white distrust of social reform grew. Working-class whites, many descended from eastern or southern European immigrants, came to despise the Johnson administration. As prices rose and the government seemed powerless to stop inflation, these white ethnics believed that their needs had been overlooked in the effort to end poverty and forge a Great Society. The urban riots and the Supreme Court's extension of protections to criminal defendants particularly infuriated white ethnic groups. Johnson seemed bereft of ideas to reconstruct his shattered consensus. After the U.S. Army had quelled the Detroit riots in July 1967, at a cost of forty-four lives, the president called for a day of prayer for "order and reconciliation among men." He created a presidential commission, headed by former judge Otto Kerner, to study the causes of urban violence. Yet when Kerner submitted his report in 1968, describing the emergence of "two nations, separate but unequal, white and black," Johnson refused to receive it.

Johnson's aides told him he needed more than prayer to restore his public standing. By the fall of 1967, his public approval rating had slipped below 33 percent, the lowest figure since Truman's dismal rating at the end of the Korean War. Assistants suggested that Johnson might revive his standing in the polls by showing support for police. In an address to the International Association of Chiefs of Police, Johnson drew prolonged applause with an attack on African American rioters: "We cannot tolerate behavior that destroys what generations of men and women have built here in America—no matter what stimulates that behavior and no matter what is offered to try to justify it."

From that point on, the Great Society ground down. The flood of legislation begun in 1965 slowed to a trickle after the new Congress assembled in 1967. The only major law passed was a housing bill, submitted in 1968, designed to replace the dilapidated dwellings devastated by riots in northern cities. This law also banned racial and religious discrimination in the sale or rental of housing. Modified during the Nixon administration, the law ultimately led to the construction of 1.3 million low-income housing units, but the building program benefited rich developers and investors more than poor people.

Other Great Society programs withered at the end of the Johnson administration. Unwilling to fund both the war in Vietnam and the War on Poverty, Congress cut back on the latter. The president lost heart too at the end of his term, when he saw his support for the poor become a liability among whites. This reduction of support for the War on Poverty further fueled the backlash over the next decade. Conservative opponents of government assistance to the poor now pointed to the failure of the Great Society to eliminate poverty as proof that such programs could not work. In fact, these programs were underfunded, often mismanaged, and had little input from poor people themselves.

Foreign Affairs in the Shadow of Vietnam

The excitement and controversy created by the Great Society, and the dramatic escalation of the war in Vietnam, left government officials with neither the time nor the inclination to think deeply about relations with the rest of the world. Essentially, the administration continued the efforts begun earlier in the Cold War to project American power around the globe. Not comfortable with foreign affairs himself, the president relied on advice from the national security experts he had inherited from Kennedy. Together with men like Secretary of State Dean Rusk, national security advisers McGeorge Bundy (1961–1965) and Walt Whitman Rostow (1965–1968), and Secretary of Defense Robert McNamara (1961–1968), Johnson involved the United States in a series of regional disputes in Latin America, the Middle East, and Europe. These controversies produced little success, and they strained relations with long-time friends. By 1968, experts inside and outside government were calling for a new direction in foreign affairs. At that point, the administration attempted to dampen the passions of the Cold War and relax tensions with the Soviet Union. But its efforts at détente were cut short, and it remained for the succeeding Nixon White House to put them into effect.

The Johnson administration reversed its predecessor's halting efforts to foster social reform in the Western Hemisphere. In March 1964 the director of the Alliance for Progress announced that the alliance would change its emphasis; instead of focusing on land reform and reducing the gap between rich and poor, it would encourage economic growth. Henceforth, he said, the United States would be neutral on social reform and would protect its private investments. The United States would not force Latin American governments to adopt democracy if they faced communist or other revolutionary movements. This policy served as an excuse for relying on Latin American military regimes to protect U.S. interests.

Besides its suspicion of social reform in Latin America, the United States also displayed insensitivity to issues of national pride and identity in the region. Early in 1964, for example, the administration had to confront a host of angry Panamanians. For sixty years, Panama had resented U.S. domination of the Canal Zone. The 1903 treaty granting the United States the rights to the zone "as if it were sovereign" offended Panamanian pride. In 1964 the Panamanians became upset when American high school students in the Canal Zone tore down the Panamanian flag and U.S. authorities refused to raise it again, despite promising to do so. Four days of rioting in Panama left twenty-four Panamanians and four American soldiers dead. Thousands of Panamanians were forced to flee their homes. Johnson took matters into his own hands. Speaking to the Panamanian president personally, he promised to discuss Panamanian grievances in detail at an upcoming summit. But when talks opened between the two nations, Washington downplayed the issue of the offensive canal treaty. Most Panamanians believed Washington was merely stalling.

Elsewhere in the hemisphere, the United States reverted to direct military intervention in the Dominican Republic. That impoverished Caribbean country had long been dominated, directly or indirectly, by the United States. A dictator, Rafael Trujillo, had ruled with American connivance from 1940 to 1961. Toward the end of his regime, however, Washington lost patience with his brutality. In May 1961 he was assassinated, and the Kennedy administration backed the democratic election of a successor. In December 1962 the Dominicans elected Juan Bosch as president. Bosch, a leftist but not a communist, soon ran afoul of the Dominican military, which overthrew him in the fall of 1963.

In April 1965 young army officers sympathetic to Bosch ousted the military-backed government. Their more conservative seniors panicked and appealed to the American ambassador for help. Shooting broke out on the streets of Santo Domingo, and the U.S. envoy wired Washington that a communist revolution was at hand. The embassy published a false press release stating that fifty-eight "identified and prominent Communist and Castroite leaders" were directing the pro-Bosch forces. President Johnson decided to send the marines and the army to quell the uprising and install another conservative government. At first, the president justified the intervention as necessary to preserve American lives and property. Two days later, on April 30, he explained instead that "people outside the Dominican Republic are seeking to gain control."

U.S. forces trounced the leftists and eventually helped put a conservative, Joaquin Balaguer, in power. But the intervention produced a furious reaction. Bosch complained that "this was a democratic revolution, crushed by the leading democracy in the world." At home, liberal opinion was discouraged that the United States had reverted to force, intervening in a way repugnant to most Latin Americans.

While the intervention in the Dominican Republic helped to dampen additional domestic consensus over foreign affairs, the war in Vietnam dealt it a fatal blow when it grew into a major controversy. At the same time, strains appeared in the NATO alliance, considered the cornerstone of American foreign policy since 1949. French president Charles de Gaulle attempted to restrain what he considered Washington's high-handed control of the alliance. Europeans were unhappy about the Cuban missile crisis of 1962, when the United States and the Soviet Union had approached the brink of war without consulting their allies. In the aftermath of the crisis, France went forward with its own atomic bomb project, and in 1966, the French president announced that his nation's forces would no longer participate in the military arm of NATO. He forced the alliance to move its headquarters from Paris to Brussels. The Johnson administration dismissed de Gaulle as a bitter old man making a futile attempt to restore France's faded glory.

Events outside Europe also challenged American leadership in international affairs. In June 1967 the Six-Day War between Israel and the Arab states of Egypt, Syria, and Jordan further strained America's foreign relations and created a bitter legacy. For ten years, Egypt had smarted from the military embarrassment it suffered at the hands of Israel during the October 1956 Suez conflict. Egypt's president Gamal Abdel Nasser wanted to restore his standing at home by erasing the stain of the Suez loss. With his army resupplied by the Soviet Union and goaded into action by other Arab states, Nasser looked for ways to threaten Israel in the spring of 1967.

He did so by demanding that the United Nations remove its emergency forces from the Sinai Peninsula, which separated Israel and Egypt. Much to his surprise, the United Nations agreed. The Soviet Union urged caution, but Nasser was trapped by his own inflammatory rhetoric. He closed the Strait of Tiran to ships bound for Israel's southern port of Eilat. At this point, the United States stepped in to head off a war. Johnson begged the Israelis not to respond to Nasser until the United States could organize an international flotilla to break the blockade. But the Europeans, fearful that the Arab states would cut off their oil, declined to join the effort.

Faced with what they believed to be a halfhearted American effort on their behalf, the Israelis took matters into their own hands on the morning of

June 5, 1967. In a pre-emptive strike, the Israeli air force destroyed Egyptian planes on the ground while Israeli tanks knifed across the Sinai. Later that day, Jordan's King Hussein ordered his artillery forces to shell the Jewish sector of Jerusalem; in response, the Israelis turned on Jordan and two days later attacked Syria as well. Within six days, Israel had taken the Sinai from Egypt, the West Bank (an area composed of the western bank of the Jordan River and the eastern part of Jerusalem) from Jordan, and the Golan Heights from Syria. After the war, the United Nations called for Israeli withdrawal from captured territories to secure and recognized borders in return for Arab recognition of Israel's right to exist. The United Nations also asked the combatants to settle the Palestinian problem, a constant source of conflict since Israel replaced the British administration in Palestine after World War II. Hundreds of thousands of Palestinians were now left homeless by Israel's conquest of the West Bank and Gaza. Neither Israel nor the Arabs implemented the U.N. resolutions, and the dispute among Israel, the Arab states, and the Palestinians, who wanted a state of their own, became more bitter than ever.

Two weeks after the Six-Day War ended in 1967, Soviet prime minister Alexei Kosygin visited New York for a special session of the U.N. General Assembly, which was called to discuss peace in the Middle East. While in New York, Kosygin accepted Johnson's invitation to meet him at Glassboro State College in southern New Jersey to discuss U.S.-Soviet relations. At this meeting, the first superpower summit since the melancholy conversations between John Kennedy and Nikita Khrushchev in May 1961, the president sought the Soviet leader's

President Lyndon B. Johnson and Soviet premier Alexei Kosygin confer at Glassboro, New Jersey, June 1968. / © Bettmann/CORBIS

help in arranging an end to the war in Vietnam. Kosygin refused because he wanted to show the North Vietnamese that the Soviet Union could do more for them than the People's Republic of China, now the Soviets' rival.

The two men did agree to begin arms control negotiations. However, steps toward détente went no further in the remaining eighteen months of the Johnson administration. In August 1968, Secretary of State Rusk planned to announce that Johnson would repay Kosygin's visit with a trip to the Soviet Union to begin talks on limiting strategic arms. But on August 20, Soviet tanks rumbled into Prague, Czechoslovakia, to crush a Czech experiment in liberalized socialism. Moscow feared that Czech leader Alexander Dubcek secretly wanted to dismantle the one-party state. *Pravda,* the newspaper of the Soviet Communist Party, explained that Communist states could not stand idly by as one of their number fell "into the process of antisocialist degeneration." Western journalists quickly dubbed this position the Brezhnev Doctrine, after Soviet party chair Leonid Brezhnev. In the climate of hostility evoked by the Soviets' crushing Czechoslovakian freedom, Johnson decided he could not afford the political risk of meeting Soviet leaders to discuss arms control. As in previous administrations, genuine détente with the Soviet Union remained only a tantalizing possibility.

Conclusion

By the end of 1968, it appeared that Lyndon Johnson's administration could be characterized largely by its failed aspirations. Johnson had done more than any other president since Franklin Roosevelt to spur Americans to reform their society. The Civil Rights Act of 1964 and the Voting Rights Act of 1965 had helped remove the legal barriers facing African Americans. The War on Poverty reduced hunger and suffering, and Medicare improved access to healthcare. Meanwhile, Johnson's appointees to the Supreme Court helped the Court expand civil liberties and ensure that electoral districts were correctly apportioned. By 1968, however, most of the public's early enthusiasm for Johnson's agenda had been lost. The Vietnam War was draining the government's funds and energy. Too many Great Society programs were underfunded or mired in administrative troubles. Race riots had erupted across the country, and a white backlash arose to block further attempts at social reform.

But it was foreign policy, not domestic affairs, that ultimately led to Lyndon Johnson's personal downfall and to the discrediting of liberalism. As demonstrated by his administration's intervention in the Dominican Republic, Johnson believed in the usefulness of military power for suppressing leftists and communists in the Third World. In this respect, he was fundamentally no different than his predecessors. As Chapter 7 explains, however, Johnson dramatically raised the stakes in Vietnam and received most of the blame for America's failure there.

F U R T H E R • R E A D I N G

On the personalities and policies of the Johnson administration, see Robert Caro, *The Years of Lyndon Johnson: The Path to Power* (1983), *Means of Ascent* (1989), and *Master of the Senate* (2002); Robert Dallek, *Lone Star Rising: Lyndon Johnson, 1908–1960* (1991) and *Flawed Giant: Lyndon Johnson and His Times, 1961–1973* (1998); Doris Kearns, *Lyndon Johnson and the American Dream* (1977); Michael Beschloss, *Taking Charge: The Johnson White House Tapes, 1963–1964* (1997) and *Reaching for Glory: The Secret Johnson White House Tapes, 1964–1965* (2001); Allan M. Matusow, *The Unraveling of America: A History of Liberalism in the 1960s* (1984); Maurice Isserman and Michael Kazin, *America Divided: The Civil Wars of the 1960s* (2000); Robert Alan Goldberg, *Barry Goldwater* (1995). **On Great Society programs,** see James M. Sundquist, *Politics and Policy: The Eisenhower, Kennedy and Johnson Years* (1968); Daniel P Moynihan, *Maximum Feasible Misunderstanding* (1970); David Reimers, *Still the Golden Door: The Third World Comes to America* (2001); John E. Schwarz, *America's Hidden Success: A Reassessment of Public Policy from Kennedy to Reagan* (1988); Michael Katz, *The Undeserving Poor: From the War on Poverty to the War on Welfare* (1989); Taylor Branch, *Pillar of Fire: America in the King Years, 1963–1965* (1998); Nicholas Lemann, *The Promised Land: The Great Black Migration and How It Changed America* (1991); David M. Chalmers, *And the Crooked Places Made Straight: The Struggle for Social Change in the 1960s* (1991); William L. Van Deburg, *New Day in Babylon: The Black Power Movement and American Culture, 1965–1975* (1992). **On the Supreme Court,** see Melvin Urofsky, *The Continuity of Change: The Supreme Court and Individual Liberties, 1953–1986* (1991); Bernard Schwartz, *Super Chief: Earl Warren and His Supreme Court* (1983); Fred Graham, *The Due Process Revolution: The Warren Court's Impact on Criminal Law* (1977). **On foreign affairs,** see H. W. Brands, *Lyndon B. Johnson and the Wages of Globalism: The Limits of American Power* (1995) and *The Foreign Policy of Lyndon Johnson: Beyond Vietnam* (1999); Diane B. Kunz (ed.), *The Diplomacy of The Crucial Decade: American Foreign Relations During the 1960s* (1994); Michael Oren, *Six Days of War: June 1967 and the Making of the Modern Middle East* (2002); Thomas A. Schwatz, *Lyndon Johnson and Europe: In the Shadow of Vietnam* (2003); Thomas Zeiler, *Dean Rusk: Defending the American Mission Abroad* (2000). **On architecture and American culture,** see Lois Craig and the staff of the Federal Architecture Project, *The Federal Presence: Architecture, Politics, and Symbols in United States Government Buildings* (1978); Robert Haddow, *Pavilions of Plenty: Exhibiting American Culture Abroad in the 1950s* (1997); Ron Robin, *Enclaves of America: The Rhetoric of American Political Architecture Abroad, 1900–1965* (1992); Annabel Jane Wharton, *Building the Cold War: Hilton International Hotels and Modern Architecture* (2001).

7

The Vietnam Nightmare

Vietnamese civilians flee the fighting in Hue during the Tet Offensive, February 1968. /
© CORBIS

In May 1964, six months into his term as president, Lyndon Johnson had a heart-to-heart talk about the looming war in Vietnam with Georgia senator Richard Russell, a man he had often relied on for advice when Johnson served in the Senate from 1949 to 1960. The two old friends agreed that Vietnam was "the damn worse mess" they had ever seen. Russell lamented that he did not see "how we're ever going to get out of [Vietnam] without fighting a major war with the Chinese and all of them down there in those rice paddies and jungles." Johnson anguished about the potential human cost of the war. He told Russell that the thought of sending one of his valets, a man with six children, to fight in Vietnam "just makes chills run up my back." But the president saw no way out. His advisers, men with far more experience than he had in foreign affairs, men who had stood beside John F. Kennedy, told him, "[W]e haven't got much choice, that we are treaty-bound [to the government of South Vietnam], that we are there," that a communist victory in South Vietnam "will be a domino that will kick off a whole list of others, that we've just got to prepare for the worst." Seeing nothing but bad alternatives, unsure of his own grasp of foreign affairs, and deathly afraid of appearing weak, Johnson took the fateful steps early in his presidency to commit the United States to fighting a major war in Vietnam.

American involvement in the war in Vietnam grew from a minor issue of little interest to most people into a frightening nightmare, affecting nearly every aspect of American life. The seemingly endless war threw the country into agony, opening deep fissures in many American political, social, cultural, and religious institutions. The war became a major cause of the American people's disillusionment with government and of their abandonment of political liberalism. Chapter 8 explores the culture of protest fostered by the Vietnam War; this chapter focuses on the war itself and its impact on American politics and foreign policy.

From the beginning of America's involvement, during the late 1940s, until the fall of Saigon in 1975, U.S. politicians, diplomats, and military leaders consistently misunderstood the rapidly changing conditions in Vietnam. Their failure to grasp the intensity of revolutionary nationalism in Southeast Asia led to a futile attempt to sustain a noncommunist regime in the southern half of Vietnam. In the devastating war that developed during the 1960s, American bombs, guns, and money ruined Vietnam physically, economically, and socially. The grueling conflict also took a profound toll on many of the American soldiers who fought it.

As the war dragged on, Americans at home became sick of the brutal, inconclusive fighting. The general consensus on U.S. foreign policy that had developed during the early Cold War eroded as the public became increasingly frustrated with the war in Vietnam. Many Americans continued to believe the United States should oppose communism, but they became disillusioned with this war because it made little progress. Other people believed the war should not have been fought at all. These misgivings about Vietnam spread into doubts about the overall principle of containment that had governed American foreign policy since World War II.

In the 1968 presidential election, Americans voted for change, hoping that a new administration could extricate them from the Vietnam morass. But more than four years—and another presidential election—would pass before a cease-fire agreement was signed.

The Growth of America's Commitment to Vietnam, 1945–1964

John Kenneth Galbraith, Harvard economist and U.S. ambassador to India, once asked President John F. Kennedy, "Who is the man in your administration who decides what countries are strategic? I would like to . . . ask him what is so important about this [Vietnamese] real estate in the space age?" The president declined to identify the planner because it was Kennedy himself who attached such importance to Indochina. Like most other high government officials in the years since 1945, Kennedy believed that the containment of communism should be the principal goal of American foreign policy. But because involvement in Vietnam represented only a small part of the larger U.S. strategy of confronting revolutionary nationalists in the postcolonial world, Americans never focused their attention on events in Vietnam until the United States was deeply involved in the war. From Truman through Kennedy, successive administrations gradually enlarged the U.S. commitment to Vietnam, setting the stage for a dramatic escalation under Lyndon Johnson.

Since 1945, the United States had backed alternatives to the Communist Democratic Republic of Vietnam (North Vietnam), established by Ho Chi Minh in Hanoi on September 2, 1945, the day World War II ended in Asia. The Truman administration, preoccupied with more pressing issues in Europe and other parts of Asia, paid little attention to Ho Chi Minh. The United States declined his pleas for diplomatic recognition. During 1946, war broke out between Ho Chi Minh's Vietminh guerrillas and French troops trying to re-establish French colonial power in Indochina. Despite some uneasiness about supporting colonial rule, the Truman administration backed France and its puppet Vietnamese regime. By the end of 1952, Washington was paying 40 percent of the cost of the war.

During the Eisenhower administration, the French required even more American aid. Despite the confident assertion of Secretary of State John Foster Dulles that an additional infusion of $400 million would help France "break the organized body of Communist aggression by the end of the 1955 fighting season," the Vietminh gained strength. By March 1954, the United States was paying 70 percent of the cost of the war. Nevertheless, the Vietminh surrounded the French military position at Dienbienphu, a strategic outpost in the northwest corner of Vietnam. Eisenhower toyed with the idea of ordering an air strike to relieve the French garrison, but ultimately he decided against it. The Vietminh overran Dienbienphu on May 7, 1954.

Although the fall of Dienbienphu was a catastrophe for France, Washington almost welcomed the defeat as a chance to demonstrate American anticommunist resolve. Unlike France, which was tainted as the colonial power, the United States could sponsor a so-called third force, composed of Vietnamese nationalists who opposed both the Communists and the French. This was the approach Eisenhower had in mind when the peace conference convened at Geneva, Switzerland. Although the United States sent representatives to the conference, it was not a signatory to the Geneva Accords. In fact, it soon helped to undermine them.

After the Geneva Accords partitioned Vietnam along the 17th parallel, the United States became more deeply involved in Southeast Asia than ever. In late 1954, the Eisenhower administration sponsored the creation of the Southeast Asia Treaty Organization (SEATO), a military alliance patterned roughly on NATO. Although the southern part of Vietnam never formally joined SEATO, the United States based its involvement in Vietnamese politics partly on its having accepted protection from the alliance. Washington helped set up Ngo Dinh Diem as prime minister of the southern section. In 1955, Diem proclaimed a new nation, the Republic of Vietnam, with himself as president. Neither the communist North nor the anticommunist South recognized each other. In 1956, the United States supported Diem when he refused to allow the nationwide unification elections, which were to include both North and South and which were promised by the Geneva Accords. The United States further assisted Diem in creating the Army of the Republic of Vietnam (ARVN) and a police force.

Eisenhower espoused what came to be known as the domino theory, which said that if Indochina fell to communism, the rest of Southeast Asia would topple like a row of dominoes. General J. Lawton Collins, the special U.S. representative to Vietnam, recommended in 1955 that Washington withdraw support from the haughty, unpopular Diem, a Catholic in a predominantly Buddhist land, but Secretary of State Dulles declared that "the decision to back Diem has gone to the point of no return."

Vowing to exterminate all vestiges of the popular Vietminh in the South, Diem had his army and police arrest twenty thousand members of the movement, killing over one thousand in a span of three years. These actions won praise from American lawmakers looking for signs of a legitimate third force. Senator John F. Kennedy, for example, glorified the new South Vietnam as "the cornerstone of the Free World in Southeast Asia, the keystone to the arch, the finger in the dike." As U.S. military and economic aid created the appearance of stability, the American government and press celebrated South Vietnam as a "success story" in Asia. It was a forlorn hope.

Despite Diem's harassment, the remnants of the Vietminh in the South, assisted by North Vietnam, managed to mount a campaign of their own. On December 20, 1960, they proclaimed a new National Front for the Liberation of Vietnam (NLF) and began guerrilla attacks against the South. By mid-1961, the NLF forces, referred to as the Vietcong by the South Vietnamese, had succeeded in gaining control of 58 percent of the territory of South Vietnam.

When Kennedy became president, he decided that the Eisenhower administration had not done enough to help Diem. And after the catastrophic Bay of Pigs invasion and his chilly summit meeting with Nikita Khrushchev,

Kennedy especially desired some measure of success against communist movements in the Third World. "How do we get moving?" he asked his staff. They suggested using the army's Special Forces, commonly called the Green Berets, against the Vietcong insurrection.

Kennedy responded with an additional $42 million beyond the $220 million already being spent each year on aid to South Vietnam. He sent hundreds more troops to advise the ARVN on how to fight, and he ordered four hundred Green Berets to lead nine thousand mountain tribesmen in an effort to stop infiltration from North Vietnam. He also had the CIA conduct commando raids against North Vietnam. The United States provided heavy weapons to South Vietnamese provincial civil guardsmen (local militias) to use against the Vietcong in rural areas. By late 1961, there were 3,205 American advisers in South Vietnam; that number rose to 9,000 the next year. The American advisers—who did not limit their activities to advising—helped the ARVN move hundreds of thousands of peasants from their homes to relocation centers, or "strategic hamlets."

The massing of peasants into strategic hamlets—separating them from land their families had tilled for generations—made it easier for the South Vietnamese government to hunt for NLF fighters. But it also gave the NLF a weapon in its propaganda war against the Saigon authorities. Once the rural South Vietnamese were relocated, the ARVN bombed and napalmed the countryside to rout out the NLF. Thousands of civilians, including women and children, lost their lives. The NLF told South Vietnamese peasants that the Saigon government was bombing and burning its own citizens. General Paul D. Harkins, in charge of the American advisory forces, dismissed warnings that this indiscriminate bombing only alienated the population from the government in Saigon, saying that napalm (highly flammable petroleum jelly) "really puts the fear of God into the Vietcong, and that is what counts."

While Harkins kept up a stream of optimistic reports flowing back to Washington, American field advisers grew disgusted with what they considered the cowardice and corruption of the ARVN and the South Vietnamese government. By mid-1963, the Kennedy administration, once so supportive of Ngo Dinh Diem, viewed him and the rest of the Ngo family as obstacles to success against the NLF. The Vietnamese peasantry despised the strategic hamlets and hated Diem's connections to the old landlord class. Leaders of the Buddhist sects, to which over two-thirds of South Vietnam's population belonged, condemned Diem's pro-Catholic policies and demanded his resignation. Buddhists and students led street demonstrations against the government in June; the police responded with clubs and tear gas. On June 11, a seventy-three-year-old Buddhist monk, Thich Quang Duc, turned the Buddhist uprising from a local affair into an international crisis by immolating himself in the middle of a busy Saigon intersection. His ritual suicide was captured on film and broadcast around the world. Americans reacted with horror. President Diem's sister-in-law, Madame Ngo Dinh Nhu, provoked further outrage against herself and her family when she scoffed that she would be "happy to provide the mustard for the monks' next barbecues."

The Kennedy administration decided that General Collins had been right eight years before: Diem's family must either change its ways and broaden its

A Buddhist monk commits ritual suicide to protest the policies of the government of South Vietnam's President Ngo Dinh Diem, June 1963. / © Bettmann/CORBIS

government to include nonfamily members and non-Catholics, or be removed from office. That summer, to secure Republican support for his policies, the president appointed an old Republican rival, Henry Cabot Lodge, as the new ambassador to South Vietnam. Lodge had been Eisenhower's ambassador to the United Nations and Nixon's vice-presidential candidate in 1960. The day after his arrival in Saigon, Lodge encouraged a plot by some of the ARVN's top generals to oust the Ngos, but the generals aborted their plans, fearful that Diem had discovered the plot. Meanwhile, American officials in Washington kept up the pressure for change in Saigon.

Diem refused invitations to go quietly into exile. He dug in his heels and turned on the Americans. His brother Nhu hinted darkly at a deal with North Vietnam that would leave the Ngo family in charge of a neutral South Vietnam. At this point, Ambassador Lodge in Saigon, along with several officials in Washington most concerned with Vietnam policy, decided to encourage the dissident ARVN generals to reactivate their plans for a coup. On November 1, 1963, the plotters seized control of the presidential palace and captured Diem and Nhu. Informed in advance of the coup, Ambassador Lodge made no attempt to protect the Ngos or offer them safe conduct out of the country. They were murdered by the plotters early on the morning of November 2, and a new government took over, headed by General Duong Van Minh. Word of Diem's death shook Kennedy, once one of the Vietnamese president's staunchest backers. He seems to have hoped that Diem would go quietly into exile. When the murder was confirmed, Kennedy turned white and retreated from the room.

At first, the existence of a new South Vietnamese government seemed to present an opportunity to wage war against the NLF with renewed vigor, but by January 1964, American officials in Saigon and Washington had grown impatient with General Minh's inability to subdue the Vietcong. Despite later claims by some Kennedy insiders that, had the president lived, he would have reduced the American commitment after the 1964 election, Kennedy remained dedicated to victory until the date of his assassination, three weeks after Diem's death. But he had not formulated a plan. Although he worried about the complete collapse of the South Vietnamese government, he thought "we'd cross that bridge when we came to it," his brother Robert recalled. The historian Fredrik Logevall concluded the following about Kennedy's intentions in the fall of 1963: "Like many politicians, he liked to put off difficult decisions for as long as possible, and he no doubt hoped that the crisis in Indochina would somehow resolve itself, if not before the 1964 election, then after."

Overall, the Kennedy administration left Lyndon Johnson a terrible burden in South Vietnam. By the time Johnson took office, sixteen thousand U.S. Army, Navy, and Marine Corps "advisers" were conducting daily operations against the NLF. Yet this effort produced diminishing returns because the NLF continued to increase its control over the countryside. The more fighting the American soldiers did, the less the ARVN soldiers and officers seemed willing to do. The government of South Vietnam enjoyed little support except from a coterie of ARVN generals, who preferred the ease of life in Saigon to fighting in the field. In the countryside, where over 80 percent of the population resided, the national government had become at best a nuisance and at worst an enemy. While Kennedy pleaded with the American public not to become weary of the war, many Vietnamese peasants had already lost patience and perhaps hope. The hated strategic hamlets and the government's widespread use of napalm and other defoliants proved powerful recruiting agents for the NLF. Johnson would have a difficult time pursuing Kennedy's vision of a victorious Republic of Vietnam.

Soon the new South Vietnamese government of Duong Van Minh proved no more receptive to American advice than had Ngo Dinh Diem and his family. The resistance of the Saigon government to American suggestions for waging the war presented the new Johnson administration with a painful dilemma, one it never resolved. The South Vietnamese authorities seemed incapable of winning the war without American assistance. Yet the more the Americans helped, the less the South Vietnamese did for themselves, thereby encouraging the Americans to get more deeply involved. The growing U.S. presence, in turn, seemed to validate NLF and North Vietnamese claims that the South Vietnamese authorities were American puppets, not genuine nationalists.

On his one trip to the region in 1961, Lyndon Johnson, then vice president, had called Diem "the Winston Churchill of Southeast Asia." When skeptical reporters questioned him about this strange exaggeration, Johnson responded, "He's the only boy we've got out there." Now new to the presidency and trying to follow Kennedy's policies, Johnson relied on the advice of his predecessor's foreign policy experts. Johnson simply wasn't comfortable with international affairs. "Foreigners," he joked, "are not like the folks I am used to." His own combative personality also led Johnson to a deeper commitment in Vietnam. At his very first meeting about Vietnam, on November 24, 1963, he told his staff: "Don't go to bed at night until you have asked yourself, 'Have I done everything I could to further the American effort to assist South Vietnam?'" A few days later, he told the new deputy chief of mission in Saigon, "Lyndon Johnson is not going down as the president who lost Vietnam." Johnson bullied and cajoled his advisers into reaching a consensus on Vietnam.

Almost to a man, Johnson's advisers believed that the United States needed to increase its presence in South Vietnam; pursue the war more vigorously; and, if necessary, replace General Minh with someone more compliant to Washington's desires. The president, facing the upcoming election, favored delay, hoping to keep Vietnam off the nation's front pages and the evening news. The president would not turn his subordinates away from their militant course, but neither did he want to disrupt the consensus that he expected to carry him to victory in the fall. Johnson had another, darker fear of the consequences of reducing the American commitment in Vietnam: he worried that if he reversed course in Vietnam, his advisers and Robert Kennedy, a man he loathed and distrusted, would accuse him of abandoning President Kennedy's militant policies in Vietnam and desert him in favor of a presidential bid by the slain president's brother.

As Johnson procrastinated, U.S. military planners and diplomatic officials moved to alter the military situation in South Vietnam. In late January 1964, the Pentagon helped engineer another coup in Saigon, replacing General Minh with General Nguyen Khanh, who the Americans thought would aggressively fight the war. Johnson ordered Lodge to do what he could to stiffen Khanh's resolve.

In June 1964 some of the president's principal advisers floated the idea of seeking a congressional resolution supporting American air or ground action against North Vietnam. Six weeks later, after the raucous Republican convention had nominated Senator Barry Goldwater for president, two controversial incidents off the coast of North Vietnam justified introduction of such a congressional resolution and provided an excuse for air strikes by U.S. forces against North Vietnamese naval bases and oil-storage facilities. Two U.S. destroyers, the *Maddox* and the *C. Turner Joy*, had been conducting so-called De Soto patrols in support of South Vietnamese naval operations along the North Vietnamese coast bordering the Gulf of Tonkin (see Map 7.1). During these patrols, American ships sailing inside the twelve-mile territorial limit claimed by North Vietnam conducted surveillance against North Vietnamese coastal radar installations. The surveillance was designed to force the North Vietnamese to activate their radar devices, revealing their location. The *Maddox* and the *C. Turner Joy* would then notify accompanying South Vietnamese patrol boats of the positions of the North Vietnamese installations, and the South Vietnamese boats would attack.

Map 7.1 ▶

Southeast Asia and the Vietnam War

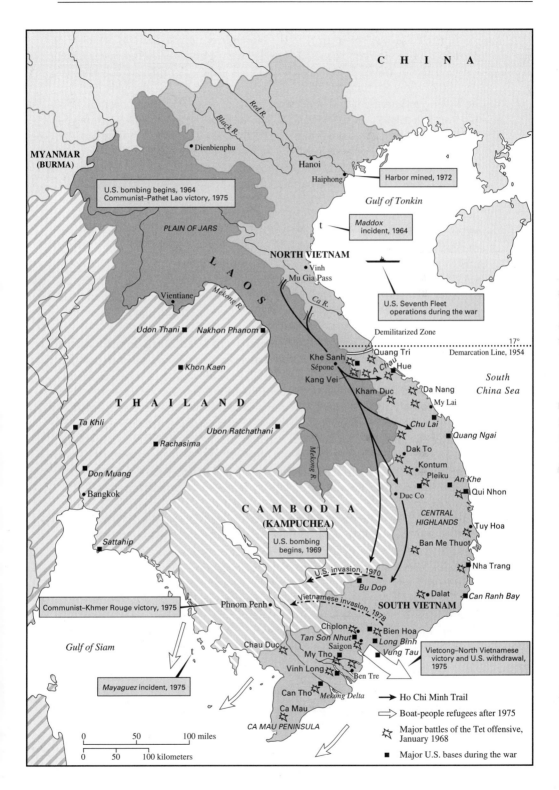

C H I N A

MYANMAR
(BURMA)

Black R.

Red R.

•Dienbienphu

Hanoi

Haiphong

Harbor mined, 1972

U.S. bombing begins, 1964
Communist–Pathet Lao victory, 1975

Gulf of Tonkin

PLAIN OF JARS

t

Maddox
incident, 1964

L A O S

NORTH VIETNAM

•Vinh
Mu Gia Pass

U.S. Seventh Fleet
operations during the war

Vientiane

Mekong R.

Ca R.

Udon Thani ■   Nakhon Phanom ■

Demilitarized Zone

17°

Quang Tri

Demarcation Line, 1954

Khe Sanh

Sépone•

Kang Vei

A Chau

Hue

South
China Sea

■ Khon Kaen

T H A I L A N D

Kham Duc   ☆•Da Nang
☆ My Lai

•Ta Khli

Ubon Ratchathani ■

Chu Lai

☆Quang Ngai

■ Rachasima

Mekong R.

Dak To

Kontum

•Don Muang

Pleiku   An Khe

•Bangkok

•Duc Co

☆•Qui Nhon

C A M B O D I A
(KAMPUCHEA)

CENTRAL
HIGHLANDS

•Tuy Hoa

Sattahip

U.S. bombing
begins, 1969

Ban Me Thuot
☆

☆•Nha Trang

U.S. invasion, 1970

Communist–Khmer Rouge victory, 1975

Phnom Penh •

Bu Dop

Vietnamese invasion, 1978   SOUTH VIETNAM

☆•Dalat   ■Can Ranh Bay

Gulf of Siam

Cholon

Tan Son Nhut ■

Chau Duc ☆

My Tho

Vinh Long ☆

☆■ Bien Hoa
■ Long Binh
Saigon
Vung Tau ■

Vietcong–North Vietnamese
victory and U.S. withdrawal,
1975

t

Ben Tre

Mayaguez incident, 1975

Can Tho ☆   Mekong Delta

Ca Mau

CA MAU PENINSULA

0   50   100 miles
0   50   100 kilometers

→ Ho Chi Minh Trail

⇨ Boat-people refugees after 1975

☆   Major battles of the Tet offensive,
     January 1968

■   Major U.S. bases during the war

The De Soto patrols provoked the North Vietnamese navy to attack the *Maddox* on the night of August 2, 1964. Two nights later, in heavy seas, the commander of the *C. Turner Joy* thought his ship was under attack and ordered his crew to return fire. They did so, but hit nothing—probably because no North Vietnamese patrol boats were in the area and there had been no hostile fire. The assault on the *Maddox* did actually occur, although Secretary of Defense McNamara was not telling the truth when he claimed, "[T]he *Maddox* was operating in international waters and was carrying out a routine patrol of the type we carry out all over the world at all times."

McNamara's false claims carried the day in Congress, which passed the Tonkin Gulf Resolution on August 7, 1964. The House voted unanimously in favor of this resolution, and in the Senate, only two members voted against it. The resolution authorized the president to "take all necessary measures to repel any armed attack against the forces of the United States and to prevent further aggression." The resolution also called for "all necessary steps, including the use of armed force, to assist" any member of SEATO that asked for American military aid. Although South Vietnam was not in fact a member of SEATO, the alliance had agreed to extend its protection to South Vietnam.

The resolution's extraordinarily broad grant of authority to the nation's chief executive included no time limit. Later, Johnson would use it to justify a greatly enlarged American presence. J. William Fulbright, an Arkansas Democrat and the chair of the Senate Foreign Relations Committee, who presented the resolution on the Senate floor, came to regret his support for the resolution. Within a year, he opposed further U.S. participation in the war. He later lamented that he was "hoodwinked and taken in by the president of the United States, the secretary of state and the chief of staff and the secretary of defense," who had lied to him about what happened in the Gulf of Tonkin.

The Tonkin Gulf Resolution effectively removed Vietnam from the political debate during the 1964 election campaign. Goldwater fully supported the resolution and the limited air raid that Johnson had ordered against North Vietnam. For his part, Johnson stood serenely in the middle of the road on Vietnam. Most people believed that he wanted to keep the United States out of a full-scale shooting war while preventing a communist victory. His major campaign speech on Vietnam sounded moderate but left considerable room for greater American involvement at a later date. He said that "only as a last resort" would he "start dropping bombs around that are likely to involve American boys in a war in Asia with 700 million Chinese." He could not guarantee the future, he said, but "we are not going north and drop bombs at this stage of the game, and we are not going south and run out and leave it for the Communists to take over."

The Americanization of the War, 1965

The year 1965 marked the point of no return for the United States in Vietnam. By July, Johnson had made a series of fateful decisions that transformed the fighting in Vietnam into an American war. Nevertheless, throughout the period of gradually increasing American military involvement in Vietnam, the Johnson administration waged a limited war. Johnson wanted to break the will of the North Vietnamese without provoking a military response from the Soviet Union or China. Officials believed that limiting the extent of the war would lessen the impact on the American public, making it easier to sustain political support for the war. It proved nearly impossible, however, to wage a limited war effectively. Every step up the ladder of escalation alarmed potential adversaries abroad and created anxiety at home. At the same time, efforts to restrict the scope of the war relieved pressure on North Vietnam and generated opposition from a different group of Americans: those who wanted to defeat North Vietnam quickly with the use of massive military force.

In the summer of 1965, Johnson took the final steps toward committing 100,000 U.S. ground troops to the war. The administration would no longer maintain the fiction that American soldiers were acting only as advisers; U.S. forces began conducting large-scale operations on their own, without accompanying ARVN units. As the South Vietnamese government grew continually weaker, the succession of military regimes nearly drove Johnson into apoplexy. News of yet another uprising provoked him to explode, "I don't want to hear any more." One of the president's assistants suggested that the coat of arms of the Saigon government display a turnstile.

In this atmosphere, Pentagon planners concluded that bombing the North would help save the South. General Maxwell Taylor, the ambassador to South Vietnam, told Johnson early in 1965 that air raids would "inject some life into the dejected spirits" of South Vietnam. The president, more prescient than some of his military advisers, worried that "this guerrilla war cannot be won from the air." Sustained bombing of North Vietnam began within a month of Johnson's 1965 inauguration. On February 7, 1965, a company of Vietcong soldiers attacked the American barracks at Pleiku, in the central highlands of South Vietnam, killing eight Americans, wounding 126, and destroying ten planes. Although the assault hardly surprised American officials, they believed that this attack on American forces would further undermine the shaky morale of the South Vietnamese government. Pleiku therefore provided the justification for sustained bombing of the North. Johnson first ordered a single retaliatory mission, similar to the one undertaken after the Gulf of Tonkin incident the previous August. But this retaliatory mission did not stop calls for harsher action. On February 13, Johnson authorized Operation Rolling Thunder, an extensive campaign of sustained bombing against the North. In April, American and South Vietnamese pilots flew 3,600 sorties against targets in the North—fuel depots, railroad yards, bridges, power plants, and munitions factories.

The initial results of the campaign disappointed the air-war advocates. Despite the expectations of Pentagon planners, the North Vietnamese quickly adapted to round-the-clock bombing. There were few industrial targets in the North, and the North Vietnamese quickly rebuilt destroyed bridges. The thick jungle provided cover for thousands of North Vietnamese men, women, and children carrying supplies by hand and bicycle to the South, along what became known as the Ho Chi Minh Trail. The North Vietnamese and NLF fighters did not capitulate, and the South Vietnamese government did not become stronger. American military officers urged even more air attacks. In response, Johnson relaxed restrictions on targets over the next several months.

Since Operation Rolling Thunder resulted in little more than temporary setbacks for the Vietcong, the American commander in South Vietnam, General William Westmoreland, called for direct American ground action throughout the South. There is no solution, he wrote the president, "other than to put our own finger in the dike." But Johnson still resisted a full Americanization of the war, and at a speech at Johns Hopkins University in April 1965, he offered "unconditional discussions" with North Vietnam to end the war.

In early May, McNamara, Taylor, and Westmoreland acknowledged that bombing alone would not win the war. They concluded that the United States had to fight the war on the ground, in the South, if the Saigon government were to have a chance of surviving. Westmoreland wanted another 150,000 troops deployed to fight the ground war throughout the South. Secretary of Defense McNamara cut Westmoreland's request to 100,000 troops and forwarded it to the president. Throughout July, Johnson consulted with his principal advisers on the future course to take in Vietnam. In these meetings, Johnson appeared skeptical of the usefulness of committing additional American troops, but he was unwilling to accept an NLF victory. The only course he could tolerate, therefore, was a continued gradual increase in the American commitment—the very policy that had failed over the previous year.

During the July 1965 meetings, he asked General Earle Wheeler, chair of the Joint Chiefs of Staff, "Tell me this. What will happen if we put in 100,000 more men and then two, three years later you tell me you need 500,000 more? How would you expect me to respond to that? And what makes you think Ho Chi Minh won't put in another 100,000 and match us every bit of the way?" To which Wheeler responded, "This means greater bodies of men from North Vietnam, which will allow us to cream them." Johnson's fear proved prophetic, and Wheeler's reply revealed the folly of the American commanders' war methods.

Eventually, nearly all the president's advisers concurred that adding 100,000 Americans to the 90,000 troops already in Vietnam would help stabilize the situation without causing a backlash in Congress or with the public. Most agreed to reject the request from the Joint Chiefs of Staff to call up the reserves. Such a move would dramatically raise the stakes, both at home and abroad, and would perhaps necessitate a presidential declaration of a state of emergency and a request to Congress for several billion dollars. In that event, Johnson worried, the Great Society would cease, and worse, "Hanoi would ask the Chinese and the Soviets for increased aid."

At the end of July, Johnson announced the plan to send an additional 100,000 troops. That afternoon, Democratic Senate majority leader Mike Mansfield wrote Johnson that most of the public approved of what he was doing because they trusted him as their president, but "not necessarily out of any understanding or sympathy with policies on Vietnam." He thought people backed Johnson for now because they sensed that "your objective [is] not to get in too deeply."

Fighting the War, 1966–1967

During 1966 and 1967, the number of U.S. troops in South Vietnam rose from 190,000 to 535,000 (see Figure 7.1). Yet even this size force could not prevail against the NLF and in fact contributed to the further deterioration of the government and armed forces of South Vietnam. The Americans were trying to apply tactics learned in World War II and Korea to a very different kind of struggle, against a guerrilla force. The "army concept" that had developed over the past twenty-five years held that wars could be won with advanced materiel and technology—aerial bombardment, tank attacks, artillery, electronic detection fences—rather than with soldiers armed with rifles. These principles seemed to make sense for a productive, industrial society that relied on conscripts. If machines could substitute for soldiers, the casualties would decline and public support would continue. But advocates of a high-tech war misunderstood the realities of the war in Vietnam. The army concept removed the

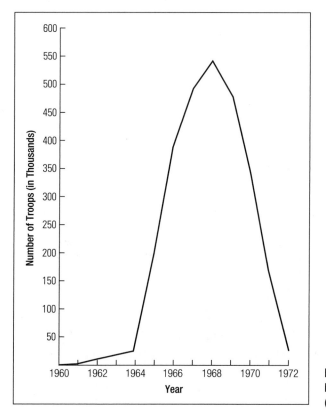

Figure 7.1
Levels of U.S. Troops in Vietnam (at year's end)

American forces from direct contact with the people they were ostensibly helping and ultimately contributed to the loss of the war.

Like most successful officers who had fought in Europe during World War II, General Westmoreland believed that American military technology could overwhelm any potential adversary; he therefore followed a strategy of attrition, or wearing down the enemy by use of massive firepower. Westmoreland never fully grasped that the NLF and the North Vietnamese fought a guerrilla war, in which they, not the Americans, determined their level of casualties. Persuaded that American technology could carry the day, Westmoreland used helicopters to send American units into the countryside on search-and-destroy missions to root out and kill enemy soldiers. Americans would fly out in the morning, pursue the Vietcong in firefights, count the dead, and return to their bases in the evening. The measure of success became "body counts" rather than territory captured, which was the standard in earlier wars. The tactic encouraged abuses. Local commanders, hoping to please their superiors in Saigon, inflated the death figures. Reliance on body counts offered an incentive to shoot first and ask no questions. One marine remembered that during his first night on patrol, "about fifty people shot this old guy. Everybody claimed they shot him. He got shot 'cause he started running. It was an old man running to tell his family. . . . Any Vietnamese out at night was the enemy." Many American GIs expressed contempt for all Vietnamese, regardless of whether they were friendly or hostile. Thrust into an unfamiliar country with a culture few Americans understood, troops used racist slurs like "gook," "slope," or "slant-eye" to refer to all Vietnamese. The U.S. army did develop rules of engagement designed to prevent indiscriminate shooting of noncombatants. But the confusion of a war without clearly defined front lines, with enemy forces who looked like civilians, with the presence of civilians on the battlefield, and with the demands of producing a satisfactory body count led to atrocities.

Before U.S. troops descended from their helicopters, giant B-52 bombers and smaller fighter jets pounded the battlefields. The United States dropped more bombs on Vietnam, a country about the size of California, each month than fell on all of Europe during all of World War II. But the air raids alerted the Vietcong and North Vietnamese forces that the Americans were on the way, giving them time to withdraw or to dive into hundreds of miles of tunnels to protect themselves from the massive firepower. Also, the Vietcong used unexploded American bombs and artillery shells as weapons against the Americans. The enemy developed shrewd booby traps using these unexploded bombs, killing or wounding thousands of inexperienced American troops. In 1966, over one thousand American soldiers died of wounds caused by booby traps, and in the first six months of the following year, 17 percent of all American casualties resulted from mines or booby traps.

The NLF kept gaining strength on the ground, using guerrilla tactics developed earlier by the Vietminh. They avoided firefights where they could, forcing the Americans to waste enormous energy and materiel for meager gains. They continued political organization in the countryside, even as American bombers flew overhead. Despite such obvious problems, the United States Army continued to rely on search-and-destroy operations. The largest oc-

Infantrymen from the 1st Cavalry Division jump from an army helicopter during a search-and-destroy operation in South Vietnam, July 1967. / © Bettmann/CORBIS

curred in late 1966 and early 1967. In one such mission, which lasted from September to November 1966, twenty-two thousand U.S. and ARVN troops, supported by B-52 bombers and massive artillery fire, pursued the NLF northwest of Saigon. In another search-and-destroy operation, from February through May 1967, American B-52s reduced the South Vietnamese landscape to the eerie bleakness of the moon, making hundreds of square miles uninhabitable by the peasants the Americans were supposedly helping. Americans entering villages to root out the Vietcong sometimes carried out so-called Zippo raids, igniting the peasants' thatched huts with tracer bullets, flamethrowers, and cigarette lighters to deny sanctuary to the enemy.

Such actions not only enraged the peasantry but also shocked Americans watching the carnage on the evening news. Yet this enormous firepower failed to eradicate the Vietcong, who would simply melt away until an assault stopped. One reporter likened each blow to "a sledgehammer on a floating cork; somehow the cork refused to stay down."

All the while, North Vietnamese commander General Vo Nguyen Giap, the victor at Dienbienphu, had the Americans playing into his hands as he waged a guerrilla war. Giap, one of the most militantly anti-French members of Ho Chi Minh's inner circle, had created an army of 250,000 in the years 1946–1954. He developed a theory of protracted war, in which a nation could throw off outside domination by patiently wearing down the colonial power, first with guerrilla raids and later with conventional battles. He welcomed the

American search-and-destroy operations, since they took American forces away from the heavily populated coastal plain, where the NLF and the North gained strength among the population. As the Americans engaged in inconclusive battles in the interior, they paid less attention to "pacification," the effort to bind the peasantry to the government in Saigon.

If anything, the Saigon government lost even more support among the South Vietnamese while the American war devastated the countryside. As part of their effort to deny sanctuary to the enemy, American forces used giant transport planes to spray trees with defoliants. Between 1962 and 1972, the Americans dropped over 1 million pounds of toxic chemicals such as Agent Orange over South Vietnam, destroying more than half its forests. Some American crews jokingly adopted the motto Only You Can Prevent Forests. But many crewmembers later suffered serious health problems, probably from contact with the toxins they dropped.

The effect of this tactic on the crops of South Vietnamese farmers—the ostensible beneficiaries of the war effort—was immediate and devastating. Deadly defoliants dropped from planes onto a suspected Vietcong area in the afternoon would soon drift over friendly villages; by the next morning, fruit fell from the trees and the leaves on rubber plants turned brown and broke off. Farmers blamed the Americans for the loss of their crops, and they feared the defoliants would harm animal and human life as well. The birth of a physically or mentally impaired infant was often blamed on the defoliation campaigns. American forces also used poisons to destroy the rice crop grown in Vietcong areas, expecting the hungry enemy to emerge and fight. The theory overlooked the NLF's practice of buying or taking rice from the peasants; in effect, the Americans ruined ten pounds of rice grown by friendly farmers for every pound of Vietcong rice that they destroyed. South Vietnam, once an exporter of rice, began importing it from neighboring countries (and even the United States) as the war ground on.

The havoc in the countryside forced hundreds of thousands of peasants to flee their homes. Between 1964 and 1969, more than 4 million South Vietnamese—one-fourth of the population—were refugees at one time or another. Those who remained on their land often did so only because they feared the Vietcong would redistribute it if they were gone. Many of those who fled the terror from the skies, the defoliants, the artillery barrages, and the Zippo raids swarmed to cities that

Vo Nguyen Giap commanded the Vietminh forces that defeated the French forces in the war from 1946 to 1954. As defense minister of the Democratic Republic of Vietnam (North Vietnam) he refined his theory of protracted war to force the United States to leave Vietnam. / © CORBIS Sygma

had neither room nor facilities for them; others languished in squalid refugee camps.

The population of Saigon, under 500,000 in the 1950s, swelled to 1.5 million by the mid-1960s. The capital and other cities near American installations—Danang, Cam Ranh Bay, Hue, to name a few—changed from Asian commercial centers, conducting business in traditional ways, to army boomtowns. Seedy bars and brothels sprang up near American bases, with women and girls as young as thirteen prostituting themselves for the GIs. Over 100,000 Amerasian children were born of liaisons between American soldiers and Vietnamese women. These children were scorned by the Vietnamese, and after the Americans departed, they suffered terrible privation.

The presence of over 500,000 Americans in Vietnam transformed the Vietnamese economy. Production of food and rubber fell as the Vietnamese concentrated on servicing the newcomers. At first, the GIs paid cash in U.S. dollars. Prices zoomed 170 percent in

American fire sometimes hurt friendly South Vietnamese. A father carries his child wounded by American soldiers who mistook him for a Vietcong fighter. / Phillip Jones Griffiths/Magnum

1966 and 1967, and many Vietnamese could no longer afford the basic necessities of life. To halt the inflation, the U.S. army started paying its soldiers in scrip, which could only be used to purchase consumer goods on U.S. bases. Vietnamese entrepreneurs responded by importing watches, tape recorders, motorcycles, radios, and the like, to sell to local people who worked for the Americans and were paid in South Vietnamese currency.

Corruption, already a problem before the Americans arrived en masse, vastly increased in 1966. The South Vietnamese government rented space to the Americans at exorbitant prices. South Vietnamese officials took bribes from contractors wishing to do business with U.S. agencies, including military bases and rural development organizations. Others demanded payment for licenses, permits, visas, and passports. Some Saigon officials traded in opium, and many engaged in the flourishing black market. Everything was for sale— U.S. government scrip, South Vietnamese piasters, Scotch whiskey, watches, hand grenades, rifles.

Americans were often aware of the corruption that eroded South Vietnamese society, but Westmoreland thought that curing it would alarm the very government the United States wanted to help. Some midranking American officials wanted to threaten the government of Saigon with loss of aid if it did not remove corrupt officials. Westmoreland overruled such advice, fearing that it would only annoy the government, without producing appropriate changes, or perhaps lead to the government's collapse.

By late 1967, the buildup had not won the war. McNamara's comment in late 1966 that he could "see the light at the end of the tunnel in Vietnam" inspired the rueful rejoinder that what he had glimpsed was the headlight of another train engineered by Ho Chi Minh. Thirteen thousand U.S. servicemen had been killed. Only the lowest American goal—denying a victory to the NLF—had been realized, and continued success was not assured. Other American war aims—creating a stable South Vietnamese government capable of waging the war on its own and winning the loyalty of its people, and forcing the North to quit—had become more elusive than ever. As American involvement intensified, South Vietnamese society dissolved. People either became dependents of the United States or went underground to join the NLF. The South Vietnamese government, once the bedrock of Washington's strategy to defeat communism in Southeast Asia, slipped into dependence and obstructionism.

Working-Class War and the Draft

Although the fighting took place far from the United States, the war deeply affected the way many Americans lived their lives. Military service became an important, life-changing experience for over 2 million American men. Combat soldiers often encountered racial tensions, boredom, drugs, and brutality against the Vietnamese. Some soldiers accepted these unpleasant realities as part of the hardships of military service, but many bore psychological and emotional scars for years after they returned from Vietnam. Nearly 80 percent of the U.S. troops in Vietnam served as support personnel, not combat troops, and their service was far less traumatic. But even those Americans who did not fight were changed by the war. Back home, millions of young men spent a substantial part of their late adolescence or young adulthood wondering whether they would be conscripted and seeking ways to avoid participating in the fighting. Far more men did not go to Vietnam than went, but the war created deep divisions among people of an entire generation. Those who fought in the war often resented those who did not, and people who did not go to Vietnam sometimes treated those who did with scorn, pity, or condescension.

Unlike World War II, for which the armed forces needed nearly every able-bodied American man, the military effort in Vietnam required less than half the eligible population. Of the 27 million available men between the ages of nineteen and twenty-six, 16 million never served in the armed forces. Of the approximately 11 million who did, 9 million enlisted more or less voluntarily, and 2.2 million were drafted under the terms of the Selective Service Act of 1947. A total of about 2.8 million men, along with 6,400 women, actually saw service in Vietnam between 1961 and 1973.

Although the draft took only about 10 percent of the men subject to its call, the Selective Service affected the lives of nearly everybody. As the war became more dangerous and American casualties rose to three hundred dead per week, many young men wanted to reduce the risk to their personal safety. Several options were available: deferments for marriage (dropped in 1965), fatherhood, or student status; enlistment in the National Guard or the reserves; enlistment in the armed forces, with a promise to serve in places other than Vietnam; and service in noncombat zones in Vietnam.

The wealthy and educated, those most aware of the intricacies of the system, knew best how to avoid the most dangerous duty. The military force that the United States sent to Vietnam consisted disproportionately of men from working-class and poor backgrounds. The best estimate indicates that 25 percent of the force was poor, 55 percent were working class, and 20 percent were middle class. Such discrepancies produced a distressing inequity in the make-up of the forces bearing the brunt of the heaviest fighting. They came from inner cities, working-class suburbs, rural areas, and medium-size towns. One enlisted man recalled who served and who did not from his small Kansas hometown: "All but two of a dozen high school buddies would eventually serve in Vietnam and all were of working class families, while I know of not a single middle class son of the town's businessmen, lawyers, doctors or ranchers from my high school graduating class who experienced the Armageddon of our generation." The fighting men were far younger than those who fought in earlier wars. The average age of the American force during World War II was twenty-six; in Vietnam, the average age was nineteen.

The Selective Service system appeared corrupt and demeaning to many of those who faced conscription. One young inductee who had the job of filing case histories at a local draft board had his eyes opened observing the ruses others used to avoid being called up. He telephoned his mother and reported, "The whole set-up is corrupt. I don't need to be here! I don't need to be here! I don't need to be here! I simply didn't need to be drafted!" Nonetheless, he went to Vietnam and became one of the fifty-eight thousand men who died. His feelings that the draft was arbitrary and unfair were common; a Harris poll concluded that most Americans believed the men who went to Vietnam were "suckers, having risked their lives in the wrong war, in the wrong place, in the wrong time."

Three-quarters of the 16 million men who did not serve in Vietnam admitted that they had changed their life plans to stay away from Vietnam, and a majority (55 percent) said that they actively took steps to avoid the draft. Even if drafted, a man had to be physically fit before he could be inducted. Some young men had their family doctor prepare false documents to keep them out of the service

A network of draft counselors, initially sponsored by churches and other pacifist organizations, arose to advise young men of their rights under the Selective Service Act and of legal ways to avoid induction. After the 1965 Supreme Court ruling in *United States* v. *Seegar* the conscientious objector status was available to anyone with a "sincerely founded reason" for opposing war. Before then, only members of recognized pacifist sects—such as Mennonites, Quakers, Jehovah's Witnesses, Brethren—had been entitled to register as

A man protesting the draft (conscription) stands in the doorway of the national headquarters of the Selective Service system, April 1967. / © Bettmann/CORBIS

CONSCRIPTION IS A MORAL EVIL AND THE HANDMAID OF WAR.

conscientious objectors. After *Seegar*, draft counselors advised young men on how to present their antiwar beliefs in a persuasive way:

Some men simply refused induction or tried to evade their draft boards. About 209,000 men were accused of a draft-related offense, but only 25,000 were indicted, and only 4,000 received prison sentences. Even those who entered the military sometimes refused to accept service in Vietnam. About 12,000 men went absent without leave (AWOL) to escape an assignment to Vietnam. About 50,000 deserters or accused draft offenders took flight during the war, with 30,000 of them going to Canada. Many of these men came home quietly over the next decade, but 11,000 remained fugitives until 1977, when President Jimmy Carter proclaimed a pardon.

For the men who went to Vietnam, life in the armed forces bore little resemblance to the experiences of their fathers or older brothers in World War II and the Korean War—and no likeness at all to the idealized versions of those wars presented in movies and television programs. For combat soldiers, Vietnam was sometimes a demoralizing, brutal experience. One day, a young man would be in the relatively familiar surroundings of a stateside military base; the next day, after eighteen hours on an airplane, he would find himself in the alien landscape of Vietnam, in a situation that provoked both frustration and terror. The enemy, often indistinguishable from the local population, could materialize suddenly from the jungle and attack with horrible efficiency. It was especially difficult to maintain the troops' morale when they saw more and more lives lost for little or no gain.

The difficulties were compounded by the military's personnel policy. Unlike earlier wars, in which soldiers served "for the duration," soldiers in Vietnam had a one-year tour of duty, spread over thirteen months, with thirty days' leave for "rest and recreation." A mixture of demographics, politics, and military management techniques prompted this arrangement. Because the pool of available soldiers far exceeded the number needed, keeping 500,000 men at the front while allowing all others to steer free of battle would cause resentment among those who fought and would erode public support for the war. Therefore, the military limited time in service and continually rotated the forces.

According to General Westmoreland, establishing end-of-tour dates helped boost morale and gave each soldier a goal. In fact, however, GIs' goal often became self-preservation: men approaching the end of their tours became reluctant to fight. No one wanted to be killed or wounded, but risking death or injury a few weeks before mustering out appeared especially pointless. One commander called the twelve-month tour "the worst personnel policy in history." To make matters worse, units did not stay together throughout their tours, which increased soldiers' and officers' feelings of isolation. Troops killed or wounded were replaced by newcomers, whose tour of duty expired later than that of the other men in their unit. Men mostly relied on themselves.

The lack of rapport between commanders and soldiers sometimes made personal hostilities difficult to control. The murder of officers by enlisted men—often with a fragmentation grenade or other anonymous weapon—became frequent enough, especially late in the war, to earn its own slang name: "fragging." The armed forces were susceptible to the same racial tensions that plagued American society as a whole. As these animosities grew in the late sixties, racial divisions rose within the armed forces. Many black soldiers had no white friends in the ostensibly integrated units. Inevitably, some of the violence between GIs took on a racial tone. These tensions became especially pronounced after the Johnson administration decided to de-escalate the war and open peace negotiations in 1968. From that point onward, more and more U.S. servicemen and -women came to see the war as pointless.

News of atrocities against the Vietnamese, whom some GIs referred to as "gooks," undermined support for the soldiers back home. In this long war against an enemy that struck without warning and then instantly melted away, soldiers sometimes disregarded the so-called rules of engagement that regulated behavior toward the enemy. Once the body count became the principal means of measuring success in the war, some soldiers became excessive and brutal. A few men chopped off the ears of dead Vietnamese for trophies. They would "take [their] dog-tag chain and fill [it] up with ears," one infantryman recalled. "If we were movin' through the jungle, they'd just put the bloody ear on the chain and stick the ear in their pocket and keep on going. Wouldn't take time to dry it off. Then when we got back, they would nail 'em up on the walls of our hootch, you know, as a trophy." Some GIs gave up the nearly impossible task of distinguishing the Vietcong from uninvolved civilians; besides burning peasants' houses, they shot any Vietnamese they saw. "If it moves, it's VC [Vietcong]" became a common slogan for American soldiers. The most dramatic atrocity of the war occurred in March 1968, when American soldiers massacred more than five hundred unarmed Vietnamese villagers, mostly women and children, at the hamlet of My Lai. The military managed to keep the incident secret until the next year. Americans were uniformly horrified when it was revealed, although like so much else about Vietnam, public opinion about the incident was divided. Some expressed sympathy for the young American soldiers, feeling that they had succumbed to the stress of combat. A smaller but significant group saw My Lai as a symbol of all the reasons why the United States should quit Vietnam.

To escape the fear and absurdity of a war without front lines, leadership, or clear goals, some soldiers turned to drugs. Marijuana, opium, and heroin were freely available and inexpensive in the cities of Vietnam because officials of the South Vietnamese government engaged in the drug trade. So did the CIA, which used profits from drugs to finance a secret counterinsurgency program in the South Vietnamese highlands and along the Laotian border. Soldiers used drugs not only on the base but also in the field. One infantryman who served from mid-1967 to mid-1968 remembered that "in the field most of the guys stayed high. Lots of them couldn't face it. In a sense, if you was high it seemed like a game you was in. You didn't take it serious. It stopped a lot of nervous breakdowns."

Overall, soldiers who experienced combat in Vietnam developed greater psychological and emotional difficulties than did the 80 percent who served in support roles. The latter readjusted relatively readily to American society once they returned home. Surveys taken ten and twenty years after the Vietnam War indicated that the subsequent careers of noncombat soldiers developed similarly to those of men who had not gone to Vietnam. The picture was darker and much more complex for combat veterans. Many experienced post-traumatic stress disorder. Symptoms included drug and alcohol abuse, difficulty sustaining family relationships, trouble finding and maintaining employment, violence, and suicide.

Rising Dissent and the Collapse of the Cold War Consensus

In addition to the soldiers in Vietnam, at least one man in Washington approached nervous exhaustion as the war expanded: President Johnson. The war had gone on longer than his military advisers predicted, and still there was no clear end in sight. Continued war threatened to wreck his cherished Great Society, and it cast doubt on his chances for re-election in 1968.

Johnson's personal crisis was deepened by mounting criticism of the war from former supporters. Arkansas senator J. William Fulbright, chair of the Senate Foreign Relations Committee and an old friend from Johnson's days as majority leader, was among the first moderate public figures to dissent. In late 1965, Fulbright undertook a crash course in American policy toward Indochina, and the following February his committee opened televised hearings on the war. Numerous foreign policy experts told the committee that the administration had headed down the wrong road in Vietnam. George F. Kennan, one of the architects of containment, worried that the "unbalanced concentration of resources and attention" on Vietnam diverted Washington from what he considered to be the proper focus of U.S. foreign policy—Europe. Fulbright expressed disbelief at Secretary of State Dean Rusk's repeated assertions that "this is a clear case of international Communist aggression." Fulbright thought that most of the world viewed the conflict in Vietnam as "a civil war in which outside parties have become involved." Two months later, Fulbright observed that the war had damaged the Great Society and hurt the nation's relations with the Soviet Union and Europe. He lamented "the arrogance of power," which he defined as a "psychological need that nations seem to have to prove that they are bigger, stronger, better than other nations."

While Fulbright and about a dozen other senators dissented from escalation of the war in 1966, more potent opposition to the war arose outside the government in the form of a citizens' peace movement. Diverse groups—peace liberals, pacifists, and social revolutionaries—joined in opposition to the war. Beginning in 1965, these groups organized "teach-ins," in which they lectured college audiences on the evils of the war. The peace movement also sponsored the 1967 "Vietnam Summer" of protests against the war and the 1968 "dump Johnson" campaign, which sought to replace the president with someone who would extricate the United States from the endless war.

Some members of the peace movement agreed with Kennan that Vietnam was diverting American attention from more serious issues. Long-time Socialist leader Norman Thomas acknowledged that more pressing problems were clamoring for attention, "but it is a practical and emotional absurdity to think that the government or people can or will deal with these and other pressing questions until it stops the war in Vietnam." By 1967, even the least radical participants in the peace movement believed that, as Seymour Melman of the Committee for a Sane Nuclear Policy (SANE) put it, "policy change now requires institutional change as well." When Students for a Democratic Society, a New Left group (see Chapter 8), organized the Vietnam Summer in 1967, one Detroit organizer reported, "I find that I am not really working here to 'end the war in Vietnam.' . . . I am working here to make people feel Vietnam, to make them realize that it is part of a pattern which oppresses them, as well as Vietnamese peasants." Along with opposition to the war, a general dissatisfaction with American government began to spread.

Public antiwar activism surged in the spring of 1967. Martin Luther King, Jr., who previously had expressed quiet misgivings about the war, openly broke with the Johnson administration. He called for de-escalation, helped organize a new antiwar group (Negotiation Now!), and endorsed the Vietnam Summer. On April 15, 1967, crowds of one hundred thousand in New York and fifty thousand in San Francisco heard speakers from both the antiwar and the civil rights movements call for an end to the war and a recommitment to the goal of racial equality at home. Johnson grew alarmed at the possibility that King and pediatrician Benjamin Spock, now an antiwar activist, might run for president and vice president, respectively, in 1968.

Federal agencies constantly observed, infiltrated, and harassed antiwar groups. The FBI compared Senator Fulbright's position during the 1966 Vietnam hearings to those taken by the Communist Party. The CIA infiltrated antiwar groups such as Women Strike for Peace, the Washington Peace Center, SANE, the Congress of Racial Equality (CORE), the War Resisters League, and the National Mobilization Committee Against the War. Agents sent phony letters to editors of publications defaming antiwar leaders; other agents infiltrated antiwar groups that called for bombings or violent confrontation with police. Eventually, the CIA opened files on over seven thousand Americans—in violation of its charter, which stipulated that it could not operate inside the United States.

The president became frantic as plans developed for a massive march on Washington in October 1967 to demand a halt to the bombing and the start of immediate negotiations to end the war. In order to discredit the antiwar movement, Johnson asked his attorney general, Ramsey Clark, to leak information about the left-wing and communist affiliations of some of its leaders. Nevertheless, on October 21, a crowd estimated at one hundred thousand assembled on the mall in front of the Lincoln Memorial to hear speeches against the war. Later, a group of about fifty thousand marched to the Pentagon, where scores crossed police lines and were arrested.

These large demonstrations helped change public attitudes toward the war. Equally important were the nightly televised newscasts showing the fighting and the devastation of Vietnamese society. Satellite technology made it possible to air footage of the war the day it was shot. Reporters and camera crews traveled with platoons into firefights in Vietnamese villages. They captured on film the flames of the Zippo raids, the moans of wounded soldiers, and the terror in the eyes of children left homeless by the fighting. What they could not show, because they did not happen, were scenes of GIs liberating villages to the cheers of grateful residents. For a public brought up on the heroic newsreels of World War II, where such images had brought tears of pride to the home front, the sharp contrast between "the good war" of 1941 to 1945 and the quagmire of Vietnam proved especially distressing.

As this "living-room war" ground on without progress, Americans at home, like the soldiers in the field, had trouble distinguishing friendly Vietnamese from the enemy—and wanted no part of either. The fighting appeared pointless, and the public longed for relief from a war it had not anticipated and no longer approved of. Distrust of the government rose sharply in 1967, as observers noted a yawning "credibility gap" between the optimism of the president and his advisers and the continuing violence shown on TV every evening.

Antiwar activities, the failure to achieve victory, and press coverage of the horrors of the fighting altered the way the public viewed the war. Throughout the country, there was a sharp division between "hawks," who supported the war, and "doves," who opposed it. In the beginning of 1967, most Americans were still hawks, willing to escalate the war if it could be

(cont. on page 270)

Wagging the Dog: "The Media-Spindustrial Complex" and American Foreign Relations

Since the Vietnam War, the executive branch of the federal government has been intent on establishing its control over the images of war presented to the American public so that presidents might retain nearly uncontested power over foreign relations decisions. Those same presidents have found that wars often increase their popularity and distract public attention away from issues they wish to obscure. In 1997, Hollywood released a film that raised unsettling questions about how American leaders manipulated public opinion in order to divert attention from the scandals and shortcomings of their public policies and private lives and used wars to create a mandate for incumbent administrations. Entitled *Wag the Dog*, the film's plot centered on a president caught in a sex scandal with a teenager.

In order to keep the president's lechery from impeding his re-election, his managers hired an expensive public relations consultant (spin doctor) to manufacture a foreign policy emergency to divert the public's attention. The consultant in turn enlisted the help of a talented film producer to help him sell the moral necessity for a war to solve a nonexistent crisis in Albania. Together, they created fake "news" footage of a young girl escaping from the violence and cruelty of unspecified "terrorists," hired a songwriter to pen a country-and-western tune hailing the American military for its "contributions" to resolving the crisis, and staged patriotic displays in order to whip the public into a flag-waving frenzy. As they discussed how to generate American fear of Albania, a country once little known to Americans, the spin doctors decided that the president should just say that it had nuclear weapons and could use them to make suitcase bombs.

Intended as parody, *Wag the Dog* seemed only slightly exaggerated, resonating as it did with the tenor of American politics in general and more specifically with the country's recent history during the Gulf War. In fact, the overt manipulation of public opinion to support the policy and electoral goals of American leaders (corporate and political) has occupied a central role in the drama of postwar America.

In the past fifty years, technology and opinion management have dramatically transformed American politics: the growth of television, with its expansive opportunities for sound-bite journalism and political advertising; the rise of political polling and the public relations industry; and a new cast of characters who exist to aid politicians, from make-up artists to pollsters and spin doctors. Given the costs of these new political props, elected officials now exist in a permanent state of candidacy, their policy decisions and their rhetoric continually focused on the next election. Because the United States has frequently used military interventions to achieve its international goals and because a state of war usually works to the advantage of an incumbent president, the packaging of foreign policy questions, in particular, has intensified in the decades after World War II. The legacy of military defeat in the Vietnam War—the war that cost Lyndon Johnson his presidency and tarnished the prestige of the United States internationally—has only intensified officials' concern with controlling the rhetoric and symbols associated with warmaking.

In 1954, when the CIA orchestrated the overthrow of the reform government of President Jacobo Arbenz Guzman in Guatemala, supporters of the intervention used a public relations campaign developed by the United Fruit Company to persuade Americans that the new policies in Guatemala revealed the communist agenda at work there. The brainchild of Edward Bernays, the public relations consultant later dubbed the "father of spin," the campaign to mold public opinion derived from

Media experts confer with a presidential adviser in a scene from the 1997 movie *Wag the Dog.* / © CORBIS Sygma

the alleged communist affiliations of the Arbenz government.

When the United States intervened in 1954, Bernays provided major media outlets with news of the brief military struggle. In a later account of the successful CIA coup, the authors determined that "Bernays outmaneuvered, outplanned, and outspent the Guatemalans. He was far ahead of them in technique, experience and political contacts." A *New York Times* reporter concluded similarly that "a hostile and ill-informed American press helped to create an emotional public opinion" that influenced Congress and the State Department. When the American-installed Armas regime failed to bring prosperity to Guatemala, Bernays orchestrated a media campaign designed to blame the previous "communist" government for all its problems.

By the 1990s, the techniques that Bernays and others had pioneered continued to serve various interests, but they did so in a transformed media and policy environment. The rise of cable television, with its all-news networks; the blurring of the boundary between news and entertainment; the importance of ratings to news broadcasts; the increasing technical sophistication of weaponry; and the determination of public leaders to lay to rest the post-Vietnam skepticism of Americans regarding military involvements abroad all shaped the techniques and politics of opinion formation. In that context, many administration officials and congressional representatives believed that the "engineering of consent" that Bernays had advocated in his books was crucial to their policy goals.

They were not the only ones. In 1983, the Reagan administration carefully controlled media access during the brief invasion of Grenada. As a result, about the only image that the public saw of this intervention was the dramatic scene of an American medical student kissing U.S. soil upon his return home. Television networks neglected to report that the Americans studying in Grenada had never been threatened. Through most

his decades of experience promoting the interests of his corporate clients. Beginning in the early 1950s, Bernays hired scholars and writers to provide information and news stories from the point of view of his client, the United Fruit Company (UFC), to American media outlets. The UFC wanted to stop the Guatemalan government's land reforms and its efforts to counter the company's monopoly on transportation facilities in the country (see pages 153–154). Bernays arranged expense paid trips to Guatemala for reporters and then used friendly journalists and editors to publish the accounts he preferred. These accounts stressed two interrelated themes: the purported benefits of the UFC monopoly to the people of Guatemala and

of the 1980s, the government and the media portrayed Panamanian leader Manuel Noriega as a democratic ally in the war against the Sandinistas. By the end of the decade, however, they represented him as a cocaine-running thug.

Within ten days of its invasion by Iraq in August 1991, the government of Kuwait hired the public relations firm of Hill-Knowlton to manufacture American support for the use of U.S. military forces against Iraq. A powerful and well-connected corporation, Hill-Knowlton had previously represented repressive political regimes from China to Indonesia to Peru. Armed with a $10.8 million retainer from the Kuwaitis, the lobbying firm organized Kuwait Information days at colleges and universities, convinced churches to hold a national day of prayer for Kuwait, and set up meetings between Kuwaitis and newspaper editors. It provided videos for television news outlets and monitored audience reactions to information on the Iraqi-Kuwaiti war.

In one of its most important media moments, the firm arranged for a young woman named Nayirah to testify before the House Human Rights Caucus, an informal group of congressmen whose official-sounding name belied their unofficial status in the House of Representatives. Stating that she feared for her safety, she refused to provide her last name. In tearful testimony broadcast repeatedly by American television news programs, the young woman told of witnessing Iraqi soldiers enter a hospital, where they stole infant incubators and left fifteen babies "on the cold floor to die." Her tale of atrocity was designed to paint the Middle Eastern war in terms of moral absolutes: savage Iraqis fighting blameless and defenseless Kuwaitis. A potent symbol of innocence, the babies made the story morally compelling. Indeed, they helped to swing public and congressional opinion in favor of U.S. intervention in the Gulf War at a time when the administration favored it, but most Americans and a large number of Democratic senators were quite hesitant to support such a policy.

The only dilemma for the architects of the public relations coup was to hide the fact that the story was a total fabrication. Nayirah, as it turned out, was the daughter of the Kuwaiti ambassador to the United States, Sheikh Saud Nasir al-Sabah. Diplomatic immunity and the fact that hers was not official testimony before a House committee (however much it looked like it to American television viewers) meant that she would not have to face perjury charges for her "testimony." As in *Wag the Dog*, the architects succeeded long enough to serve their purposes.

Determined to avoid a repetition of the Vietnam-era antiwar movement, the Bush administration moved to institute strict controls over the reporting of the war. Administration officials allowed only a specified number of reporters, chosen by the officials themselves, to enter the war zone, and they allowed those journalists access (with a government escort) only to the people and places they approved. In particular, they kept reporters away from American soldiers and almost all scenes involving casualties of war. All stories had to pass government censors before they could be published or broadcast. The government provided the media with the images it thought advantageous to administration policies. Anxious to keep their places in the small press pool, journalists provided the administration with the coverage it desired, including (in the words of scholars Susan Jeffords and Lauren Rabinovitz) "'gee-whiz' replications of Pentagon images from the war." Indeed, *Washington Post* reporter Henry Allen concluded that the Gulf War press corps looked like "fools, nit-pickers and egomaniacs . . . a whining, self-righteous upper-middle-class mob jostling for whatever tiny flakes of fame [might] settle on their shoulders."

The result, says historian Daniel C. Hallin, was a media drama of "triumphant technology" in which "the main characters—and heroes—of the [Gulf War] were the experts and the weapons themselves. . . ." Images of Patriot missiles and smart bombs detached from the images of death and injury that they inflicted helped to promote faith in American military prowess and veiled the moral issues raised in a war in which less than 400 coalition soldiers died while somewhere between 100,000 and 200,000 Iraqi soldiers and civilians lost their lives, almost always off camera. Instead of body counts, the U.S. military talked of weapons destroyed, as though the war had been one fought between machines. Even this characterization turned out to be deceptive. It was later revealed that the Patriot missile interceptor shot down almost no Iraqi missiles and that very few smart bombs were actually used in combat.

Unmarred by the images of ground soldiers slogging through the jungles of Vietnam or of little girls burned by napalm and running in terror from American planes, media coverage of the Gulf War conveyed the idea of a war without risks to Americans and without harm to others. One military officer implied that the composition of the U.S. military during the Vietnam War accounted for the differences in the outcomes of the two wars. Marine Corps General George Crist, in a CNN documentary on the Gulf War, compared the soldiers there to those of the Vietnam War. According to Crist, the latter were "an army of draftees, an army taken off the streets of ghettos," but those fighting in the Gulf War were "a professional armed force that had been trained intensely, receiving these new high-tech weapons and learning how to use them and how to use them well. . . ." President Bush, in a speech he made shortly after the American victory, exulted: "We have finally kicked the Vietnam syn-

drome." American leaders did so, however, with the assistance of the public relations industry and a compliant press.

The politics of spin in a context of "sanitized" war could create unanticipated consequences. The very small number of U.S. casualties in Grenada, Panama, and the Gulf War created an unexpected problem: the American public came to look on this situation as the norm. Thus, Clinton was bitterly criticized when eighteen U.S. peacekeepers were killed in Somalia in 1993. He was reluctant to intervene in Bosnia in the mid-1990s or Kosovo in 1998 because of concern over possible losses. Video cameras and private reconnaissance satellites could provide unauthorized images of war that could spin out of control—as happened in Somalia and in the film *Black Hawk Down*.

The panoply of resources now available to politicians and lobbyists to advance their various agendas—including advertising, polling, speechwriters, and the media—has been labeled the media-spindustrial complex by critic Randall Rothenberg. Whatever it is called, it has been an important component of international relations and domestic politics for some time. As the producers of *Wag the Dog* implied, its control over increasingly sophisticated technologies endows it with great capacities for deception. If George Orwell was right that "political language . . . is designed to make lies sound truthful and murder respectable, and to give an appearance of solidity to pure wind," then those in the media-spindustrial complex exist to make political language sound like the mother tongue.

---

decisively won. Less than one-third of the public believed the war had been a mistake. By July, that figure had risen to 41 percent, and by the time of the march on Washington in October, 46 percent thought the United States should never have entered the war. Yet the number calling for an immediate American withdrawal from Vietnam remained low. Nevertheless, in the fall of 1967, only 28 percent of the public approved of President Johnson's handling of the war. Most Americans saw themselves as neither hawks nor doves;

they simply wanted relief. As the American war entered its third year in 1968, Senator Mansfield's 1965 warning about the shallowness of public support had proved prophetic.

Although no agreement existed about what to do next, the consensus on American foreign policy had shattered. A significant number of people began to question its very basis. Did the principle of containment mean that the United States should take part in any Third World conflict in which one side identified with socialism or communism? Were the communists in places like Vietnam any worse than the regimes that the United States chose to support? Would a triumph by such communists truly weaken the U.S. position with respect to its principal Cold War opponent, the Soviet Union? Did it make sense, in any event, for the United States to fight a war with little chance of victory? Although relatively few Americans had clear answers to such questions in 1967 and 1968, the war led many people to think about them.

By the end of 1967, doubts over further escalation of the war assailed even some of the war's sponsors. The president wondered about the usefulness of bombing North Vietnam. Secretary of Defense McNamara became morose at the lack of progress. At one point, he recommended an unconditional halt to the bombing to get serious negotiations started, but Johnson refused after learning that the Joint Chiefs of Staff had threatened to resign, as one group, if the bombing was stopped. As he began to despair of winning the war through advanced technology, McNamara became emotionally distraught and wanted out. In the fall of 1967, Johnson accepted McNamara's resignation from the Defense Department, replacing him with long-time Democratic Party adviser Clark Clifford in February 1968.

Johnson tried to open negotiations with the North Vietnamese in the fall of 1967. Harvard professor Henry Kissinger secretly relayed to a North Vietnamese official an administration promise to stop the bombing, with the understanding that the pause would lead to prompt discussions. The United States would not demand that the North remove its troops from the South, but it would trust that Hanoi would not take advantage of the hiatus to raise its troop levels. As Kissinger secretly presented these conditions, the bombing continued, suggesting that the military did not know what the Johnson administration was attempting. Suffering from the bombing, the Hanoi government rejected these overtures and called once more for the United States to quit what it described as an "illegal" intervention in Vietnam's civil war.

With this rebuff Johnson sank further into gloom, wary of escalation but incapable of devising a satisfactory alternative. After McNamara announced his resignation, the president's advisers became more hawkish. The president hoped that an optimistic assessment of the war from General Westmoreland, the supreme commander in the field, might buy time with the restless public. In November, Westmoreland returned to Washington and told reporters he was "very, very encouraged" because "we are making real progress." He told Congress that the North Vietnamese and Vietcong could not hold out much longer. He thought U.S. forces had reached a point where the end of the war was in view.

While Westmoreland's rosy scenario made headlines, Johnson's civilian advisers worried about the effect of the war on domestic tranquillity and U.S. prestige abroad. Johnson assembled his so-called Wise Men, foreign policy experts who had served various administrations since 1940, to chart a future path in Vietnam. They supported Johnson's course up until that time, but they warned that "endless inconclusive fighting" had become a "most serious cause of domestic disquiet."

January 1968 brought a military embarrassment elsewhere in Asia, when the *U.S.S. Pueblo*, a navy intelligence ship, was captured off the coast of North Korea. The *Pueblo* crew would remain the North Koreans' captives for almost a year, until negotiations finally produced their release in December. But this incident was minor compared to what the North Vietnamese and the Vietcong had in store.

At 2:45 A.M. on January 30, 1968—on Tet, the Vietnamese New Year—a squad of nineteen Vietcong commandos blasted a hole in the wall protecting the U.S. embassy in Saigon, ran into the courtyard, and engaged the marine guards there for the next six hours. All nineteen Vietcong commandos were killed, but the damage they did to Washington's position in Vietnam could not be repaired. The assault on the embassy was only the most dramatic part of a coordinated offensive by North Vietnamese and NLF forces against South Vietnamese population centers over the Tet holiday. They attacked the Saigon airport, the presidential palace, and the headquarters of the ARVN's general staff. With the benefit of complete surprise, the North Vietnamese and NLF battled with the Americans and ARVN for control of thirty-six of forty-four provincial capitals, five of six major cities, and sixty-four district capitals.

In most areas, the Americans and ARVN repulsed the communists, killing perhaps 40,000 while losing 3,400 of their own. The cost to South Vietnamese civilians ran much higher, with 1 million refugees swelling the already teeming camps in two weeks. One of the most grisly scenes occurred in the old imperial capital of Hue, once noted for its serene beauty. The Vietcong succeeded in controlling the city for three weeks. By the time the battle was over, and the Americans and ARVN had recaptured Hue, their bombs and artillery had left it, according to one soldier, a "shattered, stinking hulk, its streets choked with rubble and rotting bodies." The ARVN uncovered a mass grave containing the bodies of 2,800 South Vietnamese officeholders who had been executed by the Vietcong.

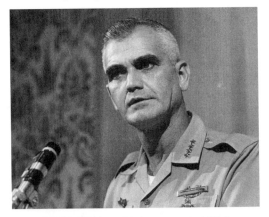

General William Westmoreland, commander of U.S. forces in Vietnam, 1964–1968. Handsome and friendly, Westmoreland got along well with the troops. But his promises of victory in Vietnam gave way to bitter public disillusionment with the war after the Tet Offensive of 1968. / © UPI/Bettmann/CORBIS

The principal American casualty was the cheery fiction of progress in

The frustration of the apparently endless war in Vietnam nearly overwhelmed President Johnson in 1968. / Jack Kightlinger/LBJ Library Collection

the war. After Tet, Westmoreland's recent assertion that an American victory could be achieved within two years sounded hopelessly unrealistic. His claims in the midst of the battle that the United States had defeated the enemy provoked derision. One of the most famous photographs of the war, showing the commander of the Saigon police shooting a Vietcong suspect in the head in the middle of a busy street, outraged the public at home.

Already discouraged by the lack of progress and by Robert McNamara's defection, Johnson grappled with Westmoreland's request for an additional 206,000 men. Failure to provide them, the general implied, meant losing the war. To Johnson, however, sending that many troops seemed a major escalation: it would risk Chinese or Soviet intervention and would shock the American public. After Tet, 78 percent of the public told a Harris poll that they thought the United States was not making progress in Vietnam, and only 2 percent approved of Johnson's handling of the war. Before he would grant Westmoreland's request, the president asked the new secretary of defense, Clark Clifford, to undertake a complete review of Vietnam policy.

Like McNamara before him, Clifford was once a hawk and now doubted whether sending more troops promised any progress. Civilian experts in the Defense Department revived a 1967 proposal by McNamara to change from a strategy of search and destroy to one of "population security." According to this strategy, American forces should protect the bulk of South Vietnam's civilian population while encouraging the ARVN to bear more of the burden of fighting the communists. American casualties would probably decline, reducing public unhappiness at home, but the hope of obtaining a military victory would vanish. Clifford therefore pressed for a negotiated settlement. In early March 1968, Johnson rejected Westmoreland's request for another 206,000 men.

Clifford persuaded the president to reconvene the Wise Men. During the last week of March, these distinguished former officials delivered some shocking opinions to the president. Dean Acheson, secretary of state under Truman, who had endured his own agony during the Korean War, asserted that the United States could "no longer do the job we set out to do in the time we have left, and we must begin to take steps to disengage." Cyrus Vance, former assistant secretary of defense, worried that "unless we do something quick, the mood in this country may lead us to withdraw." Many leading bankers and corporate executives were also in favor of a negotiated withdrawal. Although the war had initially led to an economic boom, by 1968, inflation and a shrinking dollar were causing growing problems for the economy.

Johnson did not like what he heard, but he could no longer ignore the mounting pressure to reverse course. He prepared an address to the nation to be broadcast the evening of March 31, 1968. In it, he promised a partial halt to the bombing, limiting American attacks to the region immediately north of the demilitarized zone at the 17th parallel. He promised to halt all bombing "if our restraint is matched by restraint in Hanoi." He named Averell Harriman, one of the Wise Men, as head of an American delegation to try to open peace talks with North Vietnam. Then, in a passage he wrote himself and kept secret from everyone but his wife, he withdrew from the 1968 presidential race. In order to devote himself to the negotiations he had just promised, he pledged that "I shall not seek, and I will not accept, the nomination of my party for another term as your president."

The Election of 1968

Lyndon Johnson had another reason for not seeking the Democratic nomination for president in 1968: he might not have received it. Anguish over the war had turned the Democrats against one another. For several years, many liberals and Kennedy insiders had stifled their misgivings about Johnson because they supported his domestic reform agenda; now, however, they revolted and looked for someone to challenge him for the nomination. Finding a candidate to run for nomination against a sitting president, even one as unpopular as Johnson, proved difficult. Eventually, an obscure midwestern senator, Eugene McCarthy of Minnesota, allowed himself to be drafted into running in the March 12 New Hampshire primary.

McCarthy's campaign seemed laughable at first. In its early weeks, the senator had few assistants, little money, and almost no press coverage. Everything changed in February, however, as the public reeled from the shock of the Tet offensive. Thousands of college-age volunteers hurried to New Hampshire to help the campaign. Aware that their hippie style would alienate the middle-of-the-road and the middle-aged, they cut their hair, put aside their bellbottoms, and donned coats and ties or skirts and sweaters, becoming "Clean for Gene." McCarthy made Vietnam the issue, demanding a halt to the bombing and immediate negotiations. Johnson's supporters took the bait, running TV ads warning that "the Communists in Vietnam are watching the New Hampshire primary." Johnson denounced McCarthy as "a champion of appeasement and surrender" and predicted that he would receive less than one-third of the vote. On primary day, McCarthy received 42.2 percent, coming within a few hundred votes of defeating Johnson; the Minnesota senator also took twenty of twenty-four delegates to the Democratic convention.

McCarthy's showing rattled the president and shook Robert Kennedy, who reconsidered his earlier refusal to run now that it appeared a challenge to Johnson might succeed. After consulting old supporters and trying unsuccessfully to persuade McCarthy to withdraw in his favor, Kennedy announced his candidacy for the Democratic nomination on March 16, 1968. Two weeks later, Johnson announced his own withdrawal from the race.

Aftershocks from Johnson's March 31 speech were still rumbling when, four days later, on April 4, James Earl Ray killed Martin Luther King, Jr., as King stood on the balcony of the Lorraine Motel in Memphis, Tennessee. King had gone to the city on behalf of striking sanitation workers; almost all of the workers were black, and they represented the abused, overworked, yet politically mobilized people he hoped to include in an interracial Poor People's Campaign. Seemingly prescient about his doom, King nevertheless maintained hope for the movement. The day before his assassination, he gave a speech in which he explained, "I've looked over and I've seen the Promised Land. I may not get there with you, but I want you to know tonight that we as a people will get to the Promised Land. . . . I'm not fearing any man. Mine eyes have seen the glory of the coming of the Lord." The assassination ignited another spurt of black rage. Riots erupted in more than a hundred cities; within a week, the police, the army, and the National Guard had killed thirty-seven people. Several blocks of downtown Washington, D.C., were burned and looted. The war, it seemed, had come home.

Two months later, Robert Kennedy met an assassin's bullet. Early in the morning of Wednesday, June 6, 1968, hours after he had eked out a narrow victory over Eugene McCarthy in the California primary, Kennedy was shot by Sirhan Sirhan, a Palestinian immigrant angry at the New York senator's support for Israel. Once more, the country suffered through a funeral for one of the Kennedys: a Requiem Mass in New York's St. Patrick's Cathedral, followed by a sad train ride south to Washington. Hundreds of thousands of mourners lined the tracks under a blazing sun. One senator on the train recalled that as he looked into their faces, "I saw sorrow, bewilderment." Robert Kennedy was buried next to his brother John in Arlington National Cemetery.

With Kennedy dead, McCarthy continued as the standard-bearer for the antiwar Democrats, who hoped to deny the nomination to Vice President Hubert Humphrey. Humphrey was supported by the prowar faction. The city of Chicago became an armed camp in August 1968 as the authorities prepared for antiwar protests at the Democratic national convention. Barbed wire enclosed the convention center, twelve thousand Chicago police were deployed on twelve-hour shifts, and about six thousand troops of the Illinois National Guard were called out, along with about as many army troops. The overwhelming majority of antiwar activists stayed away. On most days during the convention, there were perhaps four thousand demonstrators, with crowds peaking at possibly ten thousand on August 28. Thus, police generally outnumbered demonstrators by a factor of three or four to one, and federal records suggest that the ranks of the protesters were extensively infiltrated by government agents. Those who did come to protest were hardly a representative cross section of the antiwar movement. For example, male demonstrators at Chicago outnumbered females by eight or ten to one, imparting a particularly macho flavor to the action. The Yippies (the Youth International Party) came prepared to make a farce out of the convention by bringing along their own candidate, a live pig named Pigasus. "Our concept of revolution," said Abbie Hoffman, "is that it's fun." Paul Krassner, a prominent Yippie, terrified city residents by suggesting that demonstrators might attempt to alter people's consciousness by putting LSD into the city's water supply. An infuriated Richard J. Daley, mayor of Chicago, refused to let demonstrators camp in city parks, which guaranteed that plenty of restless people would be looking for conflict. A small minority of demonstrators—perhaps as many as three hundred—representing the extreme Left came to Chicago hoping to provoke violence.

On the same sultry night that Humphrey won the Democratic nomination, the Chicago police force went mad, clubbing and tear-gassing a crowd of ten thousand demonstrators who had come to the city to protest the war. Television cameras caught it all, including the protesters' chant, "The whole world is watching."

After this chaos, the Democratic nomination appeared worthless for Humphrey. Polls put him sixteen percentage points behind the Republican nominee, former vice president Richard Nixon. After losing a 1962 race for governor of California, Nixon had resurrected his political career by traveling the country, supporting local Republican candidates. A third candidate also ran, Alabama governor George Wallace, who had broken with the Democrats over civil rights. Some polls showed Wallace gaining 20 percent of the vote, much of it from formerly Democratic, working-class whites, largely but not exclusively in the South.

Both Nixon and Wallace fed public disgust with Vietnam. The Republican nominee, a hawk when escalation began in 1965, condemned the present stalemate. While presenting no specific way to end the war, Nixon promised an early "peace with honor" and hinted at a plan to reduce U.S. participation. Nixon also pursued a "southern strategy" of seeking the votes of southern white Democrats enraged at blacks. Promising to restore respect for law and order, he decried the race riots Johnson and Humphrey had not been able to stop. His running mate, Spiro Agnew, helped this cause by recalling the angry lecture he delivered to African American leaders after the April riots in Baltimore and on Maryland's eastern shore. George Wallace intimated that he could end the war faster than Humphrey. He named retired air force general

Curtis LeMay, an undisguised hawk, as his running mate, hoping to capitalize on nationalistic feelings. But LeMay's inflammatory remark that he would "bomb North Vietnam into the Stone Age" alarmed voters, and Wallace's campaign began to fade in late September.

Humphrey's campaign languished for six weeks after the Democratic convention. Liberals wanted nothing to do with him, even as he ran against Nixon, their old adversary. Johnson refused to release Humphrey from the political obligation to support the administration's Vietnam policy. Desperate for a way to distance himself from the stalemate in Vietnam, Humphrey announced on September 30, 1968, that he favored a total halt to the bombing "as an acceptable risk for peace, because I believe that it could lead to a success in negotiations and a shorter war." Suddenly, Humphrey began to close the gap with Nixon because many antiwar Democrats decided they preferred him to a man they despised.

Talks in Paris among the United States, North Vietnam, South Vietnam, and the NLF began in the summer, but these talks stalled over the issue of who could participate and the shape of the negotiating table. As the delegations wrangled for months, the seemingly endless talks about the talks came to sym-

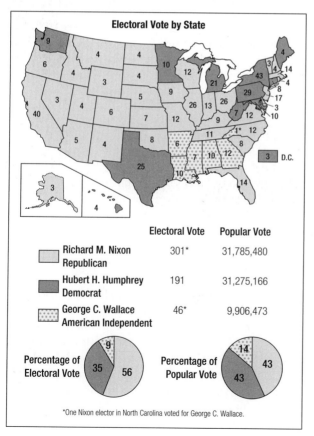

		Electoral Vote	Popular Vote
	Richard M. Nixon Republican	301*	31,785,480
	Hubert H. Humphrey Democrat	191	31,275,166
	George C. Wallace American Independent	46*	9,906,473

Percentage of Electoral Vote: 9, 35, 56

Percentage of Popular Vote: 14, 43, 43

*One Nixon elector in North Carolina voted for George C. Wallace.

Map 7.2
Presidential Election of 1968

bolize in the public's mind their frustration with the interminable war. The North Vietnamese refused to grant the Saigon government a separate place at the table, and the United States denied recognition to the NLF. The conversations finally progressed in the days before the November election because the communist side preferred a Humphrey victory to a win by the more hawkish Nixon. The Nixon camp worried that a breakthrough in the Paris talks might give the election to Humphrey. Professor Henry Kissinger, who had ties to both the Humphrey and Nixon organizations, informed the Nixon campaign that Johnson was preparing an "October surprise" to move the negotiations forward, thereby boosting Humphrey's chances. Nonetheless, the weekend before the election, Johnson announced a total bombing halt, along the lines that Humphrey had promised. Serious discussions on ending the war were scheduled to begin immediately after Election Day, on November 5, 1968.

Nixon won by a scant 510,000 votes, taking only 43.6 percent of the vote (see Map 7.2). Humphrey drew 42.9 percent, and Wallace got 13.5 percent. Humphrey's supporters believed that, given another four days, he would have won because he had made up 7 percentage points in the polls in the five days before the election. That may have been wishful thinking: the drop in the Democratic portion of the vote from the 1964 election, when Johnson took nearly 61 percent, represented a striking decline. Nearly all of the 57 percent of the public who had voted for Nixon or Wallace disagreed with Johnson's handling of the war in Vietnam, as did many of those who backed Humphrey.

The story of the events in Vietnam resumes in Chapter 9. Although Nixon took office with an apparent mandate for change, American troops continued to fight in Vietnam for another four years.

Conclusion

By the time of the 1968 election, most Americans wanted to end the Vietnam War, although they still disagreed about how to accomplish that goal. American involvement began quietly under President Truman and was gradually increased by presidents Eisenhower and Kennedy. Lyndon Johnson took the fateful step of committing the United States to a massive air and ground war. Yet the more the United States contributed to the war effort, the more the corrupt government of South Vietnam grew dependent on American support. The result was a cycle of continual frustration.

The war devastated Vietnam—its land, its people, and its society. It also proved tragic for many of the Americans who fought there. By the end of 1968, the war had already cost about thirty-seven thousand American lives, a number that would rise to over fifty-eight thousand by the time the United States withdrew its forces in 1973. And a significant number of American troops who returned physically unscathed suffered long-term psychological and emotional disabilities. Most believed that their efforts in Vietnam had been futile and were unappreciated at home. The veterans' plight contributed to the overall feeling that the nation's public institutions had failed.

At home, disagreement over the war shattered the general consensus about the proper goals of American foreign policy. Opposition became widespread and bitter, ruining Johnson's chances for re-election in 1968 and throwing the Democratic Party into turmoil. Because the war raised doubts about the power of American weapons and technology to mold events around the world, some Americans even began to question the basic doctrine of containment that had guided U.S. foreign policy since the late 1940s.

By dividing the American public, the Vietnam War also opened the deep chasms in American society that were the principal legacy of the 1960s. Chapter 8 describes how opposition to the war merged with other political and social movements to form a full-scale culture of protest. Many people became fundamentally disillusioned with American government and society. They distrusted not only the politicians in Washington, but many other forms of authority as well, and their rebellion stimulated an equally strong conservative backlash.

F U R T H E R • R E A D I N G

For overviews of the Vietnam War, see George C. Herring, *America's Longest War: The United States and Vietnam, 1950–1975* (2001); Stanley Karnow, *Vietnam: A History* (1991); Robert D. Schulzinger, *A Time for War: The United States and Vietnam, 1941–1975* (1997). **On the politics and diplomacy of the war,** see Michael Beschloss, ed., *Taking Charge: The Johnson White House Tapes* (1997) and *Reaching for Glory: Lyndon Johnson's Secret White House Tapes, 1964–1965* (2001); David Kaiser, *American Tragedy: Kennedy, Johnson and the Origins of the Vietnam War* (2000); A. J. Languth, *Our Vietnam: The War, 1954–1975* (2000); Fredrik Logevall, *Choosing War: The Lost Chance for Peace and the Escalation of War in Vietnam* (1999); Robert Mann, *A Grand Delusion: America's Descent into Vietnam* (2001); Robert S. McNamara, with Brian VanDeMark, *In Retrospect: The Tragedy and Lessons of Vietnam* (1995). **On fighting the war,** see Mark Clodfelter, *The Limits of Air Power* (1989); William Duiker, *Ho Chi Minh: A Biography* (2000); Neil Sheehan, *A Bright Shining Lie: John Paul Vann and America in Vietnam* (1988); Andrew Krepenevich, *The Army and Vietnam* (1989); Peter G. McDonald, *Giap: The Victor in Vietnam* (1993); Wallace Berry, *Bloods: An Oral History of the War by Black Veterans* (1984); Mark Baker, *Nam* (1982); Don Oberdorfer, *Tet* (1979); Ronald Spector, *After Tet: The Bloodiest Year of the Vietnam War* (1993). **On the home front during the war,** see Christian Appy, *Working Class War: American Combat Soldiers and Vietnam* (1993); Lawrence Baskir and William Strauss, *Chance and Circumstance: The War, the Draft and the Vietnam Generation* (1978); Myra MacPherson, *Long Time Passing: Vietnam and the Haunted Generation* (2002); Melvin Small, *Antiwarriors: The Vietnam War and the Battle for America's Hearts and Minds* (2002); Charles DeBenedetti, with Charles Chatfield, *An American Ordeal: The Antiwar Movement of the Vietnam Era* (1990); Tom Wells, *The War Within: America's Battle Over Vietnam* (1994); Nancy Zaroulis and Gerald Sullivan, *Who Spoke Up? American Protest Against the War in Vietnam, 1963–1975* (1984). **On the political upheavals of 1968,** see James Miller, *"Democracy Is in the Streets"* (1987); Todd Gitlin, *The Sixties* (1987); David Farber, *Chicago '68* (1988); David Caute, *The Year of the Barricades* (1988). **On media relations,** see Larry Tye, *The Father of Spin: Edward L. Bernays and the Birth of Public Relations* (1998); Susan Jeffords and Lauren Rabinovitz, eds., *Seeing Through the Media: The Persian Gulf War* (1994).

The Politics and Culture of Protest

Antiwar protester puts flowers in the guns of military police at a 1967 demonstration at the Pentagon. / Paul Conklin, © Time Magazine, Time, Inc.

n March 1968, when the *New York Times* ran a story entitled "An Arrangement: Living Together for Convenience, Security, Sex," it unleashed a firestorm of criticism at Barnard College, the all-women adjunct college of Columbia University. The article told of the lives of a few college students who were living together as unmarried couples. One interviewee, a student at Barnard, told of her success in evading Barnard's rule that its students live in campus housing, where they were subject to a set of restrictive rules, including the requirement that they be home at a specified hour. As vigilant college officials determined her identity, the newspaper and the college were inundated with letters condemning young couples who chose to "flaunt" their decision to have sex before marriage.

Barnard College charged the student, Linda LeClair, with lying about her housing arrangements and required that she appear before the student-faculty judiciary council. LeClair summarized her position in a letter to the student newspaper: "If women are able, intelligent people, why must we be supervised and curfewed?" The council recommended a minimal punishment (banishment from the college cafeteria!), but the president, who was in the middle of a fundraising campaign for the college, threatened expulsion. She did so mostly in response to a barrage of letters and editorials from an outraged public, who understood LeClair's claim to individual freedom and gender equality to be an assault on civilized morals. Many called LeClair a "whore" and claimed that she and her boyfriend were "violating the laws of decency when they flaunt their dereliction in public." Conservative columnist William Buckley said that he was not surprised "that the LeClairs of this world should multiply like rabbits, whose morals they imitate." Before the college reached a final decision in her case, LeClair dropped out of school.

LeClair's challenge to time-honored institutional practices and cultural assumptions reflected the diverse issues touched on by the volatile political and cultural energies unleashed in the 1960s. Within a few years, most colleges and universities had dropped the residence and hours rules that they had applied to women students for over a century, acceding to the demands of the students' and women's movements and recognizing that they were not equipped to monitor the private behavior of their students. Those students, indeed, by that time occupied center stage in some of the most volatile and radical social movements in U.S. history. By 1965, the spirit of protest had spread from young blacks unwilling to tolerate the slow pace of racial progress to young whites angry at government policies and sick of the bland pleasures that middle-class life offered.

Some in the baby-boom generation—those who made up the surge in the national birth rate that began in 1946—followed slightly older dissidents into the civil rights and peace crusades of the early 1960s. Some joined more radical movements, like Black Power and the Weathermen, and a few concluded that only violent revolution could bring the necessary changes. Others sought to extend the boundaries of acceptable everyday behavior, sampling the psychological challenges, sensual pleasures, and physical risks of the emerging counterculture. Many joined women's liberation groups, linking the personal and the political. Their political activism was sometimes enhanced, sometimes enfeebled by the cultural forms they created as they gloried in sexual expressiveness, musical innovation, and experimentation with drugs.

What people in the sixties would call the generation gap—the alienation of the young from the strategies and aspirations of their elders—had been brewing for some time. Among the "baby deficit" generation, born in the 1930s and 1940s, signs of discontent emerged in the 1950s. The pop-culture antiheroes of that decade, from the brooding, doomed James Dean in *Rebel Without a Cause* to the lip-curling Marlon Brando in *The Wild One*, had shown adult America the face of restless youth. Middle-class American parents in the fifties had planned ahead. They knew the price of affluence and were willing to sacrifice and save. Their children took material comfort for granted, but they wondered why so many Americans had to live in poverty. Relieved of the burden of financial worry by the growing American economy of the 1960s, the baby boomers looked to expand the boundaries of peace, justice, and spirituality as part of their quest for an ever better life.

If even the children of privilege felt distant from the American dream, others had more reason to feel disaffected and to raise their voices in increasingly angry protest. African American writer Richard Wright had sounded a note of black rage as early as 1940 with his novel *Native Son*. In the 1960s, other black writers, from Black Panther leader Eldridge Cleaver to poet June Jordan, took up Wright's legacy. From rock singer Janis Joplin to the activists of the women's liberation movement, women also began to find words to defy the restrictions that society placed on them. From these very diverse threads, the sixties wove a new politics and culture of protest.

From Civil Rights to Black Power

For about fifty years, the National Association for the Advancement of Colored People (NAACP) and the Urban League, under the leadership of careful men like Roy Wilkins and Whitney Young, had led the African American campaign for civil rights. They believed that their cause was consistent with democratic and Christian principles, and they saw their movement as instrumental to realizing the promise of American life. They used various methods to secure reforms within the system. By the early 1960s, sit-ins, boycotts, and protest marches had become widespread. But the decade would soon see the emergence of more radical goals and approaches.

By 1964, the civil rights movement had begun to focus on community organization and voter registration as primary tactics in the fight against racism. These methods were used primarily in the South, where racial segregation and hatred were particularly open and entrenched. Rank-and-file civil rights workers in organizations like the Congress of Racial Equality (CORE), founded in 1942; the Southern Christian Leadership Conference (SCLC), begun in 1957; and the Student Non-Violent Coordinating Committee (SNCC), founded at an SCLC conference in 1960, faced potential and actual white violence on a daily basis.

Black Mississippian Anne Moody joined first the NAACP, then SNCC, knowing that doing so entailed grave risks both to herself and her loved ones. One friend had been shot in the back because white townspeople suspected him of belonging to the NAACP; a local clergyman and his family had been run out of town because he had mentioned the NAACP in a sermon. While organizing blacks in the small towns of Mississippi, Moody learned to live with fear. Her uncle and three others were murdered in Woodville, Mississippi, in a campaign of what SNCC leader Robert Moses identified as "terror killings." Those who dared to speak out against the murders became targets themselves; when they asked federal authorities for protection, they were told, "We can't protect every individual Negro in Mississippi." Again and again, FBI and Justice Department officials stood by while demonstrators were beaten and illegally jailed. "I guess mostly the SNCC workers were just lucky," Moody wrote in her autobiography, *Coming of Age in Mississippi*. "Most of them had missed a bullet by an inch or so on many occasions. Threats didn't stop them. They just kept going all the time."

While Congress debated the Civil Rights Act of 1964, the SCLC's Martin Luther King, Jr., courted a national television audience, combining restraint and eloquence with the use of nonviolent boycotts, sit-ins, and demonstrations. A "conservative militant," King was a pivotal figure in the civil rights movement. He retained the support of white liberals, who provided much of the movement's financial backing, while trying to maintain ties with the increasingly frustrated younger African Americans who staffed the front-line positions in the battle. King confronted white violence with dignity, leading peaceful protest marches against segregation and injustice. He dazzled the nation with his "I Have a Dream" speech at the massive 1963 March on Washington. Rank-and-file organizers, however, found King aloof and abstract, and referred to him sarcastically as "De Lawd."

During the summer of 1964, many black and white students spent their college vacations in Mississippi, where white resistance to integration was deep and militant. These student activists sought to break the white monopoly on political power in the South by using weapons dear to the American political system: voters. The Mississippi Freedom Summer Project, organized by the SNCC-affiliated Council of Federated Organizations, attracted more than one thousand students from the North, mostly white, to join veteran black and white southern workers in a campaign to register African American voters for the newly created, racially integrated Mississippi Freedom Democratic Party (MFDP). Volunteers also walked picket lines, attended innumerable meetings, and organized "freedom schools" at community centers to teach remedial reading, government, humanities, and other academic and vocational subjects.

The Mississippi state legislature reacted to the challenge by doubling the state police force, authorizing local authorities to pool their personnel and equipment for riot-control purposes, and introducing an anti-invasion bill intended to keep civil rights workers out of the state. White vigilante groups mounted a campaign of intimidation, ranging from harassment to bombings and killings. In June 1964, civil rights workers Andrew Goodman, Michael

Schwerner, and James Chaney—two northern whites and a southern black—were murdered. Yet the volunteers kept coming, sleeping in shifts on bare mattresses, living on peanut butter, cranking mimeograph machines, and tramping the hot streets. Sustained by idealism, SNCC workers wanted not only to end segregation and political repression, but also to oppose the fury of white hatred by living out their own vision of a racially integrated "beloved community" based on respect, affection, and a shared commitment to social justice. To one young, white SNCC volunteer, African American women like Fanny Lou Hamer, Ella Baker, and Ruby Doris Smith Robinson and men like the soft-spoken Bob Moses seemed "wise, caring, courageous, honest, and full of love." Blacks living under the burden of racism inspired younger white college students from the North with their bravery and their tirelessness.

The beloved community was, however, riddled with tension. Living in fear of "nightriders," who fired shots through their windows and telephoned bomb threats, civil rights workers also had to cope with racial friction within their own ranks. Long-time black workers worried that whites were trying to take over the movement without facing the risks that blacks encountered daily. Interracial sexual relations caused conflict between black and white women and between women and men.

SNCC succeeded in mobilizing enough voters to enable the MFDP to mount a challenge to the all-white delegation that the regular state party sent to the 1964 Democratic national convention in Atlantic City. MFDP delegation leader Fanny Lou Hamer electrified a national television audience as she testified before the party's Credentials Committee that she had been denied the right to vote and had been jailed and beaten in attempting to exercise that right. "We are askin' the American people," she said, "is this the land of the free and the home of the brave?" The MFDP demanded that its delegation be seated in place of the official state delegation. White liberals like Senator Hubert Humphrey of Minnesota and southern conservatives in the party leadership worked out what they termed a compromise: the white delegation was seated, after promising not to bolt the Democratic Party later on, and two MFDP representatives received delegate-at-large status. To those who had put their lives on the line all summer, this "compromise" seemed a betrayal, a triumph of expediency over morality. Two disillusioned African American activists, Stokely Carmichael and Charles Hamilton, wrote that the lesson of Atlantic City was clear: "Black people . . . could not rely on their so-called allies."

By the time of the Atlantic City convention, African Americans throughout the country were revealing their frustration at the limited success of nonviolent tactics. Martin Luther King, Jr., framed his endorsement of civil disobedience in the language and spirit of Christian forbearance: "One who breaks an unjust law must do so openly, lovingly, and with a willingness to accept the penalty." However, the black Christian churches that King represented, which for a decade had emphasized the necessity of taking the moral high ground, were losing influence with their congregations. After a church bombing killed a group of schoolchildren during Sunday school, Anne Moody told her God,

You know, I used to go to Sunday school when I was a little girl. . . . We were taught how merciful and forgiving you are. I bet those girls in Sunday school were being taught the same as I was when I was their age. Is that teaching wrong? Are you going to forgive their killers? . . . Nonviolence is out. I have a good idea Martin Luther King is talking to you, too. If he is, tell him that nonviolence has served its purpose.

Black civil-rights workers had learned through experience that white lawlessness seldom brought penalties. Even King was aware that activists' patience was wearing thin. If nonviolent civil disobedience failed to gain justice, King warned, "millions of Negroes will, out of frustration and despair, seek solace and security in black nationalist ideologies."

King's predictions were fulfilled. Many blacks began to reject Christian forbearance altogether. Some sought new meaning in a black separatist Islamic faith. Malcolm X, the nation's most prominent and eloquent Black Muslim, spoke out for black nationalism, explicitly rejected integration, and advocated meeting violence with violence. Rioting broke out in Harlem in the summer of 1964.

After the Democratic convention, the ranks of SNCC split. One faction, which included black and white southerners and middle-class white college students, believed in participatory democracy and decision making by consensus. The other group, dominated by long-time field organizers like James Forman and Ruby Doris Smith Robinson, wanted to move away from a focus on moral and procedural issues to questions of power. Bitterly disillusioned with the fickleness of their white allies, they argued that SNCC should be black-led and black-dominated.

By the early months of 1965, the concept of "black and white together" in the civil rights movement was being eclipsed. Malcolm X had begun to tone down his antiwhite message and to seek some new solutions to the problem of racism. But he was gunned down in February 1965, allegedly murdered by less conciliatory followers of Black Muslim leader Elijah Muhammad. Ironically, his death convinced some African American activists that power came only from the barrel of a gun. Other civil rights leaders persisted in trying to channel the movement's energies into coordinated, nonviolent action, but their protests seemed inadequate in the face of white brutality. In March 1965, a national television audience watched as Selma, Alabama, Sheriff Jim Clark ordered his men to meet civil rights marchers with clubs and tear gas. Martin Luther King, Jr., and Ralph Bunche led a group of 3,200 people on a fifty-mile march from Selma to the heavily fortified state capitol at Montgomery, Alabama, where they were joined by 25,000 supporters. In the course of the Selma campaign, three activists were killed. Many Americans were struck by the contrast between the violence of the Selma police and the peaceful nature of the march. The Voter Registration Act of 1965, signed in early August, passed partly as a result of the Selma march and partly as a result of President Johnson's revulsion at the accompanying white violence. But the costs of pursuing peaceful tactics were becoming unbearable to movement veterans.

An officer harasses a woman beaten unconscious by public authorities in Selma, Alabama, for marching to protest race discrimination in voter registration. / © Bettmann/CORBIS

Around the nation, African Americans responded to the slow pace of change with increasing fury. In August 1965, five days of looting and rioting broke out in Watts, a black ghetto in Los Angeles. Residents of Watts had reason to be frustrated: although Los Angeles as a whole was booming, blacks in the area were worse off than before. Median income in the area had dropped 8 percent between 1959 and 1965. Many complained that the white-controlled businesses in Watts jacked up their prices and paid low wages to black employees. Thirty percent of adult men in Watts were unemployed, and of those who did hold jobs, many lacked the cars necessary to navigate the nation's preeminent car-culture city. Los Angeles police, mostly white and sometimes openly racist, did little to win this community's trust. By the time the rioting subsided, thirty-four people had died, four thousand had been arrested, and much of the area had been leveled. The Los Angeles police chief blamed civil rights workers; the mayor blamed communists. From the ashes arose a cry of despair that would fuel the revolutionary rhetoric of the Black Power movement and, in turn, the white backlash against African American rights: "Burn, baby, burn." In Los Angeles, a race war seemed a real possibility.

On a march through Mississippi in the summer of 1966, the message crystallized. Those who still supported the goal of integration and the tactics of nonviolence, like Floyd McKissick of CORE and John Lewis, former chair of SNCC, looked on as Stokely Carmichael, bringing news of the founding of the Black Panther Party in Lowndes County, Alabama, announced a new goal—Black Power. To his African American listeners he declared, "It's time we stand up and take over." To society at large, he issued a warning: "Move on over or we'll move on over you."

Within a year, weary veterans of the civil rights movement had been displaced in the public eye by young militants. SNCC became the organizing center of the Black Power movement. Carmichael and the new SNCC chair, H. Rap Brown, viewed the increasingly common ghetto disturbances as a dress rehearsal for revolution. Meanwhile, the federal government offered only a weak response to urban rioting. President Johnson appointed Illinois governor Otto Kerner to head a commission to study the situation. When the Kerner Commission delivered a report concluding that the United States was shot through with racism and was rapidly becoming two nations—one, black and poor; the other, white and rich—Johnson did nothing. He was too preoccupied with the Vietnam War to pursue his promised Great Society.

Urging students at black colleges to "fight for liberation by any means necessary," Carmichael declared, "[T]o hell with the laws of the United States." At a Black Power conference in Newark, New Jersey, held on the heels of a riot in which police killed twenty-five African Americans, one thousand participants approved resolutions affirming black people's right to revolt and calling for a separate black nation and black militia. In 1968, Carmichael, Brown, and SNCC were replaced by the Black Panthers as the most visible militant group. Wearing leather jackets and carrying weapons, the Panthers often resembled an elite paramilitary unit. They aimed their radical rhetoric at the American capitalist system. During the next few years, as the Panthers provoked considerable uneasiness among the white middle class, they became the objects of heavy surveillance by the FBI. They had frequent confrontations with police, including shootouts that left some Panthers dead and others under arrest.

Many African Americans, including those unwilling to embrace violence as a tactic for change, remained sympathetic to the Panthers and the black-power movement. While the vast majority of whites stated in public opinion polls that the killings had been mainly "the result of violence started by Black Panthers themselves," blacks responded that the conclusion that they drew was that "blacks have to stand together." They believed this conclusion because they expected little from whites who condoned government violence against those whom they saw as community leaders. The Panthers' "survival pending revolution" strategies had led them to provide services—including health clinics, breakfast programs for children, employment centers, and visiting programs for families of prisoners—that were of material benefit to people long ignored by white officials and charities and who were left out of significant parts of the New Deal safety net.

The SDS and the Rise of the New Left

As African American groups became more militant, so did other, predominantly white organizations that arose to challenge the structure of American politics and society. Collectively, these groups were soon called the New Left, to distinguish them from the Old Left of the 1930s to 1950s.

In contrast to the liberals and radicals of the fifties, who lived in the shadow of the Holocaust and Stalinism, those who came of age in the early 1960s were the beneficiaries of the new American affluence and the huge postwar expansion of the nation's colleges and universities. Between 1945 and 1965, public spending on higher education rose from $742.1 million to $6.9 billion per year. University life provided the chance for a small but growing group of students to imagine things as they ought to be, rather than as they are. Uneasy in the presence of the world's growing atomic arsenal and ignited by the civil rights movement, they were less wedded to older allegiances than their Old Left predecessors and more optimistic about the prospects for sweeping social change.

Some of those who came of age in the early 1960s founded the most influential and best known New Left group: the Students for a Democratic Society (SDS). At a 1962 SDS meeting in Port Huron, Michigan, Tom Hayden, one of the organization's early leaders, articulated its concerns and goals in his famous Port Huron Statement. Beginning with his Agenda for a Generation, Hayden declared, "We are the people of this generation, bred in at least modest comfort, housed now in universities, looking uncomfortably to the world we inherit." He went on to criticize college students' apathy toward politics and to deplore collegiate complacency. The country's widespread poverty and the unchallenged power of what Eisenhower had called the military-industrial complex threatened the nation's best traditions. Hayden called for a restoration of participatory democracy to make political parties, corporations, and the government more responsive to ordinary people. "America," said Hayden, "should concentrate on its genuine social priorities: abolish squalor, terminate neglect, and establish an environment for people to live in with dignity and creativeness."

Embracing Hayden's hopeful message, white students flocked into civil rights work in the early 1960s. Some SDS members went south. Others in 1964 set up the group's Economic Research and Action Project in northern ghettos, attempting to organize an interracial movement of the poor that focused on issues such as jobs and community control of social programs.

Soon this involvement in the civil rights movement propelled student activists into taking up other issues in new places. Mario Savio and Jack Weinberg, two veterans of the Mississippi Freedom Summer, returned to the University of California at Berkeley in the fall of 1964 to continue recruitment for the movement. When campus authorities forbade their efforts, the Berkeley Free Speech Movement brought active radicalism on campus. Students took over the administration building, declared a strike, and enlisted faculty support for the removal of restrictions on free expression on campus. Free Speech Movement activists expressed both their joy and their anger in words once thought inadmissible in polite company, and conservative Americans began to see Berkeley as an outpost of lawlessness and libertinism. By 1966, California gubernatorial candidate Ronald Reagan was telling campaign audiences that campus activists indulged in "orgies so vile I cannot describe them to you."

Campus protests quickly spread. By 1965, there had been disturbances at Yale, Ohio State, the University of Kansas, Brooklyn College, Michigan State, and St. John's University. Campus disputes often arose over issues of personal conduct rather than national politics. College students of the 1950s had accepted the time-honored doctrine of in loco parentis, which claimed that the institution had the right and the obligation to stand in for parents and regulate students' behavior. But by the mid-1960s, many campus regulations—particularly those attempting to preserve the conservative mating and dating rituals of the fifties—seemed quaint, artificial, and restrictive. Students began to oppose all kinds of limitations on their behavior, from dress codes and anti-smoking regulations to rules governing where they could live, what hours they could keep, and who could visit their rooms. Students at single-sex institutions agitated for coeducation. Returning from summers spent in loosely structured, sexually volatile communal households where they worked for SNCC or SDS, male and female students alike chafed at campus rules.

Even without these lifestyle issues, national politics provided more than enough cause for dissent, particularly as President Johnson escalated the war in Vietnam. As nightly newscasts brought television audiences graphic proof of the bloodiness and futility of the nation's foreign policy, official government pronouncements about the prospects for peace seemed patently false. Berkeley's Jack Weinberg admonished his fellow students not to trust anyone over thirty, and freethinking American journalists began to believe there was no point in trusting anyone in power. On campuses, in cities, and on military bases, underground newspapers sprang up to offer a more radical alternative to conventional news sources.

Even the mainstream press began to mistrust the information released by official sources. Investigative reporters like Seymour Hersh of the *New York Times* looked beyond government press releases to get at the truth of national policy. Jeopardizing his sources in the military, Hersh broke the story of the My Lai massacre in Vietnam. Hersh and other journalists were willing to accept the professional risks inherent in upsetting the previously cozy relationship between reporters and their sources. As a result, they managed to uncover many important stories that government officials had attempted to suppress.

The Vietnam War soon became the main focus of student protest. Because students—male students, at least—were directly threatened by the draft, they represented a huge new constituency for the protest effort. When the SDS endorsed draft resistance, its membership swelled. Draft-counseling centers sprang up across the country. Women joined the protests in support of their male friends. Some in the movement even tried to make resistance sexy; according to one slogan that appeared on protest signs, "Girls say yes to guys who say no." And by the late 1960s, many parents of draft-age men had changed their views on Vietnam as well.

In the spirit of participatory democracy, local SDS chapters and other draft-resistance groups tried various tactics. Some initiated draft-card burnings. Others held sit-ins at Selective Service induction centers, opposed university Reserve Officers' Training Corps (ROTC) programs, protested military recruiters' visits to campus, or demonstrated against corporations involved in defense work. Dow Chemical, the manufacturer of napalm, became a particularly hated target. According to the National Student Association, between January 1 and June 15, 1968, there were 221 major antiwar demonstrations at 101 colleges and universities, involving about forty thousand students.

Across the country, college professors and even high school teachers initiated "teach-ins" to educate curious students about Vietnamese history and politics. There were notable efforts to join student groups with other organizations to orchestrate nationwide protests against the war. In the summer of 1967, twenty thousand people participated in the Vietnam Summer, an effort modeled on the Mississippi Freedom Summer and mounted by a coalition of pacifists, liberals, and radicals to mobilize the middle class against the war. Stop the Draft Week, from October 16 to 21, 1967, culminated in a march on the Pentagon. Fifty thousand people crossed the Arlington Memorial Bridge, some to picket, some to pray, others to attempt to storm the bastion of the military-industrial complex. The march included not only students but also representatives of many other groups ranged against the war. Among those present were Berkeley Free Speech activist Jerry Rubin, childcare expert Dr. Benjamin Spock, linguistics theorist Noam Chomsky, poet Robert Lowell, social philosopher Paul Goodman, and Dagmar Wilson of Women's Strike for Peace. The coalition even had its comic aspects: Ed Sanders, leader of a rock band called the Fugs, proposed a "grope for peace"; Sanders and radical leader Abbie Hoffman coordinated an attempt to levitate the Pentagon.

Sociologist Todd Gitlin, an early president of SDS, noted that as the war became more militant, so too did the antiwar movement. Antiwar demonstrators had often tried to contrast their own peace-loving demeanor with the government's policy of violence, carrying signs reading "Make Love, Not War" and putting flowers in the barrels of the guns pointed at them by police and National Guard troops at demonstrations. By 1967, however, antiwar activists were preaching a harder line, and demonstrators began adopting a tougher posture. In Oakland, California, protests during Stop the Draft Week turned into bloody confrontations with the police.

SDS, its membership swelling, moved beyond the goals articulated at Port Huron. It adopted the slogan "From Protest to Resistance." By 1967, SDS publications had begun referring to the authorities as pigs. Insisting that the cause of justice in Vietnam—which they identified quite simply with the Vietcong and the North Vietnamese—could not get a fair hearing in the United States, some New Leftists declared free speech a sham and shouted down progovernment speakers. National Liberation Front flags began to appear at antiwar rallies, alienating many middle-of-the-road Americans. SDS leader Bernardine Dorn wanted to bring the war home, to make the American people feel Vietnam's torment; such revolutionary tactics confused and angered many Americans, including many who opposed the war. Many sympathized with the radicals' demands but found it hard to accept tactics that included violating property rights.

Nowhere was campus conflict more spectacular than at Columbia University in New York City. Columbia embodied all that campus radicals con-

Columbia University students occupy a professor's office in April 1968. / © UPI/Bettmann/ CORBIS

demned. A bastion of Ivy League privilege in the middle of the ghetto, the university was both a Harlem landlord and a holder of major defense research contracts. On April 23, 1968, the Columbia SDS chapter joined with black militants in taking over university buildings, including the president's office. Columbia students held the buildings for eight days, after which New York City police moved in with billy clubs. They arrested 692 people, three-quarters of them students. Though the siege was over, a student strike forced the university to close early for the year. The stage was set for violent confrontations between students and authorities on campuses across the nation in the next two years.

The American student protests were part of an international drive toward student militancy. The Columbia uprising had its counterpart in Paris, where angry protesters erected barricades in the streets and battled police. But not all students—and certainly not all young people—joined the protests. Some opposed only the war and the draft; some sympathized but stayed out of the streets. Many young people—political conservatives, white southerners, working-class youths who did not go to college, graduate students who had invested time and money in pursuit of professional careers—were either unaffected by the protests or opposed to them. Nevertheless, campus conflicts revealed a deep gulf between the "straight" social standards of the older generation and the beliefs of most of those who came of age in the 1960s.

The Counterculture and Mainstream Culture

At the same time that young people were becoming more radical in their political beliefs, they began to experiment with new ways of living. Many had been raised in suburban affluence, yet they condemned the materialism, conformity, and the hypocrisy of their parents' generation. The counterculture they formed derived from, transformed, and posed a threat to mainstream mass culture. Youthful dissenters relied on mass media to popularize new cultural forms and values and to communicate new political ideas. As Yippie Jerry Rubin declared in an underground newspaper, "You can't be a revolutionary today without a television set." The entertainment and communication industries were businesses that sought to sell products, especially to the huge baby-boom generation, while maintaining the economic and social system from which their enterprises had long profited. The counterculture–mainstream culture relationship in the 1960s generated conflict and uneasy accommodations in a context of mutual dependence and contradictory values.

Many young people found inspiration for new lives in the Beat writers of the 1950s. "The only ones for me," author Jack Kerouac wrote in his 1957 novel, *On the Road*, "are the mad ones, the ones who are mad to live, mad to talk, mad to be saved, desirous of everything at the same time, the ones who never yawn or say a commonplace thing, but burn, burn, burn like fabulous yellow roman candles." Along with other Beat writers, Kerouac came to symbolize the rejection of bourgeois comfort and the embrace of a life of sensation-seeking, adventure, and personal authenticity. The Beats also represented a male revolt against the middle-class family and the traditional masculine role of breadwinner. Going on drinking sprees, careening around the country, and embracing freewheeling sexuality, the Beats distanced themselves from the 1950s family man in his gray flannel suits.

While "squares" pursued the American dream in suburban comfort—drinking martinis, listening to *Hit Parade* on TV, raising their kids, and fooling around only if they wouldn't get caught—the Beats, or "hipsters," lived by another set of standards. They lived in bare apartments in urban enclaves like New York City's Greenwich Village and San Francisco's North Beach; expanded the range of recreational drugs from sweet wine to marijuana and heroin; and listened to the incendiary, experimental jazz of Charlie "Yardbird" Parker, Dizzy Gillespie, and Miles Davis. These were the beginnings of a movement that widened by the later 1960s into the counterculture, a loosely defined phenomenon that involved new types of rock music, drugs, sexual freedom, and various other emblems of a liberated lifestyle.

Meanwhile, the popular culture that the Beats despised was undergoing its own transformation. A revival of folk music—identified with the Old Left during the 1950s—meant commercial success in the 1960s for protest singers like Joan Baez and Bob Dylan. Their music sparked a yearning for social change and helped energize protesters. But it was rock 'n' roll that served as the primary musical catalyst for the counterculture.

For millions of American girls, the arrival of the Beatles in the United States in 1964 was a watershed. No musicians before or since have achieved the mass popularity or cultural influence of these four young Englishmen: John Lennon, Paul McCartney, George Harrison, and Ringo Starr. While "Beatlemaniacs" fantasized about romance with their idols, they also found much to identify with in the "Fab Four." Playful, long-haired, wacky, and talented, the Beatles personified both personal independence and a new androgynous sexual ideal. One fan recalled, "I didn't want to grow up and be a wife, and it seemed to me that the Beatles had the kind of freedom I wanted: No rules, they could spend two days lying in bed; they ran around on motorbikes, ate from room service. . . . I wanted to be like them. Something larger than life." Another wrote, "I liked their independence and sexuality and wanted those things for myself."

As they had during the Elvis Presley phenomenon of the late 1950s (see Chapter 3), parents began to worry that their children were getting out of control. But the transformation of rock music and the youth culture it represented was only beginning. By the mid-1960s, the sentimental love songs of the early Beatles gave way to the overt sexual come-ons of groups such as the Rolling Stones and the Doors. "I Wanna Hold Your Hand" gave way to the Stones' "Let's Spend the Night Together," and the Doors' "Touch Me." Many girls and women accepted these ideas, adopting a new, open, and defiant insistence on the right to sexual pleasure, for themselves as well as men. The birth-control pill, first marketed in 1960, made pleasure without procreation possible and galvanized the gradual repeal of state "blue laws" restricting the sale of contraceptives.

The ideal of sexual freedom spread rapidly, galvanized by the rock music that expressed the desires and demands of young people. As the counterculture developed, the music continued to evolve; performers invented new musical forms and hybrids, pushing folk and rock 'n' roll beyond all previous limits. Soon psychedelic music, often known as acid rock, was celebrating the use of mind-altering drugs. Groups like the Grateful Dead and Jefferson Airplane turned their sets into dizzying, deafening swirls of sound. A young white woman named Janis Joplin sang a steamy, screeching, tortured, blues-driven rock that gave her an almost legendary status within the counterculture.

Like Joplin, most of the avant-garde performers were white. Ironically, at a time when many black political leaders were turning from civil rights to Black Power, African American musicians succeeded in reaching a broad commercial audience by taking a fairly cautious approach. The best known black recording artists were associated with Motown, the Detroit music company masterminded by black songwriter-entrepreneur Berry Gordy, Jr. Motown singers like Stevie Wonder and groups like the Temptations and the Supremes combined musical virtuosity with lush production, precise choreography, glittering costumes, and a bland message. One exception to this trend was James Brown, the godfather of soul music, who marked out the frontiers of raw sex appeal. Another black innovator was guitarist Jimi Hendrix, whose incendiary playing defined the psychedelic style.

Along with sex and rock 'n' roll, the counterculture featured the abundant use of drugs. The Beatles took lysergic acid diethylamide (LSD), a psychotropic chemical better known as "acid." Their path-breaking album, *Sergeant Pepper's Lonely Hearts Club Band*, declared, "I'd love to turn you on." "More and more," former SDS president Todd Gitlin observed, "to get access to youth culture, you had to get high." Many people got "stoned" with milder drugs like marijuana, which was said at the time to impair short-term memory but had limited long-term effects. Some, like rock idols Janis Joplin, Jim Morrison, and Jimi Hendrix, sought in drugs a release from deep-seated pain. They combined alcohol with barbiturates, amphetamines, cocaine, and heroin until their drug dependence killed them. At first the term *psychedelic* referred to hallucinogenic drugs that altered perceptions. Counterculture adherents used these drugs as a means of expanding the mind to reach a higher level of experience and understanding. Drug use was also a way of expressing the antimaterialist, anti-authoritarian ethos of the era.

Soon new forms of popular behavior and expression grew up around the music and drug scenes. Adopting the Beats' notion that a posture of hipness constituted a form of social protest, counterculture devotees called themselves hippies. The hippie style, with its flowing hair and bell-bottom jeans, transformed the appearance of American youth. As part of their rejection of Western civilization's "uptight" materialism, devotees of the psychedelic culture adopted some of the trappings of Eastern mysticism, sporting bells, beads, flowing robes, and sandals. They perfumed their homes with incense and festooned them with Indian-print bedspreads. They wove flowers into their hair. They changed their diet, demanding more natural foods to enhance their spiritual health. They embraced the psychedelic art that appeared on rock posters and T-shirts, a style that used saturated colors, swirling calligraphy, and special photographic effects.

By the summer of 1967, hippie neighborhoods had sprung up in most American cities and college towns. San Francisco's Haight-Ashbury district, in particular, had become a magnet for people preaching the virtues of love, drugs, music, sex, and "flower power." While radical political activists proclaimed the summer of 1967 the Vietnam Summer, hippies announced that it was the "Summer of Love." This hedonistic interlude would transform society, not by agitating for widespread social change or an end to the war, but by encouraging individuals to drop out of the rat race and sample the pleasures of the senses. The networks and news magazines predicted the migration of thousands of young people to the Haight that summer, to "crash" in communal "pads"; "groove" at concerts in Golden Gate Park and at the Fillmore; and shower each other and the apprehensive local authorities with peace, love, and flowers. "If you're going to San Francisco," one song's lyrics advised, "be sure to wear some flowers in your hair."

At its root, the counterculture partook of the social problems and prejudices of American society in general. Crash pads, if hospitable, often recreated conventional household hierarchies. One young woman who went with a girlfriend to the Haight for a weekend reported with some disgust that her friend "moved into the first commune we entered and became a 'house-mother,' which means she did all the cooking and cleaning." Racial tensions, like gender hierarchies, persisted among the hip as well as the square. Relations between the predominantly white hippies in the Haight and the nearby black community in the Fillmore were terrible.

Although the Haight-Ashbury experience revealed contradictions in the counterculture, the music persisted, helping to keep the spirit of the cultural revolution alive. Promoters began staging large-scale, open-air rock festivals to attract the faithful. These events reached a high point with the Woodstock music festival of August 1969, a rain- and mud-soaked gathering of 400,000 rock fans in upstate New York. The unexpectedly huge crowd presented many serious problems, particularly in providing sanitation, food, and water. The audience had difficulty actually hearing the music and seeing the stage. Traffic was so bad that state authorities closed down the New York State Thruway. In spite of these troubles, however, many members of the audience would look back on Woodstock as the grandest experience of the 1960s, a demonstration that hundreds of thousands could come together for "three days of peace, love and music." The festival developed an almost mythological aura as the counterculture's finest hour.

By the late 1960s, many hippies had concluded that the only salvation for the counterculture lay in cultivating one's own garden. Across the country, disaffected hippies sought spiritual salvation and physical health by getting back to the land. College students moved out of dormitories and into rural farmhouses, bought sacks of brown rice, and planted organic gardens. Most communes were relatively short-lived, falling apart when faced with issues such as how to share expenses, whom to include or exclude, and how to divide the work. Advocates of "doing your own thing" clashed with those who saw a need for organization, and those who took on the task of collecting money for food or rent were regularly turned away with a haughty admonition to stop being so uptight and materialistic. The communes that lasted tended to be very hierarchical, like The Farm in Tennessee, or devoted to Eastern religious practices, especially various forms of Buddhism.

Hierarchy, of course, did not guarantee stability or virtue. The most infamous of the communes, the murderous Manson family, left Haight-Ashbury to settle, finally, in the dry Santa Susana Mountains of southern California. Charles Manson held his mostly female followers so completely spellbound that by December 1969, they were willing to commit murder at his orders. Even after they had been arrested for multiple homicides, including that of pregnant actress Sharon Tate, Manson's disciples continued to express their loyalty to him from their prison cells.

Hippie communes reflected a fundamental tension in American society: the tension between a longing for connectedness and a desire for personal liberty. If most of these communes lasted only a short time and seemed more dedicated to escapism than to solving the problems of a postindustrial society, they nevertheless represented a desire for a way of life dedicated not to the pursuit of consumer goods but to a vision of a meaningful existence. Often as not, those who experimented with communal living pondered not only human relations, but also the complicated connections between people and the natural world. Some who began by raising organic vegetables became pioneers of the environmental movement.

While communards sought a place apart from American consumerism and crass materialism, the counterculture spread to mainstream groups as well, becoming part of the everyday world of high school students from the mid-1960s to the mid-1970s, and extending beyond California and New York to other urban areas and even many small towns. As it spread, many people were ready to capitalize on it. Bill Graham grew fabulously wealthy promoting rock concerts. Psychedelic artist Peter Max eventually marketed his talents to about fifty companies, including Sears and General Electric. The counterculture spawned new business opportunities for purveyors of dietary and spiritual nostrums and proprietors of record stores, head shops, T-shirt stores, health-food stores, and hip clothing boutiques.

Jann Wenner, a particularly canny entrepreneur, spotted the marketing opportunity of the decade when he began publishing *Rolling Stone* magazine, a tabloid that began by covering the rock scene and soon expanded into long feature articles and investigative reporting. Wenner made a fortune while publishing some of the best of the New Journalism. On the pages of *Rolling Stone*, politics and the counterculture came together in extraordinary forms, such as Tom Wolfe's perceptive history of the space program and Hunter S. Thompson's brilliant 1972 series on presidential politics, "Fear and Loathing on the Campaign Trail."

Mass Culture and Social Critique

Wenner was not the only one who wanted to capitalize on the opportunities presented by the baby-boom market. More established businesses and their leaders, however, encountered profound challenges as they tried to sell to anti-consumerist consumers. Nowhere did the rebellion of the young create a greater crisis of legitimacy and practice than in the advertising industry. Hostile to counterculture values and aesthetics, the industry's leaders vacillated between resisting and condemning change and seeking to co-opt it. Within the industry, the battle played out between the old guard and the "Young Turks," who themselves embraced many counterculture values.

The Young Turks, who criticized 1950s advertisements as boring and unimaginative, pioneered new modes of appeal. In one of the most famous campaigns of the decade, they marketed the Volkswagen Beetle, already popular with the young, by touting its small size and its shortcomings as a status symbol. In one ad, for example, the Volkswagen Beetle, or the VW Bug, was shown sitting alone in a two-car garage with the caption, "It does all the work, but on Saturday night, which one goes to the party?" Another featured two politicians, one in a large 1950s-style convertible complete with fins and the other in the small, ugly German car, which looked the same year after year.

The ad asked: "Which man would you vote for?" The ads' use of humor to criticize consumerist excess typified one successful strategy used by advertisers to accommodate change.

In the 1960s, marketing leaders condemned those who criticized advertising's role in promoting consumption, labeling them subversives who attacked free enterprise and its benefits, while equating consumerism with liberty. As had been true in the 1950s, they singled out women as the purported beneficiaries of this freedom. Many young women began abandoning the use of cosmetics, but Revlon proclaimed that its make-up was "a great new freedom movement." The makers of Nice 'n' Easy hair coloring encouraged women to use the product, while declaring that women were "free to skip the make-up . . . free to dress any way." Increasingly, ads portrayed

A Volkswagen ad touting the small, inexpensive car as a "lemon" typifies the iconoclastic approach taken in the company's innovative ad campaign. / Private collection

women posed provocatively and dressed in miniskirts and other skimpy clothing. The new freedom promised by advertisers stopped short of freedom from objectification or freedom from worry about whether female bodies met contemporary standards for beauty. The new fashions (along with the medical community) contributed to American women's growing obsession with weight. American women joined weight-loss clubs, took amphetamines, and dieted to present themselves as youthful and slim.

Ultimately, the advertising industry decided to appropriate the symbols, music, dress, language, and aesthetics of the counterculture to distance itself from its association with mainstream or "straight" culture. This practice sometimes involved the creative assimilation of new modes and values, but more often it led to the trivialization of those values. An ad for jewelry depicted a young hippie couple with a sign saying "LOVE" in front of them; its caption proclaimed candidly that "What the world needs now is love, sweet love. It'll help our business." More than anything else, advertising sold youth, but more as a state of mind than as a chronological age. Pepsi decided it was for "those who think young," while Oldsmobile urged car buyers to "young it up" in their "youngmobile."

Television also had to accommodate the new youth market and come to terms with its political values, a challenge both to its entertainment and news divisions. CBS, for example, had numerous rural-life shows, including *Green Acres* and *The Andy Griffith Show*, in its prime-time lineup. By the late 1960s, viewers had tired of these shows, and the network decided to add more youth-oriented programs, including *The Smothers Brothers Show*, a variety show featuring two satiric folk singers, Tom and Dick Smothers. At first, CBS scheduled mainstream guests for the show, including Jim Nabors, Jack Benny, Jimmy Durante, and others. Over time, however, the show came to reflect the musical tastes and political values of the hosts.

The show battled with the network censors. Much of the conflict related to antiwar content that offended some viewers and the network brass. The episode that produced the most controversy featured leftist folk singer Pete Seeger on his first television appearance since being blacklisted in the 1950s. Seeger sang "Waist Deep in the Big Muddy," a metaphorical commentary on American involvement in the Vietnam War that includes the line "We're waist deep in the Big Muddy/And the big fool says to push on." CBS cut the song, eliciting a wellspring of protest. An internal memo from the head of Program Practices defending the decision said that a show's content should be "designed for the primary purpose of entertaining rather than to advance a point of view on a controversial subject" and claimed that the song's implication that the president of the United States was a fool was in bad taste. Ultimately, the network reinstated the segment when the show was rerun, but the censors persisted in cutting sections from other episodes, and Tom and Dick Smothers continued to explore the limits of prime-time dissent. In April 1969, CBS cancelled the program, claiming that the censors had not received a print of a forthcoming show in sufficient time to review it. The network scheduled *Hee Haw* in its time slot.

Surprisingly, the segment of the show that involved drug themes—"Share a Little Tea with Goldie"—occasioned much less criticism from viewers and network executives. A parody of afternoon programming directed at women, the segment often began with a greeting from Goldie O'Keefe (comedian Leigh French) such as "Hi! And glad of it." Although network censors cut some of her lines, her use of ambiguous language and drug terms unfamiliar to the general public meant that much of her material reached the air. In a sketch teaching viewers how to make whole-wheat bread, she enthusiastically demonstrated the proper technique: "The more you knead it, the higher it rises. The higher it rises, the lighter you feel. Ohhh—I feel good already! Ladies, ladies, ladies, get it on this way. My bread is getting high. And I'm beginning to rise!"

Despite its controversial content, the show generally had a conventional look. On NBC, however, *Rowan and Martin's Laugh-In* assimilated the counterculture aesthetic to design its sets and write its volley of one-liners. As described by one scholar, the show "abounded in hallucinogenic flashes, zooms, breathtakingly quick cuts, and a barrage of psychedelic colors. . . ." From the jokes written on the bodies of dancing women (including Goldie Hawn) in bikinis to the catchphrases fans loved, the innovative show created stock jokes that appealed to both its more hip viewers and a mainstream audience. Even president Richard Nixon made a cameo appearance, proclaiming "Sock it—to me?" The show's quick pace, which interspersed cultural and political commentary with more mainstream humor, may have defused some of the opposition. In any case, NBC seemed more at ease with its style and content than CBS had been with *The Smothers Brothers Show*.

Television also confronted volatile issues in its news divisions as it brought the Vietnam War into the nation's living rooms and covered the sometimes violent confrontations that marked American politics in these years. Beginning in 1963, the networks extended their nightly news shows from fifteen to thirty minutes, and by the time the war had escalated in the mid-1960s, the authority of well-known anchors, most notably Walter Cronkite, had increased the importance of television as an interpreter of the meanings of the war. Cronkite had almost pronounced benedictions on the war in the mid-1960s, but after the Tet offensive in 1968, he editorialized that the United States could not win and should seek a negotiated peace, and his words carried great clout.

In the print media also, reporters did not challenge political or military leaders' assertions regarding the purposes and prosecution of the war in the early years. Tom Wicker, who covered the White House for the *New York Times*, stated that at first, he did not question the official view that the war was necessary to fight communist aggression, but ultimately he grew increasingly distrustful of the government's claims: ". . . the Secretary of State tells me that, and who am I to argue with him . . . that's the view one had at the time. . . . We had not yet been taught to question the President. . . . We had not been taught by bitter experience that our government like any other in extremis will lie and cheat to protect itself."

The growing skepticism of the war on the part of the press did not mean that it offered sympathetic coverage to the antiwar and other dissident movements. In general, the media depicted opponents of the war as threats to the country's internal security, not as legitimate participants in a foreign policy debate. Indeed, they routinely ignored the political positions advanced by critics of the nation's policies. In a 1968 television feature on American deserters in France, ABC reporter John Rolfson called them misfits and emphasized, not their political objections to the Vietnam War, but the role of a "mysterious" man named Cook (a draft-resistance counselor) in "recruiting" them to desert. He concluded his story by asking rhetorically: "What do you think of the idea of the obligations of citizenship in the United States? Do these ideals mean anything to you? Obviously [these deserters are] being used against the United States."

The media also depicted the antiwar movement as a disreputable threat to social stability and law and order. Television in particular focused on the unusual, the violent, and the flamboyant when it covered dissident political movements. Although reporters tended to cover events held by middle-class people in meeting rooms (like "teach-ins" and Senate committee hearings) with more respect than student protests, they often ignored these forms of middle-class protest because they lacked drama. In the name of balance, television reports often juxtaposed long-haired hippies waving North Vietnamese flags with sober administration spokespersons protesting against the excesses of their critics. In the mid-1960s, when most violence associated with demonstrations was initiated by supporters of the war attacking peaceful marchers, the media still managed to blame antiwar activists. In one such report, CBS anchor Walter Cronkite noted that prowar spectators, angered when demonstrators displayed the NLF flag, had attacked protestors. He explained their attack on the protesters, however, by stating, "Antiwar demonstrators in New York provoked a series of clashes today with counterdemonstrators and police."

1968: A Year of Cataclysm

To some extent, the three movements—Black Power, the New Left, and the counterculture—discussed so far in this chapter represented separate strands of anti-establishment sentiment during the 1960s. They often differed from one another in both goals and methods. For instance, the Black Panthers did not wear flowers in their hair; hippies were frequently indifferent to politics, believing that salvation lay in altering the mind and spirit; and some political radicals of the New Left could not fathom how anyone could smoke marijuana when there was a rally to attend. But the membership of the three movements did overlap, and they generally shared a basic opposition to racism, social injustice, bourgeois consumerism, and the Vietnam War. As the climate of protest intensified in the late 1960s, there were more and more occasions when the various strands of the different movements came together. This was particularly true in 1968, a cataclysmic year for American society and politics.

On December 31, 1967, some important members of the counterculture and the New Left joined forces. Radical leaders Abbie Hoffman and Jerry Rubin, black activist–comedian Dick Gregory, Beat poet Allen Ginsberg, counterculture writer Paul Krassner of *The Realist* (the nation's oldest underground newspaper), and several others founded the Youth International Party, better known as the Yippies. Hoffman, a great believer in employing humor to promote serious causes, was a master at manipulating the media. Applying a combination of militant tactics, freakish pranks, and humor, the Yippies would try to make themselves the national media's front-page story. Their particular goals were sometimes hard to determine. They stood for freedom and for spontaneity; they protested against the Vietnam War, racism, and politics as usual. They planned to turn the 1968 Democratic national convention in Chicago into a "Festival of Life" featuring rock music and elaborate practical jokes, a kind of revolutionary dance party (see Chapter 7).

The Right gained momentum after the convention in Chicago, spurred on by the inflammatory rhetoric of independent presidential candidate George Wallace and Republican vice-presidential contender Spiro Agnew. The Left was transformed but not dead. SDS boomed. Some movement leaders, increasingly seduced by the romance of violent revolution, considered the convention a triumph, believing with Tom Hayden that "our victory lies in progressively demystifying a false democracy." Hayden and seven others, including Hoffman and Rubin, were indicted for conspiring to incite a riot at the Democratic National Convention. Their trial at the hands of reactionary judge Julius J. Hoffman became an emblem of the friction between radical dissidents and repressive authorities. When Judge Hoffman ordered one of the defendants, Black Panther leader Bobby Seale, bound and gagged, newspaper sketch artists had a field day depicting the fulfillment of the order. Seale was ultimately tried separately from the other defendants (all white), a judicial move that underlined the nation's persistent racial polarization.

The jurors, who were overwhelmingly white and middle class, acquitted the seven defendants on the conspiracy charges but convicted five of them of intent to incite riot. The judge added lengthy sentences for contempt of court, which resulted from the defendants' disruptive conduct. Ultimately, a federal appeals court overturned all convictions on the grounds that the judge had acted improperly when he refused to allow defense attorneys to question prospective jurors regarding their cultural biases and because of Hoffman's "deprecatory and often antagonistic attitude toward the defense." In addition, the court noted that the convictions would have also been overturned had it been known at the time of legal arguments that the FBI, with the knowledge of the judge and the prosecution, had bugged the offices of the defense attorneys during the trial.

Sports also served as a site of conflict in 1968, in part the result of the creation of the Olympic Committee for Human Rights (OCHR) by African American sociologist Harry Edwards and others. Their immediate goals were to continue the 1964 ban of South Africa from Olympic competition in protest of its policy of racial apartheid, to secure black representation on the International Olympic Committee (IOC), and to persuade the IOC to remove Avery Brundage as its chair. When the IOC announced its intention to lift the ban on South Africa, the OCHR began planning a boycott by black athletes. Brundage backed down and reinstated the ban, saying that he wanted to prevent violence at the Mexico City games. If that was his goal, however, it failed. When Mexicans demonstrated in protest of the millions spent by the Mexican government to build infrastructure for the international sports event, police opened fire, killing over three hundred people.

At the games themselves, American sprinters Tommie Smith and John Carlos used their first- and third-place finishes in the 200-meter dash as the occasion for protest. As the U.S. national anthem was played, Smith, the gold medalist, and Carlos, the bronze medalist, raised black-gloved hands in the Black Power salute and bowed their heads. In response, the U.S. Olympic Committee suspended them and ordered

As the national anthem played during their Olympics awards ceremony, dissident athletes Tommie Smith and John Carlos raised their hands and looked down in protest of racism. / AP/Wide World

them to leave Mexico City. Although many Americans reacted with outrage at the athletes' actions, some athletes and black leaders defended the dissidents. Several American athletes threatened to withdraw from competition after the suspensions. Australian Peter Norman, the silver medalist in the 200-meter dash, wore the official badge of the OCHR when he shared the victory stand with Smith and Carlos.

Smith and Carlos were not the first black athletes to test the limits of dissent in the United States. When world heavyweight champion Muhammad Ali announced that he had embraced the Black Muslim faith in 1965, FBI director J. Edgar Hoover ordered an examination of his exemption from the draft. Ali, who had apparently failed the math sections of his first mental aptitude examination, became the center of a public firestorm led by many sportswriters and politicians. South Carolina congressman L. Mendel Rivers launched a crusade to get the heavyweight champion drafted into the military: "Here he is, smart enough to finish high school, write his kind of poetry, promote himself all over the world, make a million a year, drive around in red Cadillacs—and they say he's too dumb to tote a gun! Who's dumb enough to believe that?" When the Defense Department reduced the mental aptitude percentile that it used for draft eligibility from 30 to 15, Ali (who scored at the sixteenth percentile) was reclassified as 1-A. Declaring that "I ain't got nothing against them Vietcong," Ali refused to serve and was convicted of draft evasion. His case reached the U.S. Supreme Court in 1971, when the Court ruled in his favor on narrow technical grounds.

On American campuses, confrontation became the norm by the late 1960s. In May 1969, police and demonstrators at Berkeley clashed at the battle of People's Park. The park, which belonged to the University of California, had once been a weedy meeting place for dope dealers and their customers but had since been turned into a community garden. The university, claiming that it wanted to build a soccer field on the spot, asked police to seal off the area while bulldozers razed the gardens. When marchers moved in to take back the park, the police fired with buckshot and tear gas. Governor Ronald Reagan sent in three thousand National Guard troops, who occupied the park for seventeen days. People's Park became a symbol of radical struggle and the communal alternative to private property; it also underlined the emerging importance of ecological issues, pitting organic gardeners against bulldozers, tomatoes against tear gas.

Disturbances in the spring of 1969 at Harvard, Stanford, Cornell, and nearly three hundred other campuses included more than a hundred incidents involving arson and attempted or actual bombings. The voice of the counterculture grew more militant. Jefferson Airplane, a San Francisco rock group that had risen to fame by combining powerful vocal and instrumental performances with odes to the mind-expanding power of LSD, turned to celebrating insurrection: "Look what's happenin' out in the streets/Got to Revolution!"

Meanwhile, some activists worked hard to repair the antiwar movement's damaged credibility. The New Mobilization, a coalition of moderate antiwar advocates, organized a nationwide peace demonstration in the fall of 1969, calling for a moratorium on the war. Millions of people responded, holding rallies, teach-ins, marches, and meetings. On the day of the demonstration, one hundred thousand people gathered on Boston Common; in New York City, a series of mass meetings were held, including one on Wall Street. Nationwide crowd estimates for the October 15, 1969, demonstrations ranged from 2 million to 15 million. The following month, more than half a million people gathered in Washington, D.C., for a second demonstration, the largest ever held in that city.

This huge, peaceful outcry against the war did have an impact; it demonstrated that millions of Americans supported neither the war nor the violent tactics of the extreme Left. Yet even moderate antiwar activists became angry and frustrated by their inability to stop the war. The extremists made better copy, and their frequent clashes with police drew attention away from what the moderates regarded as their more serious attempts to affect the nation's policy in Vietnam.

On December 4, 1969, Chicago police raided the local Black Panther headquarters, killing Panther leaders Fred Hampton and Mark Clark in their beds. SDS splintered, and it soon became dominated by a faction calling itself the Weathermen, after a line in a Bob Dylan song: "You don't need a weatherman to know which way the wind blows." Announcing their goal as "the destruction of U.S. imperialism and the achievement of a classless world: world communism," the Weathermen rejected coalition politics of any kind and embraced worldwide revolution. Their heroes included Chinese Communist Party chair Mao Zedong and Central American revolutionary martyr Che Guevara. Their enemies were "the pigs at home"; their vanguard was a revolutionary youth movement. "Kids used to try to beat the system from inside the army or from inside the schools," they said; "now they desert from the army and burn down the schools."

A week before the October 1969 demonstrations, two or three hundred Weathermen street fighters battled Chicago police in a showdown that came to be known as the Days of Rage. In the next year, the antiwar movement's conflicting philosophies were thrown into sharp relief. While thousands assembled to light candles and sing "give peace a chance," a relatively few shock troops fantasized about violence, trained for street fighting, and built bombs. Between September 1969 and May 1970, there were at least 250 bombings at draft boards, ROTC buildings, federal offices, and corporate headquarters. In March 1970, three bombers from the Weather Underground, as the Weathermen now called themselves, died when they blew themselves up in a New York townhouse. The following August, a bomb exploded in the University of Wisconsin mathematics building, killing a graduate student working on a research project in a facility the bombers thought to be empty.

In 1970, there were 9,408 incidents of protest; 731 involved police and arrests, 410 involved damage to property, and 230 involved violence to persons. The confrontations peaked in May, when President Nixon announced that U.S. troops had invaded neutral Cambodia, a state neighboring Vietnam. The announcement set off a wave of student strikes; at least seventy-five

A student screams in horror over the body of an antiwar demonstrator slain by the National Guard at Kent State University on May 4, 1970. In the aftermath of the Kent State killings, college students across the country staged protests and strikes. / © John Filo

campuses shut down for the rest of the academic year, and students at Northwestern University announced that their institution had seceded from the United States. About thirty ROTC buildings were burned or bombed in the first week of May, including the one at Kent State University in Kent, Ohio. Governor James Rhodes called in National Guard troops to restore order on the Kent State campus; on May 4, nervous troops opened fire on student demonstrators and passersby, killing four and wounding nine. Ten days later, police killed two more students and wounded nine at Jackson State, a predominantly black campus in Mississippi. Torn and bloody, the country seemed to be consuming its young—a cannibalism that some deplored, others embraced.

As radical Left and antiwar protests culminated in these violent confrontations, another protest movement was developing—more quietly at first, but perhaps possessing an even greater potential for long-term impact. This protest movement was for women's liberation, a product of a new feminist consciousness.

The Rise of the New Feminism

Even in the supposedly quiescent 1950s, there had been some organized and articulate attempts to come to grips with women's issues. In the period immediately following World War II, some unions had sought to organize service and clerical workers, who were mostly women, as well as female factory employees like those in California's canneries. Sometimes uniting across ethnic lines, working-class women had pushed for goals such as equal pay for equal work and had begun to consider economic and social questions that would not be articulated fully until the 1980s. Even in the heyday of domestic femininity, the idea that women belonged at home because they were nurturing, timid creatures entirely different from competitive, capable men was questioned. In the 1950s, magazines like *Ladies' Home Journal* and *Good Housekeeping* carried articles celebrating the benefits of paid work for women and featured profiles of successful career women.

By 1960, women's issues had begun to receive attention from the federal government. In 1961, President Kennedy established a Commission on the Status of Women (CSW), headed by Eleanor Roosevelt. Something of an anomaly in the masculine atmosphere of the New Frontier, the CSW took tentative positions, such as recommending new programs in adult education so that women might return to work after raising their children. Such limited goals made it clear that women should not neglect their primary responsibility in the home.

In the early 1960s, Congress began to outlaw some forms of discrimination against working women. The Equal Pay Act of 1963 made it illegal to pay women less than men for doing the same job. However, the decade's most significant piece of legislation in the area of women's rights became law almost serendipitously. As Congress debated the 1964 Civil Rights Act, a reactionary Virginia congressman, Howard W. Smith, attempted to kill the bill by introducing an amendment that he believed would reduce the whole matter of civil rights to absurdity. An amendment to Title VII prohibited discrimination on the basis of gender as well as race, religion, and ethnic background. Encouraged by business- and professional women, liberal northerners led by Representative Martha Griffiths of Michigan pushed the amendment through, and it became law along with the rest of the bill. The Equal Employment Opportunity Commission (EEOC), charged with enforcing the act's bans on workplace discrimination, did not at first take sex discrimination complaints seriously. But under increasing pressure from women's groups it ultimately began to enforce the law.

Meanwhile, as noted in Chapter 3, discontent had been brewing in the tranquil suburbs. Middle-class white women, supposedly fully absorbed in cleaning their houses and raising their children, found domestic life lacking. In 1963 came the publication of Betty Friedan's *The Feminine Mystique*, which lamented the societal waste in isolating educated, talented women in the "comfortable concentration camp" of the American home. Middle-class white American women, Friedan said, felt depressed, useless, and assailed by "the problem that has no name." Speaking for this constituency (and not, for example, for African American mothers, whose families' survival had long depended on their ability to find paid work of any kind), Friedan believed that the solution lay in giving women meaningful jobs outside the home. In 1966, Friedan was among the founders of the National Organization for Women (NOW)—the first national lobby for women's rights since the suffrage era. It was, and still is, dedicated to the goal of achieving for women political and economic opportunities equal to those enjoyed by men.

The women's movement gained momentum because it was rooted in widespread, elemental changes in American society. Among other factors, more and more women were becoming educated. Between 1950 and 1974, college enrollment for men increased 234 percent; for women, it increased 456 percent. Even more important, both married and single women were entering the paid work force. During World War II, employment of adult women increased from 27 percent in 1940 to 36 percent five years later. Female employment dropped off temporarily immediately after the war, but by the beginning of the 1960s, 37.7 percent of women age sixteen and over were employed, and they constituted 33 percent of the total work force. A decade later, 43 percent of women age sixteen and over, representing 38 percent of the civilian work force, were either working or looking for work. The numbers continued to rise steadily. More and more frequently, the working woman was a married woman: by 1962, married women accounted for 60 percent of the female work force. The working woman was also a mother: as early as 1970, one-third of women with children under six years of age held or sought jobs.

At the same time, women workers had fewer job options than their male counterparts. They generally crowded into female-dominated occupations— nursing, clerical work, teaching, domestic work—that paid less than men's jobs. In 1955, the median compensation for women in full-time, year-round employment was 64 percent of men's earnings. In 1960, the figure had dropped to 61 percent, and by 1975, full-time women workers were earning only 58.8 percent of what men earned. Even when they did the same work as men, they were paid less. The EEOC was understaffed and often reluctant to pursue complaints about violations of the Equal Pay Act. Employers could avoid the whole issue by writing slightly different job descriptions or giving different titles to men and women engaged in substantially the same activities.

Most women who worked reported that they did so out of financial necessity or to improve their family's standard of living, although some said they were seeking personal satisfaction. Still, most Americans assumed that even women who held full-time, paid jobs would continue to do most of the housework. According to figures that changed very little between 1955 and the early 1970s, full-time housewives spent between 52 and 56 hours per week doing housework. Wives who worked full-time outside the home still reported spending about 26 hours per week on housekeeping. And whether or not their wives worked, husbands spent about 1.6 hours per day, or 11.2 hours per week, doing household tasks, including yard work. Men helped at times with the shopping, cooking, and laundry, but in general they did not do the cleaning or ironing.

Perhaps most important of all, the myth of the happy nuclear family was crumbling. Greater acknowledgment of the tensions within families (signaled by a rising divorce rate), concern about women who had been widowed or abandoned, and growing alarm over family violence and abuse heralded an urgent need to re-evaluate women's place in American society. If women could no longer count on the family as a protected place, they would have to fashion new ways of making their way in the world.

The dramatic changes in women's roles in society were bound to have political consequences, particularly as civil rights activists were uncovering

(cont. on page 310)

"A Veritable Obsession": Women, Work, and Motherhood

In the spring of 2002, America's mainstream media made Sylvia Hewlett, author of a new book entitled *Creating Life: Professional Women and the Quest for Children*, the center of attention. Appearing on television talk shows from *Sixty Minutes* to *Oprah*, she promoted her new book and warned young professional women that they had to focus on marriage and childbearing if they hoped to have families in the future. Her not-so-new ideas provoked heated debate, prompting columnist Ellen Goodman to conclude that "motherhood [had] become, well, the mother of all controversies." Feminists charged that her advice was part of the larger backlash against new opportunities and enlarged lives for women, a backlash that wanted nothing more than to return women (especially middle-class women) to lives of domesticity. Antifeminists crowed that Hewlett's book had exposed "the feminists' big lie"—the idea that they could win "the war against nature" in which they had purportedly enlisted.

Hewlett's relationship to modern feminism, however, was much more complex than these debates suggested. On the one hand, she did blame "equal rights feminists," as she called them, for encouraging highly educated and ambitious women to enter the workplace and prove themselves by focusing on work in the same ways and on the same terms that high-achieving men had done. The result of this strategy, she stated, was that women either did not marry or faced age-related infertility by the time they decided to have children.

On the other hand, Hewlett credited modern feminism with expanding workplace opportunities for women and thereby giving them new ways to express their creativity and experience challenge, stimulation, and a sense of competence in the public world. She sympathetically related the views of playwright Wendy Wasserstein, who told her: "I think the women's movement saved my life. In fact, I know it saved my life. . . .The women's movement gave me the right to find my own voice—and the belief that my own voice was worth finding. It's extraordinary—that an idea can do this for someone."

Just as Hewlett's positive views of women's workplace gains generated little media attention, her criticisms of men's self-absorption or of corporate conservatism received relatively little notice compared to her warning to women that they should focus on marriage and childbearing in their twenties and thirties. Hewlett blamed men for not being willing to marry and provide emotional support to high-achieving women, and she blamed corporations for failing to adopt more "family-friendly" policies. According to Hewlett, American men still want to come home and find a nurturing, domestic woman who sees to all their needs, most particularly those needs centered on ego maintenance. As a result, women who require more egalitarian terms for relationships with men are left with poor choices. In addition, Hewlett charged that the conservative values dominating corporate culture limit employers' willingness to accommodate women's family responsibilities through policies that would enable workers to interrupt careers and then return without penalty and through policies providing flexible schedules, paid family leave, and part-time work.

The media, however, zeroed in on her findings regarding the reproductive difficulties of high-income professional women. Citing data showing that such women were much less likely to marry or have children than were men in the same circumstances, she stated her conviction that women should be able to have the same opportunities for work and family that men did. On the basis of her own selective survey of women in high-income jobs, she also concluded that this disparity in their family lives was not something women had chosen and, indeed, that it went up against powerful maternal instincts. As a woman who had spent several years and huge amounts of money so that she could have a fifth child at the age of fifty-one, Hewlett was her own best evidence. Speaking at least as much from her own emotionally-fraught experiences as from her carefully selected evidence (she did not seek women who chose to be childless for her study), she asserted, "If you're over 40, the desire to have a baby before it's too late can kick in with ferocious intensity. It can become a nonnegotiable demand—a veritable obsession—that rides roughshod over every other aspect of life." Her maternal obsession, she asserted, received little social support (even her husband was a reluctant conscript to her cause) and therefore, she concluded that "[a]ll of this must be hardwired."

Sylvia Hewlett touts her book, *Creating a Life,* and its ideas at a meeting on "Maternal Feminism." / AP/Wide World

The biology at the center of her ideas has been expressed in somewhat different ways in different historical periods. In the late nineteenth and early twentieth centuries, anxieties about women and reproduction centered on the rising numbers of women who attended college. One doctor declared, "[S]cience pronounces that the woman who studies is lost"—to reproduction, that is. Cautioning that energy drained in academic work would cost women their reproductive health, doctors and others pointed to the low numbers of college-educated women who married or had children to buttress their case.

The women's decisions, according to the critics, had dire social consequences. Popularizing an idea that developed first in academic circles, President Theodore Roosevelt claimed that the superior races (meaning whites) faced "race suicide" if women from the "better classes" had fewer children than other women. In the 1940s, S. H. Halford alerted eugenicists to "the now undoubted fact that the highly educated woman, as a direct consequence of her adoption of the student habit, very frequently loses the sexual instinct." If she then proceeded to a successful career, she also acquired "a strong economic bias to celibacy, or, if she does marry, against the bearing of children." Instead of passing her intelligence to the children she bore, she contributed to "the impoverishment of the race."

By the 1950s, experts were arguing that women who worked, especially those in demanding professions, were manifesting deep psychological problems ("masculinist strivings") and causing enormous harm to their husbands and children (see pages 101–102). Single women were, if anything, even worse. Marynia Farnham and Ferdinand Lundberg, authors of the much-discussed *Modern Woman: The Lost Sex*, proclaimed that they were "defeminized" and "deeply ill." They also blamed women's growing economic independence for rising divorce rates. Women's magazine headlines reflected the dominant pronatalist view of the period: "Have Babies While You're Young," "Birth: The Crowning Moment of My Life," and "I Will Have Another Baby. I Must Live That Divine Experience Again."

The idea that women "really" wanted domesticity and had been rendered deeply unhappy by the pursuit of careers received renewed attention in the 1980s, when the media focused intensively on the "problem" of single women. The *New York Times*, for example, claimed that single women "suffered from a sickness almost" and were "too rigid to connect." Their unwillingness to settle for just any marriage meant despair and loneliness. The title for a 1987 article in *Harper's Bazaar* provided a common answer to the question of why women were single: "Are You Turning Men Off?: Desperate and Demanding." In a 1986 television special entitled "After the Sexual Revolution," cohosts Richard Threlkeld and Betsy Aaron intoned that successful women were unlikely to have successful relationships. Aaron claimed that feminists had not warned women that the "price of revolution" would be "freedom and independence turning to loneliness and depression." As feminist critic Susan Faludi noted in her 1991 book, *Backlash: The Undeclared War Against American Women*, "It wasn't a trade-off Aaron could have deduced from her own life: she had a successful career and a husband—co-host Threlkeld."

In a highly publicized story that later proved to be greatly exaggerated, *Newsweek* warned in 1986 that single women over forty were "more likely to be killed by a terrorist" than to marry. The reason, they said, was that women were putting high-income jobs over the pursuit of husbands and that they were expecting far too much of prospective mates. Instead, they acted "as though it were not worth giving up space in their closets for anything less than Mr. Perfect." Given the very small number of American women who had managed to secure upper-income jobs, it was quite unlikely that the explanations *Newsweek* provided for national patterns of marriage had any substance. The newsmagazine drew its data from an unpublished study by social scientists at Harvard and Yale that had been severely criticized by de-

mographers on the grounds that it was based on faulty numbers. By the late 1980s, media tearjerkers focusing on miserable and apparently penitent single women had become a staple of evening news shows.

At the same time, headlines urged the small number of women holding well-paying jobs to worry that their choices would cost them their fertility and warned millions of others that their hours at work came at the expense of their children. The *Washington Post*, for example, headlined one of its 1987 stories: "The Quiet Pain of Infertility: For the Success-Oriented, It's a Bitter Pill." As with Hewlett, any infertility difficulties experienced by poor women received no notice. To underscore the view that women themselves would be happier at home, newspapers and magazines featured accounts of women who had given up highly successful careers for a happy return to full-time domesticity. While countless such stories appeared in the mainstream media, the labor-force participation rates of mothers (single and married) continued to climb, suggesting that millions of women had in fact combined motherhood and paid employment.

Increasing numbers of married women and mothers have entered the labor force in the postwar period. They have done so for a multitude of reasons. Some have sought employment to supplement family incomes. This is particularly true in working-class families, where the decline in real hourly wages for men (which began around 1970) has been especially steep, and in female-headed households, where women must provide most or all of the support for the family. Married women who have found domesticity isolating, stressful, or routine have sought work that provided them with wider experiences and social contacts, a respite from family pressures, and the opportunity to develop skills and expertise. In a 1997 book entitled *The Time Bind: When Work Becomes Home and Home Becomes Work*, sociologist Arlie Hochschild discovered that many women chose longer hours at their paid work because the emotional work

demanded of them at home left them stressed and drained. In the labor force, by contrast, they forged supportive friendships and found human relationships more manageable. This finding occurs despite the persistent discrimination and low wages that many women experience in America's workplaces and despite the stresses and work that women face as they combine long hours at their paid work and at home.

In the meantime, the debate continues, focusing attention on the decisions of individual women rather than on the economic circumstances, corporate practices, cultural values, and political decisions that create the context for their decisions.

racial injustice, liberal politicians were embracing social reform, and radical dissidents were questioning the distribution of power in American society. Although the civil rights movement and the New Left fell short of obtaining all their goals, both proved to be seedbeds for a feminist movement of lasting impact and immense scope.

In the fall of 1964, SNCC women, including Ruby Doris Smith Robinson, Casey Hayden, Mary King, and Maria Varela, drafted a paper on women's position in the SNCC. Robinson recognized that, as a woman, she shared some common ground with King and Hayden, both white, but as an African American, she also believed that the organization should be black-led and black-dominated. King and Hayden recognized that the turn toward Black Power would leave no place for them in a movement to which they had devoted years of their lives. Black Power as a political strategy might leave them out, but as an ideology focusing on difference, it provided them with a model for distinguishing the ways in which women's status diverged from men's. A year later, in the fall of 1965, King and Hayden composed "a kind of memo" and delivered it anonymously to women in the peace and freedom movements. They argued that women and blacks both "seem to be caught up in a common-law caste system . . . which, at its worst, uses and exploits women." When they raised the problem of male dominance among their fellow activists, men generally responded by laughing at them. Several months earlier, at an SNCC meeting, where the question of women's position in the movement had been raised, Stokely Carmichael had quipped, "The position of women in SNCC is prone!" Those who heard the remark, including Mary King, "collapsed with hilarity," but when the laughter faded, the serious question remained.

By June 1967, women had found a language to express their grievances. They named the problem sexism (sometimes called male chauvinism); they named the solution women's liberation. NOW activists focused on eliminating wage discrimination and fighting for legal guarantees of equality. They proposed the Equal Rights Amendment to the Constitution and pushed hard for its passage. The radical feminists, who sometimes began as NOW members but more often came out of the civil rights movement and the New Left, identified a new set of political issues, including childcare, abortion, birth control, sexuality, family violence, and the sharing of housework. Meeting in small groups to discuss not only war and racism but also problems that seemed intensely individual and private, they soon developed a new theoretical tool: consciousness-raising. By identifying their common grievances, they came to the fundamental insight of the new feminist movement—namely, that what appeared to be women's individual problems involved much larger questions of social power, or "sexual politics," in the words of feminist theorist Kate Millett. Feminist writer Robin Morgan turned this insight into the slogan, "The personal is political."

From the start, the new feminism, often called "the second wave" to distinguish it from the women's rights movement of the late nineteenth and early twentieth centuries, faced formidable obstacles. All kinds of people felt threatened by the prospect of women's liberation: conservative men, who stood to lose many privileges; middle-class women, especially housewives, who worried that men would simply abandon their breadwinner roles and that women would lose whatever protections they had; fundamentalist Christians, who believed that women's traditional role was biblically ordained; and even leftist men, accustomed to treating women as assistant radicals and sex objects. In the late 1960s and early 1970s, the mainstream press used dismissive language to ridicule the movement. Reporters for *Time* and *Newsweek* who referred to Gloria Steinem and Shulamith Firestone as "women's libbers" never called Eldridge Cleaver or Rap Brown "black libbers."

The task of building a movement based on women's common problems, interests, and objectives was deeply complicated by the very diversity of the women the movement hoped to mobilize. Certainly race made a difference in how women approached feminism. Even in the early days of SNCC, racial differences among women had raised tensions: black women had articulated grievances and goals that diverged from those of their white sisters in the "beloved community." Class, age, sexual preference, and occupational status also divided women. Middle-class housewives who had invested their lives in the idea that their husbands would protect them were far less equipped to face the challenges of economic independence than were college-age women battling discrimination in law school admissions. Lesbian activists saw their interests as diverging in significant ways from those of heterosexual women. Mexican American mothers working as migrant farm laborers or domestics had different needs from the affluent women who bought the produce they picked or hired them to clean their homes.

Some feminist activists, like Robin Morgan, took a page out of the Yippies' book and sought to create splashy media events to gain a national audience. A week after the 1968 Chicago convention, Morgan and almost two hundred other protesters at the Miss America Pageant in Atlantic City crowned a live sheep "Miss America." *New York Times* reporter Charlotte Curtis covered the protest in typically dismissive terms. Media critic Susan Douglas noted that, in Curtis's article, "[C]harges about sexism in the United States were placed in quotation marks, suggesting that these were merely the deluded hallucinations of a few ugly, angry women rather than a fact of life." Print and

The women's liberation movement brought young women into the streets to protest a variety of inequalities. / John Olson, © Life Magazine, Time, Inc.

broadcast media inevitably played up conflicts among women. Curtis devoted a full paragraph of her story to a "counterdemonstration" staged by three women. And they often went even further in demeaning feminist actions and goals. On August 26, 1970, feminists held the Women's Strike for Equality, which featured marches and rallies in major cities across the country. A march down Fifth Avenue in New York attracted between thirty thousand and fifty thousand supporters. ABC anchor Howard K. Smith led the coverage of the event that night with a quotation from Vice President Spiro Agnew: "Three things have been difficult to tame. The ocean, fools, and women. We may soon be able to tame the ocean, but fools and women will take a little longer."

Because of the enormous diversity of issues affecting women, feminists had different views on both long- and short-term goals for the movement. Some argued that the first order of business was to dismantle a capitalist system that especially oppressed women. Others believed that the movement should concentrate first on eradicating male domination. Some believed that men could be reformed and that women had an obligation to maintain relations with men. Shulamith Firestone declared that "a revolutionary in every bedroom cannot fail to shake up the status quo." Others rejected heterosexuality, some for political reasons, some because women's liberation allowed them to act on long-suppressed lesbian feelings. As visions of the women's movement proliferated, so did its tactics, victories, failures, and institutions.

By the mid-1970s, women had made inroads into male-dominated professions, mounted successful challenges to legal and economic discrimination, founded new enterprises, and claimed new rights. Yet much remained to be done. While the privileges of race and class enabled a few American women to "have it all," many more remained highly vulnerable. The wage gap between men and women persisted. If some women made strides in professional circles, many more fell deeper into poverty.

The Legacy of the Sixties

The women's movement has continued, with various shifts in emphasis, to the present day, but the other protest movements of the 1960s gradually faded or evolved into new, less sensational forms. The New Left never recovered from the cataclysmic spring of 1970, when the killings at Kent State capped a surge of bombings and confrontations. After that time, some self-proclaimed revolutionaries went underground. Moderate dissidents seemed dazed by the escalating climate of hatred. Some activists, declaring themselves burned out, retreated from politics altogether. Many left the movement to pursue other political goals. Eventually, peace came to Vietnam, removing the principal issue that had united the many factions of the New Left. But the legacy of the 1960s political protest was not forgotten. Most obviously, future administrations knew that an unpopular war abroad could provoke widespread rebellion at home.

The counterculture saw many of its distinctive attributes absorbed into the mainstream culture. Hippie styles in hair and clothing and psychedelic music became popular enough to lose some of their revolutionary impact. Society at large became more sexually permissive; indeed, the sexual revolution was a primary legacy of the 1960s. Recreational drug use spread beyond hippie enclaves, winning converts in many segments of American society. Some of the erstwhile hippies drifted into more conventional lives, or at least their habits no longer seemed extraordinary. Others founded the New Age movement, reviving ancient religions and joining experimental therapy groups in search of spiritual fulfillment and expanded consciousness. Rooting out one's inner demons—whether through meditation, confrontation, long soaks in seaside hot springs, or hard labor in religious communes—occupied some inheritors of the countercultural tradition. Inevitably, business began to capitalize on nostalgia for the wild and crazy 1960s. Nike launched a TV ad featuring the Beatles' song "Revolution." Tofu, yogurt, herbal tea, and organic rice began showing up on supermarket shelves.

Meanwhile, the civil rights movement, which had been transformed by Black Power, fragmented. Some leaders went into exile; others had died. Still others began to move into the political mainstream. SCLC workers Andrew Young and Jesse Jackson, who had stood with Martin Luther King, Jr., when he was shot in Memphis, Tennessee, led the next generation of activists. Both men became powerful in the Democratic Party. Blacks and women held more and more local and national political offices. Beginning with Carl Stokes of Cleveland, who was elected in 1967 as the first African American mayor of a major American city, blacks moved into positions of power in the nation's urban centers. By 1990, former SNCC president John Lewis would win election to the U.S. Congress, defeating a fellow movement veteran, Julian Bond.

The push for African American rights also spawned a new, multicultural politics of difference. By the late 1960s, Native Americans organized to raise public awareness of the history of their oppression by adopting both militant and moderate tactics. Members of the American Indian Movement (AIM) occupied Alcatraz Island and staged a mass protest at Wounded Knee, South Dakota, the site of a notorious massacre of Lakota (Sioux) Indians in 1890. Other Indian advocates formed organizations such as the Native American Rights Fund to pursue legal change. By 1980, Native Americans had succeeded in forcing the federal government to return some important tribal lands and to provide compensation for other lands that had been confiscated by whites.

Mexican Americans, galvanized by Cesar Chavez's charismatic leadership and his success in organizing the United Farm Workers, pressed for reform in the treatment of Latinos. Latinos shared a heritage based on their Spanish language and culture, but they had come from places as diverse as Mexico, Chile, Nicaragua, Cuba, and Puerto Rico under enormously varied circumstances. As they struggled to articulate common goals—forming organizations like the League of United Latin American Citizens (LULAC)—and to come to grips with differences among themselves, they became an increasingly important part of the American political and economic picture, especially in the Sunbelt. Latino students, particularly Mexican Americans, organized campus groups that continue to play a prominent role at universities across the country.

The protest movements of the 1960s mobilized people to seek racial justice and gender equality; they also created the possibility of a civil rights movement for homosexuals. On June 29, 1969, police raided the Stonewall Inn, a gay bar in New York City's Greenwich Village. Instead of accepting arrest, the patrons fought back with rocks and bottles. This confrontation was heralded as the beginning of the gay liberation movement. Gay and lesbian activists moved quickly to redefine homosexuality not as a perversion but as a legitimate sexual identity. If they did not reach a consensus as to whether sexual preference was inborn or chosen, they enabled millions of homosexuals to come out of the closet, redrew the boundaries of sexual identity, and organized to claim a share of political power in many American cities.

For others who carried on the political legacy of the 1960s, the fate of the earth seemed the most pressing issue. Back-to-the-land hippies became environmental advocates. Others took a more political road to the ecology movement. Peace advocates worried about the environmental threat of nuclear weapons, and activists focused on large corporations that sold shoddy and dangerous products in the United States and the Third World. In 1970, environmental activists held the first Earth Day—part teach-in, part demonstration—designed to promote awareness of the human impact on the natural environment. Books like Rachel Carson's *Silent Spring*, an indictment of the use of pesticides; Paul Ehrlich's *The Population Bomb*, a vision of demographic doom; Barry Commoner's *Science and Society*, a critique of the nuclear power industry; and Ralph Nader's *Unsafe at Any Speed*, an exposé of the automobile business, inspired a new awareness of the connections among technology, politics, personal freedom, and environmental dangers.

A huge and diverse array of organizations would press and expand the environmentalist agenda in the ensuing years. Middle-of-the-road, predominately white organizations like the Sierra Club, the Nature Conservancy, and the Audubon Society mobilized nature lovers on behalf of endangered animals and plants and against development in wilderness areas. More militant groups like Earth First! engaged in what they called "monkey-wrenching," a term taken from the title of a novel by environmentalist writer Edward Abbey. Their tactics included disabling construction equipment and driving metal spikes into trees to destroy loggers' chain saws. Other groups, like the Southwest Organizing Project, which was headquartered in New Mexico, made the connection between racism and environmental degradation. They noted developers' and policymakers' predilection for locating toxic waste dumps in minority communities, and they pointed out the seeming indifference of many white environmentalists to the ecological dangers that minority communities disproportionately faced. In time, these environmental groups became a formidable, national political force; Congress responded to their political clout by establishing the federal Environmental Protection Agency.

Conclusion

In the 1960s and early 1970s, the nation's youth launched a frontal assault on conventional behavior, smashing the barriers between public and private life, and legitimizing new ideas and new behaviors. They exposed the depth of racial oppression in the United States, catalyzed the American withdrawal from Vietnam, began a sexual revolution, helped found a lasting feminist movement, promoted recognition of the pluralist nature of American society, and pressed new concern for the environment.

But these innovations created controversy and carried troubling consequences. A small number of the young radicals contributed to the climate of violence that engulfed American society by the 1970s. By justifying their sometimes outrageous behavior in the name of personal freedom, they paved the way for what historian Christopher Lasch called "the culture of narcissism"—the retreat of many Americans into the pursuit of personal pleasure. By 1980, pundits were referring to the 1970s as the "Me Decade," contrasting that era with the more socially involved 1960s. But the cultivation of "me" was to some extent a legacy of those radical years, an outgrowth of the Yippies, hippies, rock festivals, drugs, and the Summer of Love. Values spawned by movements for social justice, it seemed, could just as easily be deployed on behalf of individualism.

Perhaps inevitably, there was a counterrevolution. President Nixon's attorney general, John Mitchell, looked at the turmoil of the late 1960s and predicted that "this country's going to go so far right, you won't believe it." That old enemy of the Left, Ronald Reagan, ultimately led the triumphal march as the Right seized power in the United States in 1980. It did so by adopting, with immense success, the grassroots organizing techniques developed by the radicals of the 1960s and 1970s.

The politics and culture of protest demanded a great deal from those who took part in the movements, and there were casualties. Drugs ended many careers too soon. Charismatic Panther leader Huey Newton died in a shootout over a drug deal. Some, like Anne Moody, simply wanted to retire from dangerous advocacy and live a quiet life.

However, not all 1960s activists burned out or rejected the politics of their youth. SNCC's John Lewis took his commitment to racial justice to Congress. Another SNCC veteran, Maria Varela, moved to northern New Mexico to create institutions promoting economic self-sufficiency for Hispanic villagers. Tom Hayden of SDS campaigned for economic democracy from the halls of the California state legislature. Feminist lawyer Ruth Bader Ginsburg was appointed to the U.S. Supreme Court. Grateful Dead member Bob Weir became a committed environmentalist, urging fans at Dead concerts to help save the Brazilian rain forest. The unruly, diverse, sometimes shimmeringly beautiful, sometimes corrosively ugly, political and cultural energies unleashed in the 1960s could not be entirely suppressed. A host of genies had been let out of a multitude of bottles.

F U R T H E R • R E A D I N G

For an overview of this period, see David Farber, *The Age of Great Dreams: America in the 1960s* (1994). **On civil rights and Black Power,** see Clayborn Carson, *In Struggle: SNCC and the Black Awakening of the 1960s* (1981); William H. Chafe, *Civilities and Civil Rights: Greensboro, North Carolina, and the Black Struggle for Freedom* (1980); David J. Garrow, *Bearing the Cross: Martin Luther King, Jr., and the Southern Christian Leadership Conference* (1986); Harvard Sitkoff, *The Struggle for Black Equality, 1954–1981.* **On the New Left and the antiwar movement,** see Wini Breines, *The Great Refusal: Community and Organization in the New Left* (1983); Todd Gitlin, *The Sixties: Years of Hope, Days of Rage* (1987); James Miller, *"Democracy Is in the Streets": From Port Huron to the Siege of Chicago* (1987); W. J. Rorabaugh, *Berkeley at War* (1989); Kirkpatrick Sale, *SDS* (1973). **On the counterculture and its relationship to mainstream culture,** see Charles Perry, *The Haight-Ashbury* (1984); Theodore Roszak, *The Making of a Counterculture* (1969); Nicholas Von Hoffman, *We Are the People Our Parents Warned Us Against* (1968); Warren J. Belasco, *Appetite for Change: How the Counterculture Took on the Food Industry, 1966–1988* (1989); Hazel G. Warlaumont, *Advertising in the 60's: Turncoats, Traditionalists, and Waste Makers in America's Turbulent Decade* (2001); Aniko Bodroghkozy, *Groove Tube: Sixties Television and the Youth Rebellion* (2001); Melvin Small, *Covering Dissent: The Media and the Anti-Vietnam War Movement* (1994). **On women's changing lives**

and the women's movement, see William H. Chafe, *The American Woman: Her Changing Social, Economic, and Political Role, 1920–1970* (1972); Beth Bailey, *Sex in the Heartland* (1999); Ruth Rosen, *The World Split Open: How the Modern Women's Movement Changed America* (2000); Flora Davis, *Moving the Mountain: The Women's Movement in America Since 1960* (1991); Susan J. Douglas, *Where the Girls Are: Growing Up Female with the Mass Media* (1994); Alice Echols, *Daring to Be Bad: Radical Feminism in America, 1967–1975* (1989); Barbara Ehrenreich et al., *Re-making Love: The Feminization of Sex* (1987); Sara Evans, *Personal Politics* (1978).

9

Illusion of Peace: America and the World During the Nixon Years

Buzz Aldrin walks on the moon, 1969. The moon walk was celebrated as a triumph at the time, but the United States abandoned the Apollo missions in 1972, soon after the Soviets ended their manned lunar program. / Courtesy of NASA

On July 20, 1969, astronaut Neil Armstrong climbed down the ladder of the Apollo 11 lunar landing module and became the first person to walk on the moon. When Armstrong radioed back to Earth, "That's one small step for man, one giant leap for mankind," the country rejoiced and temporarily set aside its bitter divisions over the continuing war in Vietnam. When the astronauts returned to Earth, President Richard M. Nixon proclaimed their seven-day journey "the greatest week in the history of the world since the Creation." Even discounting the president's hyperbole, for a moment it really seemed that a new age had dawned and that Americans had regained their faith in a technologically perfect future. Scientists predicted that Americans would be taking cheap vacations on the moon by 1990 and that astronauts would begin colonizing Mars and the outer planets by 2000. In 1972, however, after a few more missions, the Apollo program was terminated. Once the Soviets abandoned their manned lunar program, the public—and successive presidents—lost interest in the expensive, dangerous, and unproductive effort to send astronauts beyond Earth's orbit.

The Apollo 11 mission fulfilled President John F. Kennedy's pledge to "put a man on the Moon and return him safely to Earth in this decade." Kennedy had promoted space exploration as an important part of the political and scientific competition between the United States and the Soviet Union. He admitted privately early in his presidency, however, that except for the rivalry with Moscow to be first to land an astronaut on the moon, he had little interest in the space program. His vice president, Lyndon Johnson, had captured the mood of great power competition when he explained that "failure to master space means being second best in every aspect in the crucial arena of our Cold War world." But by 1969, the catastrophic war in Vietnam had sapped the Kennedy-era optimism that many Americans had felt about dominating world politics. Richard Nixon won the presidency in 1968 in part by tapping the vast public dismay over the costs of global intervention. He assailed "the policies and mistakes of the past," complaining that "never has so much military, economic, and diplomatic power been used as ineffectively as in Vietnam." Yet his own plans for solving the Vietnam riddle remained murky: his campaign speeches promised only "an honorable end to the war," rather than a policy of "cut and run."

The Retreat from Vietnam and the Search for Peace with Honor

Part of Nixon's personal and political insecurity stemmed from his difficulty in ending the conflict in Southeast Asia. He had been a vigorous hawk on Vietnam since his days as vice president, but by 1968, he had concluded that "there is no way to win the war." Of course, he added to a friend, "[W]e can't say that. We have to say the opposite just to keep some degree of bargaining leverage." Aware of the war's increasing unpopularity, Nixon agreed with many foreign affairs experts who considered Vietnam a drain on American resources and a diversion from what should be the principal focus of U.S. foreign policy—managing the dangerous competition with the Soviet Union. The new president told his staff, "I am not going to end up like LBJ, holed up in the White House, afraid to show my face on the street. I'm going to end that war. Fast." Reducing the attention paid to Vietnam and restoring the United States' freedom to act in the rest of the world became the new administration's first foreign policy goals.

Within a month of the election, Nixon began what *Time* magazine later called his "improbable partnership" with Henry Kissinger, the forty-five-year-old, German-born Harvard professor whom Nixon selected as his national security adviser. The president believed that centralizing the foreign policy apparatus in the White House would enhance his ability to cut deals with America's rivals. He did not want foreign policy to be run, as he vulgarly put it, "by striped pants faggots in the State Department." Over the next five and a half years, Kissinger had more access to Nixon than anyone else in the government, briefing him daily on world events, discussing grand strategy in foreign affairs, hammering out negotiations with other countries, gossiping about politicians, and plotting retribution on rivals at home and abroad. Under Nixon's supervision, Kissinger transformed the National Security Council (NSC) from a bureaucratic backwater into a powerful executive branch agency, mostly at the expense of the State Department.

Nixon respected Kissinger's intellect, and the professor recognized that the president's power allowed him to implement designs that most academics only dreamed of. The press seemed dazzled by their unlikely partnership and for several months barely criticized the new administration. Privately, the two men harbored a mutual suspicion that often bordered on contempt. Among close friends, Kissinger called Nixon our "meatball president" and a drunk. Nixon derisively referred to his aide as "my Jew boy." In spite of these raw edges, however, they agreed on most major policy goals and worked together effectively.

From 1969 to 1974, Nixon and Kissinger orchestrated some of the greatest reversals in U.S. foreign policy since the beginning of the Cold War. Contemptuous of the State Department bureaucracy, they worked secretly to arrange dramatic meetings with old adversaries. Together they altered the course of the war in Vietnam, reduced tensions with the Soviet Union, opened relations with China, and made the United States the dominant foreign power in the Middle East. The public cheered Nixon and Kissinger at the time, just as it had cheered the astronauts. It seemed that the United States was facing the rest of the world—not to mention outer space—with renewed imagination and purpose. A Gallup poll listed Kissinger as the most admired man in the world in both 1972 and 1973. Even long-time political foes came to believe that Nixon had a flair for foreign relations.

But by the time the president resigned in disgrace over the Watergate scandal in August 1974 (see Chapter 10), détente had soured and peace in Vietnam had proved illusory. Nixon's contempt for the nation's major allies in Western Europe and Japan strained both political and economic relations. His active support for reactionary regimes in southern Africa and in Chile had devastating consequences. What Nixon and Kissinger had heavily promoted in 1971 as their "structure of peace" appeared to have been little more than diplomatic sleight of hand. Nevertheless, the president and his chief foreign policy adviser did react positively to changes in the international environment, and some of their actions later led to the end of the Cold War.

Nixon and Kissinger hoped to clinch a deal in Vietnam within six months. They proposed that Hanoi withdraw North Vietnamese troops from the South and promise not to resume armed struggle for what they informally called a "decent interval," meaning, in effect, not until Nixon was re-elected in 1972. In return, he would pull most U.S. troops out of South Vietnam but continue to aid the Saigon regime, at least for a while. Neither Kissinger nor Nixon showed much interest in South Vietnam's long-term survival, and both assumed (incorrectly, it turned out) that the Soviet Union and China could dictate policy to North Vietnamese leader Ho Chi Minh.

Partly as a way to bring pressure on Hanoi, the Nixon administration sought to improve relations with the Soviet Union. Early on, Kissinger opened a secret, back-channel line of communication with Soviet ambassador Anatoly Dobrynin. The national security adviser circumvented Secretary of State William P. Rogers, fearing that the State Department could not be trusted to follow his blueprint for improving U.S.-Soviet relations. He tried to enlist Dobrynin's help in pressuring North Vietnam to negotiate a deal on the war. Kissinger also began exploring arms control and trade discussions with the Soviet representative.

Disarray among Democratic lawmakers and antiwar activists following the chaotic 1968 Democratic convention and the Republican presidential victory provided at least a short breathing space for the new administration. Nixon and Kissinger knew, however, that the public would not long stand for a continued stalemate in Vietnam. Both men favored a negotiated settlement, one that would preserve what they called American honor. Ultimately, the Nixon administration pursued three somewhat conflicting goals at once: reducing public attention to Vietnam, negotiating a face-saving arrangement with North Vietnam, and bolstering the military capacity of the South to enable it to stand on its own for at least a few years.

Nixon and Kissinger began what was called Vietnamization of the war in Southeast Asia. Vietnamization followed a pattern set in the last months of the Johnson administration. Because public opposition to the war rose and fell in response to reports of American casualties, the United States would reduce its ground combat operations by turning more of them over to an improved ARVN, the South Vietnamese army. At the same time, American air and naval forces would accelerate their bombing of North Vietnam in an effort to speed up the pace of the Paris peace negotiations. Also, air combat produced far fewer American casualties. "Changing the color of the [dead] bodies," one commentator observed, would reduce war opposition.

In June 1969, Nixon conferred with South Vietnamese president Nguyen Van Thieu on Midway Island. He explained his plan to turn more of the fighting over to the ARVN and to withdraw twenty-five thousand American troops from the war zone. Fewer American troops meant lower monthly draft calls, which Nixon hoped would further reduce young people's anger about the war. In 1969, he also replaced the aging, abrasive General Lewis Hershey as head of Selective Service. Hershey had becoming a symbol of a mindless war machine and his oft-quoted intolerance inadvertently mobilized millions of younger Americans against the war. The new head of the system, Curtis Tarr, promised to make the draft more fair by introducing a lottery in which men were selected for service randomly on the basis of their birth date. This was one lottery, however, no one was especially eager to win.

During his trip to Midway Island, the president announced what the press labeled the Nixon Doctrine. In the future, Nixon explained, the United States would provide military and economic assistance to foreign countries resisting communist revolution but would expect each Asian ally to assume the "primary responsibility of providing the manpower for its own defense." Put another way, the United States intended to avoid large land wars in Asia.

At the same time that Nixon selectively reduced troop levels in Vietnam, he ordered U.S. planes to expand the air war into neighboring Cambodia. For more than a year, American B-52 bombers flew thousands of bombing missions designed to stop the North Vietnamese from using Cambodian trails to bring soldiers and supplies into South Vietnam. For both moral and practical reasons, many military and diplomatic officials, even some appointed by Nixon, opposed the secret bombing.

Despite efforts to keep the attacks secret, the *New York Times* reported the bombings, asserting that they violated Cambodian neutrality. Nixon railed that he was "being sabotaged by bureaucrats," meaning civilian workers on the NSC staff whom he suspected of leaking word of the bombings to the press. Distraught over the leaks and worried that Nixon might suspect him of disloyalty, Kissinger arranged for FBI director J. Edgar Hoover to wiretap members of the NSC staff—that is, Kissinger's own aides—who were suspected of leaking information. These illegal taps uncovered little, but they set a precedent for how the Nixon administration viewed and handled dissent.

As the administration clamped down on domestic critics, it funded a vast expansion in the size and equipment of the South Vietnamese army. But it seemed unlikely that even a better-equipped and better-paid ARVN could prevail over the highly motivated guerrillas of the National Liberation Front (NLF) or the regular North Vietnamese troops who played a growing role in the South after 1969. Despite reforms, about 20 percent of the soldiers on ARVN rosters were "ghosts," men who had died or deserted but whose names were kept on the rolls so commanders could pocket their pay. High desertion rates and official corruption continued.

Meanwhile, morale among American troops declined. As it became clear that the Nixon administration wanted to get the best terms it could and then leave Vietnam, soldiers had little incentive to sacrifice themselves. Before, individual soldiers had been reluctant to fight when the end of their yearlong tour of duty approached; now, whole platoons refused to proceed with the few remaining search-and-destroy operations that were ordered. No one wanted to be one of the last Americans killed or wounded in a war that was being turned over to the Vietnamese. Drug use increased among enlisted men. In 1970, the command estimated that sixty-five thousand soldiers used narcotics. More frightening were the more than two thousand reports in 1970 of "fragging," the practice of soldiers attacking unpopular officers with fragmentation grenades. Growing problems in Vietnam made it difficult to attract volunteers or even to recruit young men into the American military academies.

In the spring of 1970, Nixon decided to pursue several dramatic military gestures in Vietnam, even as he quickened the pace of American withdrawal. In March, he announced plans to remove an additional 150,000 troops by the end of the year. At the same time, Cambodia's pro-American chief of staff, General Lon Nol, overthrew the government of neutralist Prince Norodom Sihanouk. Unlike Sihanouk, Lon Nol was eager to cooperate with the Americans and the South Vietnamese in ridding Cambodia of the North Vietnamese, who used Cambodia's border region to support insurgents in South Vietnam.

In late April 1970, Nixon decided to invade Cambodia to bolster the sagging fortunes of its new government. On the evening of April 30, he spoke to the American public to plead for their support. "If when the chips are down the world's most powerful nation acts like a pitiful, helpless giant," he said, "the forces of totalitarianism and anarchy will threaten free nations and free institutions throughout the world." The Cambodian invasion produced very modest military results. It failed completely in its larger goal of reversing the trend toward a military victory for the North. ARVN forces fought poorly, and their incompetence and unwillingness to fight were abundantly evident on evening news programs.

Worst of all, from Nixon's point of view, the Cambodian operation provoked some of the most furious antiwar demonstrations of the Vietnam era. Three members of Kissinger's staff resigned when their boss approved the move into Cambodia. Protests against the war, the draft, military-sponsored research, and the Reserve Officers' Training Corps (ROTC) erupted on hundreds of college campuses across the country. After National Guard troops killed four protesters at Kent State University, news of the killings further inflamed antiwar passions. Over 100,000 young people spontaneously converged on Washington, D.C., to petition Congress to end the war. Thousands gathered at the Lincoln Memorial, where early one morning they were astonished to receive a visit from none other than Richard Nixon, distraught over the outrage his actions had produced. Nixon did little to cool the protesters' anger with this ineffectual gesture. Uncomfortable with strangers and in situations he could not control, Nixon made small talk about college football with students who wanted the war to end. The president further strained relations with his opponents by publicly describing some protesters as "bums" who were more concerned with burning and looting their campuses than with studying.

Some members of Congress were also infuriated by the Cambodian invasion. Arkansas senator J. William Fulbright, chair of the Senate Foreign Relations Committee, thought Nixon's policies were "undermining the security of our country." Congress responded to public concern over the Cambodian invasion by repealing the 1964 Tonkin Gulf Resolution, which was used by presidents Johnson and Nixon to justify continued American participation in the war. Two Senate doves, Democrat Frank Church of Idaho and Republican John Sherman Cooper of Kentucky, introduced legislation to block additional funding of American operations in Cambodia after June 30, 1970. The amendment passed the Senate but failed in the House. In any event, Nixon had already said that the troops would leave by that date. The president responded defiantly to lawmakers' efforts to restrict his actions in Vietnam, saying, "If Congress undertakes to restrict me, Congress will have to assume the consequences."

While Nixon and the American antiwar movement denounced each other, the peace talks in Paris stalled. The North Vietnamese delegation dismissed as a farce the initial American proposals to withdraw troops only if the North Vietnamese left the South. Willing to wait for a better proposal, the North Vietnamese threatened to remain in Paris "until the chairs rot." In August 1969, hoping that North Vietnamese diplomat Xuan Thuy would be more forthcoming in private than in public, Kissinger opened secret conversations in Paris, but he returned home dispirited. The North insisted that the United States leave Vietnam and stop supporting the Thieu regime. Because North Vietnam had never acknowledged the division of Vietnam into separate countries, it would not withdraw its forces from what it considered part of its own territory.

By the middle of 1970, Nixon's honeymoon with the public over Vietnam had ended. The expansion of the war into Cambodia revived the domestic turmoil of 1968. Like Johnson before him, Nixon could not appear safely on college campuses across the country. Unlike his Democratic predecessor, however, Nixon appealed to the more hawkish section of the electorate. As long as that group was satisfied, the administration could make progress toward its other foreign policy goals. Antiwar outbursts after the Cambodian invasion polarized national opinion, making hawkish Americans even more committed to Nixon. A few days after the incident at Kent State, construction workers rampaged through New York's financial district. They beat antiwar demonstrators, forced officials at City Hall to raise the American flag (which had been lowered in mourning after the Kent State killings), and smashed windows at nearby Pace College. Two weeks later, the head of the New York Labor Council led an estimated 60,000 to 100,000 flag-waving union members in a march supporting the invasion of Cambodia and opposing the antiwar demonstrations. Nixon received their support warmly and posed for cameras wearing a hard hat presented to him by a delegation of construction workers.

The emotional exhaustion following the massive demonstrations of 1969 and the shock of the Kent State killings, combined with the American withdrawal from Cambodia in June 1970, took a toll on the antiwar movement. As another 150,000 American troops left Vietnam and casualty figures dropped below 100 per week, public concern about Vietnam fell slowly until early 1971. Then anger revived as the ARVN, encouraged by the American command, invaded another neighboring country, Laos. Once again, they were looking for a nonexistent North Vietnamese headquarters; instead, they encountered 36,000 battle-hardened North Vietnamese troops. Without the large contingent of Americans who had led them into Cambodia the year before, the ARVN forces stumbled badly. After six weeks of the bloodiest fighting of the war, in which the South Vietnamese suffered casualties of 50 percent of their forces, the ARVN retreated in disarray. Administration statements that the ARVN had exercised an "orderly retreat" from Laos seemed absurd to TV viewers, who saw film clips of terrified South Vietnamese soldiers clinging to the skids of helicopters, desperately trying to get back to South Vietnam.

For Nixon, the worst public relations problem was still to come. On Sunday, June 13, 1971, the *New York Times* began a series of articles on the origins of U.S. involvement in the war in Vietnam. "My God, there it is!" said former Defense Department official Leslie Gelb when he opened his newspaper that morning. "It" was the forty-seven-volume "History of U.S. Decision-Making Process on Vietnam, 1945–1967," popularly known as the Pentagon Papers, which Gelb had compiled at Secretary of Defense Robert McNamara's request in 1968. Daniel Ellsberg, a former marine and later Defense Department official who had grown disillusioned with the war, had leaked copies of the Pentagon Papers to *Times* reporter Neil Sheehan earlier that spring. (Ellsberg had earlier tried to give the classified documents to antiwar Senators, but they declined.) The secret history cast a dark shadow over the foreign policy of every administration from Truman through Johnson. The documents revealed that American officials had ignored international agreements; manipulated the Saigon government; and deliberately misinformed Congress and the public about the origins, progress, and purpose of the war. The Pentagon Papers convinced some people who had previously remained undecided about the war that the U.S. government had long known that its original commitment to Vietnam was a dreadful mistake and certainly was not an obligation worth prolonging.

Fearful that the information being revealed would undermine the administration's effort to negotiate a deal in Vietnam, the administration obtained, for the first time in American history, a temporary court restraining order against the *New York Times*, barring further publication of the papers. Although the *Times* stopped publishing the Pentagon Papers, it circumvented the temporary ban on publication by passing on copies for publication by the *Washington Post*, *Boston Globe*, and other major newspapers. On June 30, 1971, the Supreme Court overturned the restraining order, arguing that the government had failed to prove that publication of the documents threatened national security.

Enraged by the Court's action, Nixon ordered the Justice Department to prosecute Ellsberg for theft of government property, meaning the paper on which the Pentagon documents were printed. Nixon hoped to charge him with espionage, but this action proved difficult because the Pentagon Papers were publicly exhibited, not secretly given to an enemy. Ultimately, the legal case against Ellsberg fell apart. The trial judge dismissed charges after illegal White House efforts to "get" Ellsberg became known along with the remarkable fact that Nixon had discussed naming the judge to a high federal post if he ruled in the government's favor.

In the aftermath of the Court's decision to permit publication, Nixon added the nation's major newspapers to his growing "enemies list" and explored ways to retaliate economically against media companies who reported critically on his administration. At the president's behest, White House aide John Ehrlichman created the so-called Plumbers, a band of operatives charged with stopping leaks from government officials. The Plumbers' activities were more sinister than their playful name. One of them, a former CIA agent named E. Howard Hunt, proposed digging into Ellsberg's private life to find ways to "destroy his public image and credibility." Hunt and a squad of anti-Castro Cuban exiles with ties to the CIA then broke into the office of Ellsberg's psychiatrist to look for discrediting information to leak to the press. John Ehrlichman later went to jail for his role in the break-in. The next year, Hunt, the Cuban exiles, and G. Gordon Liddy, who had helped plan the burglary, organized the notorious break-in at the Democratic National Committee offices at the Watergate office complex (see Chapter 10). Nixon's obsession with secrecy and his effort to punish Ellsberg for his revelation played an important, if unintended, role in eventually bringing down the president.

The Road to the Paris Peace Accords

After the uproar over the Pentagon Papers, public concern over Vietnam diminished in the last half of 1971. Excitement over the diplomatic breakthrough with China (see page 332) and rapidly falling draft and casualty rates removed some of the urgency from the antiwar movement. Even though the Paris peace talks had made no progress, Nixon and Kissinger believed that improving U.S. relations with Moscow and Beijing would soon compel Hanoi to cut a deal. But North Vietnam continued to demand a complete U.S. withdrawal from the South as the price for peace. By the beginning of 1972, Nixon complained to Kissinger that he felt terrible pressure to end the war before the November election. Kissinger advised delaying any settlement until just before the election. That way, Nixon would gain timely adulation as a peacemaker without having to risk disillusioning the voters should the South Vietnamese government fall quickly to the communists.

Meanwhile, North Vietnam launched a full-scale invasion of the South in March 1972, sending in 120,000 troops. Only 6,000 of the 95,000 American troops remaining in the South were combat soldiers. The North Vietnamese met little resistance, advancing to within sixty miles of Saigon. The ARVN threw all its reserves into meeting the assault from the North, which allowed Vietcong guerrillas in the South to overrun villages in the heavily populated Mekong Delta, near the capital. In response, on May 8, 1972, Nixon ordered the largest escalation of the war since 1968. U.S. forces mined Haiphong Harbor, blockaded other North Vietnamese harbors, and engaged in the heaviest bombing of the North since the war began.

Although some politicians and other public figures condemned the escalation, it provoked less public opposition than the Cambodian invasion because it resulted in few American casualties. U.S. airpower managed to blunt the North's offensive. Then, in late summer, the Paris peace talks between Kissinger and Le Duc Tho, the North Vietnamese representative, finally moved forward. Kissinger pointed to public opinion polls that gave Nixon a thirty-point lead over Senator George McGovern, who had been nominated by a divided Democratic party to oppose Nixon in the November election. Nixon would surely win a second term, Kissinger told the North Vietnamese, and therefore they would receive the best possible offer if they reached an agreement before the November election. His strategy seemed to work: in October, the two sides agreed on an outline for a settlement. The United States would remove all its troops within sixty days of a cease-fire, and the North would release its American POWs. The United States would limit military aid to the South to replacing lost weaponry and training replacement troops. The United States also held out a promise of reconstruction assistance for North Vietnam. The North could keep its forces in the South, but it could not increase their numbers after the agreement went into effect. The Thieu regime would remain in power, but it would make a good-faith effort to include the NLF and other factions in a broader government. An international commission similar to the one created by the 1954 Geneva Accords would supervise the agreements.

On October 26, 1972, less than two weeks before the presidential election, Kissinger announced that "peace is at hand" as he made public the major provisions of his agreement with Le Duc Tho. A few hurdles remained, he

Henry Kissinger and North Vietnamese representative Le Duc Tho (*right*) confer during the Paris peace talks to end the war in Vietnam. At center is an interpreter. / © Bettmann/CORBIS

acknowledged, but he expected the end of the war to come soon. Although Kissinger's announcement almost ensured Nixon's re-election, it was not accurate in its prediction of an end to the war. The South Vietnamese president panicked: fearing abandonment by the United States and realizing that his regime had no more popular support than had earlier South Vietnamese governments, President Thieu balked at signing any agreement that permitted North Vietnamese forces to remain in the South. When no agreement had been signed by Election Day, McGovern charged that Kissinger had tricked the public. Few voters responded as McGovern had hoped: Nixon carried every state but Massachusetts and the District of Columbia.

Safely re-elected, Nixon tried to persuade Saigon to drop its objections to the October agreement. Kissinger's deputy, General Alexander Haig, traveled to Saigon with bribes and threats. If Thieu would agree to the Paris accords, the United States would provide economic and military aid to South Vietnam; furthermore, hints were dropped that the United States would resume bombing if the North violated the agreement. On the other hand, if Thieu continued to reject the agreement, the United States would sign it anyway and leave South Vietnam to fend for itself. Kissinger authorized Haig to tell the South Vietnamese leader that the president was committed to ending the war and would forge ahead with the deal, regardless of anything Saigon did to stop it. Still, Thieu would not sign the accords.

Neither would the North Vietnamese agree to consider significant modifications to the agreement in order to break the impasse. Faced with this recalcitrance, Nixon tried to bludgeon the North into reopening the talks. On December 22, 1972, the United States unleashed the heaviest bombing campaign of the war against the North. Over the next twelve days, B-52s dropped thirty-six thousand tons of explosives, more bombs than were dropped in the period from 1969 to 1971. Approximately sixteen hundred civilians were killed in Hanoi and Haiphong. Critics at home and abroad expressed outrage at Nixon's behavior. Several characterized him as a madman. The president's approval rating dropped to 39 percent. Yet Nixon and Kissinger retained a solid core of support for their overall foreign policies among journalists and foreign affairs experts.

The bombing and Nixon's eagerness to end the war restarted the stalled negotiations. Talks resumed in Paris between Kissinger and Le Duc Tho in early January 1973. They made a few cosmetic changes to the October agreement, including strengthening the boundary at the demilitarized zone, but they kept the major provisions of the earlier draft. On January 27, 1973, the two men signed a cease-fire agreement. The United States promised to withdraw its remaining troops within sixty days in return for the release of its POWs. The North promised not to increase its troops in the South above existing levels. The Thieu government would remain in power, but vague plans for "political reconciliation" would go forward in the South, supervised by an international commission. The Saigon government did not sign the agreement, but this time Thieu indicated his approval, provided the United States promised to protect South Vietnam from future North Vietnamese attacks.

Americans felt great relief at the apparent end of the war and the imminent return of the POWs. The White House press office reported gleefully,
"there is great admiration for the president, which seems to grow as we move
further from Washington." For example, an Alabama paper lauded the "patient, long-suffering efforts of the administration" in bringing about accords
that "represent in fact a much better bargain than Sen. George McGovern or
other 'dove' critics were willing to settle for."

But the peace Nixon had promised in 1968 had been a long time in the
making. Nixon's first term had seen some of the heaviest fighting and worst
suffering of the war. Officials estimated that 107,000 South Vietnamese soldiers and approximately half a million North Vietnamese and NLF fighters lost
their lives during that period. Another 20,553 American troops were killed
during those four years, bringing the total number of American deaths to over
58,000. The number of civilians killed will never be known; most estimates
place the civilian death toll at over 1 million.

There was considerable question about whether the cease-fire truly represented "peace with honor," which was the outcome Nixon had promised during the 1968 campaign. The agreement left the South Vietnamese government
in place, but it did not resolve the fundamental issue of the war: would Vietnam
be one country or two? The fact that the agreement gave official recognition to
the NLF and allowed the North to keep troops in the South ensured that
the struggle would continue. For the communists, the Paris agreement merely

On Veterans Day, November 11, 1982, the Vietnam Veterans Memorial was dedicated in
Washington, D.C. The names of the more than 58,000 Americans who died in Vietnam were
etched into the black granite. / © Susan Meiselas/Magnum.

represented another temporary delay in their thirty-year effort to unify the country under their leadership. Certain that history was on their side, they waited for the opportune moment to complete their revolution.

In the West, however, the Paris agreement appeared to be a major accomplishment. In October 1973, the Nobel Prize Committee announced that it had awarded its 1973 Peace Prize to Kissinger and Le Duc Tho for their work on the Paris agreement. Le refused his share because the political future of the South had not been resolved and fighting could resume at a moment's notice. But Kissinger and Le Duc Tho won praise from many American editorialists.

Kissinger's winning the Nobel Peace Prize marked the high point of enthusiasm in the United States for the settlement arranged in Paris. Vietnam faded as an issue for the rest of Nixon's second term as Watergate, a war in the Middle East, and relations with the Soviet Union and China took center stage. Yet the fighting in Vietnam had not come to an end. The cease-fire gradually eroded. Each side attacked the other, and the North Vietnamese reinforced their positions in the South. President Thieu refused to bargain in good faith with NLF leaders to bring them into the government. By the beginning of 1975, five months after Nixon had left the presidency in disgrace, Vietnam stood poised on the verge of a climactic struggle that would chase Thieu from power and give final victory to the communists (see Chapter 11).

Détente with the Soviet Union

Long before the cease-fire in Vietnam, the Nixon administration had taken major steps in other foreign policy arenas. One of the most significant was the administration's attempt to improve relations with the Soviet Union, which had deteriorated during the Vietnam War and since the August 1968 Soviet invasion of Czechoslovakia. Nixon and Kissinger believed that improved relations with Moscow might produce a breakthrough in Vietnam. They also hoped to expand trade with the Soviet bloc, both to help the American economy and to placate the western Europeans, who were already reaching out to make their own business deals in Eastern Europe. Finally, Nixon faced the same basic worry as all other presidents had since World War II: an expensive and destabilizing arms race that might lead to nuclear war with the Soviet Union. An arms control agreement with the Soviets that ensured, in Nixon's words, "sufficiency" rather than "superiority" would reduce the likelihood of nuclear war and demonstrate that the two powers could find common ground. In political terms, progress on arms control could help the administration quiet the scientists, editorial writers, and members of Congress who complained that the world faced grave dangers from the development of highly accurate, long-range ballistic missiles. Economically, capping the arms race would reduce the burden of developing more costly weapons systems.

The Nixon administration conducted three years of highly complicated negotiations, known as the Strategic Arms Limitation Talks (SALT), with the Soviet Union. Formal negotiations took place in Helsinki, Finland, and Vienna,

Austria, while Kissinger conducted secret back-channel conversations with Soviet ambassador Anatoly Dobrynin. Even with the best of intentions, these negotiations were complicated. Each side possessed a different mix of weapons and delivery systems—including long- and short-range missiles and manned bombers, as well as submarine-launched missiles—making it tricky to devise a fair balance. Also, both the United States and the Soviet Union were developing antiballistic missile systems (ABMs), which threatened to unhinge any agreement to cap offensive missiles. Under pressure from Congress (which nearly voted to kill a proposed ABM system in 1969), American and Soviet negotiators agreed in principle in 1971 to work toward restricting both offensive and defensive missiles.

Arms control efforts received a big assist from the improvement in U.S.-China relations beginning in July 1971. Kissinger's secret trip to Beijing and the president's dramatic visit in February 1972 (discussed below), made Moscow fear a Chinese-American alliance aimed at the Soviet Union. When Nixon visited Moscow in May 1972, he conducted a dramatic series of late-night negotiations with Leonid Brezhnev, with only Kissinger and an interpreter in attendance. These high-level talks yielded three significant agreements. An ABM treaty limited each side to only two antimissile sites, a number that made a defensive system almost useless. A SALT-I, or Interim Agreement on Limitations of Strategic Armaments, included a five-year pledge to limit the number of land-based missiles in each arsenal to about the number on hand in 1972, rather than the much higher levels both sides would build up to otherwise. The agreement also called for negotiating a more complete arms control treaty in the future. Finally, a document called the "Basic Principles of U.S.-Soviet Relations" pledged each party to deal with the other on "the principle of equality." Together, these three agreements formed the basis of détente between the two superpowers for the next two years.

When Nixon returned to Washington from Moscow, he appeared to have engineered a major turning point in U.S.-Soviet relations. Old adversaries like Democratic senators Fulbright, Church, and Claiborne Pell of Rhode Island rushed to support détente; however, other lawmakers pointed to flaws in the SALT agreement. Democratic senator Henry Jackson of Washington objected that Nixon's concept of nuclear "sufficiency"—the guiding principle that determined the U.S. position during talks—allowed the Soviets three hundred more land-based ICBMs than the United States. Kissinger emphasized that the United States retained a technological edge because its missiles were more accurate and, more important, would soon be able to carry multiple, independently targeted nuclear warheads, a system know by its acronym, MIRV. This improvement permitted a single rocket to carry as many and eight to ten nuclear warheads that could hit widely dispersed targets.

In August 1972, Congress approved the ABM treaty followed by the SALT-I agreement, but also adopted a demand from Senator Jackson that future agreements limit the Soviets to no more missiles than were allowed in the American arsenal. This represented a poison pill. Because the United States had many more manned bombers and missile-carrying submarines than did the Soviets, Moscow insisted on having a larger number of land-based missiles to offset the American advantage in other weapons systems.

Jackson and other critics of détente berated Kissinger and Nixon for failing to insist that the Soviet Union improve its poor record on human rights. In 1973, Jackson joined with Ohio Democratic congressman Charles Vanik to introduce legislation forbidding the extension of equal trading rights—so-called most-favored-nation status—to the Soviets until they permitted all citizens who wished to emigrate, mostly Jews but also other ethnic and religious minorities, to do so. In that year (1973), more than thirty thousand Soviet Jews left for the West, more than had ever before been permitted to leave; nevertheless, Jackson saw the emigration issue as one that would fuel his run for president in 1976. The passage of the Jackson-Vanik Amendment in 1974 prevented the Soviets from receiving most-favored-nation status, thereby limiting trade with the Soviets. The Soviet Union accused the United States of not treating it as an equal and legitimate power, and détente waned. Nixon met twice more with Brezhnev, in Washington in June 1973 and in Moscow in the summer of 1974, just weeks before the Watergate scandal forced his resignation. Neither summit produced new breakthroughs in arms control.

Critics of arms control efforts later complained that inadequate safeguards and Soviet cheating made a mockery of SALT and left the United States more, not less, vulnerable to nuclear attack. Although the Soviets cheated at the margins of the treaty, new technologies, more than deception, undermined SALT. During the 1970s and 1980s, first the United States and then the Soviet Union developed new weapons systems that circumvented the negotiated caps. For example, small, nuclear-tipped cruise missiles were cheap, accurate, and hard to detect. New MIRV technology allowed each side to place as many as ten independently targetable warheads on existing missiles, which dramatically expanded arsenals without violating restrictions on the number of missiles permitted. Despite these problems, however, the United States and the Soviet Union (and then Russia) continued to operate for almost thirty years within the broad parameters of SALT and the ABM accord. The framework cracked, however, in 2001, when President George W. Bush withdrew the United States from the ABM treaty as a prelude to building an antimissile defense system.

The Opening to China

Nixon's single, most dramatic foreign policy achievement was his reversal of U.S. policy toward communist China. On July 15, 1971, the president announced that National Security Adviser Kissinger had just returned from Beijing, where he had spent two days preparing the way for a presidential visit to China in 1972. Nixon and Kissinger had achieved one of the most significant diplomatic turnarounds of the twentieth century, in nearly complete secrecy. That Richard Nixon—a strident anticommunist of the early Cold War—had engineered the reversal made it all the more stunning. In 1960, for example, in a debate with John F. Kennedy, Nixon asserted that China did not just threaten Taiwan and nearby islands, "it wants the world."

Both China and the United States had much to gain by resuming regular diplomatic relations, which had been nonexistent since the beginning of the Korean War. Since 1966, China's leader, Mao Zedong, had encouraged "the great proletarian Cultural Revolution," during which thousands of young Red Guards had roamed China's cities and countryside, terrorizing the population into ideological orthodoxy. Amidst chaos, the economy faltered and the army had to restore order. Now, other Chinese officials, led by Zhou Enlai, wanted to halt the excesses of the Cultural Revolution and open better relations with the rest of the world. Part of the reason for this change was that China's once-close ties to the Soviet Union had deteriorated so badly that the two fought a series of bloody border skirmishes during 1969 and 1970. The Soviets undertook a major military buildup along the six-thousand-mile disputed border and even asked American officials if they would join or at least tolerate an attack against Chinese nuclear weapons facilities. Recognizing his own and his country's vulnerability, Mao now condemned Soviet "social imperialism" as a far greater threat to China than American "capitalist imperialism." The "Great Helmsman," as Mao called himself, recalled a Chinese proverb on the wisdom of making an alliance with "faraway barbarians" to resist nearby enemies.

For its part, Washington saw ties to China as a way of reclaiming prestige lost in the Vietnam War. Establishing a connection to China, the most populous country in the world and a huge potential market, would show the world that the war in Vietnam had not prevented the United States from pursuing a vigorous foreign policy agenda, as some critics contended. Kissinger also hoped that restoring links with Beijing would "reduce Indochina to its proper scale, a small peninsula on a major continent." An added benefit might include Beijing's persuading Hanoi to accept American peace proposals. Even if China did not help hasten the end to the Vietnam War, restoration of relations after twenty years would show that the United States had interests in Asia beyond Vietnam. The drama of opening ties to the People's Republic of China would, Nixon and Kissinger hoped, "ease for the American people the pain that would inevitably accompany our withdrawal from Southeast Asia." Closer relations with China could also help put pressure on the Soviet Union in arms control talks or regional disputes. Finally, the American policy of isolating the communist regime in China had angered U.S. allies in Europe and Asia, and they clamored for a change.

The decades-long confrontation with China had also made the United States overly dependent on Japan. Since 1949, Tokyo had wanted to trade with its giant communist neighbor, only to be restrained by a U.S.-imposed embargo. To compensate Japan for the lost China market, every president since Harry Truman had worked to expand Japanese exports to the United States. This strategy made sense when Japan was struggling to recover from wartime devastation. But by the 1960s, Japan was one of the world's most robust economies. In 1971, Japan enjoyed a then unprecedented $3.2 billion trade surplus with the United States on a two-way trade of $11.5 billion. Many

American business, labor, and political leaders accused Japan of engaging in various unfair trade practices. Magazines such as *Newsweek* and *Time* described Japan as carrying out a "business invasion" of the United States. Nixon's Commerce Secretary, Maurice Stans, reportedly told journalists that Japan was still fighting World War II, "only now, instead of a shooting war, it is an economic war. Their immediate intention is to try to dominate the Pacific and then, perhaps, the world." Complaining that the "Japanese were all over Asia, like a bunch of lice," Nixon especially resented what he called the "Jap betrayal," the failure of Prime Minister Sato Eisaku to impose promised limits on Japanese textile exports to the United States. This issue was vital to southern textile producers, who were among Nixon's biggest campaign contributors. Thus, several strategic and economic factors convinced Nixon and Kissinger that the time had come to shift U.S. interests in Asia away from exclusive reliance on Japan and toward a more balanced relationship with Tokyo and Beijing. To make sure Japan got this message, Nixon and Kissinger made their move toward China without consulting its chief Asian ally, despite longstanding promises to inform Tokyo of any policy shift.

Kissinger discussed all these issues with Zhou Enlai during his whirlwind forty-nine-hour visit to Beijing in July 1971. He found the Chinese leader to be "one of the two or three most impressive men I have ever met. Urbane, infinitely patient, intelligent, subtle." They agreed that Soviet domination of much of Europe and Asia threatened world stability; they noted that the United States, the world's leading conservative power, could preserve that stability. Although the Chinese refused to put pressure on North Vietnam (beyond encouraging Hanoi to make the best deal it could with Washington), they indicated that differences over the Vietnam War should not prevent the United States and China from making progress on other issues. Kissinger observed that American ties to Taiwan should not prevent Washington and Beijing from working together. The two countries agreed to continue talking about their mutual interests over the next seven months as they prepared for Nixon's visit.

The highly favorable public reaction to the Chinese breakthrough made the White House jubilant. Some American politicians set aside their traditional animosities toward the administration. Democratic senator Fulbright told Nixon, "I completely agree with what you are doing." Majority leader Mike Mansfield promised understanding for the "delicacy and promise of the situation." Senator Edward M. Kennedy, an archrival on whom Nixon spied, called the visit "historic." Praise also poured in from abroad.

In December 1971, war broke out between Pakistan and India over efforts by the residents of East Pakistan, known as Bengalis, to form a new state, Bangladesh. India supported the Bengalis with troops, who fought Pakistani soldiers in both the eastern and western parts of the Indian subcontinent. Public opinion in Europe and America backed the Bengalis' desire for independence from western Pakistan because the more populous but poorer easterners had suffered economically, socially, and politically at the hands of the westerners since the founding of Pakistan in 1947. Washington ignored the abuses committed by the Pakistani government against the Bengalis, however,

President Nixon and his wife Pat
visit the Great Wall during their
visit to China in February 1972. /
UPI/Bettmann/CORBIS

and tilted toward Pakistan to cement its ties with China. Beijing supported
Pakistan, whose leader, Ayub Khan, had helped arrange Kissinger's trip in July
1971. The Soviet Union supported India and Bangladesh, and the Bengali rebellion eventually succeeded.

Complaints that the United States had backed the wrong side in the conflict were drowned out by spectacular live television coverage of Nixon's
five-day visit to China, which began on February 21, 1972. The president's
handshake with Zhou Enlai at the Beijing airport erased the snub meted out
by Secretary of State John Foster Dulles in 1954, when he had refused
Zhou's hand at the Geneva conference on Indochina. Nixon and Kissinger
received a well-photographed audience with Chairman Mao Zedong. The
president toasted the Chinese in the Great Hall of the People in the heart of
Beijing's Forbidden City. He and his wife Pat walked along the Great Wall,
about which Nixon proclaimed, "[I]t truly is a great wall," while the First
Lady visited the Beijing Zoo to acknowledge its gift to the United States of
two cuddly giant pandas.

While television crews produced miles of film that would later be used in Nixon's campaign ads, Kissinger worked on the terms of the new relations between the two powers. The final communiqué, issued at Shanghai at the end of the trip, announced that each country would open an "interest section"—an embassy, by another name—in the other's capital. The United States relaxed restrictions on trade with and travel to China. The two powers agreed to disagree over Taiwan, with the United States maintaining its formal embassy there. The communiqué observed that both the Communist and the Nationalist Chinese believed China to be a single country. While warning the Soviet Union that the United States and China mutually opposed Soviet domination, the communiqué promised that their new relationship threatened no one. They did not agree to work together to end the Vietnam War, and each country expressed support for its own favorite in that conflict. Nevertheless, by its very existence, the Shanghai communiqué demonstrated that the United States had moved beyond its preoccupation with Vietnam. At Shanghai, Nixon, Kissinger, and Zhou Enlai certified that friendship between Washington and Beijing could go forward, regardless of what happened in Indochina. According to *Time* magazine, which named Nixon and Kissinger its Men of the Year for 1972, détente with the Soviets and the opening of relations with China represented "the most profound rearrangement of the earth's political powers since the beginning of the cold war."

Policies on the Margins

The breakthroughs in relations with Beijing and Moscow, combined with the Vietnam peace agreement of January 1973, established Henry Kissinger's reputation as a masterful negotiator and a brilliant innovator in foreign policy. During the summer of 1973, as Senate hearings on the Watergate scandal put Nixon in deep trouble, the president sought to recoup his flagging political standing by calling attention to his foreign affairs successes. Accordingly, in August, he nominated Kissinger to replace the ineffectual and self-effacing William Rogers as secretary of state. Kissinger also retained his position as national security adviser.

Public and congressional reaction was overwhelmingly positive, and Kissinger sailed through his confirmation hearings. *Newsweek* magazine called him "the White House genius-in-residence," and *Time* labeled him a "Super Secretary." Career diplomats were excited that the State Department would no longer be bypassed in major foreign policy decisions. As secretary of state, however, Kissinger continued his penchant for acting alone, listening to professional diplomats only when it suited his purposes. This characteristic, along with his domineering manner, eventually alienated many foreign affairs specialists.

Even their many critics concede that Nixon and Kissinger performed a valuable service by improving relations with the Soviet Union and opening a dialogue with China. Disengaging from Vietnam was also a vital accomplishment. The administration's accomplishments in solving other major problems, however, appear either fleeting or nonexistent. The Nixon administration largely ignored the western European allies and got on terribly with Japan. Neither the president nor Kissinger had much understanding of or sympathy with liberation movements in Africa, efforts at social change in Latin America, or the chronic problems of the Middle East. They tended to see instability in these regions as either communist-inspired or anti-American. In their focus on achieving a military equilibrium between the United States and its rivals, they also ignored growing economic problems that affected millions of working Americans during subsequent decades.

From 1969 through 1974, the United States not only failed to support anticolonial struggles in southern Africa but actually assisted white-ruled colonial regimes, including South Africa, Rhodesia (Zimbabwe), and Portuguese Angola and Mozambique. Discussing Africa with Kissinger in 1969, Nixon vulgarly declared, "Henry, let's leave the niggers to Bill [Rogers, the phlegmatic secretary of state] and we'll take care of the rest of the world." Nixon and Kissinger adopted a "southern Africa strategy" that resembled their domestic "southern strategy" in its appeal to whites based on the fear of black control. Kissinger's NSC decided that communists were behind liberation movements in southern Africa and that the United States should support the region's white-ruled governments. The Nixon administration weakened trade sanctions against Rhodesia, South Africa, and the Portuguese colonies of Angola and Mozambique, acts that prolonged the struggles that eventually drove the colonial and white rulers from power.

During the Nixon years, Washington also tried to block or undo social change in Latin America. The administration played a major role in efforts to prevent the election of a socialist president in Chile and, when this attempt failed, helped to finance a military coup to drive him from power. In explaining his motives, Kissinger told an interagency intelligence group (the Forty Committee), "I don't see why we have to let a country go Marxist just because its people are irresponsible." Officials in Washington feared that if a leftist took power democratically, it would inspire radicals throughout Latin America.

In the summer of 1970, Nixon and Kissinger approved a plan to block the election of socialist Salvador Allende Gossens. Although he had received a plurality of the popular vote, the Chilean congress had the final say in selecting the winner. The Forty Committee tried to bribe the Chilean congress to choose another candidate. When this tactic failed, the CIA chief in Chile, encouraged by Kissinger, worked with anti-Allende officers to assassinate the chief of staff of Chile's armed forces, General René Schneider. The prodemocratic Schneider wanted to keep the military in check and out of politics. The plotters hoped that by killing him, they could both pin the blame on Allende and provoke a coup. Despite the murder, Allende took office.

Over the next three years, the United States tried, in Nixon's words, "to make the Chilean economy scream." Washington cut off credit to Chile and pressured many allied governments and international lending agencies to do the same. The CIA spent over $20 million funding Allende's political opponents

Chilean president Salvador Allende defiantly criticizes U.S. efforts to undermine his regime, shortly before the U.S.-backed coup of 1973 toppled him. / AP/Wide World

in the Chilean press and opposition political parties. It also paid truck drivers to strike, which paralyzed the local economy and blocked food supplies. By 1973, these economic troubles, some worsened by Allende's own policies, had alienated both the middle class and the military. On September 11, 1973, a right-wing junta of military officers, led by General Augusto Pinochet, toppled the elected government. Either Allende was murdered or he committed suicide while defending the presidential palace. In the next few weeks, the junta arrested over twenty thousand socialist supporters, killed hundreds, and forced thousands into exile. Pinochet ruled with an iron fist for the next seventeen years. But the Nixon administration greeted the coup as a welcome event, lifting economic restrictions and providing military aid to the grateful generals.

The Nixon administration's effort to cultivate and work with conservative regimes was also evident in Iran. The United States had acted as the patron of Shah Mohammed Reza Pahlavi since helping to restore him to power in 1953. In June 1972, while returning from a summit in Moscow, Nixon and Kissinger stopped in Iran to enhance their ties with the Shah. "I need you," the president told the Iranian monarch. Nixon wanted Iran to act as a "surrogate" power in South Asia, as part of the regional security scheme envisaged by the Nixon Doctrine. As an inducement to protect Western strategic interests in the oil-rich region of the Persian Gulf, Kissinger offered to sell to Iran any weapon in the

American arsenal, with the exception of nuclear bombs. State Department arms experts objected that the United States might lose control of some of its most sophisticated hardware by giving the shah such free access, but Kissinger overrode the dissenters. Over the next five years, Iran bought $8 billion worth of American weapons. Ultimately, American support for the shah backfired. A revolution swept the country, and in January 1979, the shah—hated for his repressive rule—was forced to flee the country. The new leaders blamed the United States for the shah's reign of terror (see Chapter 11). But at the time of Kissinger's offer, expression of this hostility toward the United States was years in the future.

Less than a month after the Chilean coup, war broke out in the Middle East when Egypt and Syria attacked Israel on October 6, 1973. Most scholars of American Middle East policy believed that the October war, commonly called the Yom Kippur War, "completed the transformation of the Arab-Israeli dispute from a nuisance into a conflict central to American diplomatic and strategic concerns."

Since the 1967 Six-Day War, little progress had occurred in bringing Israel and its neighbors to the peace table. The United States had become the principal arms supplier to Israel and Jordan, while the Soviet Union replenished the losses incurred by Egypt and Syria in the Six-Day War. The Arab states refused to meet Israel face to face, and the Jewish state vowed to keep the territories it had taken—East Jerusalem, the West Bank of the Jordan River, the Golan Heights, and the Sinai Peninsula—until its Arab neighbors agreed to make peace. Egypt's president Gamal Abdel Nasser then launched a so-called war of attrition against Israel's forces along the Suez Canal and in the eastern Sinai in 1969 and 1970. These events formed the background to the Middle East crisis of 1973.

Of all the agencies concerned with foreign policy in the Nixon administration, the State Department paid the most attention to the Middle East from 1969 to 1972. Nixon and Kissinger concentrated on Vietnam, détente with the Soviet Union, and opening relations with China; they left the daunting task of resolving the Arab-Israeli dispute to Secretary of State Rogers. Pleased to be out from under the thumb of the imperious national security adviser, Rogers floated an ambitious plan to resolve the conflict in a single stroke. He called on Israel to withdraw from most of the territory captured in 1967 in return for full diplomatic relations with its neighbors and their pledge to maintain peace. But Israel balked at Rogers's plan as a threat to its security. Realizing that Rogers carried less weight with Nixon than did Kissinger, Israel's diplomats accurately believed that they could ignore his unsolicited proposals without offending the United States. Nevertheless, in the summer of 1970, Rogers was able to arrange a cease-fire.

Two months later, Nasser died suddenly, leaving Egypt's government in the hands of his little-known vice president, Anwar Sadat. Just as Sadat took power, King Hussein of Jordan evicted Palestine Liberation Organization (PLO) guerrillas from his country in a bloody three-day war. Nixon ordered the U.S. Mediterranean fleet to send planes and equipment to help Jordan. Thereafter,

(cont. on page 343)

"Energy Too Cheap to Meter": The Temptation of Nuclear Power

In 2001, the Bush administration followed the lead of each president since Dwight D. Eisenhower by pronouncing an "energy independence plan." Drafted by Vice President Richard Cheney in consultation with the energy industry, the program called for relaxed environmental controls on coal burning, expanded oil drilling in sensitive nature preserves, and increased reliance on nuclear energy. Nuclear power plants, once predicted to supply most of the nation's electricity, had been mired in controversy for a quarter century.

Abundant, low-priced energy would make almost any economist's short list of reasons behind America's industrial predominance. Since World War II, petroleum has played a key role in driving economic growth. Until the 1950s, most petroleum came from domestic wells. By the 1990s, however, the United States imported over half its oil from Canada, Mexico, Venezuela, Colombia, Nigeria, and countries in the Middle East. The burdens of costly imports and political complications have, for almost fifty years, prompted government calls for "energy independence." The Arab-Israeli war of 1973 and the Iranian revolution of 1979 led to embargoes and shortages that drove the price of crude oil up from $3 to $30 per barrel. Public resentment over high prices and gasoline lines played a big part in the electoral defeat of President Jimmy Carter in 1980. Ever since, periodic spikes in the price of gasoline have caused politicians to shudder.

Atomic power, unleashed in the bombs that destroyed Hiroshima and Nagasaki in 1945, remained a government monopoly for a decade. The Atomic Energy Act of 1946 placed all nuclear materials, technology, and weapons under the control of the Atomic Energy Commission (AEC), which concentrated on building more and bigger bombs. Policymakers and AEC officials disagreed over whether the agency should focus on weapons development or attempt to harness the atom's power for "peaceful uses."

In 1953, with Republicans back in control of the White House and Congress, and the Soviets and Americans running neck and neck to develop the super or H-bomb, AEC chair Lewis L. Strauss and GOP legislators launched a "nuclear power race" against the communist enemy. Democrats agreed in principle, but they favored a government-run nuclear power industry along the lines of the New Deal's Tennessee Valley Authority (TVA). Strauss, a Wall Street investment banker by trade, proposed instead to enlist the "genius and enterprise of American industry." The federal government would supply incentives and technology, but private utilities would be entrusted to develop nuclear power as a demonstration of the superiority of the free-enterprise system. President Eisenhower joined the chorus in a speech delivered to the United Nations in December 1953. His Atoms for Peace proposal called on the world's governments to cooperate to "serve the needs rather than the fears of mankind." America would take the lead and apply its nuclear technology to assist private firms in providing "abundant electrical energy in the power starved areas of the world" as well as to domestic consumers.

Although the Soviets rejected Eisenhower's proposal, it found support at home. Congress enacted the Atomic Energy Act of 1954, which instructed the AEC to promote the private ownership, construction, and operation of nuclear power plants. AEC Chair Strauss predicted a golden age when "our children will enjoy electrical energy too cheap to meter."

First, however, power plants had to be built. None could be financed or operated without hazard insurance. One initial estimate of a minor nuclear accident predicted it might kill several thousand people and destroy property valued at $4 billion. Later

Long promoted as a source of cheap, clean energy, the nuclear power industry never recovered from the near-meltdown at the Three Mile Island reactor in 1979. / AP/Harrisburg Patriot News/Wide World

studies determined that a major accident might kill forty-five thousand people and cost up to $400 billion. The AEC kept this information secret while Congress passed the Price-Anderson Act of 1957, which exempted the nuclear power industry from liability for lawsuits resulting from accidents. To compensate potential victims, Congress created a tiny fund totaling $560 million.

An industry lobbying group, the Atomic Industrial Forum (AIF), joined the AEC in a campaign to boost public support for nuclear power. Both groups adopted the goal of "developing consumer acceptance of radioactivity" and instilling a "tolerance for accidents." The campaign relied on secrecy and advertising to mold public opinion. During the 1950s, the AEC distributed over 8 million copies of a promotional pamphlet "Understanding the Atom." By 1970, about 40 million Americans had attended AEC-sponsored screenings of pronuclear films, and at least four times that number viewed them on television. One 1968 film, *The Atom and Eve*, fea-

tured "little Eve" learning to enjoy life in an "electric Garden of Eden" full of appliances powered by nuclear generators. The AEC put on promotional displays at public schools, libraries, and fairs and encouraged the Boy Scouts to offer a merit badge in atomic energy. In an especially effective pitch, the Walt Disney company televised a cartoon, *Our Friend the Atom* (1956), in which a violent, slant-eyed genie representing nuclear power is domesticated into a docile servant. When Eisenhower activated the nation's first commercial nuclear power plant, he did so by waving a radioactive "magic wand" over a control panel. In spite of these efforts, the public remained wary. Anxiety over the affects of nuclear fallout on the food chain and human health remained strong until the 1963 treaty banning the atmospheric testing of nuclear weapons.

In another public relations effort, the AEC launched Project Plowshare in 1956. Plowshare was a scheme to harness controlled nuclear explosions to excavate canals, tunnels, ports, and mines. For example, during the Suez crisis of November 1956, scientists at the AEC's Lawrence Livermore Laboratory proposed blasting a new canal through Israel with nuclear charges. Influential Plowshare boosters such as physicists Edward Teller, Glenn Seaborg, Freeman Dyson, and Harold Brown envisioned nuclear explosions that remodeled Earth's geography and propelled spacecraft filled with colonists to the moon and outer planets. They pondered blasting a "Panatomic canal" through Central America, desalinating oceans, and building ports in places like Alaska. Before Plowshare was abandoned in 1971, it explored the idea of demolishing part of the Rocky Mountains to construct a coast-to-coast waterway.

In 1974, in the wake of the Arab oil embargo that followed the Yom Kippur War with Israel, President Nixon proposed Project Independence. Nixon envisioned building two hundred additional nuclear power plants to provide 50 percent of the nation's electricity requirements by 2000, which would eliminate the need to import oil. As with all previous proposals, however, neither the economics nor the level of public support was enough.

Nixon's proposal ran headlong into a new environmental movement that saw nuclear power as wasteful and dangerous. The president himself had earlier signed into law the National Environmental Policy Act, which took effect on January 1, 1970, and he appointed the first administrator of the new Environmental Protection Agency (EPA). Meanwhile, individuals and groups critical of nuclear technology, such as Ralph Nader, Barry Commoner, the Sierra Club, and the Friends of the Earth, mobilized communities against federal efforts to build nuclear power plants.

In 1974, Congress replaced the AEC with a new Nuclear Regulatory Commission (NRC). A separate Energy Research and Development Administration (ERDA) supervised the nuclear arsenal. In 1977, President Carter merged ERDA into the new cabinet level Department of Energy.

None of this gave much traction to the civilian nuclear energy program. The fate of the Shoreham reactor in Long Island, New York, typified the industry's problem. Conceived in the late 1960s, Shoreham was budgeted to cost $75 million and come on line in 1975. Cost overruns, design changes, and inadequate safety considerations aroused public opposition and delayed completion until 1989. By then, the price tag topped $6 billion, making the plant's electricity the most expensive in the nation. The state took over the plant from the bankrupt owner and sold it for scrap in 1994.

Public opposition to Shoreham and other nuclear plants increased after March 1979 when a fault occurred in the cooling system of Unit 2 of the Three Mile Island plant near Harrisburg, Pennsylvania. A meltdown of the reactor's nuclear core was narrowly averted, but the near catastrophe (and subsequent revelations about shoddy maintenance) stopped the nuclear industry in its tracks. Two popular films, *The China Syndrome* (1979) and *Silkwood* (1983), highlighted criminal negligence in the operation of civilian reactors and their fuel production. These accounts seemed eerily similar to the Three Mile Island incident and anticipated the even bigger disaster of April 1986 at the Chernobyl reactor in the Soviet Union. That reactor suffered a catastrophic failure that killed hundreds of workers before the smoldering wreck was encased in a massive concrete coffin.

After Chernobyl, ambitious plans for nuclear plants in the United States were scaled back. No new plants were ordered after 1979. The last of those already under construction opened in 1996. As of 2002, only 103 commercial reactors were in operation, half the number projected in the 1970s, and they generated barely 20 percent of the nation's electrical energy. Many reactors are approaching the end of their approved operation period. Others have been found to suffer from unexpected corrosion and design flaws. Most communities oppose building new plants in their "back-

yard," and no one wants to accept spent fuel rods. Federal plans to store nuclear waste in the underground caverns of Yucca Mountain, Nevada, and in Utah and New Mexico have aroused bitter opposition from nearby residents.

In 1989, nuclear energy advocates took heart when two scientists at the University of Utah, Stanley Pons and Martin Fleishmann, claimed they had produced "cold nuclear fusion" at room temperature with off-the-shelf equipment and water. The university president compared this to humankind's discovery of fire and revived talk of producing abundant, pollution-free, cheap energy.

State and federal agencies rushed to fund cold fusion research, but after spending $100 million, no one could reproduce the initial result. After they were accused of deception, Pons and Fleishmann dropped from sight, and Utah officials fired the gullible university president.

Efforts by the Bush administration to revive nuclear power as the path to energy independence must overcome a troubled legacy of cost overruns, technical defects, maintenance problems, and security concerns. The production of nuclear-generated "electricity too cheap to meter" remains an elusive goal.

---

the Middle East receded from public view in Europe and the United States. Sadat consolidated his power, an uneasy calm persisted along the Suez Canal, and the PLO guerrilla raids from Jordan into Israel stopped.

By 1973, however, Sadat found the "no war, no peace" situation intolerable. He resented the presence of the ten thousand Soviet soldiers whom Nasser had invited into Egypt, and he feared that Syria's radical government threatened Cairo's preeminence in the Arab world. Despairing that the United States or the United Nations would never persuade Israel to withdraw from the captured territories, he agreed with Syria to coordinate an attack on Israeli positions in the Sinai Peninsula and the Golan Heights. On October 6, 1973, Yom Kippur, the holiest day of the Jewish religious calendar, Egyptian and Syrian forces struck. The attackers achieved more in the first three days of the conflict than Arab armies had gained in three previous wars with Israel. Egyptian troops crossed the Suez Canal and captured hundreds of stunned Israelis. In the north, Syria reclaimed a large portion of the Golan Heights and threatened to slice Israel in two. With its military position appearing desperate, Israeli prime minister Golda Meir begged Washington for a resupply of planes, tanks, and ammunition.

Nixon and Kissinger agreed to the largest airlift of equipment and armaments since World War II. Assured of new arms, Israel counterattacked, driving the Syrians off the Golan Heights and threatening Syria's capital, Damascus. In the south, Israel's tanks turned back the advancing Egyptians. A worried President Sadat asked Moscow for aid, a move that Kissinger and Nixon considered a threat to détente. Kissinger traveled to Moscow to cool the crisis. While there, he publicly rejected a Soviet call for a joint U.S.-Soviet military expedition to impose a cease-fire. It was "inconceivable," he said, for the United States and the Soviet Union to introduce enough troops to stop the fighting. He also warned the Soviets not to move their own military forces into the Middle East in any guise. Before leaving Moscow, he arranged for joint U.S.-Soviet sponsorship of a U.N. cease-fire resolution.

Now well supplied by the United States, Israel resisted an immediate end to the fighting. Its tanks crossed the Suez Canal and threatened to destroy Egypt's army and enter Cairo. The Soviets issued a warning to Jerusalem, and Nixon and Kissinger responded by ordering a full military alert of American forces in the Mediterranean and Europe. The alert occurred only days after Nixon had provoked nationwide outrage over his abrupt firing of the special prosecutor investigating White House involvement in the Watergate break-in and cover-up (see Chapter 10). One newspaper editorial speculated that "this White House may well have felt that it was necessary to display toughness on a worldwide scale to show that President Nixon was fully in command of foreign policy and in no way weakened by domestic events."

The alert passed after nine hours, and a cease-fire was finally cemented. Israeli forces occupied the east bank of the canal, Egyptian troops stood on the west bank, and Israel was in control of more Syrian territory than it had held at the beginning of the fighting. In Washington, Nixon's erratic behavior during the war and his ordering of the military alert worried politicians of both parties. Massachusetts Democratic representative Thomas P. (Tip) O'Neill, invited to a White House briefing during the height of the crisis, thought the president was unhinged. He recalled that Nixon "kept interrupting Kissinger" and acted inappropriately: "'We had trouble finding Henry,' [Nixon] said. 'He was in bed with a broad.' Nobody laughed." Peter Lakeland, an aide to New York's Republican senator Jacob Javits, informed his boss that "if, as now seems inevitable, Nixon will soon go under in what is likely to be a nasty, squalid, destructive spasm of criminal defiance, Kissinger's own . . . capacity to operate . . . will be called into doubt."

Although Lakeland's prophecy about Nixon proved accurate, Kissinger's reputation climbed in the aftermath of the Yom Kippur War. In November 1973, he commenced several rounds of negotiations—quickly labeled "shuttle diplomacy" by the press—among the capitals of Israel, Egypt, and Syria. Over the next eighteen months, he arranged the disengagement of the three countries' military forces in the Sinai and the Golan Heights. Israel's armies withdrew from the banks of the Suez Canal, permitting the reopening of that waterway. Kissinger also renegotiated the cease-fire between Israel and Syria, with the former removing its forces from the old Syrian provincial capital but retaining its control over the most strategic parts of the Golan Heights.

Although shuttle diplomacy had eased the immediate threat of renewed warfare, neither Kissinger nor anyone else developed a formula for real peace in the region. Israel insisted that its neighbors recognize its right to exist within secure borders before it returned occupied territory to them. The Arab states demanded the unconditional return of all captured territory before discussing a political settlement. Meanwhile, millions of displaced, angry, and armed Palestinian refugees languished in squalid camps in Jordan, Lebanon, and other areas near Israel. Their demand for a homeland that encompassed some or all of Israeli territory created another obstacle to peace. As American, Israeli, Arab, and Palestinian leaders discovered over the next three decades, patching together a regional settlement in the Middle East proved elusive.

During 1973–1974, as the Watergate scandal linked Nixon to illegal break-ins and fundraising practices, Kissinger's stature soared and he became a global celebrity, applauded in the American and foreign press. *Time* magazine gushed that "as he whirled through the capitals of the Middle East last week, Henry Kissinger more than ever warranted comparison to Metternich, Talleyrand or other great foreign ministers of the past. . . . No other Secretary of State in U.S. history has ever carried so much power, so much responsibility or so heavy a burden." This hero worship coincided with growing suspicion of President Nixon on the part of the press and the public. Re-elected by a landslide in November 1972, by early 1974, Nixon faced impeachment for abuse of power and obstruction of justice. An oil embargo of Europe, Japan, and the United States by the oil-producing Arab countries, in protest of Western support for Israel during the October war, doubled the price of gasoline. Nixon encouraged Americans to turn off their lights and set their thermostats at 65 degrees. Dramatizing the need to conserve fuel, he traveled on an ordinary United Airlines flight to Florida during his Christmas holiday. Although in 1973 America produced 75 percent of the oil it needed, Western Europe and Japan depended on the Middle East for over 80 percent of their oil. To prevent their economies from falling into the worst depression since the 1930s, Washington agreed to make up most of their petroleum losses. As a result, the United States had to make do with approximately 80 percent of its average fuel consumption. Unemployment rose by over two percentage points, to 7 percent, in the six months after the embargo; the stock market fell to its lowest level since 1962; and the economy was thrown into a sharp, eleven-month-long recession.

The difficulty caused by the oil embargo came on top of a larger economic problem that persisted for years. Since 1945, the American economy, its exports, and the U.S. dollar had energized world trade. U.S. assistance to and trade with West Germany and Japan had played an especially important role in fostering economic recovery and democratization. As they and other countries produced and exported growing volumes of industrial and consumer goods, this increase in economic activity inevitably cut into the surplus enjoyed by the United States. Although this broad, global, economic expansion was really a positive force in the long run, it meant that in the near term, the U.S. textile, electronics, steel, and automotive industries—along with their workers—lost their comparative advantage and customers. For low-skilled workers, finding replacement jobs proved difficult. By 1971, the United States experienced a balance-of-payments deficit of about $29 billion and its first overall merchandise trade deficit, $2.27 billion, in over a century.

Nixon and some of his economic advisers, such as Treasury Secretary John Connally, blamed the problem chiefly on the Germans and the Japanese who undervalued their own currencies, making their exports to the United States cheap and U.S. exports to them expensive. Connally, whom Nixon considered as a replacement for Vice President Spiro Agnew in 1972, summed up his economic philosophy as "all foreigners are out to screw us and it's our job to screw them first." According to one member of the NSC staff, neither

Kissinger nor Nixon cared much about monetary and trade policy until it became a crisis. Economic planning in the Nixon administration, NSC staff member Roger Morris recalled, "enjoyed equal rank with U.S. policy in Haiti, but less than Peru." Being "economic adviser to Henry Kissinger," another aide recalled, "was like being military adviser to the Pope."

Although the United States lost export markets and ran a trade deficit, it printed more dollars to pay for the Vietnam War without raising taxes. By the early 1970s, the Europeans, the Japanese, and oil-exporting countries were awash with about $25 billion in greenbacks. Since World War II, everyone wanted dollars because they were, literally, as good as gold. The U.S. Treasury would, on request, give any foreign bank or national one ounce of gold for $35.00. Increasingly, foreign banks, companies, and individuals with dollars worried about the value of the paper they held. They knew that the U.S. Treasury had only about $11 billion in gold reserves, far less than needed to cover all obligations, which would cause trouble if everyone tried to redeem their dollars. This situation made foreigners more anxious, and they increased their redemption rate.

By August 1971, the problem had become a crisis. Nixon gathered his closest aides at the presidential retreat at Camp David, where Connally announced, "We're broke—the country can't cover its obligations. Anyone can topple us anytime they want." With the gold reserve "going out by the bushel basket," the president and country would "soon be in the hands of the money changers." On August 15, 1971, without consulting America's allies or trading partners, Nixon addressed the nation to proclaim what he dubbed the New Economic Policy. He closed the gold window, stopping the exchange of dollars for gold, slapped a 10 percent surcharge on imports, and imposed temporary wage and price controls on the domestic economy.

Nixon's actions temporarily halted the run on the dollar. The import surcharge raised the cost of foreign goods, at least for a while. After a few months, the Europeans and the Japanese agreed to "float" the value of their currencies rather than peg them to a formal value. This action had the effect of valuing upward the yen, mark, pound, and other currencies. These moves slowed the growth in the U.S. trade deficit for a year or two. But by the mid-1970s, the U.S. demand for imported oil and manufactured goods resumed. With this resurge in demand came a new economic phenomenon, "stagflation," which was characterized by high rates of inflation, slow economic growth, and high rates of unemployment. Presidents Nixon, Gerald Ford, and Jimmy Carter all failed to reverse this trend, and their lack of success did much to undermine public faith in big government and Keynesian economics.

As public distrust of the Nixon administration mounted during the Watergate scandal, Congress tried to take back from the president some formerly congressional powers in foreign affairs. On November 7, 1973, Congress overrode Nixon's veto of the War Powers Act. This law capped efforts, begun with the 1970 repeal of the Tonkin Gulf Resolution, to reassert congressional influence over foreign affairs and warmaking.

Although no president had asked for a declaration of war since 1941, the United States had used military force often in the postwar era. Presidents from Truman to Nixon had asserted that events moved so quickly in the nuclear age that no time remained to consult with Congress before deploying American forces abroad. But growing public and congressional unhappiness with Johnson's and Nixon's handling of the war in Vietnam rendered lawmakers less amenable to appeals from the executive branch for complete freedom of action. Earlier versions of the War Powers Act had passed either the House or Senate; now, as the Watergate scandal undercut Nixon's political standing, the two houses agreed on a single version. Many critics of American foreign policy, both inside and outside the government, had concluded that it was vital to restrict the power of "the imperial presidency"—a phrase coined to describe the chief executive's tendency to act without regard for constitutional checks and balances.

The law that was finally adopted was the work of New York Republican senator Jacob Javits and Wisconsin Democratic representative Clement Zablocki, chair of the House Committee on Foreign Affairs. Both lawmakers were willing to grant the president wide latitude in setting foreign policy, but they also wanted Congress to play a clearly defined role. The act required that the president consult with Congress "when possible" before sending U.S. troops into combat or into a zone where hostilities were likely. If the president determined that he had to act before telling Congress, the act required him to inform lawmakers within forty-eight hours of dispatching U.S. troops. Congress would then have sixty days to approve the use of troops by a recorded vote and to state a time limit for their continued use. If Congress declined to authorize the president's action, the president would have another thirty days in which to withdraw American forces.

Some critics of the War Powers Act charged that it did not go far enough. One disgruntled legislative aide predicted, "What you'll have now is a Pentagon file full of contingency plans for ninety-day wars." Yet every president since Nixon has resisted the act, considering it to be an unwarranted restriction on the chief executive's foreign policy prerogatives. Despite subsequent complaints from lawmakers who wanted the law strengthened, and from presidents and cabinet secretaries who wanted it abolished, the War Powers Act has helped set the boundaries of the presidential use of force for three decades.

Conclusion

Immediately after Richard Nixon resigned the presidency in disgrace in 1974, analysts looking for something praiseworthy in his administration began focusing on his foreign policy record. The *Christian Science Monitor* voiced a widely held belief that Nixon had turned the country away from the damaging stereotypes of the Cold War, in which Americans saw a Soviet plot behind every world problem. The result was a more flexible and intelligent foreign policy than was ever expected from a visceral anticommunist like Nixon. The newspaper wrote that he had "risked alienating many of his longtime cold war supporters, by opening America's door to the Communist world." The authors believed that his collaboration with Kissinger had re-established White House control over the fractured apparatus of foreign policy. Kissinger's travels to China, the Soviet Union, and the Middle East represented a triumph for U.S. foreign policy, the paper said, and his shuttle diplomacy between the capitals of the Arab states and Israel appeared to lay "the groundwork for the difficult and continuing negotiations for peace" that loomed ahead. In the years following Nixon's departure, other analysts reiterated the view that Nixon conducted foreign policy well, whatever his failings in connection with the Watergate scandal. Indeed, Nixon made skillful use of his foreign policy reputation in his effort to rehabilitate his reputation in the twenty years between his resignation in 1974 and his death in 1994. He frequently wrote and spoke on foreign affairs, traveled widely, and advised his successors on what to do about contemporary issues.

In spite of some real achievements, Nixon and Kissinger failed in their central goal of reordering American foreign policy to create what they proclaimed would be "a generation of peace." They concentrated almost exclusively on issues such as the Vietnam War and relations with the Soviet Union, China, the Middle East, and Chile—all problems left over from earlier periods. They made some progress on each issue, but ten years after Nixon resigned, it seemed that his initiatives had delivered far less than was promised. Nixon and Kissinger failed to appreciate certain dramatic economic and political changes in the international arena, such as the relative decline of the U.S. position in international trade and the rise of Third World nationalism. For example, Kissinger and Nixon ignored increasing friction with Japan over trade. They tried briefly to address economic tensions with the NATO allies in 1973, but then neglected the question when crises in the Middle East intervened. Economic issues bored both Kissinger and Nixon as "low policy," in contrast to the "high policy" of military power and global politics. Nixon and Kissinger also paid little attention to Central America and Africa, where festering poverty and political repression only worsened. The costs of ignoring the Third World and the fate of individuals oppressed by foreign governments would become more apparent later in the 1970s. Nixon and Kissinger fell short even in what they considered their greatest achievements—peace in Vietnam, détente with the Soviets, and a new relationship with China. Many of these apparent successes proved short-lived, breaking down by the election of 1976. The peace agreement in Indochina—for which more than twenty thousand additional American lives had been sacrificed after Nixon took office—collapsed in 1975. The much-heralded détente with the Soviet Union, already weakened by 1974, did not survive the Ford administration. The opening to China widened in the late 1970s, but it was the Carter administration that actually made the greatest progress by resuming formal diplomatic relations with China, which was ironic because Carter was often criticized for being inept at international relations. The high hopes for peace in the Middle East had also diminished by 1974. The Carter administration exceeded Kissinger's efforts by brokering a peace treaty between Israel and Egypt in 1978 and 1979.

Nixon's and Kissinger's methods contributed to both the dazzling promise and the disappointing results of their supposedly innovative foreign policy. By concentrating power in their own hands, they could move quickly, with theatrical flair. Yet their exclusion of foreign affairs professionals and their disregard for congressional opinion came back to haunt them when support and follow-through on various initiatives became necessary. Instead of working with the permanent foreign policy bureaucracy or Congress, Kissinger mocked them. Not surprisingly, they came to resent his high-handedness. As progress toward achieving his most prized foreign policy objectives slowed toward the end of the Nixon years and during the Ford presidency, Kissinger blamed the difficulties on lawmakers, the bureaucracy, the press, an impatient public, the Democrats—almost anyone who opposed or questioned him. For all of its drama and excitement, the diplomacy of the Nixon years represented more the end of the era that began in 1945 than a new beginning for American foreign relations.

F U R T H E R • R E A D I N G

For general accounts of foreign policy in the Nixon administration, see Melvin Small, *The Presidency of Richard Nixon* (1999); Richard Reeves, *President Nixon: Alone in the White House* (2001); William Bundy, *A Tangled Web: The Making of Foreign Policy in the Nixon Presidency* (1998); Allen J. Matusow, *Nixon's Economy: Boom, Busts, Dollars and Votes* (1998); Tad Szulc, *The Illusion of Peace* (1979); Raymond L. Garthoff, *Détente and Confrontation: American-Soviet Relations from Nixon to Reagan* (1994); William G. Hyland, *Mortal Rivals: Superpower Relations from Nixon to Reagan* (1987); Richard Nixon, *RN: The Memoirs of Richard Nixon* (1978) and *In the Arena* (1990); Stephen E. Ambrose, *Nixon* (vols. 2 and 3; 1989, 1991); Herbert Parmet, *Richard Nixon and His America* (1990); Henry Kissinger, *White House Years* (1979), *Years of Upheaval* (1982), and *Diplomacy* (1994); Seymour Hersh, *The Price of Power: Kissinger in the Nixon White House* (1983); Walter Isaacson, *Kissinger: A Biography* (1992); Robert D. Schulzinger, *Henry Kissinger: Doctor of Diplomacy* (1989) and *A Time for War* (1997). **On Nixon and the Vietnam War,** see Daniel Ellsberg, *Secrets: A Memoir of Vietnam and the Pentagon Papers* (2002); David Rudenstine, *The Day the Presses Stopped: A History of the Pentagon Papers Case* (1996); George C. Herring, *America's Longest War* (1986); Arnold Isaacs, *Without Honor: Defeat in Vietnam and Cambodia* (1983); Melvin Small, *Johnson, Nixon and the Doves* (1988); Jeffrey Kimball, *Nixon's Vietnam War* (1998); Nguyen Tien Hung and Jerrold Schechter, *The Palace File* (1986); Marilyn B. Young, *The Vietnam Wars* (1990). **On China and Japan,** see James Mann, *About Face: A History of America's Curious Relationship with China from Nixon to Clinton* (1999); Patrick Tyler, *A Great Wall: Six Presidents and China* (1999); Michael Schaller, *The U.S. and China: Into the 21st Century* (2002) and *Altered States: The U.S. and Japan Since the Occupation* (1997). **On the Middle East and Africa,** see Daniel Yergin, *The Prize* (1991); Steven J. Spiegel, *The Other Arab-Israeli Conflict: Making America's Middle East Policy from Truman to Reagan* (1985);

William Quandt, *Decade of Decision* (1977) and *Peace Process* (1994); Alan Dowty, *Middle East Crisis* (1984); Douglas Little, *American Orientalism: The United States and the Middle East Since 1945* (2002); Thomas Borstelmann, *The Cold War and the Color Line: American Race Relations in the Global Arena* (2001); Gerald Horn, *From the Barrel of a Gun: The United States and the War Against Zimbabwe, 1965–1980* (2001); Andrew DeRoche, *Black, White, and Chrome: The United States and Zimbabwe, 1953–1988* (2001). **On the War Powers Act,** see John Hart Ely, *War and Responsibility: Constitutional Lessons of Vietnam and Its Aftermath* (1994); Harold Hyman, *Quiet Past and Stormy Present? War Powers in American History* (1986); Thomas Franck and Edward Wiesband, *Foreign Policy by Congress* (1979). **On nuclear power,** see Kenneth Bergeron, *Tritium On Ice: The Dangerous New Alliance of Nuclear Weapons and Nuclear Power* (2002); Joan B. Aron, *Licensed To Kill?: The Nuclear Regulatory Commission and the Shoreham Power Plant* (1997); Kenneth McCallion, *Shoreham and the Rise and Fall of the Nuclear Power Industry* (1995); Paul Boyer, *Fallout: A Historian Reflects on America's Half-Century Encounter with Nuclear Weapons* (1988).

The Use and Abuse of Power: Domestic Affairs and the Watergate Scandal, 1969–1974

10

Former White House aide John W. Dean III is sworn in before testifying in front of the Senate Watergate committee, 1973. / © Bettmann/CORBIS

Soon after Richard Nixon's 1968 campaign manager John N. Mitchell became attorney general in 1969, he tried to calm fears that the new administration intended to demolish the Great Society. "Watch what we do, not what we say," he told reporters, implying that the harsh rhetoric voiced by candidate Nixon had been misleading. Nixon and his subordinates might have stressed favorite conservative issues such as halting street crime, cracking down on campus protests, and ending the busing of schoolchildren to achieve racial balance, but in practice, Mitchell seemed to suggest, they would continue an activist government committed to intervening in most areas of American life. On one level, Mitchell proved prophetic: the new administration preserved and even expanded many of the government programs of the 1960s. Nixon and most of his principal advisers accepted the major tenet of the New Deal—that the government had a positive role to play in the economic and social life of the country. Yet Nixon owed his election to public disillusionment with government and to the race-based resentment that intensified after 1964. The Nixon administration's domestic policy both fed these resentments and consolidated the legislation of the Great Society.

Mitchell's comment contained more irony than he realized at the time. Behind the scenes, Nixon administration officials abused their power and threatened the very foundations of American democracy. As Nixon and his subordinates expanded the role of the executive branch, they intimidated critics in the press, on college campuses, and in private research organizations. The administration treated opposition politicians; writers; commentators; and even some actors, athletes, and comedians as personal enemies rather than political opponents. Nixon's obsession with secrecy, his contempt for other officeholders, and his disregard of civil liberties culminated in many violations of the law. During the episode known as Watergate, representatives of Nixon's re-election committee used illegal campaign contributions to finance burglaries and wiretaps against the Democrats. The White House then obstructed investigations of these activities; but dogged reporters, congressional committees, independent prosecutors, and federal judges brought the facts to light. Eventually, Watergate became the gravest constitutional scandal of the twentieth century, and it resulted in Nixon's resignation from the presidency in August 1974.

Recasting the Welfare State

Initially, the Nixon administration seemed to adopt the Eisenhower strategy of consolidating rather than repealing the reforms of its predecessors. During the campaign of 1968, Nixon endorsed the aims of reducing economic inequality, conquering poverty, and ending racial discrimination, but he complained that the Great Society programs of President Johnson had failed to meet these goals. Nixon claimed that the War on Poverty had been lost because of mismanagement by incompetent bureaucrats. He spoke of the principles of better management and of helping the poor and underprivileged help themselves. But in spite of these goals, the overall tendency of the Nixon administration was to de-emphasize social programs and to oppose further efforts at racial equality. The primary social initiatives in the Nixon years came from the other branches of the federal government—Congress and the courts.

Following the philosophy of many conservative thinkers, Nixon wanted to transfer much of the responsibility for social programs from the federal bureaucracy to the states and municipalities. The stated aim was to increase efficiency, make programs more responsive to local interests, and reduce federal interference. Conservatives also hoped that programs already administered at the local level would be eliminated or given a more conservative slant.

To accomplish this shift of responsibility, Nixon successfully sponsored a system of revenue sharing and block grants, a method of government funding that lasted for ten years. Under this system, funds were sliced from federally administered programs to make money available to states and municipalities for use in education, urban development, transportation, job training, rural development, and law enforcement. Few federal guidelines were attached to block grants; the specific spending decisions were to be made at the state and local levels. The program did help states and cities pay for new buildings, parks, police cars, and jails. When times were hard and resources were scarce, however, cities used the revenue-sharing and block-grant funds to meet their daily expenses. Local governments rarely used federal grants to aid the poor directly. To make certain that some funds were applied to job training, Congress passed the Comprehensive Employment and Training Act (CETA) in 1973. This law was designed to educate poor people for jobs. Over the next ten years, about six hundred thousand CETA graduates found work through its training programs.

At the same time that revenue sharing was used to transfer some responsibilities away from the federal government, Nixon created the Urban Affairs Council, a sort of National Security Council of domestic affairs. The Urban Affairs Council was designed to create new programs to be managed directly by the White House rather than by federal agencies, over which Nixon had less control. To head this new council, Nixon chose Daniel Patrick Moynihan, giving him the task of directing domestic policy and bending the bureaucracy to his will. Like Henry Kissinger, his counterpart on the National Security Council, Moynihan had been on the Harvard faculty, off and on, for nearly twenty years; he had also held several subcabinet positions since the Kennedy administration. Author of the controversial 1965 study *The Negro Family: The Case for National Action* (see Chapter 6), Moynihan was convinced that a bleak cycle of poverty kept millions of people in permanent economic bondage. He believed that the only chance to improve conditions for the poorest Americans lay in ending their dependence on welfare payments. This view appealed to Nixon, who believed that a plan that trimmed welfare would both reduce poverty and please a middle class that was increasingly resentful of the poor. Reforming the welfare system presented Nixon with an opportunity to surpass the Great Society while pursuing harsh attacks on "welfare cheats," a theme he had sounded during the 1968 presidential campaign. He promised an end to what he called the "welfare mess." His words struck a responsive chord because 84 percent of the public agreed with a pollster's statement that "there are too many people receiving welfare money who should be working."

By the end of the Johnson administration, even the advocates of the Great Society had become increasingly doubtful that the War on Poverty could be won. More and more children were growing up in poverty in the late 1960s. Inadequate funding of Great Society programs, racism, changes in the nature of work, and the cultural legacy of slavery combined to make the end of poverty an elusive goal. The largest welfare program, known as Aid to Families with Dependent Children (AFDC), had provided welfare assistance since 1935. Many poor people seemed unable to break out of an apparently endless cycle of poverty. Under AFDC, the states established the payment amounts. Eighteen of the poorest states offered less than $31 per month per welfare recipient. In all cases, every dollar earned by a working welfare recipient was deducted from his or her welfare check.

In 1969, Moynihan and the Urban Affairs Council proposed scrapping AFDC and replacing it with a Family Assistance Plan (FAP) designed to end the cycle of dependence on government assistance. Through a "negative income tax," in which poor people would receive money instead of paying taxes, the plan would end welfare by offering each poor head of household approximately $1,600 per year. A crucial distinction between the FAP and AFDC was that aid recipients would have to hold paying jobs. This provision helped deflect conservative criticism that the Nixon administration had turned into a supporter of lavish government assistance to the poor. Privately, Nixon explained to Moynihan, "I don't care a damn about the work requirement. This is the price of getting the $1,600."

The issue of revising the welfare system languished until 1972. Every time the Democrats favored welfare reform, Nixon opposed their efforts because they did too much. Every time Nixon put forward a proposal, Democrats blocked it because it did too little. Nixon told his chief of staff, H. R. Haldeman, that he wanted "to be sure it [FAP] is killed by Democrats. [W]e make a big play for it, but don't let it pass." As a result, nothing directly supplementing the low incomes of the poor became law. Welfare then became a focal point in the 1972 presidential campaign.

A few weeks before the 1972 presidential election, Congress finally passed a new welfare-reform bill, without providing a guaranteed income for poor families with children. It did, however, include a new program, Supplemental Security Income, that provided a guaranteed income for the elderly—many of whom were not poor—and for the blind and disabled of all ages. At the same time, Congress authorized automatic cost-of-living increases, tied to the consumer price index, for all Social Security recipients. Such payments went to rich and poor alike. Over the next twenty years, the annual cost-of-living adjustments to Social Security proved to be an enormously popular entitlement, one that substantially reduced poverty among the elderly. But the attempt to find a better system for helping poor people under the age of sixty-five went no further during the Nixon administration.

The government made more substantial progress in creating standards for environmental protection. A broad popular movement to protect and improve the natural environment grew in the late 1960s. Over 1 million people belonged to environmental groups advocating clean air and water and the protection of endangered species and open spaces. Fewer than 125,000 people had belonged to such groups a decade earlier. Public opinion polls indicated that a majority supported the goals. Books warning of impending environmental disasters flew off the shelves. Paul Ehrlich's *The Population Bomb*, published in 1968, sold over 3 million copies. Ehrlich warned that hundreds of millions of people would die throughout the world over the next twenty years if population growth were not restricted. Barry Commoner, a professor of biology at Washington University in St. Louis, warned of various environmental catastrophes ranging from air and water pollution to nuclear annihilation. *Time* magazine put Commoner's picture on the cover and called him "the Paul Revere of ecology." In February 1970, *Time* predicted that environmental protection "may well be the gut issue that can unify a polarized nation." On April 22, 1970, millions of people rallied across the country on the first Earth Day, showing their support for environmental causes. About ten thousand people held a festival at the Washington Monument, where they sang and danced for twelve hours in praise of the Earth. Soon after, Congress created the Environmental Protection Agency (EPA), empowering it to investigate and curtail practices destructive to the environment.

During the 1970s, the EPA brought hundreds of suits against industrial polluters of the nation's water and air. For new construction involving federal funds, the agency required environmental impact studies that clearly delineated the project's effects on traffic congestion, pollution, housing, wildlife, and a host of other concerns. The EPA set fuel-efficiency standards for cars and required manufacturers to reduce carbon monoxide emissions from automobile engines. In studies on the effects of electrical power plants on the atmosphere, the EPA determined that the burning of high-sulfur coal had created "acid rain" in the northeastern United States and neighboring Canada, harming that region's forests and fisheries. Although such reports alerted the public to environmental dangers, they also contributed to a growing sense that some problems exceeded the government's capacity to provide solutions.

Although Nixon signed the act creating the EPA, he had little use for environmentalists. He once told the secretary of the interior to "stop brown-nosing environmentalists" who pressed for more stringent safeguards on the oil pipeline under construction in Alaska. He once told his staff, "I am so sick of the goddamn environment I could die." On a more practical level, he tried to limit the amount of money that the federal government spent on environmental regulation. In 1970, to appropriate about $7 billion to clean the nation's air and water, Congress had to override the president's veto. Nixon then impounded (refused to spend) about $1 billion of the money. By 1973, concerned about excessive federal spending, Nixon had impounded about $15 billion, affecting over one hundred government programs for cleaning the environment.

Even the usually compliant Justice Department thought the president had gone too far. Assistant Attorney General William Rehnquist wrote that there was no constitutional provision justifying "a refusal by the president to comply with a congressional directive to spend." Democratic senator Sam Ervin of North Carolina, chair of the Senate Judiciary Committee's Subcommittee on Separation of Powers, held hearings on impoundment in 1971. At one point, Ervin declared that the president "has no authority under the Constitution to decide which laws will be executed or to what extent they will be enforced." Legal experts agreed, but various White House officials claimed that such congressional interference would prevent the president from doing his job. White House officials argued that the negative economic effects of a budget deficit outweighed the benefits of a cleaner environment, and Nixon continued the process of impoundment. Disagreements between the president and Congress over impoundment helped set the stage for their far larger confrontation—over the use and abuse of presidential power—that grew out of the Watergate scandal.

During the Nixon years, Congress also created the Consumer Products Safety Commission (CPSC) and the Occupational Safety and Health Administration (OSHA). Both agencies were supposed to make daily life safer and healthier. The CPSC investigated the safety of a wide variety of common household items, from televisions to kitchen appliances. It imposed rules for baby products that were highly popular with parents, but industry leaders objected to the added costs of meeting the new standards. At one point, the CPSC ruled that children's pajamas treated with Tris, a highly flammable substance, should be removed from the market. Relieved parents applauded the decision, but the manufacturer, stuck with unsold merchandise worth millions of dollars, complained that unsympathetic Washington bureaucrats had ruined the company's ability to compete. The pajamas were eventually sold in South America.

OSHA required that work sites be safe for employees and that businesses submit to unannounced inspections to ensure that safety codes were being followed. Unions and most working people believed OSHA reduced job-related accidents and saved lives. Businesses, however, found OSHA's inspectors meddlesome and imperious. Many economists and conservative commentators shared this view. Advocates of deregulation, who argued that the economy would function better if government regulations were removed, turned some of their strongest scorn on OSHA. They claimed that the government-imposed rules, regulations, and health and safety standards raised the cost of American-made products. In an era in which imports of less-expensive manufactured goods cut into the markets for American-made items, these complaints against government regulations of the workplace began to appeal to some voters.

The environmental and consumer protection agencies created in the early 1970s reflected the public concerns of the time. The Nixon administration enforced these laws, although with less enthusiasm than the laws' sponsors in the Democratic-controlled Congress. Nixon harbored grave doubts about consumer protection. "It's all crap," he told the staff of his consumer affairs office when they inquired which government department should handle consumer product safety.

Overall, the government did more to address environmental and safety concerns in the early 1970s than at any time in the next twenty years. Nevertheless, Nixon's reluctance to administer congressionally mandated environmental regulations contributed to a growing atmosphere of suspicion in Washington. Already under fire for prolonging the Vietnam War, Nixon drew little sympathy from the liberal and moderate Democrats who dominated Congress. The fight between the president and Congress over impoundment heightened the sense, on both sides, that the other branch of government could not be trusted. As economic difficulties mounted, some people began to worry about whether environmental protection came with too high a price tag. Bumper stickers reading "If you're hungry and out of work, eat an environmentalist" began appearing on cars.

The Nixon administration tried but failed to help significantly the poorest Americans, and it energetically opposed further progress on civil rights for African Americans. At first, administration officials were divided in their attitude toward civil rights. Some officials favored further advances for African Americans, but Nixon stopped them. He told his aide John Ehrlichman, "I want you personally to jump" on officials who pushed for desegregation. "Tell them to *Knock off this Crap.* I hold them accountable to keep their left-wingers in step with my express policy—Do what the law requires and not *one bit more.*" The Justice Department tried to limit the effects of the very law it was charged to enforce: the Civil Rights Act of 1964. Leon Panetta, head of the Justice Department's Office of Civil Rights, did try to enforce the law, but he was fired. Before he changed parties and won election to Congress as a Democrat, Panetta complained of "a massive retreat on civil rights" by Nixon.

In fact, the Nixon approach to civil rights came to be governed more and more by the so-called southern strategy—an attempt to woo traditionally Democratic white southern voters by appealing to their racial prejudice toward African Americans. In an unguarded moment caught on videotape during the 1968 presidential campaign, Nixon explained why he believed white Democrats would support him: "It's all about law and order and the damn Negro-Puerto Rican groups out there." Some of the Nixon administration's efforts on behalf of desegregation were designed to stir up white resentment against African Americans. One of Nixon's aides told him that it would be the "miracle of the age" if the administration could "push desegregation on the South in such a way that made sure that the courts and the Democrats," not southern republicans or the Nixon administration "received the blame."

The southern strategy was formulated by Kevin Phillips in *The Emerging Republican Majority* (1969). Phillips observed that the substantial number of people who had voted for George Wallace in the 1968 presidential election were "in motion between a Democratic past and a Republican future." Phillips actually encouraged federal promotion of African American voting rights in the South. He expected newly enfranchised blacks to vote Democratic, thereby driving more and more white southerners out of the Democratic Party and into the Republican Party. Attorney General John Mitchell, one of Nixon's key political advisers, favored the southern strategy. To appeal to southern white voters, the administration would emphasize themes such as law and order and resist further advances in civil rights.

While the Nixon administration resisted further progress on civil rights for people of color, the government responded to the activism of a revitalized women's movement (see pages 304–313). Congress passed the Equal Rights Amendment (ERA) to the Constitution and submitted it to the states in early 1972. The ERA was soon ratified by thirty-five of the thirty-eight states necessary for it to take effect. Though the ERA eventually fell short of adoption, the widespread activism of its supporters helped to focus attention on women's issues.

Along with abortion and busing, crime and drug use became major issues in the Nixon years. The Nixon administration inflamed public fears that the widespread use of drugs, especially heroin, had created a major crime wave. But the administration had no solutions to match its rhetoric.

During the 1968 campaign, Nixon had blamed the "permissiveness" of Johnson's attorney general, Ramsey Clark, for the rise in street crime. Nixon soon realized, however, that the federal government had little direct enforcement power to combat crime in the streets. Faced with a local problem that the federal government could do little to remedy, the Nixon administration tried several tactics: it tried to shift blame for drug use and crime onto its opponents; it manipulated statistics to magnify both the original problem and the effect of its own remedies; and, finally, it engaged in drug raids that disregarded the civil liberties of the accused and possibly violated the Constitution as well.

In 1969 and 1970, the administration proposed several highly repressive anticrime statutes, which it expected would fail in Congress. "The administration's position in the crime field depends on our ability to shift blame for crime bill inaction to Congress," read one White House memorandum. Much to the administration's surprise, however, the Democratic majority in Congress, not wishing to appear "soft" on crime, passed Nixon's crime package in 1970. The new laws increased sentences for federal crimes, allowed federal marshals to hold suspects for longer periods without pressing charges or setting bond, and enhanced federal officers' ability to tap telephones.

Although the federal government did not have the power to control ordinary street crime, it did have jurisdiction over the illegal sale of narcotics. By concentrating on drug crimes, the Nixon administration expected to generate popular support without having to address the sorts of crimes that had engendered public fear to begin with. Officials played with numbers to make it appear that drug use and crime had recently grown tenfold. In 1971, Nixon announced that the number of heroin addicts in the United States had soared from 69,000 in 1969 to 315,000 in 1970 and to 559,000 in 1971. In fact, the number of addicts had not changed much in those years; the Bureau of Narcotics and Dangerous Drugs had simply reworked old statistics. The administration also inflated, by about twenty-five times, the statistics on the value of property stolen by heroin addicts.

Armed with these inflated statistics about a heroin-induced crime wave, the Nixon administration declared a war on drugs. In early 1972, Nixon created the Office for Drug Abuse and Law Enforcement (ODALE), a secret police force outside the control of the FBI or CIA. ODALE recruited G. Gordon Liddy, a former FBI agent and the planner of the break-in at Daniel Ellsberg's psychiatrist's office, to organize raids on suspected drug dealers. Over the next year, ODALE agents conducted midnight raids without search warrants. They kicked in doors, grabbed people from their beds, pointed guns at their heads, and threatened them with death unless they revealed the whereabouts of drugs. If they determined that they had gone to the wrong address, the agents simply said that they had made a mistake and left.

Although the administration produced additional misleading statistics to indicate that progress had been made, the war on crime and drugs actually had a negligible impact on heroin use and street crime. The crusade did enhance Nixon's political position among middle-class Americans concerned about crime, and it put his Democratic opponents on the defensive. But most significantly, the actions of Liddy and ODALE set the stage for the Watergate scandal by establishing a precedent for how far the administration would go to bend or break the law to serve its own purposes.

The Burger Court

A major element of Nixon's appeal to southerners, whites, and conservatives during the 1968 campaign was his promise to reverse the direction taken by the Supreme Court under Chief Justice Earl Warren. He promised to appoint conservative justices that would revise the Warren Court's decisions expanding civil rights for racial minorities, civil liberties for individuals, and legal rights for criminal defendants. Nixon appointed a new chief justice, Warren Burger, and three new associate justices, Harry Blackmun, Lewis Powell, and William Rehnquist. But the new members, together with the holdovers from the Warren era, surprised both their supporters and their detractors. Instead of reversing the Warren Court's emphasis on enlarging the rights of individuals and curtailing the powers of government officials, the Court in the early 1970s consolidated the Warren Court's decisions.

For example, the Court concluded that discriminatory effects as well as intention had been outlawed by the Civil Rights Act of 1964. In *Griggs v. Duke Power and Light Co.* (1971), Burger spoke for a unanimous Court in ruling that the 1964 Civil Rights Act prohibited an employer from requiring high school diplomas or intelligence tests for job applicants if the results would be racially discriminatory. The Court reasoned that the tests and the diploma requirements had no bearing on the job to be performed. Later, in *Washington v. Davis* (1976), the Court upheld the legality of a verbal test given to applicants to the District of Columbia's police force because the questions did relate directly to

Chief Justice Warren E. Burger (1969–1986) took the Supreme Court in a more conservative direction from that of his predecessor, Earl Warren. / © Owen Franken/CORBIS

the work performed. A relevant test was permissible, even if it kept most black applicants off the capital's police force.

By far the most controversial civil rights issue to reach the Court during the Nixon years was the use of busing to achieve racial desegregation. In two important cases, *Swann* v. *Charlotte-Mecklenburg Board of Education* (1971) and *Keyes* v. *Denver School District No. 1* (1973), the Supreme Court elaborated on lower courts' rulings regarding busing. In the former case, the Court turned its attention from rural southern school districts, where students of both races lived close together, to urban schools, where only busing could achieve integration. The Court upheld a desegregation plan mandating substantial cross-town busing in a southern city. In the *Keyes* case, the justices extended busing to a northern district where legal segregation had never existed, but where the school board had divided the district along racial lines.

Both the Court and the local officials who implemented busing plans were subjected to heavy abuse from white parents. In many locations, the protests turned violent. In Lamar, South Carolina, an angry white mob attacked school buses carrying black students. Other mobs firebombed buses in Denver, Colorado, and Pontiac, Michigan. Irate whites in South Boston cursed and beat blacks who attended classes with whites under court order. Congress responded to the public anger with legislation proclaiming a moratorium on court orders attempting to achieve "a balance among students with respect to race, sex, religion, or socioeconomic status."

The Supreme Court, however, thought Congress was sidestepping the issue. If Congress had wanted to end busing, Justice Lewis Powell ruled in *Drummond* v. *Acree* (1972), "it could have used clear and explicit language appropriate to that end." In 1974, Congress did pass legislation (submitted by the Nixon administration) stipulating that busing could be used only as a last resort. But it left this determination to the courts as part of their duty to guarantee equal protection to all citizens. In the late 1970s, Congress took a further half-step by forbidding the use of federal funds to buy or maintain buses used for school desegregation.

The Nixon administration appealed to white conservatives by denouncing the 1968 Supreme Court decision in *Green* v. *Board of Education*. In this case, the Court ruled that the southern use of "freedom of choice" plans that allowed parents to select any public school within their district failed to guarantee racial balance and therefore violated the Court's earlier decision, in *Brown v. Board of Education* (1954), prohibiting segregated schools. Nixon declared that "the Court was right on *Brown* and wrong on *Green*," and administration officials tried to block implementation of the *Green* decision.

In August 1969, under heavy pressure from the White House, the Department of Health, Education and Welfare (HEW) petitioned the Fifth District Court for a three-month delay in the desegregation of twenty-three Mississippi school districts. This was the first time since 1954 that the federal government had intervened to slow the pace of desegregation. HEW's action shocked lawyers in Panetta's Office of Civil Rights. They refused to defend the administration's position and secretly supplied information to the NAACP's Legal Defense Fund.

The Legal Defense Fund appealed to the Supreme Court to reverse the delay. In a unanimous decision in *Alexander v. Holmes County Board of Education* (1969), the Court ordered that "the obligation of every school district is to terminate the dual school systems at once." The Fifth District Court responded with 166 desegregation orders over the next ten months. Legally mandated segregation ended in the South in the subsequent two years. By 1971, 44 percent of black children in the South attended schools where white students constituted a majority. In the North and West, by comparison, only 28 percent of black schoolchildren studied in schools with a majority of white students.

The Supreme Court's support for busing helped the cause of school desegregation overall, but it also contributed to a decline in middle-class white trust in public schools. Many white parents in urban districts facing court-ordered desegregation either placed their children in private schools or fled to the suburbs. Over the next decade, as this so-called white flight undermined support for public education, proposed tax increases for schools were defeated by voters. By stimulating the white exodus, the busing conflict also hastened the transformation of northern and midwestern urban centers into predominantly poor, black, and Hispanic areas. The lesser the stake that the white middle class had in the fate of the cities, the less support it gave to government programs to revitalize urban life. By reinforcing this trend with its decisions on busing, the Supreme Court unintentionally spurred an ongoing crisis in the nation's cities.

The 1970s produced an atmosphere of increased awareness of discrimination against women. The Burger Court rendered several decisions prohibiting discrimination on the basis of gender, an issue that was largely ignored by the generally more liberal Warren Court. Although they were pleased by these decisions, advocates of women's rights were worried by the Court's reasoning. Instead of finding a constitutional right to equality, the justices relied on portions of the 1964 Civil Rights Act and the 1973 Equal Pay Act to whittle away at gender-based discrimination. In *Reed v. Reed* (1971), for example, the Court invalidated an Idaho law that gave preference to men over similarly situated women as administrators of estates. The Court held that legislation differentiating between the sexes "must be reasonable, not arbitrary." The same year, the Court ruled in *Phillips* v. *Martin Marietta* that Title VII of the Civil Rights Act forbade corporate hiring practices that discriminate against mothers with small children. In *Frontiero* v. *Richardson*, (1973) the Court applied Title VII to the military, requiring the armed services to provide the same fringe benefits and pensions to women that they provide to men.

The Court went beyond issues of equal pay and job rights when it overturned all state laws restricting abortion in *Roe* v. *Wade* (1973). Feminists and civil liberties lawyers had challenged a Texas law that made any abortion a felony. The test case involved a poor, single woman who believed that she could not afford to raise a child. Justice Harry Blackmun, writing for a seven-member majority, opened a new era in reproductive law by ruling that the right of privacy established by *Griswold* v. *Connecticut* (1965) was "broad enough to encompass a woman's decision whether or not to terminate her pregnancy." Blackmun sought to balance the state's interest in the fetus with the mother's right to privacy. Therefore, the decision declared an absolute right to abortion during the first trimester of a pregnancy, when experts agreed that the fetus was not "viable"—that is, when it cannot live outside the mother's body. During the second trimester, when a fetus might possibly survive outside the womb, states could regulate, but not outlaw, abortions. Only for the last thirteen weeks of pregnancy, according to the *Roe* decision, could state laws prohibit abortion.

The *Roe* decision, along with the earlier *Griswold* decision, reversed a century of government opposition to contraception. The decision responded to a widespread public desire to make safe abortions available. Until then, many pregnant women had been forced to resort to unsafe, "back-alley" abortions. Others had turned to the so-called abortion underground, found in most cities and on many college campuses, through which they could receive information about abortion and access to safe practitioners. *Roe* changed all this by making abortion readily available, and many women soon took for granted their right to a safe, legal abortion.

However, the *Roe* decision produced more public dissent than any other Court ruling since *Brown* v. *Board of Education* struck down school segregation in 1954. The justices who wrote the *Roe* opinion, and the women's rights advocates who supported it, probably underestimated the anger it would cause. Since 1869, Catholic doctrine has held that life begins at the moment of conception; thus, many Catholics and other traditionalists assailed *Roe* as judicial sanction of murder. Over the next two decades following *Roe*, opposition to the decision became an even greater rallying point for conservatives than did the Warren Court's protection of the rights of criminal suspects.

Economic Stagnation

The behavior of the U.S. economy in the early 1970s defied the expectations of nearly all conventional economists. The perplexing economic conditions led the Nixon administration to pursue unexpected policies. Prior to that time, prices had remained steady or fallen in slow times and risen only in boom periods. But in the Nixon years, the United States experienced both inflation and slow or stagnant growth. When Nixon confronted this so-called stagflation, he abandoned long-standing conservative economic philosophy. He adopted some policies, advocated by political rivals, that he had once derided. The sudden shifts in economic policy dismayed supporters who had taken Nixon for a conventional conservative, but the changes paid political dividends.

The economy did not behave the way the rules predicted. Inflation, the scourge of the Great Society, stubbornly hovered at around 6 percent. Still worse, unemployment rose steadily, from 3.8 percent in 1968 to over 6 percent in 1971. According to orthodox economic theories, prices should decline, or at least not rise, when workers lose their jobs. In later years, economists identified some of the reasons for the stagflation: the baby boomers, representing a large population bulge, had begun to reach maturity and were thus spending more money on consumer goods; an increased proportion of entry-level workers in the work force led to a slowdown in worker productivity; the United States faced increased competition from the revived economies of Japan and Germany; and the Vietnam War had an inflationary effect on the economy. But even if economists and government officials had seen these problems clearly at the time, they could have done little about them. The causes of stagflation ran so deep, both inside and outside the United States, that government officials were limited in their ability to fine-tune the economy.

Because the experts could not explain why the economy had not followed the conventional patterns, the president decided it was time to pay less attention to the experts. In December 1970, Nixon shook up the management of economic policy by appointing John Connally, former Democratic governor of Texas, as secretary of the treasury. Connally had valuable political connections among conservative Democrats, but he had no background in economic theory. Nixon was so impressed with Connally's political skills that the president wanted Connally to be his successor, perhaps as the head of a new party made up of conservative Democrats and most Republicans.

Nixon faced more immediate problems, though, as he looked for ways out

President Nixon appointed John Connally, a conservative Texas Democrat, to serve as secretary of the treasury in 1971. Connally later joined the Republican Party, a move that signaled a political realignment in the South. / © CORBIS

of the doldrums of stagflation before the 1972 election. He acknowledged that government wage and price controls might be necessary. Early in 1971, he had told an interviewer, "I am now a Keynesian in economics." One reporter likened Nixon's embrace of Keynes, long thought to be the economist most favored by liberal Democrats, to "a Christian crusader saying 'All things considered, I think Mohammed was right.'"

Having acknowledged that it was appropriate to impose wage and price controls, Nixon had to decide when to act. Economic news worsened throughout 1971. Foreign expenditures by the government (mostly for the maintenance of hundreds of overseas military bases) and those of private citizens meant that the number of dollars going overseas exceeded the value of foreign currency coming into the United States. Such an economic situation is known as a balance of payments deficit. Since the Kennedy administration, experts had been warning that the United States could not afford to keep forever its promise to redeem its currency in gold and that a sudden rejection of dollars by overseas holders could upset the world's trading system. After a further slide in U.S. exports in mid-1971, international investors began worrying about the dollar's strength. Many bought West German marks instead of dollars. In August 1971, the Bank of England, previously supportive of U.S. economic policy, demanded that its holdings in American dollars be redeemed in gold.

Undersecretary of the Treasury Paul Volcker decided that "the jig was definitely up" when he heard the news from London. He telephoned Connally on Friday afternoon, August 13, 1971, with the grim warning that "a major crisis [was] developing in the world's monetary exchange system." Over the weekend, economic advisers huddled with the president at Camp David to devise a series of steps to save the dollar and halt inflation. Nixon, the recently converted Keynesian, was also a lifelong political animal, and he believed that wage and price controls would stop inflation before the 1972 election. His advisers agreed that wage and price controls, in conjunction with a plan to stop the international flight from the dollar, could work.

On Sunday evening, August 15, exactly one month after Nixon's startling announcement that Henry Kissinger had just returned from China, the president presented a program he called the New Economic Policy. He proclaimed a ninety-day freeze on wages and prices. Thereafter, a government wage and price commission would monitor price increases and employee contracts, rescinding excessive increases. Nixon also announced that the United States would no longer convert its currency into gold. However, he added that American citizens, who had not been able to own the yellow metal since an earlier currency reform during the New Deal, were now free to buy and sell it at the market price. Over the next year, the United States and the major trading nations ended the system, created in 1944, of fixed exchange rates among the world's currencies. By 1972, the value of currencies "floated;" that is, they were determined daily in currency exchange markets around the world.

The New Economic Policy tried to slow the escalating balance of payments deficit with a temporary 10 percent surtax on imports. Nixon also cut social spending by $4.7 billion and reduced business taxes. Coming on the heels of Kissinger's trip to China, the New Economic Policy seemed another example of pragmatic action by an administration willing to break with orthodoxy. In a Gallup poll taken a week after the speech, 73 percent of respondents approved of the new policy.

Although Nixon's policy resulted in some limited economic improvement, nothing could halt inflation after the 1973 Arab-Israeli war and the subsequent oil embargo by Arab oil producers. The price of oil rose 400 percent, and the effects of that increase caused other prices to rise sharply throughout the industrialized world. American prices rose by more than 7 percent in 1974 and 1975.

The most far-reaching consequence of the actions taken in August 1971 involved the disruption of the link between U.S. currency and gold. The United States gained in the short term because overseas banks and businesses used their dollars that were no longer backed by gold to invest in U.S. government securities. Over the long term, however, floating the dollar hastened a serious decline in American manufacturing. Investment in new plants and research in new products slowed in the 1970s and 1980s. Such investments do not pay dividends quickly, and the flexible exchange rate made it more difficult for businesses to predict the return on merchandise they planned to sell overseas.

Companies increasingly shifted their assets to predictable, often nonproductive investments that would turn a quick profit. By the end of the decade, the return on nonproductive investments like land, commodities, gold, silver, jewels, and art soared. The value of some farmland in the United States increased 500 percent, without a similar rise in the value of crops. Banks preferred to lend money for the purchase of tangibles and land rather than for investing in rebuilding factories or developing new products. Investors shied away from the stock market in the late 1970s, fearing it would not offer a profitable return in the future. This switch sapped companies' ability to raise the capital necessary to modernize American manufacturing in the late 1970s.

The New Economic Policy demonstrated both the potential and the limits of Nixon's nonideological, flexible approach to economic management at a time of rapid change. By endorsing Keynesian techniques for reducing inflation and fostering growth, Nixon followed the practices of his predecessors since World War II. Yet fine-tuning the economy proved far more difficult than sponsors had hoped. The long-term ineffectiveness of wage and price controls contributed to a growing sense that government did not work.

The Election of 1972

With the American economy in the doldrums, Democrats originally had high hopes for the 1972 election. Nixon's southern strategy had failed during the 1970 congressional election, with only one southern Democratic seat falling to a Republican candidate. On the eve of Election Day, Edmund Muskie, the Democratic vice-presidential candidate in 1968, had persuasively attacked Nixon's "politics of fear" in a televised address. In 1971, Muskie emerged as the favorite for the Democratic presidential nomination. With his rugged good looks and moderate views, Muskie appeared able to unite the Democrats. Early opinion polls showed him tied with Nixon at 42 percent.

Alarmed by Muskie's popularity rating, functionaries of Nixon's Committee to Re-elect the President (CREEP) made plans to discredit him, hoping to force the Democrats to nominate the weakest possible candidate. During the crucial New Hampshire primary campaign in early 1972, Donald Segretti, a CREEP specialist, forged a letter and sent it to William Loeb, the vitriolic editor of the Manchester, New Hampshire, *Union-Leader*. The letter accused Muskie of laughing at an ethnic slur against French Canadians, a major voting bloc among New Hampshire Democrats. Loeb printed the letter and also blasted Muskie and his wife on the front page. Outraged, the senator stood on a truck in front of the newspaper office and assailed Loeb as a "gutless coward." Muskie appeared to choke back tears as he defended his wife, and immediately the contrast between him, tearful and wounded, and Nixon, the strong world leader seen on TV that very week at the Great Wall of China, diminished his appeal. Muskie won the primary, but his margin over the runner-up, Senator George McGovern of South Dakota, was smaller than expected. Muskie's moderate, centrist opinions, which would have given him wide appeal in the general election, did not excite primary voters, and he dropped out of the race within weeks.

The McGovern campaign now took off. Unlike Muskie, McGovern had clearly articulated views demonstrating a belief in political liberalism. He expressed support for Great Society social programs; opposition to the war in Vietnam; and sympathy for the aspirations of young people, women, protesters, and other previously excluded groups. Opposition to the war in Vietnam united an army of fervent McGovern volunteers. Activists supporting McGovern opposed the Nixon administration's hostility to civil rights and its resistance to expanding the domestic welfare legislation of the Great Society. Over the next four months, McGovern won a string of primaries in a crowded Democratic race, giving him close to a majority of delegates.

McGovern's most prominent rivals during this time were George Wallace and Hubert Humphrey. Wallace won the Florida primary with white-hot rhetoric. He attacked Nixon as "a double-dealer, a two-timer, and a man who tells folks one thing and does another." Crowds roared when he complained about busing imposed by "anthropologists, zoologists, and sociologists." He did not know which was worse: the "judges who had just about ruined this country," hypocritical politicians who sent their children to private schools, or the "briefcase-totin' bureaucrats. . . . Yale Ph.D.'s who can't tie their shoelaces. . . . Hypocrites [who] if you opened all their briefcases, you'll find nothing in them but a peanut butter sandwich." But Wallace's political momentum ended abruptly in May when a gunman's bullet wounded him, leaving him paralyzed from the waist down.

By June 1972, Hubert Humphrey was the sole champion of the Anybody but McGovern coalition, an alignment of Democratic officeholders and labor union officials who feared that the South Dakota senator was too liberal and too much the representative of outsiders to win the general election. Assailing McGovern's liberal positions, Humphrey closed a wide gap to trail by only five percentage points in the June California primary.

By July, when the Democrats assembled in Miami for their national convention, McGovern's nomination depended on the interpretation of rules drafted in the aftermath of the chaotic 1968 convention. The new rules had resulted from complaints that Humphrey won the 1968 nomination because political bosses had controlled delegate selection in states that had not held primaries.

At the 1972 convention, Democrats decided on a strict interpretation of the new rules. On the first night of the convention, Chicago mayor Richard J. Daley and fifty-eight of his handpicked delegates from Cook County were booted off the convention floor for violating the guidelines, which stipulated that representatives should be selected in keeping with the racial, gender, and ethnic make-up of a district. A new group of delegates, which included more women and blacks but fewer old-time politicians or representatives from white ethnic groups, took the Daley delegation's place. Even McGovern's press secretary, Frank Mankiewicz, was startled. "I think we may have lost Illinois tonight," he grumbled.

The Democrats' endorsement of pluralism brought thousands of representatives of previously excluded groups into the party's decisionmaking process. The delegates at the 1972 convention were 38 percent female (in comparison to 13 percent in 1968), 23 percent were under the age of thirty (2.3 percent in 1968), and 15 percent were black (5.5 percent in 1968). If the groups they represented voted in November, McGovern could win through the strength of an electorate that was younger, poorer, and more racially diverse than usual. But if members of traditionally excluded groups stayed away from the polls, as they had in 1968, he would lose because he had alienated the old base of the Democratic Party—the South, labor, Catholics, the white working class, and white ethnics.

The electoral reforms hurt the men who had run the Democratic Party for decades. For instance, only eighteen of the 255 Democratic members of the House of Representatives came to Miami as delegates, whereas customarily more than half attended the convention in that capacity. No group seemed more old-fashioned and out of place than the leaders of organized labor. AFL-CIO president George Meany had led the Anybody but McGovern campaign. An old Cold Warrior, Meany found McGovern's opposition to the war in Vietnam absurd. Like most working-class men of his generation, Meany also decried the lifestyle of many McGovern supporters, blaming the senator for seeming to tolerate the open sexuality and drug experimentation of the young. Meany denied McGovern the AFL-CIO's endorsement; it was the first time organized labor had not supported the Democratic presidential nominee.

McGovern's chances declined further when he chose his vice-presidential running mate. Having given little thought to the vice presidency before the convention, McGovern selected Missouri senator Thomas Eagleton, hoping that the senator's Catholicism and moderate views would appeal to traditional

Senator George McGovern (*center*), the 1972 Democratic Party's candidate for president, is greeted at the Little Rock, Arkansas, airport by Bill Clinton (*left*), then a twenty-five-year-old campaign aide. / AP/Wide World

Democrats who were uncomfortable with the antiwar youth backing McGovern. The day after the nomination, news surfaced that Eagleton had been hospitalized three times in the 1960s for depression and exhaustion. Although perhaps 10 to 25 percent of all Americans suffer from some form of depression at one time or another, psychological or emotional dysfunction carried a much more substantial stigma in the 1970s than it does now. Initially, McGovern decided not to cater to what he considered prejudice. He said that he was "1,000 percent for Tom Eagleton" and that he did not intend to drop him from the ticket. But Eagleton then admitted that he had received electroshock therapy while he was hospitalized and that he still took medication to treat his depression. Pressure from editorialists and his campaign staff convinced McGovern to drop Eagleton. Coming so soon after his "1,000 percent" endorsement of Eagleton, McGovern's abrupt reversal made him look unpredictable, weak, and possibly foolish. The process of finding a replacement became a fiasco. After seven prominent Democratic politicians refused to run, McGovern finally selected Sargent Shriver, the Kennedy relative who had formerly directed the Peace Corps and the Office of Economic Opportunity.

In November, Nixon won a massive landslide in which he gained 61 percent of the popular vote and carried 49 states (see Map 10.1). Only Massachusetts and the District of Columbia went to McGovern. Several social and political issues contributed to the size of Nixon's victory. McGovern's support from antiwar activists and political newcomers had alarmed traditional voters. Eighteen- to twenty-year-olds, allowed to vote for the first time under the terms of the Twenty-sixth Amendment (adopted in 1971), turned out in fewer numbers than any other group, and half of them voted for Nixon after he promised that he would end the draft in 1973. White working-class Democrats deserted McGovern in droves. One long-time Democrat explained why he voted for Nixon over McGovern: "Every time he opened his [McGovern's] mouth, it came out irresponsible. Starting with the Eagleton affair. I just felt that this was a man who was not sure. So I voted for Nixon with no enthusiasm." Fifty-five percent of blue-collar workers voted for Nixon, as opposed to 34 percent in 1968. Fifty-three percent of Catholics voted for Nixon in 1972; 34 percent had voted for him in 1968. The southern strategy finally worked: three-quarters of those who voted for Wallace in 1968 supported Nixon in 1972.

Meanwhile, the New Economic Policy had tamed inflation, and unemployment had leveled off. Nixon's celebrated visits to Beijing and Moscow gave him and Kissinger the aura of successful statesmen. McGovern's opposition to the war in Vietnam faded as an issue with the public in the last two weeks of

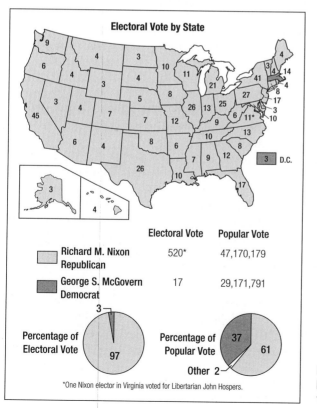

Map 10.1
Presidential Election of 1972

the campaign, when Kissinger announced (without much basis in fact) that "peace is at hand."

Watergate and the Abuse of Power

Unknown to nearly everyone but a handful of trusted CREEP operatives and White House officials, an astonishing abuse of governmental power had begun as early as 1969. Ever since he had gone to Washington as a new congressman, in 1947, Nixon had considered himself a victim, and he believed that he was never given proper respect by his political adversaries. Even the praise heaped on his foreign policy initiatives did not eliminate his feeling that he and his administration were embattled. He believed that Democrats wishing him ill occupied most of the permanent positions in the federal government. He complained bitterly about "sons-of-bitches that kick us in the ass." Feeling isolated and victimized, and taking little satisfaction in good news, Nixon lashed out at those he considered his domestic enemies. During his first term in office, he set in motion a series of events that represented serious illegal and unconstitutional abuses of presidential power. The scope of the illegalities was unprecedented, ranging from unfair campaign practices—sometimes trivialized by Republicans as "dirty tricks"—to using the Internal Revenue Service (IRS) to harass opponents, engaging in domestic espionage, and obstructing investigations into these actions by law enforcement agencies.

During the 1972 presidential campaign, George McGovern charged that Nixon ran the "most corrupt administration in history." The Democratic nominee tried but failed to arouse public interest in a curious incident: a break-in at the Democratic National Committee headquarters located in the Watergate office complex in Washington, D.C., on the night of June 17, 1972. As the public would later find out, the break-in had been perpetrated by five men employed by CREEP. Throughout the fall of 1972, McGovern expressed astonishment at White House press secretary Ron Ziegler's assertion that this had been a "third-rate burglary attempt" conducted by overzealous supporters, without direction from higher authorities.

In fact, when the Washington police apprehended the five CREEP employees on June 17, they stumbled into a complicated web of lies and paranoia. The pattern had been set early on. For many years, Nixon had considered himself undermined by various opponents: Democrats, journalists, intellectuals, academics, and even certain entertainment and sports celebrities. Early in his administration, Nixon concocted plans to derail opposition: he tapped the telephones of rivals and supporters suspected of leaking information; he ordered a break-in at Daniel Ellsberg's psychiatrist's office; he endorsed several schemes to make life miserable for his perceived enemies. Nixon saw such enemies everywhere. They included Senator Edward Kennedy; actors Jane Fonda, Gregory Peck, Tony Randall, Julie Andrews, Connie Stevens, and Steve McQueen; the Brookings Institution; columnists James Reston and Rowland Evans; New York Jets quarterback Joe Namath; and comedian Richard M.

Dixon, who did silly impersonations of Nixon. The president's lawyer, John Dean, compiled an "enemies list" at Nixon's request. The president told Dean to find ways "we can best screw" the more than one hundred people named on the list.

The White House commanded the IRS to harass political rivals. In two years, the IRS investigated 4,300 such individuals and 1,025 groups, taking legal action against forty-three people and twenty-six organizations. In addition, White House counsel Dean helped Nixon supporters who got in trouble with the IRS. Nixon insisted that "tax troubles be turned off" for his friends. When career officials resisted turning the IRS into the president's private hit squad, Nixon complained.

G. Gordon Liddy, a former FBI agent who had helped plan the Ellsberg burglary and had run the administration's drug war, joined the CREEP staff in late 1971. In early 1972, he presented to Attorney General John Mitchell—who was scheduled to leave the Justice Department soon to become chair of CREEP—a $1 million plan to disrupt the upcoming Democratic convention by kidnapping Democratic Party leaders, putting them in bed with prostitutes, photographing them, and distributing the embarrassing pictures. Intrigued but unhappy with the price tag, Mitchell told Liddy to devise a more "realistic" plan. Liddy returned with a scheme for eavesdropping on Democratic candidates during the 1972 campaign. Mitchell approved, and Liddy received $83,000 in hundred-dollar bills as a first installment for hiring surveillance operatives.

The money delivered to Liddy represented just a small part of a cornucopia of secret cash payments. Prominent individuals, corporations, trade groups, and lobbyists had curried favor with the Nixon administration by making substantial donations. During the 1970 congressional campaign, for example, Herbert Kalmbach, Nixon's personal attorney, collected another $2.8 million in cash. Donald Kendall, president of Pepsi-Cola, and H. Ross Perot, a Texas billionaire, each chipped in $250,000. These contributions were illegal and were not reported by campaign treasurers.

After the 1970 congressional election, Nixon told Kalmbach to concentrate on raising money for 1972. The desire to buy favors from the government stimulated the flow of a cash bonanza from various businesses. Dairy farmers dependent on government price supports had their lobbying arm, the American Milk Producers, pledge $2 million for CREEP. With this money in hand, Nixon overruled his own economic advisers and raised dairy price supports, which was what the milk lobbyists wanted.

In April 1972, flush with cash from Kalmbach's fundraising endeavors, G. Gordon Liddy hired James McCord and E. Howard Hunt. Both men were ex-CIA operatives who had burglarized offices of Nixon's political opponents. Liddy hired them to spy on various offices of the Democratic Party in Washington. McCord and Hunt recruited several Cuban exiles from Miami, veterans of the CIA's 1961 Bay of Pigs invasion and the burglary at Daniel Ellsberg's psychiatrist's office, to plant listening devices. In May 1972, they botched an effort to bug McGovern's headquarters. Eventually, they succeeded in planting bugs in Democratic Committee chair Lawrence O'Brien's office at the Watergate complex. Two weeks later, one of the bugs malfunctioned; the burglars returned to repair it on the night of June 16. At 1:50 A.M. on June 17, a night watchman noticed tape on the door of the Democrats' office and called the District of Columbia police. They arrived and apprehended McCord and four Cubans—Bernard Barker, Frank Sturgis, Virgilio Gonzalez, and Eugenio Martinez. Police were surprised to find the burglars carrying wads of hundred dollar bills. Howard Hunt's White House telephone number also turned up in an address book belonging to one of the suspects.

The arrests terrified Liddy, who scurried to destroy evidence linking him, CREEP, and the White House to the burglary. He asked Attorney General Richard Kleindienst to secure the release of the five men, but the request was refused. On the morning of June 17, Liddy went to his office at CREEP to shred files linking him and John Mitchell to plans to bug the opposition.

Immediately after the arrests, the White House began a cover-up. Presidential aide John Ehrlichman called H. R. Haldeman, who was with Nixon in

In the Oval Office of the White House, President Nixon confers with his top aids: (*from left*) National Security Adviser Henry Kissinger, Domestic Policy Adviser John Ehrlichman, and Chief of Staff H. R. "Bob" Haldeman. / National Archives/Nixon Presidential Materials

Investigative reporters Bob Woodward (*left*) and Carl Bernstein at work on the Watergate story at the Washington Post. / © UPI/ Bettmann/ CORBIS.

Key Biscayne, Florida, to discuss Hunt's and McCord's involvement. Because both men had recently been employed by the White House, Ehrlichman and Haldeman feared that further investigation would implicate Nixon. Ehrlichman put John Dean in charge of keeping investigators at bay. White House press secretary Ron Ziegler dismissed reporters' concerns, asserting that "certain elements may try to stretch this beyond what it is."

Over the next three months, Dean, Haldeman, Ehrlichman, Mitchell, and Nixon successfully obstructed the Watergate investigation. On June 20, Nixon told Haldeman to undertake a public relations offensive to squelch public interest in the Watergate break-in. Three days later, Nixon outlined to Haldeman a plan to have the CIA warn the FBI to "stay the hell out of this." Given Hunt's CIA connections, Nixon said, "[W]e think it would be very unfortunate, both for the CIA, and for the country, and for American foreign policy" for the FBI to pursue the origins of the money found on the burglars. Nixon's conversations with Haldeman on June 23 were caught on tape by listening devices the president had installed in the Oval Office. These conversations came to light in August 1974, providing proof of the president's efforts to obstruct justice.

Reporters' efforts to turn public attention to Watergate by following the money trail received little attention at first. Bob Woodward and Carl Bernstein of the *Washington Post* covered the story because they routinely handled relatively insignificant metropolitan news, which was what the Watergate burglary initially seemed to be. Woodward and Bernstein wrote several stories linking money laundered in Mexico to the Watergate burglars, but Nixon denied their significance. He told a news conference that "both sides" had made "technical violations" of the new campaign finance law, although he refused to say what the Democrats had done.

In mid-September 1972, it appeared that the cover-up had succeeded. A federal grand jury indicted Liddy, Hunt, and the five men arrested at Democratic national headquarters. Relieved that no one at the White House or CREEP was indicted, Nixon called Dean into his office late that afternoon and congratulated him: "The way you handled it, it seems to me has been very skillful—putting your fingers in the dikes every time that leaks have sprung here and sprung there." Nixon went on to ruminate about his plans for a second administration. He was pleased that Dean had been keeping notes on "a lot of people who are less than our friends." Those people "are asking for it," Nixon said, "and they are going to get it."

Journalists Woodward and Bernstein kept reporting details of Watergate in the months before the November election, but their stories did not have a wide impact. They followed the money trail, assisted by an anonymous source who seemed familiar with all the personalities in the White House. They called this informant Deep Throat, after a then popular pornographic movie. Deep Throat confirmed the journalists' suspicions that secret cash funds had been used for dirty tricks against the Democrats since 1970. By late October, Woodward and Bernstein believed they had traced the source of the secret funds all the way up to Haldeman. Deep Throat informed them that "from top to bottom, this whole business is a Haldeman operation."

Watergate faded but did not die in the winter following the election, while public attention was riveted on the bombing of North Vietnam and the subsequent Paris peace agreement. Democratic members of Congress kept an eye on news about Watergate because they worried that CREEP's strong-armed fundraising tactics threatened to put them out of business. Early in 1973, the Senate decided to create a select seven-member committee (four Democrats and three Republicans), chaired by the conservative constitutional expert Sam Ervin of North Carolina, to investigate the break-in and the sabotage against the Democrats in the 1972 campaign. As the Senate Select Committee on Campaign Practices—soon known informally as the Senate Watergate Committee—prepared to hold its first hearings, Nixon's staff formulated its strategy to disrupt the investigation. They would invoke executive privilege: the idea that presidential agents could not be compelled to reveal information to Congress, an equal, not superior, branch of the government. Nixon advised subordinates involved in Watergate and the subsequent cover-up to stonewall the committee by forbidding White House assistants to testify.

The trial of the Watergate burglars revealed little at first because they all pleaded guilty and denied White House involvement. The burglars continued to receive payments, and McCord heard from an agent that his wife and family would be taken care of if McCord had to go to jail for a year. Presiding over the trial, however, was U.S. District Court judge John J. Sirica, known as Maximum John for the tough sentences he handed down. Sirica expressed disbelief at prosecutors' claims that the men charged were the only ones involved in the break-in. He threatened the burglars with long prison terms. On March 19, 1973, McCord broke and wrote Sirica that he and other defendants had been under political pressure to plead guilty and remain silent, that others had lied under oath, and that higher-ups were involved in the break-in. On March 23, Sirica sentenced Liddy to six years in prison. He delayed sentencing the other defendants in the hope that they would reveal who else had participated.

As Sirica squeezed the burglars for information, Dean found it harder to maintain the cover-up. Dean told Nixon there was "a cancer growing on the presidency" because many of the people involved in the Watergate break-in and the burglary of Ellsberg's psychiatrist's office could be indicted. Demands for hush money might go as high as $1 million, Dean said. Nixon replied, "We could get that. . . . And you could get it in cash. I know where it could be gotten." Nixon instructed Dean and other aides called to testify before the Ervin committee or the grand jury investigating the break-in to avoid perjury by saying, "I don't remember; I can't recall."

Containment grew harder in April as prosecutors closed in on Dean, offering him immunity from prosecution if he divulged what he knew. Dean's possible defection frightened Nixon, who tried unsuccessfully to keep his wavering counsel in line. Fearing that Nixon might make him the fall guy, Dean decided to cooperate with the prosecutors. He began telling everything he knew about the cover-up to the Ervin committee staff. Nixon then tried to discredit Dean, claiming that he had directed a cover-up without the president's knowledge. He fired Dean on April 30. In a televised speech, he conceded that "there had been an effort to conceal the facts" about Watergate. He accepted no personal responsibility, implying instead that Dean had acted on his own. As he dismissed Dean, Nixon also decided to jettison Haldeman and Ehrlichman. He accepted their resignations, praising them as "two of the finest public servants I have ever known."

Nearly in a panic that the extent of the cover-up would be revealed, Nixon adopted a new tactic of appearing to cooperate with investigators. He bowed to public pressure and appointed Harvard law professor Archibald Cox as an independent counsel, or special prosecutor, to continue the Justice Department's investigation of Watergate. Nixon's strategy of pretending to accept responsibility for Watergate bought him a little time with the majority of the public, which did not know the extent of Nixon's involvement. However, on May 17, 1973, the Senate Watergate Committee began televised hearings, which continued throughout the summer of 1973. In the first month of the hearings, Sam Ervin, whose folksy appearance and manner could not hide a devastating wit and sharp intellect, became a celebrity. His vice-chair, Tennessee Republican Howard Baker, tried to focus attention on Nixon, repeatedly asking witnesses, "What did the president know, and when did he know it?" At hairdressing salons, muffler shops, bars, and business offices across the country, Americans interrupted their daily routines to stare at TVs tuned to the Watergate hearings.

In late June, having been granted immunity from prosecution, Dean took the stand. For two days, he read in a monotone a 245-page statement describing

(cont. on page 379)

Strange Bedfellows: The Politics of Scandal in Postwar America

While the Watergate scandal was the quintessential political scandal, the following decades witnessed the rising importance of sexual scandal. Sex and power, in fact, have long been intimately associated in American politics. Men who have occupied positions of authority have often believed that their prominence entitled them to flout conventional sexual mores. As long-time FBI director J. Edgar Hoover knew, the sexual license claimed by powerful men also made them vulnerable to public or private exposure. He systematically used the power of his office to unearth the sexual secrets of public officials in all parts of government and from all points on the political spectrum to blackmail them into supporting his own political goals. By the 1990s, the politics of sexual scandal, which focused on everyone from U.S. Supreme Court nominee Clarence Thomas to President Bill Clinton, relied on the public disclosure of wrongdoing. The American press willfully hid the sexual misconduct of President John F. Kennedy and many others in the early postwar period, but by the end of the century, it had blurred the distinction between mainstream media and the tabloids with its constant focus on such scandals.

What had changed? Increasing competition in broadcast journalism, occasioned by the rise of cable, provided incentives in the form of higher ratings for those who publicized sexual misconduct of all kinds. The rise of feminism and its New Right antagonists in the 1970s politicized areas of conduct previously regarded as private. Feminists, for example, first raised public consciousness regarding workplace sexual harassment—an abuse of power that involved unwanted sexual behaviors directed at coworkers or subordinates. By the 1980s, the U.S. Supreme Court had ruled that sexual harassment constituted an illegal violation of sex discrimination law.

On the other side of the gender wars, the New Right viewed such changes as the cause of conflicts between women and men and an unnecessary infringement on employers' rights to manage their businesses without government interference. Its desire to free businesses from government intrusion did not extend to the domains of sexuality and family, however. The Christian Right, in particular, had dedicated itself from its inception to using government as a means to enforce its moral vision on the general public. As it was publicly professed, that vision required that sexuality be confined to heterosexual, monogamous marriage; that women must dedicate themselves to domestic and family activities; and that men must support families and control public power. Some took theocratic views to an extreme. Ralph Reed, for example, believed in "legislating the ancient Jewish law laid out in the Old Testament: stoning adulterers, executing homosexuals, even mandating dietary laws."

By the late 1980s, conservative politicians had begun using the politics of scandal to expose the immorality they professed to hate and to advance their political agendas. They did so with the active cooperation of the mainstream media, which found that sex sells newspapers and provides larger audiences for television's commercials. The first prominent figure to fall victim to the new politics was Republican senator John Tower, nominated by President George Bush to be secretary of defense in 1989. Conservative activist Paul Weyrich accused him of drunkenness and adultery, thus obstructing the nomination and setting a precedent for future uses of scandal for political purposes. Democratic presidential candidate Gary Hart had suffered a similar fate in 1988, when the press revealed his extramarital affairs. Rumors that George Bush also had committed adultery received almost no press attention, either during or after his successful bid for the presidency in 1988.

In 1991, when law professor Anita Hill accused Supreme Court nominee Clarence Thomas of engaging in illegal sexual harassment while he was the chair of the Equal Employment Opportunity Commission and she was a staff lawyer there, conservatives reacted with great anger at the charges. Indeed, Republican members of the Senate Judiciary Committee went out of their way to impugn her credibility and her morality. Gossip and innuendo received its due in the hands of Senator Arlen Spector, who accused her of "flat-out perjury" and went on to say that he had been "getting stuff over the transom about Professor Hill" that said, "[W]atch out for this woman." He did not offer it in evidence. The senators also queried witnesses, including Thomas, regarding Hill's motives for her testimony, entertaining speculation that she was a woman scorned (by Thomas) whose accounts of their interactions derived from her own fantasies about him or that she suffered from thwarted career ambitions.

The hearings were an especially painful episode for African Americans, who initially rallied behind Thomas. Given the long history of whites' use of sexual slanders to denigrate and oppress blacks, any accusations of sexual impropriety caused pain and outrage in the African American community. Galvanized by Thomas's claim that the all-white (and all-male) Senate Judiciary Committee had engaged in a "high-tech lynching" when it questioned him regarding Hill's charges, many blacks supported his confirmation, putting liberal Democrats in the Senate (almost all of them opposed to Thomas) in a political quandary. The issues raised in the hearings did not die after Thomas's appointment squeaked through the Senate on a close vote.

Enter David Brock, a conservative journalist seeking to ingratiate himself with the right wing of the Republican Party. Brock, who began his reporting career at the *Washington Times* (owned by the Reverend

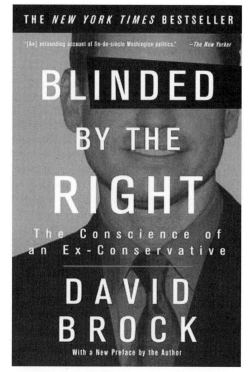

The cover for David Brock's *Blinded by the Right*, a controversial exposé of political mudslinging by New Right conservatives in the 1990s. / Courtesy of Three Rivers Press, Random House

Sun Myung Moon), had joined the staff of the *Spectator*, an archconservative Washington monthly committed to discrediting those who opposed the conservative agenda. It published an article by Brock entitled "The Real Anita Hill" in its March 1992 issue. Concluding that she was "a little bit nutty and a little bit slutty," Brock explained Hill's testimony against Thomas as the vengeful lies of a disgruntled former employee passed over for promotion. He also called Hill a "man-hater" who had "a perverse desire for male attention" and accused her of sexual harassment in her role as a law professor. He followed his opening salvo with a book by the same title, which received generally favorable reviews in the mainstream press and became a bestseller.

Brock later admitted that his *Spectator* article was a "witches' brew of fact, allegation, hearsay, speculation, opinion, and invective labeled by my editors as 'investigative journalism'" and credited his critics with identifying many of the deceptions in his work.

Buoyed by the accomplishment of his first major success as a right-wing journalist, Brock turned his attention in 1992 to Bill and Hillary Clinton. He joined an attack campaign (christened the Arkansas Project) that was financed and assisted by various conservative figures in Washington and Arkansas and dedicated to the pursuit of criminal and sexual scandals involving the newly elected First Family. His contribution was an article based on stories told by Arkansas state troopers, who claimed that they had assisted Clinton in arranging sexual liaisons with large numbers of women. Soon dubbed Troopergate, the scandal broke in a story Brock published in the *Spectator*. By his own later admission, the allegations he publicized were either false or unverified. *Newsweek*'s Joe Klein called the story "trash" and said that the troopers' remarks about Hillary Clinton were "a Neanderthal fantasy of what feminists are really like." Anthony Lewis called Brock "the man . . . who has made himself chief manure spreader for the extreme right." Nonetheless, the mainstream press published his allegations while condemning him for making them.

In the story, Brock related the tale of a woman named Paula who was brought to a Little Rock, Arkansas, hotel room so that Clinton could meet her. The story alleged that they had had a consensual sexual encounter. Recognizing herself in the story, Paula Jones came forward, with the considerable assistance of various conservative lawyers and financial backers, alleging that she had not consented to Clinton's advances and, thus, had been a victim of sexual harassment and was suing the president. According to Brock, Jones's decision not to sue the *Spectator*, the source of the remarks she saw as libelous, but to sue Clinton instead reflected the priorities of her conservative supporters. Reversing the positions they had assumed during the Thomas hearings—that sexual harassment law gave attorneys too much license to probe the personal lives of those accused—they used the Jones case to explore any consensual sexual relations Clinton may have had. They also hoped to catch him lying about his sexual encounters and thus trap him into lying about his past in court. This tactic, of course, led them to Monica Lewinsky and ultimately to impeachment proceedings based on the crime of perjury (see Chapter 14).

When faced with the charges against Clinton, feminists faced a dilemma. Angry that Anita Hill's credibility had been impugned, they nonetheless were worried that the Jones suit was based on lies and opportunism largely because of its close ties to right-wing interests. Feminists' close ties to the Democratic Party made it difficult for them to criticize a president from that party. In addition, the fact that the relationship with Monica Lewinsky was clearly consensual made its relevance to the Jones inquiry quite murky. Patricia Ireland of the National Organization for Women, for example, characterized Clinton's relationship with a young intern as "an abuse of power," but not a legal violation. Conservatives reacted by accusing feminists of being hypocritical and opportunistic.

Feminists and conservatives differed dramatically on the desirability of sexual privacy and the appropriateness of using private behavior as political cannon fodder. Indeed, the explicit questioning of Lewinsky by special prosecutor Kenneth Starr and the grand jury regarding sexual acts performed in the White House seemed to some feminists to be motivated more by a desire to humiliate the president and destroy his presidency than by legal requirements. This view was widely held by the American public as well. Conservatives, by contrast, believed that the idea of sexual privacy shields the immoral from public accountability for their actions. Conservative author David

Frum, for example, wrote that "[W]hat's at stake in the Lewinsky scandal is not the right to privacy, but the central dogma of the baby boomers: the belief that sex, so long as it is consensual, ought never to be subject to moral scrutiny at all."

Ultimately, the American people did not support impeachment. Why? For some Americans, conservatives' overt moral agenda undercut their assertions that the case was about lying and obstruction of justice. Most Americans concluded that it was about sex and did not share the conservatives' outrage about it. The means used to pursue the case seemed questionable to some. As civil rights activist Julian Bond remarked regarding the methods used by Clinton's detractors, "They had the guy and went looking for the crime." The prurience demonstrated in the Starr report and in the obsessive media attention to its sexual content also offended many Americans, who blamed Clinton's critics for confusing politics with pornography.

Meanwhile, David Brock himself was harboring his own sexual secret: he was a closeted homosexual serving as chief mudslinger for the right wing. When he believed that a *New York Times* article had "outed" him in a veiled manner, he decided to go public about his sexuality. Although he received somewhat surprising support from his conservative allies after the revelation, the homophobia of the right wing and a growing discomfort with his own hypocrisy ultimately caused him to break ranks with them. The result was a tell-all book, *Blinded by the Right: The Conscience of an Ex-Conservative*, published in 2002. In it, he admitted to the many mean-spirited and damaging deceptions he perpetrated in service to his cause. His actions, he says, were "motivated by a mix of partisanship and opportunistic careerism" that typified the new generation of young conservative leaders who were, in his words, "committed to conservatism largely as a marketing technique, not a philosophy." His description of the Arkansas Plan suggests that Hillary Clinton may not have been wrong when she claimed that her husband's legal difficulties stemmed from a "vast right-wing conspiracy."

Many have characterized the scandalmongering of the 1990s as "sexual McCarthyism." Certainly, the political invective of the 1990s and that of the immediate postwar period shared common elements. Each period saw powerful individuals use sexual charges against political opponents to bolster their political ends. Each saw some politicians abuse congressional investigative authority to discredit political opponents and advance certain ideologies and policy goals. In the case of postwar McCarthyism, some responsible journalists drew attention to its abuses and the public finally wearied of the politics of vituperation. Whether the media and the public will do so again in the future is open to debate.

the details of the cover-up. He characterized Watergate as emerging from "a climate of excessive concern over the political impact of demonstrators, excessive concern over leaks, an insatiable appetite for political intelligence."

The testimony of Nixon loyalists made matters worse for the president. They stumbled, mumbled, forgot, or fought with the senators. The hearings climaxed in mid-July, when Alexander Butterfield, the White House office manager, revealed that Nixon had tape-recorded his own conversations since 1970. Tapes existed that could show whether Dean was telling the truth. The Ervin committee, Judge Sirica, and special prosecutor Cox tried immediately to acquire the tapes. Nixon refused access to them, citing executive privilege.

Returning from the hospital after a bout with severe viral pneumonia, the president denied rumors that he was going to resign. Such talk was "just plain poppycock," he said, adding, "Let others wallow in Watergate, we are going to do our job."

Another scandal hit the White House in late August, when the *Wall Street Journal* revealed that federal prosecutors in Baltimore were investigating Vice President Spiro Agnew for bribery, extortion, and tax fraud. Prosecutors had determined that Agnew, the former governor of Maryland, had received bribes from builders and engineers in his home state for the past ten years in return for lucrative public works contracts. Agnew fought against formal indictment with a strategy that made Nixon's position more precarious because the vice president raised the specter of impeachment. The vice president's talk of impeachment angered Nixon, who did not want the notion implanted in the minds of the members of Congress. The president hinted that Agnew should step down to avoid prosecution. Agnew refused the hint, telling a cheering throng of Republican women in Los Angeles that he would never resign. But only two weeks later, he did. Prosecutors had hard evidence of bribery, and he realized he could go to jail if he did not strike a deal. He pleaded no contest to one count of income tax evasion for not reporting or paying taxes on the bribes.

Agnew's resignation left a vacancy in the vice presidency. Under the terms of the Twenty-fifth Amendment, adopted in the aftermath of John Kennedy's assassination, the president could name a successor, who would be confirmed by a majority vote in Congress. Nixon selected minority leader Gerald R. Ford of Michigan, a Republican stalwart who was well liked by his peers. He had little knowledge of or experience with foreign affairs. If Nixon's own hold on the presidency were threatened, critics might think twice about forcing him out in favor of the untested Ford.

By October 1973, even the prospect of a Ford presidency could not save Nixon from the public's wrath as the full dimensions of the cover-up began to emerge. Archibald Cox and the Watergate Committee asked Sirica for subpoenas to force Nixon to produce the tapes of key conversations he had had with aides on Watergate. Mindful of his conversations with Haldeman and Dean plotting the cover-up, Nixon realized that releasing complete tapes to Cox would be his doom. On Saturday night, October 20, 1973, Nixon asked Attorney General Elliot Richardson to fire Cox. Richardson, who had promised Cox independence, resigned rather than dismiss him. Richardson's deputy, William Ruckelshaus, also quit rather than execute the order. Only Solicitor General Robert Bork, third in command at the Justice Department, was willing to fire Cox. Nixon also abolished the special prosecutor's office and sent FBI agents to prevent Cox's subordinates from gaining access to their files.

A firestorm of protest engulfed Capitol Hill over the next forty-eight hours. Over 1 million telephone calls and telegrams flooded senators' and representatives' offices protesting the Saturday Night Massacre. People who earlier had given Nixon the benefit of the doubt, believing he would cooperate with investigators, changed their minds and thought he wanted to hide his involvement in breaking the law. The next week, eight impeachment resolutions were referred to the House Judiciary Committee. The eruption of public anger over Nixon's stonewalling on the tapes forced another White House surrender. The president's lawyer announced that the White House was willing to release subpoenaed tapes to Judge Sirica. A new independent prosecutor, Houston lawyer Leon Jaworski, resumed the investigations.

As Jaworski gathered information about the state of the Watergate inquiry, more astonishing revelations fed the public's anger about Nixon's apparent duplicity. White House attorneys cataloguing the tapes discovered that some were missing and that an eighteen-and-a-half-minute gap existed on the tape of a June 20, 1972, conversation with Haldeman. Haldeman's notes revealed that he and Nixon had discussed Watergate at that meeting and that the president had called for a "counterattack," presumably against any investigation of the break-in, during these crucial missing minutes. Soon after Judge Sirica revealed the existence of the gap, Nixon told Associated Press editors that "people have got a right to know whether or not their president is a crook. Well, I'm not a crook."

As public distrust of Nixon increased in 1974, the staff of the House Judiciary Committee carefully prepared a case for impeachment. Continual requests for tapes and documents produced White House delays or attempts to get away with half-compliance. In late April 1974, Nixon appeared on television to explain that he would make edited transcripts of the tapes available to the committee. These documents, he claimed, would show no prior knowledge of the break-in and no participation in or knowledge of obstruction of justice.

That justification crumbled within days. The House Judiciary Committee voted not to accept edited transcripts and told Nixon that he had failed to comply with the committee's subpoenas. Nixon released transcripts anyway, and excerpts were widely published in newspapers. People were appalled by the conversations that had taken place in the Oval Office. The transcripts produced angry denunciations of Nixon, even from friends. Senate minority leader Hugh Scott said they revealed a "deplorable, shabby, disgusting and immoral performance" by everyone involved in the conversations.

By late July 1974, the committee had impeachment articles ready. On July 27, in a nationally televised session, six Republicans joined all twenty-one Democrats—forming a majority of 27 to 11—in voting to adopt the first article, charging Nixon with obstruction of justice for his involvement in the Watergate cover-up. On July 29, the committee voted 28 to 10 on a second general article, charging abuse of power in connection to Nixon's harassment of domestic opponents. The next day, a narrower majority of 21 to 17 indicted the president for unconstitutionally defying its subpoenas.

The Supreme Court quickly delivered another blow to Nixon. In *United States* v. *Nixon*, by an 8-to-0 ruling, the Court demanded that the president turn over to Sirica tapes of sixty-four conversations deemed to be essential evidence in the cover-up trials of six former aides. Chief Justice Burger acknowledged that the Constitution protected executive privilege, but he ruled that "when a claim of privilege is based only on the generalized interest in confidentiality, it cannot prevail over the fundamental demands of due process of

Richard Nixon and his wife Pat leave the White House on August 9, 1974, after he has resigned the presidency. At their right are the new president, Gerald Ford, and his wife Betty. / © CORBIS

law in the administration of justice." Nixon's lawyer agreed to turn over the tapes by the August 7 deadline set by Sirica.

On August 5, 1974, Nixon released transcripts of his June 23, 1972, conversations with Haldeman. On that date, the two men had planned how to use the CIA to throw the FBI off the scent of the Watergate investigation. Here was the smoking gun his defenders had insisted did not exist: the conversations showed Nixon's early knowledge of and participation in the cover-up. Two days later, all congressional support for Nixon collapsed with release of these tapes. All the Republican members of the Judiciary Committee who had voted against impeachment said that they would now vote for it on the floor. Longtime Republican friends in the Senate told Nixon he would have fewer than ten votes in that body when it came time to decide whether to convict him on the House's bill of impeachment.

On the night of August 7, 1974, Nixon called Kissinger to the White House to tell him that he planned to resign. Nixon wept openly and clearly felt his fall from grace keenly. He hoped for some later vindication, asking Kissinger, "Will history treat me more kindly than my contemporaries?" Kissinger tried to assure him that it would.

Nixon's impending resignation became public on the evening of August 8. In a televised address, he told the nation that he intended to leave office at noon the next day. The next morning, he said farewell to his staff in a tearful, rambling, self-pitying speech; he recalled his father, his mother, his brothers' dying in their mother's arms, Theodore Roosevelt's dead young wife, and an early failure to pass the bar examination. At last, Nixon recovered some composure and bade his staff and the nation good-bye. He climbed into a helicopter on the White House lawn, flew to Andrews Air Force Base, and boarded Air Force One for a flight to California, becoming the first American president to resign the office. While Nixon was en route to the West Coast, Gerald Ford took the oath of office as the new president. Ford proclaimed that the "long national nightmare" of Watergate was over.

Conclusion

Richard Nixon's defenders, at the time of his resignation and in subsequent years, have tended to focus on his achievements in foreign policy, particularly the steps he took toward fostering cooperation with the Soviet Union and China. In some ways, his domestic record showed a similar vigor: for example, his early plan on welfare reform and his willingness to scrap his earlier economic approach in favor of wage and price controls exhibited a certain creativity and pragmatism for which he is not often remembered. He was most creative, however, in devising ways to undercut his political opponents. His presidency became dominated by his obsession with supposed enemies and his determination to get them before they could get him. President Nixon did more to divide the nation than to unite it. In the end, more of the substantive changes in domestic affairs that came about during his term in office came from Congress and the Supreme Court rather than from the executive branch: the Court extended its civil rights rulings into the controversial areas of busing and abortion rights, and Congress passed key legislation to protect the environment and to promote public health and safety.

Ironically, Nixon's resignation unified the country. No other event since John Kennedy's assassination had done more to bring Americans together. A president who had tried to exploit his power in illegal and unethical ways had failed to dominate the government and intimidate his opposition into silence. As his cynical manipulations of people and events became known during the Watergate investigations, Americans asserted their sense of justice and fair play. One of the many books that was eventually published on Watergate was entitled simply *How the Good Guys Finally Won*. Besides agreeing that justice had been done, Americans breathed a collective sigh of relief that the country's government had withstood the strain of the Watergate crisis. There was even a certain amount of national pride involved. It seemed that the American federal government, with its system of checks and balances that allowed one branch to curb the excesses of another, was fully capable of overcoming the abuse of power.

Much of this national self-congratulation was deserved, and the revulsion people felt at Nixon's duplicity was real. Nevertheless, Nixon's downfall rested more on strokes of good fortune than on the smooth workings of a system of checks and balances. Many of the White House horrors—the buggings, the dirty tricks, the break-ins—were known before the election of 1972 and shrugged off as politics as usual. Had *Washington Post* reporters Bob Woodward and Carl Bernstein not kept the story alive in the fall of 1972, the Watergate scandal would have disappeared. Judge Sirica's prickly, skeptical personality also played a major role; a more complacent jurist might well have accepted the prosecution's claim that only seven low-level CREEP officials were responsible for the break-in. The investigations by the Senate Watergate Committee and the House Judiciary Committee helped focus public attention on the affair, but the Senate committee owed its existence as much to Democrats' outrage over CREEP's obstruction of their money supply as it did to concern for justice. Finally, the impeachment process began because of the fight over the tapes. If Nixon had not taped himself, if he had destroyed the tapes, or if Alexander Butterfield had not revealed their existence, the Watergate story probably would have turned out differently.

Overall, then, the implications of Watergate are difficult to assess. Nixon's abuse of power was finally checked, but perhaps only as a result of fortunate circumstances. Will the system work again if another president tries to subvert the country's laws and institutions?

A 1982 poll of over eight hundred historians identified Nixon as one of only four outright failures in the presidency. But some of the public anger at Nixon's actions had dissipated by the late 1980s, when he achieved a sort of rehabilitation, especially with respect to his handling of foreign affairs. At the time of his death in 1994, even old political enemies praised his skill at foreign policy and his astonishing tenacity in climbing back into the public arena in the two decades following his disgrace. More lasting than the public's anger at Nixon personally was a deepening public distrust of politicians, of government in general, and of many other figures of authority in American society. This perhaps was the most fundamental legacy of Richard Nixon and Watergate.

F U R T H E R • R E A D I N G

On politics and domestic policy in the Nixon administration, see Melvin Small, *The Presidency of Richard Nixon* (1999); Allan Matusow, *Nixon's Economy: Booms, Busts, Dollars and Votes* (1998); Richard Nixon, *RN: The Memoirs of Richard Nixon* (1978) and *In the Arena* (1990); Stephen E. Ambrose, *Nixon* (3 vols.: 1986, 1989, 1991); Joan Hoff, *Nixon Reconsidered* (1994); Herbert Parmet, *Richard Nixon and His America* (1990); Monica Crowley, *Nixon Off the Record: His Candid Commentary on People and Politics* (1996) and *Nixon in Winter* (1998); William Safire, *Before the Fall: An Inside Look at the Pre-Watergate White House* (1975); Nicholas Lemann, *The Promised Land: The Great Black Migration and How It Changed America* (1991); Daniel Patrick Moynihan, *The Politics of a Guaranteed Income* (1973); Melvin Urofsky, *The Continuity of Change: The Supreme Court and Individual Liberties, 1953–1986* (1991). **On Watergate,** see Stanley I. Kutler, *The Wars of Watergate* (1990) and *Abuse of Power: The New Nixon Tapes* (1997); Kim McQuaid, *The Anxious Years: America in the Vietnam and Watergate Era* (1989); J. Anthony Lukas, *Nightmare: The Underside of the Nixon Years* (1976); Theodore H.

White, *Breach of Faith: The Fall of Richard Nixon* (1975); Bob Woodward and Carl Bernstein, *All the President's Men* (1974) and *The Final Days* (1976); H. R. Haldeman, with Joseph Dimona, *The Ends of Power* (1978); H. R. Haldeman, *The Haldeman Diaries* (1994); John Ehrlichman, *Witness to Power* (1982); John Dean, *Blind Ambition* (1976). **On the scandals of the Clinton years,** see Lauren Berlant and Lisa Duggan, eds., *Our Monica Ourselves: The Clinton Affair and the National Interest* (2001); Leonard V. Kaplan and Beverly I. Moran, eds., *Aftermath: The Clinton Impeachment and the Presidency in the Age of Political Spectacle* (2001); David Brock, *Blinded by the Right: The Conscience of an Ex-Conservative* (2002).

11

The Challenges of Change, 1974–1980

In November 1978, mourners walk in a candlelight vigil for San Francisco Supervisor Harvey Milk and Mayor George Moscone, who were assassinated earlier in the day. / © Roger Ressmeyer/CORBIS

n 1977, voters in San Francisco's Castro Street area elected Harvey Milk to the city's board of supervisors. From the time he first ran for city supervisor in 1973 until his victory in 1977, Milk had built a coalition of neighborhood activists, labor unions, and rank-and-file gay voters. At his headquarters, drag queens and leather fanciers mingled with teamsters and firefighters. Milk was not the only freshman on the board of supervisors in 1977. A former police officer named Dan White had also been elected to represent a conservative district of the city. Milk, who was always independent, thought at first that there might be some issues on which he and White could find common ground. But they began to differ when Milk more and more often voted in support of the city's liberal mayor, George Moscone, and White grew more and more frustrated and alienated.

What Milk did not know was that White was having personal problems that made him depressed and unstable. White resigned from office, then tried to have himself reinstated. Moscone opposed him; Milk offered no support. On the morning of November 27, 1978, Dan White walked into city hall with a Smith and Wesson revolver and shot Moscone four times. He reloaded the gun with hollow-headed dum-dum bullets and moved to Harvey Milk's office. White took Milk to the office he had lately vacated and shot Milk five times, twice in the head.

Harvey Milk's death brought thousands of gays, lesbians, and their supporters into the streets of San Francisco, first for a candlelight vigil and later for a massive, violent protest, dubbed The White Night Riot, when Dan White was found not guilty by reason of insanity. In October 1979, over 100,000 people participated in a gay rights march in Washington, D.C., many carrying placards bearing Harvey Milk's picture. Journalist Randy Shilts later wrote: "For years afterward, when dull moments fell over a gay demonstration and the old slogans felt thin, someone could shout, 'Harvey Milk lives,' and it would not be hollow rhetoric. Harvey Milk did live, as a metaphor for the homosexual experience in America."

Harvey Milk's life and death symbolized the emotionally fraught politics of sexuality and gender that occupied center stage in American politics in the 1970s. The growth and successes of the women's movement and the gay and lesbian movement prompted conservatives also to mobilize. They formed the Moral Majority and other groups to stem the tide of change. In particular, they resented the role of government in supporting new sexual and family values and sought to wrest political authority from the hands of liberals. The conservative backlash gained momentum partly because of the economic difficulties that Americans faced in the 1970s, when the problems of simultaneous recession and inflation (dubbed stagflation), energy crises, and rising foreign competition left American business and political leaders in a quandary. This was particularly the case for the Democrats, who could no longer rely on the kinds of solutions they had employed since the New Deal to promote economic well-being.

Changing Roles for Women and Men

In the 1970s, women's roles and status continued to change, aided by a growing feminist movement and the legal and other changes it helped to secure. The effects of the women's movement were far-reaching. They included profound changes in the legal status of and economic opportunities for women (despite relatively lax enforcement of Title VII, which prohibited discrimination on the basis of gender, race, religion, and national origin); a renewed attention to long-existing problems; new educational opportunities, primarily for middle-class women; continuing changes in basic American institutions, including churches, labor unions, schools, and to some extent the media; and greater reproductive rights, including protections against involuntary sterilizations. Feminists also created new institutions and organizations to provide services important to women and to lobby and litigate for women's interests. At the same time, institutional sexism and political resistance ensured that some institutions, including those in politics and the economy, would initiate fundamental changes only when pressured to do so and then would do so as slowly as possible. Countervailing trends included the rise of a well-organized and well-funded antifeminist movement, which began to erode some reproductive rights by the end of the decade and assisted immeasurably in the successful creation of the New Right in American politics.

Nevertheless, by 1974, profound changes in gender roles, family patterns, and personal desires had become apparent in American society. Fewer and fewer households conformed to the nuclear family idealized by middle-class Americans, with the father working outside the home and the mother caring for the children. The proportion of women who worked outside the home continued to grow. By 1970, one-third of mothers with children under six years of age held or sought jobs; 52 percent had joined the work force by 1984.

The growing numbers of divorced men and women, people who had never married, unmarried couples living together, working women, single mothers, and openly gay men and women made for a visibly more diverse society, and Americans began speaking more openly about issues of sexuality and gender. In many cases, however, those whose way of life differed from earlier norms encountered hostility and economic hardship. Some traditionalists feared for their cherished values, and they joined a growing conservative movement to reverse what they saw as threatening social trends.

Divorce became more commonplace in the 1970s, continuing a trend that had begun early in the twentieth century. By 1980, experts were predicting that one-half of all new marriages would end in divorce. For those marrying for the first time, 44 percent would divorce; for second or subsequent marriages, the figure was 60 percent. Changing attitudes toward divorce coincided with the enactment of "no-fault" divorce laws in every state but South Dakota and Illinois between 1970 and 1980. California led the way with a liberal law permitting either party to sue for divorce if he or she believed "irreconcilable differences" had caused a breakdown of the marriage. Advocates of the new laws believed they would eliminate the phony accusations of abuse or adultery, the courtroom recriminations, and the spying by private investigators that had previously made divorce a nearly unbearable experience. It was also hoped that reduced acrimony would make it easier for divorced parents to co-operate in raising their children. No-fault divorce also changed the legal focus from assessing blame to dividing assets. The new laws tried to treat men and women equally, to recognize the wife's contribution to the partnership, and to end old assumptions that women's roles were subordinate to those of men.

No-fault divorce laws achieved many of these goals, but they also had un-intended negative consequences for women and children. The divorce revolu-tion particularly hurt at least two classes of women: older women who did not work outside the home and mothers of young children. The laws supposedly treated men and women equally, but they defined equality strictly in dollar terms. Older women who had been homemakers for years found that they had few assets and limited job opportunities after divorce. The new laws often ig-nored the immense, nonmonetary contributions these women had made to their families, and they expected women to be as able to support themselves af-ter divorce as their husbands. As had been the case before, most divorced women did not receive court-ordered alimony and those who did collected rela-tively small sums for a limited period of time. In 1922, 14.7 percent of divorced women received alimony; in 1981, the figure was 14.9 percent. In the later pe-riod, however, many more of these women were trying to support children.

The economic burden of divorce fell most heavily on women with young children. In 90 percent of divorces, children continued to live with their mother, but mothers fared poorly after divorce compared to fathers. In the first year after a marital breakup, the standard of living for divorced women and their minor children declined by an average of 73 percent; that of divorced men rose 42 percent. Judges divided marital property equally. In most cases, the largest single asset was the family's house, which the court ordered sold. Thus, a mother with minor children would find herself looking for new shel-ter—with only half the proceeds from the sale of her old home—at a time of rising housing costs. Judges ordered child support, but less than half of fathers paid the full amount of child support assessed by the courts: 30 percent of di-vorced mothers received only partial payments, and 25 percent received noth-ing at all. Feminist groups, whom conservatives accused of being antifamily and blamed for the rising divorce rate, set up support and training programs for former housewives transformed into "displaced homemakers" and lobbied state governments for tougher enforcement of child support.

In taking on these issues, women's groups confronted a social problem that would become more and more critical as the century neared an end. Women had become the fastest-growing segment of poor people in America, a trend sociologist Diana Pearce described as the "feminization of poverty." Of course, this problem affected children as well as mothers. From 1970 to 1982, the proportion of children living in poverty grew from 15 to 21 percent. Most poor children lived in female-headed households.

At the same time, birth rates among unmarried women and teen-agers began to rise (although they declined among married women), placing additional burdens on both mothers and children. Unskilled, uneducated, poor, young single mothers faced serious hardships. Well-paying jobs were scarce, especially in the depressed cities of the North. Even when they found work, these mothers often discovered that their paychecks barely covered the cost of childcare, when they could find it.

Even though women experienced some improvement in their incomes in this period, America's historic pattern of paying low wages to workers in female-dominated occupations remained deeply entrenched, resulting in high poverty rates for women who were trying to support children on their own. By the end of the decade, the median income of female-headed households with children was less than 40 percent of that of all families with children. Although often debated as a welfare issue, the poverty of women and children derived in large part from the low wages typically paid to many women workers.

For some middle-class women, the enactment of Title IX in 1972, which made gender discrimination in publicly funded educational institutions illegal, opened new opportunities. Previously, many elite universities—including several Ivy League institutions, the University of Virginia, and others—had excluded women from their undergraduate degree programs, and discrimination against women in graduate and professional schools had been commonplace. These exclusions not only cost women lucrative employment opportunities, they also meant that critical institutions in American society—including law, business, the military, and medicine—remained dominated by men, their perspectives, and their concerns. The law also made employment discrimination by educational institutions illegal, opening faculty jobs to women on an equal basis for the first time.

Despite lax enforcement of Title IX in the early years, it began to have significant positive effects on women students and women who aspired to academic careers. Women entered fields previously dominated by men in large numbers. Between 1970 and 1990, the percentage of bachelor's degrees received by women went from 5.2 percent to 39.1 percent in architecture, 0.7 percent to 13.8 percent in engineering, and 8.7 percent to 46.8 percent in business. In the same time period, women also increased their share of doctorates, from 13.3 percent to 36.4 percent. Over time, these changes would also result in higher incomes for some women as they moved beyond entry-level jobs and wages in the new fields. The problem of low wages in female-dominated occupations would remain, however, consigning many women workers to economic marginality.

In addition, women's entry into new occupations occurred both because of and despite the Equal Employment Opportunity Commission (EEOC), which was created to enforce Title VII of the 1964 Civil Rights Act. In the first fifteen years of its existence, the commission experienced great instability in leadership, inadequate funding, an enormous caseload, and a lack of political support at times for serious enforcement of discrimination law. It went through eleven executive directors and an equal number of chairpersons in the period when it needed to develop legal mechanisms for challenging systemic workplace discrimination. As a result, it focused on conciliating or closing cases with as little expenditure as possible and provided only minimal investigations of the hundreds of thousands of complaints it received. The enforcement of federal antidiscrimination law was shouldered primarily by private parties bringing their own lawsuits. In this situation, the support of labor unions was crucial for some women workers seeking labor-force equity.

These suits, coupled with EEOC guidelines, managed to change the legal landscape for American employers and those workers willing and able to challenge traditional practices. More subtly, they also began to erode popular support for blatant forms of employment discrimination. By the mid-1970s, the courts had reviewed cases involving "sex-plus" discrimination—which occurred when employers created age ceilings for women workers but not men or barred married women workers or mothers from particular jobs—and declared such practices illegal. Women flight attendants, for example, sued the airline industry because it grounded them when they reached a certain age (never more than thirty-five) or got married. Aided by their unions, women flight attendants won these cases. According to EEOC guidelines, employers were also forbidden to use stereotypical assumptions about women or men, or to cite customer preferences and thus limit jobs to one gender. In 1974, the court decided that school districts could not mandate pregnancy leave for women teachers.

Litigation and lobbying from women's organizations also created other important changes in the legal status of women. In 1974, Congress passed the Equal Credit Opportunity Act, making it illegal for financial institutions to discriminate on the basis of gender when issuing credit cards or making decisions on loan applications. States passed a plethora of new laws, including laws that declared that evidence about rape victims' sexual histories would be inadmissible in rape cases. The U.S. Supreme Court also defined a new standard for reviewing cases involving gender discrimination in American law. Although its new criteria were not as rigorous as those applied in race discrimination cases, they did cause the courts to find for women litigants seeking equal treatment in some important areas of American law, including cases involving jury duty, the right to administer estates, equal benefits for servicewomen's dependents, and other issues.

Women of color also organized to secure legal and policy changes important to their well-being. In the early 1970s, they helped form a coalition of civil rights, labor, and feminist organizations to amend the 1938 Fair Labor Standards Act so that private household workers would be included under its minimum-wage provisions. They succeeded in 1974, despite strong opposition from southern Democrats, who opposed any extension of labor protections and argued that paying minimum wage for household workers would create economic hardships for the families (overwhelmingly white) who employed them. In the late 1970s, women of color mobilized civil rights and feminist organizations to make it illegal to perform sterilizations on women without their informed consent. New federal regulations also outlawed the use of various coercive measures, including threats to remove women's children or to withhold public assistance, that had become commonplace.

Throughout the 1970s, Americans adopted various alternatives to the traditional nuclear family. The number of adults living alone increased 60 percent in the 1970s; by 1980, this group constituted 23 percent of all households. At the same time, the number of unmarried couples living together tripled to 1.6 million, and one-third of them had children.

While the divorce rate and the instances of living together increased, so did the marriage rate. However their practices changed, Americans still pursued an ideal of eternal romantic attachment. Eighty percent of separated or divorced people remarried within three years. Sociologists described "blended families," in which children lived with stepparents, stepsiblings, and half siblings. Experts predicted that more than half of all children born in the 1970s would spend part of their childhood living in a household other than the traditional model, which would have been headed by their own biological mother and father and with only their biological brothers or sisters. Forty percent would spend time in a single-parent household, almost always headed by a woman. One disadvantage of such situations was their unpredictability. On the positive side, the best of these blended families offered extended networks of nurturing and affection.

Childrearing practices and expectations changed as more women entered the work force. Traditionally, mothers had borne the brunt of childcare; now nonfamily members did more of the work. A substantial part of a family's income went to babysitters or daycare facilities. Middle-class families improvised different childcare arrangements. One survey of working mothers reported that their children "may experience three, four or even more kinds of care in a single week, as they spend part of the day in nursery school, another portion with a family daycare mother, and are brought to and from these services by a parent, neighbor, or some other person." Single mothers, who were often poor, frequently left children with grandparents or other relatives. Older children let themselves into their homes after school. These so-called latchkey children had only the companionship of other youngsters or the TV until their parents got home from work. Experts said that the average child watched twelve to sixteen thousand hours of TV between the ages of two and sixteen.

Childcare advocates, including feminist leaders, worked hard to meet the growing need for daycare. Marian Wright Edelman and others formed the Children's Defense Fund, soon to become the nation's most visible advocacy group on behalf of children. Leaders like Edelman and her friend Hillary Rodham Clinton pointed out that the United States was the only nation in the developed world without a national childcare policy. Beginning in 1971, Congress considered several bills that would have provided significant federal funding for childcare, but conservatives fought the bills, which they feared would pave the way for "communal child rearing." President Richard Nixon vetoed one such bill on the grounds that it would create "Sovietized child care."

Another sign of trouble in the American family came from horrifying new reports of physical, sexual, and emotional abuse of children and spouses. Modern families may not have become more violent than earlier ones, but once feminists and child advocates insisted that the issues of wife battering and child abuse be taken seriously, behavior that had once been tolerated now invited societal intervention. Most abuse went unreported, so documented cases represented only the tip of the iceberg. Although precise figures were difficult to obtain, experts estimated that between 1.5 and 2.3 million of the 46 million children between the ages of three and seventeen who lived with both parents had been battered by one or both of them sometime during their life.

Greater attention to women's rights also brought to light the growing problems of spouse abuse, mostly committed against women, and of rape within marriage or cohabitation relationships. Reports of rapes and wife beatings soared, and women in some states lobbied successfully to allow prosecution of husbands for raping their wives. Feminists established battered women's shelters and rape-crisis centers and hotlines. The shelters provided women with housing and other forms of assistance when they decided to leave abusive husbands.

Changes in family life and the growing feminist movement met resistance in some quarters, including those women who felt that the new expectations seemed to dismiss their lives and achievements. American women did not move easily, or as a unified group, from family-centered, domestic containment to feminist self-fulfillment. Opposition to the growing assertiveness of women crystallized in a movement to prevent ratification of the Equal Rights Amendment (ERA), despite the fact that every postwar president had endorsed the principle of ERA. Masterminded by conservative Illinois lawyer Phyllis Schlafly, the anti-ERA movement sought to recruit older women, women who did not work outside the home, conservative men, and religious organizations by arguing that the ERA would diminish women's standing and leave most women unprotected. Passed by Congress and sent to the states in 1972, the ERA had to be ratified by thirty-eight state legislatures before March 1979 or it would die. After quickly gaining passage in thirty-five states, the amendment was stymied. In July 1978, sixty-five thousand women marched on Washington to pressure Congress to extend the deadline for three more years. It did so, but opponents continued to block passage in state legislatures, and the proposed amendment was never ratified.

The anti-ERA movement used women's exemption from the military draft very effectively as an example of the kinds of protections it wanted to retain for women. Their reluctance to require women's service in the military was shared by the U. S. Supreme Court. In the 1980 case of *Rostker* v. *Goldberg*, it held that restricting the draft to men was a constitutionally permissible form of gender discrimination. It was constitutional, the Court stated, because the need to maintain national security was an important policy goal and the exclusion of women was substantially related to that goal: the military could meet its need for women (largely as nurses and clerks) without a draft. It also argued that Congress had not used impermissible gender stereotypes because it had discussed that issue at length, as though the profession of good intent was sufficient proof of its existence. Citing the congressional testimony of military leaders who stated that they might not be able to secure all the servicewomen they needed without a draft, Justice Thurgood Marshall rejected the majority's conclusions. He specifically disagreed with their assertion that Congress could oppose the registration of women because it focused on "the question of military need rather than 'equity'"; he stated that "what the majority so blithely dismisses as 'equity' is nothing less than the Fifth Amendment's guarantee of equal protection of the laws which 'requires that Congress treat similarly situated persons similarly.'"

The historic limitation of women's military service (about 2 percent for most of the period since 1945) meant also that women workers lost many jobs to apparently less-qualified veterans as a consequence of veterans preference laws passed by the federal government and the states. In Massachusetts, for example, all veterans who served in a time of war (defined as the whole period between 1940 and 1975) and passed a civil-service exam were placed on the eligibility list above all other applicants, including those who had much higher scores on the exam. Tired of being passed over again and again for jobs she had sought, Helen Feeney decided to sue. The U.S. Supreme Court found in 1979, however, that there was no gender discrimination in the law because female and male veterans experienced the same treatment by the state of Massachusetts. As the decision indicates, this form of affirmative action retained a high level of popular and official support.

By the late 1970s, a sizable backlash against new roles for women had developed, orchestrated by the growing anti-abortion and profamily movement. That movement grew initially from efforts by the Catholic Church to overturn the Supreme Court's decision in *Roe* v. *Wade*. Catholic Church leaders mobilized parishioners to organize a mass-based social movement outside the purview of traditional political parties. Within a few years, ministers and others in fundamentalist Protestant, Mormon, and Orthodox Jewish congregations had joined. The churches provided key elements in the growing power of the anti-abortion, antifeminist movement: an organizational base for mobilizing voters and securing funding, the media power of the televangelists, and a moral legitimacy conferred by the association of the group with religious values. This movement, in turn, gave the New Right its apocalyptic vision of a world divided between good and evil, and the resources and voters it needed to become a potent force in American politics.

Proclaiming that "God did not ordain sex for fun and games" and that in families, "the father's word has to prevail," the New Right mobilized hostility to all nonmarital and nonprocreative sex. At the same time, they expressed and heightened public anxieties that changes in gender roles would threaten women's commitment to motherhood, domesticity, and caretaking. While promising that women would receive economic security and social approval within marriage, they concluded that those benefits would require their subordination to their husbands. Connie Marshner, one of the leaders of the profamily movement, told women that all they needed to know was "that somebody will have the authority and make the decision, and that your job is to be happy with it."

The sexual revolution of the 1960s had left a complicated legacy. Much to the surprise of both its advocates and its critics, the idea of sexual freedom had been easily absorbed into the mainstream culture. Openness about sex and the erosion of old restrictions freed women, but did so without providing women with the economic and cultural resources to claim sexual freedom without objectification. Indeed, the decline of sexual taboos and the acknowledgment of female eroticism convinced some men that women were theirs for the taking. Sales of pornographic magazines, books, and movie tickets, mostly to men, surged, reaching $4 billion per year.

The growth of the pornography industry divided old allies and created unlikely alignments. Advocates of the new freedoms had once resisted all restraints on the dissemination of sexually explicit material. In the 1970s, however, feminists became divided over the issue of pornography. Some feminists, believing that pornography incited violence against women and degraded them, joined with religious traditionalists and social conservatives to call for the regulation or banning of pornography. Other feminists joined male advocates of sexual liberation, like *Penthouse* editor Bob Guccione, to argue that restricting pornography, however repugnant the material, violated the freedom of expression guaranteed by the First Amendment and would eventually foster a backlash against sexual freedom. The courts generally upheld Guccione's point of view.

Greater openness about sexuality encouraged homosexual Americans to seek acceptance from "straight" society and an end to ingrained prejudice and stereotypes. The campaign for gay rights achieved notable gains in the 1970s. For instance, the American Psychiatric Association dropped its classification of homosexuality as a mental disorder and joined a growing call for the extension of civil rights protections to homosexuals. A major women's conference in Houston affirmed solidarity with lesbians.

In their daily lives, gays and lesbians found new self-confidence and visibility during the 1970s. Gay men established well-defined, separate neighborhoods in many American cities. Lesbians, though less geographically concentrated, nonetheless created communities for themselves in various ways, claiming a culture of their own through music, art, and literature, and founding successful businesses. Although some heterosexuals continued to oppose tolerance toward homosexuals, gays and lesbians spoke of the love and caring they experienced together. They openly acknowledged their sexual orientation, formed organizations to advance their interests, and published newspapers and magazines addressing their concerns. Gays and lesbians lobbied municipalities, states, and the federal government to guarantee equal access for homosexuals in employment, housing, and various government programs. Some laws changed, but Congress did not consider such legislation on the national level.

Opponents of gay rights mounted attacks against gays and lesbians. After Miami's city council banned discrimination against homosexuals, singer Anita Bryant began a campaign to repeal the new law. She complained that the "ordinance condones immorality and discriminates against my children's rights to grow up in a healthy, decent community." In June 1977, Bryant's Save Our Children movement organized a referendum that repealed the law by

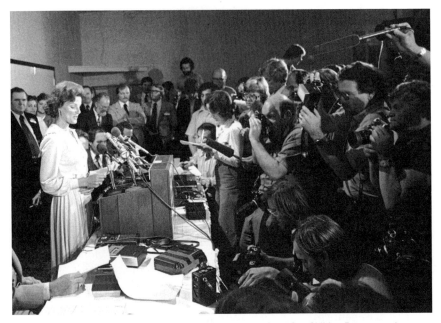

Singer-activist Anita Bryant addresses reporters after her "Save Our Children" movement won a referendum rescinding civil rights protections for gays and lesbians in Dade County, Florida. / © Bettmann/CORBIS

a 2-to-1 majority. A few years later, she and her husband divorced and she published a widely read article in a women's magazine complaining that he (and other men influenced by Christian right teachings) were dictatorial and insensitive to their wives.

The size of the vote in Miami shook gays and advocates of civil liberties across the country. The National Gay Task Force believed that the vote represented an effort to herd homosexuals back into the closet, where many had shuddered in fear of exposure before the openness of the 1960s. San Francisco mayor George Moscone, elected with the support of the city's sizable gay community, condemned the repeal as "terribly wrong." Moscone backed a march by five thousand demonstrators against Bryant and other opponents of gay rights. But in November 1978, Moscone and Harvey Milk were gunned down by Dan White, who had voted against San Francisco's gay rights law. Although the police arrested White with the smoking gun in his hand, he won acquittal on murder charges. The jury accepted White's strange claim that excessive consumption of Twinkies had left him temporarily insane. After the jury announced its verdict, about ten thousand supporters of Milk and Moscone rioted, chanting, "He got away with murder." The so-called Twinkie defense became a staple of television sitcoms and more serious discussions of law and mental illness.

Economic Problems and Social Divisions

Had the nation's economy boomed, as it had during most of the 1960s, prosperity might have assuaged the social tensions and uncertainties of the 1970s. An already sputtering economy, however, began a serious decline in the mid-1970s. Inflation took a heavy toll on Americans, making many worry about the future. Stagflation—persistent slow growth coupled with rising prices—remained a serious problem. Prices rose because American productivity had slowed and because a fourfold increase in petroleum prices produced an oil shock that rippled through the economy. The decline of industrial employment, caused by increased foreign competition and the movement of jobs abroad, combined with the weakening of the labor movement initiated a long-term decline in working-class income in the United States.

After September 1978, when a revolution in Iran sent oil prices soaring, inflation became rampant. The annual rate of increase in the consumer price index (CPI) climbed steadily from an already high 7 percent in May 1978 to 11.3 percent in July 1979. And this percentage increase represented only a cumulative average: the cost of goods people bought and used every day rose even faster. Gasoline went up 52 percent from September 1978 to September 1979. Americans panicked, fearing they would not be able to get gas no matter what they paid. Oil producers, refiners, and service stations took advantage of the fear to gouge consumers. By the summer of 1979, cars were lining up five hundred deep at some service stations. Motorists shouted, shook their fists, and even attacked one another to get gas. The apparent greed and callousness of the oil companies made people even angrier. States imposed a crude form of rationing by demanding that drivers go to the pump only on alternate days.

Fear of shortages and high prices extended beyond gasoline. As prices on home heating oil, used mostly in the Northeast and Midwest, shot up during 1979, people in these regions glumly contemplated a cold, expensive winter. Food prices also took off. Consumers felt the pinch every time they went to the supermarket, and TV news broadcasts did not let them forget it when they returned home. In 1979, the CBS evening news ran a popular weekly feature surveying the cost of a standard market basket of groceries in several cities across the country. Prices climbed everywhere; those soaring fastest included the basic staples of the American home—beer, eggs, even toilet paper.

American industry had enjoyed for some time a global edge that it believed would last indefinitely. As a consequence, many corporations, especially automakers and steel manufacturers, failed to undertake long-term planning, delayed modernizing, and underestimated their competition. Inflation made it harder for businesses to modernize. As Secretary of the Treasury Michael Blumenthal explained, "[Y]ou can't figure your rate of return, so you postpone investments." Competitors in Japan and Germany, where inflation remained below 3 percent, spent two to three times more than American firms to upgrade their manufacturing facilities. As a result, American manufacturing

An unemployed steelworker walks across the bridge near the Johnstown plant of Bethlehem Steel Corporation, where he has been laid off after sixteen years of service. Such layoffs signalled the decline of heavy industry in the United States; many workers were forced to trade well-paying skilled jobs for low-wage service work. / AP/Wide World

experienced a devastating decline. Observers began calling the industrial East and Midwest "the Rustbelt."

American workers also suffered as U.S. corporations grew more and more multinational, shifting their production facilities to Asia and Latin America, where labor was cheaper. Manufacturing jobs declined throughout the United States, especially in the large cities. New York City alone lost 234,000 industrial production jobs in the 1970s. The shrinking job market for industrial workers had a severe effect on the urban poor. In earlier decades, American cities had been a magnet for unskilled European immigrants and southern rural blacks. Poverty worsened in many American cities with the loss of industrial employment. Especially in the northern cities, deindustrialization, a declining tax base, and increased poverty nearly overwhelmed municipal services. New York City came within days of defaulting on its debt before Congress approved loan guarantees—over Gerald Ford's resistance—in November 1975. The anger many New Yorkers felt for the president was expressed in a local newspaper headline: "Ford to City: Drop Dead." In the first municipal bankruptcy since the Great Depression, the city of Cleveland actually defaulted on its bonds in 1978.

As its manufacturing industries declined, the American economy shifted toward services. The greatest job growth in the 1970s came in services such as information management, entertainment, transportation, and retail sales. While unemployed steel- and autoworkers contemplated the prospect of flipping burgers for $4 an hour instead of earning $16 plus benefits, local authorities struggled to offset the decline in manufacturing by offering direct subsidies or tax abatements for service industries to relocate to their areas. New airports were constructed in Dallas and Atlanta, increasing the growth of these Sunbelt cities. Municipalities in both the Sunbelt and the Rustbelt wooed professional sports franchises by constructing new stadiums.

To foster job development, southern states also welcomed factories that polluted and attracted new industries by promising that they would provide a low-wage, nonunion labor force. A local chamber of commerce in South Carolina, for example, sent out promotional materials pointing to what they considered a positive fact: that more than three-fourths of its workers received less than $5,000 a year for their labor. By 1980, North Carolina, which was the area's largest manufacturing employer, could also boast the lowest rates of unionization and of hourly wages in the country. Despite the state's industrial growth, its workers experienced a growing gap between their wages and those of other factory workers in the country. Clearly, the region's strategy of marketing its poverty had worked in North Carolina.

These dynamics had mixed results for African American workers. They were most likely to secure jobs in the lowest-paying industries (like textiles) or in workplaces that harbored environmental hazards. Some companies decided to locate in areas of the South with low black populations or to hold the numbers of African Americans hired to low levels so they could impede unionization. By the early 1970s, unions and employers alike had concluded that black workers were more likely to support the formation of unions than were whites. They did so because unions (even those that were previously all-white) often assisted blacks in achieving access to more skilled jobs with better pay and provided workers with an ally to help them fight against poor treatment at work. Textile worker Daisy Walker, for example, received support from her union and the EEOC when she fought her discharge for retaliating after a supervisor elbowed her in the breast. She received critical support from white workers, who corroborated her charges of racism and sexual harassment in the plant.

By the 1970s, unions confronted many problems in addition to the movement of jobs to anti-union areas in the South and the West. Nationally, they faced employers willing to go to great lengths, including violations of labor law, to defeat unionization drives. In the 1970s, the number of union cases alleging that workers had been fired for union activities more than doubled. In 1980, federal officials had ordered more than ten thousand such workers reinstated in their jobs with back pay—the only penalty levied against employers for breaking the law in this way. By the time reinstatement orders came, however, the union movement in a particular workplace had usually failed. In fact, when management was willing to break the law, it succeeded in defeating organizing efforts over 90 percent of the time. Not surprisingly, employers valued the benefits they derived from their illegal strategies. As a result, the proportions of workers fired for union activism continued to climb.

The combination of economic changes that workers experienced after 1970 caused a steady, long-term decrease in the wages of many Americans. Working-class men, especially those with limited education, found that their prospects for earning a livelihood that would enable them to support families had begun to erode. Those most affected included many men of color, who had only begun to secure better-paying blue-collar jobs in the late 1960s. The last hired, they became the first fired as employers moved their jobs to the suburbs, to the South, or outside the country. The competition for scarce jobs heightened white backlash against affirmative action, while the fundamental political and economic changes that caused the decline in good jobs received little political attention.

The competition also occasioned hostility and some violence against the new immigrants who came to the United States from Southeast Asia in the wake of the Vietnam War. In the Gulf Coast area of Texas, for example, the arrival of Vietnamese immigrants angered white Americans who viewed them as unfair economic competitors in the fishing industry. Because the Vietnamese women worked in a local plant, the men were able to secure the capital they needed to buy used, decrepit boats. As one white observer explained it, "Americans were selling them boats that were worn out—nothing but plywood glued together— for $5,000 or $6,000. I saw one piece of junk you couldn't give away. And the Vietnamese fisherman paid $7,500 for it. That boat was still fishing last year."

In Seadrift, Texas, a conflict over who was to fish a certain area escalated into violence. A white fisherman who stabbed a Vietnamese was then shot. The jury acquitted his killer, deciding that he had fired in self-defense. After the verdict, several Vietnamese were beaten and their property was vandalized. Most of them decided to move further south and start over. The conflicts over their presence on the Gulf Coast did not end, however, because whites continued to blame them for a declining shrimp harvest. Despite the fact that industrial pollution from oil refineries and chemical plants accounted for part of the decline and that the number of white fishermen had also increased in the 1970s, white fishermen found the Vietnamese a convenient scapegoat for their economic woes.

Religion and the Rise of the New Right

Confronted with social uncertainty and economic stagnation, some Americans developed a renewed interest in religion. In contrast to the earlier revival of the 1950s, when churches and synagogues had studiously avoided dogma and ritual, the most popular sects of the 1970s promised structure, authority, orthodoxy, and a return to lost moral values. The mainstream Protestant churches—Episcopalian, Presbyterian, Methodist, Congregationalist, and some Baptist groups—lost members and influence in the 1970s; so did the Catholic Church and Conservative and Reform synagogues. On the other hand, interest surged in fundamentalist, evangelical, and Pentecostal churches; Mormonism; Orthodox Judaism; and a rich variety of Eastern religions and spiritual disciplines such as Zen, Hinduism, yoga, and Tibetan Buddhism. Much of the gain in religious observance came from young people, including members of the 1960s counterculture looking for meaning and connections in their lives.

Some anguished parents whose adult children had joined cults hired strongmen to seize the young people and "deprogram" them. Cultural observers decried the proliferation of nonrational and antirational approaches to spirituality. Historian Christopher Lasch assailed the "hedonism, narcissism and cult of the self" that he said were characteristic of several new religious movements. Writer Tom Wolfe went further, putting a label on the entire culture of the 1970s: he called it the "Me Decade."

The Right also felt that the "culture of narcissism" was sapping America's vitality. Many Bible-oriented Christian leaders were particularly distraught at the direction that the country was taking. They expressed their frustration by joining the political conservatives of the New Right, which had been growing since Barry Goldwater's unsuccessful presidential campaign of 1964.

Committed to overturning liberalism and restoring traditional values, these religious leaders gave a strong impetus to the movement. Many of them took to the airwaves with "electronic churches," which quickly developed a weekly audience of millions of viewers. The popularity of their TV programs further eroded attendance at mainstream Protestant churches, which could not offer the same flashy showmanship. The TV preachers of the New Right damned liberalism, feminism, sex education, divorce, the practice of living together without marriage, homosexuality, and the teaching of evolution in the nation's schools. The most successful televangelists, as they were called, included Jerry Falwell, Pat Robertson, Jim and Tammy Bakker, and Oral Roberts. They raised millions of dollars in contributions from their viewers. More and more, they connected religion with politics. "We have enough votes to run the country," Robertson declared. In 1979, Falwell formed the Moral Majority, an organization dedicated to "pro-God, pro-family policies in government." He urged other fundamentalist ministers to abandon Jimmy Carter and help raise converts for the Moral Majority and the Republican Party.

Another member of the new political spectrum was a group of formerly liberal intellectuals, writers, and editors known as neoconservatives. Writing for small but influential magazines like *Commentary* and *The Public Interest*, neoconservatives assailed liberals for distorting the original purpose of the welfare state by changing the emphasis from promoting equal opportunity to guaranteeing equal results. They criticized affirmative action programs, which aimed to provide greater opportunity for groups that had historically been excluded from positions of economic, professional, and political power, as "affirmative discrimination." They maintained their earlier support of U.S. participation in the Vietnam War, a stance that further alienated them from most liberals, who regretted the war and urged a less assertive American foreign policy. In 1975, neoconservatives formed the Committee on the Present Danger, which spent the next five years lobbying for additional American nuclear weapons to intimidate the Soviet Union. The emerging neoconservative movement added to the strength of former California governor Ronald Reagan's campaign for the Republican presidential nomination in 1980.

(cont. on page 405)

Evangelical Christianity in American Life

Evangelical Christians, among the largest branches of conservative American Protestantism, believe that only a personal, life-altering experience that culminates with a decision to follow Jesus guarantees salvation. This decision is often referred to as being "born again." Evangelicals tend to believe it their duty as born-again Christians to guide nonbelievers toward the path of salvation and to "win" the souls of nonbelievers for Christ.

Until the controversy over evolution in the 1920s, evangelism was a stable force within American Protestantism that, if not mainstream, certainly occupied a prominent place in American society. The debate over evolution and creationism, however, pushed evangelism to the sidelines of U.S. religion for several decades. Some urban Americans, themselves unsure of their status in a fast-changing society, scoffed at evangelicals as rural primitives, unwilling to accept the insights and material benefits of twentieth-century science and technology. For their part, evangelicals responded by renouncing most political and social activity as hopelessly corrupt. Not until the 1950s did evangelists reappear as a prominent force. This upsurge in popularity owed much to the charismatic style of a North Carolina preacher, William (Billy) Franklin Graham.

Graham began his career during World War II as a traveling evangelist. In the 1950s he conducted huge public assemblies in tents, fields, and eventually sports stadiums. With his radio program, *Hour of Decision*, his newspaper column, "My Answer," and his documentary film series, Graham soon became synonymous with American evangelism. His constant denunciation of communism as a symbol of evil provided Americans with a sense of security during the early Cold War.

As Graham became more popular, he parted company with some of his more rigid earlier supporters. In the 1960s, he advocated desegregation of congregations in the South, and he opened a dialogue with Roman Catholics. Graham became a symbol of the growing integration of evangelical Protestantism into everyday life. Every president from Eisenhower to George W. Bush sought his company—and his blessing.

Also assuming prominence in the postwar years was a Pentecostal from Oklahoma named Granville (Oral) Roberts. After battling tuberculosis for five months as a young adult, Oral Roberts attended a faith healing, where he believed God had cured him. After the healing, he began his career as an evangelist at a series of southern churches. Over the next fifty years, he presided over a ministry, a university, and a television series, and he built a national reputation as a Pentecostal faith healer. Like Graham, Oral Roberts used radio, print journalism, and television to attract followers and to publicize his beliefs, which consisted of traditional Pentecostalism blended with faith healing and the supernatural. His ability to capitalize on media resources allowed him to bring Pentecostalism into mainstream conservative American religion.

The 1960s brought many obstacles to the American evangelical movement. The women's movement challenged evangelists' acceptance of the traditional Victorian ideal of women as wives and mothers. Evangelical women's associations, such as Daughters of Sarah, began to form, and they challenged the movement's male-dominated structure. Calls for racial equality and the civil rights movement also shook the belief structure of evangelism. The biggest threat, however, came from the controversy over Vietnam. The unsolvable questions of morality inspired by the war contrasted with the evangelicals' stark separation between godless communism and God's (or the American) way.

But evangelical Christianity emerged as an even more powerful force in the next

Billy Graham preaching to a crowd of tens of thousands in a Washington, D.C., football stadium. / © Bettmann/ CORBIS

decade. The election of self-proclaimed born-again president Jimmy Carter in 1976 greatly enhanced the status of evangelicals. Millions of them went to the polls for Carter in 1976. The new president's moderate views on issues such as women's rights, abortion, racial equality, and the Cold War eventually alienated many of his evangelical backers. About half of those evangelicals who had voted for him in 1976 switched to Ronald Reagan in 1980. For at least the next decade, evangelical Christians became a major element in conservative and Republican politics.

The expansion of religious television and radio consolidated the position of conservative Protestantism in American life in the 1970s and 1980s. The career of Marion Gordon (Pat) Robertson illustrates the trend. After Robertson's ordination in 1961, he purchased a small Virginia television station and began religious broadcasting. The station struggled financially until Robertson devised the idea of "faith partners." These groups enlisted seven hundred people, each of whom pledged $10 to fund the station. As money from the faith partners poured in, Robertson had enough to create the Christian Broadcasting Network (CBN) and *The 700 Club*, a nationally syndicated religious talk show.

Another prominent televangelist, Jim Bakker, began his career in 1965 as a host of Robertson's *The 700 Club*. In 1973, Bakker left CBN to begin his own show, *The PTL Club*. (PTL stands for Praise the Lord or People That Love.) Bakker occasionally encouraged viewers to use their credit cards to make donations so that the show could access the cash more quickly. Five years later, Bakker and his wife, Tammy Faye, ventured out on their own to create the first twenty-four-hour religious television network, the PTL Satellite Network.

Jimmy Swaggart, cousin of rock star Jerry Lee Lewis, was another powerful evangelistic orator. Swaggart began with a radio program broadcast on over five hundred stations, but he switched to the more lucrative medium of television in the mid-1970s. Like Graham, Roberts, Robertson, and Bakker, Swaggart relied on educational institutions to attract followers; he founded the Jimmy Swaggart Bible College in 1982.

Like the other evangelists, Swaggart was also a charismatic speaker who knew how to utilize television and radio to attract adherents and financial support.

With a president like Jimmy Carter; televangelists like Bakker, Swaggart, and Robertson; and megachurches (vast congregations with more than 10,000 members), evangelism in the 1970s became so powerful that *Newsweek* proclaimed 1976 the Year of the Evangelist.

During the 1980s, evangelism expanded into the political sphere. In 1988, Pat Robertson announced his intention to run for the Republican Party's presidential nomination, provided he received the financial and spiritual support of 3 million people. He received the money but lost the nomination to George H. W. Bush, after which he founded a political organization called the Christian Coalition. The Christian Coalition embraced a conservative agenda that opposed legalized abortion, equal rights for homosexuals, and the absence of prayer in public schools. Many critics objected to the coalition's use of "voter guides" (pamphlets, endorsing certain candidates, that were placed on windshields during church services). Despite such opposition, by the mid-1990s, the coalition had a budget of nearly $20 million and a membership of nearly 2 million. Taking credit for political victories such as Republican majorities in both houses in 1994 and the success of politicians such as Newt Gingrich, Pat Robertson's Christian Coalition was an important symbol of evangelism's shift into the political sphere.

Another prominent symbol of evangelistic politics was the Moral Majority, founded in 1979 by televangelist Jerry Falwell. Lamenting the erosion of the nuclear family, divorce, legalized abortion, pornography, and homosexuality, the Moral Majority campaigned against the Equal Rights Amendment, the gay rights movement, and the absence of prayer in public schools. An important supporter of Republican presidential candidate Ronald Reagan in the 1980 election, the Moral Majority provided the religious right with a political voice. Although less conservative alternatives to the Moral Majority and the Christian Coalition existed on the political right, Robertson and Falwell's media savvy ensured that their associations dominated the public image of political evangelism.

Scandal engulfed evangelism during the 1980s and early 1990s. In 1987, details of a sordid sexual affair involving Jim Bakker and a young church secretary from New York pervaded the media. Charges of tax evasion and financial impropriety followed these accusations, and adherents discovered that the Bakkers' urgent appeals for donations to save various branches of their religious institutions often served to finance the couple's luxurious lifestyle. In 1987, Bakker resigned and asked Jerry Falwell to take over PTL. The Bakkers' scandal was quickly followed by exposure of Jimmy Swaggart's involvement with a prostitute, which resulted in the loss of his clerical credentials.

But the airing of dirty linen did not spell the decline of evangelicalism. Cable television meant an increased number of religious television programs, the majority of which were evangelical. Evangelical radio expanded as well. Pat Robertson's empire continued to grow: by the early 1990s, he controlled a dynasty that included the cable television station The Family Channel, International Family Entertainment, MTM productions, and the Ice Capades. Evangelical organizations such as the Promise Keepers continue to form and attract supporters. Although the Moral Majority disbanded in 1989, organizations such as James Dobson's Focus on the Family ensure the continuing political voice of the religious right. Billy Graham's son, Franklin Graham, developed a wide following, and Jerry Falwell remained a powerful figure on television and in his megachurch. Although the direction of evangelism's future is unclear, the institutions created by evangelists guarantee the continued participation of evangelical Christians in American political and social life.

That campaign and the New Right in general also benefited from a growing racial backlash directed particularly against African American efforts to secure better jobs, schools, and housing. Increasingly national in scope, that backlash gained strength as white working-class men experienced job and income loss and blamed minorities for their plight. In the 1970s, the federal courts began attacking the problem of persisting school segregation in cities with high levels of residential segregation. They did so by ordering school districts to abandon neighborhood-based schools and use busing programs to move students across the divides of race. In response, many white parents throughout the country organized to oppose such plans.

Boston became the heart and symbol of the movement against busing, supplanting Little Rock, Arkansas, as an emblem of white racist resistance. In heavily Irish American neighborhoods in Boston, white mobs attacked buses filled with African American children and clashed violently with police, and incidents of racial violence occurred throughout the city, leaving two dead and many injured. Led by Louise Day Hicks, who had opposed improved schools for blacks when she served as chair of the city's school committee in

the 1960s, a diverse coalition of angry whites formed in the 1970s to fight federal court orders. Many working-class whites who joined the struggle brought their hostility toward elite city leaders who had destroyed their neighborhoods with highway and urban renewal projects in the name of progress and liberalism.

In the long run, Boston experienced many of the same dynamics as other city school districts. White school officials sometimes worked to sabotage the courts' plans, providing desegregation officials with faulty data and allowing school discipline to worsen. White families who could afford to do so often moved to the suburbs or sent their children to private schools, mostly Catholic schools. Black middle-class parents made similar decisions because they were unhappy with the social turmoil and eroding academic standards of the public schools. By the 1980s, a few schools stood out as successful models of desegregation, but most faced the problems associated with impoverished

Buses carrying African American students arrive at South Boston High School under police escort as court-ordered busing begins in 1975. / © Bettmann/CORBIS

students and middle-class flight from support for public schools, including high dropout rates and deteriorating schools.

Presidential Politics

"Gerald Ford is an awfully nice man who isn't up to the presidency," wrote John Osborne in *The New Republic*. Osborne shared the feeling of millions of Americans who at first had welcomed Ford as a relief and a breath of fresh air. But Ford alienated potential supporters—on the Right and the Left—with two decisions made within a month of his inauguration: the appointment of Nelson Rockefeller as vice president and the pardon of Richard Nixon. An experienced Republican officeholder who had served fourteen years as governor of New York, Rockefeller was widely regarded as the leader of the eastern, moderate wing of the Republican Party. But therein lay a problem: the Republican Party had grown increasingly western, southern, and conservative since 1968. The mainstream of the Republican Party now consisted of people like those who had booed Rockefeller at the 1964 convention, and these conservatives never forgave Ford for elevating Rockefeller to the vice presidency. Nevertheless, Congress acknowledged that the new president had wide latitude in choosing a vice president, and Rockefeller was confirmed in December 1974. For the first time in history, neither the president nor the vice president of the United States had been elected to their position by the voters.

If choosing Rockefeller angered the Republican Right, pardoning Nixon did huge damage to Ford's public standing with the whole country. Ford believed that a protracted trial of the former president would only stir fresh anger about Watergate, diverting attention from what Ford wanted to accomplish and hurting Republican chances in the upcoming congressional elections. On September 8, 1974, Ford announced that he had provided a "full, free, and absolute pardon" to the former president. Nixon formally accepted the pardon, an act equivalent to acknowledging guilt, but he claimed only to have made "mistakes" in the Watergate affair. The public felt betrayed by Ford and was dissatisfied that Nixon would not admit that he had broken the law. The new president's approval rating dropped from 72 percent to 49 percent.

Anger over Watergate and Nixon's pardon, combined with frustration about the sour economy, produced a strong swing to the Democrats in the 1974 elections. Ford's response to the country's worsening economic state seemed tepid and inept. Committed to voluntary action rather than government intervention, he wore a button reading WIN, for Whip Inflation Now. The president's button seemed silly, and it reminded voters of the childlike, smiling "happy face" buttons that were popular at the time.

Troubles abroad contributed to the gnawing fear that events had slipped out of control and that the country's leaders had lost their sense of direction. The National Liberation Front, which was committed to reunifying Vietnam under Hanoi's communist government, won the war in April 1975, less than nine months after Ford became president. Almost immediately after signing the cease-fire in January 1973 (which led to the withdrawal of U.S. forces), both the Saigon government and the NLF had broken it. The government of President Nguyen Van Thieu had hoped that its offensive against the communists would encourage Washington to resume direct military support. But Thieu misjudged Americans' disgust with the war and their preoccupation with Watergate and their economic difficulties. When Ford asked Congress for additional military aid in early 1975, Congress refused to advance any more money.

On April 29, 1975, the last American helicopters took off from the roof of the U.S. embassy in Saigon. The next day, the remnants of the government of the Republic of Vietnam surrendered, and North Vietnamese and Vietcong troops renamed its capital Ho Chi Minh City. The Americans evacuated about 150,000 Vietnamese, most of them high-level officials of the South Vietnamese government and their families, but they left hundreds of thousands more behind. TV viewers at home were disgusted by images of U.S. Marines clubbing screaming, terrified Vietnamese to keep them away from the American embassy and of terrified people clinging to the runners of departing helicopters. Scenes of ARVN soldiers shoving and shooting the weak, the elderly, and women with small children to secure a place on the few evacuation planes represented to many the horror, chaos, and futility of the war in Vietnam.

Détente with the Soviet Union, already strained by the October 1973 Middle East war, declined further during the Ford administration. Kissinger and his Soviet counterparts never fulfilled their promise, contained in the 1972 SALT-I agreement, to conclude a full-fledged treaty by 1977. In November 1974, Ford and Soviet president Leonid Brezhnev signed the framework for an arms control treaty to be known as SALT II, but this document never matured into a full-scale treaty. American opponents of détente complained that Kissinger had weakened the U.S. military position and ignored Soviet violations of human rights. The Kremlin considered complaints about its human rights record an unjustified interference in its internal affairs, and it believed such criticism was merely a smoke screen for American unwillingness to expand détente. Thus, while Kissinger and Ford encountered domestic pressure to demand more of the Soviets, the Soviets began to stiffen their negotiating position.

In the fall of 1975, Ford continued to appear politically vulnerable. When his widely popular wife Betty called the Supreme Court's decision in *Roe* v. *Wade* "a great, great decision" and told an interviewer that premarital sex probably reduced the divorce rate, she further alienated conservative Republicans. Most Americans thought the First Lady's views indicated a refreshing openness. But the reaction from conservative Republicans could not have been worse for Ford. The highly conservative *Manchester* (New Hampshire) *Union-Leader* headlined Mrs. Ford's remarks with "A Disgrace to the Nation."

Another champion of the conservatives, former California governor Ronald Reagan, announced his candidacy for the Republican presidential nomination in November. He charged that Ford had become part of the cozy dealmaking of official Washington and was out of touch with the concerns of ordinary Republicans. Reagan stressed his opposition to a wide variety of institutions and trends: the federal government, Social Security, busing for integration, student radicalism, sexual promiscuity, abortion, the Equal Rights Amendment, détente, and accommodating the Third World. He advocated lower taxes, prayer in public schools, and an assertive foreign policy designed to erase the stain of Vietnam. Reagan defeated Ford in a series of southern and western primaries by criticizing the Nixon-Ford-Kissinger policy of détente with the Soviet Union. He complained that "this nation has become Number Two in military power in a world where it is dangerous—if not fatal—to be second best." Reagan won his greatest support with his ardent appeals to retain U.S. control over the Panama Canal, declaring, "We bought it, we paid for it, and we ought to keep it."

Ford eked out a narrow victory over Reagan at the Republican convention in Kansas City, pleading with party regulars not to humiliate a sitting Republican president. He capitulated to the conservatives by dropping Nelson Rockefeller as his nominee for vice president and replacing him with the sharp-tongued Kansas senator Robert Dole. The president toughened his stand on arms control, thereby blocking completion of a SALT II treaty before the election, and suspended work on the Panama Canal treaty. Ford also accepted a conservative platform that adopted many of Reagan's positions—"less government, less spending, less inflation." The platform called for constitutional amendments prohibiting abortion and permitting prayer in public schools. The party did retain its support for the ERA, a fixture of Republican platforms since 1940.

Democratic voters chose Jimmy Carter, former governor of Georgia, to oppose Ford in the fall election. A graduate of the Naval Academy at Annapolis, Carter had served in a nuclear submarine before leaving the navy in 1953 to take over his family's peanut farm in the southern Georgia town of Plains. He won election to the Georgia state legislature and ran for governor in 1966, but lost to segregationist Lester Maddox. Like many other moderate southern politicians defeated by ardent segregationists in the twenty years after *Brown v. Board of Education*, he vowed never to be "out-segged" again; he won the governorship in 1970 in part by accusing his moderate opponent of excessive friendliness to blacks.

Once elected governor, Carter became a model advocate of the New South, which claimed it was too busy attracting modern industry to dwell on the racial divisions of its past. He declared in his inaugural address that "the time for racial segregation is over," and he ordered a portrait of Martin Luther King, Jr., hung in the state capitol. His governorship drew business to Georgia and healed many racial wounds of the previous decade. After the catastrophic Democratic defeat in the 1972 presidential election, Carter decided to run for president. Massachusetts senator Edward Kennedy and Alabama governor George Wallace were the two candidates believed most likely to run, and Carter realized that each generated strong animosity among large segments of Democratic voters. A gap existed that could be filled by a moderate southerner unsullied by recent controversies.

A deeply religious man, Carter stressed old Protestant virtues in his campaign for the presidency. Nearly unknown at the beginning of 1976, he followed the advice of political professionals who grasped what the public wanted in the wake of Watergate and Vietnam. Specific programs mattered less than confidence in the rectitude and competence of their leaders. At a time when nearly all Washington politicians were under suspicion, Carter effectively used his status as an outsider, untouched by the failures and scandals of the federal government. "I'm not a lawyer, I'm not a member of Congress, and I've never served in Washington," Carter told responsive audiences as he traveled the country in the winter of 1975–1976 looking for support in caucuses and primaries.

When forced to take a stand on specifics—abortion, busing, amnesty for draft evaders—Carter tried to occupy the middle ground. He was "personally opposed to abortion" and did not want the government to fund abortions for poor women, yet he also did not want to overturn the Supreme Court's judgment that abortion was a right. He opposed mandatory busing to achieve racial balance, but he also opposed a constitutional amendment outlawing the practice. He favored a pardon for draft evaders, but he did not want to grant amnesty because accepting a pardon meant acknowledging having done wrong.

By April 1976, Carter had emerged as the clear front-runner. Carter's preeminence distressed some Democratic leaders. Part of the uneasiness about Carter derived from regional or religious snobbery: big-city liberals had little in common with southerners and evangelical Christians. But Carter also raised doubts among African Americans when he explained his opposition to low-income housing in mostly white suburbs. He said, "I see nothing wrong with ethnic purity being maintained. I would not force racial integration of a neighborhood by government action." Carter's long-time support for the Vietnam War, his skepticism about many Great Society programs, and his disdain for Washington also seemed a slap in the face to Democratic Party liberals.

Despite these strains, Carter wrapped up the nomination, and the Democrats met in optimism and harmony at their July convention, a sharp contrast to their last two gatherings. To appease traditional liberals, Carter chose one of them, Minnesota senator Walter Mondale, as his vice-presidential nominee. Martin Luther King, Sr., who delivered a benediction, declared that "surely the Lord sent Jimmy Carter to come on out and bring America back where she belongs."

Ford gave Carter a boost in the second of three televised debates when he mishandled a question on détente and U.S. relations with Poland. He claimed that "there is no Soviet domination of Eastern Europe, and there never will be under a Ford administration." The camera then focused on Carter, whose face broke into a broad grin. "I would like to see Mr. Ford convince the Polish-Americans and the Czech-Americans and the Hungarian-Americans in this country," Carter replied. *Time* magazine labeled Ford's remark "The Blooper Heard Round the World" and questioned his "grasp of foreign policy and even his mere competence." On a more substantial level, Carter continued his denunciations of Republican foreign policy, claiming it had ignored the human rights abuses of other nations and turned the United States into "the arms merchant of the world."

On Election Day, Carter defeated Ford by a slender margin in the popular vote and in the electoral college. The narrow victory revealed a divided and troubled electorate. Ford carried a majority of the white vote. Carter won all the states of the old Confederacy except Virginia. In the South, black voters turned out in substantial numbers, joining rural whites proud to vote for one of their own. But many Americans remained indifferent. Turnout was only 54.4 percent, then the lowest of any presidential election since World War II.

As president, Jimmy Carter relied on the advice of the pollsters and media specialists who had helped him win the White House. They told him to continue emphasizing his outsider status, to keep the Democrats who dominated Congress at arm's length, and to do whatever he could to demonstrate his closeness to ordinary people. Following this advice made Carter popular temporarily, but it severely strained his relationship with the professional politicians of the party he ostensibly led.

Deeply divided, the Democratic Party could not help the president, and it often hurt him when the country encountered hard times. Competing factions—southerners, blacks, urban ethnics, supporters of organized labor, feminists, former antiwar protesters, consumer advocates, environmentalists, educated professionals, traditional liberals, traditional conservatives—coexisted in an uneasy coalition, broader but less secure than the one assembled by Franklin Roosevelt. The New Deal alignment had made the Democrats a majority party for thirty years, but the war in Vietnam and racial tensions had broken old political ties. The Democratic Party of 1977 remained dominant, but it presented various conflicting programs and approaches to government and society.

Carter's efforts to follow through on his campaign promises showed how difficult it was for the president to occupy a middle position. On his first day in office, he offered a "full, complete and unconditional pardon" for all draft resisters. With this generous offer, he established a pattern of trying to bridge the chasms separating Americans on divisive issues—and of winning little gratitude for his efforts. The pardon announcement helped retire lingering controversies over Vietnam, but it diminished the president's sparse political capital. The director of the Veterans of Foreign Wars called it "the saddest day in American history." The Senate came close to passing a resolution of disapproval.

Many of Carter's early policy initiatives sparked congressional hostility. He offended important Democrats in February 1977 by abruptly canceling nineteen water projects in the South and West. These dams, river diversions, and irrigation systems were of dubious economic value in relation to their cost. They also represented tangible evidence of the wastefulness of the despised "Washington buddy system," in which legislators spent years building alliances by agreeing to support one another's pet construction projects. To Carter, who was committed to reducing waste and to judging each government program solely on its economic and social merits, the cancellations seemed logical. Politically, however, the decision angered many Democrats whose local support hinged on their ability to deliver public works projects to their districts.

Carter's effort to compromise on divisive social issues dissatisfied important groups within his party and left an impression of a confused president
who did not know where he wanted to lead the country. For example, he
sought a middle ground on abortion where none existed; he attempted to
bridge the gap between Joseph Califano, head of the Department of Health, Education and Welfare (HEW), who opposed all abortions, and Midge Costanza,
the White House liaison to women's groups, who favored a woman's unre-
stricted right to terminate a pregnancy. When the Supreme Court upheld a
congressional action forbidding the use of Medicaid funds for abortion except
in cases where the mother's life was threatened, supporters of reproductive
choice complained that the decision unfairly penalized poor women. Carter's
response—"life is unfair"—evinced no sympathy for poor women facing unwanted pregnancies.

The Carter administration also failed to resolve the nation's deep divisions
on the question of affirmative action programs. These programs represented
an effort by businesses, universities, and other organizations to compensate
the victims of generations of prejudice by giving them preference for jobs or
educational opportunities. To guarantee fair representation of minorities,
many such programs established minimum quotas for minority groups and
women, but this arrangement began to provoke strong resentment among
those who did not benefit.

Carter supported the Supreme Court's effort to solve the dilemma in *University of California Board of Regents v. Bakke* (1978). Allan Bakke, a white man who
had been denied admission to the university's medical school, argued that the
university's affirmative action policy had produced a reverse form of discrimination, admitting less qualified black applicants in his place. Although the
Supreme Court decided in Bakke's favor, the ruling was highly ambiguous. A
majority of the justices allowed affirmative action programs based on race but
invalidated rigid quota systems. Because many Democrats disagreed about affirmative action, the issue threatened to split the president's fragile coalition. The
Court's sharply divided ruling failed to still the controversy about what steps, if
any, institutions should take to redress previous discrimination. The Carter administration tried to apply the *Bakke* ruling by insisting that agencies awarding
federal grants and contracts adopt affirmative action programs but not require
set quotas for specific classes of people. Neither supporters nor opponents of affirmative action considered Carter's position satisfactory. Disagreements about
affirmative action and about "set-aside" programs for certain groups persisted
long after *Bakke*, dividing the Democratic coalition as feminists and racial minorities found themselves supporting the broad-based affirmative action policies
opposed by many white ethnics and some labor unions.

As politicians squabbled in Washington and the president's popularity fell,
a public backlash against government at all levels began to grow. In June
1978, Californians ignored the objections of Governor Brown and nearly
every other prominent political figure, education professional, and busi-
nessperson in the state and voted by a 2-to-1 ratio to roll back property taxes
to the levels of the mid-1960s. The popularity of Proposition 13, as the tax

limitation measure was called, was due to several factors. Because of the rapid inflation in the value of real estate, taxes on California homes had tripled in the preceding decade. Despite warnings that the proposition's restrictions on future tax increases would damage the state's schools, universities, parks, libraries, and highways, voters responded to the plan's sponsor, seventy-five-year-old gadfly Howard Jarvis, when he urged them to "take control of the government again or it will control you."

The passage of Proposition 13 alarmed officials across the country. Governor Brown quickly reversed himself and supported the tax rollback because it was "the strongest expression of the democratic process in a decade." Elections in other states confirmed the extent of public anger but also demonstrated its limits. Measures similar to Proposition 13 passed in four states that had experienced sharp rises in housing prices in the previous decade, but tax limits or spending caps were defeated in four others.

Officeholders in both parties lost primaries to conservative insurgents who accused incumbents of supporting taxes. In Massachusetts, liberal Democratic governor Michael Dukakis, elected in the post-Watergate Democratic landslide of 1974, lost to a conservative who promised to reduce state taxes. Ronald Reagan, preparing for another run at the White House, told supporters that opposition to taxes was "a little bit like dumping those cases of tea off the boat in Boston Harbor."

Democrats felt the sting in Washington. Patrick Caddell, Carter's pollster, reflected that "this isn't just a tax revolt, it's a revolution against government." Opposition to new federal spending scuttled plans for national health insurance. Despairing of Carter's timidity and his increasing conservatism, Democrats took heart from Senator Edward Kennedy. At a Democratic "miniconvention" in December 1978, he encouraged support for traditional social welfare programs. "Sometimes," Kennedy said, "a party must sail against the wind." Kennedy's powerful speech thrilled Democrats embarrassed by Carter. By the spring of 1979, many Democrats wanted Kennedy to challenge Carter for the 1980 nomination, and the senator seemed ready to run. Public opinion polls taken among Democrats showed Kennedy defeating Carter by a 2-to-1 ratio.

By July 1979, President Carter's approval rating had fallen to a dismal 29 percent, about where Nixon had stood on the eve of his resignation. The president knew he had to do something, but what? He acknowledged that the complaint that he had been "managing, not leading" the country had merit, and he begged citizens to "have faith in our country—not only in the government, but in our own ability to solve great problems." The next day he fired or accepted the resignation of five cabinet members.

During the cabinet shakeup, the president appointed Paul Volcker, a twenty-year veteran of the Treasury Department and the New York Federal Reserve Bank, to chair the Federal Reserve Board. Volcker was confronted with an economic crisis consisting of high prices, slowed production, and mounting unemployment. Volcker responded by driving interest rates above 15 percent to stop inflation; but by the beginning of 1980, prices were still rising and 8 million Americans were out of work. In April 1980, the economy entered the sharpest recession since 1974. Americans wondered if people could buy a house with mortgage rates at 18 percent. Could they fill up their cars to drive to work? Would there be a job to drive to?

The public at large thought Carter was ineffectual. After one of his attempts to reassure his fellow citizens that the nation's problems could be solved with time and careful planning, a Boston newspaper mocked his speech with the headline, "More Mush from the Wimp."

Energy and the Environment

Despite rising public skepticism, the Carter administration made serious attempts to confront long-term challenges. In April 1977, Carter unveiled a major legislative initiative promising a national energy policy. Like Carter's other programs, his energy policy sought to satisfy various competing and antagonistic regional and economic interests. In the process, it offended more people than it pleased. He asked for the creation of a Department of Energy. He called for tax incentives and penalties to encourage consumers to conserve energy and producers to drill more oil and gas wells. As a last resort, he said, he favored further development of nuclear power.

Carter delivered his first energy speech at the height of his popularity. He warned that "the energy shortage is permanent." He encouraged his fellow citizens to turn their thermostats down to 65 degrees, and he called his energy program "the moral equivalent of war." Critics quickly pounced on the contradictory nature of the program. Speaking for conservatives, Ronald Reagan complained that "our problem isn't a shortage of oil, it's a surplus of government." Liberals objected that too much had been offered to oil companies and too little to the poor.

Congress finally passed a greatly modified version of Carter's energy program in November 1978, about the time oil prices began another sharp rise following the revolution in Iran. The final law gave more benefits to both oil companies and their opponents. At the federal, state, and local levels, governments sponsored research on multiple alternative energy sources and conservation programs, and offered programs to make it easier for individuals to be environmentally responsible; for example, it gave homeowners tax breaks for insulating their homes. But there was also more than a little something for corporate America, such as government investment in the giant Synthetic Fuels Corporation—controlled by Exxon, Occidental Petroleum, and Union Oil of California—to extract petroleum from rocks in Colorado, Utah, and Wyoming.

As Congress struggled to craft an energy policy that would be acceptable to diverse regions and economic interests, Americans became increasingly skeptical about the ability of technology and engineering to improve their lives. Indeed, they feared that modern technology might not be safe. In the early 1970s, residents of the Love Canal neighborhood in Niagara Falls, New York, began to notice foul air; blackened trees; and increased numbers of cancer cases, miscarriages, and babies born with birth defects in their locality. For several years,

The Organization of Petroleum Exporting Countries (OPEC) increased oil prices several times in the 1970s, fueling the rise of inflation and signalling the end of an era of easy abundance. / Don Wright, © 1976, reprinted by permission of Tribune Media Services

terrified residents demanded explanations, but they received no satisfaction. Experts eventually traced the problems to toxic wastes buried thirty years earlier by the Hooker Chemical Company. The federal government declared an emergency in the area and ordered the people in the neighborhood to move. None could sell their homes, and few thought the compensation offered by the government was adequate. The Environmental Protection Agency (EPA) warned that the hazardous materials poisoning the land, polluting the water, and fouling the air of Love Canal might be found in hundreds of locations across the country. "There are time bombs ticking all over," one EPA officer proclaimed. "We just don't know how many potential Love Canals there are."

Fears about the safety of nuclear power, which was heavily promoted in the 1950s as the cleanest, cheapest form of electricity available, expanded in March 1979 when a reactor at Three Mile Island near Harrisburg, Pennsylvania, badly malfunctioned. A stuck cooling valve overheated the reactor core, and a meltdown of the deadly nuclear fuel was barely avoided. One hundred thousand residents fled their homes, and many did not believe officials who told them two weeks later that it was safe to return. The power plant remained permanently disabled, its interior deadly to anyone who might enter it. In the wake of the incident, electric companies canceled over thirty proposed nuclear power plants.

The near catastrophe at Three Mile Island also fed more general fears about the degradation of the environment. Washington created a $1.6 billion "superfund," paid for by extra taxes on industries that pollute the environment, to clean up toxic waste sites. The Carter administration also placed over 100 million acres of Alaskan land under federal protection, barring mining or petroleum development. But such actions could not reverse the public's concern over the deterioration of the nation's land, air, and water. The environmental movement grew, and many environmentalists expressed increasing skepticism about the benefits of unrestrained economic growth.

At the same time, conservatives in the West gained new support for the "Sagebrush Rebellion" against federal control of vast amounts of land. As much as 60 percent of the land in Nevada, Utah, Arizona, Idaho, Montana, and Colorado belonged to the federal government. Several Rocky Mountain state legislatures passed laws demanding that the state take charge of its federal lands to allow more grazing, logging, mining, petroleum drilling, or recreational development than the federal Bureau of Land Management or the U.S. Forest Service would permit. Earlier generations of westerners had often approved of the federal government as a good steward, whose efforts protected local resources for future generations. But advocates of the Sagebrush Rebellion saw Washington as the enemy, the home of haughty bureaucrats indifferent to the economic well-being of the West.

Foreign Affairs in the Carter Years

Despite Jimmy Carter's troubles on the domestic front, his administration initially succeeded in redirecting American foreign policy, turning it away from Cold War confrontation and toward advocacy of human rights abroad and sensitivity to the needs of poor nations. Early in his term, the president explained that "we are now free of the inordinate fear of communism which once led us to embrace any dictator in that fear." But Carter's foreign policy momentum stopped in 1979, and the last eighteen months of his administration saw a series of foreign policy setbacks and catastrophes.

The Cold War returned with a vengeance as the Soviets became more assertive on their southern borders, in the Middle East, and in Africa. Americans who had opposed détente felt vindicated. Distrustful of the Soviets and fearful of U.S. conservatives, Carter and his advisers dropped détente, and America became more hostile toward the Soviet Union than at any other time since the early 1960s. Meanwhile, a revolution in Iran culminated in the seizure of the American embassy on November 4, 1979. Iranian revolutionaries held fifty-two U.S. citizens captive for 444 days. The Iranian hostage crisis nearly paralyzed Carter, undermined public confidence in his foreign policy, and eventually cost him re-election.

Carter achieved his greatest triumph in foreign affairs by arranging the first peace treaty between Israel and one of its Arab neighbors, Egypt. Carter believed that Egyptian president Anwar Sadat became a "man who would change history" when he courageously flew to Jerusalem in November 1977 to address Israel's parliament and offer an end to the thirty-year war. Israelis were euphoric in the wake of Sadat's trip, but the Palestinians and most other Arab states damned him as a traitor. The excitement faded in 1978 as Egypt and Israel made little progress in their talks. At that point, President Carter became personally involved as a mediator.

Carter invited Sadat and Israeli prime minister Menachem Begin to a series of conversations in Washington, and in September 1978, he arranged a joint meeting with them at Camp David, the presidential retreat in the Maryland mountains. A planned three-day conference lasted thirteen days. Carter dropped all other work to concentrate on bridging the gap between Egypt and Israel. The difficult details of the negotiations included Israel's withdrawal from the Sinai Peninsula and the future of the 1.5 million Palestinians living under Israeli control in the West Bank and Gaza Strip. Although these issues were not resolved, Carter's determination paid off with the signing of a framework for peace that promised a future treaty between Egypt and Israel, establishment of a five-year transitional authority in the West Bank and Gaza, and additional negotiations on the status of the occupied territories.

However, the initial congratulations gave way to suspicion and recriminations. The Israeli-Egyptian treaty, which was supposed to be completed in three months, took six months and another round of personal diplomacy from Carter before it was signed in Washington in March 1979. The other Arab states and the Palestine Liberation Organization (PLO) ostracized Egypt and refused to join the Camp David peace process. Israel did not offer real autonomy to the Palestinians and continued its policy of not dealing with the PLO.

Like many other critics of Nixon's and Ford's foreign policy, Carter believed that the United States had ignored the fate of ordinary people in foreign countries who suffered mistreatment at the hands of their own government. Carter promised to pay far greater attention to promoting human rights abroad, hoping thereby to restore the United States' moral standing in the world, which had been badly tarnished by the war in Vietnam. The new administration made significant progress in promoting human rights during its first two years. Congress created a new State Department office, assistant secretary of state for human rights, and required the State Department to report on the status of individual rights around the globe. Governments that violated basic standards of decency might be shamed into altering their behavior by appearing on a list of abusive authorities. Congress might also reduce foreign aid to nations appearing on the list.

But the administration soon found it was difficult to apply standards of human rights strictly and impartially. The State Department did criticize some old friends in Latin America, but political expediency caused the administration to temper its criticism of other long-term partners in important areas of the world. For example, Carter went out of his way to praise the shah of Iran, and the United States continued its strong support for the corrupt regime of Ferdinand Marcos in the Philippines.

Similar inconsistencies arose as the government grappled with the escalating pace of immigration and refugee flight to the United States. War and its aftermath in Southeast Asia, combined with poverty and repression in Latin America, brought millions of people to the United States. Modifications of the 1965 immigration law led to the planned entry of almost half a million Asian and Latino immigrants annually. But this number accounted for only a small part of the total immigration flow.

In March 1980, for example, thousands of Cubans took refuge in foreign embassies in Havana. President Carter believed that he could embarrass Castro by offering these people asylum in the United States, but the Cuban strongman trumped his hand by announcing that any Cuban could leave from the port of Mariel. The United States organized a flotilla to transport the Marielitos, but a public relations disaster ensued when Castro emptied Cuba's jails and mental hospitals and ordered the inmates to board the boats for America. The criminals and mentally ill composed only a small number of the 130,000 fleeing Cubans, but opponents of immigration pointed to them in an effort to fan resentment against all refugees.

A refugee act passed in 1980 offered asylum in the United States to anyone facing a "well-founded fear" of persecution for religious, political, or ethnic reasons. In practice, people fleeing left-wing or communist countries were usually granted asylum, but those escaping right-wing regimes found their entry to the United States barred. About fifty thousand Haitians were excluded during the Carter years, and this inconsistency prompted criticism of the administration's refugee policy. Each year during the 1970s, several million Mexicans crossed the border without official permission. Some left after a time, but enough stayed to create a permanent pool of between 5 and 15 million undocumented aliens—another indication of a serious gap between administration policy and reality.

The influx of millions of non-European immigrants in the 1970s had a significant impact on the American population, hastening the development of a more multicultural society. Overall, the economy benefited from the new arrivals, but many Americans feared the economic competition from them. Others responded to the newcomers with fear and prejudice, fueling a movement to enact more restrictive immigration laws that would reduce the overall number of immigrants and stem the flow of undocumented aliens.

Although it was becoming an increasingly multicultural nation at home, the United States continued to operate abroad within a Cold War context. Détente continued to decline. Carter first tried to reduce tensions with the Soviet Union and to demonstrate that it could conclude a better arms control agreement than the SALT II treaty, which the Ford administration had abandoned in 1976. In March 1977, Secretary of State Cyrus Vance took to Moscow proposals to reduce strategic nuclear weapons on each side by 33 percent. Much to his surprise, the Soviets scornfully turned him down, suspecting a trick because the proposals went so far beyond what Kissinger had offered. Deeply embarrassed, the Americans resumed bargaining with the Soviets on the basis of the foundation laid previously. Two years later, in June 1979, Carter and Soviet leader Leonid Brezhnev signed the SALT II treaty, limiting each side to 2,400 nuclear launchers. Had the SALT II treaty been ready earlier in Carter's term, the Senate might have ratified it. By 1979, however, Carter was a weak president, with little political pull on Capitol Hill. That fall, the Senate Armed Services Committee voted against ratification.

In December 1979, the Soviets invaded Afghanistan to quell an uprising by Islamic fundamentalists against the Soviet-sponsored Afghan government. Carter used the invasion to justify shelving the SALT II treaty, calling the invasion the "gravest threat to peace" since the end of World War II. In January 1980, Carter withdrew the treaty from Senate consideration, where it faced certain defeat anyway. To punish Moscow for the invasion, he refused to send athletes to the upcoming Moscow Olympics, a decision that upset hundreds of would-be American participants. He also embargoed grain shipments to the Soviet Union, which infuriated thousands of American farmers, and he revived registration for the draft, which alarmed millions of young men. The president's moderate supporters felt abandoned, whereas neoconservatives and other Cold Warriors did not trust his newfound toughness.

Americans would likely have tolerated Carter's reversals had it not been for the rage and frustration they felt after the capture of the U.S. embassy and its staff in Teheran, Iran, on November 4, 1979. The revolution in Iran had simmered beneath the surface for decades. In 1953, the United States had restored Shah Mohammed Reza Pahlavi to power in a CIA-sponsored coup against a government that had forced the shah into exile. The monarch then embarked on an expensive effort to modernize his country. Flush with oil revenue, the shah built the largest military force in the region with billions of dollars in weapons purchased from the United States. Along with the weapons and the development of the oil fields came fifty thousand American technicians and military advisers. The shah's revolution from above elevated a new class of merchants and technicians, who adopted Western mores and lifestyles. But many Iranians resented the shah's iron-fisted rule. The shah's secret police jailed and tortured thousands of dissenters. Among those most hostile to the rapid social changes were Islamic fundamentalists. One of the men most eager to sweep out Western influences, depose the shah, and create a society based on the Koran was an elderly *ayatollah*, or religious leader, Ruholla Khomeini. A long-time opponent of the shah, the exiled Khomeini fervently encouraged revolution. By February 1979, Khomeini's followers ruled the streets, evicted the shah, and greeted the returning ayatollah as a savior.

The Iranian revolution affected American lives directly in the spring of 1979, when the new Islamic government raised its oil prices, thus causing long lines at gas stations in the United States. Throughout the summer of 1979, the United States tried to maintain a stable relationship with the new Islamic leadership in Teheran. But when President Carter admitted the deposed shah to New York for medical treatment in October, he infuriated the Iranian revolutionaries. Khomeini told his followers that the admission of the shah represented a plot by "the Great Satan"—the United States—in collaboration with "American-loving rotten brains" in Teheran to restore the shah to power. Khomeini demanded that the United States deliver the shah to Iran for trial and that he restore his "stolen wealth" to the Islamic regime. A week later, revolutionary students seized the American embassy.

The initial reaction in the United States to the capture of about seventy Americans—a group that included diplomats, marines, CIA agents, and a few private citizens doing business at the embassy—helped to temporarily revive Carter's flagging reputation. Showing his dogged energy, he froze Iran's assets in the United States, growled that American "honor" had been besmirched by the militants, and vowed not to travel out of Washington until the hostages came home. After some of the hostages were released, the number in captivity declined to fifty-two, but news broadcasts kept nerves raw by ticking off the number of days they had languished in Teheran since November 4, 1979. Relatives and friends of hostages tied yellow ribbons around trees, mailboxes, and telephone poles to keep the plight of the captives firmly in the public mind. Senator Kennedy assailed Carter for

Angry mobs in Teheran, November 1979, ridiculed and demonized President Carter. / AP/Wide World

"lurching from crisis to crisis," and Ronald Reagan, who was running for the Republican nomination, implied that "our friend" the shah would not have lost his throne if the Carter administration had not betrayed him by criticizing his secret police for torturing political opponents. Reagan also suggested that Carter's inability to free the prisoners reflected his general lack of competence.

In April 1980, Carter accepted the advice of National Security Adviser Zbigniew Brzezinski to mount a military mission to rescue the hostages. Secretary of State Vance objected; he had promised European allies that the United States would not use force, and he believed the complicated plan would not work. He told Carter that he would resign after the operation, whether it succeeded or failed. On April 24, eight helicopters took off from an aircraft carrier in the Persian Gulf and headed for a desert rendezvous with transport planes. One chopper malfunctioned, and the remaining seven flew into a dust storm. Two of these helicopters were abandoned, and the site commander decided that the five remaining helicopters were not enough to mount a successful rescue operation. He telephoned the White House that he was withdrawing the rest of the force. After receiving orders to leave the desert landing site, another helicopter collided with a refueling plane, killing eight servicemen. The White House announced the mission's failure, Vance resigned, and some Americans believed that the aborted mission was yet another demonstration of the limits of American military superiority.

Carter finally left the White House to campaign actively for re-election. Diplomacy proceeded behind the scenes, and the administration tried to arrange a deal with Iran for the captives' release before Election Day, November 4, 1980. Unfortunately for Carter, the efforts did not bear fruit until early 1981. The Iranians may have received promises of future favors from the Reagan camp if they kept the hostages until Carter left office. Gary Sick, a staff member on Carter's National Security Council, charged in 1991 that the Reagan campaign promised Teheran arms if it retained the American prisoners beyond the election. The hostages finally flew to freedom on January 20, 1981, half an hour after Ronald Reagan took the oath of office.

The failure to gain the release of the hostages sealed Carter's fate with the electorate. He defeated Kennedy for the Democratic nomination, but the fact that 35 percent of the convention delegates favored the challenger sent an ominous sign for the fall. Carter's advisers believed he could overcome Ronald Reagan by portraying him as a dangerous reactionary. They feared that an in-

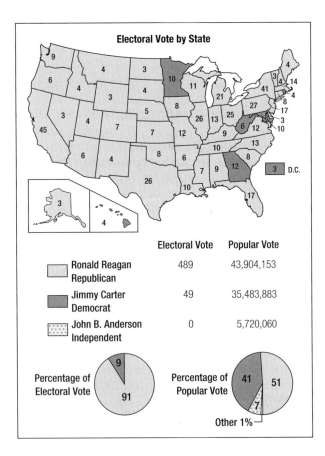

Map 11.1
Presidential Election of 1980

dependent candidate, former Republican congressman John Anderson, presented the greater danger because he could appeal to middle-of-the-road voters. But Anderson's support dribbled away in October 1980 as voters concentrated on the only viable choices—Carter and Reagan.

Late in the campaign, Carter and Reagan debated head to head. Carter believed that his greater intelligence and command of the facts would make his conservative challenger appear unworthy, but the president badly miscalculated. In the debate, Carter stressed the severity of the last few years: "We have demanded that the American people sacrifice, and they have done that very well." Reagan, on the other hand, reminded voters how much austerity hurt: "We do not have to go on sharing in sacrifice," he said. In his summary remarks, Reagan looked directly into the camera with his cheerful blue eyes and urged Americans to "ask yourself, are you better off than you were four years ago?"

A week later, voters answered with a sharp no. Opinion surveys showed Carter's support collapsing in the weekend before Election Day as it became clear that the hostages would not be coming home.

Voters believed that whatever Reagan did would be an improvement over Carter's hand-wringing, sermons, and demands for sacrifice. Reagan won 51 percent of the popular vote, Carter won 41 percent, and Anderson received 7 percent (see Map 11.1). For the first time since 1954, the Republicans carried the Senate, and they gained 33 seats in the House. "It's a fed-up vote," observed Pat Caddell, Carter's pollster.

Conclusion

In the aftermath of Watergate, the Vietnam War, and the upheavals of the 1960s and early 1970s, Americans confronted changes in the late 1970s that demanded creativity and perseverance on an everyday basis. Disillusionment and disorientation from the recent past ran so deep that politicians found it almost impossible to restore public faith in government. Gerald Ford, an unelected leader, lacked both a base of popular support and a clearly articulated vision of how to restore public confidence. Jimmy Carter had some advantages over his predecessor because he could credibly claim to be an outsider and that he was not responsible for the disappointments of the Johnson and Nixon years. By 1980, it became apparent, however, that Carter's good intentions, intelligence, and firmly rooted moral values had not been enough.

Although many ordinary Americans continued to work hard to consolidate and extend the gains of the social justice movements of the 1960s, the economic and social developments of the times frustrated both the nation's leaders and the public. Increasing competition from foreign business, particularly from Japan; soaring inflation; and a decline in manufacturing put the country's economic future in doubt. These trends, combined with a successful corporate campaign against unions, initiated a decline in real wages that would continue for many Americans. The oil shock stimulated worries about scarce resources, and at the same time Americans became more aware of the environmental costs of industrial and nuclear development. The cultural changes of the 1960s had brought a new sense of freedom in personal relationships, but the growing diversity of American households presented new and sometimes bewildering challenges. Women demanded respect, but pornography boomed. Gay men and lesbians achieved greater legitimacy, but the New Right singled out homosexuals with virulent attacks. Many alienated people took refuge from these bewildering trends in new religious sects, some of which were authoritarian or violent. Others turned to a reaffirmation of traditional churches, and some were galvanized by televangelists who denounced liberalism, divorce, and all the new social and sexual freedoms.

Articulating many of the public's frustrations, the television preachers and other conservatives formed political organizations that helped mobilize support for conservative candidates. When President Carter failed to resolve the Iranian hostage crisis before the 1980 election, the public found a final reason to reject him. They turned instead to Ronald Reagan, a conservative champion who promised Americans that the future could still be bright.

F U R T H E R • R E A D I N G

On general accounts of society and politics in the 1970s, see Peter N. Carroll, *It Seemed Like Nothing Happened* (1982); Bruce J. Schulman, *The Seventies: The Great Shift in American Culture, Society, and Politics* (2001); Steve Fraser and Gary Gerstle (eds.), *The Rise and Fall of the New Deal Order, 1930–1980* (1989); Michael Barone, *Our Country* (1990); Theodore H. White, *America in Search of Itself, 1956–1980* (1982). **On public policy,** see Gerald Ford, *A Time to Heal* (1977); Robert T. Hartmann, *Palace Politics: An Inside Account of the Ford Years* (1980); A. James Reichley, *Conservatives in an Age of Change* (1980); Jimmy Carter, *Keeping Faith: Memoirs of a President* (1981); Mary Berry, *Why the ERA Failed* (1986); Nathan Glazer, *Affirmative Discrimination* (1975); J. Harvey Wilkerson, *From Brown to Bakke* (1979); William Julius Wilson, *The Truly Disadvantaged: The Inner City, the Underclass, and Public Policy* (1987). **On women and the family,** see Ruth Rosen, *The World Split Open: How the Modern Women's Movement Changed America* (2000); Flora Davis, *Moving the Mountain: The Women's Movement in America Since 1960* (1991); Winifred D. Wandersee, *On the Move: American Women in the 1970s* (1988); Judith Stacey, *Brave New Families: Stories of Domestic Upheaval in Late Twentieth-Century America* (1990). **On the emerging gay community,** see John D'Emilio, *Sexual Politics, Sexual Communities: The Making of a Homosexual Minority in the United States, 1940–1970* (1983). **On economic changes,** see Barry Bluestone and Bennett Harrison, *The Deindustrialization of America* (1982); John P. Hoerr, *And the Wolf Finally Came: The Decline of the American Steel Industry* (1988); David Halberstam, *The Reckoning* (1986); Lester C. Thurow, *The Zero Sum Society* (1980); Daniel Yergin, *The Prize* (1991); Patricia Cayo Sexton, *The War on Labor and the Left: Understanding America's Unique Conservatism* (1991); James C. Cobb, *Industrialization and Southern Society, 1877–1984* (1984). **On the new immigrants,** see Jeremy Hein, *From Vietnam, Laos, and Cambodia: A Refugee Experience in the United States* (1995). **On foreign affairs,** see Raymond L. Garthoff, *Detente and Confrontation: American-Soviet Relations from Nixon to Reagan* (1985); William Hyland, *Mortal Rivals: Superpower Relations from Nixon to Reagan* (1987); Gaddis Smith, *Morality, Reason and Power: American Diplomacy in the Carter*

Years (1986); Zbigniew Brzezinski, *Power and Principle: Memoirs of the National Security Adviser* (1983); Cyrus Vance, *Hard Choices: Critical Years in American Foreign Policy* (1983); James Bill, *The Eagle and the Lion: The Tragedy of American-Iranian Relations* (1987); Gary Sick, *All Fall Down: America's Tragic Encounter with Iran* (1986); William Quandt, *Camp David* (1987). **On evangelical Christianity,** see Steve Bruce, *Pray TV: Televangelism in America* (1990); Jerry D. Cardwell, *Mass Media Christianity: Televangelism and the Great Commission* (1984); Linda Kintz and Julia Lesage, eds., *Media, Culture, and the Religious Right* (1998); Robert Kraphol and Charles Lippy, *Evangelicals: A Historical, Thematic, and Biographical Guide* (1999); David Snowball, *Continuity and Change in the Rhetoric of the Moral Majority* (1991).

Right Turn: Conservatism Ascendant, 1980–1993

Freed American hostages return from captivity in Iran, January 21, 1981. The public credited the just-inaugurated Ronald Reagan for their release. / © Bettmann/CORBIS

At his inauguration on January 20, 1981, President Ronald Reagan looked marvelous. Standing tall, elegant in his formal attire, his persona defied Jimmy Carter's talk of limits. To millions of Americans watching on television, the incoming and outgoing presidents were a study in contrasts. Reagan slept well the night before he took the oath of office and seemed poised for action. Carter appeared stooped, almost shrunken, with hooded eyes. Unknown to the public, Carter had not slept for days as he tried desperately to negotiate the final details for the release of hostages from Iran.

Speaking from both deep conviction and utilizing his acting skill, Reagan declared that Americans were not people to dream "small dreams." The new president recalled past heroes who overcame earlier crises. Then, reversing the central tenet of national politics since the New Deal, Reagan declared, "In the present crisis . . . government is not the solution to our problem, government *is* the problem." To prove the point, his first presidential act was temporarily freezing federal hiring.

Over the next twelve years, Republican presidents Reagan and George Bush promoted policies designed to halt or roll back many of the New Deal's accomplishments and legacies. Reagan proved especially adept at forging a powerful bond with the public that transcended voters' opinions about his specific policies. He tapped a popular yearning to restore a sense of community, real or imagined, that had been lost since the 1960s. With his ruddy good lucks, a tremor in his voice, and a twinkle in his eye, Reagan fulfilled an ideal of what a president should be. Whether or not they agreed with his programs, people enjoyed hearing his jokes and inspirational stories—which also served to deflect criticism and prevent serious introspection. Bush, who lacked comparable charm, was elected in 1988 largely on the goodwill he had earned as Reagan's vice president. As long as the "good times" continued, including the end of the Cold War and a victory over Iraq in the Gulf War, President Bush enjoyed high levels of voter approval. But when economic troubles began in 1991, he quickly lost the trust of the American public, and Republicans suffered major setbacks.

The Republican agenda during the 1980s and early 1990s focused mostly on reducing many government programs initiated by Democrats. The Reagan and Bush administrations worked to shrink the social welfare system; limit the role of the federal courts and agencies in promoting civil rights and liberties; reduce government regulation of business and protection of the environment; slash income taxes; and foster a conservative social ethic in areas such as abortion rights, gender relations, premarital sex, drug use, and the role of religion in public life. The two Republican presidents rejected the belief that the federal government should foster greater equality, insisting that market forces would create new wealth and ensure its equitable distribution.

Ronald Reagan and the New Conservatism

Reagan's election in 1980 culminated a long journey for the sixty-nine-year-old candidate. He was born in 1911 and had grown up poor in a small Illinois town along the Mississippi River. His speeches and stories recaptured the rural ideal of the past. Although he spoke with nostalgia about his childhood, he experienced many hardships. His religiously devout mother struggled to hold the family together while his alcoholic father had trouble keeping a job. The family moved frequently, often just ahead of the bill collector. In spite of these difficulties, Reagan made the most of his life. He attended a local religious college and, in the midst of the Great Depression, found work as a sports announcer at an Iowa radio station. When visiting Hollywood in 1937, Reagan took a screen test and won a contract with the Warner Brothers film studio. Although never a first-rank star, he enjoyed a successful movie career for more than a decade.

Reagan's personal political journey paralleled that of many other Americans: from New Deal liberal in the 1930s to antigovernment conservative by the late 1960s. During the Depression, Reagan's father fed his family by working for a federal relief agency. Not surprisingly, as a young man, Reagan idolized President Franklin D. Roosevelt, memorizing his speeches so well that, forty years later, he incorporated many of FDR's best lines into his own addresses—even as he called for rolling back the New Deal!

During World War II, Reagan served in an Army Signal Corps unit in Hollywood that made training and morale films. This service was honorable but perhaps not heroic enough. In later years, Reagan implied that he served in the front lines, even liberating a concentration camp. Perhaps he sought to solidify a bond with the millions of other GIs who had served abroad.

In the late 1940s, as his film career waned, Reagan became active in the Screen Actors Guild, serving as the union president from 1947 to 1952. In this position, he cooperated both publicly and secretly with the FBI to frustrate what he called a "Communist plot to take over the motion picture business" and thus brainwash American movie audiences. As with millions of other Americans, Reagan's zealous anticommunism and fervent patriotism pushed him to the political right. During the 1950s, these conservative leanings were bolstered by his growing hatred of high income taxes for wealthy people like himself. In 1952, three years after the dissolution of his marriage to actress Jane Wyman, he married Nancy Davis. This alliance also shaped his political outlook because his new father-in-law was a wealthy physician and conservative activist.

In 1954, Reagan applied his storytelling skills to a new career as a corporate spokesperson for the General Electric Company (GE). He worked for GE for eight years, making hundreds of speeches warning about the dangers of communism abroad and creeping socialism at home. Somehow, Reagan managed to deliver these warnings in an upbeat fashion that left audiences more hopeful than despondent. In 1962, he formally joined the Republican Party. He justified his political migration by joking, "I didn't leave the Democratic Party, it left me."

Reagan first achieved national political notoriety from a spirited television speech he delivered in support of Barry Goldwater's doomed 1964 presidential bid. Two years later, backed by wealthy friends, he ran for governor of California as an "ordinary citizen" fed up with big government that overregulated business and raised taxes while "coddling criminals" and supporting "welfare cheats." Reagan linked the popular Democratic incumbent, Edmund (Pat) Brown to riots in the Watts ghetto of Los Angeles and to radical politics and "sexual perversions" at the University of California at Berkeley. Dismissed by most Democrats and journalists in 1966 as a lightweight, he beat Brown by 1 million votes.

During his two terms as governor, Reagan governed more from the center than the right. He combined pragmatic policies with conservative rhetoric. He blamed his predecessor for spending and taxing too much, then doubled the state budget and raised taxes. Reagan signed into law the nation's most liberal abortion rights bill, but when he was criticized by religious conservatives, he defended himself by claiming that he had never read it. Several times, he sent state police to quell disturbances on the Berkeley campus, claiming it was a hotbed of subversion and perversion. Despite threats to do so, however, he did not slash education funds. By the time he left office in 1974, Reagan had become a conservative icon, "the man who can enunciate our principles to the people," according to a leading conservative publication.

In 1974, after Nixon resigned and Ford became president, Reagan criticized Ford's selection of liberal Republican Nelson Rockefeller as vice president and challenged Ford for the presidential nomination in 1976. In primary contests, Reagan proposed slashing federal social programs and returning others to state control. When this issue fell flat, he attacked Ford and Secretary of State Kissinger for pursuing arms control and détente with the Soviet Union and for negotiating a giveaway of the Panama Canal. In the end, however, Ford won renomination but lost the general election to Jimmy Carter.

Reagan possessed a keen ability to communicate a point of view and to smooth over differences between warring conservative factions. He also found a way to appeal to Americans who disagreed with his right-wing politics. Conservatives as varied as Herbert Hoover and Barry Goldwater came across as gloomy, uncompassionate, and sanctimonious. By contrast, Reagan presented a softer, more affable image that enabled him to say harsh things in a good-natured manner.

Economic stagnation, the collapse of détente, and the Iranian hostage crisis made the public receptive to Reagan's call for a dramatic change in leadership in 1980. Although his chief rival for the Republican nomination, George Bush, ridiculed his tax-cutting scheme as "voodoo economics" and his social views as "backward thinking," Reagan secured the nomination handily and then, to build bridges to Republican moderates, chose Bush as his running mate. In the general election campaign, he downplayed his more extreme beliefs, such as his long-time dislike of the Social Security program; instead, he focused on themes of renewal, strength, and national pride. "This is the greatest country in the world," he declared. "We have the talent, we have the drive, we have the imagination. Now all we need is the leadership." Most Americans, he believed, hungered for "a little good news" and for a leader who promised renewed American strength and success. Reagan projected common sense, spoke of heroes, and—in contrast to Carter's public hand-wringing—offered simple, reassuring answers to complex questions.

Whether Reagan's victory represented an ideological mandate or not (only one-tenth of those voting for Reagan told pollsters they picked him because he was a "real conservative"), conservatives had in fact won considerably more power. Republicans picked up twelve Senate seats (and knocked off key liberals such as George McGovern, Frank Church, and Birch Bayh) to take control of the upper chamber of Congress for the first time in nearly three decades. They also added a net of thirty-three House seats. By allying with mostly southern conservative Democrats—nicknamed boll weevils—the GOP achieved working control of the House of Representatives.

As he assumed the presidency, Reagan relied on a triumvirate of top policy advisers who served him well. In an astute move, he reached outside his inner circle of conservative Californians to appoint James A. Baker III, a close friend of Vice President Bush, as White House chief of staff. The more conservative and abrasive Edwin Meese, a close associate from Reagan's time as governor, became a presidential "counselor," an amorphous post without clear responsibility. Michael Deaver, a skilled public relations expert personally close to the president and First Lady Nancy Reagan, worked as deputy chief of staff and was responsible for managing the president's image.

Reagan's first cabinet consisted almost entirely of white, male Republicans who had served in the Nixon and Ford administrations or with him in California. Only two posts, in the departments of the Interior and Energy, went to members of the New Right—James Watt and James Edwards. Watt's provocative criticism of liberals and non-Christians as "un-American," as well as his effort to speed development of protected federal land, forced the president to replace him. Initially, no women served in the cabinet, although U.N. ambassador Jeane Kirkpatrick received honorary cabinet status. In 1983, after midterm elections in which GOP candidates fared poorly among women voters, Reagan named Margaret Heckler as secretary of Health and Human Services and Elizabeth Dole as secretary of Transportation. The new president appointed an African American, Samuel Pierce, as secretary of Housing and Urban Development, but cared so little about housing policy that he failed to recognize Pierce the few times they met. Reagan usually skipped cabinet meetings and often dozed off when he did attend.

Chief of Staff James Baker persuaded Reagan to push Congress for two items on his agenda that were popular and that the president wanted most: tax cuts and a defense buildup. "If we can do that," Baker maintained, "the rest will take care of itself." Following this advice, the president gave token support to proposals by New Right activists to amend the Constitution to ban abortion and permit school prayer but expended little energy on their behalf.

Reagan had long been critical of the progressive income tax. He believed that people should be rewarded for achieving wealth, not taxed at higher rates for doing so. He embraced conservative "supply-side" economics, which held that cutting the tax rate would pay for itself by stimulating business activity and economic growth. The Republican mantra against taxes also served to hamstring new government programs (by reducing funding sources) and to attract voters fed up with perceived giveaways.

Ronald Reagan made strategic use of TV in pledging to cut taxes, inflation, and wasteful social programs. / Ronald Reagan Presidential Library: TV courtesy of Zenith Electronics Corporation

As the keystone of his agenda, Reagan asked Congress in January 1981 to cut federal business tax rates by 25 percent over three years and to lower the top income tax rate from 70 percent (though the wealthy seldom paid this much because of numerous shelters) to 50 percent. To reduce federal power and expenses, he called for shifting many social programs to control by the states, trimming Social Security benefits, and eliminating many business regulations and environmental protections. Many of these proposals reflected ideas broached by economists Arthur Laffer and Milton Friedman. Reagan assured the public that these measures would balance the budget, create jobs, cut inflation, make government less intrusive, and leave the American people with more money to spend.

Reagan denied that he was secretly "trying to undo the New Deal." Rather, he told himself in a diary entry that he wanted to "undo the Great Society. It was LBJ's war on poverty," he insisted, "that led us to our present mess." Reagan complained that the Democrats' excessive deficit spending had "mortgaged our future and our children's future for the temporary convenience of the present." As the national debt approached $1 trillion, he believed reduced social spending would save money and encourage people to help themselves.

The president subscribed to the so-called supply-side theory, conceived by economist Arthur Laffer, which held that tax cuts would stimulate growth and actually boost tax revenue. But as his budget director, David Stockman recognized, without big spending cuts, Reagan's program would generate huge budget deficits. To make matters worse, the new administration intended to increase defense spending significantly without making cuts in popular programs such as Social Security and Medicare. As a result, Stockman privately predicted a "budget hemorrhage," with annual shortfalls of $100 billion or more for the next four years. This figure represented greater peacetime deficits than any run up by Democratic presidents. The president ignored these concerns. He guessed, correctly, that most Americans would happily trade big deficits that had to be paid off by future generations for current tax cuts that they could enjoy.

Reagan rallied support for his program in direct appeals to the public and the press. Organized labor feared opposing him after Reagan summarily fired twelve thousand striking federal air-traffic controllers whose work stoppage had violated their contract. The president's stature also benefited from the humor and optimism he displayed on March 30, 1981, just six weeks into his presidency, when he was gravely wounded in an assassination attempt by a mentally unstable gunman. Although holding a majority, House Democrats hesitated to block popular tax cuts. Reagan also won support from sixty-three conservative, mostly southern Democrats (the boll weevils).

On August 13, 1981, President Reagan signed two major laws, the Economic Recovery Tax Act and the Omnibus Budget Reconciliation Act. The former slashed federal income tax rates by 25 percent over three years. The budget bill cut about $40 billion in domestic spending but left intact most popular big-ticket programs like Social Security and Medicare. Funding for programs such as Amtrak, synthetic fuels, low-income housing, school lunches, and other social services for the poor received small to medium cuts. Reagan spoke of pruning additional social programs, but Congress balked at making unpopular reductions after this first round. In effect, the president's early victory in reducing federal appropriations turned out to be his last. In fact, by June 1982, as the budget deficit ballooned, Reagan bowed to congressional pressure and raised taxes.

The income tax cut received by most working- and middle-class taxpayers proved elusive. In April 1983, Reagan and Congress approved a bipartisan panel's proposal to shore up the Social Security trust fund that paid retirement benefits to millions of elderly Americans. The plan included a small reduction in benefits and an increase in the payroll tax. For most workers, this increase exceeded the small income-tax reduction they received in 1981. But the plan stabilized Social Security and removed it from partisan debate.

Reaganomics had a wobbly beginning in 1981–1982. The nation slipped into a deep economic recession soon after Congress approved the president's program. The economic downturn was partly the result of decisions made by Federal Reserve Board chair Paul Volcker to raise interest rates as high as 21.5 percent to stifle inflation. This increase drove unemployment rates to 10.8 percent, representing more than 11.5 million jobless workers. Business failures, farm foreclosures, and homelessness increased dramatically. Conditions were especially difficult in the Midwest's so-called Rustbelt.

The recession affected the election of 1982, in which congressional Democrats made substantial gains. Reagan's approval ratings declined from 61 percent to only 41 percent by the end of 1982. Media pundits described him as a likely one-term president. Reagan, however, refused to alter his priorities and predicted economic recovery by 1984.

This prediction proved partially correct. The high interest rates gradually squeezed inflation out of the economy and in turn allowed the Federal Reserve to reduce interest rates. World oil prices began to fall, reducing the cost of imported fuel. Massive defense spending created a boom in the high-technology and aerospace industries of New England, the Southwest, and the West Coast. By the end of 1983, the worst of the recession had passed and the subsequent economic expansion lasted until 1991.

Supply-siders took credit for creating over 18 million new jobs, spurring economic growth, lowering federal tax rates, and tripling the average price of stocks. Many Americans agreed that the final six years of Reagan's term and the first three years of the Bush administration marked a period of broad prosperity.

Reagan used television more effectively than any of his predecessors to gain public support for his programs. With his experience as a film star and television host, he proved to be a master of the electronic media, earning the nickname "the Great Communicator." Each presidential action was designed "as a one-minute or two-minute spot on the evening network news"; every presidential appearance was conceived "in terms of camera angle." With his uncanny ability to turn clichés into winning phrases, he fostered in his audience a sense of joint purpose even as he rallied them against government. In times of uncertainty, Reagan projected a reassuring decisiveness.

The large tax cuts and defense buildup laid the foundations for Republican governance in the 1980s, but the so-called Reagan Revolution and Bush aftermath reflected perception more than reality. When Reagan left office in 1989, the federal government collected about the same percentage—19 percent—of the nation's gross national product (GNP) in federal taxes as it had throughout the previous twenty years. Federal spending actually increased under Reagan, from about 7 percent of GNP to 8.2 percent. The biggest increases occurred in defense outlays, Medicare, and Social Security. The gap between tax revenues and rising spending under presidents Reagan and Bush produced the largest budget deficits in U.S. history. Annual shortfalls ranged from $100 billion to over $250 billion. The cumulative national debt soared from $1 trillion in 1980, to $2 trillion in 1989, to $3 trillion in 1993. To make up the shortfall, Washington turned to foreign investors, who financed much of the debt by purchasing Treasury bonds and notes. The United States began the twelve years of Republican presidential rule as the world's leading creditor; it ended the era as the world's largest debtor.

Re-election and the Second Administration

By 1984, as the economy climbed out of recession and into its long expansion, Ronald Reagan loomed as a formidable opponent for any Democratic challenger. Most voters enjoyed a few more dollars in their pockets from the tax cut, inflation had practically disappeared, and abstract difficulties such as the growing budget deficit had little immediate impact on individuals. Reagan's 1983 decision to invade the tiny island of Grenada (see Chapter 13) was a whopping success with the public. In 1984, he even managed to share the glory of American athletes at the Los Angeles summer Olympics, where they won a large number of gold medals in the absence of Soviet athletes, who were boycotting the games.

By 1984, the Democratic Party was struggling to mobilize an electorate no longer attuned to the New Deal legacy. To both inside and outside observers, the Democrats often appeared to be a loose coalition of special-interest groups, running the gamut from blue-collar union members to gay and African American civil rights activists. It seemed like Humpty Dumpty—after the fall.

After bruising primaries, former vice president Walter Mondale defeated rivals Gary Hart and Jesse Jackson. At the end of a highly visible search for an "appropriate" running mate, Mondale finally selected New York representative Geraldine Ferraro as his vice-presidential candidate. As the first woman nominated for the national ticket by a major party, Ferraro excited millions of Americans. She was a smart, articulate candidate who easily held her own in a debate with Vice President George Bush. Questions about her husband's financial dealings, however, obscured her critique of the Reagan presidency. Many voters concluded that, having served only three terms in Congress, Ferraro was untested. Ultimately, her presence on the ticket did not affect the election outcome.

Mondale tried valiantly to run a campaign based on issues. He warned the public about runaway spending, an out-of-control arms race, environmental disasters, and the unfairness of Reagan's economic policies. His most famous campaign line was "He'll raise taxes, so will I. He won't tell you, I just did." Commentators briefly praised Mondale's political courage, but within a week, they decided he had committed political suicide. U.N. ambassador Jeane Kirkpatrick, a conservative Democrat who served Reagan, dubbed him "bad news Fritz Mondale," leader of the "blame-America-first crowd."

The president's speeches and commercials emphasized the themes of redemption, patriotism, and family. Borrowing a slogan from an automobile ad, he proclaimed it was "morning again in America." In 1980, Reagan had run against government; in 1984, he *was* the government, but it made no difference. His campaign theme, summarized by a newspaper as "don't worry, be happy," carried him to a landslide sweep of forty-nine states. Democratic candidates nonetheless did much better at the congressional and state levels: they retained their majority in the House and pecked away at the slim Republican majority in the Senate.

Reagan's second administration got off to a slow start, with the president giving his aides little policy direction. He regained his poise by the summer of 1986. As the stock market surged to record highs, Congress passed a major tax-reform bill, the economic centerpiece of Reagan's second-term legislative agenda. The new tax law, a modification of the flat-rate income tax system proposed by Democrats Bill Bradley and Richard Gephardt, was presented as a way to restore simplicity and fairness to the complex tax code. It closed many tax loopholes and reduced the code's multiple tax brackets to just three, at rates of 15, 28, and 33 percent, respectively. Even though most taxpayers ended up paying about the same total as before, Reagan convinced middle-class voters that the law had reduced their taxes.

On July 4, 1986, the president hosted a celebration in New York Harbor that showed him at his best. The extravaganza featured a renovated Statue of Liberty, the biggest fireworks display ever assembled, and Ronald Reagan. Leslie Stahl, a White House reporter for CBS, commented, "Like his leading lady, the Statue of Liberty, the president, after six years in office, has himself become a symbol of pride in America." Despite his immense popularity, however, Reagan failed to achieve any realignment in national politics. In the 1986 congressional elections, even as Reagan rode high in the polls, the Democrats regained control of the Senate and increased their majority in the House. Democrats blocked administration proposals to make additional cuts in social programs, expand defense spending, and intervene more directly in Central America.

By late 1986, the Iran-contra scandal—which involved a series of weapons-for-hostage deals with Iran and illegal arms transfers to a group of Central American "freedom fighters"—was becoming public, and during the next year, it proved a profound embarrassment to the administration (see Chapter 13). A year later, in October 1987, a collapse in stock prices jolted the confident economic mood that had prevailed since 1983. After the Dow Jones Industrial Average hit a record high of 2,700 points in August 1987, it slumped. In mid-October, it fell 600 points in a few days, losing almost one-fourth of its value and reviving memories of the 1929 stock market crash that had ushered in the Great Depression. Although Wall Street soon recovered most of its losses, the minicrash created economic anxiety that proved impossible to shake.

The combined impact of the Iran-contra scandal and Wall Street jitters in 1987 might have been Reagan's undoing. But the president's ability to adjust to circumstances once again surprised Americans. During 1988, relations between the United States and the Soviet Union improved dramatically, creating the possibility for an end to the Cold War. The public proved quite willing to forget the Iran-contra affair. Reagan left office with an overall 68 percent approval rating, higher than that of any president since Franklin D. Roosevelt.

Economic Realities of the Reagan-Bush Era

Reagan's high public approval rating, along with his remarkable success at communicating his ideas and his faith in America, gave the impression that the nation's problems were vanishing before an onslaught of new pride and optimism. Often, however, the reality did not match the administration's glowing rhetoric. When Reagan took office, he was bitterly critical of Carter's

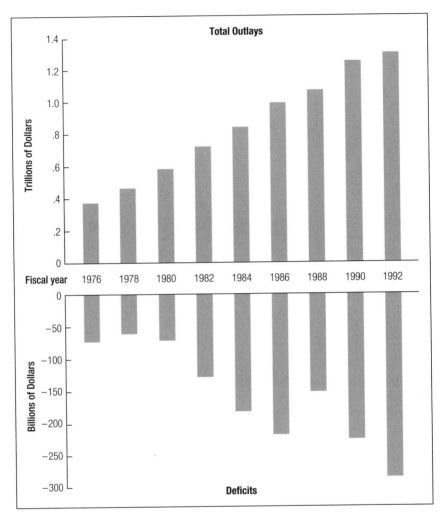

Figure 12.1
Federal Budget Expenditures and Deficits, 1976–1992

"runaway deficit of nearly $80 billion" and the cumulative national debt of al-
most $1 trillion. Over the next eight years, however, his administration ran up
annual deficits that ranged from $128 billion to well over $200 billion (see
Figure 12.1). The national debt tripled, to almost $3 trillion. The $200 billion
annual interest tab became the third-largest item in the budget. By the end of
the Bush years, the debt grew by another $1 trillion.

Reagan denied responsibility for any of these economic realities, accusing
Congress of squandering funds on new social programs. In fact, he never submitted a balanced budget proposal to Congress and few new programs were
enacted. Most of the red ink resulted from Reagan's insistence on increasing

defense spending at the same time that tax rates were reduced. When the president endorsed a constitutional amendment mandating a balanced budget, he stipulated that it should apply only to his successors.

Because the U.S. Treasury had to borrow so much at home and abroad to fund the deficit, fewer dollars were available for private investment in research, new plants, and machinery. Although the country began the 1980s with a positive trade balance in manufactured goods, the balance soon turned negative. The foreign trade deficit grew dramatically, surpassing $150 billion per year by the second half of the decade. Every week during the Reagan years, American consumers spent an average of about $2 billion more on foreign goods than foreigners spent on American products. The cumulative imbalance for the decade approached $1 trillion.

In 1986, financier Ivan F. Boesky addressed adoring graduating business students at the University of California at Berkeley. Celebrated for his success at buying shares of stock in companies about to be acquired in lucrative mergers, Boesky told his audience on a campus once renowned for its social activism that "greed is healthy." He explained that earning and flaunting great wealth was the driving force of capitalism, the key to its growth and prosperity. In the fall of 1986, however, the Justice Department charged Boesky with multiple violations of security laws. He pled guilty to buying inside information from corporate officials, which he used to manipulate stock prices, acquire companies cheaply, and make billions in profit. Film director Oliver Stone chronicled the rise and fall of Gordon Gecko, a Boeskylike tycoon played by actor Michael Douglas in the 1987 movie *Wall Street*, a cautionary tale about the era's glitter and deceit.

The economic expansion of the 1980s was highly selective. Prosperity and wealth tended to flow to both coasts, partly because of defense spending. The Northeast and California boomed. After severe doldrums in the 1970s, Boston and Manhattan blossomed again during the 1980s. In these boom areas, real estate prices skyrocketed for both residential and commercial property.

Meanwhile, much of the upper Midwest experienced a loss of high-paying industrial jobs, continuing the decline that began in the 1970s. Small farmers abandoned the land in accelerating numbers, while cities like Houston, buffeted by falling energy prices, faced economic disaster. As Reagan spoke of "morning again in America," the sun set on many traditional industries and small farms, and the Southwest experienced a prolonged recession.

Even in national terms, the long economic expansion of the later Reagan years was less impressive than it looked. It was a marked improvement compared to the late 1970s, but compared to the entire period from 1945 to 1980, the recovery appears more modest. During most of the 1980s, the inflation rate was twice as high as the average for the years from 1947 to 1967. Unemployment also remained higher than in most years between 1947 and 1973. Overall, the economy grew no faster in the 1980s than it had during the 1960s and 1970s.

Continuing a trend that began in the 1970s, real wages—that is, wages adjusted for inflation—remained stagnant; in fact, salaries declined slightly on average during the 1980s, although the impact was hidden by an increase in the number of working wives and mothers, whose earnings boosted total family income. Incomes were not stagnant for the richest Americans. In 1980 a typical corporate chief executive officer (CEO) made about forty times the income of an average factory worker; nine years later, the CEO made ninety-three times as much. Reagan-era policies nearly doubled the share of the national income going to the wealthiest 1 percent of Americans, from 8.1 to about 15 percent. Over 60 percent of income growth during the 1980s belonged to the top 1 percent of Americans. By the end of the decade, the top 1 percent, about 834,000 households, was worth more than the bottom 90 percent, or 84 million American households. In the early 1990s, the gaps among the rich, the middle class, and the poor were bigger than at any time since World War II.

A "merger mania," fueled by the 1981 tax law and the Reagan-era Justice Department's relaxed attitude toward enforcing antitrust laws, gripped Wall Street for most of the decade. Many of the nation's biggest companies bought out competitors or were themselves swallowed up in leveraged buyouts financed by huge loans bearing high interest rates. Colorful Wall Street operators like Carl Icahn, T. Boone Pickens, Ivan Boesky, and Michael Milken, and real estate speculator Donald Trump earned billions of dollars buying and merging companies and constructing new office towers, apartment complexes, and resorts. Corporate raiders argued that these deals rewarded stockholders and eliminated incompetent management, thus increasing industrial competitiveness.

In addition to the Wall Street wizards, the decade celebrated "yuppies"—an extended acronym for young urban professionals—a group that exulted in its upward mobility during the 1980s. Journalists used the term lavishly in 1983 and 1984, partly to describe Gary Hart's unexpected following among young Americans as he campaigned for the Democratic presidential nomination. *Newsweek* dubbed 1984 the Year of the Yuppie and applauded the group's eagerness to "go for it" as a sign of the "yuppie virtues of imagination, daring and entrepreneurship." Yuppies existed "on a new plane of consciousness, a state of Transcendental Acquisition."

Despite the hoopla, yuppies were easier to describe or parody than to find. Fewer than 2 million Americans were bona fide yuppies—people born between 1945 and 1959, earning over $40,000 as professionals or managers, and living in a city. As candidate Hart learned, they were not a big constituency for Democratic liberals. Even though they rejected restrictive ideas on abortion and enjoyed recreational drugs, most supported Reagan's economic policies. Yuppies aspired to become investment bankers, not social workers. They spent and overspent on leisure products like Porsches and BMWs, designer sneakers, state-of-the-art electronic equipment, and gourmet foods. They also embraced the fitness craze, shunned cigarettes, wore natural fibers, took up jogging, patronized health spas, and ate high-fiber diets.

Early in his presidency, President Reagan joked that the federal government had fought poverty for twenty years and that "poverty won." As proof, he cited the nearly identical rate of poverty—about 13 percent in 1963 and 1980. But Reagan's humor obscured the facts. Before the Great Society reforms of Medicare, Medicaid, food stamps, and Social Security expansion, the elderly and disabled comprised the bulk of the poor. By 1980, these groups were much better off materially than before. Women and children made up most of the "new" poor.

As the gap between the richest and poorest Americans widened to the largest it had been since 1945, poverty increasingly became the lot of women and children. The so-called feminization of poverty grew more severe during the 1980s, partly because of the rising rate of children born to single mothers. The rate of children living with a never-married mother soared by 70 percent between 1983 and 1993. In the early 1980s, 3.7 million children under age eighteen lived with a single parent who had never married. A decade later, 6.3 million children, or 27 percent of all American children, lived with a never-married parent. As many as 7 million children lived with single, divorced parents (see Figure 12.2).

By the early 1990s, one of every four births in the United States was to an unwed mother; the rate for African American and Hispanic women was about 50 and 33 percent, respectively. Compared to married women, unwed mothers were less likely to receive prenatal care, finish high school, or hold a paying job. The Reagan administration made the situation worse by slashing funds for the Women, Infants, and Children (WIC) program and other programs that provided prenatal and postnatal care to poor women.

Although some of these funds were restored under the Bush administration, by 1992, 22 percent of all American children under the age of eighteen lived in poverty, including 47 percent of all African American children

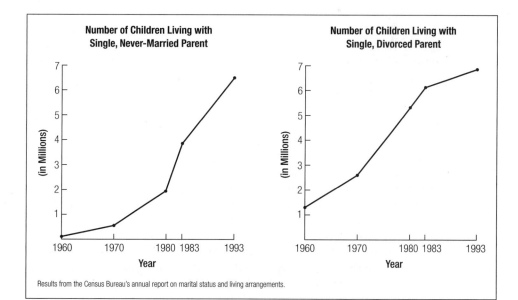

Results from the Census Bureau's annual report on marital status and living arrangements.

Figure 12.2
Children in Single-Parent Households, 1960–1993

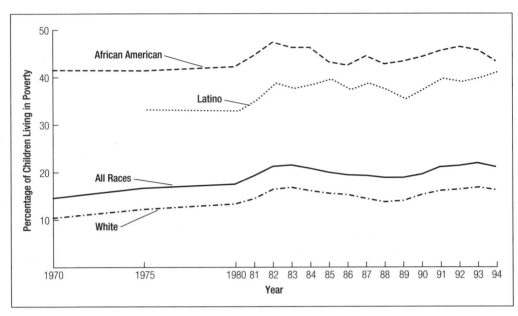

Figure 12.3
Percentage of American Children Living in Poverty, by Ethnicity, 1970–1994

and 29 percent of young Hispanics (see Figure 12.3). Just over one-third of the 37 million Americans living below the poverty line resided in female-headed households.

One of the most troubling economic trends of the 1980s and early 1990s was the sharp increase in the number of people who worked full-time but could not lift themselves and their families out of poverty. The percentage of all Americans working full-time but earning less than a poverty-level income—about $13,000 a year for a family of four in 1991—rose by 50 percent between 1979 and 1992, from 12 percent of the work force to 18 percent. The trend toward lower wages was particularly sharp for young workers and those without college degrees.

The growing phenomenon of homelessness and the worsening plight of a seemingly unreachable "underclass" alarmed both conservatives and liberals during the 1980s. The homeless included all kinds of people, from women fleeing abusive spouses to the chronically mentally ill displaced by the closing of mental institutions. Many lived on urban streets or in subway stations, begging for money and food. The plight of the homeless and urban underclass shocked public sensibilities, but it did not affect policy. Conservatives who saw poverty as the mark of personal failure believed that government efforts to help only worsened the situation. Liberals argued that government was obliged to help, but they had few new ideas to offer.

Government regulation of business, the environment, and banking had been one of the most important innovations of the New Deal. Conservative economists and some business leaders criticized government interference with market forces, even though regulators argued that they had improved markets by keeping them honest. Now, as the public expressed its own doubts about the competence of government, the Reagan administration initiated a major assault on the regulatory powers of the federal government.

As noted earlier, the Carter administration began eliminating regulations that interfered with competition in the transportation and communication sectors, lowering prices in the airline, railroad, and trucking industries. Reagan carried this policy even further because he and his advisers saw almost all government regulation as anticompetitive. In February 1981, Reagan issued an executive order requiring federal agencies to perform cost-benefit studies of proposed new regulations to find the least costly alternatives. New appointees to federal agencies abolished many rules, ranging from stronger car bumpers to environmental restraints on offshore oil drilling. Existing regulatory agencies, such as the Environmental Protection Agency (EPA), the Occupational Safety and Health Administration (OSHA), and the Securities and Exchange Commission (SEC), struggled to operate on reduced budgets with smaller staffs.

The savings and loan (S&L) debacle that struck in the early 1990s resulted directly from policies of mindless deregulation. Since the 1970s, savings and loan institutions, S&Ls or "thrifts," had lost depositors because unregulated money-market funds paid higher rates of interest. To make commercial banks and S&Ls more competitive and to attract new deposits, in 1980 Congress raised the federal insurance level to $100,000 on individual accounts and allowed S&Ls to pay depositors any interest rates they wanted. Two years later, Reagan convinced Congress to deregulate S&Ls further. Previously, S&Ls made only low-risk loans, usually for the purchase of single-family homes. Under the new rules, they could invest depositors' funds in commercial real estate, shopping malls, or almost anything else. By creating more profitable S&Ls, the argument ran, these lenders could then make more home loans. If bad loans caused an S&L to collapse, depositors' accounts would be protected by a government insurance pool and corporate owners had little personal liability.

S&L deregulation sparked a commercial construction boom during the mid-1980s as the thrifts loaned money

A mother begs for work and food—an increasingly common sight during the 1980s and 1990s. / © David Butow/Black Star

to what they hoped were high-yield, but were in reality risky, ventures. Some S&L executives, such as the notorious Charles Keating, head of Lincoln Savings and Loan in California, colluded with builders to drive up the cost of commercial projects, producing bigger fees for all the principals. Unscrupulous S&L executives also made dubious loans to business partners or paid themselves exorbitant salaries.

Then, in 1986, the major change in federal tax laws designed to close tax-avoidance loopholes reduced the inflated value of commercial properties built with S&L funds. This change threatened to bury the industry under a mountain of bad debt. Timely intervention by federal regulators might have limited the cost of the debacle by closing down badly run institutions. But S&L executives with close ties to both the White House and influential members of Congress—such as Keating and the vice president's son, Neil Bush—lobbied to keep business going as usual.

Fortunately for Reagan, the bottom did not fall out of the S&L industry until he retired. Shortly after President Bush took office in 1989, hundreds of S&Ls failed. To prevent a broader and costlier collapse, Congress created the Resolution Trust Corporation to take over a huge inventory of vacant buildings and obligations from the failed thrifts. At a cost to taxpayers of several hundred billion dollars, the S&L collapse was the biggest "bank heist" in the nation's history.

Civil Rights and Conservative Justice

"Conservatives have waited over thirty years for this day," commented Richard Viguerie, a leading New Right fundraiser, when President Reagan nominated Judge Robert H. Bork in July 1987 to a vacant seat on the Supreme Court. Like most conservatives, Reagan and, to an extent, Bush had criticized many Supreme Court decisions since the 1950s. Republican leaders complained that rulings by liberal judges had encouraged a decline in morals, coddled criminals, promoted premarital sex and abortion, and banished religion from public schools.

Reagan was especially critical of efforts by the federal courts and Congress to promote civil rights for minorities and equal rights for women. He had opposed landmark legislation such as the 1964 Civil Rights Act and the Voting Rights Act of 1965. Reagan was not "racist" in the narrow meaning of the term. He often recalled that he and his family had befriended black athletes shunned by teammates while he was in high school. But his perception of race focused on his personal feelings, not on the realities of life faced by minority groups.

Reagan and many other Republicans supported "conservative egalitarianism," the notion that government should oppose *both* racial discrimination and legal efforts to advance the rights of any group—even if members of a particular group, such as African Americans or women, had suffered past injustice in areas like education, housing, and employment. They also opposed "reverse discrimination" against whites and men. The 1980 Republican Party platform stated that true "equal opportunity should not be jeopardized by bureaucratic regulation and decisions which rely on quotas, ratios, and numerical requirements to exclude some individuals in favor of others, thereby rendering such regulations and decisions inherently discriminatory." Conservative Republicans used the language of equality to justify doing nothing about challenging the racial and economic inequality inherent in the status quo.

Reagan's own discomfort with addressing racial problems and his implicit support for the Nixon-era "Southern strategy" of expanding the GOP appeal among white southerners showed in several ways. He endorsed a constitutional amendment to outlaw school busing; opposed a federal holiday honoring Martin Luther King, Jr.; attempted to restore tax benefits to private, segregated schools; and called for gutting the 1965 Voting Rights Act. Only opposition by congressional Democrats and several Supreme Court rulings blocked these initiatives.

Reagan had better luck implementing his views opposing affirmative action through his executive appointments to the Justice Department and other federal agencies. The president's choice for attorney general, William French Smith, and head of the Justice Department Civil Rights Division, William Bradford Reynolds, reflected Reagan's opposition to affirmative action and similar programs. They vehemently opposed any special protection for groups or remedies based on rectifying past mistreatment, including voluntary school busing programs based on race. Presidents Reagan and Bush also changed the direction of the federal Equal Employment Opportunity Commission and Commission on Civil Rights by appointing conservative members who opposed most efforts to challenge racial or gender discrimination or its legacies.

GOP leaders faulted the federal courts for a series of decisions since the 1960s that expanded protections for criminal defendants, including informing defendants of the right to remain silent and their right to have an attorney, and limits on evidence that police could use at trial. Public fear over rising crime rates in the 1980s prompted both Republican and Democratic legislators at the state and national levels to mandate longer, mandatory prison sentences for many crimes, especially those related to the possession or sale of drugs. As noted in the next section, presidents Reagan and Bush did not create this harsh reaction to the crime wave, but they rode it skillfully for partisan purposes.

Reagan appointed nearly four hundred federal judges—a majority of all those sitting in 1988—as well as a chief justice of the Supreme Court and three associate justices. Bush appointed two justices to the Supreme Court and many other federal judges. Especially under Reagan, the Justice Department carefully vetted potential judicial appointments to ascertain their conservative views. When Republicans controlled the Senate from 1981 to 1986, it easily confirmed Reagan's first three Supreme Court appointments: Sandra Day O'Connor, the first female justice; the staunchly conservative Antonin Scalia; and William Rehnquist, who was promoted to chief justice.

The situation changed after the Democrats regained control of the Senate in 1987. That year, Reagan nominated Robert Bork to fill a Supreme Court vacancy. Bork was an outspoken conservative. In 1973, as solicitor general, he had carried out Nixon's firing of the Watergate special prosecutor Archibald Cox. He argued that the Constitution offered little protection for privacy, free speech, women, and minorities. Offended by his arrogant demeanor as well as his views, a majority of senators voted against his nomination. Reagan then nominated Anthony Kennedy, a respected conservative judge whom the Senate easily confirmed.

As the number of conservative justices increased after 1984, the Supreme Court whittled away at previous decisions making police responsible for alerting suspects to their constitutional rights. The Court also approved limitations on bail, affirmed most state death-penalty laws, and allowed prosecutors to present certain illegally seized evidence to juries. In addition, a conservative majority issued rulings that made it harder for women, minorities, the elderly, and the disabled to sue employers for job discrimination.

Society, Culture, and New Americans in the 1980s

In the social and cultural sphere, as in the judicial system, the 1980s were a decade when conservative values re-emerged. President Reagan and many of his supporters stressed family values, clean living, religion, attention to the basics in education, and cultural unity. At the same time, however, the nation experienced a renewed drug crisis, a decline in the reputation of public education, a series of scandals among right-wing television evangelists, an AIDS epidemic, and a large influx of immigrants that made the United States even more culturally diverse.

During the 1980s, as the scourge of AIDS and increased drug use aroused public concern, a health and fitness craze swept the nation. Americans paid increasing heed to warnings that their health suffered from their often sedentary life; high-fat diet; and use of alcohol, tobacco, and caffeine. Exercise became popular, even fashionable, along with natural foods. When the popular press warned about "deadly white powder," it was often unclear if the term referred to salt, sugar, or cocaine. Groups such as Mothers Against Drunk Driving (MADD) campaigned to stiffen state laws against driving under the influence of alcohol and other substances. Antitobacco groups pressed state and local governments to mandate smoke-free workplaces and restaurants, while Surgeon General C. Everett Koop escalated the ongoing federal campaign to warn the public about the health and addiction risks of smoking. Even conservative presidents generally opposed to government regulation authorized their deputies to take stronger steps to move toward what Koop called a "smoke free society."

During the Reagan and Bush administrations, the war on crime merged with the war on drugs. Nearly every president since Woodrow Wilson had launched some type of war on drugs. During the 1980s and early 1990s, an estimated 40 million Americans consumed an illegal substance each year. A

1987 survey revealed that half of all citizens under age forty-five had smoked marijuana at least once. In the first part of the decade, public concern about illegal drug use remained low. In 1985, barely 1 percent of Americans surveyed listed drugs as a major national problem. But four years later, more than half of those surveyed described drug use as the gravest threat to national security.

What had happened to alter the public attitude? Much of the change stemmed from the appearance of crack cocaine, an inexpensive cocaine derivative that became widely available by the middle of the decade. Newspapers, magazines, and television news reports carried frightening stories: robberies inspired by addicts' need for money to buy crack, crack-using pregnant women and parents who ignored or abused their children, preteen dealers, turf wars in which rival dealers shot not only each other but innocent bystanders as well. Also, as the Cold War receded, government and public anxieties focused on new subjects.

Although accurate numbers are hard to come by, many experts believe that drug use among white Americans and the middle class peaked in the late 1970s or early 1980s. When cocaine and its derivatives became popular, the greatest concentration of users was among poor, inner-city, minority youth. For some of these young people, staying high relieved the miseries of daily life. For others, selling drugs provided one of the few avenues of economic and social mobility available to them. The drugs themselves killed surprisingly few people, about four thousand to five thousand in a typical year during this period. About eight thousand died in drug-related violence. In comparison, annual alcohol- and tobacco-related deaths totaled about 200,000 and 400,000, respectively.

Claiming that the nation faced an unprecedented threat, President and Mrs. Reagan urged the public to "just say no" to drug use. Reagan, then Bush, continued to treat drug use as primarily a criminal problem, not a social symptom. Antidrug efforts focused on intercepting supplies, arresting dealers, and jailing users. By 1992, the federal and state war on drugs cost about $16 billion annually, mostly for police and prisons. As in Vietnam, the war produced its own grim body count—millions of small-time users in prison with little change in drug-use patterns.

Another of the nation's periodic episodes of self-flagellation regarding the education system began in the 1980s. Since the Sputnik scare of 1957, Americans had worried about how the nation's schools compared to those of its Soviet rival. Concern mounted during the 1980s, when stories appeared about American high schools turning out functional illiterates while Japanese and South Korean students (the new "threat" as the Soviets faded) outperformed Americans on standardized tests. The Department of Education's 1983 study, *A Nation at Risk*, reported that "if an unfriendly foreign power had attempted to impose on America the mediocre educational performance that exists today, we might well have viewed it as an act of war."

Ironically, Reagan's own secretary of education, Terrel Bell, issued the report in the hope of generating opposition to the president's deep cuts in school

(cont. on page 447)

"Dumber Than We Thought We Were": The Politics of Education

After World War II, American public schools began their first serious attempts to provide at least a high school education for all children. Not surprisingly, this change and others prompted heated debates over the proper goals of education and over a range of other issues, including curriculum content, school discipline, and proper teaching methods. As before, educational reformers of all stripes lamented the perceived shortcomings of the nation's schools, worrying that too many Americans lacked the skills and knowledge necessary for basic competence in an increasingly complex society. In particular, they focused on the lack of fit between Americans' educational achievements and the economy. To take a recent example, a 1993 study demonstrated that almost half of American adults could not read a bus schedule or decipher the numbers on their pay stubs, a finding that prompted Secretary of Education Richard Riley to sound a warning heard many times before: "[T]he vast majority of Americans . . . do not have the skills to earn a living in our increasingly technological society and international marketplace." Most of those who had participated in the 1993 study believed that their skills in English were good. William Bennett, a conservative critic of education who had served in Riley's position under President Ronald Reagan, said, "Yeah, we're dumber than we thought we were."

Spurred by the conviction that the country was failing to educate future citizens properly, postwar critics of the schools have offered everything from a "return to basics" to a diversified curriculum as solutions for the problem. At the same time, federal officials have expanded their role in local education, a trend opposed by conservatives when it involved policies designed to equalize schooling for racial minorities and girls and embraced by those conservatives when it promised national standards for academic performance, invariably measured by standardized tests.

Broader political concerns have shaped the debates about education and the policies adopted to address them in the postwar period. In the 1940s and 1950s, the Cold War provided the context within which Americans interpreted the role of education in their society and in politics. The emergence of the modern civil rights movement in the 1950s placed the needs of racial minorities and poor children on the national agenda for the first time, leading to greater federal involvement in local schools. The passage of Title IX in 1972 not only gave women students more access to all kinds of academic programs but also enabled educated women to choose from a much wider range of employment opportunities. As a result, many talented women left the female employment ghetto of teaching, librarianship, and nursing for other fields. Schools faced increasing difficulties recruiting enough high-quality teachers to serve the growing student population. By the 1980s, the power of the New Right in American politics and growing concerns about the economic consequences of the global economy for education once again shifted the terms of the discussion as many embraced the movement for national standards of performance. At the same time, officials tried to reduce violence, drug use, and disorders in the schools.

Throughout the postwar period, however, commentators have lambasted America's educational system, claiming it was plagued by low academic standards and violence. In 1940 journalist Walter Lippmann worried that educational changes over the previous decades had "progressively removed from the curriculum . . . the western culture which produced the modern democratic state." Business leaders concluded that recent high school graduates were not as skilled in

Since the 1980s, state and federal agencies have linked educational reform and funding to requiring students to take a growing number of standardized tests. / © Will & Deni McIntyre/CORBIS

mathematics, writing, geography, and other academic subjects as their parents had been. Benjamin Fine wrote in his 1947 book, *Our Children Are Cheated*, that the public schools, the main "bulwark of the democratic way of life . . . have deteriorated alarmingly since Pearl Harbor." Calling on Americans to join in a crusade on behalf of quality public education, he warned that otherwise, "we will suffer the consequences of our present neglect of education a generation hence." Claiming that students in urban schools "terrorize teachers," *Life* magazine in 1958 advanced the concern about school violence fictionalized in the 1953 book, *Blackboard Jungle*, by former teacher Evan Hunter.

After World War II, conservative critics particularly emphasized the issue of "subversion" in the public schools. They viewed progressive educators' goal of developing "cooperative democratic character," which stressed the social development of students and the use of group work in the schools, as

a communist plot. In Pasadena, California, for example, the chair of the School Development Council, a local conservative group linked to national right-wing organizations, asserted that progressive education there was "leading to Socialism, and there isn't much difference between Socialism and Communism." He further alleged that the teaching of sex education to mixed-gender classes would lead to free love, which would also cause communism. In response to conservative pressures, the school authorities decided in 1950 to fire Superintendent Willard Goslin, a former president of the American Association of School Administrators and a leader in educational reform.

America's struggle over race also shaped the politics of education. Confronted by the Supreme Court's insistence in 1954 that they admit African Americans to previously all-white schools, some southern school districts devised plans to close the public schools and use public funds to support private, all-white schools. In Little Rock,

445

Arkansas, for example, the public high schools were closed in the 1958–1959 academic year to avoid the minimal integration achieved in the previous year. Under the leadership of Governor Orval Faubus, state officials provided tuition grants (now called vouchers) to displaced high school students attending public or private schools elsewhere in the state. Although the courts ruled against Little Rock's use of public funds to support all-white private schools, white-flight academies with private funding took root throughout the South in the 1960s and 1970s.

Beginning in the 1960s, various movements from outside the schools promised radical changes if only schools privatized or adopted business methods or new technologies. As historian David Tyack noted, these reformers viewed history as "something to be overcome, not a source of insight." Often openly contemptuous of public school teachers and administrators, they preferred "to bypass teachers and to produce teacher-proof instruction." Performance contracting, which involved providing public money to private companies to deliver instruction, came to fruition in Texarkana, Arkansas, in the late 1960s. Hailed as the "mecca of the educational world," the Texarkana school district used federal funds to hire a private company that promised students would make substantial progress on standardized tests. The company would be paid only if it achieved specified results. In turn, it offered the students various incentives to raise their test scores, including everything from Green Stamps to a portable television. The experiment became a scandal when a local school official found out that the "instructional manager" hired by the company had provided students with test questions and answers the day before the test.

The search for solutions from outside the schools continued late in the twentieth century. The New American Schools Development Corporation (NASDC), formed by President George Bush in the late 1980s to "unleash America's creative genius to invent ... the best schools in the world, . . . to achieve a quantum leap in learning," defined an ambitious set of goals published as *America 2000*. They included having all students demonstrate proficiency in basic subjects at grades 4, 8, and 12 and making U.S. students the best in the world in science and mathematics. Not surprisingly, NASDC failed to achieve its utopian goals, in part because it saw teachers more as obstacles than as partners in the endeavor. In its "Who Does What?" section, *America 2000* described parents, government officials at the state and federal levels, and business leaders as key actors. Teachers appeared later on a list of people who had an impact "at the community level."

By the 1980s, support for desegregation had subsided in the executive branch, as had its willingness to enforce Title IX. This shift led to a change in the terms of the debate about improving schools for children, especially those from poor communities. During this period, an ideology of accountability developed, and it centered on the use of standardized tests and on vouchers, charter schools, and homeschooling as mechanisms to hold specific schools and school districts accountable for students' performance and to provide more choices for parents. The reliance on national tests, often developed by commercial providers seeking to supply what the market demanded, sparked intense conflict. Critics claimed that the tests did not measure critical thinking or imagination and created incentives for educators to narrow curriculum content and "teach to the test."

The issue of vouchers, which ostensibly gave parents of students in poor schools a means to choose other schools for their children, also generated controversy. According to a representative of the conservative Heritage Foundation, "It's an idea that, for the first time, shifts the focus of federal education policy from inputs to outcomes, zeroes in on closing the achievement gap between rich and poor students, and rewards success while punishing failure."

The use of public money to support students in religious schools, however, raised important constitutional issues regarding the separation of church and state. In a June 2002 decision, the U.S. Supreme Court found that school-voucher programs that provide money for students to use in private religious schools are constitutional. Writing for the majority, Chief Justice William Rehnquist stated that the Cleveland, Ohio, program reviewed by the Court was "neutral in all respects toward religion," despite the fact that 97 percent of the money involved was going to religious schools. The Court also stated, however, that as long as students had secular choices available, the state was not promoting religion unconstitutionally. Four of the justices disagreed emphatically, reflecting the divisions in American society over the issue. In a dissenting opinion, Justice John Paul Stevens accused the five majority justices of forgetting the lessons of religious unrest in other parts of the world, including the Balkans and the Middle East; he wrote that "[w]henever we remove a brick from the wall that was designed to separate religion and government, we increase the risk of religious strife and weaken the foundation of our democracy."

Other critics agreed. Prior to the decision, the Anti-Defamation League worried that the privatization of education would undermine the role of education in creating unity in a diverse society and that it would make it "difficult to prevent schools run by extremist groups like the Nation of Islam or the Ku Klux Klan from receiving public funds to subsidize their racist and anti-Semitic agendas." Detractors also noted that the inability of poor parents to raise the rest of the money required to send their children to private schools meant that state governments were subsidizing the school choices of the affluent and therefore intensifying educational inequality. Such subsidies, they argued, would threaten the very future of public schools because affluent taxpayers would withdraw their political support for them, causing schools for poor children to deteriorate even further.

It appears that many citizens of postwar America have agreed with H. G. Wells that their history has become "more and more a race between education and catastrophe." If Americans fail to find meaningful remedies, we will prove to be, in William Bennett's words, "dumber than we thought we were."

---

aid. Americans sympathized with the tone of the report, but few agreed on a remedy. Conservatives blamed school problems on teachers' unions, wasteful spending, and a lack of attention to "basics." Liberals complained that public schools were chronically underfunded even as they were called upon to provide a growing list of services. Unlike other industrialized countries, over 90 percent of all U.S. public school funding came from local, not federal, taxes. Also, educational policies were set by local school boards. The federal government played only a limited role. Thus, schools in affluent areas tended to be relatively well funded and successful, while those in poor areas struggled to make ends meet.

Reagan soothed public anxiety by posing for "photo ops" with honor students—and firing Education Secretary Bell after the 1984 election. Bush promised to be "the education president," but he did little to bolster federal support for public education. To complicate educational matters, the urban middle class abandoned public schools in growing numbers. Continuing the trend of the 1970s, middle-class parents enrolled their children in private and parochial schools with selective admission policies. With many of their more affluent and motivated students gone, the public schools struggled to educate a larger proportion of poor, minority, and non-English-speaking children. The flight of middle-class students reduced the ability of school districts to raise needed revenues. Parents paying tuition for private education were reluctant to support new taxes. The gradual aging of the American population also contributed to the school crisis because the elderly—with no young children of their own to educate—tended to oppose additional expenditures on schools. These problems in turn accelerated the decline of faith in public education, making it still harder to fund schools adequately.

Continuing a phenomenon that surfaced in the late 1970s, evangelical Christianity became both a national political issue and a movement closely linked to the Republican Party. With approximately 40 percent of Americans describing themselves as born again, Reagan and his advisers recognized the immense impact that a large number of disaffected Christians could have if they supported national and local candidates. Republican officials capitalized on the ability of television ministers, or televangelists, to mobilize an audience of millions on behalf of the Republican cause.

Reagan had been raised in a deeply religious home, but as an adult he seldom attended church. Nevertheless, he spoke with verve and certainty on religious matters. In 1980, he told a meeting of self-described, fundamentalist Christian leaders that he considered himself born again and that "it was a fact that all the [world's] complex and horrendous [problems] have their answer in that single book—the Bible." He criticized federal courts for not permitting "creation science" to be taught as a scientific alternative to the theory of evolution, and he urged amending the Constitution to permit the return of prayer to public schools. "You can't endorse me," he told cheering preachers, "but I endorse you."

Opinion surveys revealed that younger and socially liberal voters believed that the once-divorced Reagan, who had many gay friends in Hollywood, was "winking" at them when he denounced homosexuality, divorce, premarital sex, etc. Yet self-described Christian conservatives took his statements at face value. As a group, they voted for Reagan over his opponents by almost a 4-to-1 ratio. The religious right never felt as comfortable with George Bush as they had with Reagan, but he received the same proportion of votes from Christian conservatives in 1988. Equally important, religious voters formed a growing proportion of participants in Republican primaries that selected candidates.

By 1985, the electronic ministries such as Jerry Fallwell's Moral Majority, Pat Robertson's 700 Club, and Jim Bakker's PTL (Praise the Lord) club were raising well over $1 billion annually. The most successful televangelists preached two basic sermons. One fulminated against the threat posed to America by immorality, communism, abortion, and secular humanism (the belief that humans, not God, were the basis of moral law). The other celebrated a gospel of wealth, a belief that money and possessions represented a form of divine grace. The Reverend Jimmy Swaggart epitomized the former style, and the Reverend Jim Bakker represented the latter. Both implied that grace was readily available to those who demonstrated their faith by making large donations.

Many televangelists were honest and sincere, and were less inclined to the flamboyant exaggeration and flagrant fundraising conducted by Swaggart and the Bakkers. The Reverend Billy Graham, for example, had used television to preach the gospel since the 1950s. While a conservative who befriended powerful Republican politicians, Graham did not demonize Democrats or those who did not follow his faith, and he showed no hint of financial impropriety. For their part, not all viewers accepted the political dogma put forth by the more strident media preachers.

Televised ministries suffered a major setback in 1987, when several of the most outrageous televangelists were tainted by scandal. A federal jury convicted Jim Bakker on numerous counts of fraud and conspiracy for bilking followers out of $158 million that they had invested in a scheme involving his ministry's religious theme park, Heritage USA. In addition, a rival TV preacher revealed that Bakker had forced a female church member to have sex with him and had used donation funds to pay her hush money. Oral Roberts became an object of derision when he locked himself in a prayer tower, claiming that God would "take" him in thirty days unless his flock mailed him $8 million—which they promptly did. Jimmy Swaggart admitted that he had paid for sex with prostitutes, who in court depositions described him as "really weird." Pat Robertson's crusade for the 1988 Republican presidential nomination collapsed amid ridicule after he announced that he would use prayer to divert a hurricane from Virginia to New York, where God would presumably vent his wrath on those of little faith.

President Reagan and his top aides had pressured government agencies to overlook charges of lawbreaking by certain televangelists because they had supported the administration. During the 1990s, many politically active televangelists and Christian conservatives refocused their attention on local rather than national campaigns, throwing their support behind candidates for school boards, city councils, county governments, and Congress.

In the 1987 film *Fatal Attraction*, actress Glenn Close portrays a thirty-something career woman who has a weekend affair with a married colleague, played by Michael Douglas. Douglas's philandering comes back to haunt him when the distraught Close stalks him, threatens his wife and children, and slaughters the family pet. The film echoed themes voiced by conservative politicians and their religious allies: feminism and sexual independence harmed women's mental health and endangered families. In this view, single, childless career women were social misfits and potential moral outlaws who threatened society. Marriage, monogamy, and motherhood, like faith, prevented women from becoming homicidal maniacs and kept society stable.

At the 1980 Republican convention, two issues evoked real passion among delegates to the party's platform committee: repealing the fifty-five-mile-per-hour highway speed limit and implementing the New Right social agenda on women and reproductive rights. In a symbolic sense, GOP activists wanted men to drive faster and women to drive slower down the highway of life. This approach reflected Republican efforts to woo white southern men and northern blue-collar Catholic voters as well as religious conservatives. The platform committee adopted a plank calling for a constitutional amendment to ban abortion and also came out against ratification of the Equal Rights Amendment (ERA) to the Constitution. In an effort to put a positive spin on their agenda, Republican activists did not proclaim an overtly antifeminist agenda. Instead, they called their party the advocate of "traditional family values." But the tradition carried a clear message: women should stay at home, obey their husbands, and raise children.

During the 1980s and early 1990s, American society seemed to pull in two directions regarding gender issues. At one level, the nation appeared increasingly liberal and tolerant. Most single and married women now worked outside the home in various professions. Sexuality in general was depicted much more openly in the arts and entertainment, and homosexuality was widely acknowledged, if not fully accepted, as part of the human experience. At the same time, religious conservatives and other members of the New Right in and out of the Republican Party denounced gays, abortion, gender equality, pornography, and a host of other "sins" as the progeny of secular humanism.

Ronald Reagan and the religious right celebrated the "traditional family," which consisted of a breadwinning husband and a wife who served as mother and homemaker. Many Americans found this image of family life appealing. Yet the so-called traditional household continued to decline in the 1980s. In 1970, 40 percent of the nation's households still conformed to that ideal; by 1980 that proportion had dropped to 31 percent, and by 1990, to 26 percent. (Part of this trend stemmed from an aging population in which women outlived men and lived alone after their partner's death.) In 1983, the proportion of adult women with jobs outside the home surpassed 50 percent for the first time in the country's history, and it continued to rise over the next decade.

With women holding so many of the nation's paying jobs, feminists continued to press harder for affordable childcare, approval of the Equal Rights Amendment, and an end to gender discrimination by employers. Despite the administration's verbal support for a "profamily" agenda, Reagan and his aides opposed efforts to develop a national childcare policy, and Republicans in Congress blocked any reconsideration of the Equal Rights Amendment when the deadline for ratification expired in 1982.

The administration's focus on the family often seemed to settle on the unborn. The president endorsed an anti-abortion constitutional amendment, ordered that no federal funds go to domestic or foreign family-planning organizations that tolerated abortion as a means of birth control, and backed legislation that created "chastity clinics" to encourage teenagers to avoid sex. At the urging of the White House, Congress continued to ban Medicaid-funded abortions as well as some forms of birth control and counseling. Support for children, however, seemed to end at birth because the administration cut funds for infant nutrition programs, opposed the expansion of federally funded daycare, and ignored calls to establish a national family-leave policy for new parents.

In 1983, the Justice Department urged the Supreme Court to limit the guarantees of Title IX of the 1972 Education Act. This law barred sex discrimination by educational institutions receiving federal funds. Title IX had opened a wide variety of athletic and academic programs to women. But the Court ruled in the 1984 *Grove City College* case that the law had a narrow application and that institutions could skirt its provisions by using nonfederal money to support a potentially discriminatory program. Congress tried to restore broader federal protection against sex discrimination by passing a civil rights restoration act in 1988, but Reagan vetoed the bill. As discussed below, Reagan's appointees to the Supreme Court struck down civil rights legislation that would have facilitated women's ability to sue employers for gender discrimination. In 1989 and 1992, the Court also ruled that states could impose a wide array of restrictions on abortions.

Many commentators proclaimed that the 1980s were witnessing the end of the sexual revolution that had begun during the 1960s. This pronouncement was probably premature, but the outbreak of the AIDS epidemic in the early 1980s brought a health crisis that would indeed make Americans more cautious about sexual relations. The result of a virus apparently originating in Africa, AIDS (an acronym for acquired immune deficiency syndrome) destroyed the immune system and left victims vulnerable to opportunistic infections. The deadly human immunodeficiency virus (HIV) that caused AIDS was transmitted from one person to another through the exchange of body fluids, particularly blood and semen. In the early years of the epidemic, sexual transmission was especially prevalent among gay men. Intravenous drug users who shared needles were also at grave risk, as were their sex partners. Before tests were developed to check the nation's blood banks, many

The fight against AIDS included a public education campaign to alert people to the danger. / Courtesy of Saatchi & Saatchi

hemophiliacs caught the virus through transfusions. By the end of 1993, about 200,000 Americans had died from the disease, and an estimated 1 million others carried the deadly HIV infection. AIDS struck even harder in other countries, especially in Africa, Brazil, and Asia.

Because many of the first people with AIDS were gay men or drug abusers, President Reagan was uncomfortable even discussing the disease. Along with his conservative backers, he opposed spending much federal money on AIDS research or preventive education during his first term. The president remained silent on the subject, while televangelists spoke of God's sending a "gay plague" to punish sinners. Scientists urged public officials to endorse a safe-sex program that promoted the use of condoms to reduce transmission of the virus. But many religious authorities and cultural conservatives fought against the idea, arguing that promoting safer sex—just like educating teenagers about contraception— encouraged promiscuity.

In October 1985, Rock Hudson, a popular film star and a personal friend of the Reagans, died from AIDS, an event that humanized the disease for both the president and the public. The president appointed a commission that recommended much higher levels of funding for government and private research, education programs, and treatment. The virus had been identified by 1984, and now a search for ways to prevent or cure the disease began in earnest. Although Reagan urged compassion for people with AIDS, he seldom spoke on the subject and he refused to endorse his own surgeon general's call for widespread publicity encouraging the use of condoms.

Immigrants continued to be a major part of the American experience. In fact, about as many foreign-born (25 million) entered the country in the fifty-five years since 1945 as came during the years from 1880 to 1940. Most came following the 1965 immigration law reform that abolished restrictive rules dating from the 1920s. During the 1980s, 7 million immigrants arrived, and 9 million more came in the 1990s. In 1990, Congress authorized nearly 700,000 regular entry slots per year, with an additional 100,000 visas for refugees. In addition to legal entrants, as many as 300,000 undocumented immigrants arrived each year, and they totaled at least 5 million in the mid-1990s. Because of its proximity, Mexico was the country of origin for about half of the undocumented immigrants.

Since 1980, about 45 percent of immigrants came from Asia and the Middle East, and about as many came from Latin America and the Caribbean (see Figure 12.4). Only about 10 percent came from Europe. Mexicans and South Americans raised the Latino portion of the U.S. population to 13 percent during the 1990s, surpassing the number of African Americans. By the early 1990s, the Asian American population doubled with the arrival of 3.5 million Filipinos, Chinese, Koreans, Indians, Vietnamese, Cambodians, and Laotians. These newcomers settled everywhere, but they concentrated in the cities of California, New York, Florida, Texas, New Jersey, and Illinois. Even though New York City's Chinese population increased from 33,000 to 400,000 between 1960 and 2000, Los Angeles replaced New York as the ma-

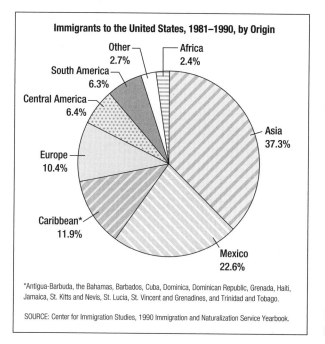

Immigrants to the United States, 1981–1990, by Origin

Other 2.7%
Africa 2.4%
South America 6.3%
Central America 6.4%
Europe 10.4%
Caribbean* 11.9%
Asia 37.3%
Mexico 22.6%

*Antigua-Barbuda, the Bahamas, Barbados, Cuba, Dominica, Dominican Republic, Grenada, Haiti, Jamaica, St. Kitts and Nevis, St. Lucia, St. Vincent and Grenadines, and Trinidad and Tobago.

SOURCE: Center for Immigration Studies, 1990 Immigration and Naturalization Service Yearbook.

**Figure 12.4
Moving to America, 1981–1990**

jor port of entry for Asian and Latino immigrants. By 1992, one-fourth of its 9 million inhabitants were recent arrivals.

In addition to the large Latino and Asian migration to the states named above, many immigrants found their way to places like Minnesota, North Carolina, Georgia, and Arkansas. For example, Hmong from Laos resettled in Minneapolis. Mexicans and Central Americans, sometimes as whole groups of villagers, moved to small cities in the South where they worked in textile, furniture, and food-processing plants. Without these new workers, the region could not have sustained its economic base.

New immigrants worked in all areas of the economy, from unskilled agricultural labor to running small shops, to staffing hospitals, to designing computer software. They filled American cities with the sounds of new languages and diversified religious life as millions of Muslims, Buddhists, Hindus, and Sikhs joined the traditional mix of Protestants, Catholics, and Jews.

The increase in immigration aroused mixed feelings among the general public, even though the new arrivals often filled jobs shunned by other Americans and helped to revitalize the cores of many cities. In Florida, for example, many African Americans resented what they saw as favored treatment given to those coming from Cuba. The large number of undocumented Mexicans living in the United States aroused special concern. With the proliferation of new cultures and tongues, some whites feared the erosion of English as the national language. Voters in California, Arizona, and Florida passed laws declaring

English the official state language. Some states denied driver's licenses to non-English speakers and moved to limit social service to the undocumented.

Refugee policies also aroused debate. The Reagan and Bush administrations, like Congress, continued preferential treatment for those fleeing Cuba. Refugees streaming out of Haiti and Central America, however, were deemed economic migrants, even though they often fled civil war and harsh repression. In the mid-1980s, some church leaders and lay activists defied Washington by assisting Central American refugees on their own. The so-called Sanctuary Movement functioned like the Underground Railroad in pre-Civil War America, helping to transport and relocate individuals and families.

After years of debate about how to control immigration, Congress passed the 1986 Simpson-Rodino Act. It offered legal status to several million undocumented aliens living in the United States, but it imposed fines on employers who hired new undocumented workers. Despite hopes that the new law would ensure orderly immigration procedures, it had little impact on undocumented immigrants or on those who hired them. By the mid-1990s, close to 1 million people immigrated legally to this country each year, historically a very high number.

George H. W. Bush, Michael Dukakis, and the 1988 Election

As Ronald Reagan approached the end of his second term, Democrats once again hoped to win back control of the White House by restoring the New Deal coalition that had splintered in the late 1960s and 1970s. But the Democratic Party's divisions had not healed, and a majority of the public still viewed the party's presidential nominee with suspicion.

Despite serving eight years as vice president, George Bush remained relatively unknown to the public. He was not close to Reagan personally and had not played much of a role in setting the domestic or foreign policy agenda. Until being tapped as Reagan's running mate in 1980, Bush had angered conservatives by supporting abortion rights and ridiculing their tax-cutting plans as "voodoo economics." These past lapses, along with his "preppy mannerisms" and what some viewed as a wimpy, Mr. Rogers personality, made Bush the object of mistrust and derision among the Republican right wing. In the contest to succeed Reagan, more conservative challengers, such as Reagan aide Patrick Buchanan, televangelist Pat Robertson, and Senator Robert Dole accused Bush of being an unauthentic conservative, more of an "Eastern Establishment liberal" than a rugged individual. One wag dismissed his claim to being a Texan as "all hat and no boots."

In fact, Bush was a capable and ambitious politician who had long sought the presidency. The son of a wealthy Republican senator from Connecticut, Bush left college during World War II to become the youngest fighter pilot in the U.S. navy. After the war, Bush graduated from Yale, moved to Texas, and made a fortune in the oil business. As a moderate in an increasingly conservative Republican Party, he served two terms in the U.S. House of Representatives from 1967–1971. His strong support for funding family-planning programs earned him the nickname "rubbers" among House members. In fact, until his selection as Reagan's vice president in 1980, Bush continued to support a woman's right to choose and the ERA. After he failed to win a 1970 election bid for a U.S. Senate seat in Texas, presidents Nixon and Ford appointed Bush to several posts, including chair of the Republican National Committee, U.S. representative in China, and director of the Central Intelligence Agency.

After Bush had secured the 1988 GOP nomination, he worked to highlight his conservative credentials. He selected Senator Dan Quayle of Indiana, a favorite among Christian conservatives but otherwise considered a lightweight, as his running mate. At the Republican convention, Bush brought delegates to their feet by paraphrasing a line spoken by actor Clint Eastwood. "Read my lips," he declared (in a line which came back to haunt him), "No new taxes."

Eight Democrats battled for their party's nomination, and by the spring of 1988, two remained in play. The Reverend Jesse Jackson, the first African American presidential candidate to win a substantial following, led the Rainbow Coalition, which championed traditional liberal causes. But Massachusetts governor Michael Dukakis, a relative unknown, eventually outpolled Jackson, who was dogged with a "radical" image. Dukakis shunned the "liberal" label and promised to achieve nationally the rapid economic growth that his state had experienced during his efficient stewardship. With the hope of attracting white southern males back to the Democratic fold, he chose Texas senator Lloyd Bentsen as his running mate.

Once the presidential race began, Bush adopted a slashing campaign plan crafted by his adviser, Lee Atwater. Bush promised to oppose abortion, cut taxes, promote prayer in public schools, and get tougher on drug users. He caricatured Dukakis as an "unrepentant liberal" and a "high tax, high spending, pro-abortion, card-carrying member of the American Civil Liberties Union." Bush also denounced his opponent for his veto of a Massachusetts law requiring schoolteachers to lead students in the Pledge of Allegiance to the American flag, and he blamed Dukakis for granting a prison furlough to a murderer named Willie Horton, who then raped a woman.

Dukakis proved to be a wooden candidate, slow to respond to Bush's charges or to articulate a program designed to regain the support of conservative Democrats who had voted for Nixon and Reagan. Bush won the election with 54 percent of the popular vote and majorities in forty states, running especially strong among white men and in the South. Yet Bush was also the first candidate since John F. Kennedy to win the presidency while his party lost seats in Congress. Democrats made a net gain of two House seats, for a majority of 260 seats compared to the Republicans' 175. In Senate races, Democrats won 19 of 33 contested seats and retained their ten-seat majority (55 seats compared to the Republicans' 45). Democrats improved their state standings slightly, showing that GOP dominance of national politics centered on the White House.

The Bush Presidency at Home

As a candidate, Bush had pledged to preside over a "kinder, gentler America." From 1989 through 1991, continued economic expansion, the collapse of the Soviet Union, and quick success in the Panama intervention and the Gulf War (discussed in Chapter 13) sustained Bush's popularity. The president's abrasive chief of staff, former New Hampshire governor John Sununu, worked hard to keep the White House on good terms with the religious right, while Bush himself cooperated with the Democratic majority in Congress during 1990–1991 to pass several important pieces of legislation for the environment and the disabled.

The Americans with Disabilities Act was designed to ensure that government, business, and educational institutions provided equal access to the physically disabled. It expanded opportunities—and often opened physical access—in private employment, schools, public services, and travel to a broad class of people who had frequently been excluded from participating fully in national life. The act required the redesign of many public and private buildings as well as public transport to accommodate the disabled. The Supreme Court, however, limited the scope of the act in a series of rulings in the late 1990s and in 2001–2002 that narrowed the definition of disability and made it easier for employers to deny certain kinds of jobs to the disabled.

Congress and the president agreed to revisions of the Clean Water Act and the Clean Air Act, laws first enacted in the 1970s that set federal and state standards for water and air purity, regulated automobile and industrial emissions, and funded sewage systems. The Radiation Exposure Compensation Act provided payments for victims of atomic mining and testing during the Cold War. The Native American Graves Repatriation Act forced museums to return certain bones and cultural artifacts to American Indian tribes. In 1991, Bush signed a civil rights bill that permitted racial and gender goals in hiring. He also cooperated with a group headed by Arkansas governor Bill Clinton that called for new federal initiatives to raise local education standards. The president's support for these "good-government measures" infuriated more conservative Republicans.

Their anger intensified when economic circumstances forced Bush to retreat from another pillar of the Reagan revolution, his commitment not to raise taxes. Faced with a federal deficit climbing toward $300 billion and complaints from foreign creditors worried about the value of the dollars owed to them, the president and the Democratic leadership of Congress agreed to a budget deal late in 1990. It called for modest tax hikes along with small spending cuts in social programs and defense. Conservatives led by Representative Newt Gingrich of Georgia condemned Bush for breaking his "no new taxes" pledge. Meanwhile, some liberal Democrats balked at approving a plan that imposed regressive sales taxes on beer and cigarettes that hit the poor hardest. Together, this unlikely coalition blocked the budget deal and forced a three-day shutdown of the federal government in October 1990. Congress soon approved a reconfigured budget that included small tax hikes for high-income Americans and a small reduction in spending. Bush's compromise outraged Gingrich and his right-wing followers, and the president never regained their trust.

By now it was clear that Bush, unlike Reagan, did not really believe that government was the enemy. He also tried to work with the Democratic majority to pass needed legislation. Unlike the president, Gingrich and a group of younger, more conservative House Republicans advocated a "take no prisoners" strategy of politics, denouncing Democrats' motives and opposing everything they attempted to accomplish. (Republican governors who controlled many of the largest states tended to be more centrist than national party leaders.) As the newly selected Republican Whip (a party officer charged with enforcing discipline) in the House, Gingrich favored confrontation as the best way to undermine the Democrats' built-in advantage of incumbency.

In 1989, Democrats provided unintended assistance to Gingrich when the Senate rebuffed Bush's nomination of former Texas senator John Tower as Secretary of Defense. Tower, who had enemies in both parties, faced embarrassing criticism from Democrats for his problems with alcohol, womanizing, and business ethics. Gingrich used Tower's rejection to rally House Republicans and to justify his own blistering attack on the ethics of House Speaker Jim Wright, a Democrat from Texas. Wright, a flamboyant personality who had violated House procedures, resigned under pressure in 1989. Over the next several years, charges of legal and ethical transgressions became common.

Despite growing partisan rancor in Congress, voters returned nearly all incumbents on Election Day in November 1990. Only one of thirty-two Senate incumbents seeking re-election—Republican Rudy Boschwitz of Minnesota—lost his seat, and nearly all House incumbents won re-election. Democrats increased their majority in the Senate by one seat (they held fifty-six seats compared to the Republicans' forty-four) and they gained eight seats in the House. Although most incumbents were returned, public distaste for congressional feuding expressed itself in other ways. Colorado became the first state to impose term limits on federal officeholders. Voters in California, Colorado, and Oklahoma placed similar caps on service by state legislators.

Controversies over individual rights continued to strike discordant notes. Abortion rights remained an especially charged issue. Before 1980, Bush had supported a woman's right to choose, but in 1988, he declared, "abortion is murder." Two Supreme Court decisions, *Webster* v. *Reproductive Services of Missouri* (1989) and *Planned Parenthood* v. *Casey* (1992), held by 5-to-4 votes that states could strictly regulate, but not absolutely ban, abortions.

Liberal concerns and conservative hopes for the future direction of the Supreme Court intensified when associate justices William Brennan and Thurgood Marshall retired from the Court. The departure of these stalwart liberals gave Bush an opportunity to tip the ideological balance of the Court. To replace Brennan in 1990, the president nominated the nearly unknown David Souter of New Hampshire, who had served for only a few months on the federal bench. Unlike Robert Bork, Souter had not expressed himself publicly on controversial issues such as abortion, the right to privacy, and the death penalty. He maintained silence on these matters during the Senate confirmation process and easily won confirmation. To the surprise of nearly everyone, Souter emerged as a voice of moderation on abortion and other issues.

After disappointing conservatives with Souter, Bush filled the Supreme Court vacancy left by the retirement of Thurgood Marshall—the Court's first African American—with a high-profile conservative. The "most qualified American" to replace Marshall, Bush claimed, was Clarence Thomas, a forty-three-year-old African American federal appeals court judge. Thomas, a staunch conservative, had criticized many past Supreme Court rulings on abortion, school prayer, privacy rights, and the death penalty. As a member of the Equal Employment Opportunity Commission appointed by Reagan, he had dismissed most complaints brought by women and minorities. But he appeared headed for speedy confirmation until a journalist revealed that he had been accused of sexual harassment by law professor Anita Hill, among others.

The all-male Senate Judiciary Committee reluctantly interviewed Hill (but ignored other women prepared to testify about Thomas's behavior) in a tense, televised hearing. Hill's detailed allegations, Thomas's vehement but vague denial that the hearings were a "high tech lynching," and the committee's condescending treatment of Hill were sorry spectacles. The Senate confirmed Thomas and he proved to be a reliable conservative. But the episode aroused strong misgivings, especially among feminists, over Bush's judgment in making the nomination. It also brought into the mainstream the larger issue of sexual harassment in the workplace.

As discussed in Chapter 13, his success in toppling General Manuel Noriega in Panama and in mobilizing a twenty-eight-nation coalition to liberate Kuwait from Iraq made Bush an extremely popular president through mid-1991. But once the excitement of victory in the Gulf War faded, Americans refocused their concern on the deteriorating economy. President Bush,

When President Bush nominated Judge Clarence Thomas to fill a Supreme Court vacancy, law professor Anita Hill, his former assistant, accused him of sexual harassment during riveting Senate testimony. / Left: AP/Wide World; Right: © Reuters/Bettmann/CORBIS

who appeared so dynamic and resourceful in managing foreign military ventures, came across as lethargic and disengaged from domestic problems. After first denying that America was experiencing a recession, he insisted that economic problems would solve themselves. But American voters preferred an activist president, certainly on issues that affected their economic livelihood. This contrast set the stage for a political transformation as the 1992 election neared.

George H. W. Bush, Bill Clinton, and the 1992 Election

In spite of the president's boast that the United States had finally "kicked the Vietnam syndrome," the victory in the Gulf War was a limited one. Saddam Hussein remained in power in Iraq partly because Bush's advisers feared that Islamic fundamentalists would fill the void created by his elimination. But during the remainder of the Bush presidency and for the next decade, the Iraqi tyrant continued to threaten his neighbors and frustrate U.N. arms inspectors. By 1992, a growing number of Americans criticized Bush's failure to "finish off" Saddam.

The lack of clear direction after the end of the Cold War and the murky outcome of the Gulf War were somewhat abstract problems. The onset of a deep economic recession in 1991 proved far more tangible and damaging to the Bush administration and GOP fortunes. Conservative Republicans angrily attributed the downturn to the president's reversal of Reagan's tax policies. Bush felt trapped between the massive federal deficit of almost $300 billion and GOP conservatives prepared to denounce him for any display of moderation. Afraid to raise taxes (to reduce the deficit) or to boost spending (to stimulate the economy), the president appeared paralyzed and an easy target.

As the recession extended into 1992, the public blamed different villains. With the unifying demon of the Soviet Union gone, some Americans condemned the nation's own allies for unleashing a barrage of automobiles and electronic goods against the United States. Paul Tsongas, a Democratic senator from Massachusetts, popularized this sentiment with a joke: "The good news is that the Cold War is over, but the bad news is that Germany and Japan won."

By early 1992, the fading glow of the Gulf War victory and the worsening recession tarnished Bush's halo. Criticism by Democrats of the president's apathy toward domestic issues, along with harsh denunciations by conservative Republicans for breaking his 1988 "read my lips, no new taxes" pledge, drove down Bush's job approval rating from about 91 percent in March 1991 to 44 percent in February 1992. That spring, over 80 percent of Americans told the Gallup poll that they were unhappy with the state of the nation. Despite plummeting popularity and bitter attacks on his record by GOP rival Patrick Buchanan, Bush won renomination for a second term in the summer of 1992.

Prior to 1992, Democratic presidential candidates had lost five of six elections since 1968, including three straight landslide trouncings in the 1980s. Political pundits and academic specialists speculated that the GOP had secured a lock on the White House, given Republican strength in the South and southwestern Sunbelt states, the Rocky Mountain region, and the upper Midwest.

These states possessed about 250 electoral votes, just twenty less than the 270 needed for victory. A related argument held that a majority of voters were strongly attracted to the symbolic and cultural positions held by GOP candidates, such as their appeals to patriotism and support for tax cuts.

Beginning in the late 1980s, a small but influential group of Democrats worked to reshape their party's positions on issues of patriotism and moral values, challenging the perceived GOP advantage. Calling themselves "New Democrats," these reformers organized the Democratic Leadership Council (DLC). Most DLC members came from the moderate and conservative wings of the party, from the South, and had close ties to corporations. They included senators Al Gore of Tennessee, Joseph Lieberman of Connecticut, Sam Nunn of Georgia, Joseph Biden of Delaware, and Bill Clinton, governor of Arkansas.

New Democrats worked to distance the party and its candidates from their traditional embrace of liberal policies and their close identification with labor unions and racial and ethnic minorities. Through past efforts to satisfy these constituencies, they argued, Democrats had alienated a larger group of white voters, especially males, who lived in the nation's suburbs and in the South. To win the presidency, a Democrat would have to attract these centrist voters—along with corporate contributions—by adopting relatively conservative proposals on issues such as welfare reform, crime, free trade, and defense. More traditional party leaders like Jesse Jackson viewed New Democrats as GOP clones and joked that DLC stood for "Democrats for the Leisure Class."

Unlike Republicans, however, New Democrats still believed that the federal government should play a major role in many areas of American life, including job training; national service; environmental protection; and investments in education, health, transportation, and housing. New Democrats also supported a woman's right to choose an abortion. Republicans since Reagan had identified the federal government as the problem and called for eliminating or privatizing many of its functions. New Democrats spoke of reinventing government to make it smaller and more effective.

Arkansas governor Bill Clinton based his 1992 presidential campaign on New Democrat themes. He stressed economic mobility rather than wealth transfers and adopted tough-minded lines on crime, welfare dependency, and international security issues. Clinton won most of the Democratic state primaries and secured the nomination, despite rumors of marital infidelity and draft avoidance during the Vietnam War. As the recession worsened, he added an element of economic populism to his campaign, which appealed to organized labor; liberals; and nonunion, working-class Americans who felt passed over by both Bush and the New Democrats. Clinton led a unified party and focused on an economic message. In reply to what the election was about, his campaign declared, "It's the economy, stupid."

Ross Perot, a flamboyant Texas billionaire who personally disliked Bush, entered the presidential race as a self-funded independent. Promising to slash the soaring deficit and shake up the system, his mercurial campaign attracted slightly more Republican than Democratic voters.

President Bush ran a lethargic re-election campaign. Clinton's relatively conservative position on issues such as the death penalty and crime made it hard to paint him as a bleeding-heart liberal. The end of the Cold War and the Soviet threat also muted the effectiveness of the standard GOP charge that Democrats were soft on communism and defense. Bush's relentless attacks on Clinton's character defects, such as his rumored womanizing, youthful marijuana use, and avoidance of the Vietnam-era draft, fell flat. Instead, the public responded enthusiastically to Clinton's pledge to improve the economy.

On Election Day, voters turned Bush out of office. Clinton carried thirty-two states, won 370 electoral votes, and received 43 percent of the popular vote, compared to Bush's 38 percent. Perot, who had quit and then reentered the race, received 19 percent of the popular vote, nearly the most ever for an independent candidate. Democrats maintained control in both houses of Congress, but races there showed a desire for change; the congressional races were marked by the election of record numbers of women, African Americans, and Hispanics. Voters in fourteen states endorsed limits on congressional terms.

Clinton's victory and the re-election of Democratic majorities to both houses of Congress dashed GOP hopes of institutionalizing the Republican ascendancy begun under Nixon and solidified during the Reagan and Bush administrations. In retaking the White House, Clinton owed a great deal to the high unemployment rate during the 1992 recession, which followed twenty years of stagnant incomes for 80 percent of American families. Reversing a trend begun in the 1960s, Clinton won six southern and border states and swept the Pacific West, becoming the first Democrat since 1964 to secure California's fifty-four electoral votes. As a moderate, southern Democrat, Clinton restitched the tattered but resilient New Deal coalition. Reduced racial tension, the end of the Cold War, and economic recession caused millions of working-class, southern, and Catholic whites to return to the Democratic presidential fold. Whether or not the Democrats could hold onto these voters remained unclear. As Clinton's tart-tongued campaign strategist James Carville remarked, "We didn't find the key to the electoral lock . . . we just picked it."

Conclusion

The Reagan-Bush era represented a major turning point in American politics. The fracturing of the Democratic Party was matched by the rise of an assertive, conservative Republican Party that directly challenged the New Deal legacy. For the first time since the 1930s, national leaders not only questioned the value of a large, powerful federal government but also began to dismantle it. While ordinary Americans did not always agree with the specific programs pushed by the Reagan and Bush administrations, many shared their skepticism toward social programs and appreciated Reagan's efforts to restore national pride. But the economic and social policies of the Reagan-Bush era failed to reverse many negative trends.

While Reagan's charm and political magic overwhelmed most naysayers, George Bush proved a weak second act to the Reagan revolution. Where Reagan denounced government as the cause of most problems, Bush valued public service and hesitated to crusade against established institutions. Trying to occupy the middle ground between the New Right and the New Deal, he found no place to stand. Officeholders in the 1990s discovered that the American people's tolerance for their elected leaders—like the "sound bites" those leaders used to get elected—had become increasingly brief.

F U R T H E R • R E A D I N G

On Reagan's background and the rise of New Right conservatism, see Matthew Dallek, *The Right Moment: Ronald Reagan's First Victory and the Decisive Turning Point in American Politics* (2000); Lisa McGirr, *Suburban Warriors: The Origin of the New American Right* (2000); Garry Wills, *Reagan's America* (1988); Lou Cannon, *President Reagan: The Role of a Lifetime* (1991); Michael Rogin, *Ronald Reagan: The Movie, and Other Episodes in Political Demonology* (1987); Haynes Johnson, *Sleepwalking Through History* (1991); Michael Schaller, *Reckoning with Reagan: America and Its President in the 1980s* (1992). Robert Dallek, *Ronald Reagan: The Politics of Symbolism* (1984); William Pemberton, *Exit With Honor: the Life and Presidency of Ronald Reagan* (1997). **On the politics and the economic and social policies of the 1980s and early 1990s,** see James A. Farrell, *Tip O'Neill and the Democratic Century* (2000); Donald T. Regan, *For the Record: From Wall Street to Washington* (1988); David Stockman, *The Triumph of Politics: How the Reagan Revolution Failed* (1986); Benjamin Friedman, *Day of Reckoning: The Consequences of American Economic Policy Under Reagan and After* (1988); Herman Schwartz, *Packing the Courts: The Conservative Campaign to Re-write the Constitution* (1988); Jane Mayer and Jill Abramson, *Strange Justice: The Selling of Clarence Thomas* (1994); Randy Shilts, *And the Band Played On: Politics, People, and the AIDS Epidemic* (1987); William Julius Wilson, *The Truly Disadvantaged: The Inner City, the Underclass and Public Policy* (1987); Barbara Ehrenreich, *The Worst Years of Our Lives: Irreverent Notes from a Decade of Greed* (1990); Nicolaus Mills (ed.), *Culture in an Age of Money* (1991); Mark Hertsgaard, *On Bended Knee* (1988); Leonard Dinnerstein, Roger L. Nichols, and David M. Reimers, *Natives and Strangers: A Multicultural History of America* (2002); Susan Faludi, *Backlash: The Undeclared War Against American Women* (1991); Sidney Blumenthal, *Pledging Allegiance: The Last Campaign of the Cold War* (1990); Jack Germond and Jules Witcover, *Wake Us When It's Over: Presidential Politics of 1984* (1985) and *Whose Broad Stripes and Bright Stars? The Trivial Pursuit of the Presidency, 1988* (1989); James D. Hunter, *Culture Wars: The Struggle to Define America* (1991); William C. Berman, *America's Right Turn: From Nixon to Clinton* (1998); E. J. Dionne, *Why Americans Hate Politics* (1992); Tanya Melich, *The Republican War Against Women* (1996); Kevin Phillips, *The Politics of Rich and Poor: Wealth and the American Electorate in the Reagan Aftermath* (1990); Michael Katz, *The Underserving Poor: From the War on Poverty to the War on Welfare* (1989); Martin Mayer, *The Greatest Bank Job Ever: The Collapse of the Savings and Loan Industry* (1990); Jeffrey K. Hadden and Anson Shupe, *Televangelists: Power and Politics on God's Frontier* (1988); Dan Baum, *Smoke and Mirrors: The War on Drugs and the Politics of Failure* (1996); John R. Greene, *The Presidency of George Bush* (2000). **On school policy and education reform,** see Joel Spring, *The Sorting Machine: National Educational Policy Since 1945* (1976); Diane Ravitch and Maris A. Vinovskis, eds., *Learning from the Past: What History Teaches About U.S. School Reform* (1995).

13

From the Cold War to the New World Order

In 1987, President Reagan spoke in a divided Berlin and called on the Soviets to "tear down this wall." Just over two years later, the wall came tumbling down. / © Wally McNamee/CORBIS

In August 1984, engaging in some banter before delivering a Saturday morning radio commentary, President Reagan spoke into a microphone he did not know was on. "My fellow Americans," he began, "I am pleased to tell you today that I've just signed legislation that will outlaw the Soviet Union forever. We begin bombing in five minutes." The president laughed off criticism of his remark as if it were merely something his friend John Wayne might have said while acting in a Hollywood western. But many people in the United States and abroad thought that this incident confirmed that Reagan had not only restored national pride, but had made America all too ready to end the long-standing stalemate with the Soviets by provoking a showdown. Soviet leaders took the off-the-cuff joke seriously enough to instruct KGB intelligence officers in Washington to report indications of war preparation, such as the stockpiling of food and blood in federal buildings.

To everyone's surprise, however, less than eight years later, legislation was signed abolishing the Soviet Union. On Christmas 1991, Soviet president Mikhail Gorbachev issued a decree dissolving the U.S.S.R. and turning over authority to the elected leader of a democratic Russia. Reagan and his successor, George H. W. Bush, were eager to claim and happy to accept credit for victory over America's Cold War rival. But the causes and consequences of this event are still being debated.

As a presidential candidate, Reagan had insisted that "there are simple answers" to complex questions. He complained that America suffered from a Vietnam syndrome: an inability or unwillingness to use force to resist Soviet pressure and defend U.S. friends and foreign interests. This situation, he argued, explained why Americans had been seized as hostages in Iran. Attributing this weakness to misplaced guilt over the Vietnam War, Reagan repeatedly praised that struggle as a "noble cause." His first secretary of state, General Alexander Haig, echoed this sentiment, declaring that the time had come for Americans to "shed their sackcloth and ashes." The new administration pledged to restore America's military superiority, defend its allies, and support anticommunist movements throughout the world. It was no accident, Reagan and his supporters suggested, that Iran released its American captives just as the new president took the presidential oath of office on January 20, 1981.

Unlike Dwight Eisenhower, who had campaigned on a promise to roll back communist rule but had actually restrained defense spending, Reagan pushed through Congress the largest military budgets the United States had ever adopted in peacetime. Between 1981 and 1989, total defense spending ballooned from less than $200 billion to over $300 billion per year. At its peak in 1984, the Pentagon spent over $30 million per hour.

Beneath the rhetoric, however, the president pursued old policies more vigorously than he initiated new ones. His talk of restraining Moscow's "evil empire" harked back to the Truman Doctrine—the policy of containment— and the birth of NATO. His willingness to intervene in Central America and the Caribbean echoed the policies of Dwight D. Eisenhower, John F. Kennedy, and Lyndon Johnson. He even forged ties with conservative Democrats who had chafed under the Carter administration, appointing several of them to top diplomatic positions.

Midway through his second term, when the Iran-contra scandal erupted and the president's popularity plummeted, it appeared that Reagan's foreign policy legacy would consist mostly of escalating tensions with the Soviet Union while subverting Congress and hiring individuals who engaged in secret wars, illegal fundraising, and black-market arms deals. By the end of his second term, however, Reagan had presided over the most dramatic thawing in the relations of the United States with the Soviet Union since the collapse of the World War II era Grand Alliance in 1945. The two countries agreed to eliminate an entire class of nuclear-tipped missiles and build confidence in other ways. Like their president, most Americans no longer thought of the Soviet Union as an "evil empire" and expressed more positive attitudes toward it than at anytime since World War II.

George H. W. Bush also reaped the benefits of this political thaw during his tenure as president. As the Soviet Union's domestic problems multiplied, Gorbachev withdrew Soviet military forces and permitted the nations of Eastern Europe to go their own way. Most of these countries quickly toppled their communist regimes in peaceful revolutions. Even the most well-known symbol of the Cold War, the Berlin Wall, came down on the eve of German reunification. By the end of 1991, a democratic Russia and several successor states replaced the Soviet Union.

As the world's sole remaining superpower, the United States was free to fight a regional war in the Persian Gulf with Soviet assistance in place of opposition. It also invaded Panama to topple its dictator. The United States achieved a quick victory in both struggles, prompting President Bush to proclaim the dawn of an American-led "new world order." In fact, the post–Cold War era proved far more chaotic—at home and abroad—than most Americans could have imagined.

Reagan's Foreign Policy Style

The new president spoke forcefully about the divide he saw between the "free world" of America and its allies, and all other governments. The former were peaceful, democratic, and prosperous; the latter were aggressive, oppressive, and poor. The Soviet Union, he remarked on more than one occasion, "underlies all the unrest that is going on. If they weren't engaged in this game of dominoes, there wouldn't be any hot spots in the world." This belief underlay his talk of abolishing what he often called the "evil empire." As critics pointed out, this analysis of the sources of world violence failed to explain conflicts that began before 1917, lasted after 1991, or had little to do with superpower rivalry.

Reagan modified his harsh view of communism when he applied it to China. As a candidate, he had praised Taiwan as an American ally and hinted that he would restore diplomatic ties to the anticommunist island if he were elected. But Reagan's aides convinced him that the People's Republic of China (PRC) was a key ally in containing the Soviet Union and aiding anti-Soviet guerrillas in Afghanistan. He then agreed to maintain formal ties with only the communist PRC, limiting American contact with Taiwan to informal relations and defensive weapons sales. The Chinese regime accepted this arrangement and hosted the president on a tour of China in 1984, where he visited the Great Wall, saw the giant pandas in the Beijing Zoo, and complimented his communist hosts.

Reagan had an even more tolerant attitude toward pro-American anticommunist dictators. He popularized an idea broached by Georgetown University political scientist Jeane Kirkpatrick (whom he appointed as his ambassador to the United Nations) that right-wing dictatorships could, with encouragement, evolve toward democracy. Left-wing regimes, however, could never reform. Reagan used this argument to justify economic and political support to oppressive governments in Haiti, Chile, El Salvador, Guatemala, South Africa, Pakistan, and the Philippines. Democratic change eventually came to some of these countries, but often despite, not because of, American support for their oppressive governments. Kirkpatrick's prediction notwithstanding, the Soviet Union and China did evolve toward democracy during the 1980s.

Overall, the Reagan administration continued a trend begun during the Nixon years. As a proportion of its gross national product (GNP), the United States provided a much smaller percentage (one-third of 1 percent) of nonmilitary foreign aid than nearly every other industrialized country. Most foreign assistance went for military purposes, and 75 percent went to just six nations—Israel, Egypt, the Philippines, Turkey, Pakistan, and El Salvador.

As even the president's strongest admirers admitted, Reagan lived in a world of myths and symbols rather than facts and programs. Jimmy Carter, with his emphasis on details and process, had failed to articulate any overarching vision, but Reagan excelled in evoking sunny images of unity and purpose without stipulating the difficult steps for achieving those goals. He let his subordinates handle unpleasant or complicated announcements while he spoke reassuringly of America as a divinely blessed "city on a hill" protected by a "space shield" he hoped to build.

Although Reagan articulated a strong belief in the perfidy of communism and the Soviet Union, he provided little specific direction to his foreign policy advisers. Before 1983, there is little evidence that he even thought in terms of a coherent military and diplomatic strategy. In fact, for most of his first term, stockpiling new weapons and launching covert attacks in Central America and the Middle East passed for a foreign policy. When advisers approached him for guidance, he exhibited what aides called "that glassy look" and changed the subject. Reagan believed that "negotiating from strength" would yield results, but he never indicated how to build this strength. After the collapse of the Soviet Union, some of Reagan's aides claimed that he promoted a costly arms race to "bankrupt" his communist rival. But this claim appeared more an after-the-fact rationale for what occurred, not an intentional plan.

Reagan appointed former Kissinger aide General Alexander Haig as secretary of state in 1981, promising him full authority to conceive and implement foreign policy. As Haig soon learned, however, Reagan and his inner circle of advisers had no interest in pursuing the secretary's bellicose plans, such as his talk of turning Cuba "into a parking lot." Frustrated by his lack of influence, Haig later described the Reagan policymaking apparatus as a "ghost ship." You heard the "creak of the rigging and the groan of the timbers and sometimes even glimpsed the crew on deck . . . but which of the crew had the helm . . . was impossible to know for sure." By 1982, Haig was replaced at the State Department by George Shultz.

Although a skilled team player, Shultz had limited influence before 1986 and had to compete for the president's attention with Defense Secretary Caspar Weinberger as well as six successive national security advisers (Richard Allen, William Clark, Robert McFarlane, John Poindexter, Frank Carlucci, and Colin Powell). Each pursued separate and sometimes competing policies toward different parts of the world. Shultz favored an arms buildup primarily as a negotiating tactic with the Soviets. Weinberger hoped more arms would force a Soviet collapse. Several of Reagan's other advisers, such as the director of the Central Intelligence Agency, William Casey, promoted covert wars in Latin America and the Middle East. Shultz believed it was better to fight an open, not a secret, war against guerrillas in Central America, but Weinberger opposed any military commitments in peripheral areas. This opposition led an exasperated Shultz to snap at him, "[I]f you are not willing to use force, maybe we should cut your budget." Rather than impose his will, the president urged his advisers to compromise, but they ignored him.

In addition to the large arms buildup discussed below, the Reagan administration emphasized paramilitary operations in the Third World. The president appointed his friend and campaign manager, William Casey, to head the Central Intelligence Agency. During World War II, Casey had served in the Office of Strategic Services (OSS), the CIA's predecessor, and hoped to make the CIA a major player in the struggle against Soviet influence in the Third World. This plan meant shifting the agency away from intelligence gathering and analysis and toward paramilitary action. A victory in a contested area, he believed, would help unravel the entire Soviet empire.

After Congress agreed to remove many Carter-era restrictions on CIA operations, Casey poured money, weapons, and agents into anticommunist guerrilla movements active in Angola, Mozambique, Afghanistan, Lebanon, and Central America. The results of these interventions were quite mixed. Through at least 1986, the administration boasted that "low-intensity warfare" (its pet term for counterinsurgency operations) was a cheap and relatively safe way to battle Moscow for global influence. Covert warfare minimized the risk of a direct confrontation with the Soviets while giving the administration freedom to act with minimal public knowledge or congressional oversight.

More Bang for More Bucks: The New Arms Race

"Defense," Reagan was fond of saying, "is not a budget item. You spend what you need." Taking his cue from the president, Defense Secretary Weinberger proposed early in 1981 to increase defense spending 10 percent annually, using the 1980 budget as a base. Over the next five years, defense expenditures totaled almost $1.5 trillion.

To justify these increases, Weinberger displayed impressive charts at a White House meeting shortly after Reagan took charge. These charts showed Soviet nuclear and conventional forces dwarfing those of the free world. As David Stockman, director of the Budget Office and a skeptic about the need for such large increases recalled, Weinberger showed the president a poster depicting three cartoon soldiers. One was a pygmy who carried no rifle; he represented the Carter budget. The second was a wimp wearing glasses and who looked like Woody Allen; he was Stockman's proposed military budget. Finally, there was G.I. Joe himself, 190 pounds of fighting man, decked out in helmet and flak jacket and pointing an M-60 machine gun. Stockman objected to these portrayals, arguing that Weinberger "thought the White House was on Sesame Street." But the defense secretary knew exactly how to appeal to Reagan, and the G.I. Joe display became the basis for defense budgeting.

During the arms buildup, the Department of Defense spent lavishly to purchase advanced weapons systems, mostly intended for use in a nuclear war with the Soviet Union. These weapons included enhanced neutron bombs and artillery designed to irradiate enemy tanks and troops; one hundred MX intercontinental missiles, each capable of carrying ten nuclear warheads; the B-1 intercontinental bomber, which was designed to replace the aging fleet of B-52s; the B-2 Stealth bomber capable of evading enemy radar; D-5 submarine-launched nuclear missiles; and several shorter-range cruise and Pershing missiles that could carry nuclear or conventional warheads against various targets. In addition, the Pentagon planned a navy with six hundred ships, the biggest naval flotilla since World War II.

These weapons systems were immensely powerful, expensive, and controversial. Although justified as necessary to close what Reagan called a "window of vulnerability," they promised to give the United States strategic superiority over the Soviet Union. This strategy sounded good but hid several pitfalls. For example, the MX missiles were so powerful and accurate that they could destroy unlaunched Soviet missiles in their protected silos. In a crisis, Soviet commanders might feel impelled to launch their missiles before they could be knocked out. Expecting this outcome, American strategists might be tempted to launch the MX even earlier, before the Soviets fired. This hair-trigger scenario, in which both sides might turn to nuclear war early in a crisis, reflected the logic of "use it or lose it." Thus, rather than enhancing stability, the new weapons could actually reduce it.

In spite of some misgivings, nearly all Republicans and many Democrats in Congress supported the Reagan-era buildup. Although still in the majority for most of the 1980s, Democrats remained disorganized and insecure in the wake of Reagan's two election victories. Also, like much of the public, many admired the president's tough rhetoric and believed that two decades of negotiating arms control agreements with the Soviets had produced few positive results.

During Reagan's initial arms buildup, however, public opinion wavered. At the grassroots level, many Americans continued to express anxiety over the risks of nuclear war. In 1982, journalist Jonathan Schell published a best-selling book, *The Fate of the Earth*, describing what might happen if New York City were hit by a hydrogen bomb. A year later, over 100 million American television viewers watched *The Day After*, a chilling drama portraying the devastation of a nuclear war as experienced by a handful of survivors. These media events coincided with the activities of the Nuclear Freeze Movement, a citizens alliance that organized large demonstrations calling on both superpowers to cease building new weapons of mass destruction. In 1982, 128 members of the House of Representatives and seventeen senators voted for a nuclear-freeze resolution. The next year, a majority of the House voted in favor of a nuclear weapons freeze.

The president and his aides voiced contradictory views on arms control. Reagan sharply criticized the efforts by Nixon, Ford, and Carter to negotiate with the Soviet Union. He particularly disliked Carter's unratified SALT II treaty. Its "fatal flaws," he argued, left America vulnerable to Soviet nuclear blackmail. In practice, however, the SALT II cap on missiles (which permitted small increases on both sides) was actually observed by Reagan. Meanwhile, each side put forward arms control proposals they knew were mutually unacceptable and used the other side's rejection as a reason to deploy new weapons.

By 1983, Reagan grew concerned that nuclear-freeze advocates in the United States and Europe, who included influential bishops in the Catholic Church, might succeed in restraining the American arms buildup. The administration suggested again proposals from the 1950s to build a nuclear fallout shelter system, but the public proved no more accepting than it had been decades earlier. The president then promoted a new approach to the problem that he hoped would reassure the public and further isolate the Soviets. Beer brewer and Reagan friend Joseph Coors had previously introduced the president to physicist Edward Teller. Teller, a prominent hard-liner, told Reagan that a space-based, nuclear-powered X-ray laser could produce energy beams capable of shooting down Soviet missiles after they were launched but before they deployed their nuclear warheads. An array of these lasers, mounted on orbiting platforms, could provide a virtual shield over the United States.

The president, who harbored a genuine horror of nuclear weapons, quickly embraced this concept as a way to protect civilians. It also appealed to him as a high-tech way to neutralize enemy missiles. (At the time, some observers noted that as a young actor, Reagan appeared in a film that depicted an "inertia ray" that immobilized airplane engines, causing enemy bombers to fall.) The president revealed his vision to the public in a speech in March 1983, in which he called on the nation's scientists to join in building a strategic defense initiative (SDI) that would render nuclear weapons "impotent and obsolete." Supporters and critics immediately began to debate the idea, dubbing the president's plan "star wars."

SDI, or star wars, proved something of a "Rorschach test" in which proponents and opponents saw their hopes and fears expressed. (The Rorschach test involves the classic inkblots whose shapes psychologists ask patients to describe.) Reagan perceived it as a pure, defensive means to protect America without the need to negotiate or compromise with others. Some administration officials considered it a bargaining chip to maneuver the Soviets. Defense contractors and some university researchers envisioned it as a gold mine that would keep federal dollars flowing. Critics dismissed it as a dangerous boondoggle that would militarize space and merely encourage the Soviets to overwhelm it by building additional missiles.

SDI was not a workable system. When selling Reagan on the concept, Teller had neglected to mention that the X-ray laser was merely a theory, not a fact. Other SDI concepts faced daunting technical challenges and fell by the wayside. By the time Reagan left office in 1989, at least $20 billion had been spent on missile defense with little to show for it. During the next twelve years, the Bush and Clinton administrations spent an additional $40 billion on antimissile research but failed to design a workable system. Still, the concept would not die. In 2001, President George W. Bush committed his administration to building and deploying a missile-defense system, even though no workable model existed and cost estimates had skyrocketed.

The Soviet government denounced SDI as a violation of the anti-ballistic missile (ABM) treaty of 1972 and condemned Reagan as a warmonger. Until 1985, however, Moscow failed to mount an effective response to American initiatives. The old and ailing Leonid Brezhnev, in power since 1964, presided over a lethargic and increasingly corrupt administration. For several years before his death in 1982, he was unable, as an aide put it, "to engage in conceptual thinking." Upon his death, Communist oligarchs selected Yuri Andropov, the Soviet security chief, as the nation's leader. Although Andropov was actually something of a reformer, he suffered from kidney disease and spent most of his brief term in office on a dialysis machine. Following Andropov's death in 1984, party elders tapped Konstantin Chernenko, a lackluster timeserver, as the general secretary of the Communist Party. Suffering from severe emphysema, Chernenko died after only a year in the post. When asked why he had refused to meet with his Soviet counterparts, Reagan quipped, "[T]hey keep dying on me." Only in 1985, when the vital, fifty-four-year-old Mikhail Gorbachev emerged as head of the Communist Party, did the Soviet Union have an effective leader.

In the interim, Soviet actions alienated much of the noncommunist world. In December 1981, as the Solidarity labor movement in Poland threatened to topple the communist government there, Moscow persuaded the Polish army to impose martial law. Reagan denounced the Soviets for imposing the "forces of tyranny" on Poland and called on Americans to light "candles of freedom" on their windowsills as a sign of support for Poles. More important, he ordered the CIA to cooperate with the influential Polish Catholic Church to provide secret financial and moral support for Solidarity activists.

Two years later, in September 1983, a tragic error further tarnished Soviet fortunes and outraged world opinion. A series of pilot navigational errors had led a Korean Airlines jumbo jet—KAL 007—to stray far off course en route from Alaska to Seoul. After flying unknowingly for some time over Soviet territory that included a secret missile test site, the passenger plane was shot down by a Soviet fighter plane. All 269 people, including an American congressman, on board KAL 007 were killed.

Electronic intercepts of Soviet air defense communications quickly revealed to American intelligence that Soviet commanders mistakenly thought they were attacking a U.S. spy plane masquerading as a civilian aircraft. They attacked without investigating the situation, but without premeditation. Even though he was informed of this mistake, Reagan immediately branded the attack a "crime against humanity" and an "act of barbarism."

The incident hardened American perceptions of the Soviet Union and bolstered congressional support for the president's arms buildup and tough rhetoric. When voices were raised in Congress or by private citizens about huge cost overruns in defense contracts or the fact that a single B-2 bomber cost $1 billion or more to produce, the administration responded by describing the crushing of Solidarity in Poland and the KAL shootdown. Also, ordinary citizens did not know whether spending $1 billion on a single plane was a fair price. They did recognize the folly of the Pentagon paying $500 for a toilet seat or a utility hammer on the B-2 bomber. In the end, much of the criticism of the Reagan-era arms programs focused on these trivial problems, not the larger question of whether or not the weapons worked well or if they were even needed.

America and the Middle East

As it confronted the Soviet Union with a massive arms buildup, the Reagan administration also tried to address some of the thornier problems in the Middle East and South Asia. But, like his predecessors, the president found it difficult to impose any solution, American or otherwise, on these volatile regions. Conflicts between the Israelis and Palestinians, among Lebanese factions, and within Afghanistan remained unresolved. In addition, a bloody war between Iran and Iraq lasted most of the 1980s and set the stage for future problems in the Persian Gulf. Making these issues especially urgent was the rise in terrorist attacks around the world, many of them against American targets.

In the early 1980s, Lebanese religious and political factions had resumed their periodic civil slaughter. Israel joined the fray by bombing parts of Lebanon under the control of the Palestinian Liberation Organization (PLO), a guerrilla group composed of Palestinians displaced from Israel in the late 1940s. Encouraged by Secretary of State Haig, Israeli forces invaded Lebanon in June 1982, hoping to destroy the PLO. But Haig acted before clearing the mission with Reagan, and he resigned in a huff when the president's inner circle criticized him.

By August, Israeli forces surrounded Beirut. At this point, the Reagan administration arranged for the evacuation of the same PLO fighters Haig had hoped to see destroyed. The new American secretary of state, George Shultz, urged Israel to compromise and permit the PLO to establish a homeland on the West Bank of the Jordan River (then occupied by Israeli forces) in return for the PLO making peace with Israel. But neither side agreed. To make matters worse, on September 14, 1982, assassins killed Lebanese Christian leader Bashir Gemayel, sparking Christian massacres of Palestinians living in refugee camps around Beirut.

As Lebanon approached complete chaos, the United States, France, and Italy sent in "peace keepers." In reality, these troops helped shore up Christian militias fighting Muslim forces backed by Syria. Lebanese Muslims bitterly resented this interference and on April 18, 1983, a suicide squad attacked the American embassy in Beirut, killing sixty-three people. U.S. navy ships off the coast responded with a series of artillery barrages aimed at Islamic strongholds. On October 23, Muslim fighters counterattacked by driving a truck filled with explosives into a U.S. Marine barracks near the Beirut airport, killing 241 marines. French troops were also attacked.

Reagan offered a moving tribute to the fallen Americans, but he could not explain their mission or the reason for their deaths. The marine presence in Lebanon, he declared in his 1984 State of the Union address, was "central to our credibility on a global scale." Only two weeks later, with no explanation, he ordered all American troops out of Beirut and turned aside while Lebanese factions resumed their communal slaughter.

Like the conflict in Lebanon, the problem of Palestinian refugees and guerrillas living in refugee camps or under Israeli occupation defied an American solution. In 1987, Palestinians living in territories seized by Israel during the 1967 war began an *intifadah*, or uprising, against Israeli authorities. In response to riots, rock throwing, and shooting, Israeli troops and police killed seven hundred Palestinians over the next three years. The

The scene after a terrorist bombing leveled part of the American embassy in Beirut, killing sixty-three people in April 1983. / AP/Wide World

violence sputtered on until 1994, when PLO leader Yasir Arafat and Israeli prime minister Yitzhak Rabin reached a tentative accord in which the PLO would be permitted to establish a state on the West Bank and Gaza Strip in return for recognizing Israel's right to exist. But implementing the so-called Oslo accord proved exceedingly difficult. Six years later, the intifadah resumed and the prospects for peace seemed dimmer than ever.

The Iranian hostage crisis of 1979–1980 had focused public attention on the vulnerability of Americans abroad. Throughout the 1980s, sporadic incidents of hostage taking, airplane hijacking, and bombings were on the rise. The risk affected diplomats and military personnel and, to a lesser degree, businesspeople and tourists.

Terrorism is a slippery concept. As some have noted, one person's terrorist is another person's freedom fighter. Terrorism has also been called the "atomic bomb of the weak." During the 1980s, terrorism became the weapon of choice for many frustrated groups, especially those in the Middle East. When assessed objectively, the various politically motivated hijackings, kidnappings, and bombings carried out against Americans during the 1980s were marginal acts affecting relatively few people. On average, throughout the decade, more American civilians were killed each year by lightning while playing golf than by terrorist acts. However, the fear generated by terrorism, the intense media coverage given these attacks, as well as the responses by President Reagan, made terrorism a major issue.

State-sponsored terrorism, as opposed to that carried out by informal groups, further complicated matters. In an effort to expand its influence in contested areas, the Soviet Union and its satellites sometimes provided financial, technical, and military assistance to violent anti-American or anti-Israeli organizations. But Moscow was not alone. The Reagan administration sometimes matched this behavior, arming Christian militias in Lebanon and anti-leftist groups in Central America that often used terror and assassination against civilian opponents.

Washington focused much of its antiterrorist sentiment during the 1980s on Libya's demagogic strongman, Muammar Qaddafi. Flush with cash from oil exports, Qaddafi bought Soviet military equipment and funded several terrorist groups in the Middle East. The United States deployed naval vessels close to Libya and fought several aerial battles with Libyan planes. In April 1986, after Libyan agents were implicated in the bombing of a Berlin nightclub frequented by American soldiers, Reagan called Quaddafi the "mad dog of the Middle East." He sent planes to bomb Tripoli and Qaddafi's residence. Although the Libyan strongman survived, the attack killed his infant daughter.

After the bombing, Libya and the United States confined their hostility to a war of words. American officials boasted that they had put Qaddaffi "back in his box." In fact, the drop in oil prices and feuds between Libya and its North African neighbors had much to do with restraining Qaddafi's behavior. Two years later, in December 1988, Libyan agents played a role in planting a bomb that destroyed a U.S. passenger plane flying over Scotland, killing several hundred Americans.

The most devastating violence in the Middle East had nothing directly to do with the United States or Israel. It occurred during a nine-year war between Iraq and Iran that started in 1980. The conflict, fought for regional influence and control of deep-water ports, claimed nearly 2 million lives before a cease-fire took effect in 1988. The war put the United States in an awkward position. American officials feared both the secular greed of Iraq's Saddam Hussein as well as the religious ambitions of Iran's Ayatollah Khomeini. A victory by either side threatened the stability of the entire region as well as its immense oil reserves. To prevent this instability, Washington went back and forth in providing aid to Iran and Iraq, with the aim of blocking a lopsided victory. Until 1986, most U.S. aid went to Iran, which appeared to be losing the war. After 1986, American help went to Iraq's Saddam Hussein. The two war-weary states finally agreed to a cease-fire in August 1988. However, each side continued until 2003 to hold tens of thousands of prisoners of war. Meanwhile, as the United States continued its attempt to balance the rivals by providing aid to both, it managed to alienate both Iran and Iraq.

When Soviet forces invaded neighboring Afghanistan in December 1979, the Kremlin sought to sustain in power a procommunist Afghan regime whose hold had been weakened by civil war. They became trapped in a brutal guerrilla conflict against *mujahidin*, or freedom fighters, inspired by fundamentalist Islam. To frustrate the Soviets, the Reagan administration (through the CIA) poured weapons and money into both Pakistan (as a base of operations) and Afghanistan. American support and advice went to the mujahidin guerrillas, most of whom were Afghani but many of whom came from Pakistan and Muslim countries in the Middle East. Among the latter was a wealthy Saudi named Osama bin Laden, who viewed the anti-Soviet struggle as the first phase in a wider war against Western infidels. At the time, however, the Reagan administration asked few questions about the beliefs or goals of its allies.

By the late 1980s, the reform-minded Soviet leader Mikhail Gorbachev ended the disastrous intervention by withdrawing his forces from Afghanistan. This move did not end the country's agony. The victorious mujahidin factions began fighting each other and destroyed much of what had survived the war with the Soviets. Operating in part from bases in Afghanistan, Osama bin Laden created a terror network—Al Qaeda—that targeted "enemies of Islam," including moderate Arab regimes and the United States. This Al Qaeda network played a major role in the bombings of the World Trade Center in New York City in 1993, two U.S. embassies in Africa in 1998, and a U.S. navy ship in Yemen in 2000. In the mid-1990s, the Taliban, an extreme fundamentalist Islamic faction, gained the upper hand in most of Afghanistan and gave Al Qaeda free reign. On September 11, 2001, nineteen of bin Laden's followers hijacked four American airliners, flying two into the World Trade Center's twin towers, one into the Pentagon, and crashing a fourth in rural Pennsylvania. Nearly three thousand civilians perished in this most deadly act of terrorism in American history.

Adventures South of the Border

During the 1980s, the Reagan administration became obsessed by what it perceived as a communist threat to the Western Hemisphere. It hoped to alleviate this danger and to erase the memory of Vietnam with some old-fashioned muscle flexing. By doing so, it revived the century-long tradition of military intervention in Central America. Some of these nations were derisively called "banana republics." In the 1980s, the United States invaded Grenada, financed civil wars in El Salvador and Nicaragua, propped up hard-line military rulers in Honduras, and used economic pressure in an effort to topple the government of Panama.

American officials warned of a "Moscow-Havana" axis in which Fidel Castro's agents tried to spread revolution throughout Latin America. Their arguments maintained that, by creating several Cubalike regimes from Panama to Mexico, the Soviet Union would gain control of vital sea lanes and threaten the United States.

Critics of this scenario, such as Connecticut's Democratic senator Christopher Dodd, complained that Reagan and his advisers "knew as much about Central America" in the 1980s as "we knew about Indochina in 1963." Dodd, who had served as a Peace Corps volunteer in Latin America, argued that the region's instability stemmed from its chronic poverty and the exploitation of its peasants by rich landholders and their military allies. Poverty, he insisted, caused revolution, not a Cuban-Soviet plot. Nevertheless, Reagan continued to maintain that military aid to friendly forces in Central America was the key to stability.

Despite a constant stream of rhetoric, the usually persuasive president failed to mobilize public or congressional support for active intervention in Central America. According to opinion polls, most Americas simply did not care who held power in, say, Tegucigalpa or Managua. This apathy led Reagan to authorize a program that relied heavily on military aid and covert warfare in Central America. Between 1981 and 1985, Washington provided a remarkably large sum of money, nearly $5 billion, to the tiny nation of El Salvador. A terribly poor country in which 2 percent of the people controlled nearly all the wealth, El Salvador had been racked by rural rebellions since the 1920s. Although a civilian served nominally as president, right-wing military officers held real power.

In spite of massive American aid, the Salvadoran military could not defeat the leftist rebels and their allies. The military squandered much of the money and devoted its energy to terrorizing unarmed critics of the regime. Army and paramilitary death squads, some trained by Americans, killed as many as seventy thousand peasants, teachers, union organizers, and church workers. Congress placed a cap on the number of American military advisers permitted to operate in El Salvador but otherwise approved the funds Reagan requested and asked few questions. The civil war continued until 1992. By then, the collapse of the Soviet Union had shifted American concerns away from the region. El Salvador remained a poor and violent country, but it was no longer of great interest to the United States.

In contrast to the drawn-out struggle in El Salvador, the Reagan administration achieved a quick victory through conventional warfare in Grenada. Grenada was a tiny Caribbean island and former British colony whose economy relied on the export of nutmeg. It had been ruled by a Marxist regime since 1979. Neither the Carter nor the Reagan administrations had paid any attention to it. The only American presence on the island consisted of five hundred students enrolled at St. George's University School of Medicine, a profit-making enterprise that recruited aspiring doctors unable to gain admission to U.S. medical schools. A contingent of armed Cuban construction workers labored nearby, building an airport designed to boost tourism (according to Grenada) or to serve as a possible Soviet base (according to Washington).

On October 12, 1983, a more militant faction of the Marxist New Jewel movement seized power on the island. General Hudson Austin killed the incumbent president, Maurice Bishop, and imposed martial law. The Reagan administration did not respond dramatically until October 23, when terrorists attacked the marine barracks in Beirut, killing several hundred Americans. Unable to identify or retaliate against the bombers in Lebanon, the president and his aides felt intense frustration. At this point, they turned their attention to the medical students in Grenada. Although none had been harmed or faced obvious danger, officials in Washington described them as potential hostages. After consulting with the leaders of some nearby Caribbean islands, on October 25, 1983, Reagan ordered thousands of marines and army troops to storm ashore and liberate Grenada and the American students from what he called a "brutal gang of thugs."

More of a comic opera than a war, the invasion quickly succeeded in defeating the tiny Grenadian military and securing the American students. The Pentagon awarded an unprecedented eight thousand medals to members of the assault force. Free elections soon restored representative government to Grenada. Washington lost interest in the island, which returned to its normal obscurity. News coverage of the crisis alerted many Americans to Grenada's unspoiled beaches and eventually spurred a tourist boom.

Carefully controlled television news coverage of the invasion assured public support. Pictures of returning students falling to their knees and kissing American soil trumped interviews with the medical school's director, who noted that the students had never been in danger. Opinion polls found that most Americans were simply pleased that the United States had "won one for a change." President Reagan used pictures of the triumphant marines and happy medical students to great effect in his 1984 campaign against Democratic nominee Walter Mondale, who had initially condemned the invasion as a violation of international law.

Popular enthusiasm for this kind of muscle flexing appeared in the mass media throughout the 1980s. Numerous adventure novels and Hollywood films portrayed American heroes who refought and won the war in Vietnam,

(cont. on page 480)

The Prison/Industrial Complex

At the beginning of the new millennium, the United States had much to be proud of and thankful for. Its political institutions, economic power, cultural vibrancy, and military strength were the envy of much of the world. But one "growth industry" proved more a source of embarrassment than pride. With just 5 percent of the world's population, the United States accounts for over 2 million, or one-fourth, of the world's 8 million prisoners. In addition to the nearly 161,000 federal and 1.85 million state and local prisoners, another 4.5 million people are on some form of parole or probation. On any given day in 2003, the criminal justice system supervised around 6,500,000 Americans, or one in thirty-two adults. Put another way, 3.1 percent of the adult population was in the correction system, compared to 1 percent in 1980. In recent decades, only two nations approached these numbers: the Soviet Union before its collapse in 1991 and the white-ruled regime of South Africa before it relinquished power to the black majority in the middle 1990s.

The explosion in the size of the prison system followed increased public resentment over rising crime rates during the 1960s and 1970s. In that period, the number of reported crimes quadrupled, and the rate of violent crimes grew even faster. Fear of crime became especially severe in cities and merged with issues of race. African Americans, for example, made up about 12 percent of the population in this period, but in victim surveys, they represented 30 percent of the perpetrators of assault and 62 percent of the perpetrators of robberies.

This increase was attributed to many factors, including a surge in the number of teenage boys and young men most likely to engage in criminal behavior, the loss of blue-collar urban jobs, and the growing number of single-parent families. Conservatives often blamed the problem on a "permissive" attitude among liberal Democrats

and judges who worried more about the rights of criminals than the violence perpetrated against honest citizens. This criticism took hold in the public mind. For example, in the mid 1960s, 48 percent of Americans described courts at all levels as too lenient toward defendants. By 1980, that number soared to 83 percent. This outlook made crime a political issue. Presidents Ronald Reagan and George Bush pledged to appoint federal judges who favored tougher sentencing.

State legislatures, which had jurisdiction over most crime, joined Congress in passing laws to mandate longer prison terms, limit access to parole, treat younger offenders as adults, and impose three-strike laws. In California, for example, a voter-passed initiative stipulated that a third conviction for even a minor, nonviolent felony would result in a twenty-five-year to life sentence. As a result, hundreds of men and women have received lengthy sentences for stealing items such as golf clubs, videocassettes, and, in one case, a pizza. In 2003, the U.S. Supreme Court upheld these laws.

During the 1980s and 1990s, the war on crime merged with the war on drugs. Nearly every president since Woodrow Wilson had proclaimed a campaign against narcotics, and Reagan, Bush, and Clinton did the same. Middle-class Americans feared not only drug use by their children but also the violence associated with the sale of crack cocaine in the 1980s. Although the rate of overall drug use did not rise after 1980, several high-profile deaths among celebrities and violence among drug dealers created a climate of fear. National and local politicians rode this wave to escalate the war on drugs by devoting more funds to law enforcement and prison construction. When Congress imposed new mandatory minimum prison sentences for drug offenses in the 1980s and 1990s, it did not hold substantive hearings on the subject before passing legislation.

477

Back to the future: as prison populations surged in the 1980s and 1990s, state officials reintroduced classic chain gangs, designed to humiliate inmates and assign them useful labor. This group maintains a highway near Phoenix, Arizona. / © Bergsaker Tore/CORBIS Sygma

In 1980, federal facilities housed about twenty-five thousand prisoners. That number grew to 161,000 in 2003. Drug offenders account for 60 percent of the growth in the federal prison population over the last twenty years. African Americans and Latinos constitute 75 percent of these new federal prisoners. The number of women in federal custody has increased ninefold since 1980, with two-thirds of them imprisoned for drug offenses. After the terrorist attacks of September 2001, a growing number of federal prisoners were charged with violating immigration law.

State and local prisons and jails held about 475,000 people in 1980 and about 1.85 million in 2003. Drug offenses account for about one-third of this increase, and mandatory minimum sentences account for most of the remainder. Among the approximately 4 million Americans on probation or parole, about half were convicted of felonies, mostly driving under the influence of alcohol, followed by drug offenses. Only about one-third of prisoners and those under court supervision have committed physical violence.

By 2003, the cost of running local, state, and federal corrections facilities surpassed $50 billion, at least half of which is spent on housing nonviolent offenders. States pay most prison costs; since 1995, they have spent more annually on prisons than on higher education. In 1995, for example, all fifty states spent $2.6 billion building new prisons and $2.5 billion constructing new college campuses. Between the mid-1980s and mid-1990s, overall prison spending grew by 200 percent in California compared to a 15 percent increase for higher education funding. During 2002, after twenty years of steady increases, the rate of state prison growth leveled off. The federal prison population, however, has continued to increase, and authorities plan to add capacity for fifty thousand additional inmates in the coming decade.

Defenders of strict sentencing argue that despite the high cost of prison maintenance (reaching $25,000 or more per prisoner per year), the public is well served by this system. More convictions and longer sentences, they claim, account for the steady drop in the crime rate during the 1990s. In

other words, doing more time kept criminals out of circulation and deterred others. But little evidence supports this assertion. New York, for example, experienced a significantly greater *drop* in violent crime rates than did California, even though New York had the second slowest growing prison system in the country. California, on the other hand, had one of the fastest and imposed harsher penalties for similar crimes. Whether or not a state imposed the death penalty for capital crimes or longer terms for drug offenses did not affect the rate at which murders or drug crime occurred.

America's incarceration policies have disproportionately affected minorities, especially African Americans and Latinos. During the 1990s, for example, African Americans accounted for about 12 percent of the overall population, but they represented almost 50 percent of those in prison. One in three black men between the ages of twenty and twenty-nine were under some form of criminal justice control. At current levels of incarceration, black males born in the 1990s have about a 1 in 4 chance of going to prison in their lifetimes, Hispanic males have a 1 in 6 chance, and white males have a 1 in 23 chance of doing time.

Harsher drug laws account for some of this trend. Either because of less effective legal representation or prior offenses, blacks and Hispanics receive longer state and federal sentences than whites convicted of similar offenses. State and federal laws also punish those possessing or selling crack cocaine far more harshly than those arrested with powder cocaine. Under federal guidelines, 1 gram of crack is treated like 100 grams of powder. Since African Americans used crack more commonly than did whites, courts routinely sentenced them more harshly. In 2002, the Bush administration responded to criticism of this practice by proposing to treat powder cocaine offenders more severely.

Incarceration carries other social stigmas. Most states bar voting by convicted felons, while in custody, on probation, or on parole. Several states disenfranchise felons for life. As a result, about 13 percent of the black adult male population has lost the right to vote. In a few states, nearly 40 percent of African American men may be permanently disenfranchised.

The expansion of the prison system during the past twenty years has created a web of public and private economic interests eager to collect some of the $50 billion to be made in the prison industry. These groups range from prison guards to construction firms; private correctional companies; and businesses that supply meals, uniforms, and other institutional staples. Organizations that have a financial stake in expanding the prison system, including the American Correctional Association, an industry trade group, and labor unions representing prison guards in California, Texas, and New York routinely lobby state legislatures to promote tougher sentences.

To control the high costs of incarceration, state and federal officials often turn to the private sector. Since the 1980s, several for-profit correctional companies have broken what had traditionally been a government monopoly. Among the largest is the Corrections Corporation of America (CCA), which by 2002 ran the sixth largest prison system in the United States, after Texas, California, the federal government, New York, and Florida. CCA's sixty-three privatized prisons, based loosely on the model of publicly funded, privately managed charter schools, hold sixty-three thousand inmates. Other private firms supervise about eighty thousand state and federal prisoners. In an effort to reduce costs, both publicly and privately managed prisons have eliminated many education, counseling, and drug-treatment programs.

The rising costs of prisons, the social problems they create as well as solve, and changing public views about crime and drugs have begun to alter policies. For example, in 2000, voters in California and Arizona passed initiatives mandating treatment rather than incarceration for many people arrested a first or second time on drug offenses. Recognizing that rehabilitation rather than punishment is more appropriate (and cheaper) for ordinary drug users will likely reduce the number of new prisoners in those states. If this shift marks a new trend, the prison/industrial complex may have reached its zenith. Hundreds of thousands of prisoners still face years of incarceration, however, based on current policies.

---

defeated Soviet troops in the Third World, and crushed upstarts such as Libya's Colonel Qaddafi. The best known of these films starred Sylvester Stallone. As Rocky the prizefighter, Stallone punched out Soviet heavyweights in the ring; as the commando Rambo, he decimated Vietnamese communists and freed American POWs from Red captivity. Similarly, actor Chuck Norris kickboxed his way through Vietnam to rescue Americans; Tom Cruise in *Top Gun* blasted Soviet and Libyan pilots from the sky. Tom Clancy's immensely popular novel, *The Hunt for Red October*, portrayed the American navy humbling the Soviets.

For many Americans, the 1984 Olympic Games held in Los Angeles provided further confirmation of national superiority. With the Soviet Union and its allies boycotting the contest, American athletes triumphed in an unusually large number of events. Boisterous crowds waved banners proclaiming "We're Number One" and chanted "USA! USA!" American TV coverage often skipped victory ceremonies in which other countries took top honors or declined to broadcast the national anthems of other teams. The Chrysler Corporation ran ads that proclaimed the same slogan as Reagan's 1984 re-election campaign: "America is back."

Ronald Reagan's landslide victory over Walter Mondale that November prompted House Speaker Tip O'Neill to tell the president, "[I]n my fifty years in public life, I've never seen a man more popular than you are with the American people." But Reagan lacked any compelling set of foreign policy goals for his second term. When his national security adviser, Robert McFarlane, asked him to select a couple of priorities from a long list that included issues such as arms control, the Arab-Israeli conflict, and proxy wars in the Third World, Reagan simply replied, "Let's do them all!"

The Iran-Contra Debacle

During Reagan's eight years as president, nothing tarnished his reputation so greatly or called into question his judgment so seriously as his decision to sell weapons to Iran as part of a scheme to ransom U.S. hostages in Beirut and fund anticommunist guerrillas in Central America. As the moving force behind the scheme, Reagan nearly destroyed his own administration.

During his 1980 campaign, Reagan denounced Jimmy Carter for not standing by a long-time American client, Nicaraguan dictator Anastasio Somoza. In 1979, a group of Marxist guerrillas called the Sandinistas (after a nationalist hero from the 1920s, General Sandino) overthrew Somoza.

Reagan accused the Sandinistas of being communist stooges and turning Nicaragua into a "Soviet alley on the American mainland" and a "safe house and command post for international terror."

The Sandinistas certainly disliked the United States and sought aid from Cuba and the Soviet Union. They harassed opponents and blocked demo-cratic elections. But Sandinista human rights abuses paled compared to the gory record of American allies in neighboring El Salvador and Guate-mala. Nicaragua was a tiny country with fewer people than the population of many American cities. To speak of it as a hemispheric threat was grossly exaggerated.

Nevertheless, in 1981, Reagan ordered CIA director William Casey to or-ganize and support an anti-Sandinista force called the *contra-revolucionarios*, or contras, among Nicaraguan exiles. By 1985, the ten to twenty thousand contras (or freedom fighters, as Reagan often called them) survived almost en-tirely on American aid. With some exceptions, most of the leaders were veter-ans of the Somoza dictatorship.

The president told Congress that the contras helped intercept Sandinista aid to guerrillas in neighboring countries. The CIA, he assured the lawmakers, was not using them as a force to overthrow the Sandinistas. But as evidence linking the contras to thousands of civilian killings and many acts of terror-ism mounted, Congress responded in 1982 by strictly limiting the amount and purpose of American assistance to the guerrillas.

To circumvent this so-called Boland Amendment, as well as tougher re-strictions imposed in 1984, the Reagan administration asked foreign govern-ments, including Taiwan, Israel, Honduras, Panama, and Brunei, to provide money to the contras in return for increases in American aid. This effort soon merged with secret approaches to Iran. Reagan had condemned the govern-ments of Iran and Libya as "outlaw states" run by the "strangest collection of misfits, Loony Tunes, and squalid criminals since the advent of the Third Reich." He was moved by the plight of kidnapped Americans, nearly all of whom were private citizens who had ignored warnings to leave Beirut, who were be-ing held by Islamic militias allied to Iran. In an attempt to win their release, the Reagan administration began a series of deals with Iranian intermediaries that started in the summer of 1985, despite Reagan's pledge "never to negoti-ate with terrorists." The president and some of his aides justified these con-tacts by convincing themselves that they were assisting "moderate" Iranians poised to assume power after the death of Ayatollah Khomeini. In fact, they were Khomeini loyalists out to hoodwink the United States.

The Iranians wanted arms and replacement parts for U.S. weapons al-ready in their arsenal. If the United States sold weapons to them, the Iranians promised to help free Americans held in Beirut. In making the secret deal, Rea-gan violated the law against selling arms to a "terrorist state" without con-gressional approval. He authorized several more shipments of short-range missiles and anti-tank and anti-aircraft weapons during 1985–1986.

Marine Lieutenant Colonel Oliver North, a deputy to National Security Adviser Robert McFarlane, played a key role in the transactions. North pushed

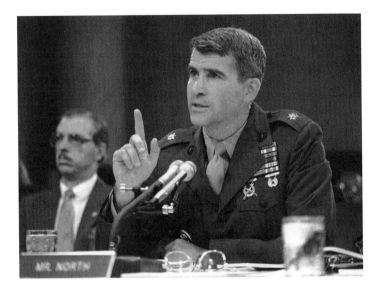

In 1987, an unrepentant Lieutenant Colonel Oliver North defends before Congress his secret effort to sell weapons to Iran, win the release of American hostages in Lebanon, and arm the anticommunist contras in Nicaragua. / AP/Wide World

the arms sales, even though only three of the dozen or so captive Americans in Beirut were released. In fact, the hostages were North's secondary concern. His main interest lay in helping the contra guerrillas fighting the Sandinistas in Nicaragua.

After Congress limited funding for the contras in 1984, North prevailed on wealthy foreigners and Americans, such as the sultan of Brunei and Joseph Coors, to donate money secretly to the contras. When these funds were expended, he searched for new sources. North devised the idea of charging the Iranians inflated prices for American missiles and other equipment and using the profits to fund the contras. Reagan may not have known the details of North's plan, but he gave him his enthusiastic approval, even though both understood the action violated American law.

The bizarre scheme began to unravel on October 5, 1986, when Sandinista gunners shot down a CIA-chartered plane ferrying weapons to the contras bought with Iranian profits. One American crewmember, Eugene Hasenfus, survived the crash and promptly confessed all he knew about the secret program to his captors. On November 2, 1986, a Lebanese magazine printed an account of the arms-for-hostages deal. Iranian officials then announced that the alleged "moderates" dealing with Oliver North were actually agents of the Ayatollah Khomeini. Although the story broke just two days before the November 4 midterm election, it probably still helped the Democrats recapture control of the Senate.

President Reagan, CIA director William Casey, North, and other officials tried to cover up the scandal by lying to the press, to Congress, and to the American people about what had occurred. Attorney General Edwin Meese mounted a halfhearted probe in which he nearly encouraged North and his staff to destroy incriminating documents before Justice Department lawyers found them. Despite the large-scale destruction of evidence by North and the National Security Council (NSC) staff, investigators discovered documents revealing the link between illegal arms sales to Iran and the diversion of up to $20 million to the contras. This discovery forced Meese to ask a federal court to appoint a special prosecutor and compelled Congress to begin a probe of its own.

As the scandal unfolded, Reagan insisted that he knew nothing about any arms-for-hostages deal or the secret funding of the contras. The public, which had stood by the president, no longer believed him. Reagan's approval rating plummeted below 50 percent. Desperate to shift responsibility, the president blamed the Israelis (who played a bit part in the operation), and then North and National Security Adviser John Poindexter. When these actions failed to restore public faith, Reagan appointed a blue-ribbon panel, chaired by former senator John Tower, to examine the affair.

The Tower Commission report in February 1987 shed some light on the Iran-contra scandal. It showed how the arms deal had devolved into a sordid ransom scheme designed mostly to raise illegal funds for the secret war in Nicaragua. The president's actions, the commission concluded, "ran directly counter" to his public promises to punish terrorists. The most damaging aspect of the report was its portrayal of Reagan as disengaged, uninformed, and easily manipulated. The president sidestepped these criticisms by firing several more aides and giving a speech on March 4, 1987, in which he appeared to accept the criticisms of the Tower report without really doing so. The "facts" might suggest that he had approved ransom payments, he said, but in his heart he never meant to trade arms for hostages or to violate the law.

Through the summer of 1987, congressional committees continued to investigate the actions of the National Security Council staff, the CIA, and the State Department in the Iran-contra scandal. But the probe suffered from an unclear focus, lack of access to crucial documents, and outright lying by many of the principals, including Oliver North and John Poindexter. CIA director William Casey died of a brain tumor before his role could be analyzed.

In March 1988, special prosecutor Lawrence Walsh indicted North, Poindexter, and several lesser-known CIA and State Department officials for complicity in the affair. Most pleaded guilty or were convicted. The Supreme Court later overturned the convictions of North and Poindexter on technical grounds. Later, both men insisted that Reagan had known about and approved all their actions, including the destruction of evidence. As North put it, "Reagan knew everything." Trials of lesser-known figures in the affair carried over into the 1990s. One of President George H. W. Bush's last actions as president in 1993 was to pardon many of the participants, some of whom, such as Poindexter, reappeared in his son's administration after 2001.

Reagan survived the Iran-contra scandal and avoided impeachment for several reasons. First, despite the public's disillusionment with him, he retained a fair measure of approval. The congressional and judicial investigations lacked focus and often showed a reluctance to connect the president directly to lawbreaking, even when the evidence pointed toward him. The probes tended to stress the illegal funding of the contras rather than the illegal arms sales to Iran. Because so few Americans paid attention to Latin American affairs, this detail made little impression on them. Most Americans had a visceral dislike for Iran's Ayatollah Khomeini, but investigators did not play up this angle. Ultimately, the public decided that Reagan was more befuddled than criminally culpable.

But perhaps the most important reason why this scandal faded was the sudden change in Soviet-American relations that began in 1987. Reagan, who had spent the previous six years denouncing the "evil empire," suddenly showed great interest in negotiating with the new Soviet leader, Mikhail Gorbachev. The Democrats, who controlled both houses of Congress after the November 1986 election, as well as the public applauded this change of heart and encouraged Reagan's new approach.

As for Nicaragua, the problem solved itself shortly after Reagan left office. To everyone's surprise, once the United States stopped funding the contras, the Sandinista regime agreed to hold free elections. In February 1990, a moderately conservative coalition won a majority of votes and formed a new government. The Sandinistas reconstituted themselves as a peaceful opposition party. As happened with El Salvador and Grenada, Washington soon lost interest in an impoverished Nicaragua that was no longer vital to U.S. interests.

Ratcheting Down the Cold War

As the Iran-contra scandal unfolded, dramatic changes took place within the Soviet Union and between it and the United States. Ironically, Reagan's strident opposition to communism accounted for his initial popularity, but his turn toward cooperation with the Soviet Union helped salvage his presidency. Unlike all his predecessors since Franklin D. Roosevelt, Reagan had refused during his first term to meet his Soviet counterpart. Between November 1985 and December 1988, however, Reagan met Mikhail Gorbachev on five separate occasions.

When Gorbachev became general secretary of the Soviet Communist Party in March 1985, he was the best-educated, most worldly, and least dogmatic leader of his country since Lenin. He blamed his three predecessors for presiding over twenty years of stagnation and acknowledged that the Soviet Union had fallen far behind the economic and technological level of most other industrialized nations. Apart from the defense sector, Soviet industry produced shoddy and insufficient goods. The Soviet Union was, in the words of one cynic, "Mexico with H-bombs." The old methods of central planning and authoritarian control succeeded in carrying out rudimentary industrialization but could not compete in an age where international competition and technological innovation drove progress. As a result, corruption and despair permeated Soviet society.

In an effort to reform the Soviet Union before it collapsed, Gorbachev proclaimed new policies of *perestroika* (social and economic restructuring) and *glasnost* (openness and democracy). He nudged his colleagues toward accepting market economics and democratic principles as the only way to pull the country out of its torpor. The new leader traveled widely, telling foreign governments that he represented a new type of communism. Britain's conservative prime minister, Margaret Thatcher, whom Reagan admired, described Gorbachev as "charming" and someone with whom "the west can do business."

Reagan and Gorbachev held a brief get-acquainted session in Geneva in November 1985. Their conversation alternated between arguments over star wars and anecdotes about Hollywood film stars. They met a second time at a hastily called meeting in Reykjavik, Iceland, in October 1986. Gorbachev proposed a 50 percent cut in long-range missiles and their eventual elimination. In return, the United States must not deploy an antimissile shield. Reagan responded with an even more radical proposal: why not eliminate all the world's missiles within ten years and also scrap all forms of nuclear weapons? In return, however, the Soviets must agree to American deployment of an antimissile system—even though none had been developed! Both American and Soviet officials were flabbergasted by Reagan's idea. They were especially confused by his seemingly contradictory proposal to eliminate all missiles and nuclear weapons and to build a vast antimissile system. Many American and European strategists considered this idea dangerous, if only because it would guarantee a Soviet advantage in conventional weapons. The summit broke up in confusion with nothing settled.

The swiftly breaking Iran-contra scandal superseded questions about the Iceland summit. Early in 1987, faced with a collapse of public approval, Reagan replaced most of his hard-line, anti-Soviet advisers. Former senator Howard Baker took over as White House chief of staff from the abrasive Donald Regan. The death of William Casey led to the appointment of FBI director William Webster to head the CIA. National Security Adviser John Poindexter was replaced by Frank Carlucci. A few months later, when Caspar Weinberger resigned as defense secretary, Carlucci took over at the Pentagon. This change cleared the way for Lieutenant General Colin Powell to succeed Carlucci as head of the NSC. Secretary of State George Shultz, one of the few senior advisers to have opposed the Iran-contra scheme, now had the president's ear.

This new foreign policy team stressed pragmatic results over ideological purity. They shared Prime Minister Thatcher's opinion of Gorbachev as someone prepared to get down to business. For the first time, the Reagan administration set about pursuing realistic arms control accords with the new Soviet leadership. Finally, both sides approached the issue from similar vantage points.

By the autumn of 1987, Soviet and American negotiators agreed on a treaty to remove all intermediate-range nuclear (INF) missiles from both sides of the Iron Curtain in Europe. These weapons comprised only a small part of the superpower arsenal, but an agreement to eliminate them entirely (not just cap their number) represented a symbolic breakthrough. Equally important, to preclude cheating, Gorbachev agreed to mutual, on-site inspections. The Soviets, realizing that Reagan's SDI proposal was going nowhere, dropped their demand that the INF agreement include a promise not to deploy star wars.

The fact that the Soviets made most of the concessions on the INF treaty convinced American hard-liners that six years of confrontation had paid off. What probably brought Gorbachev around, however, was an internal economic crisis building for decades. The Soviet economy had been in trouble since at least the 1970s. Previous leaders had relied on deception, intimidation, and gutting the civilian economy to maintain a high level of military spending. Gorbachev recognized that continuing this policy would cripple the entire economy. Instead, he favored structural changes that required a reduction in military spending as well as an infusion of Western and Japanese investments and technology. This change in emphasis required a new relationship with the noncommunist world.

Soviet leaders, like the Russian Czars before them, had always measured national security by the degree to which Moscow dominated or intimidated its neighbors and potential rivals. In a reversal of long-standing cultural and strategic perceptions, Gorbachev sought to enhance Soviet economic and military security through cooperation with the outside world.

This transformation involved personality as well as ideology. When Gorbachev visited Washington in December 1987 to sign the INF treaty, he reached out to Americans through the media and in person. He hosted a party for prominent actors and politicians and, while driving around the city, continually bound out of his limousine to shake the hands of startled pedestrians. "I just want to say hello," he gushed to gawking Americans, who were more familiar with Soviet leaders pounding shoes on lecterns and declaring, "[W]e will bury you."

During the year that remained in Reagan's presidency, few substantive Soviet-American agreements were signed. Both leaders recognized, however, that the dramatic change in atmosphere provided a welcome political boost. As cooperation with the Soviets became the order of the day, most Americans overlooked the Iran-contra scandal. For Gorbachev, the promise of Western economic aid and the ability to shift spending from defense to the civilian sector bought him time in his struggle to reform the Soviet system before it imploded. Reagan gave Gorbachev his formal blessing by visiting Moscow in June 1988 and embracing him in front of Lenin's tomb. When asked by a reporter if he still considered the Soviets the "focus of evil" in the world, the president answered, "They've changed." The superpowers still had thirty thousand nuclear weapons aimed at each other, but in the spirit of the time, few people feared their use.

During 1988, the Soviets withdrew their troops from Afghanistan and supported American efforts to end civil conflicts that had festered for years in

Africa and Southeast Asia. Reagan met Gorbachev a final time in December in New York, where the Soviet leader announced plans to reduce the size of his conventional forces unilaterally. Taking a cue from the president's public relations advisers, Gorbachev arranged for pictures to be taken of himself, Reagan, and president-elect George H. W. Bush in front of the Statue of Liberty.

The New World Order

The improvement in Soviet-American relations helped Vice President Bush coast into the White House in 1988. Clinging to Reagan's coattails, Bush parlayed his own substantial foreign policy expertise (while disparaging the patriotism of Democratic nominee Michael Dukakis) into an electoral triumph in the November 1988 election.

The years 1989 through 1991 witnessed some of the most dramatic changes in global politics since 1945. The world order envisioned by Franklin Roosevelt near the end of World War II seemed finally to be emerging as the Cold War waned and the United Nations began to function as a forum for global cooperation. The United States and the Soviet Union ended their rivalry, and communism rapidly collapsed in Eastern Europe. In a dramatic reversal, Washington and its NATO allies provided billions of dollars of aid to promote reform in the former Soviet empire.

Bush assembled an experienced group of policymakers at the onset of his administration. National Security Adviser Brent Scowcroft; Secretary of Defense Richard Cheney; Secretary of State James Baker III; and General Colin Powell, chair of the Joint Chiefs of Staff, had all held senior posts during the Ford and Reagan administrations. As a group, they favored the kind of pragmatic policies that Reagan adopted in his final years. But the new president's greatest accomplishments in foreign policy were more passive than active. He had the good luck to preside over the peaceful collapse of the Soviet empire and the demise of global communism, and he claimed credit for the good things that happened on his watch. In some ways, he resembled his Soviet counterpart, Mikhail Gorbachev. Both recognized the need to move their countries beyond the limits of the Cold War. Like Bush, Gorbachev did not push change but rather declined to block internal pressure for reform.

Shortly after Bush took office, Gorbachev permitted free elections to the Soviet parliament. This move transformed the Soviet system in profound ways. In July 1989, the Soviet leader stunned members of the Warsaw Pact by announcing that Moscow would no longer impose its will on Eastern Europe. The Soviet satellite states were free to run their internal affairs without Soviet interference. Boisterous but peaceful demonstrations quickly brought down nearly all the unpopular communist regimes throughout the region. Only in Bulgaria and Rumania did the old order put up futile armed resistance.

The most dramatic change occurred in Germany. In November 1989, after several months of street protests, the East German regime opened the

In November 1989, exuberant crowds in Berlin tear down a section of the hated wall as East German border guards look on. / © AFP/CORBIS

Berlin Wall. Soon, wrecking balls and sledgehammers battered down this icon of East-West division. Street vendors began a thriving trade selling concrete chunks of the dismal barrier to tourists. Then, on October 2, 1990, Germany reunited, ending the division that epitomized the Cold War.

The speed and relatively peaceful nature of these political upheavals caught both American and Soviet leaders by surprise. President Bush and his advisers were uncertain how to respond to such rapid change in the communist world. When he visited Eastern Europe during 1989, Bush encouraged a more cautious approach. There was, he said, "big stuff, heavy stuff going on" and pushing things too quickly in Poland and Germany might "be more than the market can bear."

But political ferment even spread to the Soviet heartland. Gorbachev hoped to nudge economic and political transformation toward a market economy and democracy while preserving a major role for the Communist Party and the Soviet state. But many Russians preferred to jettison the old structure, and the demand for change was even stronger among the disparate ethnic groups that comprised a majority in nearly twenty republics under Moscow's control. In 1990, the Baltic republics of Lithuania, Estonia, and Latvia asserted their independence (see Map 13.1). Soon, other regions with non-Russian majorities (including Ukraine, Belarus, Moldova, Armenia, Azerbaijan, Georgia, Turkmenistan, Tajikistan, Kazakhstan, Kyrgystan, and Uzbekistan) demanded sovereignty. The Communist Party's old guard blamed Gorbachev for unleashing chaos, while reformers, such as Boris Yeltsin, accused him of moving too slowly. Yeltsin, a former Communist Party official, won election as president of the Russian republic in June 1991 and immediately began challenging Gorbachev's authority.

After some hesitation about how to respond to these developments, the Bush administration threw its full support behind Gorbachev by the end of 1989. The president held the first of six meetings with the beleaguered Soviet president. In November 1990, the two leaders issued a joint statement declaring an end to the Cold War. Bush praised Gorbachev, criticized Yeltsin's effort to bring down the Soviet government, and urged the restive republics to remain under Moscow's umbrella.

Map 13.1
Democratic Movements in Eastern Europe, 1989–1991

Despite American assistance, Gorbachev's hold on power grew shakier during 1991. Communist hard-liners and military leaders demanded a reassertion of central control and called for action to suppress independence movements among the republics. But Gorbachev insisted on pursuing reforms. That summer, he dissolved the Warsaw military pact and signed a wide-ranging missile reduction agreement with Washington. In August, just as he prepared to sign a treaty giving the republics a large measure of autonomy, communist hard-liners struck. On August 18, they arrested Gorbachev at his vacation villa in the Crimea and proclaimed a new government. The coup failed when Boris Yeltsin and hundreds of thousand of Muscovites took to the streets in defense of democratic reform. After three days, the plot collapsed and Gorbachev returned to power.

Nevertheless, the botched coup signaled the end of the communist era. Gorbachev quit the Communist Party but continued to insist that the Soviet Union could reform itself. By now, however, he lacked the authority to do much aside from issuing decrees. In the final months of 1991, Boris Yeltsin and leaders of other republics simply ignored the powerless Soviet president. On Christmas day, Gorbachev bowed to reality. He signed a final decree dissolving the Soviet Union, turned power over to Boris Yeltsin, and resigned from office. As president of the large Russian Republic, Yeltsin ruled over 75 percent of the territory of the former Soviet Union.

China, the other large communist state, also underwent a profound transformation during the 1980s and 1990s. But its experience did not follow the Soviet script. Communist leader Deng Xiaoping reversed Gorbachev's priorities, promoting economic reform while preserving a communist power monopoly. China's economy began to grow rapidly in the late 1980s, and material life for most Chinese improved greatly. Even though individuals enjoyed a far freer life than at any time since the communist revolution of 1949, they were still not allowed to organize opposition political parties or labor unions, practice religion freely, or openly dissent from government policy.

Dissatisfied with these half-steps, Chinese students and workers in several cities began to demonstrate in favor of democratic reform in the spring of 1989. The largest gathering occurred in Beijing's Tiananmen Square, a vast plaza in front of the old imperial palace. During May, as many as 1 million protesters demanded change while tens of thousands took up a permanent vigil on the square. In front of Western television cameras, they erected a "goddess of democracy" (modeled on the Statue of Liberty) and refused orders to disperse.

On June 4, 1989, Deng ordered military units to scatter the demonstrators and restore order. Anywhere between one thousand and three thousand Chinese civilians may have been shot or crushed by tanks in the ensuing violence. Thousands more were arrested or fled the country. Americans who saw pictures of the repression were appalled. But President Bush, like his predecessors since Nixon, concluded that China's importance in Asia and its surging economy were so important to the United States and world stability that Washington should not impose stiff sanctions on the regime. Instead, American officials hoped that a moderate response would buy time for the old guard to pass from the scene and make way for political reformers. They also believed that by promoting China's foreign trade, they could encourage greater political pluralism. This stance proved at least partially true. During the 1990s, as China's economy grew at a record pace, material life for its people improved substantially and the sphere of personal freedom expanded modestly.

Post–Cold War Interventions

The end of the Cold War did not usher in a golden age of peace. Even without a Soviet enemy, the world possessed no shortage of problems or threats. When the United States felt impelled to use force abroad, it justified its actions as a defense of human rights, a humanitarian intervention to alleviate famine and disease, protect world energy supplies, or suppress the drug trade. These reasons resembled the justifications great powers gave for foreign ventures in the century before the Cold War.

The first foreign intervention by the Bush administration took place in Panama. Manuel Noriega, a military officer and long-time CIA informant, assumed power in 1983 following the death of nationalist leader Omar Torrijos, who had negotiated the treaty restoring the canal to Panama. Noriega was a notorious thug who had at various times cooperated with Fidel Castro, the CIA, Colombian drug lords, and foreign bankers seeking a place to stash tainted money. During the 1980s, he permitted the CIA to use Panama as a conduit to aid the contras in Nicaragua. In return, Washington ignored his drug running.

But by the end of the Reagan administration, as the armed conflicts in Central America wound down, Noriega became an embarrassment and Washington applied financial pressure to drive him from power. This effort continued under Bush, who saw Noriega's continued cooperation with Colombian cocaine barons as an impediment to the expanded war on drugs. In May 1989, Noriega called an election but cancelled it when vote counting showed a likely victory by the opposition.

During the next six months, Bush authorized several plans to depose Noriega, but none succeeded. Finally, in December 1989, the president sent a force of twelve thousand American soldiers into Panama with the goals of arresting Noriega and installing as president the likely winner of the aborted election. In three days of fighting with Noriega loyalists, twenty-three Americans died. Several hundred Panamanian civilians perished in the crossfire and accidental bombings. Noriega was captured and later convicted of drug smuggling in a Miami court. The jury ignored his claim that past U.S. presidents had tacitly consented to his crimes. The American public overwhelmingly supported the intervention and its aftermath.

The United States faced a far greater challenge after August 2, 1990, when Iraq invaded the tiny, oil-rich sheikdom of Kuwait in the Persian Gulf region. Iraqi leader Saddam Hussein had long coveted his wealthy neighbor and insisted that Kuwait was really a "lost province" of Iraq. By annexing Kuwait, he could enrich his regime and play a major role in setting global petroleum prices. The fact that Saudi Arabia, with its huge oil reserves, lay just beyond Kuwait, worried Arab states as well as industrialized nations.

Saddam Hussein probably expected the Bush administration to react to the conquest of Kuwait with only a token protest. After all, during the 1980s, both Reagan and Bush had occasionally armed Iraq in its war with Iran; had provided generous loans and agricultural credits to Baghdad; and had even stood by silently while Iraq developed chemical, biological, and nuclear weapons. The Iraqi leader had, with impunity, used poison gas against Iranians and rebels within his own country.

To his dismay, Saddam Hussein finally overreached. He discovered that America's indifference to his murderous behavior at home did not mean a free pass to seize a major portion of world petroleum reserves. Kuwait, of course, was no democracy. But it was a sovereign state and a member of the United Nations. If Iraq's conquest went uncontested, Bush, along with European and Japanese leaders, feared that Saddam would next target Saudi Arabia.

To prevent this outcome, Bush prevailed on the United Nations to impose an economic blockade on Iraq. He also sent nearly half a million American troops to Saudi Arabia as part of a twenty-eight nation coalition force. Even the Soviet Union, Iraq's former military supplier, joined in the collective action. By January 15, 1991, it was clear that diplomatic efforts to compel an Iraqi withdrawal had failed. Congress debated the president's request to authorize military action and gave its assent by a narrow margin. Senators Al Gore of Tennessee and Joseph Lieberman of Connecticut were among a handful of Democrats who supported the use of force.

On January 17, Bush ordered American planes to begin attacking Iraqi targets. In launching the so-called Desert Storm assault, the president paraphrased the words of President Woodrow Wilson uttered in World War I when he declared, "[W]e have before us the opportunity to forge for ourselves a new world order." For five weeks, allied planes pounded targets in Iraq and Kuwait. The military permitted only limited and carefully controlled press coverage. On February 23, 1991, U.S. ground forces and those of several coalition members quickly liberated Kuwait and pushed on halfway to the Iraqi capital of Baghdad in less than one hundred hours. When Bush accept Saddam Hussein's plea for a cease-fire on February 27, only 223 allied troops had been killed, compared to many thousands of Iraqis. American troop commander, General Norman H. Schwarzkopf, became a media star and then a bestselling author. A Gallup poll reported that 90 percent of Americans, a record high number, supported the president.

Kuwaiti sovereignty (not democracy) was restored and Saudi Arabian energy supplies were protected. But most Americans were surprised to discover that Saddam Hussein remained very much in power. The Bush administration feared that if he were removed, Islamic fundamentalists in Iraq or from Iran might fill the power vacuum, posing an even greater threat than the vicious dictator. For this reason, the president halted the offensive before Saddam was crushed. Whether justified or not, Bush's decision created a host of later prob-

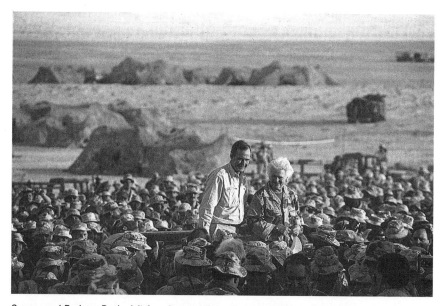

George and Barbara Bush visit American soldiers after the Gulf War. / Diana Walker/Gamma Liaison/Getty Images

lems. Many Americans came to fault Bush for leaving the job half done. Meanwhile, Saddam Hussein turned his wrath on Iraqi dissidents and ethnic minorities, such as the Kurds. Despite his pledge not to rebuild weapons of mass destruction, within a few years the Iraqi tyrant was again arming to the teeth and threatening regional mayhem.

The war against Iraq had one positive, if unintended, consequence. PLO chief Yasir Arafat had, as usual, bet on the wrong horse. By supporting Iraq, he infuriated the wealthy Arabs of Saudi Arabia and the Persian Gulf states who subsidized the PLO. Suddenly abandoned by his patrons, Arafat had no choice but to adopt a more conciliatory attitude toward Israel and the United States. He soon entered into peace talks with Israeli officials that culminated in a tentative peace plan in 1994.

The triumphs in the Cold War, along with easy victories against unsavory enemies in Panama and Iraq, propelled George Bush to unprecedented levels of popularity. Just eight months after Desert Storm, however, polls revealed that only 39 percent of Americans approved of the direction in which he led the country. His recent 90 percent approval rating had evaporated in record time. The "new world order," a phrase first used optimistically after victory in World War I, proved no better a guide for the 1990s than it had for the 1920s. The collapse of communism had, of course, reduced the danger of nuclear war. But it also allowed long-suppressed ethnic, religious, and regional conflicts to resurface in areas previously under Soviet control. In other parts of the world, such as the Middle East and Africa, superpower rivalry had imposed a kind of lid on these long-standing resentments. After 1991, with the disappearance of a Soviet enemy, the American public and its leaders were far less eager to play the role of world police officer.

As the victories over Panama and Iraq faded from memory, and as the economy faltered during 1991–1992, the president's palpable apathy toward domestic problems took a toll. By the spring of 1992, over 80 percent of Americans told the Gallup poll that they were dissatisfied with the state of the nation. Bush's two most memorable phrases, "Read my lips: no new taxes" and "new world order" became objects of popular derision.

Challenged by conservative Patrick Buchanan in the 1992 Republican primaries, Bush struggled to show empathy with financially pressed citizens. To counter what critics called his indifference, Bush told New Hampshire voters in a speech, "Message: I care . . . don't cry for me Argentina," but the tortured syntax made it seem as if it were written by *Saturday Night Live* Bush impersonator Dana Carvey.

A growing number of Americans sensed that victory in the Cold War had come at an unexpectedly high price. At first, the decline in defense spending sent major shock waves through the economy. California, the "buckle" on the Gunbelt, received a particularly severe jolt. Defense contractors, along with many other large employers, began "downsizing," a euphemism for laying off workers.

The sense of despair felt by many midcareer engineers and other defense workers was portrayed in the 1993 film, *Falling Down*. The story follows actor

" CONGRATULATIONS ....YOU WON THE COLD WAR! "

The Cold War had overshadowed U.S. domestic problems, such as unemployment, economic troubles, and the poor and homeless. / Reprinted with special permission of King Features Syndicate

Michael Douglas, playing an anonymous aerospace engineer, who on one awful day loses his job, his marriage, and his hope. The unnamed hero abandons his car on a jammed Los Angeles freeway and begins a violent trek through the urban underworld that culminates in a shootout with police outside the home of his estranged wife. The character's fate seemed to mirror Paul Tsongas's joke: the "good news" is that the Cold War is over; the "bad news" is that the Germans and Japanese won.

In the run-up to the 1992 election, as trade deficits mounted and millions of American workers feared losing their jobs in obsolete factories, George Bush unleashed a barrage of accusations against Democratic presidential candidate Bill Clinton. He berated Clinton's avoidance of military service in Vietnam, his admission about smoking marijuana in his youth, and his alleged womanizing. Similar accusations had served GOP candidates well in earlier elections. Now, they fell flat.

Conclusion

In his farewell address delivered in January 1953, President Harry Truman voiced a question that was undoubtedly on the minds of millions of Americans: "Some of you . . . may ask when and how will the Cold War end?" Nevertheless, the president whose term of office coincided with the emergence of the global struggle between East and West had no doubt that change would eventually come. "I have a deep and abiding faith in the destiny of free men," Truman concluded. "With patience and courage, we shall some day move on into the new era." In light of the events of the late 1980s and early 1990s, these words proved prescient. In the long run, the growing economic strength of the United States, Western Europe, and Japan and the allure of democracy overwhelmed the Soviet communist system. For nearly half a century, American policies of promoting world trade and guaranteeing the security of U.S. allies created the context for this triumph. Along the way, however, the United States sometimes strayed from the priorities of containment set in the early years of the Cold War. Interventions in the Third World, especially in Vietnam, now seem to many historians to have been irrelevant and costly diversions from the strategies that secured eventual success.

New economic and security challenges in Europe, Asia, the Middle East, and Latin America characterized the post–Cold War world. Sometimes, as with Iraq, American leaders were swift and sure in their response. But in areas such as Yugoslavia and Africa, where bitter ethnic rivalries led to genocidal attacks, Bush and his advisers were hesitant to intervene. The public, like its president, pondered what kind of influence they wished the United States to exercise abroad. The world remained full of economic challenges, political trouble spots, and natural disasters. Determining the national interest and deciding on appropriate responses to these hazards fell to a generation that had to look beyond the simple truths of the Cold War.

F U R T H E R • R E A D I N G

On foreign policy during the 1980s and early 1990s, see Alexander Haig, *Caveat: Reagan, Realism, and Foreign Policy* (1984); Caspar Weinberger, *Fighting for Peace* (1990); George Shultz, *Turmoil and Triumph* (1993); Constantine Menges, *Inside the National Security Council* (1988); Strobe Talbot, *Deadly Gambits* (1984); Bob Woodward, *Veil: The Secret Wars of the CIA, 1981–1987* (1987); Steve Emerson, *Secret Warriors: Inside the Covert Military Operations of the Reagan Administration* (1988); William Broad, *The Star Warriors* (1985); Beth A. Fischer, *The Reagan Reversal: Foreign Policy and the End of the Cold War* (1997); Frances Fitzgerald, *Way Out There in the Blue: Reagan, Star Wars, and the End of the Cold War* (2000); Kenneth Oye et al., *Eagle Defiant: U.S. Foreign Policy in the 1980s* (1983); John Tower et al., *The Tower Commission Report* (1987); Theodore Draper, *A Very Thin Line: The Iran-Contra Affairs* (1991); Jane Mayer and Doyle McManus, *Landslide: The Unmaking of the President, 1984–1988* (1988); Jonathan Kwitny, *The Crimes of Patriots: A Tale of Dope, Dirty Money, and the CIA* (1987); Raymond Bonner, *Weakness and Deceit: U.S. Policy and El Salvador* (1984); Roy Gutman, *Banana Diplomacy* (1988); Mark Donner, *Massacre at El Mozote: A Parable of the Cold War* (1994); Michael Schaller, *Reckoning with Reagan: America and Its President in the 1980s* (1992); John R. Greene, *The Presidency of George Bush* (2000); George Bush and Brent Scowcroft, *A World Transformed* (1998); James Baker III, *The Politics of Diplomacy: Revolution, War and Peace, 1989–1992* (1995); Michael R. Beschloss and Strobe Talbot, *At the Highest Levels: The Inside Story of the End of the Cold War* (1993); John L. Gaddis, *The United States and the End of the Cold War* (1992); Alan Friedman, *Spider's Web: The Secret Story of How the White House Illegally Armed Iraq* (1993); Rick Atkinson, *Crusade: The Untold Story of the Persian Gulf War* (1993); Stephen R. Graubard, *Mr. Bush's War: Adventures in the Politics of Illusion* (1992); Don Oberdorfer, *The Turn: From the Cold War to a New Era, The U.S. and the Soviet Union, 1983–1990* (1991); Gale Stokes, *The Walls Came Tumbling Down: The Collapse of Communism in Eastern Europe* (1993). **On the prison/industrial complex,** see Eric Schlosser, *Reefer Madness: Sex, Drugs, and Cheap Labor in the American Black Market* (2003).

On the Edge: 1993 to the Present

The Silicon Valley headquarters of Oracle Corporation, a major software manufacturer. / ©
Ed Kashi/CORBIS

14

In January 1993, Marc Andreesen was a twenty-year-old computer science major earning $6.85 as an intern at the National Center for Supercomputing Applications (NCSA) at the University of Illinois. Bored with work one day, he started tinkering with a new information exchange system called the Internet, which had been developed in the previous couple of years at the European Center for Nuclear Research (called by its French acronym CERN). The Internet could transfer almost limitless amounts of information from one computer to another. Users could retrieve text, images, video, and sound, and they could respond with information of their own. But the Internet was more like a toy for computer geeks than anything else, and Andreesen became frustrated with the complex process for gaining access to it. The software used for this purpose was at least ten years behind the times. A user had to be an expert at the operating system UNIX. Andreesen thought, what if he could develop a program that would allow even novice computer users to point and click their way onto the Internet? He went to Eric Bina, a programmer with some seniority at NCSA, and together they began working on a "killer application" that would make the Internet accessible to everyone. The two immediately started working, writing computer code for three or four days straight, resting a day, and then starting all over again. Three months later, they produced Mosaic, the first World Wide Web browser that would enable anyone to get information from the Internet and to exchange files electronically. And thus the Web was born.

Andreesen soon left the University of Illinois for Mountain View, California, a once sleepy town in the burgeoning high-tech promised land called Silicon Valley. There he and Bina teamed up with Jim Clark, the founder of Silicon Graphics. Silicon Graphics made highly prized computer display terminals. They created a new company called Netscape, which soon began selling a new Internet browser called Netscape 1.0. The founders went on to earn hundreds of millions of dollars as the World Wide Web took off.

The Internet, the Web, and Silicon Valley became catchphrases of what seemed almost like a golden age. The gloom hanging over the American spirit since the Vietnam War and the Watergate scandal of the 1970s lifted. The Cold War had ended. The economy boomed. Cities revived and sparkled. Crime rates plunged. New technologies promised unimaginable riches. Tens of thousands of people made millions of dollars in the stock market. The 1990s saw the largest migration to the United States of any decade since the early twentieth century. Both rich and poor came for employment opportunities unavailable anywhere else in the world. The federal government, an object of suspicion and derision for a decade, seemed to get its house in order. The largest budget deficits in history gave way to the largest surpluses. People spoke without irony of the United States as the world's indispensable nation.

Bill Clinton, the president for eight of these years, proved to be one of the most enigmatic figures to occupy the White House. A man of enormous knowledge, empathy, and interest in public policy, he was loved and hated. Clinton connected with his many supporters as a man who cared about them and wanted to use the powers of the federal government to improve their lives. Yet a sizable minority despised Clinton. Many social and political conservatives viewed him as the embodiment of everything that was wrong with the 1960s. They considered him to be morally weak, self-indulgent, dishonest, and radical. Some liberals also distrusted him for opposite reasons. They bridled at his efforts to move the Democratic Party to the center of the political spectrum. They believed his relentless focus on the aspirations of the middle class and away from the party's traditional identification with labor unions slighted the needs of the poor. They lamented that he was too quick to compromise with his political opponents.

But public policy and government process captured little of the American imagination in the 1990s. Public life, such as it was, became a source of endless, superficial entertainment. People fixated on the personal lives of the famous. Celebrity hairstyles, marriages, divorces, and murders absorbed attention. Scandal became the staple of endless TV talk shows. Whether it was the trial of former football star O. J. Simpson for the murder of his ex-wife or the impeachment of President Clinton for lying about a tawdry affair with a young female intern, the mixture of sex, fame, celebrity, and trivia dominated the news. As the new millennium approached in 2000, Americans worried that the very computer technology that had led the prosperity would crash, leaving the country cold, hungry, and afraid.

Americans were prosperous in the 1990s, but they were not all that content. An edgy air of anxiety hung over the decade. Representatives of some religious groups and conservative talk show hosts fed the fears of some people that morality and ethics had plummeted. These fears were reinforced by widespread worries that money had corrupted the political system. Although the overall crime rate dropped, several deadly explosions in public buildings at home and military installations abroad shook public confidence. In 1999, when two students opened fire with automatic weapons at Columbine High School near Denver and killed thirteen people, Americans again worried that something was seriously amiss with their society.

The presidential election of 2000 ended with one of the most unusual outcomes in the history of the republic. For only the fourth time since 1788, the candidate with the fewer popular votes gained the White House. But even that remarkable fact did not tell the whole story of an election in which the eventual winner, Republican George W. Bush, defeated Democratic vice president Al Gore because of a botched voting system in Florida and a highly controversial decision by the U.S. Supreme Court.

The first eight months of the Bush administration seemed to be a continuation of the 1990s: scandal, trivial entertainment, and bitter partisan political bickering. Then catastrophe struck on September 11, 2001. Many things seemed to change after terrorists hijacked four commercial airliners and slammed two of them into New York's World Trade Center and another into the Pentagon. In the aftermath of the attack that killed nearly three thousand people, the United States was at war—even though the enemy was not a state and the war aims were indistinct. After September 11, many Americans came to believe that the 1990s represented an unreal interlude. The present was tense, and the future unknowable.

The Technology Decade

The Internet boom of the 1990s reminded people of the 1920s. In the earlier decade, Americans basked in the warmth of a new era, one in which amazing new technologies heralded a period of unimaginable prosperity. Financial experts proclaimed that stocks had reached a permanently high plateau. Such sentiments proliferated again in the 1990s. The Internet, the network of networks that enables computers to communicate with one another, seemed to revolutionize commerce and industry. Financial markets became truly global for the first time. With the stroke of a key and a click of a mouse, global financial transactions worth billions of dollars took place instantly. The computer terminals may have been in New York; Chicago; San Jose, California; Singapore; Hong Kong; or London, but the actual exchange of funds occurred somewhere in a place called cyberspace.

By the late 1990s consumers ordered books, clothing, garden supplies, cars, airplane tickets, groceries, pets, and almost anything else ingenious marketers could manage to display over the Internet. Commentators thought this trend was just the beginning. Enthusiasts for the Internet predicted that it would create a vast global village. Over 1 billion people worldwide would log on regularly. Boosters of the Internet and the World Wide Web proclaimed a new era in which information would flow freely. The Web, they promised, would liberate ordinary people from governmental restrictions. Information would be free for all, thereby breaking the stranglehold of highly paid and often arrogant experts. National boundaries would disappear, and old national, regional, religious, and ethnic differences would melt away. In 1999, Andrew Grove was the chair of Intel, the leading manufacturer of the microchip processors powering desk and laptop computers. He predicted that within five years all companies would be Internet companies or they would not be companies at all. Government data were just as intriguing. As the economy surged in the four years between 1995 and 1998, the U.S. Department of Labor reported that more than one-third of the growth came from the Internet. Government experts predicted that by 2006, about half of the nation's workers would work for companies producing or using information technology.

The work of the Internet may have taken place in cyberspace, but the boom had several local addresses—the San Francisco Bay area, Los Angeles, Atlanta, Boston, Austin, Seattle, New York, and many other cities close to major research universities. The most prominent was Silicon Valley, which stretched about twenty miles from Palo Alto to San Jose, California. Over 400,000 high-tech jobs were created in Silicon Valley during the 1990s. Many people worked for companies where the *average* salary was $72,000 per year. Many made far more. College graduates received $30,000 signing bonuses. A survey reported that sixty-four new millionaires were created each day. They were remarkably young—in their twenties and thirties. They spent freely on Porsches, Rolls Royces, mansions, and jewels.

They didn't have much time to enjoy these toys. They worked eighty to one hundred hours a week. Their workplaces resembled the college campuses where they had recently spent their younger years. The millionaire executives and new technical workers scorned the hierarchies of older companies. Dress was casual. No man wore a tie; no woman wore hose. Many high-tech workers came to the office in the same jeans or shorts, T-shirts, and sneakers or sandals they had worn as college or graduate students. Workers brought their dogs to the cubicles where they spent most of the day. When these workers needed a break, they skateboarded down sunny corridors to lounges equipped with pool tables, TVs, and exercise equipment. Some of the high-tech companies in Silicon Valley saved money by furloughing their workers for a week every March or April. Of course, the companies called these unpaid vacations "spring break."

Throughout Silicon Valley and other centers of the high-tech industry (in Seattle, Boston, Austin, and New York, to name only a few) people talked constantly of the riches to be made in the stock market. Men and women in their twenties made hundreds of millions of dollars listing their companies on the NASDAQ stock exchange. By 1997 panic buying had taken over the market for initial public offerings (IPOs) of companies ending in dot-com. Henry Blodget, the Internet analyst for Merrill Lynch, predicted that the stock of Amazon.com, a major online bookseller that first issued stock at $2 a share, would soar from $280 to over $400. (It did, but by 2001, it sold for $8.) Thousands of eager investors hung on Blodget's every word, as their holdings soared from 1996 to 2000. During the boom in the late 1990s, venture capitalists vied for the right to fund dot-coms. Few if any of these start-ups made money, but that did not matter to many of the stock market analysts who touted them to an eager stock-buying public. Financial analysts and venture capitalists encouraged dot-com companies to spend millions on advertising in the hope of gaining a greater share of the market. The peak of excess took place on the Sunday night when the Super Bowl was televised in January 1999. Dot-com ads promising limitless, immediate commercial opportunities in cyberspace went for $1 million a minute.

The stock-market boom went on and on. The NASDAQ average, heavily weighted with shares of high-tech companies, went from 800 to 5000 from 1993 to 2000. Microsoft, the Seattle-based software manufacturer, had not even existed twenty years before, but it briefly became the biggest company in the world in terms of its market value in 1999. Bill Gates, one of Microsoft's founders, became the richest person in the world. In the mid-1990s, day trading, the buying and selling of stock over the Internet, became the latest craze. Thousands of people, often in their twenties and thirties, quit their jobs to trade stocks over the Internet with borrowed money. Despite the lionization that some of the day traders enjoyed in the mass media, over 80 percent of them lost money.

The sharp rise in stock prices had no relationship to profits, and that fact alarmed Alan Greenspan, chair of the Federal Reserve Board. In December 1996 Greenspan warned against "irrational exuberance" among stock-market investors. No one paid much attention. The NASDAQ and the Dow Jones Industrial Average, composed mainly of old industrial stocks, powered

(cont. on page 505)

The Stock Market

It took twenty-five years, but in 1954, the Dow Jones Industrial Average finally climbed back to the level where it had been before the crash of 1929. A postwar boom took off as families began spending money that they had saved during the war years. Memories of old stock-market swindles and crashes faded, and optimism ruled on Wall Street and among the American middle class. For some newly prosperous Americans, having a stockbroker became almost as much a symbol of success as a car, a washer and dryer, a dishwasher, or a TV.

Although the stock market experienced a resurgence of popularity, holders of a few shares here and there remained largely on the sidelines in the 1950s. To attract more retail investors, Wall Street brokerage houses began training employees to cater to the smaller investor. Merrill, Lynch, Pierce, Fenner and Bean (it later shortened its name to Merrill Lynch), the biggest Wall Street firm, proclaimed that their smaller clients would receive the sort of detailed information previously reserved for experienced investors. By the 1960s, financial writers began touting the Nifty Fifty, the fifty stocks most favored by brokerage houses and mutual funds in the pages of the *Wall Street Journal*, *Business Week,* or *Fortune* magazine.

Investing in mutual funds, previously a small part of the investment industry, took off in the 1960s. One legendary mutual funds manager, Peter Lynch, launched the Fidelity Magellan Fund in 1963. For most of twenty years, Magellan's returns surpassed those of the major market averages. Lynch reassured investors that the stock market made sense. He explained that he bought the shares of companies whose products he used and whose businesses he understood. Most people were too busy to explore the inner workings of most businesses, but they could give the chore of choosing stock to professional experts. Most mutual funds

managers, like Lynch or Warren Buffet (a spectacularly successful investor based in Omaha, Nebraska, whose advice earned him the nickname "the Oracle of Omaha"), were scrupulously honest and committed to the well-being of their clients. But the huge amounts of money to be made naturally attracted shady characters in the 1960s. One star manager of the 1960s who became infamous was Bernard ("Bernie") Cornfield. He began marketing his Investors Overseas Services (IOS) to international consumers interested in making money on the American stock market. Operating a sort of chain letter or Ponzi scheme (where early contributors are paid from the proceeds of later participants but no money is actually invested in going concerns), Cornfield bilked his clients of hundreds of millions of dollars.

The 1960s saw frantic merger and acquisition activity. Big companies went looking for bargains frequently, but they paid little attention to the possible advantages offered by acquiring similar lines of business. It was the period of the conglomerate. Litton Industries, International Telephone and Telegraph (ITT), and Ling-Temco-Vaught were among the best-known conglomerates. Investors happily accepted inflated earnings reports of conglomerates at face value, and stock prices soared. When the market began to soften later in the decade and continued gains failed to materialize, the value of many conglomerates' stocks dropped quickly.

By the end of the 1960s, the stock market absorbed more attention and money than ever before. Market indices had increased fourfold, and trading volume had risen 500 percent. Over 20 million individual investors had put their faith—and money—in the market. The breadth and depth of money in the market and the steady returns over two decades helped create an atmosphere in which large-scale panic seemed improbable. The Dow Jones Industrial Average closed above 1000 for the first time on

The trading floor of the New York Stock Exchange. / © John Marshall Mantel/CORBIS

November 14, 1972, breaking through what many had thought to be an insurmountable obstacle, but the 1970s proved rather bleak. Rising inflation, soaring interest rates, the decline of the dollar, and world economic miseries all deterred investments. *Business Week*, for decades one of the stock market's greatest boosters, ran a cover story in 1979 with the ominous question "Are Common Stocks Dead?" Even during these dark days, however, entrepreneurs busily devised new investment products and strategies that yielded extraordinary gains for some. Early in the 1970s, an unknown named Michael Milken began pursuing the idea that high-yield ("junk") bonds could be good investments for the average consumer; by the middle of the decade, his thesis had been proven correct. Milken later went to jail and paid an astonishing fine of $1 billion for cheating on the price of the bonds he sold.

The 1970s also marked the advent of large-scale retirement planning based on mutual funds investing. Congress began privatizing retirement with the authorization of 401(k) plans and individual retirement accounts (IRAs). Employees welcomed the opportunity to control the direction of their own retirement funds. Businesses were even happier to see the risk of a worker's retirement costs fall on the employee, not the employer. The system worked well when stock prices rose. The outsized returns of many individual accounts encouraged a movement among brokerage houses and some officeholders to advocate privatizing the Social Security system. When the market fell or stayed flat for a prolonged period, some holders of 401(k) or IRA plans were left wondering if they had been sold a bill of goods.

The difficult years of the 1970s gave way to a bull market in the 1980s. After a deep recession in 1981–1982, the economy grew for the rest of the decade. Wall Street renewed its dedication to attracting individual investors. International money poured into Wall Street, especially from Britain,

Germany, Switzerland, Japan, and the oil-rich Middle Eastern states.

In the 1980s, mergers returned to dominate financial dealings, and accounting scandals once again made headlines. Many mergers and acquisitions became known as hostile takeovers. A potential buyer would accumulate stock in the target company until it held a dominant position. Takeover specialists such as T. "Boone" Pickens, Kirk Kerkorian, and Carl Icahn became famous—and rich. As merger mania picked up speed, anticipation over prospective merger activity drove much of the stock market's advance. Investors bought firms hoping they would be taken over.

The second major market collapse of the twentieth century occurred in 1987. Rising interest rates at home sparked increases by other countries, and fears of worldwide rate hikes roiled the markets. In September 1987, the market began to slip; difficulties culminated on October 19, "Black Monday." The Dow Jones lost over 500 points, 22 percent of its total value, and the NASDAQ composite slid 30 percent. In contrast to the stock-market crash of 1929, however, the market slowdown of 1987 did not trigger any bank collapses or widespread panic in the long run. The market regained its losses within eighteen months.

The prosperity of the 1960s and merger frenzy of the 1980s paled in comparison to that of the 1990s. Between 1995 and 1999, the value of the Dow Jones doubled, from 5000 in November 1995, to an astonishing 10,000 by March 1999. The Dow Jones reached its highest point to date—a breathtaking 11,722.98—on January 14, 2000. At the outset of the 1990s, over 50 million Americans owned stocks. By 1999, this number had almost doubled to 95 million. The stock market became entertainment. Financial news proliferated on television. Fitness clubs and sports bars that once had daytime soap operas or baseball on their TV screens found their clientele demanding that the sets be tuned to the fast-talking announcers on the ubiquitous all-day financial news channels. The sky was the limit when two exuberant stock market aficionados published a manifesto in 2000 promising that the Dow would hit 36,000 in the next decade. Hundreds, maybe thousands, of mostly young men and women quit their regular jobs to trade stocks for a living. Despite stories of a few overnight millionaires among these day traders, more than 80 percent lost money. During the height of the frenzy, two unhinged, bankrupt day traders shot and killed other speculators on trading floors in Atlanta and San Francisco.

Many investors were attracted by the steady upward climb of nearly all stocks, but the most exciting story was the growth of the Internet. Rapid adoption of Internet technologies promised to revolutionize the international marketplace, and investing in the Internet began in earnest late in 1997. Savvy investors at first purchased direct Internet companies such as Yahoo!, Netscape, and America Online; then enthusiasm for Internet-related equities spread across the entire technology sector. The heights to which stocks soared astonished amateurs and long-time professionals alike, and more money flooded into the market.

In the rush to cash in on the potential of the Internet, corporations and individuals alike made foolish financial decisions. Once again, accounting issues eventually spelled disaster for several firms. Energy trader Enron hid its huge losses and grossly inflated its miniscule profits before it succumbed to bankruptcy in 2001. In 2002, similar types of fraud were uncovered at Global Crossing, WorldCom, and Qwest Communication (three telecommunication companies); Tyco International (a conglomerate); and Adelphia (a cable TV operator). Some of the young companies entering the marketplace in the 1990s barely had business models, and many were not expected to earn profits for years. At the height of the mania, analysts attempted to valuate the stocks with absurd new measures. Some proclaimed that profits were actually bad in the amazing new economy.

It could not last, and it didn't. In 2000, valuations of stocks across the entire technology sector plummeted, and many other groups followed suit. The New York attorney general forced Merrill Lynch to pay a huge fine of $100 million for dumping onto the public shares of companies that it believed were worth little or nothing.

In 2001, following the terrorist attacks on New York City and Washington, D.C., the markets closed for an unprecedented four trading days in a row. When trading resumed, the market—already in bear territory—declined further until September 21. Then prices turned around once more, and even the battered NASDAQ index climbed nearly 40 percent over the next four months. These gains evaporated in the unfolding accounting scandals of 2002. In the winter of 2002–2003 the market settled into a narrow trading range. The major indices of established companies—the Dow Jones and the Standard and Poor's 500—were forty to fifty percent off their highs of early 2000. The high tech NASDAQ average was off seventy percent from its highs. The mania of the late 1990s faded, replaced by a new sobriety about the limits to the riches available in the stock market. But the millions who owned shares, either directly or through mutual funds, continued to look to the stock market as a major source of their financial well-being.

---

forward in the greatest bull market in history. Soon, however, even Greenspan became caught up in the enthusiasm for the so-called new economy. The productivity of American workers, long a problem during the tough economic times of the 1970s and 1980s, doubled during the 1990s. Greenspan believed that the technological revolution represented by the personal computer, the Internet, cell phones, fax machines, personal digital assistants, digital cameras, and scores of other new gadgets dependent on the computer chip meant that the economy could grow faster than at any time since the 1960s.

Greenspan convinced the Federal Reserve Board to lower interest rates from 1993 until 1999. Unemployment fell from 7 percent in 1993 to 3.8 percent, the lowest in over thirty years, in mid-2000. At the same time, inflation remained tame. This "virtuous circle" of high productivity, low unemployment, and low inflation defied the theories of many conventional economists who believed the United States could not sustain low inflation and low employment at the same time.

While the Internet captured most of the headlines, equally significant innovations took place in medicine. Many of the most sought-after start-up companies during the fantastic stock-market boom of the 1990s used technological advances to formulate new drugs. Instead of the traditional mode of using various chemical compounds to fight diseases, the new processes concentrated on the breakthroughs in genetic engineering. A massive Human Genome project, funded by the federal government, sought to map the entire structure of the human gene. Researchers expected that the knowledge gleaned from such a map would lead to future treatments for diseases as diverse as Alzheimer's, diabetes, arthritis, and Down syndrome.

Genetic research and genetic engineering also raised serious ethical questions. Religious figures, philosophers, and anyone else who thought seriously about the ethical implications of technology expressed concerns about where the science would lead. Some wondered whether genetic research would lead to the creation of flawless bodies or superior brains. While either or both might be desirable, would the engineering of "perfect" human beings some-how demean others? Medical research also became enmeshed in the bitter controversy over abortion.

Some of the most promising avenues for genetic research involved tissues developed from stem cells in human embryos. Researchers could obtain such stem cells from embryos frozen for possible use by in vitro fertilization of a woman who could not conceive in other ways. Opponents of abortion de-manded a complete halt to all research using stem cells. Patients with diseases for which cures might be found through stem-cell research and the re-searchers themselves were just as adamant that such research continue. The potential payoff in relieving human suffering could prove to be greater than it had for earlier breakthroughs, such as the development of antibiotics or the polio vaccine. The Clinton administration favored pursuing stem-cell research that stopped short of cloning human beings. The Bush administration, how-ever, paid far more heed to the adamant opposition to such research from abortion foes. The Bush administration halted stem-cell research on every-thing but the dozen or so stem-cell lines used in labs in 2001. Angry doctors and patients predicted that the United States would lose its preeminence in ge-netic research within five years.

Both the Internet and biotechnology had significant downsides. The eco-nomic promises of the so-called new economy seemed greatly exaggerated. The NASDAQ average hit 5000 in March 2000, and then the bubble burst. Over the next three years, the average fell to as low as 1100. The NASDAQ crash also destroyed the reputation of many of the prominent stock analysts of the late 1990s. In 2002, New York's attorney general revealed that analysts had earned millions publicly lauding stocks while they privately dismissed them in their email messages with terms such as "crap," "dogs," or "hot air." Many of the high-flying dot.com companies like Pets.com (an Internet pet store) or Webvan.com (an Internet grocery service) simply closed their doors, throwing more than 600,000 workers into the unemployment lines. Even worse, financial and accounting scandals engulfed several of the darlings of the 1990s stock boom. WorldCom, Global Crossing, Qwest Communications (three telephone companies), Enron (a Houston-based energy trading com-pany), Xerox (the once-proud document-imaging company), and Adelphia Communications (a cable TV operator), to name a few, revealed that they had cooked the books to the tune of tens of billions of dollars.

A small segment of the American population took home most of the ben-efits of the new economy. The top 1 percent of households took home more than 90 percent of the increase in family income. In 1999, 80 percent of households took home a smaller portion of the national income than had been the case in 1977. The income of the poorest 20 percent of the population rose less than 1 percent in the 1990s, while that of the richest 20 percent grew 15 percent (see Figure 14.1). A huge gap opened between the income of

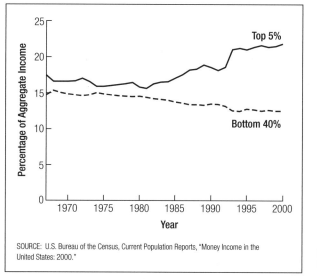

Figure 14.1
The Income Gap, 1965–2000

SOURCE: U.S. Bureau of the Census, Current Population Reports, "Money Income in the United States: 2000."

corporate CEOs and that of industrial workers. By 2000, the salary earned by a typical CEO was *419 times* that of the average worker.

At the same time, a digital divide opened between Americans who had access to the Internet and those who did not. The Commerce Department noticed that the divide was actually a "racial ravine" that separated prosperous whites from poorer people of color. By 2000, over 75 percent of white families used home computers to access the Internet, while fewer than 40 percent of African American and Hispanic households enjoyed the same kind of access. Government officials feared that the digital divide would make it even harder for children of poor families and racial minorities to find work in the Internet economy. The federal government thus imposed a tax on telecommunication companies, and the money collected was earmarked for the wiring of all public schools to the Internet.

The Changing Face of America

During the 1990s the American population grew by 13.2 percent, to 281 million people, the largest increase since the baby-boom decade of the 1950s. The country was more racially and ethnically diverse than ever. Seventy-five percent were white, 12 percent were African American, and 3.6 percent were Asian–Pacific Islander. Hispanics, many of whom could identify with different racial groups, made up 13 percent of the population. The booming American economy of the 1990s attracted the largest immigration into the United States in a century. The foreign-born population increased more that 27 percent throughout the decade. In 2000, more than10 percent of the American population, about 31 million people, was foreign-born. In 1970 only 4.7 percent

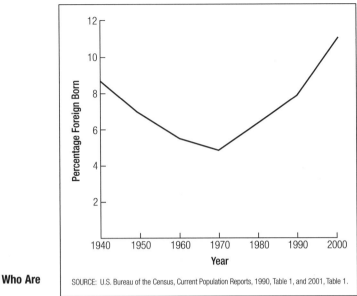

Figure 14.2
Percentage of Americans Who Are
Foreign Born, 1940–2000

SOURCE: U.S. Bureau of the Census, Current Population Reports, 1990, Table 1, and 2001, Table 1.

of the population was foreign-born (see Figure 14.2). The change was the most dramatic in major cities. Forty percent of New York City's population was foreign-born. Immigrants to the city made New York City's population increase for the first time in forty years.

Immigrants from Spanish-speaking countries made up the largest contingent. The 1990s saw an increase of nearly 13 million in the nation's Latino population, to 35.3 million people. The Mexican American population reached 20.6 million. Latinos continued to migrate to localities with large Spanish-speaking populations, such as California, Texas, Illinois, Florida, and the New York metropolitan area. Just as significant, however, was a surge in the Latino population in other places—North Carolina, Ohio, Iowa, and Minnesota—where they took jobs in chicken-processing plants, light manufacturing, domestic service, food service, and hospitals. Asian–Pacific Islanders made up the second largest group of immigrants during the decade. They also concentrated in areas that had sizable Asian populations in major cities on both coasts. For the first time in American history, no racial group made up a majority of the population in the largest state: California.

The 1990s also saw a vast upsurge in immigration among wealthier and well-educated people, often from Asia. Indians, Pakistanis, and ethnic Chinese played an especially large role in the burgeoning Internet industries. Foreign-born doctors and nurses worked in urban hospitals, Public Health Service clinics, and rural medicine.

These new immigrants had an enormous impact on daily life, culture, and politics. Ethnic food became available in previously insular places like Greenville, South Carolina; Des Moines, Iowa; Tulsa, Oklahoma; or Little Rock,

Signs in English, Korean, and Spanish along a shopping street in Los Angeles show some of the impact of the new immigration. / © Michael Newman/PhotoEdit

Arkansas, not just in major cities on the East and West coasts. When people spoke of an American cuisine it could just as easily be tacos or burritos, or Asian stir-fry, or dim sum, or falafels, as such traditional American staples as hamburgers, French fries, chicken-fried steak, bagels, pizza, or potato salad. Salsa surpassed ketchup as the best selling condiment in the United States.

Non-English-language media boomed. Newspapers appeared in Chinese, Russian, Vietnamese, Hindi (India), Tagalog (the Philippines), and Creole (Haiti), to name a few. Spanish-language media dwarfed all other non-English-language media. In addition to scores of daily papers, weekly Spanish news and style magazines flourished. Spanish-language versions of bridal magazines reached the millions in circulation. Across the country, hundreds of radio stations broadcast music, news, talk, and information in Spanish. Televiso and Telemundo, two Spanish-language TV networks with audiences in the millions, were bought for billions of dollars by major media conglomerates.

Latino culture often crossed over into Anglo or other non-Latino venues. Selena reached the top of the pop charts in the mid-1990s with Tejano music, which included Mexican themes with a Texas flavor. Young Latina actresses like Jennifer Lopez and Cameron Diaz gained huge followings. Other performers who had long kept quiet about their Hispanic heritage now proudly embraced it. Raquel Welch (whose father was Bolivian) or Charlie Sheen (whose mother was Mexican) learned Spanish and sought roles emphasizing Spanish characters or themes that they earlier had avoided.

Immigrants influenced professional sports like never before. Spanish-speaking professional baseball players outnumbered African American players. Baseball teams noticed that attendance among Mexican Americans or immigrants from the Dominican Republic or Cuba surged whenever pitchers from these countries took the mound. The team owners marketed baseball aggressively to Spanish-language radio and TV stations. They encouraged tourists from Latin American countries to make quick trips to American cities to watch their heroes in person at the ballparks. Baseball also stepped up its efforts to find players outside the United States. In addition to sending scouts throughout the Caribbean and Central America to find new talent, major league baseball recruited players from Japan and Korea, where the sport is immensely popular.

Professional hockey, football, and basketball also began recruiting players worldwide. Players from Africa, Eastern Europe, the former Soviet Union, and China joined the National Hockey League (NHL) and the National Basketball Association (NBA). The National Football League (NFL) recruited talent in the Pacific Islands and Africa. The migration of players went both ways. Dozens of American basketball players joined teams in Europe. Basketball became an international sport rivaling what Americans call soccer and what people in the rest of the world call football. Michael Jordan, an African American basketball player whose graceful leaps and keen shooting led the Chicago Bulls to six championships, became one of the most popular Americans in the world. American tourists in remote Chinese, Indian, Iranian, South African, or Bolivian villages were occasionally surprised to see children in Air Jordan sneakers, which are made by Nike. They were even more bewildered when adults in the same towns asked them if they knew Mike.

The new immigrants had the greatest impact in education. Some urban school districts reported that as many as eighty languages were spoken in schools whose student bodies included a large proportion of immigrants. Schools taught English as a second language (ESL). Students who knew little or no English were taught basic subjects for a few years in their native language. They also received instruction in English. Research showed that these methods helped non-English-language speakers keep up with, or at least not fall hopelessly behind, their English-speaking classmates. But ESL became a flashpoint for some old anti-immigrant sentiments. Critics of ESL charged that the procedure kept immigrant children from learning English, thereby preventing their assimilation into American culture.

A political backlash against immigration developed in the 1990s, but it proved to be less virulent than earlier outbreaks of nativism. About a dozen states passed legislation declaring English as their official language. The courts and the U.S. Justice Department insisted that an "official" language could not be an exclusive language. States had to continue to provide ballot information and social services in languages comprehensible to all American citizens.

Immigrants were most vulnerable to nativist antagonism early in the 1990s, when memories of the 1990–1991 economic recession remained sharp. In 1994, voters in California passed Proposition 187, which prohibited the state from paying for the education or medical care for undocumented immigrants. Pete Wilson, the Republican governor of California, hoped to ride a wave of anti-immigrant feeling into the White House. Proposition 187 became a nightmare, however, for its sponsors. The courts invalidated most of its punitive provisions. Over the next several years, Mexican American voters turned against the California Republican Party, and Wilson's hopes for a presidential bid were dashed.

In 1994, the same year that California adopted Proposition 187, George W. Bush was elected governor of Texas, another state where Mexican Americans made up more than one-quarter of the population. Bush wooed Mexican American voters, spoke some Spanish, and steered clear of immigrant bashing. When he won the Republican presidential nomination in 2000, he steered the party away from its earlier flirtation with nativism. By that time, the soaring economy had whittled away at the platform supporting the advocates of strict immigration restrictions.

The 2000 census also revealed great changes in the look of the American family. In 1960, 45 percent of all households were identified as "nuclear families," which consisted of married couples living with children under the age of eighteen. By 2000 only 23.5 percent of households qualified as nuclear families. Single-parent households, mostly headed by women, grew five times faster during the decade than the number of couples with children. Single-mother families tended to be poorer. One positive sign was a sharp drop in the birth rate to teen mothers. Still, teen mothers were far more likely than older women to be unmarried. Two-thirds of white and Hispanic teen mothers were unmarried. Ninety-five percent of African American teen mothers were unmarried.

Various trends contributed to the multiple forms of U.S. households. Men and women delayed marriage and having children. The number of unmarried couples living together rose from 3.2 million in 1990 to 5.5 million in 2000. People lived longer, too. Life expectancy at birth rose to 78 years for women and 75 years for men. The fastest-growing segment of the population was the elderly—people over 85. The consequences of these trends were just as varied. With more childless households, public school districts continued to encounter difficulty in attracting support. Early in the decade, housing experts predicted that the aging of the baby boomers would reduce demand for homes. Exactly the opposite happened because the number of households proliferated. By 2000, middle-class Americans joined the poor in lamenting the dearth of affordable housing. One of the largest population increases occurred in the nation's prison population, which soared 77 percent, to over 2 million people. Incarceration rates for young men of color were especially depressing. One in eleven African American men in their late twenties was serving a sentence of a year or more. Many were casualties of the war on drugs. More Americans were jailed for drug offenses than the entire prison population of Europe.

Trivial Pursuits

In the midst of the economic boom, the bull market, and Internet mania, Americans felt little inclination to pay attention to politics and world affairs. In Silicon Valley and the other centers of the high-tech world, politics and government were among the least important topics anyone talked or cared about. The trivial and the scandalous, especially when they involved sex, physically attractive people, or children, captured the most attention.

From June 1994 to October 1995, many Americans became engrossed in the story of the murder of Nicole Brown Simpson, the former wife of football star and actor O. J. Simpson, and her friend Ron Goldman. Nicole Simpson was white; O. J. Simpson was black. On the evening of Friday, June 17, 1994, millions watched for two and a half hours as Los Angeles police cars chased a slowly moving, white Ford Bronco down the 5 Freeway to O. J. Simpson's $2-million Brentwood mansion. Simpson emerged from the Bronco to be arrested for the murder of his former wife and Ron Goldman. The media spotlight then shone on Simpson for fifteen months. He went on trial for the murders in October 1994. Talk radio buzzed with fevered rants about the case. As the trial went forward, the trial participants took their turns in the spotlight.

Finally, on October 3, 1995, the mostly black jury acquitted Simpson on all charges, even though all the evidence pointed to his guilt. Reactions to the verdict split along racial lines. A vast majority of whites believed that Simpson had played upon the sympathies of a jury consisting mostly of people of color

Robert Shapiro, one of O. J. Simpson's defense attorneys, walks through a crowd of newspeople outside the Los Angeles Criminal Courts building during Simpson's trial for murder, September 1995. / AP/Wide World

to get away with murder. Many African Americans approved of the verdict. They thought that either the police had framed O. J. or his acquittal represented just a small down payment on the centuries of indignities imposed upon African Americans by whites. But the story did not end. Ron Goldman's and Nicole Brown Simpson's survivors sued O. J. Simpson for wrongful death. In February 1997, an all-white jury in Orange County, California, found O. J. Simpson responsible for the deaths and ordered him to pay millions to the Goldman and Brown families.

The media soon had a new grisly murder to attract audiences. On December 26, 1996, the body of six-year-old Jon-Benet Ramsey was found strangled in the basement of her home in Boulder, Colorado. The story was irresistible. Her parents were wealthy, the child was adorable, and there were dozens of hours of videotapes of her dressed in adult clothes, heavily made up, singing and dancing in child beauty pageants. No charges were ever filed, but that fact could not stem the flow of endless speculation about who was responsible. Had the authorities been intimidated by the wealth and influence of the Ramsey family? Did the mother's relentless promotion of Jon-Benet as a Las Vegas showgirl represent a form of child abuse? To many Americans, these questions seemed to be the most important questions of the day.

Sentimentality affected most of the fascination with celebrity. For six months, during late 1999 and early 2000 another beautiful child, five-year-old Elian Gonzalez, became the centerpiece of media frenzy. Elian, a Cuban refugee, was rescued after a shipwreck in the Caribbean in which his mother drowned. He was brought to Miami, where the boy's relatives took him in, but his father wanted him back home in Cuba. American tradition and legal precedent clearly awarded custody to the father. But Cuban Americans demanded that Elian remain in the United States. The Justice Department, led by Attorney General Janet Reno, a long-time fixture in Miami politics, tried to arrange Elian's return to Cuba. "The boy belongs with his daddy," Reno said. The Miami relatives disagreed, and they turned the house in Little Havana where Elian was staying into a shrine. There, they vented their grievances against the government of Fidel Castro and their resentments against the Democratic administration in Washington that looked for ways to reverse the forty years of hostility between the United States and Cuba. The Justice Department tried for months to arrange an amicable settlement, but the Miami relatives would not budge. Finally, on the day before Easter in 2000, Justice Department agents raided the house, grabbed Elian, and flew him to Washington, D.C. He was reunited there with his father, who had come to Washington to retrieve his son. They soon left the country for Cuba. In Miami, Cuban Americans erupted in fury against Reno; the Justice Department; the Clinton administration; and Vice President Al Gore, who was running for president on the Democratic ticket. That fall Florida's Cuban Americans voted overwhelming against Gore and for George W. Bush, the Republican candidate. Their ballots helped Bush squeeze out a narrow and disputed victory in the Sunshine state, and with that, win the presidency.

The Clinton Presidency

While national politics seemed to matter less than ever before in the 1990s, President Bill Clinton attracted enormous attention. Elected with barely 43 percent of the vote in a three-candidate race in 1992, Clinton proved to be an enormously successful politician because he connected instinctively with his constituents. The first president born after World War II (1946) he embodied the hopes, aspirations, achievements, and shortcomings of the baby-boom generation. Clinton was well educated (Georgetown, Oxford, and Yale), intelligent, articulate, curious, empathetic, and notoriously undisciplined. Before assuming the presidency, he had served for ten years as governor of Arkansas, where he had emphasized education and economic development. He had chaired the Democratic Leadership Council (DLC), a group of moderate officeholders, many of them from the South and West, who sought to steer the Democratic Party away from its traditional liberalism in the hopes of attracting the votes of suburban middle-class whites.

After a shaky start in 1993 and 1994, Clinton achieved the DLC's goal. His first eighteen months proved to be a political disaster, even though many of his policies worked. In the summer of 1993, Congress passed a tax increase on a strict party-line vote. Opposition Republicans predicted that raising the top income-tax rate from 36 to 39.6 percent would throw a weak economy into a depression. Despite these pessimistic forecasts, the economy took off after passage of Clinton's first budget. The federal deficit began to fall, and by 1997, the U.S. government began to amass annual surpluses. Holders of government bonds took heart, and interest rates dropped dramatically. As a result, money began to flow to new industries, and the boom was on.

It took a couple of years, however, before people became aware of improvements in the economy. In the meantime, critics took aim at other Clinton initiatives. His decision to alter the Defense Department's ban on gays serving in the military unleashed a barrage of complaints. Instead of letting gays and lesbians serve openly, the administration constructed a compromise in which the military would not aggressively investigate sexual preferences, and uniformed personnel would not reveal them. This "don't ask, don't tell" policy disappointed supporters of gay rights for doing too little, and it enraged opponents for recognizing that gays had any rights.

Clinton lost even more support when he introduced an elaborate plan to provide health insurance for the 37 million Americans without coverage. He put his wife, Hillary Rodham Clinton, in charge of an administration task force to develop a national health-insurance plan. As a candidate for president, Clinton had won support by promising a prominent role for his wife, an accomplished lawyer. "You get two" (Bill and Hillary) became a prominent slogan of the Clinton campaign. For every person drawn to the Clintons and the prospect of a strong, professional woman committed to public policy, however, about the same number of people found Mrs. Clinton threatening and irritating. She quickly became a lightning rod for opponents. They condemned the Clinton administration for bringing to Wash-

ington hundreds of people who had adopted the mores of the counterculture of the 1960s.

These complaints reached a crescendo in the summer of 1994, when
Hillary Clinton's task force revealed its plans for a major overhaul of the way
in which healthcare would be provided in the United States. The program
would rely on employers paying premiums to private insurers, but the government would exercise overall supervision. People would be encouraged to join
health maintenance organizations (HMOs), employers would be required to
provide health insurance, and the government would become the insurer of
last resort. Various government boards would exercise overall control over the
cost of medical care. The plan ran into vigorous opposition. The insurance industry mounted a highly effective advertising campaign to convince the 85
percent of the public who had health insurance that the Clinton plan would
limit their choice of doctors and hospitals. Conservative talk-show hosts had a
field day deriding Hillary Clinton as arrogant and controlling. The Democratic
chairs of congressional committees also resisted direction by the White House.
Finally, in the fall of 1994, the plan failed in Congress.

The medical system seemed to stabilize for about five years after the failure of the Clinton healthcare-reform plan. More and more Americans joined
HMOs, which recruited new members by promising lower premiums and at
the same time maintaining benefits. Managed care, as it was called, did
squeeze costs for a while. But it did so in ways guaranteed to annoy and eventually enrage both patients and healthcare providers. The HMOs limited access
to the costliest procedures. They demanded that doctors, hospitals, nurses,
and all other healthcare providers do more with smaller payments. By 2001,
HMOs were raising premiums at double-digit annual rates, and the healthcare
crisis, which had prompted the healthcare reforms in the first place, had returned with a vengeance.

By the time Congress dropped healthcare reform in 1994, the Republican opposition sensed weaknesses in the Democratic platform. They assailed Democratic representatives and senators who had voted to raise taxes
in 1993. They lambasted Hillary Clinton for the health plan and accused
her of ethical misconduct as a lawyer in private practice in Arkansas in the
1980s. Newt Gingrich, the second-ranking Republican in the House of Representatives, developed a ten-point Contract with America for Republican
candidates to run on in 1994. The contract called for lower taxes, lower
deficits, higher defense spending, and restrictions on welfare and term limits for officeholders. In the November election, demoralized Democrats
stayed home while angry Republicans came to the polls. The result was a
political earthquake. Republicans gained control of both the House and the
Senate for the first time since 1954. Gingrich became Speaker of the House
and Robert Dole of Kansas took over as Republican majority leader in the
Senate. Republican candidates for governor also won across the country. In
New York, Democratic governor Mario Cuomo lost to Republican George
Pataki. In Texas, George W. Bush, son of the president ousted by Clinton, de-
feated Democrat Ann Richards.

The triumphant Republican Congress of 1995 came to Washington confident that it could render Clinton irrelevant and orchestrate his defeat two years later. For the first few months of 1995, Gingrich became the most prominent public figure in the country. He was everywhere complaining about Clinton and promoting the Contract with America. He also advocated various idiosyncratic projects from additional research on dinosaurs and outer space to more personal computers for poor schoolchildren and legislation prohibiting women in the military from serving in combat.

But Gingrich overreached. Clinton began to recover his standing with the public after Timothy McVeigh and Terry Nichols, two army veterans furious with the federal government, planted a bomb outside the federal office building in Oklahoma City on April 19, 1995, killing 169 people. In the wake of the Oklahoma City bombing, Clinton's genuine empathy for the victims shone through. Alternately compassionate and reflective, Clinton summoned Americans to wonder whether the angry antigovernment rhetoric of the past several years had created a climate in which people had come to consider their own government the enemy. Such thinking might "take us to a dark place we do not want to go," he said.

After Oklahoma City, Clinton seemed to recover his political footing. He adopted a strategy of "triangulation," in which he would stand midway between congressional Republicans and Democrats. Gingrich and the emboldened Republican majority played into his hands by forcing two shutdowns of the federal government in November 1995 and January 1996 when Congress refused to pass a budget. Gingrich believed that antigovernment sentiment ran so high that the public would welcome, or at least ignore, the closing of federal office buildings. Instead, Americans were furious, and they perceived Gingrich and other Republicans as petty and vindictive.

Clinton pressed his advantage in 1996. He adopted some of the most popular aspects of the Republican program. At the same time, he let it be known that his administration was more compassionate and cared more about the needs of ordinary Americans than did his Republican critics. In his State of the Union address, he announced, "The era of big government is over." He presented a balanced budget. In the summer of 1996, he signed a welfare-reform law that required welfare recipients to seek work, limited them to two years of consecutive benefits, and put a lifetime limit of five years on welfare. Passage of welfare reform enraged some of Clinton's erstwhile liberal supporters who viewed it as punitive. They voiced fears that millions of welfare recipients would be thrown into utter destitution after they exhausted their five years of eligibility. At least in the first five years after the enactment of welfare reform, these fears were unrealized. The number of people on the welfare rolls fell by 25 percent across the country because many recipients found work.

Clinton won re-election easily in 1996 over Senator Robert Dole, the Republican candidate, and Ross Perot, who ran once more as an independent. The economic boom was at it height. Clinton seemed far more attuned to the needs of the suburban middle class than did either of his opponents. Dole, a well-regarded lawmaker, was a seventy-three-year-old World War II veteran.

Reporters chuckled at Dole's acerbic wisecracks, but most voters considered him grossly out of touch with the concerns of the 1990s. Perot's angry denunciations of the federal budget deficit also resonated far less in prosperous times. Clinton coasted to an easy victory with 49 percent of the popular vote. He came tantalizingly close to an outright majority, something he desperately wanted. He probably would have reached the magic 50-percent mark and the Democrats probably would have recaptured the House of Representatives if criticism of Clinton's and the Democrats' fundraising had not developed two weeks before the election.

Throughout 1997, congressional committees with Republican majorities investigated foreign contributions to Clinton's re-election campaign. Conservative talk shows and newspaper editorials denounced Clinton, but the public took little notice. Then, in January 1998, a sex scandal exploded over the White House. The sordid tale of the president's involvement with Monica Lewinsky, a twenty-one-year-old White House intern, dominated conversation for a year.

Clinton had a lengthy reputation for womanizing, but the Lewinsky affair became public knowledge because of an investigation by a Justice Department special counsel into the president's and his wife's involvement fifteen years before in a failed Arkansas real estate deal. Kenneth Starr, the special prosecutor, had an impeccable Republican Party pedigree. As he delved more deeply into both Clintons' finances, he became convinced they were not telling the truth. But the scrutiny of the land deal revealed no breaches of the law. As Starr wound down his investigation, lawyers for Paula Jones, a woman suing Clinton for sexual harassment while he was governor of Arkansas, learned that the president had had an affair with Lewinsky. Jones's lawyers demanded that Clinton admit having sex with Lewinsky. They also got in touch with Starr, who pressured Lewinsky to reveal details of her relationship with Clinton. The now twenty-four-year-old woman was shocked to discover that her former friend, Linda Tripp, had taped their telephone conversations in which Lewinsky spoke in graphic detail about everything she and Clinton had done.

Reporters heard of the Lewinsky-Tripp tapes in mid-January, and they began peppering Clinton with questions about the nature of his friendship with the intern. Commentators assured newspaper readers and television viewers that he would resign within days. In a panic, Clinton consulted a pollster, who told him that the public would never forgive him for an affair with a woman less than half his age. The president then went on television, turned red, wagged his finger, and asserted, "I did not have sex with that woman, Monica Lewinsky." The next day, his wife told a television interviewer that she believed her husband's denial of the affair, and that the two of them were victims of a "vast right wing conspiracy."

Over the next year, the public came to believe both that Clinton *had* had a sexual affair with Lewinsky and that he and his wife *had* been the victims of a vast right-wing conspiracy. Most people were appalled at Clinton's conduct, but they also thought that Starr's pursuit of Clinton was petty, vindictive, and, most of all, smutty. Starr's office subpoenaed Clinton to testify about his relations with Lewinsky. Attorneys demanded that he answer specific, detailed questions about every intimate physical act he had done with Lewinsky. They compared his answers to his earlier deposition in the Jones sexual harassment case and concluded that he had lied. In August 1998, Clinton went on television once more and retracted his earlier denial of a sexual affair with Lewinsky. He apologized for misleading his family, his supporters, and the public. Clearly furious at Starr, he concluded, "Even presidents are entitled to privacy."

Clinton's poor performance in his August address emboldened his Republican critics. They had been surprised that Clinton had not resigned in January, and they were mystified that the public continued to support the way he conducted the presidency even as they expressed strong disapproval for his personal behavior. Now that Clinton had admitted what he called his "inappropriate relationship" with Lewinsky, congressional Republicans thought they could force him from office. Starr submitted a report to Congress outlining in elaborate detail what Clinton and Lewinsky had said and done to each other. House Speaker Gingrich quickly arranged for the report and thousands of pages of supporting documents to be released to the public. He expected that revulsion at Clinton's lack of judgment, his immaturity, and even his immorality would lead to a call for his resignation.

The public had other ideas. However angry people might have been with Clinton, they were even more outraged with Starr for having chased down these prurient details and at the House Republicans for broadcasting what had happened between Clinton and Lewinsky. Clinton's approval ratings remained in the mid-60-percent range. In a major political miscalculation, Gingrich encouraged Republican congressional candidates to assail Clinton and the Democrats for the president's misconduct. The speaker expected huge gains in the 1998 off-year congressional elections. Voters reacted differently. By November they were sick of hearing about Clinton's sex life, and they blamed his opponents for keeping the subject alive. Democrats actually gained five seats in the House of Representatives. A few days later, Gingrich stunned the political world by resigning from Congress.

On the surface, it appeared as if Gingrich had fallen on his own sword after failing to increase the Republican House majority. The same politics of personal destruction aimed at Clinton also brought Gingrich down. Gingrich had spent much of 1998 assailing Clinton's sexual misconduct, but it turned out that the speaker had carried on an affair with a younger woman on his own office staff. House Republicans then turned to Louisiana representative Robert Livingston as their choice for speaker. A few weeks later, he too resigned after confessing to a series of sexual affairs with staff members. The public was disgusted with these witch hunts, but numerous members of Congress feared that they too might have their careers ruined by revelations of sexual misconduct.

Clinton's opponents were relentless. In December 1998, the House of Representatives voted along party lines to impeach him before the Senate. In the midst of the House deliberations over impeachment, Henry Hyde, chair of the Judiciary Committee, admitted that he too had had an affair with a married woman thirty years before. He called it a youthful indiscretion. (He was forty-three at the time.) In January 1999, the upper chamber of the House commenced a trial of the president on the charges of perjury and obstruction of justice. Clinton's standing with the public was as high as ever. Eighty-one percent of those polled judged his presidency a success. Sixty-nine percent approved of his performance on the job, and approximately 66 percent did not want the Senate to convict him.

When he delivered a seventy-seven-minute State of the Union address in January 1999, Clinton received high marks from the public for his specific suggestions. He wanted to use the growing federal budget surplus to shore up Social Security. He advocated permitting workers to divert part of their Social Security contributions to private accounts. He favored better schools, improved Medicare, higher defense spending, and federal money for crime prevention, and he promised a federal suit against tobacco companies for having misled smokers about the dangers of smoking tobacco. Commentators sneered that the speech, like his presidency, lacked a consistent ideological approach or an overarching vision. But that was precisely what the public liked about the ideas in his speech.

Senators understood that the public thought the charges against the president did not amount to the kinds of offenses requiring his dismissal from office. The Senate Republican leadership demanded that the House managers of the Clinton impeachment wrap up their work quickly. In February 1999, the Senate voted to acquit Clinton. On the charge of perjury, forty-five Democrats and ten Republicans voted against conviction, while forty-five Republicans voted in favor. On the charge of obstruction of justice, the Senate split 50-50. Both votes were well short of the two-thirds needed to convict.

The public felt relieved that the sordid ordeal had ended. Both Clinton and Congress seemed exhausted. The president's Republican foes continued to revile him as dishonest and illegitimate. Many Democrats alternated between a sense of betrayal by Clinton and fury at Republicans, whom they believed had misused the constitutional process of impeachment to overturn an election. As the *Economist*, a British newsweekly, observed, "[T]he end of this awful tale still leaves in place the elements that spawned it: a diminished presidency, a bitterly divided Congress, an over-mighty prosecutor, and a media pack that is proud to seek out scandal wherever it can."

Clinton served out the remainder of his term. He remained popular with the public for the specific proposals he made to better the lives of the middle class. African Americans expressed special affection for a president who empathized more with their concerns than any president since Lyndon Johnson. Many blacks also believed that Clinton had suffered injustices at the hands of his political opponents that were similar to the discrimination they had all too often experienced. As for Clinton, he maintained a sunny optimism in public. He promised to work till that last hour of his term for the interests of working families. Privately, he was morose. The strain between him and his wife, whom he deceived about the nature of his relationship with Lewinsky for months, was obvious. His relationship with Vice President Al Gore, with whom he had been especially close, was almost as tense as the one with his wife. Clinton also resented the criticism leveled at him by his fellow Democrats. While Democratic officeholders thought Clinton had lied to them, the president lamented that they were ungrateful for everything he had done to reposition the Democratic Party into the center of American politics.

Foreign Affairs in the Post–Cold War Era

The Clinton administration followed a centrist agenda in foreign affairs. The United States often deployed armed forces to dampen ethnic tensions, and U.S. officials tried to mediate apparently intractable conflicts. Clinton promoted free trade and open markets, a position that often put him at odds with important constituencies in the Democratic Party.

The Clinton administration succeeded in having Congress ratify the North American Free Trade Agreement (NAFTA) in 1993. This treaty, negotiated by the Bush administration, drew criticism from organized labor and environmentalists. The former feared the loss of jobs to lower-wage workers in Mexico. The latter worried that Mexico would not enforce strict standards to protect the air and water. The Clinton administration believed that the process of globalization was irreversible. For the remaining years of his term, Clinton continued to press for free trade in goods, services, ideas, and finance.

During the Clinton administration, the United States went further than it ever had before in taking international action to protect the environment. The United States signed the 1997 Kyoto agreement, in which 150 nations agreed to reduce the worldwide release of carbon-based gases to 5.2 percent below the 1990 level. (Scientists maintained that carbon-based gases were responsible for global warming.) Europe pledged to cut its level to 8 percent below 1990 levels, Japan pledged to cut to 6 percent, and the United States pledged to cut to 7 percent. But the Clinton administration faced strong congressional opposition to the Kyoto agreement, and it never submitted the agreement for ratification by the Senate.

The United States actively intervened to promote human rights abroad. Clinton inherited from Bush a major U.S. military humanitarian intervention in the East African country of Somalia. Heartbreaking television pictures of mass starvation in Somalia prompted Bush in December 1992 to dispatch twenty-eight thousand U.S. ground troops to help distribute food. Clinton supported the humanitarian mission, and the new administration turned the relief effort over to a U.N. force in May. By June 1992, only four thousand U.S. troops remained in Somalia. In October, the mission ended in catastrophe as eighteen U.S. army rangers lost their lives in a firefight with Somali soldiers. Television, the medium that had convinced Americans to send forces to feed Somalis, now showed grisly scenes of the body of one of the Americans being dragged through the streets of Mogadishu. Americans quickly lost heart, and Clinton removed the remaining U.S. troops.

(cont. on page 524)

Labor Conflict, Capital Movement, and the Rise of Global Capitalism: The Case of RCA

In 1998, RCA announced that it was closing its television assembly plant in Bloomington, Indiana, and transferring those jobs to its already large production facilities in Juarez, Mexico. Bill Breedon, a trucker whose job depended on the Midwest factory, observed, that "a lot of people have built their dreams and their houses and their families around working for that company." And they had done so "under poor working conditions . . . to build a television, a product, that made a lot of people rich." Unlike some of the American workers displaced by the change, he did not blame Mexican workers for "taking American jobs." Instead, he understood that they, like the people in Bloomington, took the best jobs they could find. In fact, when the electronics colossus built its Indiana plants in the late 1930s, it did so in order to close down its assembly plants in Camden, New Jersey. When the company once again decided to relocate some of its operations in the 1960s, it looked to the American South and to Mexico for new plant sites.

In each case, moves by RCA were management's response to workers' efforts to organize and pressure the company for better wages and working conditions. Instead of bargaining with workers, RCA searched for a place where it might find compliant workers willing to work for less money. In most cases, it also preceded its moves with efforts to get workers to agree to substantial wage cuts in order to keep their jobs.

In the 1930s, RCA workers in New Jersey, inspired by the rising labor movement and the New Deal's labor politics, organized to force the corporation to abandon its company union and extend exclusive bargaining rights to the United Electrical Workers (UEW), a radical CIO union, and to make concessions on wages and other issues. The company responded to the ensuing strike with violence and by demonstrating a cavalier attitude to the new federal laws designed to protect workers' right to organize. RCA's alliance with local officials, who sided openly with the company, prompted one union leader to state that the actions of law enforcement made it look "as if the RCA Company had purchased the city of Camden outright, and was trying to develop cowboys from the city police."

The company, which had amassed over $6 million in profits in the Great Depression year of 1936, took out newspaper ads threatening to move its company elsewhere if the workers prevailed. The workers ignored this threat as well as the other forms of intimidation practiced by the company as it tried to undermine the certification election conducted by the National Labor Relations Board. In 1936, the company lost its fight against the UEW, which was certified to represent its workers. The workers' victory, however, proved short-lived because the company began moving its production work to other states in the late 1930s. When its white-collar workers organized in the 1940s, the company also shifted their work.

No one benefited more from these decisions than did the workers in Indiana, where new plants took over most of RCA's assembly-line production. The company hoped that depression-ravaged southern Indiana, with its rural traditions, economic hardships, and weak union tradition, would provide the cheap and tractable workers it sought. As before, most of these workers were to be young, single women.

The rigors of assembly-line work, which required that workers go through the same motions repetitively at high speed, and managerial intransigence in the face of worker complaints prompted the midwestern employees to unionize in the 1940s. Faced with the possibility that the CIO-affiliated UEW would represent the workers, RCA decided to recognize the more

RCA workers in Mexico celebrate union victory. / © Keith Dannemiller/ CORBIS SABA

conservative International Brotherhood of Electrical Workers, an affiliate of the American Federation of Labor. In the postwar period, a growing demand for new televisions fueled company profits and reduced management-labor conflict.

By the 1960s, the labor surplus in southern Indiana had evaporated, encouraging worker militancy. This led to wildcat strikes and a formal strike in 1967 when the two sides could not agree on terms for a new contract. From the company's point of view, the workers were spoiled by a full-employment economy and they lacked the work ethic of the past. Managers complained that "the people who were old employees lived through a period [the Depression] and had some appreciation [for work]." It would not be the last time the company waxed nostalgic for the low wages and worker desperation of the Great Depression. The company also threatened to move jobs elsewhere if workers rejected its terms. Over the next thirty years, it did exactly that: reducing jobs in Indiana and transferring them to Memphis, Tennessee, and to Juarez, Mexico.

The company used the same reasoning for its move to Memphis as it had used for the move to Indiana. The Memphis area had a weak industrial base, low wages, an in-effectual labor movement, and a labor surplus. In addition, the local government was willing to provide financial incentives to the company. For area workers, the new jobs seemed like a godsend. One stated: "When I hired on at RCA it looked like it was straight from heaven. It was more money than I'd ever seen. . . . And the best thing, it was the first time me and the family ever had any hospitalization. I thought the world had finally opened up for us."

Within one year of the opening of the Memphis plant, however, workers were picketing, angry at the very fast pace of the assembly line, the requirement that workers had to sign up in order to go to the bathroom, and managerial imperiousness. Grievance complaints to their union were ignored by the company and frustrations mounted. RCA, which was facing greater foreign competition, pushed the workers in order to keep its profit margins high. One worker noted that after two years on the job, she hardly knew anyone and had to struggle to keep up with the work: "The line was so fast I could hardly do my own job. It seemed like I was always sitting in the lap of the woman next to me just trying to finish a set before another was coming at me. . . ." Within a short period of time, the company confronted a resurgent union movement and growing racial conflicts in its work force. The dream of cheap and tractable southern labor evaporated fast. The company closed the Memphis plant in 1970, leaving large numbers of workers without work. Many of the unemployed were African American women with families to support. Their hardship was exacerbated when area employers refused to hire former RCA workers because of their history of union activity.

For the next thirty years, RCA focused its labor search in Mexico, hoping once again to find workers who would toil on the company's terms. Indeed, the level of poverty and underemployment in Mexico led RCA to assume that they had found a permanent source of low-wage labor. When the Juarez plant opened in 1968, RCA found that its total labor costs per worker amounted to $20 U.S for a forty-eight-hour, six-day workweek. The U.S. government's 1964 agreement with Mexico, which created the Border Industries Program, ensured that companies would pay tariffs only on the value added to their products, marginally increasing the incentives for American employers to relocate. The Mexican government's desire to attract these industries and its control over labor unions created greater barriers to worker organization than existed in the United States. The Mexican government's willingness to devalue the peso, which automatically drove wages down, also assisted the companies' efforts to keep labor costs at very low levels. The companies made it clear to the Mexican government that they would move elsewhere if it did not cooperate with them.

For a while, it seemed as though RCA might have achieved its goal. Sporadic slowdowns and worker protests did not succeed in ousting the unions favored by the Mexican government and U.S. employers and did not threaten corporate profits. RCA and others deliberately fired women who had more than five years on the job or who reached the age of twenty-five because they feared that older and experienced workers would be more likely to contest corporate policies. In the four years after the devaluation of the peso in 1982, companies expanded their facilities in Juarez, doubling the number of industrial workers there to over 300,000. After the last devaluation in 1994, an economist reported that the Mexican government's action made the always profitable border industries into an amazingly lucrative enterprise, observing that they were "making so much money down there that running a factory in Mexico now . . . is like running a mint. They are making tons of money." At the same time, however, the scale of operations in Juarez had increased so drastically that the local labor surplus had been exhausted.

When RCA announced a cut in paid vacation time from two weeks to one week, the exasperated workers organized en masse. They formed their own labor organization and demanded a 30 percent increase in wages, the restoration of their vacation time, and the dismissal of the union officials, whom they believed to be mere agents of the Mexican government and RCA. Management responded with a lockout, which only increased worker protests. In response, the company threatened to move its operations to Asia, where wages were lower than in Mexico. The Mexican government opposed the workers on the grounds that wage hikes along the border would lead to inflation in Mexico. Workers agreed to return to work, but then held a sit-down strike inside the plant. Ultimately, the workers won a new union of their choice and a 20 percent raise. Their success meant that they would be making about $24 a week for six days of labor.

As RCA's history suggests, however, this victory would be but another episode in an enduring story of management-labor conflict and capital flight. That history also reminds us that, although this process has now moved onto a global stage, it has its roots in interregional movements in the United States. As the American economy accelerated its shift from industrial production to a service and technical economy in the last thirty years of the twentieth century, real hourly wages for American workers began a steady decline. The deindustrialization of the U.S. economy has occasioned a rising debate over the effects of the global economy on the well-being of American workers and that of the low-wage workers of the Third World who have replaced Americans on the assembly line.

Disheartened by and criticized for the loss of American lives in Mogadishu, the Clinton administration did not respond effectively to a humanitarian calamity in the East African country of Rwanda in 1994, when over 750,000 people were slaughtered in fighting between rival ethnic groups. Finally, in the summer of 1994, the United States sent a contingent of fewer than one thousand troops to ferry other nations' soldiers to restore order in Rwanda. One of the great humanitarian catastrophes of the twentieth century could have been averted had the United States and its European allies responded more quickly and with greater courage.

The program of humanitarian intervention faced its most severe test in the former Yugoslavia. During the 1992 presidential election campaign, Clinton harshly criticized the Bush administration for ignoring the "ethnic cleansing" committed by Serbs against the mostly Muslim population of the former Yugoslav republic of Bosnia. Once in office, however, Clinton was reluctant to get the United States more deeply involved in the ancient ethnic rivalries of the Balkans. The festering conflict between mostly Muslim Bosnian and mostly Orthodox Christian Serbs intensified in the summer of 1995. A Serb attack on the Muslim town of Srebrenica culminated in the massacre of up to four thousand Bosnian men and boys, whose bodies were found a few months later in shallow graves. Bosnian Serb soldiers raped thousands of Muslim women and girls. American leaders were sickened by the massacre and the violence. Deputy Secretary of State Strobe Talbott characterized the conflict as "another European holocaust."

In August 1995, the United States and its NATO allies Britain and France launched air strikes against Serb artillery, tanks, and ammunition dumps. In Yugoslavia's capital of Belgrade, the Serb leader Slobodan Milosevic worried about the complete collapse of Serb power. He agreed to attend a peace conference in Dayton, Ohio. On November 21, 1995, Serbs, Croats, and Bosnian Muslims agreed to share political power in an independent state of Bosnia. The United States agreed to contribute twenty thousand troops to an International Implementation Force of about sixty thousand soldiers to maintain the peace in Bosnia. The U.S. deployment in Bosnia was the first time that NATO forces went to war since the founding of the alliance in 1949.

For seven weeks in the spring of 1999, NATO aircraft bombed Serbia, one of the remaining provinces of Yugoslavia. U.S. warplanes carried out over 80 percent of the bombing in an operation designed to force Yugoslav president Slobodan Milosevic to remove his armed forces from the southern province of

Kosovo. Ninety percent of the Kosovar population was Albanian Muslim, and they suffered gross discrimination at the hands of the Serb minority.

On March 24, 1999, NATO planes bombed Serbia. At the very beginning of operation Allied Force, Secretary of State Madeleine Albright, National Security Adviser Samuel R. ("Sandy") Berger, and President Clinton all believed that Milosevic would surrender in a matter of days; however, these hopes evaporated within days. Instead, Milosevic sent the Yugoslav army on a rampage inside Kosovo. Serbs burned Albanian crops and villages. Thousands of Albanians fled their homes, and within a month over 1 million Muslim refugees had left Kosovo for camps in neighboring countries.

In May and June 1999, NATO stepped up the bombing. Russia, one of Yugoslavia's long-time allies, pressed Milosevic to submit to NATO's demands. In mid-June, a Kosovo Force (KFOR) consisting of sixty thousand troops from the United States and European NATO countries entered Kosovo to supervise the return of the refugees and keep the peace. The end of the Kosovo war brought little celebration in the United States. The war lasted far longer than anyone had predicted. Clinton seemed shocked by the endurance of Yugoslavia's resistance.

The Clinton administration came close to resolving the Israeli-Palestinian-Arab dispute, but its efforts ended in failure at the very end of Clinton's term. The disappointment proved especially bitter because the parties almost reached an agreement that would have ended a century-old conflict. In September 1993, Clinton hosted a ceremony on the south lawn of the White House, where Israeli prime minister Yitzhak Rabin and Palestine Liberation Organization (PLO) leader Yasir Arafat shook hands over an agreement. The terms included a phased withdrawal of Israeli troops from the Gaza Strip and much of the West Bank over the next five years. PLO chair Arafat would rule over a Palestine National Authority (PNA) in the areas to be evacuated by Israel. Israel and the PLO promised to reach a final agreement settling the status of Jerusalem and the political standing of the Palestine National Authority within five years.

The road to peace turned much rockier than anyone expected in the heady days after that fateful handshake. Extremists among both the Palestinians and the Israelis killed scores of people in the next two years. A Jewish nationalist opposed to making peace with the Palestinians assassinated Rabin in November 1995. Six months later, Benjamin Netanyahu, leader of the nationalist Likud Party, was elected Israel's prime minister. The United States continued to mediate between Israel and the PNA, but the original deadline of September 1998 for reaching a final status agreement passed. In July 1999, the Labor Party returned to power in Israel under the leadership of Prime Minister Ehud Barak. The new Israeli leader promised to reach an agreement with Arafat. Clinton threw himself into the negotiations, hosting Barak and Arafat at a sixteen-day marathon meeting at Camp David in July 2000.

The meeting failed. Barak offered far-reaching concessions to Arafat, including the return of the entire Gaza strip and most of the West Bank. The

On September 13, 1993, President Bill Clinton presided over the signing of the peace accord between Israel and the Palestine Liberation Organization. Israel's Prime Minister Yitzhak Rabin (*left*) and PLO chair Yasir Arafat shake hands. / AP/Wide World

Palestinian leader declined to engage in give-and-take bargaining. He demanded sovereignty over East Jerusalem so that it could serve as the capital of an independent state of Palestine. He also insisted on the right of Palestinian refugees and their descendents to return to their homes in Israel. Barak offered Palestinian control over Arab sections of East Jerusalem, but would not accept the return of any Palestinian refugees. Two months later, the worst violence in a decade broke out between Israelis and Palestinians.

Nearly three thousand people, two thirds of them Palestinian, one-third Israeli, lost their lives in the violence that continued into 2003. In the last months of Clinton's presidency, he spent hours on the phone with Barak and Arafat, sent numerous officials around the globe, and went himself to the region, desperately trying to hammer out a peace between Israel and the PNA, but conditions went from bad to worse. In February 2001, Ariel Sharon of the nationalist Likud Party defeated Barak and became prime minister. The violence between Israelis and Palestinians plunged to new depths. The new U.S. administration of President George W. Bush took less interest in mediating the Israeli-Palestinian dispute. By the fall of 2001, as the United States fought its own war against terrorism, the Bush administration reluctantly stepped up its efforts to mediate. Until the war between the United States and Iraq in 2003 (see pages 532–535 for the war on terrorism and the conflict with Iraq), the Bush administration declined to become deeply involved resolving the deadly strife between Israel and Palestine.

The Clinton administration tried to help the states of the former Soviet Union and communist Eastern Europe complete their transition toward democracy and market economies peacefully. The United States sympathized with Russian president Boris Yeltsin's difficulties when ultranationalists and Communists in parliament tried to oust him in the fall of 1993. The United States openly backed Yeltsin when he ran for re-election in 1996. The Clinton administration heaved a sigh of relief when he won. The Russian economy had revived in time for the 1996 election, but it nearly collapsed in the late summer of 1998 when Russia defaulted on its foreign debt. This debt crisis set off a plunge in world financial markets. Only quick intervention by the U.S. Federal Reserve Board prevented an international financial catastrophe. Debilitated from heart disease, Yeltsin resigned as Russia's president on December 31, 1999. His successor, Vladimir Putin, a former secret service operative, won election in his own right in March 2000. Putin pursued a more nationalist foreign policy than had Yeltsin. Clinton and Putin had cordial but never friendly relations. In 2001, however, presidents Bush and Putin established a genuine rapport. Bush hosted Putin at his Texas ranch. Russia strongly backed the American war on terrorism.

The Election of 2000

Both Democrats and Republicans had high hopes for the presidential election of 2000. Democrats boasted that the country had seen eight years of peace and prosperity in the two Clinton administrations. Clinton's policies were largely popular, and he occupied the center of the American political spectrum, the best place to be for electoral success. Republicans acknowledged Clinton's mastery of the political process, but they knew he could not run again. Vice President Al Gore, his chosen successor, lacked Clinton's deft, personal touch. Ernest and eager to please, Gore was wooden on the platform. He seemed to be uncomfortable in public, alternately pedantic and supercilious. For his opponents, his very name invited rhyming comparisons with *bore*.

Republicans also believed that, however much the public supported Clinton's policies, they remained disgusted with his personal behavior in the Lewinsky scandal. If given a credible alternative, Republicans hoped voters would punish Clinton by voting for the Republican candidate. Throughout late 1999, public opinion polls gave a substantial lead to the Republican front-runner, Texas governor George W. Bush, son of ex-president George H. W. Bush, over the likely Democratic nominee, Vice President Gore.

Bush did prevail over Gore, but only after one of the strangest presidential elections since the Civil War. Both candidates had a more difficult path to the nomination than expected. On the Republican side, Bush adopted some of the most conservative positions in his party to fend off challenges from right-wing party elements. Eyeing the substantial federal surplus projected over the next decade, Bush called for a $1.8-trillion income-tax cut. He received the support of the religious right with his proclamations of faith and strong opposition to abortion rights. His strongest challenge in the primary campaign came not from more conservative candidates, but from Arizona senator John McCain. In the late winter and spring of 2000, McCain captured the hearts of the news media by his apparent candor and openness. He would answer questions on almost any subject for hours. Reporters thought he was fresh and "authentic," a word they used repeatedly to contrast his spontaneity with the scripted evasions they had come to despise in other candidates. McCain defeated Bush in the New Hampshire primary by a large margin. But the Texas governor quickly recovered and guaranteed himself the nomination with a string of victories in March.

Gore also had to overcome a challenge to the nomination. Most prominent Democrats declined to enter the primaries, but former New Jersey senator Bill Bradley did. Bradley attracted support among Democratic liberals who believed Clinton and Gore had gone too far toward the center. Bradley, like McCain on the Republican side, assailed the campaign finance system, which allowed both political parties to raise unlimited sums of money from wealthy donors. Gore won every primary, but Bradley's barbs stung. The vice president tacked to the left to blunt Bradley's appeal to liberals.

During the fall campaign, Bush and Gore remained very close in public opinion surveys. Both men chose vice presidential candidates to address their perceived weaknesses. Bush selected Dick Cheney, a veteran of his father's administration. Since leaving Washington, Cheney had amassed millions as the CEO of Halliburton, a Dallas-based oil-services firm. Cheney proved to be an uninspired campaigner, and critics pointed to his and Bush's ties to the oil industry as evidence that a Bush administration would serve the interests of big business. Nevertheless, Cheney's long career in Congress and previous Republican administrations gave the ticket the experience and depth that Bush clearly lacked. Cheney also did well in his debate against the Democratic vice-presidential nominee, Connecticut senator Joseph Lieberman. Gore's choice of Lieberman, an Orthodox Jew who had publicly reprimanded Clinton for immorality during the Lewinsky scandal, revived Gore's flagging campaign. Gore won high marks for choosing the first Jew to run on a major party ticket. The choice of the pious and straitlaced Lieberman also signaled Gore's own disapproval of Clinton's sexual misadventures.

Gore faced an exquisite dilemma in dealing with Clinton's record. The vice president clearly wanted voters to remember the good times: the stock-market boom, the plunging crime rates, and the full employment. But he also wanted to put distance between himself and Clinton. "I'm my own man," he reminded voters. The obvious warmth of his marriage contrasted with Clinton's philandering. Gore seldom referred directly to Clinton, and he never invited the president to campaign with him. Some of Clinton's most ardent admirers condemned Gore for wasting such a superb campaigner. Clinton chafed at being relegated to the sidelines, but Gore probably made a wise choice. Clinton would have overshadowed Gore, and his presence on the campaign trail would have reminded some undecided voters of a scandal they wanted to forget.

Gore also faced a challenge from a third candidate: Ralph Nader, the consumer advocate. Throughout the fall campaign, Nader registered about 5 percent of the voters' choice for president in public opinion polls. Nader appealed to some liberals disgruntled with the centrism of the Clinton record. Nader insisted that there were no significant differences between Bush and Gore. The vice president, desperate for votes that might go to Nader, downplayed his moderate credentials and appealed directly to workers, the poor, and racial minorities. Some middle-class suburbanites, a central constituency of Clinton's 1996 re-election victory, felt slighted.

By Election Day, November 7, 2000, Bush and Gore were running neck and neck in the public opinion polls. Voters supported Gore on the issues, but they liked Bush better. When the votes were counted, Gore won the popular vote by 537,000, but Bush took the electoral college (see Map 14.1). Nader

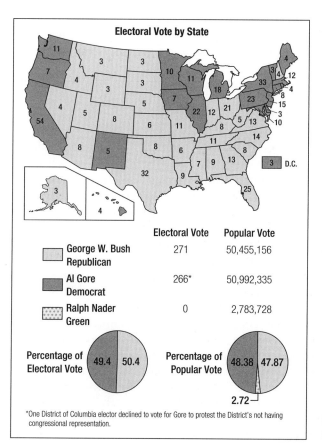

Electoral Vote by State

	Electoral Vote	Popular Vote
George W. Bush Republican	271	50,455,156
Al Gore Democrat	266*	50,992,335
Ralph Nader Green	0	2,783,728

Percentage of Electoral Vote: 49.4 / 50.4

Percentage of Popular Vote: 48.38 / 47.87 / 2.72

*One District of Columbia elector declined to vote for Gore to protest the District's not having congressional representation.

Map 14.1
Presidential Election of 2000

gained barely 2.7 percent of the vote. For the first time, the outcome hinged on the result in a single state: Florida. For thirty-six days after November 7, the nation held its breath to see which candidate would receive Florida's twenty-five electoral votes, and which candidate would win the election with those electoral votes. It was clear that more voters went to the polls on Election Day intending to vote for Gore than for Bush. But because of poor ballot design and defective voting machines, thousands of Gore's votes were actually recorded for other candidates or discarded from the final tally. Both Gore and Bush filed lawsuits in state and federal courts.

Finally, the U.S. Supreme Court decided the outcome of the presidential election in a 5-to-4 decision. The majority in *Bush* v. *Gore* stopped the recount that Gore had requested. With that, Bush was proclaimed the victor in Florida by 537 votes out of millions cast. Gore graciously accepted the results. Many of his supporters were bitter about the Supreme Court's decision and questioned the legitimacy of Bush's presidency. Some Democrats were also angry at Gore for having squandered the enormous advantages of the positive attributes of the Clinton presidency. Clinton chose to see the results as more of a failure of Gore's campaign than a repudiation of his own legacy. The outgoing president also had a reason to cheer the election. His wife, Hillary Rodham Clinton, now more or less reconciled with her husband, was elected senator from New York. Other Democrats also did well in the congressional elections. When the new Congress convened in January 2001, the Senate was split evenly: fifty Democrats and fifty Republicans. Republicans retained control, with Vice President Cheney breaking the tie. In the House, the Republicans had a tiny six-seat majority.

Into the Twenty-first Century

The first eight months of the Bush administration seemed to continue the partisan bickering of the previous few years. Many Democrats remained bitter at the way Bush had won the presidency. Many people expected Bush to govern as a centrist and reach out to Democrats, but he surprised these people by pursuing a conservative agenda in his first months. His public approval rating hovered around 50 percent through August. In the spring of 2001, Congress passed his large tax cut of approximately $1.2 trillion over the next decade. Eighty percent of the benefits went to the wealthiest 5 percent of Americans. The tax reductions promised to eat up a substantial amount of the predicted budget surpluses. What remained of the budget surpluses was promised for Social Security, leaving few government resources for any other projects. (By the fall, even those surpluses had disappeared and the federal government began once more to run a deficit.) Bush favored drilling for oil in the Arctic National Wildlife Refuge in Alaska, and he reversed several popular environmental initiatives of the Clinton administration. Bush's conservatism proved too much for Vermont Republican senator James Jeffords, one of the most moderate of the Senate Republicans.

In May, Jeffords bolted the GOP, declared himself an independent, and voted with the Democrats, giving them control of the Senate.

Politics in Washington seemed to matter very little throughout the summer of 2001. President Bush contributed to the general lack of interest in government by spending as much time as he could at his Texas ranch. People were more concerned with falling stock prices, rising gasoline prices, and the possibility of electricity shortages. The economic boom stopped, and unemployment began to rise. For the most part, however, people were content, and they thought little about public affairs. Trivia again dominated the news. The most gripping stories of August 2001 involved a missing Washington, D.C., intern who had had an affair with a congressman and reports of sharks attacking swimmers off the East Coast.

The idyll broke suddenly at 8:46 A.M. on Tuesday morning, September 11, 2001, when a hijacked jetliner slammed into the north tower of the World Trade Center (WTC) in lower Manhattan. Twenty-six minutes later, another hijacked plane crashed into the south tower; a third crashed into the Pentagon; and a fourth, headed for public buildings in Washington, D.C., crashed in western Pennsylvania. Across America, people watched in horror as both WTC towers collapsed: the north at 10 A.M., the south tower twenty-five minutes later. The carnage was horrific, and three thousand people died.

Almost everyone who was in the towers above the floors where the hijacked planes hit perished. Nearly all who were below the point of impact managed to walk down the stairs to safety before the buildings collapsed. In the ninety minutes between the impact of the hijacked planes and the collapse of the buildings, frantic office workers used their cell phones to call family and friends. Some left heartbreaking messages of love on answering machines. Others assured their loved ones that they were safe because WTC building authorities had told workers to remain at their desks in the north tower after the south tower was hit. The fortunate workers were those who began climbing down the stairs to the street immediately. Many bravely led or carried disabled colleagues to safety. The unluckiest were the workers who climbed *up* in the vain hope that helicopters might rescue them from the roofs of the towers. As the flames

Pedestrians flee as the south tower of New York's World Trade Center collapses after the terrorist attack on the morning of September 11, 2001. / AP/Wide World

engulfed the upper floors, dozens threw themselves from the windows to certain death below.

The political and social climate changed immediately in the wake of the September 11 attacks. Flags flew everywhere, some even displayed by aging baby boomers who had protested against the Vietnam War. Expressions of sympathy for New York flowed in from around the country and around the world. The firefighters who had rushed into the burning trade towers before they collapsed won praise worldwide. Baseball caps with the logos FDNY (Fire Department of New York), PAPD (Port Authority Police Department), and NYPD (New York Police Department) appeared in the most unlikely places. The *New York Times* began running daily profiles, called "Portraits of Grief," of the thousands of victims. Each short biography, no more than three hundred words, told the tale of a life caught short. Many of these biographies were about women and men in the prime of life. Some had recently been married or were planning their weddings. Many had young children.

The nineteen men of Middle Eastern origin who had hijacked the planes were identified as members of Al Qaeda, a terrorist network led by Osama bin Laden, a wealthy Saudi angry at the United States and the West who lived in exile in Afghanistan. Within days, the Bush administration declared war on terrorism. For the first time in its history, the NATO alliance invoked a clause declaring that the attack on one ally (the United States) had been an attack on all NATO members. On October 7, 2001, the United States began bombing Afghanistan. U.S. ground troops arrived in that country to hunt down bin Laden and root out his terrorist network. In December, the military campaign overthrew the Taliban government, the Islamic fundamentalist regime led by Mullah Mohammed Omar, which had given sanctuary to bin Laden. The United States and the NATO allies sponsored a new provisional government in Afghanistan led by Hamid Karzai, a modernizer strongly opposed to the fundamentalist policies of the Taliban. A U.N. peacekeeping force went to Kabul, the capital of Afghanistan, to provide physical safety for Karzai's new government. Children (including girls, who previously had been denied education) returned to school, and international aid rebuilt Kabul's infrastructure. But most of the rest of Afghanistan remained a damaged and dangerous place. By early 2003 the United States had killed or captured several Al Qaeda commanders in Afghanistan and other countries, but bin Laden himself remained at large.

Bush's public approval rating soared immediately to approximately 90 percent. (From mid-2002 to early 2003 it settled in a range between 55 and 70 percent, still high by historical standards.) The president, who once seemed to drift through life and who seemed so disdainful of Washington, seemed now to have found his calling—wartime leader. In a well-received speech to Congress and the nation on September 20, 2001, he carefully distinguished between a war on terror and a war on Islam. He demanded that Afghanistan's Taliban government turn over bin Laden to the United States. Speaking of Al Qaeda, he said, "[E]ither we will bring them to justice or we will bring justice to them." He received nearly unanimous support in Congress for the war. The public, recently so disengaged from political life, expressed the highest faith in American government institutions since the early 1960s.

Cracks opened later in the widespread endorsement of the Bush administration's conduct of the war. Some advocates of civil liberties criticized the government's plans to try suspected terrorists before military tribunals. The U.S. military brought over five hundred suspected Taliban and Al Qaeda fighters to a prison at the U.S. naval base at Guantanamo, Cuba. They remained there indefinitely, neither charged as criminals nor officially designated as prisoners of war. The military, the CIA, and the FBI interrogated these captives (called detainees), but the U.S. government remained tight-lipped about what information they had revealed. The government also provided little information about the status of over one thousand foreign nationals that it had detained in the United States, mostly on visa violations, in the aftermath of September 11.

Political debate gradually returned after September 11. Congressional Democrats complained that the Bush administration was not doing enough to reverse the economic recession begun in March 2001 and intensified by the terror attacks. This criticism mounted in 2002 with the revelation of billions of dollars in accounting fraud by the energy trading firm Enron and the telecommunications company WorldCom. In 2002 Bush alarmed critics of his war policies when he identified an "axis of evil," which included Iran, Iraq, and North Korea and might soon possess nuclear or other weapons of mass destruction. Bush implied that the United States might take pre-emptive military action against these states. In June 2002, Bush declared that the military strategy of deterrence and the political path of deterrence were outmoded. In the future, he said, the United States might strike first when dealing with terrorist groups and states that sponsored them.

Preemption became a reality as the United States confronted Iraq. In the late summer and fall of 2002, Secretary of Defense Donald Rumsfeld, CIA Director George Tenet, Vice President Dick Cheney, and President Bush demanded that Iraqi president Saddam Hussein account for and destroy his nation's weapons of mass destruction—stocks of chemical, biologicial, and nuclear weapons—as the United Nations required after the Gulf War of 1991. In October, Congress authorized Bush to use force to disarm Iraq. The resolution passed each house with greater than two-to-one majorities, with Republicans voting overwhelming in favor and Democrats split down the middle. Supporters of confronting Iraq considered the conflict to be part of the wider war on terrorism. Skeptics believed it was just the opposite, a diversion from the paramount goal of defeating Al Qaeda. Critics of Bush's foreign policy also expressed misgivings about the president's apparent willingness to confront Iraq alone, thereby squandering the reservoir of international goodwill the United States had developed after the September 11, 2001, terrorist attacks. During the fall 2002 congressional election campaign, Republicans were united in their support of Bush, and they accused Democrats of being soft on national security. Democrats foundered. They feared being perceived as soft on homeland security, and yet many of their most ardent backers opposed going to war with Iraq. Republicans increased their slim majority in the House and recaptured the Senate they had lost the previous May when Vermont Republican James Jeffords became an Independent and allied with the Democrats.

International tensions surged in the months following the congressional election. The United States and Britain sent nearly 300,000 troops to the region in preparation for a war to disarm Iraq. In stark contrast to the events leading to the Gulf War in 1990–1991, the United States had far fewer allies willing to launch a war. Secretary of State Colin Powell, unlike some of his more hawkish colleagues, advocated approaching the U.N. Security Council to disarm Iraq. Powell believed a multilateral approach would strength the American position in any potential war and in the reconstruction that would follow. He succeeded in persuading Bush to pursue a diplomatic track before launching a war on Iraq.

In November, the Security Council unanimously adopted a resolution requiring Iraq to list and destroy its weapons of mass destruction or face "serious consequences," a phrase generally understood to mean war. U.N. weapons inspectors went to Iraq after the passage of the resolution. They did not find the banned weapons of mass destruction, but they also reported limited Iraqi compliance with U.N. demands that they declare and destroy them. The United States grew increasingly frustrated with the slow pace of inspections.

At the same time, many governments and people around the world grew alarmed with what they perceived to be an impatient rush to war on the part of the United States. Antiwar protests drew tens and sometimes hundreds of thousands to cities in Europe, the Middle East, and Asia. The largest antiwar rallies since the Vietnam War also took place in cities across the United States in January and February 2003. By early March 2003 public opinion polls in the United States showed declining support for Bush's handling of the crisis with Iraq. Majorities favored military action to disarm Saddam Hussein, but similar majorities also favored waiting for a war until the U.N. Security Council enacted another resolution finding that Iraq had not lived up to its commitment to disarm. Americans also expressed uncertainty about the justification for war. The Bush administration offered various explanations for why military confrontation was in the national interest. Sometimes it was Iraq's violation of its obligations to destroy its weapons of mass destruction. At other times, administration officials expressed the concern that Saddam Hussein had ties to Al Qaeda or other terrorists. Increasingly, United States officials stated that the reason to fight Iraq was to bring about regime change, the replacement of Saddam Hussein's dictatorship with a democratic government.

In March 2003, American efforts to win another U.N. Security Council Resolution failed. On March 17, Bush delivered an ultimatum for Saddam Hussein to leave Iraq within forty-eight hours. Two days later (the evening of March 19 U.S. time and just before dawn on March 20 in Iraq), the United States and Great Britain began bombing Iraq. The next day, U.S. and British ground forces crossed into Iraq. The well-trained coalition forces, armed with sophisticated high-technology weapons, overwhelmed the Iraqi troops, many of whom shed their uniforms and melted into the civilian population. The

British secured Iraqi cities in the south while the Americans raced toward Baghdad. On April 9, 2003, three weeks after the war began, U.S. Marines and Army soldiers captured the capital and Iraq's government disintegrated. Iraqis, happy to be free of Saddam Hussein's brutal rule, tore down statues of their tyrant, ransacked the palaces he had constructed for himself and his family, and looted government offices.

The results of the war were mixed at press time, in May 2003. Casualties among American and British forces, approximately two hundred dead, were lower than they had been in the first Gulf War of 1991. Iraqi losses were probably also lower than they had been twelve years earlier, but thousands of Iraqi soldiers and civilians died. The United States searched for, but did not find, the chemical and biological weapons that had been the original justification for the war. The military did discover protective suits and antidotes to germ agents, which strongly suggested that Iraq had developed a weapons program. The U.S. also did not find Saddam Hussein. Iraqis were glad that the arrests, torture, and executions of Saddam's regime were over. They were less sure what they thought of the victorious Americans and British. Were the Westerners there as liberators, intending to stay in Iraq only long enough to promote a popular, stable, democratic government, as President Bush and British Prime Minister Tony Blair asserted? Or did they come as conquerors with more selfish motives?

Most people in the United States supported Bush's conduct of a war that was shorter, less costly, and less destructive than some skeptics had feared. As the brutality of Saddam's regime became evident, many Americans believed that the United States had properly gone to war. Yet a significant portion of the American public remained troubled by the doctrine of preemption, or war by choice. These people detected an arrogant disregard for other nations in the way in which the United States went to war without explicit backing from the U.N. Security Council. They also expressed doubts about America's ability to foster democracy in the Middle East.

Conclusion

The American economy did better during the post–Cold War years than at any period since the 1960s. The ethnic and racial diversity of American society seemed to be more a sign of strength than people had feared in previous decades. The stock-market boom created a new category of heroes in finance, the Internet, and biotechnology. Americans enjoyed the prosperity, but many of the anxieties of the recent past continued. People expressed a vague sense of dissatisfaction with their political leaders. But for most of the 1990s, Americans did not think that politics mattered very much. Americans continued to concentrate on their own personal affairs or the lives of celebrities. This placidity was broken with stunning suddenness on September 11, 2001.

The aftermath of the terrorist attacks made the 1990s appear to be almost an unreal interlude. Less than two years after the destruction of the

World Trade Center, the United States fought wars in Afghanistan and Iraq, and it pursued a global campaign against terrorism. Americans were on edge at the beginning of the twenty-first century.

F U R T H E R • R E A D I N G

For general works on the 1990s and the Clinton presidency, see William C. Berman, *From the Center to the Edge: The Politics and Policies of the Clinton Presidency* (2001);Sidney Blumenthal, *The Clinton Wars* (2003); Haynes Johnson, *The Best of Times: America in the Clinton Years* (2001); Joe Klein, *The Natural: The Misunderstood Presidency of Bill Clinton* (2002); Elizabeth Drew, *On the Edge: The Clinton Presidency* (1994); Bob Woodward, *The Agenda: Inside the Clinton White House* (1994). **On the Lewinsky scandal,** see David Brock, *Blinded by the Right* (2002); Jeffrey Toobin, *A Vast Conspiracy: The Real Story of the Sex Scandal That Nearly Brought Down a President* (1999); Joe Conason and Gene Lyons, *The Hunting of the President: The Ten-Year Campaign to Destroy Bill and Hillary Clinton* (2000). **For the election of 2000,** see E. J. Dionne and William Kristol, eds., *Bush v. Gore: The Court Case and the Commentary* (2001); New York Times Staff, *36 Days: The Complete Chronicle of the 2000 Presidential Election Crisis* (2001); Jeffrey Toobin, *Too Close to Call: The Thirty-Six-Day Battle to Decide the 2000 Election* (2001). **For changes in the American economy and society,** see Janet Abbate, *Inventing the Internet* (1999); Tim Berners-Lee with Mark Fischetti, *Weaving the Web: The Original Design and Ultimate Destiny of the World Wide Web by Its Inventors* (2000); Jefferson Cowie, *Capital Moves: RCA's 70-Year Quest for Cheap Labor* (1999); John Cassidy, *Dot-Con: The Greatest Story Ever Told* (2002); James Cramer, *Confessions of a Street Addict* (2002); James Gilles and Robert Cailiau, *How the Web Was Born: The Story of the World Wide Web* (2000); Charles R. Geisst, *Wall Street: A History* (1997); Michael Lewis, *Liar's Poker* (1989); John Naughton, *A Brief History of the Future: From Radio Days to Internet Years in a Lifetime* (2000); Neil Randall, *The Soul of the Internet: Net Gods, Netizens and the Wiring of the World* (1997); Robert Shiller, *Irrational Exuberance* (2000); Bob Woodward, *Maestro: Greenspan's Fed and the American Boom* (2000). **On foreign affairs,** see Andrew J. Bacevich, *American Empire: The Realities and Consequences of U.S. Diplomacy* (2003); William Hyland, *Clinton's World: Remaking America's Foreign Policy* (1999); Thomas Lippman, *Madeleine Albright and the New American Diplomacy* (2000); Lester Brune, *The United States and Post–Cold War Interventions: Bush and Clinton in Somalia, Haiti and Bosnia, 1992–1998* (1998); Ivo Daalder and Michael E. O'Hanlon, *Winning Ugly: NATO's War to Save Kosovo* (2000); Thomas Friedman, *Longitudes and Attitudes* (2002); David Halberstam, *War in a Time of Peace: Bush, Clinton, and the Generals* (2002); Robert S. Litwak, *Rogue States and U.S. Foreign Policy: Containment After the Cold War* (2000); Strobe Talbott, *The Russia Hand: A Memoir of Presidential Diplomacy* (2002); Bob Woodward, *Bush at War* (2002).

Index

Credits